METHOD MATTERS

Resources for Biblical Study

Susan Ackerman
Editor (Old Testament/Hebrew Bible)

Number 56

METHOD MATTERS

Essays on the Interpretation of the Hebrew Bible in Honor of David L. Petersen

METHOD MATTERS

ESSAYS ON THE INTERPRETATION OF THE HEBREW BIBLE IN HONOR OF DAVID L. PETERSEN

Edited by

Joel M. LeMon

and

Kent Harold Richards

Society of Biblical Literature
Atlanta

METHOD MATTERS
Essays on the Interpretation of the
Hebrew Bible in Honor of David L. Petersen

Library of Congress Cataloging-in-Publication Data

Method matters : essays on the interpretation of the Hebrew Bible in honor of David L. Petersen / edited by Joel M. LeMon and Kent Harold Richards.
p. cm. — (Society of Biblical Literature resources for biblical study ; no. 56)
Includes bibliographical references and indexes.
ISBN 978-1-58983-444-6 (paper binding : alk. paper)
1. Bible. O.T.—Hermeneutics. 2. Bible. O.T.—Criticism, interpretation, etc. I. Petersen, David L. II. LeMon, Joel M. III. Richards, Kent Harold, 1939–.
BS476.M35416 2009
221.6'01—dc22 2009037237

17 16 15 14 13 12 11 10 09 5 4 3 2 1
Printed in the United States of America on acid-free, recycled paper conforming to ANSI/NISO Z39.48-1992 (R1997) and ISO 9706:1994 standards for paper permanence.

Over twenty years of collaboration—OTFS

Contents

Abbreviations

AB	Anchor Bible
ABD	*Anchor Bible Dictionary.* Edited by David Noel Freedman. 6 vols. New York: Doubleday, 1992.
ABRL	Anchor Bible Reference Library
AEL	*Ancient Egyptian Literature*, by Miriam Lichtheim. 3 vols. Berkeley and Los Angeles: University of California Press, 1971–1980.
ANET	*Ancient Near Eastern Texts Relating to the Old Testament.* Edited by James B. Pritchard. 3rd ed. Princeton: Princeton University Press, 1969
AOAT	Alter Orient und Altes Testament
AOTC	Abingdon Old Testament Commentaries
ARM	Archives royales de Mari
ASTI	*Annual of the Swedish Theological Institute*
ATANT	Abhandlungen zur Theologie des Alten und Neuen Testaments
ATD	Das Alte Testament Deutsch
BA	*Biblical Archaeologist*
BASOR	*Bulletin of the American Schools of Oriental Research*
BDB	Brown, Francis, Samuel R. Driver, and Charles A. Briggs, *A Hebrew and English Lexicon of the Old Testament.* Oxford: Clarendon, 1907.
BEATAJ	Beiträge zur Erforschung des Alten Testaments und des Antiken Judentums
BETL	Bibliotheca ephemeridum theologicarum lovaniensium
BHS	*Biblia Hebraica Stuttgartensia.* Edited by Karl Elliger and Wilhelm Rudolph. Stuttgart: Deutsche Bibelgesellschaft, 1983
Bib	*Biblica*
BibInt	*Biblical Interpretation*

BibOr	Biblica et orientalia
BibS(N)	Biblische Studien (Neukirchen, 1951–)
Bijdr	*Bijdragen: Tijdschrift voor filosofie en theologie*
BJRL	*Bulletin of the John Rylands University Library of Manchester*
BJS	Brown Judaic Studies
BR	*Biblical Research*
BSOAS	*Bulletin of the School of Oriental and African Studies*
BZAW	Beihefte zur Zeitschrift für die alttestamentliche Wissenschaft
CAD	*The Assyrian Dictionary of the Oriental Institute of the University of Chicago*. Chicago: University of Chicago Press, 1956–.
CBET	Contributions to Biblical Exegesis and Theology
CBQ	*Catholic Biblical Quarterly*
CBQMS	Catholic Biblical Quarterly Monograph Series
CC	Continental Commentaries
CCSL	Corpus Christianorum: Series latina. Turnhout, 1953–
CHANE	Culture and History of the Ancient Near East
ConBOT	Coniectanea biblica: Old Testament Series
COS	*The Context of Scripture*. Edited by William W. Hallo and K. Lawson Younger. 3 vols. Leiden: Brill, 1997–2002.
CQR	*Church Quarterly Review*
CSHJ	Chicago Studies in the History of Judaism
CurBS	*Currents in Research: Biblical Studies*
CurTM	*Currents in Theology and Mission*
DBI	*Dictionary of Biblical Interpretation*. Edited by John H. Hayes. 2 vols. Nashville: Abingdon, 1999.
DJD	Discoveries in the Judaean Desert
DMBI	*Dictionary of Major Biblical Interpreters*. Edited by Donald K. McKim. Downers Grove, Ill.: InterVarsity Press, 2007.
DOTHB	*Dictionary of the Old Testament: Historical Books*. Edited by Bill T Arnold and H. G. M. Williamson. Downers Grove, Ill.: InterVarsity Press, 2005.
EHAT	Exegetisches Handbuch zum Alten Testament
ERE	*Encyclopedia of Religion and Ethics*. Edited by James Hastings. 13 vols. Edinburgh: T&T Clark, 1908–1926. Repr., 7 vols. New York: Scribners, 1951.
ErIsr	*Eretz-Israel*

FAT	Forschungen zum Alten Testament
FOTL	Forms of the Old Testament Literature
FRLANT	Forschungen zur Religion und Literatur des Alten und Neuen Testaments
GBS	Guides to Biblical Scholarship
HAL	Koehler, Ludwig, Walter Baumgartner, and Johann Jakob Stamm. *Hebräisches und aramäisches Lexikon zum Alten Testament*. 5 vols. Leiden: Brill, 1967–1995. ET: *HALOT*.
HALOT	Koehler, Ludwig, Walter Baumgartner, and Johann Jakob Stamm. *The Hebrew and Aramaic Lexicon of the Old Testament*. Translated and edited under the supervision of M. E. J. Richardson. 5 vols. Leiden: Brill, 1994–2000.
HAR	*Hebrew Annual Review*
HBT	*Horizons in Biblical Theology*
HKAT	Handkommentar zum Alten Testament
HOTTP	Hebrew Old Testament Text Project
HR	*History of Religions*
HTR	*Harvard Theological Review*
HUCA	*Hebrew Union College Annual*
IBT	Interpreting Biblical Texts
ICC	International Critical Commentary
Int	*Interpretation*
IRT	Issues in Religion and Theology
JAAR	*Journal of the American Academy of Religion*
JAOS	*Journal of the American Oriental Society*
JBTh	*Jahrbuch für Biblische Theologie*
JBL	*Journal of Biblical Literature*
JDT	*Jahrbuch für deutsche Theologie*
JHS	*Journal of Hellenic Studies*
JPS	Jewish Publication Society
JQR	*Jewish Quarterly Review*
JRitSt	*Journal of Ritual Studies*
JSOT	*Journal for the Study of the Old Testament*
JSOTSup	Journal for the Study of the Old Testament Supplement Series
JSS	*Journal of Semitic Studies*
KAT	Kommentar zum Alten Testament
KEH	Kurzgefasstes Exegetisches Handbuch zum Alten Testament

KHC	Kurzer Hand-Commentar zum Alten Testament
L.A.B.	*Liber antiquitatum biblicarum* (Pseudo-Philo)
LHBOTS	Library of Hebrew Bible/Old Testament Studies
LTQ	*Lexington Theological Quarterly*
MANE	Monographs on the Ancient Near East
NABU	*Nouvelles assyriologiques breves et utilitaires*
NEA	*Near Eastern Archaeology*
NIB	*The New Interpreter's Bible*
NIDB	*New International Dictionary of the Bible.* Edited by J. D. Douglas and Merrill C. Tenney. Grand Rapids: Zondervan, 1987.
NJPS	*Tanakh: The Holy Scriptures: The New JPS Translation according to the Traditional Hebrew Text.* Philadelphia: Jewish Publication Society, 1985.
Numen	*Numen: International Review for the History of Religions*
OBO	Orbis biblicus et orientalis
OBT	Overtures to Biblical Theology
Or	*Orientalia* (NS)
OTE	*Old Testament Essays*
OTG	Old Testament Guides
OTL	Old Testament Library
Proof	*Prooftexts: A Journal of Jewish Literary History*
PSB	*Princeton Seminary Bulletin*
PTA	Papyrologische Texte und Abhandlungen
PTMS	Pittsburgh Theological Monograph Series
RA	*Revue d'assyriologie et d'archéologie orientale*
RB	*Revue biblique*
RBL	*Ruch biblijny i liturgiczny*
RevQ	*Revue de Qumran*
RIMA	The Royal Inscriptions of Mesopotamia, Assyrian Periods
RTAM	*Recherches de théologie ancienne et médiévale*
SAA	State Archives of Assyria
SBL	Society of Biblical Literature
SBLABS	Society of Biblical Literature Archaeology and Biblical Studies
SBLBSNA	Society of Biblical Literature Biblical Scholarship in North America
SBLCP	Society of Biblical Literature Centennial Publications
SBLDS	Society of Biblical Literature Dissertation Series

SBLMS	Society of Biblical Literature Monograph Series
SBLRBS	Society of Biblical Literature Resources for Biblical Study
SBLSBS	Society of Biblical Literature Sources for Biblical Study
SBLSCS	Society of Biblical Literature Septuagint and Cognate Studies
SBLSP	Society of Biblical Literature Seminar Papers
SBLSymS	Society of Biblical Literature Symposium Series
SBLTT	Society of Biblical Literature Texts and Translations
SBLWAW	Society of Biblical Literature Writings from the Ancient World
SBS	Stuttgarter Bibelstudien
SBT	Studies in Biblical Theology
SEÅ	*Svensk exegetisk årsbok*
Semeia	*Semeia*
SemeiaSt	Semeia Studies
SHANE	Studies in the History of the Ancient Near East
Shofar	*Shofar*
SJOT	*Scandinavian Journal of the Old Testament*
SNTSMS	Society for New Testament Studies Monograph Series
ST	*Studia theological*
STK	*Svensk teologisk kvartalskrift*
TB	Theologische Bücherei: Neudrucke und Berichte aus dem 20. Jahrhundert
ThTo	*Theology Today*
ThViat	*Theologia viatorum*
ThWAT	*Theologisches Wörterbuch zum Alten Testament.* Edited by G. Johannes Botterweck and Helmer Ringgren. Stuttgart: Kohlhammer, 1970–.
TLZ	*Theologische Literaturzeitung*
TRE	*Theologische Realenzyklopädie.* Edited by Gerhard Krause and Gerhard Müller. 36 vols. Berlin: de Gruyter, 1976–2004.
TRu	*Theologische Rundschau*
TZ	*Theologische Zeitschrift*
UBL	Ugaritisch-biblische Literatur
UF	*Ugarit-Forschungen*
VF	*Verkündigung und Forschung*
VS	Vorderasiatische Schriftdenkmäler der Staatlichen Museen zu Berlin

VT	*Vetus Testamentum*
VTSup	Supplements to Vetus Testamentum
WBC	Word Biblical Commentary
WMANT	Wissenschaftliche Monographien zum Alten und Neuen Testament
WOO	Wiener Offene Orientalistik
WTJ	*Westminster Theological Journal*
WW	*Word and World*
YNER	Yale Near Eastern Researches
ZAW	*Zeitschrift für die alttestamentliche Wissenschaft*
ZTK	*Zeitschrift für Theologie und Kirche*

Preface

Joel M. LeMon and Kent Harold Richards

> "Reading maketh a full man, conference a ready man, and writing an exact man." (Sir Francis Bacon)

Contemporary biblical scholarship has seen a proliferation of interpretive approaches and methodologies. This phenomenon has contributed to a growing consensus that the field will never be dominated by one, two, or even a handful of methods. As biblical studies keeps expanding to accommodate new modes of inquiry, there is a pressing need for methodological clarity. Put simply, in order to evaluate and engage an interpretation of a biblical text, one must understand the governing principles and fundamental presuppositions that lie behind each mode of inquiry.

David L. Petersen's teaching, research, and service to the guild are marked by a commitment to such methodological clarity—a focus that ultimately promotes scholarly exchange. Petersen's emphasis on methodological clarity is thus an expression of his consummate collegiality. In that spirit of collegiality, the authors in this volume have contributed essays in his honor that are characterized by sustained reflection on the panoply of contemporary methods. Taken together, the essays constitute an authoritative and up-to-date handbook of methods in scholarship on the Hebrew Bible.

The handbook contains essays of two types: essays on discrete methods of biblical interpretation; and "reflection essays" that treat larger classes of interpretive approaches. The contributions of the first type have a common, two-part structure. (1) Each begins by addressing a series of questions about the method, including but not limited to the following: What are the distinguishing characteristics of this approach? How is this method related to other methods? What and who has contributed to the development of this form of inquiry? Many authors have also chosen to provide a brief history of the method in this section as a way of approaching these critical questions. (2) The second part of these essays provides a worked example of the method on a particular biblical text. The case studies—which come from a variety of texts throughout the biblical corpus—demonstrate how the fundamental methodological issues govern the results of particular interpretative enterprises. In sum, these essays provide a representative sampling of the full range of contemporary methods in Hebrew Bible scholarship.

The second type of essay provides an even more comprehensive view of the field by reflecting on the taxonomies of critical approaches. In short, these essays describe what unites and distinguishes certain families or classes of methods, specifically: historical criticism; sociological criticism; literary criticism; ideological criticism along with postcritical perspectives; and the history of interpretation/consequences. In the course of these essays, the authors explore how the larger interpretive categories superintend the array of contemporary methods and identify the intellectual currents that have generated and guided these forms of inquiry in both past and present.

We have designed this handbook to appeal both to specialists and students of all levels seeking to apprehend the current landscape of biblical scholarship. For the scholarly audience, the Festschrift of a valued colleague already has an intrinsic appeal. We trust this volume will be particularly appealing to Hebrew Bible scholars because of the quality and utility of the essays. The plurality of voices within the book provides a certain balance to the presentation of methods. Since no single scholar can write an authoritative essay on every method currently employed—much less provide worked examples of each from throughout the canon—the many voices in this volume assure the quality of the descriptions, analyses, and examples of the methods.

Motivated students will also find the volume useful. Indeed, our decision to organize this Festschrift as a handbook reflects Petersen's sustained investment in the formation of undergraduates, seminarians, and graduate students. So, in addition to its value for the guild, we envision this text as a helpful resource for introductory biblical studies courses in seminaries and colleges, especially those courses that deal carefully with traditional and newly emerging methods of interpretation. Since a large portion of the volume is dedicated to worked examples, the book is more than a reference work; students will encounter methods both carefully described and self-consciously employed.

For the past several years, the bulk of Petersen's teaching load has been devoted to the large two-semester Introduction to the Old Testament course at the Candler School of Theology and a required seminar on methods in Emory's Graduate Division of Religion. Petersen's lively and rigorous courses orient students to critical issues arising from the texts of the Hebrew Bible. Moreover, the courses place a heavy emphasis on analyzing and employing various methods of biblical interpretation. By the end of those courses, Petersen's students have come to understand that method *matters*. Some teachers might argue that such extensive discussion on specific methods is atomizing and pedagogically unproductive. Petersen's students would disagree—especially those who serve as religious leaders in churches and synagogues. Petersen's focus on method enables students to face the challenges of speaking clearly within those communities of interpretation. Religious activities rely on interpretations of biblical texts—be it a sermon, a hymn, a rite, or an act of piety—and every interpretation relies (if only unconsciously and implicitly) upon a method. When students become sensitive to this fact, they are better equipped to respond adequately and intelligently to these various forms of interpretation and practice in any context. We hope the same will be true for readers of the present volume and its constituent essays.

Finally, a word of thanks is due to several individuals who assisted with the preparation and publication of this manuscript. We are grateful to Bob Buller, editorial director of the Society of Biblical Literature, who saw fit to include this project in Resources for Biblical Studies and who affirmed that Petersen's Festschrift deserved to be the first such honorary volume to be published by the Society in many years. We also thank the publications staff at the Society of Biblical Literature, especially Leigh Andersen, Billie Jean Collins, and Kathie Klein, who assisted us at various points in the project with characteristic graciousness and carefulness. Among David's colleagues at Emory, we thank Carol Newsom, Brent Strawn, and Rex Matthews, who provided numerous helpful suggestions as we conceptualized and initiated this project. We also benefited greatly from Emory's deep pool of diligent graduate students, several of whom helped ready the manuscripts for publication: Brennan Breed, Ryan Bonfiglio, Travis Bott, Michael Chan, Kelly Murphy, and John Quant. The quality of this cohort is yet another testament to Petersen's reputation as a scholar and his pedagogical skill.

The last word of thanks goes to David himself, whose work and work ethic have challenged and inspired us. It is an honor to present this volume to our distinguished colleague.

David L. Petersen: A Tribute

S. Dean McBride Jr. and James Luther Mays

This volume of essays has been created by its editors and authors as a tribute to a colleague in the scholarly study of the Old Testament whose career has graced the field by its quality, cooperativeness, and productivity. Its publication by the Society of Biblical Literature is a signal of the Society's appreciation and gratitude for his personal and intellectual contributions to our common endeavors. Since his first academic appointment in 1972, he has labored as a teacher, author, editor, and administrator with distinction for himself and profit for us all. Now as his career approaches its maturation, these essays are presented to him as a collective "Well done!" on behalf of all who know and applaud his exemplary diligence, congeniality, and scholarly achievements.

The influences that shaped the future scholar and teacher began early. David Petersen was a p.k. (preacher's kid). Both his father and his grandfather were Presbyterian ministers. He grew up in the manses of a succession of pastorates in which his father served, all in the state of Illinois. Towns such as Elton and Galesburg were the scenes of his childhood and early youth. During his high school years he had already begun to develop an interest in the intellectual side of religion, an interest that was fostered and encouraged by his parents and social environment. In the career that was to unfold out of this heritage, he would always, no matter its institutional setting, realize a vocational dimension in the work he would undertake.

It was not surprising for a person of his biographical setting that he selected Wooster as his college and that in an environment that fostered the Presbyterian tradition he selected the Department of Religion as the context of his major. The Department had an outstanding faculty in biblical studies, and their competence led him to emphasize the biblical field as he worked in the Department of Religion. It is interesting that he began with a particular engagement with the New Testament, attracted to courses taught by J. Arthur Baird. During his latter college years he was befriended and influenced by the college chaplain, Beverly A. Asbury, whom he remembers as a particularly good preacher, philosopher, and pastor. Asbury was a graduate of Yale Divinity School, and it was in the context of his influence that Petersen selected Yale for further studies in the field of religion.

David Petersen entered the Yale Divinity School in 1965 and began work on his Bachelor of Divinity. This was a halcyon era at the Divinity School. The distinguished senior faculty included, among others, Jaroslav Pelikan, James Gustafson, Julian Hartt, Paul Minear, Nils Dahl, Marvin Pope, and Brevard Childs. There was also a young and energetic "junior" faculty, among them Rowan Greer, David Kelsey, David Little, Dean McBride, Sibley Towner, and Don Saliers—several of whom became Petersen's close personal friends as well as influential mentors. At the college of Wooster, Petersen had already been introduced to classical historical criticism in the interpretation of biblical literature and religion. This approach to textual scholarship was also emphasized at Yale, where Petersen developed complementary technical skills in classical Greek and Hebrew and cognate Semitic languages. He studied New Testament and patristic texts with Rowan Greer, Biblical Hebrew and Aramaic texts with McBride and Towner, Ugaritic texts with Pope, Akkadian with Harry Hoffner, and rabbinic texts with Judah Golden. In exegesis courses taught by Brevard Childs and Rowan Greer, he encountered form criticism and the ways of newer literary and theological scholarship that were then still sweeping into the American scene from Continental Europe. This intensive focus on texts, analyzed in their ancient linguistic, sociohistorical, and comparative contexts—and interpreted using a variety of critical methods—became a hallmark of Petersen's own scholarship.

After finishing his B.D. work in 1968, David Petersen decided to remain at Yale for his doctoral work. While Petersen was engaged in his doctoral studies, the scholarly interests of Brevard Childs began to turn away from historical criticism and related disciplines toward canon-oriented exegesis and theology, closely informed by the history of Jewish and Christian scriptural interpretation. Petersen, however, chose to continue working with more traditional textual sources and methods of biblical criticism. With McBride as his primary advisor, he concentrated on the history, phenomenology, and literature of ancient Israelite prophecy, thus laying the groundwork for some of his most significant contributions to biblical scholarship. His doctoral dissertation examined the development of late Israelite prophecy as attested in exilic and postexilic sources. Here, too, can be seen the beginnings of his sensitivity to social-scientific issues of interpretation. Prompted by Brevard Childs, he spent a year of work on the dissertation abroad at the University of Tübingen (1970–71), where he was in contact with Hartmut Gese. Between 1968 and 1972, when he completed his dissertation, Petersen pursued the doctoral degree in an unusually disciplined, ordered, and timely manner, which proved indicative of his professionalism ever since.

The year his graduate work was completed, David L. Petersen was ordained to the ministry of word and sacraments in the Presbyterian Church by the Presbytery of South East Illinois. The "call" required by the Church for ordination was to teach at the University of Illinois, where the young doctoral graduate had found a position as assistant professor of religious studies in the Department of Religion. The ordination sermon was delivered by Sibley Towner. Petersen would fulfill his call by years of biblical teaching and working on publications produced to help pastors and laity in the use and interpretation of the Bible.

His tenure at the University of Illinois was to continue until 1983. During his career in the department he rose to the position of Director of the Program in Religious Studies, a progress that was an augury of his ability to assume institutional as well as professional responsibility. Undergraduate students at this large public university were predominantly Jewish and Christian, but a wide spectrum of denominational and other religious affiliations was represented, as were nonreligious persuasions. A number of them came under his encouraging influence and choose careers in his field, including Alan Avery-Peck, Naomi Steinberg, and Marvin Sweeney. The departmental curriculum was accordingly designed to be non- or multiconfessional and comprehensive, influenced particularly by the comparative and social-scientific approaches to religious studies developed at the University of Chicago. This lively, diversified, open academic environment broadened Petersen's own intellectual horizons and sharpened his acumen as a teacher, even as he continued to offer courses in conventional biblical subjects such as the History of Ancient Israel, Classical Hebrew, and Introduction to the Hebrew Bible. Among his faculty colleagues at the University of Illinois, Petersen found another good friend and mentor in William Schoedel, a prominent patristic scholar who shared and encouraged his primary commitment to the critical studies of classical texts. Petersen spent a sabbatical year 1977–78 as a Fulbright senior lecturer in

Hebrew Bible studies at Aarhus University in Denmark, where he enjoyed the association with Kirsten Nielsen and Benedikt Otzen, among others. The time there brought another opportunity for him to become familiar with the methods and contributions of Continental biblical scholarship. A season with the dig at Bab edh Dhra directed by Walter Rast and Thomas Schaub gave him first-hand experience in field archeology.

In 1983 Petersen was called to the faculty of Iliff School of Theology in Denver, where he would spend almost two decades of his career. With this move he left the diversified humanistic ethos of a university department of religious studies for a Methodist seminary whose principal mission is to train women and men for ecclesial service and educational ministries. Petersen thus became reacquainted in his seminary teaching with the homiletic and theological dimensions of biblical education. In cooperation with the University of Denver, Iliff also offered a Ph.D. program, allowing Petersen to teach advanced courses in the field of Old Testament/Hebrew Bible. He served as the program's director for two terms, 1985–89 and 1993–96. He was awarded a full professorship at Iliff in 1985 and was installed as the Clifford E. Baldridge Professor of Biblical Studies in 1999.

Iliff's faculty during Petersen's tenure there was stimulating and strong. He especially enjoyed the intellectual company of his colleagues, Dennis MacDonald in New Testament and Delwin Brown in theology. His Old Testament colleague was Kent Richards, with whom he began to collaborate productively in a number of professional enterprises. It was also during these years that Petersen began his extensive involvement in the work of the Society of Biblical Literature, first as chair of the research section on Israelite Prophetic Literature and later in various editorial, administrative, and executive capacities.

In 2002 Petersen heeded the call of the Candler School of Theology and assumed the professorship of Old Testament in that faculty of Emory University. Once again he was in a situation that combined seminary and university contexts for pedagogy. He has had an extensive involvement in the Ph.D. program of the university, but his primary interest and investment has been the M.Div. program with its hundreds of students. His most influential contact with students has been the annual introductory course to Old Testament, usually with around 170 students enrolled. His obvious competence with the material, his effectiveness as a lecturer, and his ability to engage individual students in the midst of such numbers has made him a popular and effective teacher; in two successive years he has been chosen as "the Professor of the Year." He has also received the Emory William award for distinguished teaching, awarded by the university.

In 1977 Petersen's dissertation at Yale, *Late Israelite Prophecy: Studies in Deutero-Prophetic Literature and in Chronicles* (Scholars Press), was published. Its sequel, *The Roles of Israel's Prophets* (JSOT Press), followed in 1981. Both works illustrate his inclination to engage in orderly definition and classification of biblical data. His approach, emphasizing social forms and functions, along with the work of his colleague and fellow student at Yale, Robert Wilson, had great impact on other, especially younger, scholars working with Israelite and Near Eastern forms of prophetism and divination. Petersen's two publications initiated almost a lifetime of work that has been a continuing contribution to the study of prophecy in general and particularly in the postexilic period in Israel's history. Since the dissertation was published, he has pursued the subject in articles and contributions to books, study Bibles, and dictionaries. A survey of his bibliography turns up at least thirty-five items dealing with many facets of prophecy in the postexilic period and steadily broadening the field of concern to Israelite prophecy in general.

His work on prophecy in Israel culminated in two ways. The first is the major commentaries in the Old Testament Library series (Westminster John Knox). His commentary on Haggai and Zech 1–8 appeared in 1984, followed by the volume on Zech 9–14 and Malachi in 1995. It is fair to say that Haggai, Zechariah, and Malachi together, though relatively small in size, constitute one of the most challenging assignments for an interpreter of the Old Testament, but Petersen's doctoral work and subsequent research and writing had prepared him for the challenge. The commentaries when published filled a virtually empty space in English-language work as a full-scale study of these books. They are, as well, a valuable resource for the study of prophecy in Israel and for the understanding of important areas in the postexilic period in Israel's history. The commentaries offer an exercise in all the disciplines that comprise critical biblical studies, leaving hardly a question unasked and discussed. More than most in the series in which they appear, the comment is written in discussion with other scholars at work on the material, especially British and Continental.

The second culmination is his introductory volume, *The Prophetic Literature* (Westminster John Knox, 2002). In many ways this volume is a summation of his writing and teaching. It is an ideal textbook for instructional work and reflects the many years he has spent teaching the prophets.

It comprehends both the subject and all aspects of its scholarly study. It is a parade example of what "critical biblical study" should be. As one reads the volume, one encounters repeated illustrations of the characteristics of Petersen's scholarship and writing. Precision and clarity are hallmarks of his work. The recognition of diversity in the materials with which he deals and attention to the various approaches that recognize that diversity are standard features. His writing is disciplined by the texts under study. The questions with which he deals are those raised by the texts themselves. There are no generalizations or overinterpretations that blur and commandeer the text to purposes alien to them.

Students and colleagues who have worked with him say that, in one way or another, his interests in what might be called methodology emerges in virtually every academic encounter. His interest in "method" clearly is an extension of his concern for respectful and orderly discourse. This is explicitly apparent in his contribution on Gen 12–50 to *A Theological Introduction to the Old Testament* (Abingdon, 2005). Before his own theological assessment of these chapters, he reviews the many approaches to this material that have been employed in discerning its meaning as religious literature. He chooses to interpret them as composed of a particular kind of narratives arranged in a redactional pattern. But he is at pains to make clear that there are other perspectives from which this material has been viewed and valid useful methods associated with those perspectives. He wants his reader to know his approach and how his interpretive conclusions are generated by it. In fairness to and respect for other scholars, he avers with a typical irenic spirit that different methods respond to different aspects of the biblical material. All of them can be useful to interpreters in exploring the many religious and theological dimensions of the material. But it is crucial to know what one is doing and how one reads the text. It can be noted that Petersen's list of methods is composed of the disciplines that address features in the texts themselves, but not approaches that intentionally incorporate concerns with uses of the text or their dogmatic identity.

An attempt to summarize the characteristics of Petersen's scholarly work and writing would surely include such characteristics as the following. It is generally focused on and concerned with specific texts. He largely practices the scholarly disciplines involved in the explanation of texts. He always sets a high value on an understanding of texts that is accountable to the elements of a text explained by "critical biblical study." An interest in the usefulness of social studies in construing biblical texts surfaces episodically in his work. He approaches his field of study primarily in its identity as "Hebrew Bible" rather than "Old Testament." For him the professions of biblical scholar and constructive theologian are distinct and separate in method and purpose. He takes the theology of biblical texts to be the view of God and God's way with the world expressed or implicit in particular texts in their individuality and variety. This theology is discernible apart from confessional and dogmatic considerations. He rather finds the usefulness of biblical texts as Scripture in the ways that a critical understanding of particular texts intersects and engages human life in history. A parade example of his characteristic approach is evident in his Presidential Address to the Society of Biblical Literature, "Genesis and Family Values" (*JBL* 124 [2005]). For him, the meanings of texts emerged from their ancient literary, social, and cultural contexts, and their theological relevance is always a function of those settings as well as our own context of church, academy, and society. However, he always works with an irenic awareness that other approaches and methods could be used than those that he employs, and he would argue that the critical issue in the employment of various methods and perspectives in reading texts is that the scholar should work with an accurate awareness of the assumptions and reasoning inherent in the approach being followed.

David Petersen's career has, more than that of most academics, featured various kinds of group projects. Those who have worked in various contexts with him consider him the consummate colleague. The many collaborative projects to which he has been assigned and which he has undertaken are a massive testimony to his aptness and responsibility as a partner at work. He has served as the co-editor of four one-volume commentaries on the Bible and an annotated edition of the Bible. He has been co-editor and author in a number of collaborative works. The range and number of these shared projects say much about the confidence of the scholarly guild in his work, demeanor, and availability. Many of these projects have been designed as resources, not only for students, but as well for a larger public of the church. They are together one impressive indication of his concern that scholarship should serve a general audience.

His students across the years talk of him in terms that portray him as a "model teacher." In him they have found an instructor whose lectures and discussions were characterized by a clarity that provided access and order to complex materials. His lectures are always supremely organized and delivered in an engaging manner. His presentations give the impression of thorough preparation and a broad command of the subject at hand.

His students say that he sooner or later communicated the high expectations he held for excellence in their work, but always in a manner that was encouraging. They experienced from him a combination of support and criticism that enhanced what was to be learned.

His written works display the same characteristics. He is a master of the well-chosen vocabulary to suit the material. Clarity is a hallmark of his style. As one reads there is the impression of an unrelenting concern to be clear and precise so as to leave no doubt what is being claimed and communicated. There is about his composition an earnest intention to be correct, to be right. The material he authors is always based on a wide and considered knowledge of the subject at hand, and what he has to say is the expression of a serious deliberation on possibilities and positions in the search for those that are most accurately based on the subject and its material. The reader is left in no doubt that research has been done. It is even reported, when he was working on his commentary on Zechariah with its reference to horses, that he made several trips to the Agricultural School of the University of Illinois to check on the hues of horses and to learn about the livers of sheep in connection with their use in divination.

With all, in his teaching, writing, collegial relationships, and personal deportment, there is a reflection of a person whose life is ordered and intentional. He lives and works in an organized, structured manner. He gives others the impression that in ordinary and professional matters of life he is executing detailed plans carefully thought through. When others speak of him they use terms such as rational, thorough, efficient, precise, consistent, particular, orderly, thoughtful, decisive, fair, considerate, disciplined, and reserved. Those who know him best depict him as "a methodical person." His focus on the clarity and logic of thought involved in the scholarly enterprise is a theme of everything he does. It is this central characteristic of Petersen that has suggested the subject of this volume dedicated to him.

During his entire career, beginning in the days of graduate study, David Petersen has been an indefatigable member of and participant in the Society of Biblical Literature. In the last two decades he has served in thirteen different roles in the organization and work of the Society. He has been particularly active in the Society's publications program. In 2004 the Society recognized his distinguished career and rich service to the Society by his election as president.

Though this Festschrift and its introductory tribute are designed to be a recognition of David Petersen's scholarly career, an introductory article about him would be seriously flawed if it spoke of him only in the realm of the academy, the study, and the classroom. In his childhood and youth, Petersen discovered the consummate pleasure of being and doing out in the world of nature. He learned to balance the formal occupations of mind and energy with a harmonious engagement of consciousness with woods and streams. When his vocational life took him west, he found in the slopes and valleys, steams and lakes of the high Rockies a second environment. He realized a special resonance of self with water, frozen and flowing. The fly rod became an instrument of aspiration for excellence. He was even able to bring his scholarly vocation into a unity with the piscatorial as a founding member of the OTFS (Old Testament Fishing Society). Those who have practiced with him in this second environment can testify that he brings to its endeavors the same purposive concentration and execution that characterizes his academic work.

Bibliography of the Works of David L. Petersen

A. Books

The New Interpreter's One Volume Bible Commentary. Co-edited with Beverly Gaventa. Nashville: Abingdon, forthcoming.

Theological Bible Commentary. Co-edited with Gail R. O'Day. Louisville: Westminster John Knox, 2009.

A Theological Introduction to the Old Testament. Co-authored with Bruce C. Birch, Walter Brueggemann, and Terence E Fretheim. 2nd ed. Nashville: Abingdon, 2005.

The Prophetic Literature: An Introduction. Louisville: Westminster John Knox, 2002. (Chinese edition published in 2007).

HarperCollins Bible Commentary. Co-edited with James L. Mays et al. Rev. ed. San Francisco: HarperCollins, 2000.

A Theological Introduction to the Old Testament. Co-authored with Bruce C. Birch, Walter Brueggemann, and Terence E. Fretheim. Nashville: Abingdon, 1999.

The SBL Handbook of Style: For Ancient Near Eastern, Biblical, and Early Christian Studies. Co-edited with Patrick Alexander, John F. Kutsko, James D. Ernest, and Shirley Decker-Lucke. Peabody, Mass.: Hendrickson, 1999.

The Access Bible. Co-edited with Gail R. O'Day. New York: Oxford University Press, 1999.

Contemporary Biblical Studies (in Russian). Edited and Translated by E. Stepanova. Ekaterinburg: Ural University Press, 1998.

Old Testament Interpretation: Past, Present, and Future, Essays in Honor of Gene M. Tucker. Co-edited with James L. Mays and Kent Harold Richards. Nashville: Abingdon, 1995.

Zechariah 9–14 and Malachi. OTL. Louisville: Westminster John Knox, 1995.

The New Interpreter's Bible, Senior Old Testament Editor, vols. 1–7. Nashville: Abingdon, 1994–2001.

Interpreting Hebrew Poetry. Co-authored with Kent Harold Richards. GBSOT. Minneapolis: Fortress, 1992.

Harper's Bible Commentary. Co-edited with James L. Mays et al. San Francisco: Harper & Row, 1988.

Canon, Theology, and Old Testament Interpretation. Co-edited with Gene M. Tucker and Robert R. Wilson. Philadelphia: Fortress, 1988.

Prophecy in Israel: Search for an Identity. Issues in Religion and Theology 10. Philadelphia: Fortress, 1987.

Haggai-Zechariah 1–8. OTL. Philadelphia: Westminster, 1984.

The Roles of Israel's Prophets. JSOTSup 17. Sheffield: JSOT Press, 1981.

Late Israelite Prophecy: Studies in Deutero-Prophetic Literature and in Chronicles. SBLMS 23. Missoula, Mont.: Society of Biblical Literature, 1977.

B. Articles, Chapters in Books, and Major Dictionary Entries

"Brevard Childs and Form Criticism." In *Brevard Childs Memorial Volume.* Edited by Kent Harold Richards and Christopher R. Seitz. Atlanta: Society of Biblical Literature, forthcoming.

"Introduction and Notes on Joel," "Introduction and Notes on Haggai," "Introduction and Notes on Zechariah," and "Introduction and Notes on Malachi." In *The New Oxford Annotated Bible.* Edited by Michael Coogan et al. New York: Oxford University Press, forthcoming.

"Remembering the Prophets." In *Robert R. Wilson Festschrift.* Edited by John Ahn and Stephen L. Cook. New York: T&T Clark, forthcoming.

"Exegetical Perspectives: Ps 23; 30; 138." In *Feasting on the Word: Preaching the Revised Common Lectionary: Year C.* Edited by Barbara Taylor and David Bartlett. Louisville: Westminster John Knox, forthcoming.

"The Genesis of Genesis." In *Congress Volume: Ljubljana, 2007.* Edited by André Lemaire. VTSup. Leiden: Brill, forthcoming.

"Prophet, Prophecy" and "Prophecy, False." Pages 622–48 and 620–21 in vol. 4 of *The New Interpreter's Dictionary of the Bible*. Edited by Katharine Doob Sakenfeld et al. 4 vols. Nashville: Abingdon, 2009.

"Haggai and Zechariah 1–8: Some Reflections." Pages 319–26 in *Tradition in Transition: Haggai and Zechariah 1–8 in the Trajectory of Hebrew Theology*. Edited by Mark J. Boda and Michael H. Floyd. LHBOTS 475. New York: T&T Clark, 2008.

"Exegetical Perspectives: Isa 42:1–9; 49:1–7; 50:4–9." Pages 187–91, 211–15, and 235–39 in *Feasting on the Word: Preaching the Revised Common Lectionary: Year B, Vol 2*. Edited by Barbara Brown Taylor and David Bartlett. Louisville: Westminster John Knox, 2008.

"The Ambiguous Role of Moses as Prophet." Pages 311–24 in *Israel's Prophets and Israel's Past: Essays on the Relationship of Prophetic Texts and Israelite History in Honor of John H. Hayes*. Edited by Brad E. Kelle and Megan B. Moore. LHBOTS 446. New York: T&T Clark, 2006.

"Prophecy." Pages 145–46 in vol. 10 of *Encyclopedia of Language and Linguistics*. Edited by Keith Brown et al. 2nd ed. 14 vols. Elsevier: Oxford: 2006.

"Shaking The World of Family Values." Pages 25–32 in *Shaking Heaven and Earth*. Edited by Christine R. Yoder et al. Louisville: Westminster John Knox, 2005.

"Polities in Genesis." Pages 75–88 in *Constituting the Community: Studies on the Polity of Ancient Israel in Honor of S. Dean McBride, Jr.* Edited by John T. Strong and Steven S. Tuell. Winona Lake, Ind.: Eisenbrauns, 2005.

"Genesis and Family Values." *JBL* 124 (2005): 5–23.

"Creation and Hierarchy in Ezekiel." Pages 169–79 in *Ezekiel's Hierarchical World: Wrestling with a Tiered Reality*. Edited by Stephen L. Cook and Corrine L. Patton. SBLSymS 31. Atlanta: Society of Biblical Literature, 2004.

"The Basic Forms of Prophetic Speech." Pages 269–75 in *The Changing Face of Form Criticism for the Twenty-First Century*. Edited by Marvin A. Sweeney and Ehud Ben-Zvi. Grand Rapids: Eerdmans, 2003.

"Abhorrence, Abhorrent, Abomination, Abominable," "Clean, Cleanse, Defile, Impure, Profane, Pure, Unclean," "Devote, Devoted," "Holy, Holiness, Consecrate, Dedicate, Holy Place, Holy of Holies, Saint, Sanctify," and "Perfect, Perfection." Pages 2–3, 74–79, 106–7, 202–8, and 366–67 in *The Westminster Theological Wordbook*. Edited by Donald E. Gowan. Louisville: Westminster John Knox, 2003.

"Zechariah 9–14: Methodological Reflections." Pages 210–24 in *Bringing Out the Treasure: Inner Biblical Allusion in Zechariah 9–14*. Edited by Mark J. Boda and Michael H. Floyd. JSOTSup 370. Sheffield: Sheffield Academic Press, 2003.

"Haggai." Pages 607–10 in *The Oxford Bible Commentary*. Edited by John Muddiman and John Barton. Oxford: Oxford University Press, 2001.

"Introduction to Prophetic Literature." *NIB* 6:1–23.

"The World of Creation in the Book of the Twelve." Pages 204–14 in *God Who Creates: Essays in Honor of W. Sibley Towner*. Edited by Susan Dean McBride and William P. Brown. Grand Rapids: Eerdmans, 2000.

"Zechariah." Pages 677–82 in *HarperCollins Bible Commentary, Revised Edition*. Edited by James L. Mays et al. San Francisco: HarperSanFrancisco, 2000.

"A Book of the Twelve?" Pages 3–10 in *Reading and Hearing the Book of the Twelve*. Edited by James D. Noglaski and Marvin A. Sweeney. SBLSymS 15. Atlanta: Society of Biblical Literature, 2000.

"Defining Prophecy and Prophetic Literature." Pages 33–44 in *Prophecy in Its Ancient Near Eastern Context: Mesopotamian, Biblical and Arabian Perspectives*. Edited by Martti Nissinen. SBLSymS 13. Atlanta: Society of Biblical Literature, 2000.

"Zechariah's Visions: A Theological Perspective." Pages 188–99 in *Prophecy in the Hebrew Bible*. Compiled by David E. Orton. Brill's Readers in Biblical Studies. Leiden: Brill, 2000.

"Creation in Ezekiel: Methodological Perspectives and Theological Perspectives." Pages 490–500 in *Society of Biblical Literature 1999 Seminar Papers*. SBLSP 38. Atlanta: Society of Biblical Literature, 1999.

"Promises Made, Threatened, and Fulfilled," "Prophecy and Reform: From Jeroboam to Josiah," and "New Life, Renewed Community, Renewed Crises." Pages 67–98, 283–318, and 417–48 in *The Old Testament: A Theological Introduction to the Old Testament*. Edited by Bruce C. Birch. Nashville: Abingdon, 1999.

"What Is Bible Study?" Pages 4–16 in *The Oxford Access Bible*. New York: Oxford University Press, 1999.

"The Book of the Twelve/The Minor Prophets." Pages 95–126 in *The Hebrew Bible Today: An Introduction to Critical Issues*. Edited by Steven R. McKenzie and M. Patrick Graham. Louisville: Westminster John Knox, 1998.

"Malachi: The Form-Critical Task" Pages 269–27 in *"Lasset uns Brücken bauen…": Collected Communications to the Congress of the International Organization for the Study of the Old Testament, Cambridge, 1995*. Edited by Klaus-Dietrich Schunck and Matthias Augustin. BEATAJ 42. Frankfurt: Lang, 1998.

"Rethinking the Nature of Prophetic Literature." Pages 23–40 in *Prophecy and Prophets: The Diversity of Contemporary Issues in Scholarship*. Edited by Yehoshua Gitay. SemeiaSt 33. Atlanta: Scholars Press, 1997.

"Ecstasy and Role Involvement." Pages 279–88 in *The Place Is Too Small for Us: The Israelite Prophets in Recent Scholarship*. Edited by Robert P. Gordon. Sources for Biblical and Theological Study 5. Winona Lake, Ind.: Eisenbrauns, 1995.

"The Formation of the Pentateuch." Pages 31–45 in *Old Testament Interpretation: Past, Present, and Future, Essays in Honor of Gene M. Tucker*. Edited by James L. Mays, David L. Petersen, and Kent Harold Richards. Nashville: Abingdon, 1995.

"Exegesis." *Lectionary Homiletics* 5 (1994): 1–2, 7–8, 14–15, 22, 29–30.

"Introduction and Notes on Ezekiel." Pages 1222–1301 in *The New Revised Standard Version: Harper's Annotated Edition*. Edited by Wayne A. Meeks et al. San Francisco: Harper & Row, 1993.

"Old Testament Eschatology." *ABD* 2:575–79.

"Zechariah 9–14." *ABD* 6:1065–68.

"The Social World of the Old Testament." Pages 68–78 in *The Oxford Study Bible: Revised English Edition with Apocrypha*. Edited by M. Jack Suggs et al. New York: Oxford University Press, 1992.

"Hebrew Bible Form Criticism." *Religious Studies Review* 18 (1992): 29–33.

"Old Testament Personalities." *Adult Bible Studies* (1992): 7–95.

"Israelite Prophecy: Change versus Continuity." Pages 190–203 in *Congress Volume: Leuven, 1989*. Edited by J. A. Emerton. VTSup 43. Leiden Brill, 1991.

"The Temple in Persian Period Prophetic Texts." Pages 125–44 in *Second Temple Studies 1: Persian Period*. Edited by Philip R. Davies. JSOTSup 117. Sheffield: JSOT Press, 1991.

"The Temple in Persian Period Prophetic Texts." *Biblical Theology Bulletin* 21 (1991): 88–96.

"Statistical Differences among Documentary Sources: Comments on 'Genesis: An Authorship Study.'" *JSOT* 50 (1991): 3–14 (co-authored with Stephen L. Portnoy).

"Hebrew Bible Textbooks: A Review Article." *Critical Review* 1 (1988): 1–18.

"Zechariah." Pages 747–752 in *Harper's Bible Commentary*. Edited by James L. Mays et al. San Francisco: Harper & Row, 1988.

"Yahwism and Monotheism: The Unfinished Agenda." Pages 92–107 in *Canon, Theology and Old Testament Interpretation: Essays in Honor of Brevard S. Childs*. Edited by Gene M. Tucker, David L. Petersen, and Robert R. Wilson. Philadelphia: Fortress, 1988.

"Rethinking the End of Prophecy." Pages 65–71 in *Wünschet Jerusalem Frieden: Collected Communications to the XIIth Congress of the International Organization for the Study of the Old Testament, Jerusalem 1986*. Edited by Matthias Augustin and Klaus-Dietrich Schunck. BEATAJ 13. Frankfurt: Lang, 1988.

"Portraits of David: Canonical and Otherwise." *Int* 40 (1986): 130–42.

"Old Testament Survey: Sacred Diversity." *New Ventures in Bible Study* 8.2 (1985–86): 1–48.

"The Prophetic Process Reconsidered." *The Iliff Review* 41 (1984): 13–19.

"Genesis, Wellhausen and the Computer: A Response." *ZAW* 96 (1984): 421–25 (co-authored with Stephen L. Portnoy).

"Zechariah's Visions: A Theological Perspective." *VT* 34 (1984): 195–206.

"Biblical Texts and Statistical Analysis: Zechariah and Beyond." *JBL* 103 (1984): 11–21 (co-authored with Stephen L. Portnoy).

"Isaiah 28, A Redaction Critical Study." Pages 101–22 in vol. 1 of *Society of Biblical Literature 1979 Seminar Papers*. 2 vols. SBLSP 16–17. Missoula, Mont.: Society of Biblical Literature, 1979.

"Genesis 6:1–4, Yahweh and the Organization of the Cosmos." *JSOT* 13 (1979): 47–64.

"Max Weber and the Sociological Study of Ancient Israel." Pages 117–49 in *Religious Change and Continuity: Sociological Perspectives*. Edited by Harry M. Johnson. San Francisco: Jossey-Bass, 1979.

"Covenant Ritual: A Traditio-historical Perspective." *BR* 22 (1977): 7–18, 35–37.

"Northwest Semitic Religion: A Study of Relational Structures." *UF* 9 (1977): 233–48 (co-authored with Mark Woodward).

"The Yahwist on the Flood." *VT* 26 (1976): 438–46.

"The Oracles against the Nations: A Form-Critical Analysis." Pages 39–61 in vol. 1 of *Society of Biblical Literature 1975 Seminar Papers*. 2 vols. Missoula, Mont.: Society of Biblical Literature, 1975.

"Zerubbabel and Jerusalem Temple Reconstruction." *CBQ* 36 (1974): 366–72.

"A Thrice-Told Tale: Genre, Theme, and Motif." *BR* 18 (1973): 30–43.

Form Criticism: The Question of the Endangered Matriarchs in Genesis

Marvin A. Sweeney

Form criticism is a foundational, dynamic, and continually evolving exegetical method employed in modern critical interpretation of biblical texts.[1] It analyzes the formal features of a text, including its unique syntactical and semantic form or literary structure and its typical linguistic genres that give shape to the text and function within it to facilitate its expression. Form criticism functions both synchronically to analyze the present literary form of the text and diachronically to ascertain and examine its compositional history in relation to its postulated written and oral stages. It works in tandem with other critical methodologies, such as rhetorical criticism, redaction criticism, tradition-historical criticism, textual criticism, canonical criticism, newer literary criticisms, social-scientific analysis, and linguistics in the interpretation of biblical texts. Form criticism is intimately concerned with the societal, historical, literary, and conceptual settings in which the biblical texts function, in which they were produced, and in which they are read.

The purpose of this paper is to (1) describe contemporary form-critical theory and (2) apply contemporary form-critical theory to a reading of the endangered matriarch texts in Gen 12; 20; 26; 34; and 38. David Petersen was among the first scholars to expand form-critical analysis beyond its standard preoccupation with structure, genre, setting, and intent to include theme and motif as well.[2] This paper builds on Petersen's analysis to consider the formal, thematic, and motivic functions of these texts in relation to the broader literary context of Genesis. It argues that the endangered matriarch narratives cannot be limited to the so-called wife-sister texts in Gen 12; 20; and 26 but must include the Dinah and Tamar texts in Gen 34 and 38 as well. The proposed reading of these narratives demonstrates Genesis's preoccupation with the question of ancient Judah's national and ethnic self-understanding.

Introduction to Form-Critical Theory

A full understanding of the technical terminology employed in contemporary form-critical theory is essential. "Form" (German, *Form*) refers to the unique formulation of an individual text or communication, whereas "genre" (German, *Gattung*) refers to the typical conventions of expression or language that appear within a text. Genre does not constitute form, as many early form critics presupposed;[3] rather, it functions within the unique form of a given text. Other key terms include *Sitz im Leben*, "setting in life" or "societal setting"; *Sitz im Literatur*, "setting in literature" or "literary setting"; *Formkritik*, "form criticism" or the analytical study of the formal features of a text; and *Formgeschichte*, "the history of form," which refers to the historical development and function of forms and genres in texts.

Each text is uniquely formulated and constitutes a singular event of communication in relation to the language in which the text is written or translated.[4] Like all language systems, Biblical Hebrew employs a combination of typical semantic, syntactic, and generic linguistic features and elements that are combined to produce its unique textual expressions.[5] Thus, analysis of the formal literary structure of a biblical text requires a full understanding of the semantic and syntactical dimensions of Biblical Hebrew in order to enable the interpreter to grasp the means by which a text organizes and presents its contents. Such formal literary structure appears in the seven-day creation pattern in Gen 1:1–2:3, in which six days are devoted to creative acts and the seventh day is reserved for the Sabbath as a day of rest and renewal in all creation. It also appears in the sequence of *tôlĕdôt* (i.e., "generations") formulae that define the literary structure of Genesis and the Pentateuch at large, which traces the emergence of the people of Israel, including the Levitical priesthood, from among all the nations of creation.

Although each text is unique, it employs typical linguistic patterns or genres that function within a specific social, literary, or historical context to facilitate the presentation of its contents and ideas. An example of a modern genre is the contemporary novel, which employs typical elements, including a lengthy narration, well-developed plot lines and characterizations, and some challenge that must be addressed by the fictional or semifictional characters in an effort to entertain, stimulate, and influence the reader. Alternatively, the ubiquitous credit card or loan offer, which emphasizes favorable interest rates, low monthly payments, and easy acceptance, is a well-known standard form or genre in contemporary American society. Biblical texts likewise employ typical genres that were easily recognized by ancient readers. The etiological legend, in which the origins and significance of a contemporary practice, social identity, or institutional structure is explained, is well-known in biblical narrative (see, e.g., Gen 28, which explains the origins of the Beth-El sanctuary).[6] Likewise, the vision report, in which a character experiences a vision (usually from the divine realm) that discloses otherwise hidden knowledge that enables the character to face the challenges of the present or future (see Abram's vision of the future of his descendants in Gen 15 or Jacob's vision of YHWH's promise of covenant and descendants again in Gen 28).[7] Each of these examples employs typical patterns of linguistic expression, but each is a unique formulation that conveys specific contents in relation to the social, literary, and historical settings in which it functions.

Early form critics focused especially on the analysis of short, self-contained texts, identification of their typical structural elements or generic characteristics, and their societal function or *Sitz im Leben*, "setting in life," but the development of form criticism over the course of the twentieth and twenty-first centuries has prompted interpreters to recognize a variety of contexts in which a text is produced and in which it functions. Thus, the societal, historical, and literary settings of a text are key factors in influencing both the composition of a text and its function or interpretation in the contexts in which it is employed and read.

Societal setting is frequently a very challenging aspect of form-critical research, insofar as the early literary and historical settings of a text must be reconstructed as part of the larger effort of reconstructing societal setting. The use of creation narratives to explain the origins, structures, and presuppositions of present-day social and political orders is well-known in the ancient Near Eastern world.[8] Examples such as the Enuma Elish (the Babylonian creation epic) or the Ugaritic Baal Cycle explain the origins of the major cultic institutions, societal structure, and political roles in the world of Babylon and Ugarit, respectively, and each myth functioned as part of a larger cultic liturgy and an educational system that celebrated and reinforced the worldviews articulated therein. Pentateuchal narrative displays similar patterns of reflection on creation to explain the origins and early history of the nation Israel, its civil and religious laws, and its institutional cultic structure. Yet modern interpreters do not possess sufficient knowledge of the specific liturgical or educational means that were employed to impart such knowledge and worldview to the people or its leaders.[9]

The historical setting of a text is a crucial aspect of composition. The Wellhausenian paradigm of four foundational sources or strata for reading the Pentateuch—J (the Yahwist), E (the Elohist), D (the Deuteronomist), and P (the Priestly source)—has played a dominant role in modern readings of the Pentateuch throughout the late nineteenth and twentieth centuries.[10] But recognition of the role that Wellhausen's anti-Semitic and anti-Catholic theological biases have played in the construction of his system, coupled with recognition of Assyrian or Babylonian influence in the J stratum, have prompted interpreters to reconsider past historical paradigms for reading pentateuchal texts. Such reconsideration has major implications for reconsidering the purportedly monolithic reading of P; interpreters have come to recognize that monarchic-period elements may well appear within the P literary stratum, pointing to a much longer and a far more reflective process of Priestly engagement, interpretation, and composition within the pentateuchal narratives.[11] Such reconsideration also points to the emerging consensus concerning the dating of the J stratum to the late monarchic period as well, which has important implications for the reading of the pentateuchal narratives.[12] The identification of Abraham and Sarah as the founding ancestors of Israel and the placement of their narratives prior to those concerning Jacob and Joseph points to the Judean character of the so-called JE narrative and indeed of the pentateuchal narrative at large. The presentation of Abraham is especially informed by Davidic interests from the late monarchic period, such as the concerns for the continuity of the dynasty, its association with Hebron in Judah, the definition of its role in relation to Assyrian or even Babylonian patterns of expression, and its role in ruling over all of the tribes of Israel. Likewise, the presentation of Jacob and Joseph, including all of their flaws, points to an underlying E tradition that addressed problems faced by the northern monarchies in relation to their Aramean and Edomite neighbors and in relation to tensions within the internal tribal structure or balance of power in the ninth and eighth centuries B.C.E. Such an E stratum that focused on the key eponymous ancestors of Israel, namely, Jacob and Joseph, would have been taken up and edited in Judah following the collapse of the northern kingdom in 722/721 B.C.E. in an effort to demonstrate Judean priority by focusing on Abraham as the ideal and founding ancestor of all Israel.

The literary setting of a text also plays a key role in interpretation.[13] Modern interpreters are accustomed to read the pentateuchal narratives according to the standard Wellhausenian pattern of sources or strata—J, E, D, and P—which frequently results in a fragmented reading of the pentateuchal text. But contemporary concerns with broader synchronic literary patterns (e.g., concern with plot analysis and narrative poetics) and rethinking of the standard historical paradigms for the reading of the Wellhausenian sources or strata has prompted interpreters to recognize the larger narrative patterns and concerns that inform the present form of the pentateuchal narrative rather than a narrow focus on reading, dating, and interpreting individual narratives.[14] Examples include the questions of divine fidelity, especially with regard to the birth and well-being of Sarah's son, Isaac, that inform the Abraham-Sarah narratives in Gen 11–25; Jacob's identity as the eponymous ancestor of Israel and his struggles with his likewise eponymous neighbors and relatives, Esau/Edom and Laban/Aram, to define his own national integrity in Gen 25–35;[15] and Joseph's process of challenge and maturation as he transforms from a self-absorbed adolescent to a worthy leader for his brothers, eponymously representing the tribes of Israel in Gen 37–50.

Endangered Matriarchs in Genesis

In order to illustrate the application of contemporary form-critical theory to the interpretation of biblical texts, this paper focuses on the endangered matriarch narratives in Gen 12; 20; and 26 as well as the associated narratives concerning the rape of Dinah in Gen 34 and the Tamar narrative in Gen 38.[16] This choice is made for three reasons: (1) Petersen's own form-critical work on these texts, which emphasizes the need to consider the intrinsic literary character of the narratives in relation to the form critical enterprise;[17] (2) the interrelations between the similarly formulated wife-sister texts, which are so frequently discussed in relation to each other, and the very different texts concerning Dinah and Tamar, which are generally treated in isolation; and (3) the general inability or unwillingness of interpreters to examine the interrelationships between these texts and their larger literary context, viewing them instead as isolated narratives that contribute little to the development or hermeneutical outlook of the ancestral narratives in Genesis.

From the work of Hermann Gunkel on, interpreters have treated the three wife-sister narratives in Gen 12; 20; and 26 as a *sui generis* group of narratives that must be interrelated with each other but have little to do with their larger literary context. But despite the obvious perception of commonality among these narratives, interpreters have had a very difficult time in classifying these narratives according to a common generic character. Thus, Gunkel classifies Gen 12 as *Sage* (legend),[18] which is concerned with the exemplary or etiological portrayal of persons or events; Gen 20 as *Legende*, which glorifies YHWH and divine assistance;[19] and Gen 26 as a narrative without clear generic characteristics.[20] Klaus Koch claims to follow Gunkel in arguing that all three represent the *ethnologische Sage* (ethnological legend) but suggests that the unique characteristics of Gen 20 indicate its origins in prophetic circles.[21] Claus Westermann argues that all three are variants of the same narrative but notes that each is unique insofar as Gen 20 is a reflection on Gen 12 and Gen 26 takes up elements of both of its predecessors.[22] Gerhard von Rad and Martin Noth likewise consider the three to be variants of the same narrative but note the reflective character of Gen 20 while positing that the disparate character of Gen 26 marks it as the oldest of the three.[23] George Coats maintains that all three are tales but follows Koch in positing that Gen 20 gravitates toward prophetic legend.[24]

Although his paper was published prior to the commentaries by Westermann and Coats, Petersen's work must be considered in relation to this discussion because he points to problems in employing genre classification to interpret this literature.[25] He recognizes that the generic classifications presuppose distinct societal settings—*Sage* represents style characteristics of nomadic life, whereas *Legende* represents those of the monarchic period—which has the effect of highlighting the social background of the narratives more than the literature itself. In proposing a focus on theme and motif, Petersen aims to achieve greater understanding of each narrative as literature. In his analysis, Gen 12, 20, and 26 must be considered as episodes in the patriarchal saga (i.e., legend), and each narrative episode has a unique set of concerns. Genesis 12:10–13:1 employs the wife-sister motif to demonstrate how Abraham's plan in 12:10–16 saved his life but left Sarah in jeopardy, whereas YHWH's plan in 12:17–20 resolved the issue of Sarah by visiting plagues on Pharaoh in order to illicit his understanding of proper behavior. Genesis 20 employs the wife-sister motif to portray recognition of divine moral authority or "fear of G-d" on the part of the Philistine monarch Abimelech. Genesis 26 employs the wife-sister motif to emphasize Gerarite envy of Isaac, who becomes wealthy under the protection of Abimelech.

Petersen's analysis is especially useful in developing a deeper understanding of the interrelationship between the common or typical elements of each narrative and their unique formulations and concerns. His observations highlight the contemporary debate on genre: To what degree do the typical elements of generic entities function within a text to facilitate the uniquely formulated expression of its concerns and worldview? But questions still remain, particularly since the field has developed since the publication of Petersen's study. To what extent does the typical motif of the endangered matriarch necessarily depend on the four-part wife-sister motivic pattern identified by Petersen in these texts: (1) travel to the place in which the husband and wife are unknown; (2) a claim that the man's wife is his sister; (3) discovery of the ruse; and (4) resolution of the situation created by the false identity? It seems that the question of danger to the matriarch is lost to a degree in the development of another set of concerns: the question of the patriarch's deceptive act in asking the matriarch to identify herself as his sister rather than as his wife. To what extent must the motif of danger to the matriarch be differentiated from the wife-sister motif with its focus on the patriarch's deception in these narratives?

One may further ask: To what degree is the motif of danger to the matriarch necessarily dependent on the wife-sister motif? After all, Dinah faces very clear danger when she is raped in Shechem in Gen 34. Tamar faces danger as well insofar as her status in the family of Judah—and indeed the future of the tribe of Judah itself—is brought into question when she remains barren following the deaths of her husband Er and his brother Onan and failure of Judah to marry her to Shelah. As a barren woman, she could be sent back to her father's family, where she would have a very questionable future. Unlike Sarah (or Rachel or Leah, for that matter), Tamar is not able to protect herself by offering a handmaiden to her husband because her husband is dead and no levirate substitute is forthcoming. Indeed, the question of the endangered matriarch is a question of her progeny, insofar as each matriarch—Sarah twice; Rachel, Dinah, and Tamar once each—are placed in situations of sexual compromise that has implications for the identities of their respective progeny (or lack thereof) as well as implications for the future of the people Israel/Judah. Insofar as each instance of the endangered matriarch, including both the three wife-sister narratives as well as those concerned with Dinah and Tamar, raises question concerning the identity of the matriarch's progeny, the interrelationship of these narratives with the larger context of the ancestral narratives must also be considered. Petersen's observation that these narratives must be viewed as episodes within the larger ancestral saga demands further consideration.

In order to facilitate such consideration, two fundamental issues must be addressed. The first is the formal literary structure of the larger Genesis or pentateuchal narrative in which the endangered matriarch texts appear, and the second is the place and function of each narrative within that larger literary framework. Each narrative, Gen 12:10–20; 20; 26; 34; and 38, will be considered in sequence. Three essential questions will guide the discussion: (1) What is the nature of the danger in which each matriarch is placed? That is, to what degree does the narrative display an interplay between typical generic elements and unique narrative concerns? (2) What implications does the danger in which each matriarch is placed have for the larger narrative context in which each episode appears? In other words, why is each narrative placed in the larger narrative context? And (3) what implications do the observations made on the basis of the first two questions have for the interpretation of the ancestral narratives at large?

Contemporary interpreters are beginning to recognize that the formal literary structure of Genesis or even the Pentateuch at large cannot be based on broad thematic concerns, such as the primeval history in Gen 1–11, the ancestral narratives with their constituent foci on Abraham, Jacob, and Joseph in Gen 12–50, the exodus and wilderness traditions in Exodus–Numbers, and Moses' last speeches to Israel in Deuteronomy. Such broad strokes do not account adequately for concerns with minor figures such as Isaac, Esau, Dinah, and Tamar, on the one hand, and the complicated questions of the interrelationships between the exodus, wilderness, and Deuteronomy narratives, on the other. Instead, interpreters are paying closer attention to the formal literary features of the text, particularly the so-called *tôlĕdôt* formulas: *ʾēlleh tôlĕdôt* PN, "these are the generations of PN," that appear throughout Genesis in 2:4; 5:1; 6:9; 10:1; 11:10, 27; 25:12, 19; 36:1; 37:2 and in Num 3:1 as introductions to narrative blocks that recount the histories of the descendants of the party named in the *tôlĕdôt* formula.[26] Of less concern for the present discussion is the related focus on the so-called itinerary formulas in Exodus–Numbers that recount the movement of Israel by stages from Egypt through the wilderness and on to the border of the land of Israel in Moab and that play an important role in discerning the formal literary structure of Exodus–Deuteronomy. When the structural role of the *tôlĕdôt* formula is taken into consideration, the formal literary structure of Genesis and the Pentateuch at large emerges as a history that traces the early history of

Israel/Judah and its Levitical priesthood in twelve major segments from the time of creation and within the larger context of the history of humankind. The progressively focused narrative begins with Adam and Eve as the descendants of the creation of heaven and earth (see Gen 2:4), and it continues with the descendants of Adam (Gen 5:1); Noah (6:9); the sons of Noah (10:1); Shem (11:10); Terah (11:27); Ishmael (25:12); Isaac (25:19); Esau (36:1); Jacob (37:12); and Aaron and Moses (Num 3:1). By culminating with the descendants of Aaron and Moses, the pentateuchal narrative points to the emergence of YHWH's sanctuary and priesthood within Israel—and thus within humankind—as the holy center of the creation that is first described in Gen 1:1–2:3. The pentateuchal narrative at large must therefore be recognized generically as a saga, insofar as it constitutes a long, prose narrative with an episodic structure developed around stereotyped themes or objects. Insofar as those themes or objects include the formation of the people of Israel around YHWH's sanctuary within the context of creation, the pentateuchal narrative might best be termed a saga or history of creation focused on the formation of the people of Israel. The following diagram illustrates the resulting literary structure of Genesis and the Pentateuch at large, and it takes account of the itinerary formulae in the substructure of Exodus–Deuteronomy:[27]

Synchronic Literary Structure of the Pentateuch:
Saga/History of Creation: Formation of People Israel

A.	Creation of Heaven and Earth	Gen 1:1–2:3
B.	Human Origins	Gen 2:4–4:26
C.	Human Development/Problems	Gen 5:1–6:8
D.	Noah and the Flood	Gen 6:9–9:29
E.	Spread of Humans over the Earth	Gen 10:1–11:9
F.	History of the Semites	Gen 11:10–26
G.	History of Abraham (Isaac)	Gen 11:27–25:11
H.	History of Ishmael	Gen 25:12–18
I.	History of Jacob (Isaac)	Gen 25:19–35:29
J.	History of Esau	Gen 36:1–37:1
K.	History of the Twelve Tribes of Israel	Gen 37:2–Num 2:34
	1. Joseph and His Brothers in Egypt	Gen 37:2–50:26
	2. Deliverance from Egyptian Bondage: Rameses	Exod 1:1–12:36

	3. From Rameses to Succoth: Consecration of Firstborn	Exod 12:37–13:19
	4. From Succoth to Etham: Pillar of Fire and Cloud	Exod 13:20–22
	5. From Etham to the Sea (Pi-hahiroth/ Baal-zephon): Deliverance at Sea	Exod 14:1–15:21
	6. From Reed Sea to Wilderness of Shur/ Elim: Water in Wilderness	Exod 15:22–27
	7. From Elim to Wilderness of Sin: Quails and Manna	Exod 16:1–36
	8. From Sin to Rephidim: Amalek and Jethro	Exod 17:1–18:27
	9. From Rephidim to Sinai: Revelation of Torah	Exod 19:1–Num 10:10
	a. Arrival at Sinai	Exod 19:1–2
	b. Revelation from mountain: Ten Commandments; Covenant Code; building of the tabernacle	Exod 19:3–40:38
	c. Revelation from tabernacle: laws of sacrifice and Holiness Code	Lev 1–27
	d. Census and organization of people around tabernacle	Num 1:1–2:34
L.	History of Israel under the Guidance of the Levites	Num 3:1–Deut 34:12
	1. Sanctification of the People Led by the Levites	Num 3:1–10:10
	2. From Sinai to Wilderness of Paran/ Kibroth-hattaavah: Rebellion in the Wilderness	Num 10:11–11:35a
	3. From Kibroth-hattaavah to Hazeroth	Num 11:35a–12:15
	4. From Hazeroth to the Wilderness of Paran	Num 12:16–19:22
	5. From Paran to Wilderness of Zin/ Kadesh: Water from Rock	Num 20:1–21
	6. From Zin/Kadesh to Mount Hor: Death of Aaron	Num 20:22–21:3
	7. From Mount Hor to Edom/Moab: Defeat of Sihon and Og	Num 21:4–35

8.	Arrival at Moab: Balaam; Census and Organization of People	Num 22:1–36:13
9.	Moses' Final Address to Israel: Repetition of the Torah	Deut 1:1–34:12

When the formal literary character of the Pentateuch is taken into consideration, it is clear that the endangered matriarch narratives appear within a much broader literary context concerned with the formation of Israel. In order to determine the function of each narrative within that broader context, discussion must turn to the analysis of each narrative.

Genesis 12:9–20 appears within the context of 11:27–25:11, which recounts the history of the descendants of Terah: Abraham and his wife Sarah. Although many interpreters define the unit as Gen 12:10–13:1, this definition is based on a diachronic construction of the narrative as an element of the J stratum. Although such a view is likely correct, synchronic analysis points to Gen 12:9 as the introduction to the present episode and 13:1 as the introduction to the following episode insofar as both verses signal the movement of the ancestral figures from the land of Israel to Egypt and back again.

Genesis 12:9–20 constitutes an episode that focuses on the question of the endangered matriarch in Egypt. Following Coats, the narrative may be classified generically as a tale, insofar as it displays a relatively short and simple plot based upon a tension and its resolution. The formal literary structure of the narrative begins with an introduction Gen 12:9, which signals Abram's and Sarai's travel in the Negev. The second major subunit of the narrative then turns to the exposition of tension in three parts: Gen 12:10 recounts famine in the land of Canaan, which prompts Abram and Sarai to move to Egypt; Gen 12:11–13 recounts Abram's fear of the Egyptians and his request to Sarai that she identify herself as his sister rather than as his wife so that his life will be spared; and Gen 12:14–16 recounts the actions of the Egyptians in taking Sarai for Pharaoh's harem and in rewarding Abram handsomely for his new status in relation to the royal court. The third major subunit of the narrative in Gen 12:17–20 focuses on resolution of the tensions, when Pharaoh, responding to the plagues unleashed against Egypt by YHWH, questions Abram and learns Sarai's true status as Abram's wife and then expels both of them from Egypt together with their possessions under military escort.

Several features of this narrative must be considered. First, the initial threat comes from YHWH, and it is directed to Abram and Sarai in the form of a famine in the land of Israel that calls into question all of YHWH's promises in the preceding episode (Gen 12:1–8) that Abram will become a great nation. If they die of starvation, there will be no great nation. Second, the next threat comes from the Egyptians. Whether justified or not, Abram clearly believes that the Egyptians will kill him to take his wife and concocts the ruse that she is his sister because of his perception of that threat. Third, the threat to Sarai does not include any possibility of bodily harm. As part of Pharaoh's harem, she is in the safest possible place for her in the world. When viewed from the perspective of a patriarchal society, Abram has sacrificed his own interests and honor to protect his wife. The danger to Sarai does not lie in the potential for bodily harm. Rather, it lies in the potential identity of her descendants as Egyptian sons of Pharaoh and the implications such births would have for the promises made by YHWH to Abram and Sarai in Gen 12:1–8. Although many interpreters charge Abram with acting churlishly to place his wife in danger so that he might become rich, there is no indication that he acts to enrich himself. His statement to Sarai in verse 13 that she should identify herself as his sister so that "it may go well with me because of you" immediately precedes his statement, "and that I may remain alive because of you." Abram fears for his life, first from YHWH and now from Pharaoh. With Sarai safely placed in the royal harem, Abram now turns to the question of survival. Even if he dies, Sarai will remain safe, but if he lives, he might still have a chance to recover her. In the end, he does so through divine intervention.

But the major result of the resolution of the tensions in this narrative must be recognized. Sarai's children will not be Egyptian but Israelite. Indeed, the literary context makes the importance of this outcome clear. The narrative has already noted Sarai's barrenness (Gen 11:30) immediately before articulating YHWH's promises to Abram that he will become a great nation in 12:1–8. The narrative will continue with Abram's vision of Israel's subjugation to Egypt and YHWH's deliverance in 15:13–16, again in the context of YHWH's promises of descendants and land. Genesis 16 and 21 will again raise the question of Abram's descendants, insofar as his first son, Ishmael, is born to him by the Egyptian handmaiden, Hagar, before his son Isaac is finally born to him by Sarah. Throughout the Abraham and Sarah narratives, the question of the identity of their descendants is paramount: Will they have descendants? And will their descendants be Egyptian, whether born to Sarah or to Abraham? The narrative in Gen 12:9–20 plays an important role in raising questions concerning the character of Abraham's and Sarah's descendants—and indeed YHWH's promise that they will become a great nation—in the broader context of Gen 11:27–25:11.

When considered diachronically, Gen 12:9–20 (or 12:10–13:1) must be placed in the historical setting of the late monarchic period of the seventh century B.C.E., when Egypt emerged as the major threat to Judah following the decline of the Assyrian Empire.

Genesis 20:1–18 likewise appears as an episode in the larger narrative block concerning the descendants of Terah in 11:27–25:11, although it appears much later in the narrative sequence. The setting for the encounter has shifted from Egypt to Gerar, presumed to be located in the western Negev near Philistine Gaza, and the identity of the foreign monarch has shifted from the pharaoh of Egypt to King Abimelech of Gerar. Again, the narrative may be characterized generically as a tale, although it is ascribed to the E stratum of the Pentateuch, and many interpreters note the presence of prophetic influence. The formal literary structure of the narrative begins with the introduction in Gen 20:1, which notes Abraham's journey to Gerar in the Negev. The tension of the narrative emerges in the second major unit in 20:2, when Abraham instructs Sarah without any explanation to identify herself as his sister, prompting Abimelech to send for her, presumably so that he might marry her. The third major unit appears in 20:3–18, which resolves the narrative tension in three subunits: 20:3–7, in which G-d appears to Abimelech to inform him that Sarah is Abraham's wife before Abimelech has the opportunity to touch her; 20:8–13, in which Abimelech demands an explanation from Abraham, who only then expresses his fear of death at the hands of nation that does not fear G-d; and 20:14–18, in which Abimelech restores Sarah to Abraham and grants him wealth and land, prompting Abraham to pray to G-d on Abimelech's and Gerar's behalf to restore the birth of children to the land.

Interpreters tend to focus on the interpretative aspects of this narrative, insofar as it explains Abraham's deception in Gen 12:9–20 by pointing out that Sarah is actually his half-sister. Nevertheless, the reconsideration of the dating of the pentateuchal strata suggests that Gen 20:1–18 might actually be the oldest narrative and that 12:9–20 might have been deliberately composed to raise narrative tension to highlight questions concerning YHWH's promises to Abraham. As for Gen 20, the questions of Abraham's fear and Sarah's descendants remain paramount. Genesis 20 makes it clear that Abraham's fears are unfounded: Abimelech and the people of Gerar fear G-d, much as Pharaoh proves to do in Gen 12:9–20.

Again, Sarah would be protected as a woman in the royal harem, but the identity of her descendants again comes into question. Following upon the Sodom-Gomorrah narratives in Gen 18–19, Gen 20 raises the question of Sarah's descendants immediately after YHWH has reiterated intentions to grant her a son even though she is an old woman. Finally, of course, Gen 20 appears immediately prior to Gen 21, in which Isaac is finally born. Like Gen 12:9–20, Gen 20 provokes narrative tension over the question as to whether YHWH will fulfill promises to grant Abraham and Sarah a son and thereby to fulfill the promise to make them a great nation.

As for the diachronic dimensions of this narrative, Gen 20 appears to reflect tensions on the borders of Israel/Judah and Philistia in the late ninth and early eighth centuries B.C.E., when Libnah (and Edom) revolted against Judah during the reign of Joram ben Jehoshaphat (2 Kgs 8:22), and Hazael of Aram captured Gath, which would prompt the Philistines to free themselves from Judean control, prior to his attack against Jerusalem during the reign of Jehoash ben Amaziah (2 Kgs 12:18–19). In both cases, the Judean kings were vassals of Israel at the time.

Genesis 26 appears as an episode within the context of the account of the generations of Isaac in 25:19–35:29. This block of material concludes with the death of Isaac, but it focuses especially on Isaac's sons, Jacob and Esau. Jacob, of course, becomes the dominant figure for the future of Israel, whereas Esau will marry Hittite women and become the ancestor of Edom. The endangered matriarch and wife-sister motif narrative appears as part of a larger narrative framework that examines the tensions in Isaac's relations with the Philistines and his role in founding major Judean cities in the Negev, such as Beer-sheba, Esek, Sitnah, and Rehoboth. The narrative may again be classified generically as a tale, although the tensions and resolutions of this unit encompass far more than only the endangered matriarch or wife-sister motif. The formal literary structure of the text is determined by the movement of its major characters. Genesis 26:1–17 discusses Isaac's move to Gerar in 26:1–5 and his continued sojourn there in 26:6–17; his move to the wadi of Gerar in 26:18–21; his move to Rehoboth in 26:22; his move to Beer-sheba in 26:23–33; and the concluding notice of Esau's marriage to two Hittite women.

Noteworthy concerns in Gen 26:1–17 include YHWH's reiteration of the promises to make Isaac into a great nation and the jealousy of the Philistines over Isaac's success, which would provoke the water disputes that appear throughout the balance of the narrative. The subunit concerning the endangered matriarch or wife-sister motif in 26:6–11 never actually places Rebekah in danger, although the narrative does emphasize Isaac's fears as the motivation for his action. His fears prove to be unfounded when Abimelech recognizes that Rebekah is Isaac's wife and decrees that Isaac and Rebekah are not to be molested, but royal decree ultimately proves to be a major factor in the Philistines' jealousy of Isaac. When Isaac prospers as a result of YHWH's promises and Abimelech's protection, the Philistines stop up the wells, which prompts Isaac to leave. The subsequent units of the narrative focus on the tensions between Isaac and the Philistines as he moves from place to place to escape their efforts to thwart his success by stopping up his wells until Abimelech comes to him to settle the matter. As part of the resolution of their relationship, Abimelech affirms YHWH's blessing as a factor in Isaac's success.

Although Rebekah is never taken as wife by Abimelech or the other Philistines, the threat of such an outcome underlies the narrative. Because the narrative appears immediately after Gen 25:19–34, which discusses the birth of her sons, Esau and Jacob, the identity of her children does not come into question. Thus, the question of the identity of Rebekah's children becomes a more distant question, but one that is nevertheless present in the narrative. The placement of the brief notice concerning Esau's marriages to Hittite women at the conclusion of the narrative signals a larger concern with the identity of the progeny of Isaac. Indeed, the tensions between Esau and Jacob are at least temporarily resolved in the following narratives when Rebekah sends Jacob to Haran in order to find a wife from his extended family instead of from the Hittite women, as Esau had done (see Gen 27:46). The question of Isaac's and Rebekah's progeny through Jacob is ultimately resolved in a satisfactory matter, but the larger narrative makes it clear that the question of their progeny through Esau is not.

The diachronic background of this J narrative, which is clearly aware of Gen 12:9–20 (see 26:1), would lie in the movement of the Judean population away from Philistia and into the Negev in the seventh century B.C.E., when Judah began to build up major Negev sites, such as Beer-sheba, Tel Ira, Tell Masos, and others.

The narrative concerning the rape of Dinah in Gen 34 differs markedly from the wife-sister narratives already considered insofar as Dinah is the first matriarchal figure actually to suffer harm when she is raped by Shechem son of Hamor. The narrative may be classified once again as a tale, although Coats notes the presence of other generic elements.[28] The literary structure of the narrative focuses on the initial tension: the rape of

Dinah and Shechem's proposal to marry her in 34:1–3; continued tension in expressed throughout 34:4–24, when Hamor and Shechem come to negotiate the terms of the marriage; the resolution of the issue in 34:25–29, when Simeon and Levi kill the Shechemites for the outrage committed against their sister; and the introduction of a new source of tension, when Jacob upbraids his sons for their action. The wife-sister motif is not explicit, although readers should note the emphasis placed on her identity as the sister of Simeon and Levi, who ultimately kill the Shechemites and take their property for the crime perpetrated against their sister. Readers should also note the emphasis placed on Shechem's desire to marry Dinah following the rape and thus the potential that she might become a wife. Thus, the question of Dinah's progeny and her potential marriage to a Canaanite man remain of paramount concern throughout the narrative. This concern appears together with the immoral character of the Canaanites who would allow such an outrage to take place and the possibility that such a people would become a part of Israel by circumcising themselves so that a marriage could take place.

But a key element is Jacob's silence throughout the narrative in the face of his daughter's rape. As the patriarchal figure and father of Dinah, he is responsible for her welfare and protection. Traditional Jewish commentators have noted his failure to supervise his daughter when she went out to visit the daughters of the land, leaving her in a position in which the rape could take place.[29] Jacob's silence following the rape and his at least implied acquiescence to a marriage with the perpetrator also raises questions about his exercise of paternal authority and his concern for the welfare of his own daughter. The narrative does not mention Dinah again, so readers never learn if she ever married or had children. But this narrative appears immediately prior to the narratives concerning Jacob's return to Bethel, YHWH's reiteration of the covenant promises to him, and the death of his beloved wife Rachel while giving birth to Benjamin. It also notes Reuben's act of lying with Bilhah, his father's concubine, to illustrate the fact that there are continued problems within the family of Jacob. Indeed, these problems will emerge once again in the narrative block of Gen 37:2–Num 2:34, in which the Joseph narratives of Gen 37:2–50:26 will figure so prominently.

Genesis 34 is a J narrative, which indicates that its diachronic background may be found in Judean critiques of northern Israel, which would focus on Jacob as the patriarchal figure most closely associated with the north, during the late monarchic period. Jacob is an inadequate father, and this has consequences for the future of his children.

The narrative concerning Tamar in Gen 38 appears within the context of the account of the generations of Jacob in Gen 37:2–Num 2:34, within the segment in Gen 37:2–50:26 devoted to Joseph. Commentators have struggled to ascertain why this narrative appears in its present position, immediately following the introductory exposition of Joseph's character and his strained relationship with his brothers in Gen 37:2–36, who were ultimately responsible for his sale into Egyptian slavery. But interpreters note that Judah's efforts to talk his brothers out of their original plan to kill Joseph (Gen 37:25–27) might justify the focus on Judah in the Tamar narrative. Indeed, Judah's efforts to save Benjamin from Joseph later in the Joseph narrative would also play a role.

Again, Gen 38 is not the typical endangered matriarch or wife-sister narrative seen above in Gen 12; 20; and 26. Nevertheless, Tamar is a matriarch who is placed in danger, although the danger is somewhat more subtle. Tamar is married to Er son of Judah, who was born of a Canaanite mother. When Er dies, Tamar is given to his brother Onan, also born of the Canaanite mother, who dies after refusing fully to consummate the levirate marriage with Tamar. Although Tamar is to be married to Shelah, the third son of Judah and Shua, when he grows up, Tamar sees that Judah does not follow through in arranging the levirate marriage, prompting her to take action on her own. In order to see to the proper disposition of the levirate marriage, she disguises herself as a prostitute, has relations with Judah, and ultimately gives birth to a son.

Coats describes the genre of the narrative as a novella, apparently under the influence of his decision to label the entire Joseph narrative a novella,[30] but the relatively limited scope of the Tamar narrative indicates that it is simply another tale. Its formal literary structure includes an introduction in 38:1–5, which describe the births of Judah's sons to Shua, a Canaanite woman; 38:6–11, which describes tension in the narrative when Judah's sons die before having a son with Tamar; 38:12–23, in which Tamar resolves the issue by disguising herself so that she might have relations with Judah to produce a son; 38:24–26, in which the situation is resolved when Judah recognizes Tamar's righteousness and his own failure to act properly in the matter; and the conclusion in 38:27–30, which relate the births of Tamar's twin sons to Judah.

The significance of this narrative in relation to the narrative context of Genesis becomes evident when the identities of Judah's sons are compared to those of Joseph much later in the narrative. Although Tamar's ethnicity is never named, the Canaanite identity of Shua, Judah's first wife, is made clear. Judah's sons are therefore born of a Canaanite woman, making YHWH's displeasure with Er and Onan's despicable actions clear in the minds of Israelite or Judean readers. The failure to mention Tamar's identity suggests that she is Israelite/Judean, insofar as she presents no problem. Following the deaths of Judah's half-Canaanite sons, Tamar's actions ensure that Judah has Israelite/Judean progeny.

The identities of Judah's sons through Tamar stand in striking contrast to those of Joseph. Interpreters rightly focus on Joseph's efforts to overcome the challenging circumstances in which he is placed and his maturation from the self-centered adolescent of Gen 37 into the judicious leader of Egypt and of his brothers in the subsequent development of the narrative. But as part of Joseph's "success story," he marries an Egyptian woman, Asenath daughter of Potiphera, priest of On, which would make his sons Manasseh and Ephraim half-Egyptian (Gen 41:45; 46:20). The narrative recognizes the problem and attempts to resolve the issue by portraying Jacob's adoption of Joseph's sons prior to his death (48:8–20).

Although Jacob's adoption of Joseph's half-Egyptian sons would seemingly resolve any problems associated with their identity, readers must recognize that Joseph and Jacob, the leading patriarchal figures of their time, have now done what Abraham and Sarah and Isaac and Rebekah avoided despite the repeated threats of marriage into the Egyptian and Philistine royal families: Joseph marries into an Egyptian priestly family at the behest of Pharaoh, and his sons are formally accepted by Jacob, who adopts them as his own.

But the matter is not one of simple family relations. Joseph (as well as Jacob) is the eponymous ancestor of the northern kingdom of Israel, which was built around the central tribes of Ephraim and Manasseh. Judah is the eponymous ancestor of the tribe of Judah and thus of the southern kingdom of Judah, which becomes the central component of the nation of Israel after the destruction of the northern kingdom. Judah's descendants ultimately survive as the southern kingdom of Judah even beyond the Babylonian exile; Joseph's descendants, who become the core of the northern kingdom of Israel, do not survive in any meaningful or recognizable form beyond the Assyrian destruction.

When the diachronic character of Gen 38 is considered, the issue is even more pronounced. As a J narrative, Gen 38 constitutes an element of the J redaction of the underlying E Joseph novella in the late monarchic period. The redaction highlights Judah's leadership role both when he faces Reuben in attempting to save Joseph from death at the hands of his brothers and against Simeon when he acts as guardian and protector of Benjamin during the audience with Joseph. The placement of the Tamar narrative in the Joseph novella makes an important polemical point: Joseph, or the northern kingdom of Israel, is compromised by the Egyptian identity of the core sons/tribes, which underlies the syncretistic character of northern Israel as portrayed in biblical sources. Judah, although threatened with similar tendencies as exemplified by Judah's first marriage, is saved from such compromise and can emerge as the heir to the covenant with Abraham and Sarah (and Isaac and Rebekah), who for their own part avoided such compromise despite the many challenges that they faced.

Conclusion

As this case study shows, contemporary form-critical theory differs markedly from early expressions of the methodology in the early through mid-twentieth century. Whereas earlier form critics such as Gunkel tended to focus on short, self-contained texts in an effort to reconstruct the earliest oral stages of the development of a text, the influence of literary studies and text linguistics in particular have prompted form-critical analyses to take account of a much broader textual purview: the place and function of individual texts in their larger literary context. While past form critics struggled to discern the place and function of the so-called endangered matriarch or wife-sister texts in Genesis, contemporary form-critical theory enables interpreters to recognize that the endangered matriarch motif includes texts beyond the three wife-sister narratives in Gen 12; 20; and 26 to include the rape of Dinah in Gen 34 and the Tamar-Judah narrative in Gen 38 as well. The method also enables interpreters to discern the function of these texts in their larger literary setting: they function to highlight the question of the social, religious, and ethnic identities of the progeny of the ancestors in relation to YHWH's promises that the descendants of the ancestors will become a great nation in relation to YHWH. Furthermore, the analysis highlights a polemical factor. The ancestors and their descendants through Judah, which eventually formed the core of the southern kingdom of Judah, were able to protect the identity of the people by avoiding intermarriage with the Egyptians, Philistines, and other Canaanite peoples, whereas the descendants through Joseph, who would eventually form the core of the northern kingdom of Israel, were descended from Egyptians, with consequences for the religious integrity of the northern Israelite kingdom in later times.

For Further Reading

Buss, Martin J. *Biblical Form Criticism in its Context*. JSOTSup 274. Sheffield: Sheffield Academic Press, 1999.

Hayes, John H., ed. *Old Testament Form Criticism*. San Antonio, Tex.: Trinity University Press, 1974.

Knierim, Rolf. "Old Testament Form Criticism Reconsidered." *Int* 27 (1973): 435–68.

Koch, Klaus. *The Growth of the Biblical Tradition: The Form-Critical Method*. Translated by S. M. Cupitt. New York: Scribner, 1969.

Sweeney, Marvin A. "Form Criticism." Pages 227–41 in *Dictionary of the Old Testament Wisdom, Poetry and Writings*. Edited by Tremper Longman III and Peter Enns. Downers Grove, Ill.: InterVarsity Press, 2008.

Sweeney, Marvin A., and Ehud Ben Zvi, eds. *The Changing Face of Form Criticism for the Twenty-First Century*. Grand Rapids: Eerdmans, 2003.

Tucker, Gene M. *Form Criticism of the Old Testament*. GBS. Philadelphia: Fortress, 1971.

Notes

1. The theoretical portions of this paper are adapted and revised from my "Form Criticism," in *Dictionary of the Old Testament Wisdom, Poetry and Writings* (ed. Tremper Longman III and Peter Enns; Downers Grove, Ill.: InterVarsity Press, 2008), 227–41. For additional discussion of form-critical theory, see Marvin A. Sweeney, "Form Criticism," in *To Each Its Own Meaning: An Introduction to Biblical Criticisms and Their Applications* (ed. Steven L. McKenzie and Stephen R. Haynes; Louisville: Westminster John Knox, 1999), 58–89; Marvin A. Sweeney and Ehud Ben Zvi, eds., *The Changing Face of Form Criticism for the Twenty-First Century* (Grand Rapids: Eerdmans, 2003); Martin J. Buss, *Biblical Form Criticism in Its Context* (JSOTSup 274; Sheffield: Sheffield Academic Press, 1999); John H. Hayes, ed., *Old Testament Form Criticism* (San Antonio, Tex.: Trinity University Press, 1974); Rolf Knierim, "Old Testament Form Criticism Reconsidered," *Int* 27 (1973): 435–68; idem, "Criticism of Literary Features, Form, Tradition, and Redaction," in *The Hebrew Bible and Its Modern Interpreters* (ed. Douglas Knight and Gene M. Tucker; BMI 1; Chico, Calif.: Scholars Press, 1985), 123–65; Klaus Koch, *The Growth of the Biblical Tradition: The Form-Critical Method* (trans. S. M. Cupitt; New York: Scribner, 1969); idem, *Was Ist Formgeschcihte? Methoden der Bibelexegese* (Neukirchen-Vluyn: Neukirchener, 1974); Gene M. Tucker, *Form Criticism of the Old Testament* (Philadelphia: Fortress, 1971).

2. David L. Petersen, "A Thrice-Told Tale: Genre, Theme, and Motif," *BR* 18 (1973): 30–43.

3. See, e.g., Claus Westermann, *Basic Forms of Prophetic Speech* (trans. Hugh C. White; repr. with new foreword by Gene M. Tucker; Louisville: Westminster John Knox, 1991).

4. For discussion of the communicative and rhetorical functions of biblical texts, see esp. Phyllis Trible, *Rhetorical Criticism: Context, Method, and the Book of Jonah* (Minneapolis: Fortress, 1994); Patricia K. Tull, "Rhetorical Criticism and Intertextuality," in McKenzie and Haynes, *To Each Its Own Meaning*, 156–80.

5. For discussion of the linguistic character of Biblical Hebrew texts, see esp. Harald Schweizer, *Metaphorische Grammatik: Wege zur Integration von Grammatik und Textinterpretation in der Exegese* (Arbeiten zu Text und Sprache im Alten Testament 15; St. Ottilien: EOS, 1981).

6. Marvin A. Sweeney, "Legend," *NIDB* 3:631–33; see also George W. Coats, *Genesis, with an Introduction to Narrative Literature* (FOTL 1; Grand Rapids: Eerdmans, 1981), 206–9, 318.

7. Marvin A. Sweeney, *Isaiah 1–39, with an Introduction to Prophetic Literature* (FOTL 16; Grand Rapids: Eerdmans, 1996), 542.

8. See esp. John Van Seters, *Prologue to History: The Yahwist as Historian in Genesis* (Louisville: Westminster John Knox, 1992), 1–103. See also his *The Life of Moses: The Yahwist as Historian in Exodus–Numbers* (Louisville: Westminster John Knox, 1994).

9. See David M. Carr, *Writing on the Tablet of the Heart: Origins of Scripture and Literature* (Oxford: Oxford University Press, 2005), who lays the groundwork for such study.

10. For contemporary discussion of pentateuchal research, see Ernest Nicholson, *The Pentateuch in the Twentieth Century: The Legacy of Julius Wellhausen* (Oxford: Oxford University Press, 1998); Joseph Blenkinsopp, *The Pentateuch: An Introduction to the First Five Books of the Bible* (New York: Doubleday, 1992); Jean-Louis Ska, *Introduction to Reading the Pentateuch* (trans. Pascale Dominique; Winona Lake, Ind.: Eisenbrauns, 2006); Thomas P. Dozeman and Konrad Schmid, *A Farewell to the Yahwist? The Composition of the Pentateuch in Recent European Interpretation* (SBLSymS 34; Atlanta: Society of Biblical Literature, 2006).

11. E.g., Israel Knohl, *The Sanctuary of Silence: The Priestly Torah and the Holiness School* (Minneapolis: Fortress, 1995).

12. See esp. the work of Van Seters, *Prologue to History*; *The Life of Moses*.

13. For discussion of the impact of the *Sitz im Literatur* in form-critical research, see esp. Wolfgang Richter, *Exegese als Literaturwissenschaft: Entwurf eineralttestamentlichen Literaturtheorie und Methologie* (Göttingen: Vandenhoeck & Ruprecht, 1971).

14. See, e.g., Robert Alter, *The Art of Biblical Narrative* (New York: Basic Books, 1981); Meir Sternberg, *The Poetics of Biblical Narrative: Ideological Literature and the Drama of Reading* (Bloomington: Indiana University Press, 1985).

15. See my "Puns, Politics, and Perushim in the Jacob Cycle: A Case Study in Teaching the English Hebrew Bible," *Shofar* 9 (1991): 103–18.

16. For major commentaries, see Hermann Gunkel, *Genesis* (trans. Mark E. Biddle: Macon, Ga.: Mercer University Press, 1997); Gerhard von Rad, *Genesis: A*

Commentary (trans. W. L. Jenkins; rev. ed.; OTL; Philadelphia: Westminster, 1972); Claus Westermann, *Genesis 12–36: A Commentary* (trans. John J. Scullion; CC; Minneapolis: Augsburg, 1985); idem, *Genesis 37–50: A Commentary* (trans. John J. Scullion; CC; Minneapolis: Augsburg, 1986); Coats, *Genesis*.

17. Petersen, "A Thrice-Told Tale."

18. Hermann Gunkel, *Genesis* (1901; repr.; Göttingen: Vandenhoeck & Ruprecht, 1977), 168–69, 225–26 ; see also the English edition of Gunkel, *Genesis* (1997), 168, 223–25, which translates German *Sage* as "legend." On the problems of these terms, see my "Legend," *NIDB* 3:631–33; "Saga," *NIDB*, forthcoming. For discussion of saga, see also Coats, *Genesis*, 319.

19. Gunkel, *Genesis* (1977), 220, where he labels Gen 20 a *Sage*, but cf. 226, where he labels it a *Legende*; see also Gunkel, *Genesis* (1997), 218. For discussion of legend, see also Coats, *Genesis*, 318.

20. Gunkel, *Genesis* (1997), 224, 293–94.

21. Koch, *Growth of the Biblical Tradition*, 120; idem, *Was Ist Formgeschcihte*, 145–49.

22. Westermann, *Genesis 12–36*, 161–62.

23. Von Rad, *Genesis*, 167–68, 226, 269–70; Martin Noth, *A History of Pentateuchal Traditions* (trans. Bernard W. Anderson; Englewood Cliffs, N.J.: Prentice-Hall, 1972), 22–23.

24. Coats, *Genesis*, 109–13.

25. Petersen, "A Thrice-Told Tale."

26. See, e.g., Frank Moore Cross Jr., "The Priestly Work," in idem, *Canaanite Myth and Hebrew Epic* (Cambridge: Harvard University Press, 1973), 293–325; Matthew Thomas, "These Are the Generations: Identity, Promise, and the Toledoth Formulae" (Ph.D. diss.; Claremont Graduate University, 2006); Marvin A. Sweeney, *Reading the Hebrew Bible after the Shoah: Engaging Holocaust Theology* (Minneapolis: Fortress, 2008).

27. Sweeney, *Reading the Hebrew Bible*.

28. Coats, *Genesis*, 235.

29. See Nahum Sarna, *Genesis* (JPS Torah Commentary; Philadelphia: Jewish Publication Society, 1989/5749), 233, who makes similar observations but does not cite the traditional sources.

30. Coats, *Genesis*, 274–75.

Source Criticism: The Miracle at the Sea

Christoph Levin

Definition of the Method

"Source criticism" is the name given to the analytical method that, starting from the (more or less) final form of the text as it can be reconstructed from transmitted textual versions, goes on to enquire about the preliminary literary stages. Strictly speaking, source criticism is not a single method, in the sense of a precisely defined text-analytical technique. It is an approach that scans the surface of today's text in order to discover its historical deep structure, insofar as this has developed in the course of the literary transmission. Earlier oral stages are not necessarily excluded, but they are reconstructed in a different way, particularly on the basis of their genres and their *Sitz im Leben*.

Like all established exegetical methods, source criticism has a long history. At its beginning—as it is today—source criticism was prompted by the conspicuous phenomena in the text that inescapably demanded an explanation, such as unmotivated repetitions, irregular grammar, a change in linguistic usage, a sudden mingling of different genres, the interruption of one and the same speech through multiple introductions, and so forth. The variants in the transmitted text not infrequently reflect disturbances originating in its literary history that have been solved by the different textual traditions in various ways.

In the last 250 years, biblical scholars have learned with increasing clarity that a text that displays irregularities of this kind does not, as a rule, derive from a single author's intention. Rather, such a text reflects a process of literary growth, in the course of which many hands worked on it from varying viewpoints until it arrived at its present form. Long before the critical thrust of modern times, there were indications that the traditional view that the Torah was written by Moses could not be correct—any more than that the Psalms were written by David, the wisdom books by Solomon, and the prophetic books by the prophets under whose names they go.

In the book of Genesis, people became aware of literary incoherence because there are noticeably double accounts that use different names for God: two accounts of creation; double genealogies in Gen 4–5 and 10–11; two interwoven but opposing versions in the story of the flood; two great promises to Abraham in Gen 17–18; two accounts of the danger to Sarah (Gen 12; 20); and more. The initial explanation was a naïve one: it was suggested that Moses had had recourse to older sources—that is to say, that he had worked not just as an author but as an editor, too.[1] Though the initial explanation has not survived, the premise that Moses himself used written sources still lives on in the term "source criticism."

Classifying texts based on the varying names given to God proved to be conclusive because texts separated on the basis of this criterion fit together into more or less coherent sequences. In this way the *Documentary Hypothesis* developed. According to this hypothesis, underlying the Pentateuch are at least two previously independent historical works. In spite of numerous attempts to replace it by other models, this hypothesis has held its ground for 250 years, down to the present day.

At the same time, there were good reasons for the alternatives that were put forward. The Documentary Hypothesis on its own is not sufficient. The text has far too many strata for it to be explained on the basis of only a few sources, and the comprehensive historical works are themselves based on sources of their own. Consequently, the *Fragmentary Hypothesis* can also claim to be correct to some degree. We can assume that in the historical works many short individual texts have been collected, many of which survive only in fragmentary form.

The basic presupposition of the literary analysis has to do with genre criticism: it is the presumption that the Old Testament as the traditional religious literature of the Jewish community of the Second Temple was not only transmitted and received but actually came into being as precisely that. Its beginnings were the holdings of the royal archives in Jerusalem, those texts that had survived the conquest of the city and had been preserved: relatively slim collections of prophetic sayings; cult poetry; wisdom sayings; collections of laws; annals; and stories that had been passed down at the court. In addition, soon after the downfall of the monarchy, the first two great compilations came into being as a way of coming to terms with the new situation. One, known today as the Deuteronomistic History, was the historical work that constitutes the nucleus of the books Joshua to Kings and that propagandizes the return of the Davidic monarchy.[2] The other was the history that forms the basis of Genesis, Exodus, parts of Numbers, and the close of Deuteronomy. This work, known as the Yahwist's History, grapples with the experience of the exile and dispersion.[3]

With this as its basis, the Old Testament in its present form developed over the course of the Persian and the Hellenistic periods. The guiding concern was to relate the transmitted text, which was understood as the word of God, to the changing conditions in the ongoing history of Judaism. This concern found expression through an innertextual interpretation that overlaid the already-existing material with commentary and increasingly expanded the text. In this way the Old Testament is to a great extent its own interpretation—we might say, a great midrash. The hypothesis that best does justice to this literary fact is the *Supplementary Hypothesis*.

The aforementioned growth generally followed no rules. That was in accordance with the material: a sacred text is not "made"; it is received from tradition and interpreted only for the needs of the present time. Redactional interventions such as organization and rearrangement of the written material were the exception. Occasionally scrolls that had become too large were split up, and texts that belonged together were amalgamated into greater conglomerations. It was only from the Hellenistic period onward that the text gradually crystallized into fixed form, beginning with the Torah. The process out of which the Old Testament emerged forbids us from seeing the final shape that the text reached in one or another linguistic form (Hebrew or Greek) as anything more than a provisional result, one that awaits further interpretation and contemporary reference.

The tradition—which in each given case provides the foundation for the literary process—was fundamentally sacrosanct; consequently, the scholar can work on the text like an archaeologist. If one clears away later strata, one can in each instance expect to come upon an older, intact form of the text.

In all work in the humanities, argument is to a certain degree circular. If there is progress in what we know, it develops in the form of a spiral. Work on the literary history of the Old Testament also proceeds from the decisions at which the field has previously arrived. These decisions have developed in the course of our scholarly tradition and rest on the experience of many generations of biblical scholars, but they are not a dogma. In work on an individual text, the decisions are continually reexamined, and their validity has to be tested.

The Miracle at the Sea

The story about the miracle at the sea in Exod 14 is one of the traditional examples that shows that the pentateuchal narrative has been put together from several sources. "The lack of unity in the account of the sea event has been recognized for well over a hundred years."[4] With the Documentary Hypothesis as a presupposition, from early on scholars generally accepted the separation of the narrative into two formerly independent strands of tradition. In 1869 Theodor Nöldeke summed up earlier research on this topic by indicating that Exod 14:1–4, 8, 9, 10 (in part), 15–18, 21 (in part), 22, 23, 26, 27 (in part), 28, 29 all belong to the "Basic Document," which we today call the Priestly Code.[5] With some small modifications, this classification still holds today.[6] The rest of the text was assigned to what we today call the Yahwist (or J, from the German *Jahwist*), which was considered the later source in the period before Karl Heinrich Graf (1867), Abraham Kuenen (1869), and Julius Wellhausen (1876).

The story about the miracle at the sea is also a good example of the literary-critical approach because it shows that the separation into two sources is too simple a solution to do justice to the complex nature of the text. This, too, was already realized in the nineteenth century. Hermann Hupfeld believed that he had additionally identified the "Elohist" as a third document,[7] so Julius Wellhausen was able to reckon with *three* sources. From verse 21 onward, he assigned to this Elohist the text that until then had been allocated to the Priestly Code.[8] Rudolf Smend Sr. went further still and disputed that the story included any part of the Priestly Code; instead, he differentiated between two levels (J^1 and J^2) within the Yahwistic text.[9] A three-source hypothesis would, of course, presuppose that the sources have been mutilated in the course of their amalgamation, since the number of repeated statements is not sufficient for three complete versions. This is a fundamental weakness of the three-source hypothesis; besides, there have always been good reasons for doubting the existence of the "Elohist."[10]

In spite of the considerable evidence suggesting the separation of the two sources—the Priestly Code and the Yahwist—we must not overlook the fact that the amalgamation of such parallel accounts is exceptional in the highest degree. It probably took place only once in the whole history of the Old Testament literature.[11] Its goal was to bring together two hitherto separate accounts of God's history with God's people in order to make its unity visible in literary terms as well.[12] If some external occasion was required for this literary synthesis, it could well be found in the development of the Jewish Diaspora. The religious community that had been dispersed throughout the world needed a common text to keep it together.[13]

The *normal* supposition about the literary history of the Old Testament, however, was the Supplementary Hypothesis. Abraham Kuenen already pointed to this with special emphasis. It also holds good for the Pentateuch. Literary additions can be found in almost every text. They can be brief explanations ad hoc, taking the form of marginal or interlinear glosses, which are even occasionally encountered as catchword glosses that are provided with lemmas. Frequently, however, the literary additions go back to more or less purposeful revisions that can also include more extensive literary complexes. This can best be shown by the following example.

The Supplementary Hypothesis (1): Late Revisions and Expansions

In the form in which it has been passed down, the story about the miracle at the sea cannot simply be distributed between two sources; for the version that emerged through the amalgamation of the Yahwist and the Priestly Code was extensively revised. Before the narrative is analyzed on the basis of the Documentary Hypothesis, the later expansions must be cleared away.

As a rule, additions of this kind are the work of many hands and introduce varying standpoints. We also, however, come across revisions with a deliberate aim. In the story about the miracle at the sea in Exod 13:17–18a, 22; 14:2 (only one word: *wĕyāšūbû*), 3, 11, (12), 14b, 19a, 25a, and 31, a shared tendency can be detected.[14]

> 13:17 When Pharaoh let the people go, God did not lead them by way of the land of the Philistines, although that was near, for God said, "Lest the people repent when they see war, and return to Egypt." 18a But God led the people round by the way of the wilderness toward the Reed Sea.
> 22 The pillar of cloud by day and the pillar of fire by night did not depart from before the people.
> 14:2 that they turn back
> 3 Pharaoh will say of the Israelites, "They are wandering aimlessly in the land; the wilderness has shut them in."
> 11 They said to Moses, "Was it because there were no graves in Egypt

> that you have taken us away to die in the wilderness? What have you done to us, taking us out of Egypt? [12 Is not this what we told you in Egypt would happen, when we said, 'Leave us alone; we will serve the Egyptians?' For it is better for us to serve the Egyptians than to die in the wilderness."]
> 14b Yet you may keep still.
> 19a The angel of God who went before the host of Israel moved and went behind them.
> 25a He <clogged>[15] the wheels of their chariot so that they drove heavily.
> 31 When Israel saw the great work that YHWH had done against the Egyptians, the people feared YHWH and had faith in YHWH and his servant Moses.[16]

The reason for this revision is that the Israelites call YHWH's promise into question and doubt his saving power.[17] This doubt has evidently befallen the contemporary Jewish community to whom the reviser addresses the revised text. Consequently, the reviser presents the event in such a way that the saving act that YHWH performed in early times proves that the doubt is unfounded: "When Israel saw the great work that YHWH had done against the Egyptians, the people feared YHWH and had faith in YHWH and his servant Moses" (v. 31). The intention is to strengthen the belief that YHWH is able to help in time of need. It is easy to see that this theological conclusion has been tagged on to the story at a later stage. Rudolf Smend Jr. notes that the beginning of this phrase ("When Israel saw") already appeared at the beginning of verse 30b, this noticeable doublet leading to the plausible conclusion that verse 31 is a postscript.[18] The linguistic usage suggests a very late origin.[19] As in Num 21:5, 7, the divine demonstration goes hand in hand with the rehabilitation of Moses.[20] What is at stake is not only God's power but also the credibility of his cultic and theological agents, who therefore comment on the text.

The doubts that are overcome by the end of the story are put into the mouths of the Israelites in verses 11–12. According to Erik Aurelius, "The complaint can be a later interpolation, inserted between v. 10 and 13; in this case vv. 13–14 would originally have been an answer not to 'murmuring' Israelites but only to fearful ones."[21] The peoples' complaint that Moses had led the Israelites out of Egypt so that they might die in the wilderness (*lāmût bammidbār*) does not refer to the immediate pursuit by the Egyptians but to the dangers of the march that are still to come: thirst and hunger (see 16:3; 17:3).[22] YHWH's help now also has the aim of silencing this complaint: *wĕʾattem taḥărîšûn* "yet you may keep still" (v. 14b).

In verse 12 the objection is even intensified. Doubt is replaced by negative certainty: "It is better for us to serve the Egyptians." That statement is tantamount to open rebellion, for the command "Let my people go that they may serve *me*" was given to Pharaoh again and again.[23] Now that the people have been freed, they are close to disclaiming the promise and returning to Egypt (see Num. 14:2–3). The verse is set apart as a further addition through the pointer *hălōʾ-zeh* "is not this" and the resumptive repetition *mimmutēnû bammidbār* "than to die in the wilderness."

Yet God's solicitous care for his people goes so far that he foresees their disobedience and prevents it. He does not lead them on the direct route, the Philistine road (*derek ʾereṣ pĕlištîm*), which would have brought them into certain conflict with the Philistines; he takes them through the desert to the Reed Sea, that is, to the Gulf of Aqabah (*derek hammidbār yam sûp*, 13:17–18a). God knew that, if faced with the belligerent Philistines, the Israelites would have been tempted to return to Egypt. So God forced them to make a detour far away to the southeast. In this way, the reviser simultaneously presents himself and his readers with a solution to the question as to why the wanderings of the Israelites did not take them straight from Egypt into the (west Jordan) land of Israel. The theologian writing here even sees himself in a position to pass on God's thoughts, word for word. The explanation, which begins with "a subordinate clause … which … serves as a connection,"[24] originally joined on to the departure described in Exod 12. It differs from the rest of the account in that it avoids the name of God (YHWH) and uses *Elohim* instead.

In order to combine the deviation with the events that follow, in 14:2 Moses has to be given the command to make the Israelites turn back again (*wĕyāšūbû*). At the same time, God uses the Israelites' detour as a way of deceiving Pharaoh, whose thoughts the reviser passes on in 14:3 in the same way as he does the thoughts of God in 13:17b.

In the same move, God's help is underlined. The explanations in 13:22 about the function of the pillar of cloud and fire emphasize the unceasing presence of God among his people. The repetitions of what has been said in 13:21a show that the verse is a later addition. In 14:19a *Elohim*'s angel has been added in the same way. Finally, YHWH's solicitude is also shown in 14:25a by the way he puts the Egyptian chariots out of action. Heinrich Holzinger contends that "14:25b joins on to 14:24; 14:27aβγb (from *wayyāšob* onwards) knows nothing about difficulties with the wheels but lets the Egyptians be driven to destruction in panic and wild flight."[25] Martin Noth adds, "Within this closely knit sequence of events the observation in v. 25a has a disruptive effect."[26]

The other late additions can less clearly be put down to a common thrust or intention:

> 13:18b And the Israelites went up out of the land of Egypt equipped for battle.
> 19 And Moses took the bones of Joseph with him, for Joseph had solemnly sworn the Israelites, saying, "God will visit you; then you must carry my bones with you from here."
> 21b That they might travel by day and by night.
> 14:5b The mind of Pharaoh and his servants was changed toward the people, and they said, "What is this that we have done in letting Israel go from serving us?"
> 7 He took six hundred choice chariots [and all the chariots of Egypt] with officers in charge of them all.
> 8b The Israelites were going forth defiantly.
> 20aβγ [And there was the cloud and the darkness.] And it gave light by night.

The explanation in 13:18b that the Israelites left Egypt *ḥămūšîm* "in parties of fifty" "has the character of a commentary."[27] This can be seen from the syntax, too, which deliberately puts the phrase outside the *consecutio temporum*. The number given, 600,000 men, is taken up from 12:37b and explained, perhaps in the sense of a military order. The participial clause in 14:8b is comparable, where it is said that the Israelites went out *bĕyād rāmâ* "with raised hand." Further, the details about the strength of the Egyptian troops in verse 7 could also belong to this context. The verse is "parallel to verse 6"[28] and adds that the chariots were six hundred in number, each of them carrying a team of three. The size of the pursuing force makes the defeat of the Egyptians all the greater. A further addition in verse 7aβ involves the *whole* chariot power of the Egyptians in the downfall.

The asyndetic infinitive clause in 13:21b ("so that they might travel by day and by night") offers an explanation about the pillar of cloud and fire. The possibility of marching day and night is a subsidiary aspect that was not originally intended. Further explanations of this kind can be found in 14:20aβγ, which wrenches apart the connection between 14:20aα and b. The syntax of these marginal exegeses, which present interpreters with a puzzle, is faulty.

On the occasion of the departure in 13:19, the bones of Joseph are mentioned in order to make it clear that the Israelites fulfilled the oath that they swore to Joseph in Gen 50:25. Moses, who is otherwise not mentioned, is the active subject. The factual continuation can be found in Josh 24:32.

Exodus 14:5b subsequently establishes a cross connection to the series of plagues.[29] That Pharaoh turns against the people is, according to Noth, "an extremely surprising statement after everything which we have been told up till now."[30] We could agree with Rudolf Smend Sr. when he claims, "The real follow up to v. 5a is v. 6: after hearing the news about the Israelites' flight, Pharaoh immediately sets out in pursuit."[31]

The Documentary Hypothesis: The Separation of the Yahwist's History and the Priestly Code

Given the occurrence of doublets and contradictions, the text of the narrative as we have it, after the various late additions have been separated out, rests on two independent versions that have been fused together into a single account at a later stage. Both these accounts have been retained complete.

The way in which the sources were bound together parallels the composition of the flood story.[32] Over against the practice of the redaction of the Pentateuch, which normally places the sources P and J one after another, section for section (e.g., Gen 1–3), the flood and the sea miracle are exceptions.[33] It is easy to see why. Since the Egyptians (and, in the flood, the whole of humanity) could not have been drowned twice successively, the redaction was compelled to dovetail the two versions into a single account. In the following text, the later additions already discussed are eliminated and indicated by bracketed ellipses. Italics mark additions by the redactor who united the two parallel narratives.

J 13:20 And they moved on from Succoth and encamped at Etham, on the edge of the wilderness. 21a And YHWH went before them by day in a pillar of cloud to lead them along the way and by night in a pillar of fire to give them light. [...]

P 14:1 YHWH said to Moses, 2 "Tell the Israelites, [...] that they encamp in front of Pi-hahiroth, between Migdol and the sea, in front of Baal-zephon. You shall encamp facing it, by the sea. [...] 4 Then I will harden the heart of Pharaoh so that he will pursue them, and I will gain glory over Pharaoh and all his host; and the Egyptians shall know that I am YHWH." And they did so.

J 5a When the king of Egypt was told that the people had fled, [...] 6 he made ready his chariots and took his army with him. [...]

P 8a Then YHWH hardened the heart of Pharaoh, *king of Egypt*, and he pursued after the Israelites. [...] 9 The Egyptians pursued them and overtook them encamped by the sea, all the horses and chariots of Pharaoh, his horsemen and his army, by Pi-hahiroth, in front of Baal-zephon.

J 10 *And Pharaoh drew near.* When the Israelites lifted up their eyes, behold, the Egyptians were pursuing after them, and they were in great fear. And the Israelites cried out to YHWH. [...] 13 But Moses said to the people, "Fear not! Stand firm and see the deliverance of YHWH, which he will work for you today; for as you see the Egyptians today, you shall never see them again. 14a YHWH will fight for you." [...]

P 15 YHWH said to Moses, "*Why do you cry to me?* Tell the Israelites to go forward, 16 and you, raise your rod and stretch out your hand over the sea and divide it, so that the Israelites may go on dry ground into the sea. 17 Then I will harden the hearts of the Egyptians so that they go in after them, and I will gain glory over Pharaoh and all his host, his chariots and horsemen. 18 And the Egyptians shall know that I am YHWH, when I have gained glory over Pharaoh, his chariots, and his horsemen." [...]

J 19b And the pillar of cloud moved from before them and stood behind them, 20 coming between the host of Egypt and the host of Israel. [...] And neither came near the other all night.

P 21 Then Moses stretched out his hand over the sea.

J And YHWH drove the sea back by a strong east wind all night and made the sea dry land.

P And the waters were divided. 22 And the Israelites went into the sea on dry ground, the waters being a wall to them on their right hand and on their left. 23 The Egyptians pursued and went in after them, all of Pharaoh's horses, chariots, and horsemen, right into the sea.

J 24 At the morning watch, YHWH looked down upon the host of Egypt in the pillar of fire and cloud and threw the host of Egypt into panic. [...] 25b And the Egyptians said, "Let us flee from before Israel, for YHWH is fighting for them against Egypt."

P 26 YHWH said to Moses, "Stretch out your hand over the sea, that the water may come back upon the Egyptians, upon their chariots, and upon their horsemen." 27 So Moses stretched out his hand over the sea.

J And the sea returned to its normal course when the morning appeared, and the Egyptians fled before it, and YHWH shook the Egyptians into the sea.

P 28 And the water returned and covered the chariots and horsemen that belong to the whole host of Pharaoh, those who had followed them into the sea, not one of them remaining. 29 But the Israelites walked on dry ground through the middle of the sea, the waters being a wall to them on their right hand and on their left.

J 30 Thus YHWH delivered Israel that day from the hand of the Egyptians, and Israel saw the Egyptians dead upon the seashore. [...]

In the linking of the two sources, the Priestly Code provided the foundation, because its account is clearly structured through the three divine commands in 14:1, 15, and 26. The Yahwistic source was inserted into this sequence.[34]

The two sources divide most clearly at the crowning moment. The return of the water is described twice: "and the sea returned" (*wayyāšob hayyām*, 14:27aα^2); and "and the waters returned" (*wayyāšūbû hammayim*, 14:28). In the J account, the Egyptians *flee* from the *sea*, which had been forced back during the night and returns in the morning. YHWH "shakes them off" into the waves. In the P account, the Egyptians *go through* the divided sea. When the *water* returns, they are overwhelmed by the waves.

The return of the water in 14:28 follows on the command that YHWH gave to Moses in 14:26: "YHWH said to Moses, 'Stretch out your hand over the sea, that the water may come back upon the Egyptians, upon their chariots, and upon their horsemen.' So Moses stretched out his hand over the sea. ... And the waters returned." The other version, which is thereby passed over, is linked through the catchword *nûs* "flee" with what the Egyptians say in 14:25b: "And the Egyptians said, 'Let us *flee* from before Israel; for YHWH is fighting for them against Egypt.' ... And the sea returned to its normal course when the morning appeared, and the Egyptians *fled* before it, and YHWH shook the Egyptians into the sea." Verse 24 also belongs to this version, since it mentions the terror of God that drives the Egyptians into the sea according to v. 27a$\alpha^2\beta$b.

It is clear that the sequence of command and obedience belongs to the Priestly Code. We find the same sequence in the creation account Gen 1:1–2:4a as well as in the Priestly Code's version of the flood and in the story about the plagues in Exod 7:8–13, 19, 21aα^1, 21b–22; 8:1–3, 11aβb–15; 9:8–12. The sea miracle as told in the Priestly Code reads like another plague; the other version belongs to the Yahwist's History. The reasons will emerge below.

The interplay between command and obedience also comes out in 14:15–16 and 21aα^1, b. When YHWH orders, "raise your rod and stretch out your hand over the sea and divide it, so that the Israelites may go on dry ground into the sea," Moses obeys: "then Moses stretched out his hand over the sea, … and the waters were divided." Here, too, the Yahwist's version is interpolated: "And YHWH drove the sea back by a strong east wind all night and made the sea dry land" (v. 21a$\alpha^2\beta$). Again there is the same contradiction: in the Priestly Code Moses divides the sea so that the Israelites can pass through; in the Yahwist's History YHWH drives the sea back through a wind during the night. In the morning the Egyptians think that the sea bed is dry land and flee into it. Between the command and its implementation stands the report in 14:19b–20 that the pillar of cloud placed itself between the armies, in order to protect the Israelites from the Egyptians during the night. This detail belongs to the Yahwist version, for it is only there that the night has to pass before the sea can retreat. In the Priestly Code the whole incident takes place by day.

YHWH's first command is given in 14:1–2, 4a. YHWH lets Moses set out and predicts the way the Egyptians will behave, just as they accordingly do in 14:4b, 8a, 9. This part of the story also belongs to the Priestly Code. If we put the three stages together, we have a complete, clearly structured progression. (1) YHWH orders Moses to make the Israelites start out, and they comply. The Egyptians pursue and catch them as they camp at the sea (14:1–2, 4, 8a, 9). (2) YHWH commands Moses to divide the sea and then to guide the Israelites through: these events occur as commanded. The Egyptians follow the Israelites through the divided sea (14:15–17, 21aα^1, b, 22–23). (3) YHWH commands Moses to let the water return; that, too, takes place, and the Egyptians drown (14:26–27aα^1, 28–29).

On the other hand, the verses that have been eliminated also form a complete account. It begins with the departure into the wilderness from Succoth (13:20–21a). The pillar of cloud and fire guides the Israelites on their way. When Pharaoh learns what has happened, he mobilizes his army of chariots (14:5a, 6). The Israelites are overcome by fear and appeal to YHWH (14:10b). Moses proclaims to them the oracle of salvation and predicts the destruction of the Egyptians (14:13–14a). In the form of the pillar of cloud, YHWH protects the Israelites during the night (14:19b–20aα, b) and dries out the sea (14:21aα^{2}β). In the morning, he causes terror to fall on the Egyptians out of the pillar of cloud and fire (14:24). The Egyptians flee in the direction of the returning sea and are destroyed (14:25b, 27aα^{2}βb). At the end comes the summing up: "Thus YHWH delivered Israel that day from the hand of the Egyptians, and Israel saw the Egyptians dead upon the seashore" (14:30). What Moses proclaimed in 14:13 has come to pass.

At three of the joints between the accounts, the redactor has intervened in order to harmonize the two versions. In 14:5 the Yahwist refers to the "king of Egypt" (*melek miṣrayim*), as he does elsewhere (see Exod 1:8, 15; 3:18). The Priestly Code, however, uses the title "Pharaoh" (14: 4, 8, 17, 18, 23, 28). In order to bridge the difference, in 14:8 the redactor has introduced the title *melek miṣrayim* "king of Egypt" into the Priestly Code's account. Conversely, in 14:10a the redactor has added *Pharaoh* in order to make the concentration on his personality (which pervades the Priestly Code's account) apply to the Yahwistic version as well. The addition can easily be detected because of the inversion *ûparʿōh hiqrîb* "and Pharaoh drew near," which disturbs the sequence of tenses. Finally, the question in 14:15aβ *mah tiṣʿaq ʾēlāy* "why do you cry to me?" which disrupts the pattern of the Priestly Code (see 14:1–2, 26) and only finds support in the Yahwistic text (14:10), is also a harmonizing addition to be attributed to the redactor (R). It marks YHWH's command to Moses in the Priestly Code as being an answer to the Israelite cry for help that the Yahwist relays in 14:10.

The Supplementary Hypothesis (2): Supplements within the Priestly Code

After the Yahwist and the Priestly Code have been separated, numerous doublets still remain in the Priestly Code. That is why scholars assumed for a time that there was a third source and ascribed parts of the text to the so-called Elohist.[35]

However, the solution is not to be found in a second application of the Documentary Hypothesis but, once again, in the Supplementary

Hypothesis: the basic version of the Priestly Code (P^G) was expanded by supplements (P^S). In the text below, italics indicate these supplements. Still later additions are given in brackets. Bracketed ellipses indicate the non-Priestly text eliminated already above.

> 14:1 YHWH said to Moses, 2 "Tell the Israelites, [...] that they encamp before of Pi-hahiroth, between Migdol and the sea, in front of Baal-zephon. *You shall encamp facing it, by the sea.* [...] 4 *Then I will harden the heart of Pharaoh so that he will pursue them, and I will gain glory over Pharaoh and all his host, and the Egyptians shall know that I am YHWH."* And they did so. [...] 8 *Then YHWH hardened the heart of Pharaoh,* [...] *and he pursued after the Israelites.* [...] 9 The Egyptians pursued them and overtook them *encamped by the sea* [all the horses and chariots of Pharaoh, his horsemen, and his army] by Pi-hahiroth, in front of Baal-zephon. [...] 15 YHWH said to Moses, [...] "Tell the Israelites to go forward, 16 *and you, raise your rod* and stretch out your hand over the sea and divide it, so that the Israelites may go on dry ground into the sea. 17 *And I, behold, I will harden the hearts of the Egyptians so that they go in after them, and I will gain glory over Pharaoh and all his host,* [his chariots and horsemen]. 18 *And the Egyptians shall know that I am YHWH* [when I have gained glory over Pharaoh, his chariots, and his horsemen]." [...] 21 Then Moses stretched out his hand over the sea. [...] And the waters were divided. 22 And the Israelites went into the sea on dry ground, *the waters being a wall to them on their right hand and on their left.* 23 The Egyptians pursued and went in after them [all of Pharaoh's horses, chariots, and horsemen] right into the sea. [...] 26 Then YHWH said to Moses, Stretch out your hand over the sea, that the water may come back upon the Egyptians [upon their chariots, and upon their horsemen]. 27 So Moses stretched out his hand over the sea. [...] 28 And the waters returned and covered [the chariots and horsemen that belonged to the whole host of Pharaoh], those who had followed them into the sea, [not one of them remaining]. 29 *But the Israelites walked on dry ground through the middle of the sea, the waters being a wall to them on their right hand and on their left.* [...]

The expansion shapes the event into a historical proof of the universal power of God. Before all eyes, YHWH shows that he is the God who rules the world. The purpose of YHWH's acts is clearly stated: "you shall know that I am YHWH" (14:18). This theologumenon is especially common in the book of Ezekiel,[36] and it is genuinely prophetic.

The proof of YHWH's power develops in the sequence of prediction and fulfillment. The religious evidence is shown to the non-Israelites, who are simultaneously the witnesses and the victims of YHWH's acts. This manifests the experience of the multireligious world in which Judaism was living in the Persian and Hellenistic periods. The same kind of proof is found in the stories about the plagues (Exod 7:5, 17; 8:6, 18; 9:14, 29). Since none of these instances goes back to the basic version of the Priestly Code, we probably see the same revision at work in all of them.

Strictly speaking, the Egyptians—and Pharaoh first and foremost—should have immediately converted to Judaism and ended their hostility to the Israelites. But that would have marred the sequence of events and would have deprived YHWH of the occasion for his victory. In order to avoid the contradiction to which this was bound to lead, the revision picks up the "hardness of heart" motif (14:4, 8, 17), which regularly comes into play in the plague narrative as well[37] (Exod 4:21; 7:3, 13, 14, 22; 8:11, 15, 28; 9:7, 12, 34–35; 10:1, 20, 27; 11:10).[38] Thus the text stresses a sharp distinction between Jews and non-Jews in relation to the God of the whole world (see Exod 8:19; 9:4; 11:7).

Right at the beginning of the narrative, it emerges that the theme of the proof of God's power did not belong to the basic version of the Priestly Code. Wellhausen writes, "Verses 3 and 4 are neither in substance nor formally a good continuation of what Moses is supposed to say to Israel; *wyʿśw kn* at the end of 14:4 rather joins directly on to 14:2."[39] The comment "and they did so" refers solely to the command to set out in 14:2. Meanwhile, the prediction about what is going to happen to the Egyptians, which has been inserted in 14:3–4a, is fulfilled in verse 8. There is another noticeable doublet in 14:8–9: "he [Pharaoh] pursued them"//"The Egyptians pursued them."[40] This, too, is extraneous to the strict structure of the original account.

YHWH's second command to Moses in 14:15–16 is again followed by a prediction (14:17–18). This corresponds exactly to 14:4. The two statements belong together and are the work of one and the same hand. This time the expansion can be detected from the prophetic *futurum instans*:[41] *waʾănî hinĕnî mĕḥazzēq* "and I, behold, I will harden."

This speech form indicates the way in which the interpretive crux in 14:16a¹ should be understood: *wĕʾattâ hārēm ʾet maṭṭĕkā* "and you, raise your rod." Most exegetes recognize that the rod is an alien element that destroys the balance of the exact correspondence between the command 14:16a²b and the performance 14:21aα¹, 21b–22a. The only possible solution is that the rod is an addition. Moses uses the rod as he does in the case of the plague of blood (Exod 7:19–22) and in the miracle in which he strikes water from the rock (Num 20:2–13). Apparently the detail is intended to emphasize that the real author of the miracle is YHWH.[42] The correspondence between *wa'ănî* "and I" and *wĕ'attâ* "and you" is deliberate.[43]

Verse 29, at the end of the passage, stresses the marvelous character of the rescuing act and appears to be a gloss.[44] By way of the inverted verbal clause *ûbĕnê yiśrā'ēl hālĕkû* ("And as for the Israelites, they went"), it purports to be an external reference to the course of events. Not only the Egyptians but the Israelites too—that is, the readers and hearers of the text—are intended to see and understand the saving power of their God. The verse refers back to 14:22a, but here verb *hlk* "go, walk" has taken the place of *bw'* "go in." It is a sign of the miraculous rescue that the water forms *lāhem ḥōmâ* "a wall to them" (14:29b). This nominal clause appears word for word in 14:22b and was perhaps subsequently added there by the same hand.

The description of the scene in 14:2bβ can probably be ascribed to this hand, too: "you shall encamp facing it." This has an origin different from the rest of the verse, where YHWH talks about the Israelites in the third person, whereas in 14:2bβ YHWH speaks to the Israelites in the second person.[45] The description *ḥōnîm 'al hayyām* "encamped by the sea" in 14:9aα is apparently connected with this.

The lists in 14:9aβ, 17bβ, 18b, 23aβγ, 26bβ, 28aαβ (from *'et* onward), and 28b were probably added by a later hand still. They stress that YHWH destroyed the whole Egyptian army, "the chariots and the horsemen … not one of them remaining" (14:28b), in order to manifest his glory (*kbd* 14:18b). This magnification of the concept of the YHWH war is highly reminiscent of the theology of Chronicles.

The Redaction Hypothesis: The Narrative within the Yahwist's History

The version of the narrative that is not part of the Priestly Code belongs to a second continuous source: the Yahwist's History. Earlier research rightly assumed that this was so. The proof is not merely negative, depending on a subtraction from the Priestly Code's text; on the contrary, there are positive criteria for the existence of this historical work. In recent times, it has become possible to identify an overriding redaction that under particular aspects selected a number of previously independent narrative cycles and amalgamated them into a new whole.[46] The work begins with Gen 2:5 and probably ends with the death of Moses in Deut 34:5–6. The distinction between the source and the redactional text (here given in italics) is a special form of the Supplementary Hypothesis.

> 13:20 And they moved on from Succoth and encamped at Etham, on the edge of the wilderness. 21 *And YHWH went before them by day in a pillar of cloud to lead them along the way and by night in a pillar of fire to give them light.* [...] 14:5a *When the king of Egypt was told that the people had fled,* [...] 6 *he made ready his chariot and took his army with him.* [...] 10b When the Israelites lifted up their eyes, behold, the Egyptians were pursuing after them, and they were in great fear. *And the Israelites cried out to YHWH.* [...] 13 But Moses said to the people, "Fear not! *Stand firm, and see the deliverance of YHWH, which he will work for you today; for as you see the Egyptians today, you shall never see them again.* 14b YHWH will fight for you." [...] 19b *And the pillar of cloud moved from before them and stood behind them,* 20 *coming between the host of Egypt and the host of Israel.* [...] *And neither came near the other all night.* [...] 21aα^2 And YHWH drove the sea back by a strong east wind all night and made the sea dry land. [...] 24 At the morning watch, YHWH looked down upon the host of Egypt *in the pillar of fire and cloud* and threw the host of Egypt into panic. [...] 25b And the Egyptians said, "Let us flee from before Israel, for YHWH is fighting for them against Egypt." [...] 27aα^2 And the sea returned to its normal course when the morning appeared, and the Egyptians fled before it, and YHWH shook the Egyptians into the sea. [...] 30 *Thus YHWH delivered Israel that day from the hand of the Egyptians, and Israel saw the Egyptians dead upon the seashore.* [...]

Two different sources underlie the account. The one is the itinerary describing the wanderings of the Israelites through the wilderness (13:20), which continues in 15:23; the other is the story about the miracle at the sea. This derives from the Moses tradition.[47] The differing origin of the two sources emerges from the style, from the scenes of the action (the desert and the sea), which cannot simply be made to agree, and the actors themselves. Moses originally played no part in the wanderings through the wilderness.

Just as at other points in the Yahwist's History, here the editor puts at the center YHWH's assistance and the rescue he brings about. The assistance is given visual form in the pillar of cloud and fire.[48] It is the form in which YHWH hides himself (see Exod 34:5) and in which he, at the same time, reveals himself. As a pillar of cloud and fire, he guides his people on their wanderings (13:21a) and protects them during the night from the pursuing Egyptians (14:19b–20aα, b), and as a pillar of cloud and fire he appears to the Egyptians in order to destroy them (14:24aγ). It can be seen from 13:21 that this motif has been added. The resumptive stative clause, *wĕyhwh hōlēk lipnêhem* ("but YHWH was going before them"), which picks up the pillar of cloud and fire and brings it into play for the first time, interrupts the *consecutio temporum*.[49]

The rescue that the miracle signifies is emphasized by the cry for help with which the Israelites articulate their fear in 14:10bβ. The repetition of the subjective ("the Israelites") after the verb *wyṣʿqw* is evidence that the clause comes from a different hand than the earlier part of the verse.[50] A unified text would not have repeated the unchanged subject: the sequence that is brought about through the redactional addition is deliberate. It corresponds to the promise that the editor has put into YHWH's mouth on the occasion of Moses' call: "I have seen the affliction of my people who are in Egypt and have heard their cry, and I have come down to deliver them out of the hand of the Egyptians" (Exod 3:7–8). Here the overriding redactional cohesion of the work emerges. YHWH also reacts similarly to the cries that follow the murder of Abel (Gen 4:10) and also the atrocity in Sodom (Gen 18:20–21; 19:13).[51]

The cry for help is answered in Moses' words. Here the editor has expanded the original reassuring formula "fear not": "Stand firm and see the deliverance of YHWH, which he will work for you today; for as you see the Egyptians today, you shall never see them again" (14:13*). Introduced in this way, the miracle at the sea becomes the proof of "YHWH's deliverance" (*yĕšûʿat yhwh*). This is the editor's message to his contemporary readers: Israel is promised deliverance from its enemies for all future time.

At the end of the story the editor establishes that the announcement to the Egyptians has been fulfilled: "Thus YHWH delivered Israel that day from the hand of the Egyptians, and Israel saw the Egyptians dead upon the seashore" (14:30).[52] The temporal interlocking *bayyôm hahûʾ* "on that day" shows that this summary sentence has been subsequently added. In the overall structure of the Yahwist's History, the story about the miracle at the sea is parallel to the flood in Gen 6–8, as well as to the story about the destruction of Sodom in Gen 19.

The Fragmentary Hypothesis: The Transmitted Sources

As soon as the analysis of the Yahwist's account reaches the level that preceded the editorial work, the Fragmentary Hypothesis also comes into play. This is the third great hypothesis about the Pentateuch, and it was originally introduced by Alexander Geddes.[53] The sources that the editor has passed down have been extracted from narrative complexes that have only partially been preserved.

> 13:20 And they moved on from Succoth and encamped at Etham, on the edge of the wilderness. [...]
>
> 14:10b When the Israelites lifted up their eyes, behold, the Egyptians were pursuing after them, and they were in great fear. [...] 13 But Moses said to the people, "Fear not! [...] 14 YHWH will fight for you." [...] 21aα^2 And YHWH drove the sea back by a strong east wind all night and made the sea dry land. [...] 24 At the morning watch, YHWH looked down upon the host of Egypt [...] and threw the host of Egypt into panic. [...] 25b And the Egyptians said, "Let us flee from before Israel, for YHWH is fighting for them against Egypt." [...] 27aα^2 And the sea returned to its normal course when the morning appeared, and the Egyptians fled before it, and YHWH shook the Egyptians into the sea. [...]

One of the two sources is the itinerary of the march through the desert. The note at 13:20 belongs to the series of notes about the itinerary that begins when the Israelites set out from Rameses to Succoth in 12:37a. Its continuation is found in 15:22aβ, 23: "And they went into the wilderness of Shur and came to Marah."[54]

The story about the miracle at the sea, which the editor of the Yahwist's History has interpolated, is the account of a YHWH war.[55] Compared with other examples of this genre, it appears as its positive prototype. The deity alone fights with the enemies and destroys them completely. Before the fight begins, Moses (who is here presented as priest, as he is in Exod 2–3 and 19–34) pronounces an oracle of salvation in the purest style of the genre: "Fear not! YHWH will fight for you" (14:13aα^1, 14a). The Egyptians are overcome by fear ("Let us flee from before Israel") and confess that the oracle has been fulfilled ("YHWH fights for them against the Egyptians," 14:25b). In headless flight, they turn toward the sea, which now flows back, "and YHWH shook the Egyptians into the sea" (14:27b). With the proof that the remaining text still offers a meaningful unity, source criticism has completed its work and passes the baton on to genre criticism.

For Further Reading

Carr, David M. “Controversy and Convergence in Recent Studies of the Formation of the Pentateuch.” *RSR* 23 (1997): 22–31.
Dozeman, Thomas B., and Konrad Schmid, eds. *A Farewell to the Yahwist: The Composition of the Pentateuch in Recent European Interpretation*. SBLSymS 34. Atlanta: Society of Biblical Literature, 2006.
Kratz, Reinhard Gregor. *The Composition of the Narrative Books of the Old Testament*. Translated by J. Bowden. London: T&T Clark, 2005.
Levin, Christoph. *The Old Testament: A Brief Introduction*. Translated by M. Kohl. Princeton: Princeton University Press, 2005.
Nicholson, Ernest. *The Pentateuch in the Twentieth Century: The Legacy of Julius Wellhausen*. New York: Oxford University Press, 1998.
Ska, Jean-Louis. *Introduction to Reading the Pentateuch*. Winona Lake, Ind.: Eisenbrauns, 2006.

Notes

1. The title of Jean Astruc's fundamental work reflects this assumption: *Conjectures sur les mémoires origineaux dont il paroit que Moyse s'est servi pour composer le livre de la Genèse* (Brussels: Fricx, 1753).

2. Typically, the book of Deuteronomy is also assigned to it. It is, however, more probable that Deuteronomy was later interpolated between Numbers and Joshua; see Reinhard G. Kratz, *The Composition of the Narrative Books of the Old Testament* (trans. J. Bowden; London: T&T Clark, 2005), 115. Because the guiding intention of the Deuteronomistic History was the reinstatement of the monarchy, it must be assigned to the period after the monarchy's downfall. Many American scholars from Frank Moore Cross onward (see his *Canaanite Myth and Hebrew Epic* [Cambridge: Harvard University Press, 1973], 274–89) have maintained the view that the first version was written under Josiah, but this was refuted by Erik Aurelius, *Zukunft jenseits des Gerichts* (BZAW 319; Berlin: de Gruyter, 2003), 39–57. What is correct in Cross's thesis is that the excerpt from the synchronistic annals that forms the basis of the books of Kings derives from the period of the monarchy. See Christoph Levin, “Die Frömmigkeit der Könige von Israel und Juda,” in *Houses Full of All Good Things: Essays in Memory of Timo Veijola* (ed. Juha Pakkala and Martti Nissinen; Publications of the Finnish Exegetical Society 95; Helsinki: Finnish Exegetical Society; Göttingen: Vandenhoeck & Ruprecht, 2008), 129–68, esp. 131–38.

3. See Christoph Levin, “The Yahwist: The Earliest Editor in the Pentateuch,” *JBL* 126 (2007): 209–30; idem, *Der Jahwist* (FRLANT 157; Göttingen: Vandenhoeck &

Ruprecht, 1993). Contrary to John Van Seters (*The Edited Bible: The Curious History of the 'Editor' in Biblical Criticism* [Winona Lake, Ind.: Eisenbrauns, 2006]), it can be shown that the Yahwist worked as an editor. This does not necessarily refute the concept of the Yahwist as historian. However, this historian did not retell traditional material but compiled his work from written sources.

4. Brevard S. Childs, *The Book of Exodus: A Critical, Theological Commentary* (OTL; Philadelphia: Westminster, 1974), 218.

5. Theodor Nöldeke, "Die s. g. Grundschrift des Pentateuchs," in idem, *Untersuchungen zur Kritik des Alten Testaments* (Kiel: Schwers, 1869), 1–144, esp. 45–46. Nöldeke agrees with August Wilhelm Knobel, *Die Bücher Exodus und Leviticus* (KEH 12; Leipzig: Hirzel, 1857), 137–39.

6. See Martin Noth, *A History of Pentateuchal Traditions* (trans. B. W. Anderson; Englewood Cliffs: Prentice-Hall, 1972), 19; and idem, *Exodus: A Commentary* (trans. J. S. Bowden; OTL; London: SCM, 1962), 105. The analysis maintained in what follows takes its own slightly deviating path only in regard to vv. 9–10.

7. Hermann Hupfeld, *Die Quellen der Genesis und die Art ihrer Zusammensetzung* (Berlin: Wiegandt & Grieben, 1853).

8. Julius Wellhausen, "Die Composition des Hexateuchs," *JDT* 21 (1876): 391–450, 531–602; 22 (1877): 407–79, esp. 545–47; later idem, *Die Composition des Hexateuchs und der historischen Bücher des Alten Testaments* (4th ed.; Berlin: de Gruyter, 1963), 75–77. Adolf Jülicher, "Die Quellen von Exodus VII, 8–XXIV,11: Ein Beitrag zur Hexateuchfrage," *Jahrbücher für protestantische Theologie* 8 (1882): 79–127, 272–315, esp. 119–24, takes over the three-source hypothesis from Wellhausen but reckons with a much greater share on the part of P. Abraham Kuenen, *An Historico-Critical Inquiry into the Origin and Composition of the Hexateuch* (London: Macmillan, 1886), 71–72, rejected a threefold division.

9. Rudolf Smend Sr., *Die Erzählung des Hexateuch auf ihre Quellen untersucht* (Berlin: Reimer, 1912), 137–43. This hypothesis provided the foundation for Otto Eissfeldt, *Hexateuch-Synopse* (Leipzig: Hinrichs, 1922), 133*–37*.

10. See already Nöldeke's objection to Hupfeld: "It would be much more difficult to assume that this Elohist and the Yahwist were independent of one another and were only integrated into a whole by an earlier redactor, and that this work was in front of the redactor of the pre-Deuteronomistic Pentateuch in addition to the Basic Document" ("Die s. g. Grundschrift des Pentateuchs," 3–4; unless otherwise noted, all translations of German works are my own). The criticism of Paul Volz and Wilhelm Rudolph, *Der Elohist als Erzähler: Ein Irrweg der Pentateuchkritik?* (BZAW 63; Gießen: Töpelmann, 1933), is fundamental.

11. Smend takes a quite different view: "This remarkable procedure was continually repeated in the history of the Hexateuch" (*Die Erzählung des Hexateuch*, 343).

12. For the theological presuppositions of the synthesis of these sources, see esp. Herbert Donner, "Der Redaktor: Überlegungen zum vorkritischen Umgang mit der heiligen Schrift," in idem, *Aufsätze zum Alten Testament* (BZAW 224; Berlin: de Gruyter, 1994), 259–85.

13. In recent times the hypothesis has been put forward that the amalgamation of the documents was intended to serve as legal argument for the official recognition

of the Jewish community by the Persian overlord, but analysis of the books of Ezra and Nehemiah has made this improbable. The biblical account probably dates from the Hellenistic period. The Jewish authorities cited the great Persian king in order to claim religious and legal privileges from the Ptolemaic and Seleucid kings.

14. See Thomas Krüger, "Erwägungen zur Redaktion der Meerwundererzählung (Exod 13,17–14,31)," *ZAW* 108 (1996), 519–33, who, however, attributes much more text to this revision and identifies it with redaction R^{JP}. He at least admits: "It is quite conceivable that this redactional work was carried out in several stages" (524). If this is the case, a clear distinction should be made between redaction and revision!

15. Read *wayyeʾĕsōr* with Samaritanus, Septuagint, and Peshitta instead of Masoretic *wayyāsar* "he removed."

16. Bible translations here and throughout the rest of the essay follow the Revised Standard Version with some alterations.

17. The revision was certainly not confined to Exod 13:17–14:31. Its extent could have been quite considerable. At the same time, it goes beyond what can be proved if it is identified with the so-called "Pentateuch redaction" or even the "Enneateuch redaction," as Hans-Christoph Schmitt has proposed ("'Priesterliches' und 'prophetisches' Geschichtsverständnis in der Meerwundererzählung Exod 13,17–14,31: Beobachtungen zur Endredaktion des Pentateuch," in idem, *Theologie in Prophetie und Pentateuch* (BZAW 310; Berlin: de Gruyter, 2001), 203–20; idem, "Das spätdeuteronomistische Geschichtswerk Genesis I bis 2 Regum XXV und seine theologische Intention," in *Theologie in Prophetie und Pentateuch*, 277–94.

18. Rudolf Smend Jr., "Zur Geschichte von *hʾmyn*," in idem, *Die Mitte des Alten Testaments: Exegetische Aufsätze* (Tübingen: Mohr Siebeck, 2002), 244–49, esp. 246.

19. Ibid. In the context, the motif is also found in Exod 4:1–9, 31; 19:9; Num 14:11; 20:12; Deut 1:32; 9:23.

20. Pointed out by Erik Aurelius, *Der Fürbitter Israels: Eine Studie zum Mosebild im Alten Testament* (Stockholm: Almqvist & Wiksell, 1988), 147, with reference to an observation by Martin Noth, *Numbers: A Commentary* (trans. J. D. Martin; OTL; London: SCM, 1968), 157.

21. Aurelius, *Der Fürbitter Israels*, 184 n. 238.

22. See also Num 11:20; 14:2–3; 16:13–14; 20:4–5; 21:5.

23. Exod 4:23; 7:16, 26; 8:16; 9:1, 13; 10:3, 7.

24. Noth, *Exodus*, 106–7.

25. Heinrich Holzinger, *Exodus* (KHC 2; Tübingen: Mohr Siebeck, 1900), 44.

26. Noth, *Exodus*, 117.

27. B. D. Eerdmans, *Alttestamentliche Studien III: Das Buch Exodus* (Gießen: Töpelmann, 1910), 40.

28. Jülicher, "Die Quellen von Exodus," 121.

29. Fujiko Kohata, *Jahwist und Priesterschrift in Exodus 3–14* (BZAW 166; Berlin: de Gruyter, 1986), 176–77.

30. Noth, *Exodus*, 111.

31. Smend, *Die Erzählung des Hexateuch*, 140.

32. See Nöldeke, "Die s. g. Grundschrift des Pentateuchs," 45.

33. Contrary to Hermann Gunkel, *Genesis* (trans. M. E. Biddle; Macon, Ga.:

Mercer University Press: 1997), 139, (referring to the flood story): "The beginner can learn the proper way to distinguish the sources from this pericope." This statement led the opinion about the Documentary Hypothesis astray.

34. This procedure is often viewed as being the general rule, but that is erroneous: between Gen 12 and Exod 5 the Yahwist's History provides the basis of the source synthesis, the Priestly Code being complementary.

35. See Wellhausen, *Die Composition des Hexateuchs*, 75–77.

36. See Walther Zimmerli, "Erkenntnis Gottes nach dem Buche Ezechiel," in idem, *Gottes Offenbarung: Gesammelte Aufsätze* (2nd ed.; Munich: Kaiser, 1969), 41–119.

37. See Franz Hesse, *Das Verstockungsproblem im Alten Testament* (BZAW 74; Berlin: Töpelmann, 1955).

38. These instances, too, do not belong to the basic version of the Priestly code (P^G).

39. Wellhausen, *Die Composition des Hexateuchs*, 75. Similarly, Wilhelm Rudolph, *Der "Elohist" von Exodus bis Josua* (BZAW 68; Berlin: Töpelmann, 1938), 29: "14:3 and 4a divide 14:4b from 14:2 in an unhappy way."

40. See Wellhausen, *Die Composition des Hexateuchs*, 75.

41. See GKC §116p.

42. See Horacio Simian-Yofre, "מַטֶּה," *TDOT* 8:241–49, esp. 244.

43. As a rule, *wĕʾattâ* is assigned to the basic text, the copula before *ûnĕṭēh* being eliminated instead. But this separation, which does violence to the word, is inadmissible.

44. See Jülicher, "Die Quellen von Exodus," 123.

45. Smend, *Die Erzählung des Hexateuch*, 140.

46. See Levin, "The Yahwist"; idem, *Der Jahwist*, 341–44.

47. The earliest tradition about Moses is otherwise to be found in Exod 2:1–23*; 3:1–5*; 4:20* and Exod 19:2b–3a; 24:18b; Num 20:1b; Deut 34:5–6*. An asterisk after a verse number indicates an earlier layer found in that verse.

48. In Gen 26:3, 28; 28:15; 31:3; 39:2–3, 21; Exod 34:9 the editor of the Yahwist's History has also interpolated the motif of YHWH's assistance into the older sources he has taken over.

49. Noth, *Exodus*, 109.

50. See Jülicher, "Die Quellen von Exodus," 122.

51. In the further episodes that also tell of YHWH's help in the wanderings in the wilderness, the editor of the Yahwist's History has introduced the cry for help (Hebrew root *ṣʿq*); see Exod 15:25; 17:14; Num 11:2.

52. See Ps 98:3; Isa 52:10.

53. Alexander Geddes, *Critical Remarks on the Hebrew Scriptures, Corresponding with a New Translation of the Bible* (London: Davis, Wilks & Taylor, 1800).

54. The itinerary can be followed in Exod 12:37a; 13:20; 15:22aβb, 23, 27; 16:1*, 13b, 14*, 15a, 21, 31; 17:1abα*; 19:2a; Num 10:12a*; 11:31aα*, 32aα*, b; 20:1aβ; 25:1a.

55. See esp. Gerhard von Rad, *Holy War in Ancient Israel* (trans. Marva J. Dawn; Grand Rapids: Eerdmans, 1991), 88–90.

Redaction Criticism: 1 Kings 8 and the Deuteronomists

Thomas Römer

What Does "Redaction Criticism" Mean? A Short History of the Method

The idea of redactors and redaction is probably as old as the historical and critical investigation of the Bible. It can be traced back to Richard Simon's critical history of the Old Testament, where he claimed that the original texts of the Bible had been altered by "public scribes" who added new ideas to, or sometimes shortened, the text they were rewriting.[1] According to the Documentary Hypothesis as established by Abraham Kuenen and Julius Wellhausen, redactors are distinguished from the original authors of the documents, or "sources." The original sources of the Pentateuch, or the Hexateuch, are: JE (the Jehovist); D (the first edition of the book of Deuteronomy); and P (the Priestly document). These documents were put together, in the light of this model, by different redactors who worked more or less mechanically.[2] They neither invented the chronological framework of the first books of the Bible, which already existed in the oldest document (J [Yahwist]), nor did they add new stories. Their main concern was to harmonize the different sources by intermingling the parallel accounts (as, e.g., in Exod 14) or putting them side by side (in Gen 1:1–2:3; 2:4–3:25). As Otto Eissfeldt puts it: "There is a distinction, for the most part clearly recognizable, between the author, organically shaping the material, and the redactor working mechanically."[3]

Until the middle of the twentieth century, biblical scholars were not much interested in the work of the redactors. They were concerned with discovering the oldest sources in the narrative books or the *ipsissima verba* in the prophetic books. The focus on the "authentic" prophetic words led Bernhard Duhm in his commentary on Jeremiah to disqualify more than 60 percent of the book as stemming from *Ergänzer* (supplementers), who were unqualified scribes. The opposite of talented authors, these confused the clear thoughts of Jeremiah.[4] Duhm rightly recognized the importance of later revisions of older texts or documents, but the time was not yet ripe for a positive or even neutral evaluation of such redactional activity.

In a sense, Martin Noth was not only the "father" of the Deuteronomistic History; he may also be considered the earliest promoter of redaction criticism, even though he titled his book about the Deuteronomistic History *Überlieferungsgeschichtliche Studien* (*Studies in the History of Transmission/Tradition*).[5] The interest in transmission of written or oral traditions is less concerned with the exact reconstruction of the oldest sources. Rather, its focus is to explain the development and the formation of larger units such as the Pentateuch, the Former Prophets, the Latter Prophets, Chronicles, and so on. It must be noted that the importance of Noth's Deuteronomistic History hypothesis does not reside in the identification of Deuteronomistic texts in the books of Deuteronomy, Joshua, Judges, Samuel, and Kings. Such texts had been identified since the time of Heinrich Ewald and Wellhausen, but no one really took interest in them, since they were just "late additions." Noth was the first to emphasize that those Deuteronomistic texts belonged to a coherent and unified redaction, due to one redactor, whom Noth called the Deuteronomist (Dtr). According to Noth, Dtr wrote the first history of Israel, by making use of older traditions and documents, which he arranged in a coherent chronology and narrative. In this view, the Deuteronomist's attitude toward his traditions was that of an "honest broker": he integrated in his work all of the older documents available to him, even when they contradicted his own theology.[6] Noth is indeed convinced that "Dtr's transmission of old traditional documents and accounts makes his work a most valuable historical source."[7] Thus for Noth, Dtr was not only a redactor but also an author who "brought together material from highly varied traditions" and "apparently arranged the material according to his own judgment."[8]

Thus, Noth's view of Dtr parallels the conception of the Evangelist Mark advanced by Willi Marxsen (who is often considered the real founder of redaction criticism).[9] Noth's Dtr and Marxsen's Mark were both redactors, but not in the sense that they mechanically edited the former traditions. On the contrary, as mentioned above, in the view of redaction criticism a redactor can almost be considered an "author," but not, of course, according to the meaning of modern authorship, which does not apply to the historical context of the Hebrew Bible.

With regard to the Deuteronomistic History, the emphasis on redaction-critical approaches grew in light of two major modifications that succeeded Noth's theory.[10] Frank Moore Cross's model of the double redaction of the Deuteronomistic history, which still dominates scholarship in the Anglo-Saxon world, distinguishes two blocks or layers. The first redactor—which Cross, contrary to Noth, locates under Josiah—organizes the older material in order to write a work of propaganda for the Judean king and its politics of centralization. After 587 B.C.E., a later redactor added 2 Kgs 24–25, as well as other texts, in order to update the history in the light of the downfall of Jerusalem and the Babylonian exile. The model of the "Göttingen school," which is now very popular in European biblical research, distinguishes three Deuteronomistic redactors, each of them having his own theological profile: (1) the Deuteronomistic Historian (DtrH), who is a diminished version of Noth's Deuteronomist and who wrote Israel and Judah's history in order to explain the reasons for Judah's fall; (2) the Prophetic Deuteronomist (DtrP), who added prophetic stories and was eager to show that everything that YHWH announced through the prophets finally did come true; and (3) the Nomistic Deuteronomist (DtrN), who was responsible for those passages that emphasize obedience to the law. Both models, even if they seem to be contradictory, are interested in investigating the different intentions of the Deuteronomistic redactors. On the other hand, recent criticisms of the Deuteronomistic History fail to explain the function of Deuteronomistic texts in Deuteronomy and the Former Prophets, whose existence is not denied by the opponents of the Deuteronomistic History.

Space does not allow for a comprehensive discussion of the growing importance of redaction criticism. Suffice it to underline the frequent use of this method in current research on the prophetic books, the Pentateuch, and the Psalms.

There is some evidence for one or several Deuteronomistic redactions of the book of Jeremiah that organized and edited prior editions of the book, and the same may apply to Hosea and Amos.[11] The book of Ezekiel seems to have been edited with a "Golah-oriented" redaction.[12] The current debate on the Book of the Twelve also emphasizes the possibility that the scrolls of twelve Minor Prophets were not just juxtaposed in order to obtain one big scroll. One may observe an important number of cross-references and themes (e.g., "the Day of YHWH") that indicate the existence of comprehensive redaction(s) of the Twelve.[13]

The same focus on redaction criticism applies to recent pentateuchal research. Since (at least in European scholarship) the traditional Documentary Hypothesis has been radically modified or even given up,[14] several recent models attribute the chronological framework of the Pentateuch (and the Hexateuch) not to the Yahwist but to redactors of the Persian period.[15] Generally speaking, there is a shift of interest from the reconstruction of the oldest units to the understanding of the methods and intention of the (latest) redactors of the Pentateuch, the Hexateuch,[16] and even the Enneateuch (the so-called Primary History).[17] If the framework of the Torah is the work of redactors working during the Persian period, special attention needs to be given to their work, to their literary strategies, to their editorial techniques and the way they used and transformed older material.

This development in biblical research has been sharply criticized by John Van Seters, who refutes the idea that redactors or editors (Van Seters uses both terms promiscuously) played any part in the formation of the Hebrew Bible. According to him, the method of redaction criticism should be given up altogether: "all talk of 'redactors' and 'redactions' should be scrupulously avoided in biblical studies."[18] For Van Seters, the formation of the Pentateuch and the Former Prophets may be ascribed to three authors: the Deuteronomist; the Yahwist; and the Priestly writer. Van Seters considers Dtr and the Yahwist to be historiographers and authors who freely composed their works; therefore, any attempt to reconstruct documents or traditions they may have had at their disposal is entirely useless. For P, the case is a bit more complicated, because Van Seters argues "that P merely supplemented the older tradition as he received in the written form of J."[19] Contrary to Van Seters's claim, editors and redactors were as real in the biblical world as they were in the ancient Near East. We have material evidence for the editing of the Gilgamesh Epic that can hardly be denied.[20] The Hebrew Bible (except perhaps the book of Qoheleth) does not result from the work of individual authors who signed their writings; it is anonymous literature that has been transmitted in several literary stages.[21] Therefore, redaction criticism remains a major method in biblical scholarship.

How Does One Do Redaction Criticism?

The tools of redaction criticism are those of diachronic analysis. These can be found in several introductory handbooks and do not need to be detailed here, but let us recall some important points.

Some redactional techniques reveal that redactors did not necessarily want to hide their activity. For instance, when they wanted to add something to an existing speech in the text, there is little effort to reduce literary and historical dissonance. In Gen 16, the original narrative of the encounter between Hagar and the divine messenger focused on the birth oracle: "The angel of YHWH said to her, 'Behold, you are with child, and will bear a son. You shall call his name Ishmael, because YHWH has heard your affliction'" (16:11). A later redactor added to this speech an order that Hagar should return to Sarah (16:9), because the redactor needed to prepare the second expulsion story in Gen 21. When introducing this addition, the introduction to the speech was repeated, juxtaposing the addition and the older discourse: "The angel of YHWH said to her, 'Return to your mistress, and submit yourself under her hands'" (16:9).[22]

Redactional reworking may also be detected by literary incoherencies that can result from the insertion of a new passage. Such a case is created by the insertion of Exod 11:1–3, which interrupts the last encounter between Pharaoh and Moses. In Exod 10:28–29 the reader is informed that Moses will never see the king of Egypt again, and in 11:8 Moses leaves the palace. Through the insertion of the divine speech to Moses in 11:1–3, however, 11:4–10 appears to relate a new encounter, contradicting the assertion of 10:29.

Another famous redactional technique is the so-called *Wiederaufnahme* (resumption). At the end of the passage that the redactor has inserted, the text that precedes the insertion is repeated, either in order to strengthen the coherence of the new text or to inform the reader about the extent of the insertion. A good example can be found in the story about Jephthah, in which the episode of the sacrifice of his daughter has clearly been added by a (post-Deuteronomistic) redactor who repeated the final words of Judg 11:29 in 11:32a.[23] This repetition marks the passage about Jephthah's vow as a redactional interruption. Another example can be found in Josh 1:7–9. These verses, which clearly are an addition to the Dtr speech of YHWH to Joshua, are framed by the phrase "be strong and courageous," which repeats the formula from the original end in 1:6. It thus modifies the royal oracle of victory, turning it into an exhortation to follow above all YHWH's law transmitted by Moses.[24] This is a good example showing that we should distinguish different redactional layers inside the so-called Deuteronomistic History.

This is also the case in Deut 12, where the redactors worked by juxtaposition. As in a new edition of a book, the more recent introduction precedes the older ones. There is no doubt that the primitive text of this chapter, dealing with the centralization of the cult, is to be found in 12:13–18*.[25] These verses are mainly concerned with the practical consequences of the centralization law and address an audience that is supposed to live in the land. There is no clear indication in these verses of the fiction of Deuteronomy as a Mosaic testament spoken before the conquest of the land.[26] A later redactor has added a new introduction in 12:8–12 where the addressees are clearly identified as the generation of the desert that has not yet entered the land. These verses try to give a new meaning to the idea of cultic centralization in the context of the Babylonian exile. To this new edition, another introduction has been added in 12:2–7. In this last addition, the theme of the unique sanctuary becomes mainly a pretext for an ideology of strict separation from the "other people" dwelling in the land.

The technique of juxtaposing a more recent text to an older one can also be observed at the end of a book or a longer passage, where the later redactors prefer to put their additions at the very end in order to "have the last word." Examples of this can be found in the two endings of the book of Joshua: chapter 23 is the Dtr ending of the book, whereas chapter 24 is a later addition made when the link between Joshua and Judges was cut off. The redactor who added Josh 24 wanted to separate that chapter from the following book to underline its close link with the foregoing Pentateuch.[27] One could also mention the double ending of the book of Leviticus, where a redactor supplemented the original conclusion in Lev 26 with an appendix in Lev 27.

A good method for distinguishing the work of redactors is to look for changes in style and vocabulary that may indicate redactional reworking of a former text. Judges 6:7–10 interrupts the connection that exists between the cry of the Israelites in response to the Midianite oppression (6:6) and the story about the call of Gideon, whom YHWH establishes as Israel's savior (6:11–24). The speech of an anonymous prophet inserted in 6:7–10 betrays a late Dtr style and also introduces the Dtr idea that, in spite of YHWH's delivery of the people and the gift of the land, they did not obey the divine commandment. The conclusion that this passage is a late insertion is fostered by the fact that the passage is missing in a manuscript of Judges found at Qumran.[28]

One of the clearest examples of redactional reworking of older documents is the so-called Deuteronomistic History. Even though there is no consensus at the moment on how to modify (or even reject) Martin Noth's hypothesis, there is no doubt that inside the Former Prophets one can distinguish between texts that show Dtr style and topics and those that do not and that may be older documents reworked and edited by the Deuteronomists.[29] There is also much evidence that the abbreviation "Dtr" should not be understood as referring to one individual but to a group or "school" (see above). There were several Dtr redactions of the books of Deuteronomy to 2 Kings, probably starting in the seventh century (under Josiah?) and ending in the Persian period.[30]

I would like to illustrate the diversity of Dtr redactional activity through an analysis of Solomon's inauguration of the temple of Jerusalem, related in 1 Kings 8.

Redaction Criticism of 1 Kings 8

1 Kings 8 and the Three Deuteronomistic Editions of the Story of Solomon

In its actual shape, 1 Kings 8 is built around the number seven: Solomon summons the people on the seventh month (8:2), feasts last fourteen days (Heb.: seven days and seven days; 8:65), the "fathers" are mentioned seven times, Solomon calls David his "father" seven times, and Solomon enumerates seven prayer occasions. This final redaction took place at the end of a long redactional process, which most exegetes accept. There is, however, less consensus on the precise identification of Deuteronomistic and other layers.

It is clear that the oldest pre-Dtr account should be detected in the narration about the introduction of the ark into the temple in 8:1–13, although these verses underwent an important Priestly and post-Dtr reworking[31] that makes it impossible to reconstruct in detail the oldest account. Inside this account, an even older tradition may be detected in the dedication of the temple in 1 Kgs 8:12–13, which the LXX (3 Kgdms 8:53) puts after Solomon's great prayer.The LXX preserves an older version of this dedication whose Hebrew *Vorlage* seems to reflect the installation of the storm-god YHWH by the solar-god who grants him a place in the Jerusalem temple, in which the two deities co-existed.[32]The primitive story, which had integrated this poetic piece and was probably among the annals of the Jerusalem palace or temple (the "Book of the Acts of Solomon"? see 1 Kgs 11:41), was first used by a Dtr redaction in Josiah's time. This story underwent a redaction after the destruction of Jerusalem and its temple in 586 B.C.E., then another new Dtr redaction in the first half of the Persian period, and finally a rereading of priestly type from the Second Temple period.[33] The three Dtr redactions are distinguished by their themes, by their different interpretations of the temple, and partly by their style. Roughly, 8:14–20 can be attributed to the Josianic text; 8:22–26, 28–40, 46–51 (?), 54–56 to the Babylonian period; and 8:52–53, 57–61 to the rereading of the Persian period. Verses 41–45 probably belong to a later period, since they presuppose the Diaspora and the idea of proselytes coming from the whole world to Jerusalem; the scene of the sacrifices in 8:63–64 belongs to a Priestly redaction.[34]

1 Kings 8:14–21: Solomon, Worthy Successor of David and Forerunner of Josiah

This prayer shows a parallel between God's choice of David and his dynasty and the choice of the temple. Verse 16 seems to establish the chronological priority of the election of royal lineage: "Since the day that I brought my people Israel out of Egypt, I have not chosen a city from any of the tribes of Israel in which to build a house, that my name might be there, but I chose David to be over my people Israel." The MT probably suggests that the Davidic election precedes the choice of Jerusalem. In the parallel version of Chronicles, Jerusalem as temple location is mentioned before David: "I have chosen Jerusalem in order that my name may be there, and I have chosen David" (2 Chr 6:6).[35] In any case, the first part of the Solomonic prayer suggests an indissoluble link between the Davidic dynasty and the election of the temple of Jerusalem. This points favors the attribution of 8:14–21 to a Josianic edition of the book of Kings. The insistence on God's choice "of a single tribe" recalls the formulation of Deut 12:14.[36] In turn, 8:20 takes up 1 Kgs 3:7 and asserts the Davidic dynasty's stability. By carrying out the building of the sanctuary chosen by YHWH, Solomon acts according to the Deuteronomic law; thus, he is in some way a forerunner of Josiah, who will completely carry out the law of centralization.

The quite triumphant tone of 1 Kgs 8:14–21* makes perfect sense in the context of the Josianic period. This tone changes in the central prayer that follows.

1 Kings 8:22–40*, 46–56*: From the Temple Builder to the Foreseer of Exile

The first part of the prayer added in the Babylonian period (8:22–26) provides a transition. It mentions again the "David the father" who will no longer appear in the discourse: 8:25 takes up the promise of an everlasting dynasty but makes it conditional, a result of reflection on the situation after 587 B.C.E. The same situation is presupposed in the verses that preceded the presentation of prayer occasions (8:27–30). Solomon declares that YHWH does not really dwell in the temple but in the heavens; the temple is the place where his name dwells. The same ideology appears in the exilic redaction of Deut 12 (vv. 8–12). Another link with Deut 12:8–12 is found in the theme of rest; as Deut 12:8 states that YHWH has not given his people "rest," Solomon concludes his prayer by thanking God for this rest:

> Deut 12:9: "for you have not yet come into the *rest* and the possession that YHWH your God is giving you."

> 1 Kgs 8:56: "Blessed be YHWH, who has given *rest* to his people Israel according to all that he promised; not one word has failed of all his good promise, which he spoke through his servant Moses."

These are the only two texts in the Hebrew Bible that express the idea that YHWH gives Israel rest.

The very strong link between Deut 12 and 1 Kgs 8:22–56* indicates that for the Deuteronomists of the Babylonian period YHWH gave the land only after the building of the temple. That is why the expression "the land given to the fathers" appears for the first time in the Deuteronomistic History in 1 Kgs 8 (vv. 34, 40, 48), while in the books of Deuteronomy and Joshua the land "promised to the fathers" appears constantly. It is only after the building of the temple that the divine oath is fulfilled. But in spite of the importance of the temple, Solomon emphasizes in his prayer YHWH's freedom from the sanctuary: YHWH could be worshiped outside of the temple. This is obvious in the description of occasions for prayer in 8:31–51. Contrary to the always identical call to YHWH ("hear from heaven"), the place from which the prayer is spoken varies in an interesting manner. In the first case, it is clearly the temple, before the altar (8:31). Then (8:35), the prayer is addressed toward the sanctuary. Finally, people pray from another country, raising their request toward the ancestral land, the city, and the temple (8:46–51). During the dedication of the temple, Solomon predicts the loss of the land and the deportation. It is significant that prayer occasions in 8:33–40 and 46–51 correspond to the curses of Deut 28: defeat (1 Kgs 8:33; Deut 28:23); no rain (1 Kgs 8:35; Deut 28:25); famine, plague, blight, mildew, locusts or caterpillars, and enemies (1 Kgs 8:37; Deut 28:21–22, 25, 38); and deportation and exile (1 Kgs 8:46; Deut 28:64–65).[37] In this speech, Solomon is thus dressed up with the garments of the Deuteronomistic History redactors from the Babylonian period, since he shows that God kept his commitments. The exile is thus entirely the fault of the people and its kings. At the same time, Solomon gives the temple a new role: from its dedication, it becomes a *qibla*, and sacrifices are replaced by prayers toward the temple.

1 Kings 8:52–53, 57–61: Solomon, Preacher of the Torah

While there is a strategy of distancing in the central prayer, Solomon's last blessing makes the temple completely disappear. These are the laws and commandments (8:58, 61) that in some way replace the temple and the land. This passage also insists on the opposition between Israel, YHWH's people, and other peoples (8:59–60, see also 8:53); this brings these verses closer to the later Dtr layer of Deut 12:2–7, which are also about a very strict separation between Israel and other peoples. Israel's identity is no longer expressed through the temple but through its election and observance of the Torah. The election of the temple and king is definitively supplanted in later texts by the election of the people.[38]

Solomon's prayer thus allows the astute redaction critic to discern the preoccupations of various editions of the Deuteronomistic work: Solomon as king in the image of Assyrian rulers; as an ambiguous king responsible for the collapse of the "united kingdom"; and, finally, as a king who fades away to leave room for the law.

Conclusion

Redaction criticism allows us to retrace the formation of biblical texts (but also of other ancient texts[39]) from their oldest textual forms to their "final" form. Biblical research in the twenty-first century has shifted from fascination with the *Ur*-text to the reconstruction of the work of the biblical redactors, since it is their activity that preserved the texts and transmitted them from generation to generation, showing at the same time that these texts are not static but need constant actualization and interpretation. This necessity of interpretation already occurs within the Hebrew Bible. A famous example is the story of the patriarch pretending his wife is his sister, which is transmitted three times (Gen 12:10–20; 20; 26:1–14). Apparently, Gen 20 can be understood as a revision and interpretation of Gen 12, but the older text is preserved. The same holds true for the transmission of the Covenant Code in Exod 20–23 and the Deuteronomic Code in Deut 12–26 or for the two versions of the story of the monarchy in Samuel–Kings and in Chronicles. These examples also give insight into the hermeneutics of the biblical redactors. They did not want to hide their work, since redactional reworking was simply a way to transmit and actualize older traditions by giving them a new meaning.

For Further Reading

Dozeman, Thomas B., and Konrad Schmid. *A Farewell to the Yahwist? The Composition of the Pentateuch in Recent European Interpretation.* SBLSymS 34. Atlanta: Society of Biblical Literature, 2006.

Nicholson, Ernest. *The Pentateuch in the Twentieth Century: The Legacy of Julius Wellhausen.* Oxford: Clarendon, 1998.

Nogalski, James D., and Marvin A. Sweeney, eds. *Reading and Hearing the Book of the Twelve.* SBLSymS 15. Atlanta: Society of Biblical Literature, 2000.

Perrin, Norman. *What Is Redaction Criticism?* London: SPCK, 1970.

Petersen, David L. “The Formation of the Pentateuch.” Pages 31–45 in *Old Testament Interpretation: Past, Present, Future: Essays in Honor of Gene M. Tucker.* Edited by James Luther Mays, David L. Petersen, and Kent Harold Richards. Nashville: Abingdon, 1995.

Römer, Thomas. *The So-Called Deuteronomistic History: A Sociological, Historical and Literary Introduction.* 2nd. ed. London: T&T Clark, 2007.

Stone, Lawson G. “Redaction Criticism: Whence, Whither, and Why? Or, Going Beyond Source and Form Criticism without Leaving Them Behind.” Pages 77–90 in *A Biblical Itinerary: In Search of Method, Form and Content: Essays in Honor of George W. Coats.* Edited by Eugene E. Carpenter. JSOTSup 240. Sheffield: Sheffield Academic Press, 1997.

Notes

1. Richard Simon, *Histoire Critique du Vieux Testament* (1678; new ed. annotated and introduced by Pierre Gibert ; Montrouge: Bayard, 2008), 3. Simon does not speak of "redactors" but of "public scribes." See further idem, *A Critical History of the Old Testament* (London: Walter Davis, 1682), 3.

2. For more details, see John Rogerson, *Old Testament Criticism in the Nineteenth Century : England and Germany* (London: SPCK, 1984); David L. Petersen, "The Formation of the Pentateuch," in *Old Testament Interpretation: Past, Present, Future: Essays in Honor of Gene M. Tucker* (ed. James Luther Mays, David L. Petersen, and Kent Harold Richards; Nashville: Abingdon, 1995), 31–45; Ernest Nicholson, *The Pentateuch in the Twentieth Century: The Legacy of Julius Wellhausen* (Oxford: Clarendon, 1998).

3. Otto Eissfeldt, *The Old Testament: An Introduction* (New York: Harper & Row, 1965), 240.

4. Bernhard Duhm, *Das Buch Jeremia* (KHC 11; Tübingen: Mohr Siebeck, 1901), xix–xx.

5. Martin Noth, *Überlieferungsgeschichtliche Studien: Die sammelnden und bearbeitenden Geschichtswerke im Alten Testament* (1943; 3rd ed. ; Darmstadt: Wissenschaftliche Buchgesellschaft, 1967); idem, *The Deuteronomistic History* (trans. Jane Doull, John Barton, and Michael D. Rutter; 2nd ed.; JSOTSup 15; Sheffield: Sheffield Academic Press, 1991).

6. Noth, *Deuteronomistic History,* 84.

7. Ibid., 121.

8. Ibid., 26.

9. Willy Marxsen, *Der Evangelist Markus: Studien zur Redaktionsgeschichte des Evangeliums* (FRLANT 49; Göttingen: Vandenhoeck & Ruprecht, 1956); idem, *Mark the Evangelist: Studies on the Redaction History of the Gospel* (trans. James Boyce; Nashville: Abingdon, 1969). Norman Perrin (*What Is Redaction Criticism?* [London: SPCK, 1970], 33) points out that Marxsen "is responsible for the name Redaktionsgeschichte," even if he had some forerunners.

10. For details, as well as for bibliographical references for the works and authors quoted, see Thomas Römer, *The So-Called Deuteronomistic History: A Sociological, Historical and Literary Introduction* (2nd ed.; London: T&T Clark, 2007), 21–43.

11. For Jeremiah, see Thomas Römer, "How Did Jeremiah Become a Convert to Deuteronomistic Ideology?" in *Those Elusive Deuteronomists* (ed. Steven L. McKenzie and Linda S. Schaering; JSOTSup 268; Sheffield: Sheffield Academic Press, 1999), 189–99.

12. For the recent discussion, see Karl-Friedrich Pohlmann, "Forschungen am Ezechielbuch 1969–2004 (III)," *TRu* 71 (2006): 265–309. "Golah" refers to the community that returned to Judah after Cyrus's conquest of the Neo-Babylonian Empire.

13. For an overview, see James D. Nogalski and Marvin A. Sweeney, eds., *Reading and Hearing the Book of the Twelve* (SBLSymS 15; Atlanta: Society of Biblical Literature, 2000), especially the contribution of David L. Petersen, "A Book of the Twelve?" 3–10.

14. Thomas B. Dozeman and Konrad Schmid, eds., *A Farewell to the Yahwist? The Composition of the Pentateuch in Recent European Interpretation* (SBLSymS 34. Atlanta: Society of Biblical Literature, 2006).

15. Interestingly, Christoph Levin, who maintains the idea of the Yahwist as the first creator of a "Pentateuch" (without Leviticus and Deuteronomy), considers this Yahwist more a redactor than a "source" ("The Yahwist: The Earliest Editor in the Pentateuch," *JBL* 126 [2007]: 209–30).

16. For the existence of those redactions, see Thomas Römer and Marc Z. Brettler, "Deuteronomy 34 and the Case for a Persian Hexateuch," *JBL* 119 (2000): 401–19.

17. Thomas Römer and Konrad Schmid, eds., *Les dernières rédactions du Pentateuque, de l'Hexateuque et de l'Ennéateuque* (BETL 203; Leuven: Peeters, 2007).

18. John Van Seters, *The Edited Bible: The Curious History of the "Editor" in Biblical Criticism* (Winona Lake, Ind.: Eisenbrauns, 2006), 398.

19. John Van Seters, *Abraham in History and Tradition* (New Haven: Yale University Press, 1975), 285.

20. Jeffrey H. Tigay, *The Evolution of the Gilgamesh Epic* (Philadelphia: University of Pennsylvania Press, 1982).

21. See also the critical remarks against Eckart Otto in his review of Van Seters's book (*RBL* online: http://bookreviews.org/pdf/5237_5516.pdf) and Jean-Louis Ska, "A Plea on Behalf of the Biblical Redactors," *ST* 59 (2005): 4–18.

22. Verse 10 is another redactional insertion, using the same literary technique by repeating the introduction to the angel's discourse.

23. For more details, see Thomas Römer, "Why Would the Deuteronomists Tell about the Sacrifice of Jephthah's Daughter?" *JSOT* 77 (1998): 27–38.

24. Rudolf Smend, "The Law and the Nations: A Contribution to Deuteronomistic Tradition History," in *Reconsidering Israel and Judah: Recent Studies on the Deuteronomistic History* (ed. Gary N. Knoppers and J. Gordon McConville; Sources for Biblical and Theological Study 8; Winona Lake, Ind.: Eisenbrauns, 2000), 95–110.

25. An asterisk after a verse number indicates an earlier layer found in that verse.

26. It could be argued that v. 14 ("but in the place that YHWH chooses in one of your tribes") is alluding to a perspective of the Mosaic fiction. This, however, is not necessary. Be that as it may, our purpose is to show the threefold redaction of Deut 12.

27. Richard D. Nelson, *Joshua: A Commentary* (OTL; Louisville: Westminster John Knox, 1997), 266–69.

28. Birgit Lucassen, "Josua, Richter und CD," *RevQ* 18 (1998): 373–96.

29. Even those scholars who do not accept the idea of a Deuteronomistic History recognize the presence of "Deuteronomistic" texts in the Former Prophets. Contrary to Noth, they have some difficulties in explaining the existence and especially the purpose of those texts.

30. For a history of research and overview of the current discussion, see Römer, *So-Called*; Jeffrey C. Geoghegan, *The Time, Place and Purpose of the Deuteronomistic History: The Evidence of "Until This Day"* (BJS 347; Providence, R.I.: Brown University, 2006).

31. Compare vv. 10–11 and Exod 40:34–35 [P]; see also Ernst Würthwein, *Die Bücher der Könige: 1Könige 1–16* (ATD 11.1; Göttingen: Vandenhoeck & Ruprecht, 1977), 84–91.

32. Othmar Keel, "Der salomonische Tempelweihspruch: Beobachtungen zum religionsgeschichtlichen Kontext des Ersten Jerusalemer Tempel," in *Gottesstadt und Gottesgarten: Zur Geschichte und Theologie des Jerusalemer Tempels* (ed. Othmar Keel and Erich Zenger; Freiburg: Herder, 2002), 9–22.

33. Voir Eep Talstra, *Solomon's Prayer: Synchrony and Diachrony in the Composition of I Kings 8, 14–61* (CBET 3; Kampen: Kok Pharos, 1993). He distinguishes, after the ancient document, the following layers: three Deuteronomistic redactions (one centered on the character of David, another on the place of worship, the third on the explanation of the deportation) and a post-Deuteronomistic redaction from the Second Temple period.

34. The diachrony of prayer occasions is difficult. Verses 44–51 are often considered a late insertion since they exhibit stylistic differences with vv. 33–40. It is, however, quite plausible that vv. 41–51 (and not vv. 44–51) are interpolated. Contrary to other cases, these verses, with mention of a stranger coming from afar to worship YHWH (the word *nokrî* is rare in Deuteronomistic History: only Deut 14:21; 15:3; 17:15; 23:21; 29:21; Judg 19:21; 2 Sam 15:19; 1 Kgs 11:1, 8), do not have any parallel in Deut 28. In all these texts, the word had a negative connotation, with the possible exception of a late text (Deut 29:21), coming from afar to worship YHWH. This is not a Deuteronomistic concept but better fits the Hellenistic period, when proselytism developed. The mention of war is not very logical after v. 33, where Israel is already defeated. Verses 46–51 mention the idea of a return to YHWH and thus recall Deut 30, which probably dates from the Persian period. But contrary to Deut 30, there is no mention of a gathering from among the peoples and return to the land. This could also be explained by the acceptance of the Diaspora situation, in which case it could also favor a Persian setting. The question can hardly be settled.

35. Either the Chronicler tried to correct a difficult text or the MT of 1 Kgs 8:16 was corrupted by a scribal error (*homoioarkton*). According to A. Graeme Auld, the Chronicler's version would be primitive (*Kings without Privilege: David and Moses in the Story of the Bible's Kings* [Edinburgh: T&T Clark, 1994], 59).

36. According to the LXX. The MT has a plural. 1 Kgs 8:16 clearly reflects Deut 12:11, 14, and 18; see Albert Šanda, *Das erste Buch der Könige* (vol. 1 of *Die Bücher der Könige*; EHAT 9; Münster: Aschendorff, 1911), 221.

37. Charles Fox Burney, *Notes on the Hebrew Text of the Book of Kings* (Oxford: Clarendon, 1920), 112–15.

38. The affirmation that YHWH alone is God and that there is no other god recalls Deut 4, another late Dtr text from the Persian period.

39. I have already mentioned the Gilgamesh Epic. A more recent example are some writings from Qumran, such as the Rule of the Community, which copies biblical passages and provides a new context with new comments.

Textual Criticism: Recovering and Preserving the Text of the Hebrew Bible

Ralph W. Klein

Introduction[1]

The standard critical edition of the Hebrew Bible used today, *Biblia Hebraica Stuttgartensia* (hereafter *BHS*), contains as its text a virtually unchanged copy of a medieval manuscript, Codex Leningradensis, whose colophon dates it to 1009 C.E. This codex was produced in Cairo by Shemu'el ben Ya'aqob. The vocalization (use of vowels and accents) in this manuscript follows the Ben Asher tradition, which reached its final form under Aaron Ben Moses ben Asher, who died about 960 C.E. Another medieval manuscript, the Aleppo Codex, whose consonants were written by Shĕlomo ben Buya'a, was vocalized and accented by Aaron Ben Asher himself about 925 C.E. Unfortunately, about one fourth of this manuscript has been lost, including its copy of the Pentateuch.

The Hebrew Bible was written originally without vowels or accents. So as to preserve traditional readings, three systems of vocalization arose between 500 and 700 C.E., namely, the Tiberian, the Palestinian, and the Babylonian systems. After several centuries, the Tiberian system eventually prevailed. Altogether, the completed Masoretic Text (MT) consists of the consonants, as well as instructions on how the text is to be laid out on the page, the vocalization of the text, the addition of accents, and the Masorah. The Masorah contains even more information designed to ensure that special care would be taken in transmitting the text. It consists of three parts: Masorah parva; Masorah magna; and Masorah finalis.

The Masorah parva notes specific occurrences of spellings, vocalization, or forms (e.g., it tells us that the phrase "in the beginning" [*bĕrešit*] in Gen 1:1 occurs five times in the Hebrew Bible, of which three are at the beginning of a verse). As for the Masorah magna, it gives detailed information about the particulars noted in the Masorah parva. With regard to the phrase "in the beginning," the Masorah magna refers the reader to verses now known as Gen 1:1 and Jer 26:1; 27:1; 28:2; 48:34, which are the five places where this form appears. The Masorah magna contains more than four thousand such lists. In turn, the Masorah finalis gives lists of the phenomena already cited and provides information about the number of letters, words, and verses in each biblical book. At the end of Genesis, the Masorah finalis reads: "The total number of verses in the book is 1,534."

Although there is no scholarly consensus on when the compositional phase of Old Testament books came to an end, most scholars would date the consonantal MT, the traditional text of the Hebrew Bible, to the end of the first century C.E. or early in the second century at the latest.[2] Thus, about a millennium separates our earliest complete copy of the Hebrew Bible, Codex Leningradensis, from the consonantal form of the MT in the late first or early second century C.E. During that millennium, this text seems to have been copied with extreme care and with very few changes.

Evidence for Variant Readings

The discovery of ancient Hebrew texts in the Judean Desert, popularly known as the Dead Sea Scrolls, between 1947 and 1956, that date from approximately 250 B.C.E. to 135 C.E., revealed that in this period we should speak of textual plurality, in that the variants from MT are of far greater number than had been known from medieval manuscripts.[3] Emanuel Tov has identified five groups of texts among the two hundred fragments of biblical scrolls from Qumran itself:[4] (1) proto-Masoretic texts whose consonants are very similar to MT; (2) pre-Samaritan texts whose expansionistic and harmonistic characteristics are similar to those noted earlier in the Samaritan Pentateuch (SP)[5] but without its ideological changes; (3) texts copied in the Qumran scribal practice (variations in orthography, morphology, and the like);[6] (4) texts close to the Hebrew source of the Septuagint (LXX); and (5) nonaligned texts that follow an inconsistent pattern of agreements and disagreements with MT, SP, and the LXX. His third category is somewhat dubious, since the variations in orthography and morphology noted in these texts were probably widespread in Palestine and not restricted to the Qumran community, but his point about the manifest textual plurality at Qumran is well taken.

Before the discovery of the texts from the Judean desert, scholars were primarily dependent on variant readings known from medieval Hebrew manuscripts, those reflected in the Samaritan Pentateuch, and those reconstructed on the basis of the ancient translations of the Old Testament: LXX, including the Old Latin, which is an ancient translation of the LXX; the Aramaic Targumim;[7] the Peshitta (the Syriac translation);[8] and the Latin Vulgate, translated by Saint Jerome between 390 and 405 C.E., from a copy of the Hebrew Bible in the MT tradition. Of the ancient versions, the LXX was and is the most important, containing more variants than all the rest of the ancient versions combined. The LXX translation was originally made in the third and second centuries B.C.E., and the translation stemming from this era is called the Old Greek. From time to time in antiquity the Old Greek was revised to agree with the current Hebrew text. Two of these recensions are known as the proto-Lucianic recension and the *kaige*-Theodotion recension. A third type of recension is the result of the creation of the Hexapla by Origen in the third century C.E. All three of these recensions will be defined in the following paragraphs.

Origen's Hexapla

Origen's Hexapla was a mammoth manuscript, arranged in six columns, four of which contained Greek translations.[9] The first column held the consonantal Hebrew text of Origen's day, which was not always the same as the consonantal text of the Dead Sea Scrolls or the Hebrew text used by the translators of the LXX, while the second column represented the transliteration of that Hebrew text into Greek letters. This Greek transcription also included representation of Hebrew vowels and thus gives us some indication of how the Hebrew Bible was read or vocalized in the third century C.E. The third, fourth, and sixth columns contained, respectively, the translations of Aquila, Symmachus, and Theodotion (or *kaige*-Theodotion [see below]). Aquila and Symmachus are either second-century C.E. Jewish revisions of the Old Greek or new translations into Greek. Aquila, the most literal of the ancient translations, attempted to represent every word into Greek, including the Hebrew sign for the definite direct object. Both Aquila and Symmachus seem to have based their revisions on *kaige*-Theodotion. At one time Theodotion was classified as another late second-century revision, but the Greek scroll of the Minor Prophets found in Naḥal Ḥever in 1952 contains an early Greek revision of the Old Greek (middle first century B.C.E.) that is now known as *kaige*, because of its distinctive translation of the Hebrew word *gam*, and this revision is thought to be identical with Theodotion, or, according to others, it should be called proto-Theodotion. This recension is also found in parts of the LXX in Samuel–Kings (2 Sam 11:1–1 Kgs 2:11; 1 Kgs 22:1–2 Kgs 25:30), the Theodotion text of Daniel, and elsewhere.

The discovery of this early date for *kaige*-Theodotion solves an old interpretive problem: How is it possible that, when the New Testament book of Revelation cites the book of Daniel, it follows the recension of Theodotion rather than the Old Greek? Since Revelation is usually dated to the last decade of the first century C.E., this created an anomaly: a first-century C.E.. document seemed to cite a second-century C.E. translation, namely, Theodotion. Now that *kaige*-Theodotion or proto-Theodotion has been shown to come from pre-Christian times, the textual basis for Revelation's citations from Daniel is no longer a mystery.

The fifth column of the Hexapla contained the LXX of Origen's day, which was a derivative of the Old Greek. Origen's methodology was to compare the quantitative differences between the first and the fifth columns. When an element was present in Greek and not in the Hebrew, he marked it with an *obelos*; when an element was extant in Hebrew and not in Greek, he added the Greek from one of the other columns, usually *kaige*-Theodotion, and marked it with an *asterisk*. Origen's purpose was apparently to make the Greek Bible used by the Christians agree as closely as possible with the Hebrew Bible used by Jewish scholars so that disagreements between Christians and Jews would not be based on alternative readings. Origen, of course, was unaware of Hebrew textual fluidity in the centuries prior to the end of the first century C.E. and assumed instead that the Hebrew text had always been the same. In emending the fifth column, he was destroying some of its ancient and more original readings.

Most manuscripts of the LXX that have survived from antiquity are based on Origen's fifth column, but when this column was later copied into another manuscript, without the other five columns, the *obeloi* and *asterisks* were usually dropped, resulting in an expanded form of the text of the LXX that is called Hexaplaric. Despite this unintended negative effect of the Hexapla, the editors of the Göttingen Septuagint, a modern critical edition of the LXX, have been able to use standard text-critical methodology and surviving non-Hexaplaric manuscripts in their attempt to approximate the best text of the Old Greek for each book. The other modern critical edition of LXX, called the Cambridge Septuagint, on the other hand, is a diplomatic edition, printing one manuscript at the top of the page, usually the fourth-century manuscript Vaticanus (abbreviated as LXX^{B}), and providing readers with a series of apparatuses that list all the variants that were known at the time the volumes were published. It is generally thought that LXX^{B} represents a pre-Hexaplaric form of the text. The two volume abridged edition of the LXX edited by Alfred Rahlfs follows the Göttingen system but is based primarily on three manuscripts: Vaticanus and Sinaiticus from the fourth century and Alexandrinus from the fifth century.[10] Advanced text-critical work requires use of one of the two larger critical editions, the Göttingen or Cambridge Septuagint.

The most important post-Hexaplaric revision is that of Lucian, who died in 312 C.E. Lucian is known to have made a number of linguistic changes to the text of the LXX, but now scholars have identified within Lucianic manuscripts (called b, o, c^2, and e^2 in the Cambridge Septuagint) a substratum that seems to reflect another revision of the Old Greek toward a Hebrew text like 4QSam^{a}, which is dated to the first century B.C.E. The importance of this proto-Lucianic recension will be demonstrated in the discussion of 2 Sam 24 and 1 Chr 21 at the end of this chapter.

Even when a text approximating the Old Greek has been identified through the use of a critical edition, such as the Cambridge Septuagint or the Göttingen Septuagint, the reconstruction of the Hebrew that lay before the LXX translator is difficult, since the translator's translation technique and exegesis of the Hebrew text played a role in the translation that was produced. Scholars therefore attempt to distinguish between true Hebrew variants lying behind the LXX and variant readings introduced by the translator.

Biblia Hebraica Stuttgartensia

While professional exegetes and writers of biblical commentaries will use one of the critical editions of the LXX, all students will depend, at one time or another, on a textual apparatus such as that in *BHS*. The editors of the individual books in this edition, listed on the reverse side of the title page, have approached the task in somewhat different fashions and do not use the abbreviations employed in the apparatus with absolute consistency. Nevertheless, a wealth of textual data is contained in the apparatus to *BHS*, based on medieval Hebrew manuscripts, the ancient versions mentioned above, and variants attested in the Dead Sea Scrolls that were available when this edition was produced (1967–1977). The editors often offer the reader advice (though written in Latin) that directs one to read another manuscript's alternate version of a text or to add or delete a certain reading on the basis of such evidence. At other times, the editors merely list variants and expect readers to make their own judgments. *BHS* has been criticized for resorting too often to conjecture and for including literary-critical judgments in the textual apparatus. As a result, users of the apparatus in *BHS* are required to exercise their own critical judgment about the data and recommendations cited therein.

Biblia Hebraica Quinta

A new edition of the Hebrew Bible called *Biblia Hebraica Quinta* (*BHQ*) *is* now being produced, and four preliminary volumes have appeared: the Megilloth; Ezra-Nehemiah; Proverbs; and Deuteronomy. *BHQ* prints an unchanged copy of Codex Leningradensis that is based on newer and superior photographs of the manuscript. This edition will eventually appear in two large volumes: the first will contain the text of the Hebrew Bible, the Masorah, and a neutral critical apparatus; the second will include introductions to the text history of individual books, translation of the notes to the Masorah, and commentaries on the Masorah and on data contained in the textual apparatus. For the first time, the Masorot will be easily understood by nonspecialists. The information provided in the textual apparatus itself will be neutral, simply listing the variants, with no indication of editorial preferences. The variants included in the apparatus must meet two criteria. The variants must represent a Hebrew text differing from Leningradensis, and they must be potentially significant for translation or exegesis. This edition will be able to make full use of all the extant Dead Sea Scroll manuscripts, and its citations from the Peshitta will be based on the Leiden Peshitta project, which is publishing a multivolume critical edition of the Peshitta. It is in the second volume where the editors of each book will make specific comments on variant readings recorded in the apparatus.[11]

Representative Types of Textual Variants

Variants in the textual evidence for the Hebrew Bible arose both by accident and by intention. Accidental variants depend in part on the competence and attentiveness of the copyist. The following types of variants often occur.

Haplography occurs when a scribe writes one letter or one word instead of two, as in Judg 20:13, where the Kethib[12] is *binyāmin* (Benjamin), and the Qere is *bĕnê binyāmin*[13] (sons of Benjamin, or Benjaminites). The longer reading is clearly preferable because the verb in this sentence has a third-person common plural ending rather than the singular form, as would be expected if the subject were Benjamin. In writing the sequence of letters *bny bny,* a scribe accidentally omitted one of them.

Dittography is the writing two letters or two words or two clauses instead of one, as in Lev 20:10: "And as for the man who commits adultery with the wife of *a man who commits adultery with the wife of* his neighbor, he shall be put to death, both the adulterer and the adulteress." The italicized works are dittographic in the MT and are lacking in various minuscule manuscripts of LXX.

Conflation denotes the inclusion of both of two variant readings. For example, 2 Sam 22:43 MT ("I crushed them and stamped them down") is a conflation of alternate readings. "I crushed them" is attested by LXX[B], and "I stamped them down" is attested by 4QSam[a]. Another example is 2 Sam 21:22 MT "of the giants in Gath" (*lhrph bgt*), compared to LXX "of the giants in Gath, to Rapha a house" (based on a Hebrew *Vorlage*[14] *lhrph bgt lhrph byt*). *Byt* (house) arose originally as a corruption of *bgt* (in Gath), and the two expressions were conflated in the *Vorlage* of the LXX.

Glossing, or adding details or comments to a text, can be seen in Josh 2:15: "She [Rahab] let them down *with a rope* through the window, *for her house was in the city wall, and it was in the wall that she lived*." The italicized words, lacking in the LXX, explain more fully Rahab's strategy in letting the Israelite spies escape.

Homoioteleuton refers to the omission of a word or words because a scribe's eye skipped from the ending of one word to the ending of another word, as in 1 Sam 12:8 MT "When Jacob went to Egypt..." compared to LXX "When Jacob went to *Egypt*, the *Egyptians* oppressed them...." In Hebrew, the words "Egypt" (מצרים) and "Egyptians" (מצרים) come at the end of the clauses, with the result that the second clause was lost in the MT, because the copyist's eye skipped from "Egypt" to "Egyptians."

Homoioarcton refers to the omission of a word or words because a scribe's eye skipped from the beginning of one word to the beginning of another word and left out all of the intervening words. For example, Gen 31:18 MT reads, "And he drove all his livestock and all his property that he had gained, the livestock in his possession that he had gained in Paddan-aram," while the LXX omits "that he had gained, the livestock in his possession." The Hebrew *Vorlage* of the LXX had been damaged by homoioarcton.

Expansion due to the influence of other parts of the passage can be observed in Josh 2:16: MT HAS "until the pursuers returned," while LXX reads "until those who pursued after you returned." The addition of "after you" may have been influenced by the expression "those who were pursuing after them" in Josh 2:7.

Interchange of similar letters also takes place.[15] In the "square" script, such as that used in *BHS*,[16] the following letters are similar: *d*/*r* (ד/ר); *b*/*m* (ב/ם); *b*/*k* (ב/כ); *k*/*m* (כ/ם); and *h*/*ḥ* (ה/ח). In the earlier Hebrew script, in which some of the biblical books were composed, or in the Paleo-Hebrew script that is present at Qumran, the following letters are similar: *ʾ*/*ṭ*; *ṣ*/*y*; and *n*/*p*.

Metathesis is the transposition of adjacent letters. For example, Deut 31:1 MT reads "and Moses went [*wayyēlek*] and spoke," while LXX has "and Moses finished [*wayyēkel*] speaking." Clearly, the position of *kāp* and *lāmed* has been interchanged, a change that would have been easier before the use of final letters and vowel points in Hebrew.

Incorrect word division. Spaces between words in the Dead Sea Scrolls were very narrow, and some early forms of biblical books may have been written with no word division at all. An example of such an incorrect word division is in a conjectural emendation in Amos 6:12. MT reads: "Can one plow with oxen [*babbĕqārîm*]?" *BHS* proposes a different division of the letters of the last word (*babbāqār yām*) "with oxen sea," taking the noun "oxen" as a collective noun. If one then revocalizes the verb "plow" from *qal* to *nipʿal*, the result is a superior translation: "Can the sea be plowed with oxen?" In this case, two reasonable conjectures created a far superior text.

Differences involving vowel letters (*matres lectionis*). Often the presence or absence of vowel letters does not affect the meaning; thus, Judg 1:19 *wayyōreš* and 1:20 *wayyôreš* both mean "and he took possession." In 1 Sam 1:24, however, there is a significant difference between MT "with three bulls" (*bĕpārîm šĕlōšâ*) and LXX "with a three-year-old bull" (*bpr mšlš*). The variant in MT shows incorrect word division, the addition of an internal *yôd* vowel letter as part of the masculine plural noun "bulls," and the addition of the final *hê* on the number "three."

Alternate vocalizations. The MT of Isa 9:7 contains the reading *dābār* ("word"), but the LXX reads *thanaton* ("death"), which may presuppose a different vocalization of the consonants *dbr* as *deber* ("pestilence" or the like). "The LORD sent a word/death against Jacob." While in the vast majority of cases the vocalization in MT seems correct, there are a significant number of cases where the word found in the MT has to be revocalized, such as Isa 7:11, "whether it is deep, ask" (*haʿmēq šĕʾālāh*), or "whether it is deep as Sheol" (*haʿmēq šĕʾōlāh*). The latter vocalization is supported by Aquila, Symmachus, and Theodotion and favored by the editor of *BHS*. The consonants are the same in either reading.

Synonymous readings. The translations of one clause in 2 Sam 22:1 and Ps 18:1[17] in the NRSV are identical: "on the day when the LORD delivered him from the hand of all his enemies." In Samuel, the word for hand is *kāp,* while in Psalms it is *yād*. This change may have arisen consciously or unconsciously, and there is no easy way to determine which reading is preferable.[18]

Some accidental variants do not reflect any of these categories but arose truly accidentally, based on factors such as scribal fatigue or lack of competence.

Intentional changes include replacing rare words with more common ones, harmonizing tendencies (a scribe adapted a reading to other elements in the same verse, the same context, the same book, or in another book of the Bible), addition or expansion of personal or divine names, theological changes (e.g., using the word "shame" in place of the name Baal);[19] euphemistic changes, changing details of the text to agree with biblical laws, and interpolations. An example of a euphemistic change is found in 2 Sam 12:9. The MT reads: "Why do you treat the word of the LORD with contempt?" LXX^{L}, on the other hand, reads: "Why do you treat the LORD with contempt?" The addition of "the word" softens the insult to the deity, so it seems that the MT represents a euphemistic change. The Masoretes recorded some eighteen "corrections of the scribes" where they recognized that a change in the text had been deliberately made, often for euphemistic reasons. For example, 1 Sam 3:13 indicates that the sons of Eli were cursing for themselves (*lhm*), but the corrections of the scribes recognized that these sons had originally been blaspheming God (*ʾlhym*). The original reading in this case is also preserved in the LXX.

DECIDING BETWEEN ALTERNATIVE READINGS

What are the bases for a text critic's decisions between individual variant readings? The collecting of ancient variants, whether from Hebrew manuscripts such as the Dead Sea Scrolls or by retroversion from the ancient versions, is a relatively objective procedure. However, as I have indicated, retroversion from Greek or another ancient language into Hebrew requires high linguistic skills, and there is always a danger that the variant reconstructed into Hebrew was a change made by the translator in the course of translating. Choosing which is the preferable reading, however, is a much more subjective activity; it is an art rather than a science. Textual critics have formulated "rules" for making textual decisions, but these rules are far from absolute.

Rule 1: The more difficult reading is to be preferred (*lectio difficilior praeferenda est*). If the variation is between a rare word and a more common word, the textual critic may decide that the rare word has been replaced by a common one in the course of textual transmission. But every scribal spelling error would also be the more difficult reading, and such misspellings are hardly to be preferred.

Rule 2: The shorter reading is to be preferred (*lectio brevior potior*). This rule assumes that scribes are likely to combine ancient variants known to them, fill out divine and human personal names, or otherwise expand the text. Texts generally get longer rather than shorter, but omissions caused by haplography or by homoioarcton and homoioteleuton are also shorter readings and are not to be preferred. In Jeremiah, the shorter text attested by the LXX is usually considered superior by scholars, whereas the many shorter readings in MT of Samuel are thought to result from various forms of textual corruption.

Rule 3: That reading is original if its presence suggests how all the variant readings arose. This rule can be slightly reformulated by asking which reading is more likely to have given rise to the other. For example, text from a parallel passage is occasionally added, creating a harmonized form of the text. The MT of Exod 32:10b reads: "I will make you [Moses] a great nation." At this point, the Samaritan Pentateuch adds text from a parallel passage in Deut 9:20: "But against Aaron the LORD was exceedingly angry [enough] to destroy him, so Moses prayed on behalf of Aaron." This addition, called a "plus," is already attested in 4QpaleoExod^{m}, demonstrating that many of the pluses in SP were not made for sectarian reasons but merely reflect a harmonizing form of the text. The SP, which harmonizes Deut 9:20 and Exod 32:10b, is clearly not the original reading.

None of these rules works in every case, and perhaps not even in the majority of cases. Therefore, the textual critic makes judgments based on detailed knowledge of the writing style or theology of a given writer and chooses that reading as preferable that is contextually most appropriate.

The textual critic tries to support his or her decision by marshalling as many arguments as possible, but we should not be surprised if two competent textual critics differ on how to interpret individual variant readings.

Despite the evidence offered by the scrolls, the LXX, and other ancient versions, much ancient evidence has been lost: we do not have in any case the hypothetical final text that existed at the end of the composition process, and the Dead Sea Scrolls themselves are highly fragmentary for most books (1QIsa[a], containing the complete text of Isaiah, is a notable exception). There may well be texts that the exegete perceives as corrupt even without any manuscript or versional evidence to support that conclusion. In such cases, the only resort may be conjecture, but this practice should be used very sparingly and with full awareness of all of its uncertainties.[20]

Sometimes there is no sure way to emend a difficult or impossible text. In 1 Sam 13:1, the MT text is surely corrupt when it states that King Saul was one year old when he became king and that he reigned for two years over Israel. Saul is clearly an adult in every mention of him in 1 Samuel, and the many events in his life seem to require a length of reign far in excess of two years. The verse is lacking in LXX[B], perhaps intentionally. It could be that the entire verse was dropped by the translator or was already missing in the Hebrew *Vorlage* lest this error be perpetuated. An error can only be *identified* in this case. The reconstruction of an original, superior reading is pure guesswork. As such, the NRSV puts three dots for the age of Saul at his accession, and a note on the two-year length of his reign states: "Two is not the entire number; something has dropped out." That suggests, but does not prove, that Saul reigned for twelve, twenty-two, or thirty-two years.

The Goal of Textual Criticism

A major text-critical study of the Old Testament called the Hebrew Old Testament Text Project (HOTTP) was supported by the United Bible Societies and involved an international team of outstanding scholars. The purpose of this project was to provide aid to Bible translators on some five thousand passages that had proved troublesome to translators. Eventually that list was expanded to six thousand passages. The team produced a bilingual (English and French) five-volume work entitled *Preliminary and Interim Report on the Hebrew Old Testament Text Project* (1976–1980).[21] Its final report has appeared in a four-volume work, published only in French, entitled *Critique textuelle de l'Ancien Testament*.[22]

These scholars noted four phases in the history of the transmission of the text of the Hebrew Bible. (1) Early literary forms of various blocs of texts were in the hands of editors and schools before they became community texts. At this stage the biblical works were in the process of formation, and the investigation of this stage is beyond the province of textual criticism. (2) Thereupon the text entered a period of fluidity and diversity, as attested at Qumran and in the LXX. This is the first stage of textual transmission and is the earliest stage in which text-critical work can be done. The scholars involved in HOTTP note that there is some overlap between the phase of textual formation and the phase of textual transmission. (3) Then follows the phase of proto-MT, which is evidenced by the Hebrew manuscript finds at Murabbaʿat and Masada and in the second-century C.E. Greek translations of Aquila and Theodotion. The Greek Minor Prophets scroll, mentioned above, is transitional between phases 2 and 3. (4) Finally, we find the full MT present in the Aleppo Codex and Codex Leningradensis of the tenth and eleventh centuries C.E.

While the team originally hoped to establish the text that had emerged at the beginning of phase 2, they found increasingly that they could not discover a text that was stable and unified before the time of the Old Greek translators. At the conclusion of their work, they chose the proto-MT of phase 3 as the basis for an edition of the Hebrew text of the Bible. The team identified three tasks for textual criticism. (1) Textual criticism must first determine which form of the text is most authentic to the classic Tiberian text. (2) It must then attempt, with the aid of other proto-Masoretic text witnesses, to restore the consonantal form that is most likely to represent the standard proto-Masoretic edition, as well as the vocalization and accentuation corresponding to it. (3) Finally, it must discern those corruptions and accidental mutilations suffered by the pre-Masoretic text and correct them to the extent that they have not produced literary restructurings. By means of this last point the team notes that some early variants required literary restructuring by ancient scribes to accommodate them, and therefore the corruption could not be removed without removing the restructuring as well.[23]

Emanuel Tov has discussed at some length the question whether there once was an original text (called an Ur-text) from which all subsequent texts derived or whether there were various pristine texts of the Bible that did not derive from one another but had equal status. He adopts a modified form of the original text theory and distinguishes between the various stages of literary composition of the biblical books (one might think of the gradual development of the books of Isaiah and Jeremiah and the final status of a book such as Isaiah or Jeremiah). Textual criticism, he proposes, deals with the transmission of the text after its final authoritative status had been achieved. But Tov also proposes that some books, like Jeremiah, achieved a final status more than once, that is, a final status in MT and an earlier "final status" in the shorter form of the text known from LXX and from manuscripts 4QJer[b] and 4QJer[d] that were discovered at Qumran. The survival of this form of the text alongside the proto-Masoretic 4QJer[a] and 4QJer[c] is thus explained. Textual criticism of Jeremiah, based on the LXX, 4QJer[b], and 4QJer[d] enables students to distinguish between these editions of Jeremiah. Tov goes on to argue that textual criticism of the "final and canonical edition," that is, of the MT, is the objective of textual criticism.[24] The final MT form of Jeremiah may also contain corrupt readings that arose during the course of textual transmission and that can be corrected on the basis of the Dead Sea Scrolls or the ancient versions.

Eugene Ulrich takes issue with Tov on the purpose and function of textual criticism.[25] In his view, the MT is merely the text of the edition of each book of the Bible that rabbinic Judaism eventually chose, but this choice was not based on careful collation of available manuscripts and creation of a perfected text. In the case of the books of Samuel, the final MT text chosen is notably inferior and must frequently be corrected on the basis of the scrolls and the LXX. Unfortunately, the textual apparatus for the books of Samuel in *BHS* does not mention all of the variants from the MT that can be reconstructed from the LXX, or when it does cite them it does not provide enough information for the student to know the exact nature of the variation. The text of MT varies in quality from book to book, as does the value of the LXX. Ulrich proposes that the purpose or function of textual criticism is to reconstruct the history of the texts that eventually became the biblical collection in both their literary growth and their scribal transmission. Ulrich calls attention to a number of double editions of biblical accounts that are now available to us: 1 Sam 1–2 (Hannah and Samuel); 1 Sam 17–18 (David and Goliath); the shorter (LXX) and the longer (MT) texts of Jeremiah; and Dan 4 and 6, which are shorter in MT, and Dan 5, which is shorter in LXX. The shorter and longer texts provide evidence for literary growth that can be identified by textual criticism. Scholars also make judgments about literary growth based on other criteria, such as in the putative preexilic and exilic editions of the Deuteronomistic History. But in the cases cited above, the evidence for literary growth comes from textual criticism itself. Textual criticism in Ulrich's view is *not just* to judge individual variants in order to determine which readings were superior or original, although of course it must at times make judgments on such individual variants, but textual criticism is also to make distinctions between the shorter and longer versions of Jeremiah or the shorter and longer versions of the Goliath story on the basis of text-critical evidence.

What unites Tov and Ulrich is that the idea of "the original text" is in some ways a distracting concept. In classical studies, one often speaks of an autograph, that is, the finished literary product of a single author. Ulrich prefers to speak of the base text, which is the form of the text, or the literary edition, of any particular book that was current (during any given period) prior to a new, creatively developed literary edition. His approach to the history of the biblical text, therefore, is that it was *diachronic* (changing over time) and *pluriform*. The differences among MT, LXX, and SP in the Pentateuch demonstrate that numerous individual variant readings arose in these three texts. The SP contains a number of harmonistic readings that were also typical of some pentateuchal manuscripts at Qumran, in addition to its specifically sectarian Samaritan readings themselves, which favor Mount Gerizim rather than Jerusalem as the preferred worship center.

Case Study: The Chronicler's *Vorlage*

In addition to the question about what form of the text a textual critic should try to reconstruct, textual criticism also helps in other aspects of biblical exegesis. The author of Chronicles (first half of the fourth century B.C.E.) based his work in large part on the text of Samuel and Kings (whose final literary formation is probably to be dated to the mid-sixth century B.C.E.). But the text of Samuel-Kings that lay before the Chronicler was not identical with MT. Hence a number of differences between Samuel–Kings, on the one hand, and Chronicles, on the other, do not reflect changes introduced by the Chronicler but merely the fact that the Chronicler was using an alternate *Vorlage* of Samuel–Kings. Representative examples from 1 Chr 21, based on 2 Sam 24, are cited below to illustrate one of the important uses of textual criticism.[26] The readings cited from Samuel after "cf." reflect the alternate form of the *Vorlage* that the Chronicler used. LXX^{L} is the proto-Lucianic recension from the first century B.C.E. discussed above.

Examples of Non-mt Readings of Samuel That Were Known by the Chronicler

1 Chr 21:1: “the commanders of the people”; cf. 2 Sam 24:2 LXX^{L}. Samuel MT: “the commander of the people” (referring to Joab).

1 Chr 21:2: “bring me a report”; cf. 2 Sam 24:2 LXX^{L}. This clause is lacking in Samuel MT and LXX.

1 Chr 21:3: “to his people”; cf. 2 Sam 24:3 LXX^{L}. Samuel MT: “to the people.”

1 Chr 21:8: “in that I have done this matter”; cf. 2 Sam 24:10 LXX. Samuel MT: “in what I have done.”

1 Chr 21:9: “Gad the seer of David”; cf. 2 Sam 24:11 LXX^{L}. Samuel MT: “Gad the prophet the seer of David.”

1 Chr 21:10: “saying”; cf. 2 Sam 24:12 LXX and LXX^{L}. Lacking in Samuel MT.

1 Chr 21:11: “take your choice”; cf. 2 Sam 24:13 LXX. Lacking in Samuel MT.

1 Chr 21:12: “three years of famine”; cf. 2 Sam 24:13 LXX. Samuel MT: seven years of famine.

1 Chr 21:12: “in the land”; cf. 2 Sam 24:13 LXX^{L}. Sam MT: “in your land.”

1 Chr 21:12: “and now”; cf. 2 Sam 24:13 LXX^{L}. Sam MT: “now.”

1 Chr 21:13: “let me fall”; cf. 2 Sam 24:14 LXX^{L}. Samuel MT: “let us fall.”

1 Chr 21:13: “exceedingly”; cf. 2 Sam 24:14 LXX. Lacking in Samuel MT.

1 Chr 21:15: “God sent an angel to Jerusalem”; cf. 2 Sam 24:16 LXX: “And the angel of God extended his hand.” Samuel MT: “The angel extended his hand to Jerusalem.” The word “God” was added secondarily in the *Vorlage* of Samuel LXX, and this word shows up in a different position in Chroni-

cles, where it became the subject of the sentence and turned the angel into the direct object, with the consequent omission of "his hand."

1 Chr 21:15: "was standing"; cf. 2 Sam 24:16 4QSam[a]. Samuel MT: "was."

1 Chr 21:16: "David looked up and saw the angel of the LORD standing between earth and heaven with his drawn sword in his hand stretched out against Jerusalem. David and the elders, covered with sackcloth, fell on their faces"; cf. 4QSam[a], which contains this long reading with minor variants. The whole verse is lost in Samuel MT and LXX by homoioarcton (a scribe's eyes skipped from "And David looked up" to And David said" in 2 Sam 24:17, leaving out everything in between).

1 Chr 21:17: "And I acted very wickedly" (*whrʿ hrʿwty*); cf. 2 Sam 24:17 4QSam[a]: "I the shepherd did wrong" (*hrʿh hrʿty*). These two readings are closely related, and 2 Sam 24:17 4QSam[a] may be superior. 2 Sam 24:17 MT: "I have acted iniquitously" (*hʿwyty*).

1 Chr 21:18: "an altar for the LORD"; cf. 2 Sam 24:18 LXX[L]. 2 Sam 24:18 MT: "for the LORD an altar."

1 Chr 21:19: "which" (*ʾšr*); cf. 2 Sam 24:19 LXX[L]. Samuel MT: "just as" (*kʾšr*).

1 Chr 21:20–21: "Ornan was threshing wheat. As David came closer to Ornan, Ornan got a better look and recognized David"; cf. 2 Sam 24:20 4QSam[a], which adds "and his servants covering themselves with sackcloth coming…." Lacking completely in 2 Sam 24:20 MT and LXX.

1 Chr 21:23: "take" (imperative); cf. 2 Sam 24:22 LXX[L]. Samuel MT: "May he take."

1 Chr 21:23: "May my lord the king do"; cf. 2 Sam 24:22 LXX[L]. Samuel MT: "May my lord the king offer up."

Conclusion

Textual criticism seeks to recover and preserve the authentic text of the Bible. Scholars can choose to recover the text of the proto-MT, removing errors that emerged after it arose at the end of the first century C.E. or errors that had emerged earlier and were therefore present when the MT came into existence; they can also seek to recover and preserve alternate forms of the text as we know them from the Dead Sea Scrolls, the LXX, and other ancient versions. The different opinions about the goal of textual criticism noted above (by HOTTP, Tov, and Ulrich) have not been conclusively resolved.

In a sense, text criticism is always one of the first steps in biblical exegesis, right after the initial translation of the text, but preliminary decisions about textual criticism may need to be adjusted when the passage has been thoroughly studied and the criteria for deciding between alternate readings have been clarified by a deeper knowledge of what the text was trying to say. In a similar way, a preliminary translation will always need to be revised during the course of exegesis. It is a pleasure to offer this essay in tribute to David L. Petersen, who has consistently demonstrated text-critical expertise in his publications.

For Further Reading

Hendel, Roland. "The Oxford Hebrew Bible: Prologue to a New Critical Edition." *VT* 58 (2008): 324–51.

McCarter, P. Kyle, Jr. *Textual Criticism: Recovering the Text of the Hebrew Bible*. GBS. Philadelphia: Fortress, 1986.

Talmon, Shemaryahu. "Textual Criticism: The Ancient Versions." Pages 141–70 in *Text in Context: Essays by Members of the Society for Old Testament Study*. Edited by A. D. H. Mayes. Oxford: Oxford University Press, 2000.

Tov, Emmanuel. *Textual Criticism of the Hebrew Bible*. 2nd ed. Minneapolis: Fortress, 2001.

Ulrich, Eugene. *The Dead Sea Scrolls and the Origins of the Bible*. Studies in the Dead Sea Scrolls and Related Literature. Grand Rapids: Eerdmans, 1999.

Weis, Richard. "*Biblia Hebraica Quinta* and the Making of Critical Editions of the Hebrew Bible." *TC: A Journal of Biblical Textual Criticism* 7 (2002). Online: http://rosetta.reltech.org/TC/vol07/Weis2002.html.

Notes

1. For further, authoritative information on aspects of textual criticism, see the

magisterial work of Emanuel Tov, *Textual Criticism of the Hebrew Bible,* (2nd ed.; Minneapolis: Fortress; Assen: Van Gorgum, 1992). References to this work will often be given within the text: Tov, *Textual Criticism,* followed by page number(s).

2. An early form of this text, called proto-MT, is present at Qumran and at other sites in the Judean Desert. Tov estimates that 35 percent of the manuscripts from Qumran are proto-MT. At other first- and early second-century C.E. sites in the Judean Desert, the proto-MT is the only text.

3. Thousands of relative minor textual variants were collected by B. Kennicott and J. B. de Rossi in the eighteenth century, and they are frequently cited in the apparatus of *BHS.* The majority of these readings arose after the end of the first century C.E. and rarely reflect earlier traditions (Tov, *Textual Criticism,* 35–39).

4. There are fragments of every Old Testament book except Esther. For the number of scrolls extant for each book, see Tov, *Textual Criticism,* table 19, 104–5. The scrolls have been published in the series Discoveries in the Judaean Desert (of Jordan) by Oxford University Press (1955–).

5. The Samaritan Pentateuch is a consonantal text of the first five books of the Old Testament preserved by the Samaritan community that split off from the rest of the Jewish community in the second century B.C.E. Variants from the MT in SP are of two types. (1) Ideological changes indicate that sacrificial worship should take place on Mount Gerizim instead of at Jerusalem. In Deut 27:4 the SP reads Mount Gerizim instead of Mount Ebal as the name of the place where the Israelites were to erect an altar after the crossing of the Jordan. From the Samaritan perspective, Shechem had already been chosen at the time of the patriarchs as the place for cultic worship. Hence, in Deut 12:5, 14, the text refers to the place YHWH *has* chosen rather than the place YHWH *will* choose. See also the addition of a commandment to the Decalogue at Exod 20:17 and Deut 5:18 referring to the sanctuary of Mt. Gerizim instead of Mt. Ebal. This addition is drawn from Deut 27:2b–7 and 11:30. (2) Other differences from MT, dealing with features such as harmonization, linguistic corrections, and expansions, are also attested in the pre-Samaritan manuscripts from Qumran. That is, this second kind of variant was not introduced by the Samaritan community itself.

6. See Tov, *Textual Criticism,* 107–11

7. Text critics recognize that there is much midrashic material in the Targumim that is not directly relevant to textual criticism itself. The Hebrew text presupposed by the Targumim is very close to the MT, with the exception of the Job Targum from Qumran.

8. The Peshitta also is close to the MT, showing fewer variants than the LXX but more than the Targumim and the Vulgate. Its greatest deviations from the MT are in Chronicles.

9. For a few books there were additional Greek columns called Quinta and Sexta.

10. Alfred Rahlfs, *Septuaginta, id est Vetus Testamentum graece iuxta LXX interpretes* (Stuttgart: Württemberg, 1935).

11. Advanced students may also choose to use the volumes in the Hebrew University Bible Project. This edition has four separate apparatuses based on the ancient versions, the Dead Sea Scrolls and rabbinic citations, medieval codices containing

consonantal differences, and medieval codices containing differences in vocalization and accents. This exhaustive edition does not contain conjectural emendations and does not take a position on the comparative value of readings. So far volumes on Isaiah, Jeremiah, and Ezekiel have been published.

12. The Kethib/Qere variants are recorded in Masorah parva and usually also in the textual apparatus of *BHS*. Kethib refers to the consonants that are written in MT, while Qere refers to vowels that are to be read. The Qere readings often presuppose a different consonant or consonants or a different vowel letter (See Tov, *Textual Criticism*, 58–63).

13. In this case the Qere in MT has no consonants, only the vowels necessary to spell the word "sons of." The longer reading is supported by many medieval Hebrew manuscripts, LXX, Syriac, and the Targum.

14. *Vorlage* is a German word referring to the Hebrew text that lay before the LXX translator.

15. For several examples, see Tov, *Textual Criticism*, 244–48.

16. Sometimes this script is called Aramaic or even Assyrian.

17. Here, as frequently in Psalms, the English and Hebrew verse numbers differ. What is considered v. 1 in Hebrew is construed as an unnumbered superscription to the psalm in English versions.

18. For other examples, see table 16 in Tov, *Textual Criticism*, p. 94

19. 1 Kgs 18:19, 25: "the Baal"; LXX: "the shame" in both cases. Compare Jer 11:13 "to shame" and LXX "to Baal."

20. Tov, *Textual Criticism*, 351–69.

21. United Bible Societies, *Preliminary and Interim Report on the Hebrew Old Testament Text Project = Compte rendu preliminaire et provisoire sur le travail d'analyse textuelle de l'Ancien Testament hebreu* (5 vols.; New York: United Bible Societies, 1976–1980).

22. Dominique Barthélemy, ed., *Critique textuelle de l'Ancien Testament* (4 vols.; OBO 50; Fribourg: Editions Universitaires; Göttingen: Vandenhoeck & Ruprecht, 1982–1985). Those who do not know French can access most of the results of this project in the preliminary bilingual publication. Fortunately, the outstanding introductions written by Dominique Barthélemy in the first three volumes of the final report and covering both the history of textual criticism and the text-critical methodology of the HOTTP itself will be published in English by Eisenbrauns. This is not the place to review the individual judgments made by the team in these thousands of cases, but it needs to be noted that their decisions are, at least in my judgment, exceedingly cautious, declining to change the text in many cases where change seems to me to be necessary.

23. For example, Gen 24:67 reads, "Isaac was comforted after his mother" (presumably implying after his mother's death). The critical apparatus of *BHS* suggests that this verse should be emended to read Isaac was comforted after "his father's death." HOTTP admits that this may indeed have been the reading in a precanonical form of the text, such as in the document J of the Documentary Hypothesis. But in the canonical text, Abraham dies only in Gen 25:8, so that in this structuring of the text no change should be made.

24. Tov, *Textual Criticism*, 189.

25. *The Dead Sea Scrolls and the Origins of the Bible* (Grand Rapids: Eerdmans, 1999).

26. For a complete list, see Ralph W. Klein, *1 Chronicles* (Hermeneia; Minneapolis: Fortress, 2006), 414–17.

Traditio-Historical Criticism: The Development of the Covenant Code

Douglas A. Knight

The various historical-critical methods contributing to the exegesis of the Hebrew Bible do not necessarily exclude or oppose each other, even though as discrete approaches they arose in different periods, under different assumptions, and with different chief proponents. In some sense, each was developed to complement its predecessors by extending the discussion to additional subjects or questions not sufficiently addressed until then. Supposing that the various methods are sharply distinct from each other or even in conflict with each other can mislead exegetes into thinking that the exegetical steps are neater and more controllable than is actually the case. A certain fluidity and elasticity needs to guide the interpreter of texts.

During the eighteenth and nineteenth centuries, biblical scholars tended to assume that the creative period in the production of the Hebrew Bible occurred at the written stage, and they occupied themselves with identifying the literary sources on which the biblical texts were thought to be based. The written documents underlying the Pentateuch and the historical books were, in their view, especially evident, and they engaged in the painstaking task of reconstructing each source, describing its stylistic and ideological features, and situating it in time and space. Without disputing this source-critical work, Hermann Gunkel and others introduced a new exegetical method in the early twentieth century: form criticism. It sought the conventional genres, the "forms," that circulated among the people and were rooted in very specific settings of their life. In many cases these forms were known in oral contexts, and thus form critics began to move the focus away from the written process as the most creative stage in the production of the Hebrew Bible. At the same time, though, considerable interest persisted in trying to determine the redactional process whereby the written sources were combined and edited into their final form; hence redaction criticism arose as a complement to source criticism but not in opposition to form criticism.

Two prominent features of these approaches eventually led to the rise of traditio-historical criticism:[1] (1) the sense that it took a long process, at least several decades and often centuries, for most of the literature to arise—quite in contrast to our modern understanding of writing novels, short stories, poems, laws, and records within a relatively short period of days, months, or years; and (2) the recognition that, for all of the importance of writing, significant literary components could be produced, remembered, and circulated orally. The role of the solitary "author" receded, and in its place specific groups, the "community" at large, and generations appeared as the creators of the literature.

Tradition, according to this critical method, is not a vague, amorphous entity inherited from the past, such as ways of behaving, customary practices, or basic perspectives within a lineage or group or culture. The famous appeal to "tradition" in *Fiddler on the Roof*[2] evokes the sense of identity derived from one's heritage, while at the same time disclosing the past's control over later generations and the inclination of many to resist it. These issues play a role in the discussions of tradition historians but are not their primary subject matter. Rather, the "tradition" under scrutiny for exegetes is *the text*, a specific portion of literature that may have come into being over a period of time but now exists in finished form as a written passage. The goal of the traditio-historical critic is to retrace this formation of the literary piece from its initial composition through its later stages of revision and to its final form in the text.

History of the Method

As indicated, traditio-historical criticism arose in the wake of source criticism, form criticism, and redaction criticism. With roots in these methods and the research results they produced, traditio-historical criticism developed in somewhat distinct manner in two different contexts: Germany and Scandinavia. Most scholars elsewhere tended to follow the German direction, although with some influences from Scandinavian circles as well. It would be fair to say that, as currently practiced, traditio-historical criticism is now more of a uniform method, less distinguished by school lines than was earlier the case.[3]

Among German scholars, Martin Noth and Gerhard von Rad are the two most significant progenitors of traditio-historical criticism. Beginning in the 1930s and working separately, they began a series of studies that eventually resulted in the traditio-historical method as we know it. Noth's first study in this area did not focus on a specific text in the Hebrew Bible but rather on the historical context in which traditions could have arisen and been preserved.[4] During the premonarchic period while the land was being settled, he maintained, the twelve Israelite tribes formed a type of confederacy, termed an amphictyony, with its center in a specific cultic site (variously Bethel, Shechem, Gilgal, or Shiloh) where the tribal leaders gathered annually to coordinate their joint interests and develop common practices, including maintenance of a central sanctuary, adherence to the divine law, governance by "judges," and conduct of the holy war. For Noth, this amphictyony remained active, though in modified form, through the monarchic period until the fall of Jerusalem in 586 B.C.E., and it constituted the seedbed for many of the tribal traditions that eventually formed the Pentateuch and other "historical" literature.

The next major step was taken by von Rad in 1938 with his publication of "The Form-Critical Problem of the Hexateuch."[5] The lead sentence in the essay reveals von Rad's dissatisfaction with the exegetical methods and theological discussions available to him at the time: "No one will ever be able to say that in our time there has been any crisis in the theological study of the Hexateuch. On the contrary, it might be held that we have reached a position of stalemate which many view with considerable anxiety. What is to be done about it?"[6] The word "form-critical" in his title is itself a indication of the limitations: "tradition history" was scarcely used by exegetes in that period, and von Rad could only consider his own work as a continuation of the line begun by Gunkel. More explicitly than Noth, however, he focused on a biblical text, albeit a very extensive one: the whole of the Hexateuch, including both the Pentateuch and the book of Joshua. He shifted the ground under Wellhausen's source-critical findings by positing that each source must necessarily have gone through complex stages of development before reaching the *Endstadium*, its final stage.[7] In von Rad's view, the entirety of the Hexateuch appears to have been organized according to an Israelite creed, a summary of fundamental beliefs about key moments in their history, such as is preserved in Deut 26:5b–9. The Yahwist, the composer/compiler of the J source in the Pentateuch, played the key role in assembling the various traditions into a coherent narrative whole: placing the primitive history (Gen 2–11) at the beginning; following it with the ancestral stories (Gen 12–50); sequencing the exodus, wilderness, and conquest traditions in a series; and, finally, inserting the account of the giving of the law at Sinai. While the Yahwist completed this work during the early monarchy, according to von Rad, it was clearly preceded by an intricate process in which independent traditions circulated before being incorporated into the initial composition of the Hexateuch. In von Rad's words: "Many ages, many people, many traditions, and many theologians have contributed to this stupendous work.… None of the stages in the age-long development of this work has been wholly superseded; something has been preserved of each phase, and its influence has persisted right down to the final form of the Hexateuch."[8]

Noth followed with several studies that significantly advanced the development of this method. In 1943 he published a two-part treatment of the two large historical sections of the Hebrew Bible, which he called the Deuteronomistic History (Dtr, comprising Deuteronomy, Joshua, Judges, 1–2 Samuel, and 1–2 Kings) and the Chronicler's History (Chr, comprising Ezra, Nehemiah, and 1–2 Chronicles).[9] Both are probably best understood as redaction-critical studies, although Noth adamantly argued that, especially for the first, an editor was not in play: "Dtr. was not merely an editor but the author of a history which brought together material from highly varied traditions and arranged it according to a carefully conceived plan."[10] He focused on the work of the Deuteronomist, whom he placed in the exilic period, but in so doing he also drew attention to the stock of older traditions on which the Deuteronomist drew, many of them already collected into literary complexes. At the same time, Noth also pursued the ways in which the historical context, especially the fall of Jerusalem and the exile, affected the Deuteronomist's perspective and ideology. Although there are similarities between Noth's study of Dtr and his analysis of Chr, his findings vary in several ways. For both he focuses on the compositional stage of each work as a whole, and he regards the Chronicler as an author, not a redactor, just as he did for the Deuteronomist. Also, in both cases the authors draw on a sizable store of older materials to incorporate into their works; in fact, the Dtr version of the books of Samuel and Kings serves as one of the primary bases for Chr. In addition, both authors are influenced by the conditions of their respective times, which for the Chronicler is some three hundred years after the Deuteronomist.

However, Noth perceives some differences between them. The Chronicler took considerably more freedom with the sources than did the Deuteronomist, resulting in nearly half of Chr being new materials.

Further, while the Deuteronomist sought with Dtr to cope with the fall of the kingdom and the exile, the Chronicler used Chr to underscore the legitimacy of the Davidic monarchy and the Jerusalem temple.

With his 1948 monograph on the Pentateuch, Noth made his most significant contributions to traditio-historical research.[11] Acknowledging the 1938 study by von Rad, he pushed the creative period for the origin of the pentateuchal themes into the premonarchic period, thus prior to the dating of von Rad's Yahwist. According to Noth, five themes—ancestors, exodus, wilderness wandering, Sinai, and conquest—were all known during the period of Israel's settlement, and in fact they had already been brought together with each other in that period in a source he called the *Grundlage*, the "groundwork" or "foundation" of the Pentateuch. Yet a wide range of separate, independent traditions also circulated, presumably in oral form, before they were finally incorporated into the whole, filling out these themes and interconnecting them. Much of Noth's study is devoted to tracing the history of these materials.

Other studies by both Noth and von Rad—as well as by several others who joined this task of uncovering the traditions that led to the final biblical text—contributed to the development of the traditio-historical method.[12] Rather than following those details further here, a different kind of question is worth noting at this point, one that both Noth and von Rad pioneered in probing: What significance does traditio-historical criticism have for two key projects in biblical studies: the writing of Israel's history and the understanding of the theology of the Hebrew Bible? Noth, for his part, focused on matters of history, while von Rad pursued the implications of tradition history for theology. Noth's overview of Israel's history appeared in 1950, drawing especially on his proposals regarding the Pentateuch.[13] His treatment of Israel's early period differs markedly from other historical surveys. He basically dismisses any Israelite history prior to 1200 B.C.E. as unrecoverable. Even the archaeological record delivers no clear picture of an "Israel" prior to that point, so his account starts with the inception of the Iron Age in the southern Levant. He treats the preceding period only in terms of the traditions that circulated among the settlers after 1200 B.C.E.: the narratives about the ancestors, the exodus from Egypt, the wilderness wanderings, the covenant at Sinai, and the entrance into the land of Canaan. These traditions, in his view, do not provide reliable information about the periods and events they describe, but they do reveal what the Israelites believed during the early Iron Age. The tribal confederacy with its cultic centers served as the incubator of these traditions as well as those about the "judges," preserving them for centuries until the Babylonian exile.

Theological implications of traditio-historical research occupied von Rad's attention. His two-volume theology of the Old Testament/Hebrew Bible represented a novel approach to the subject, characterized as it is by traditio-historical perspectives.[14] Rather than follow the usual approach of organizing a theology according to traditional rubrics such as God, world, humanity, sin, salvation, and eschatology, von Rad thought it more in keeping with the biblical record to examine the theological testimonies or affirmations of the people. Just as his 1938 study of the Hexateuch had focused on the creedal statements, here he pursued the variety of ways in which the Israelites viewed and discussed their history with their God. To access these testimonies, he turned to the traditions, both their content and their process of transmission. The overriding concept for him was *Vergegenwärtigung*, the practice of interpreting, retelling, or reactualizing old traditions in new eras. A process occurring throughout Israel's history and in essentially all contexts, it reveals the people's efforts to understand their past and apply it or reinterpret it for their own times. Thus tradition history and theology are intertwined: "In general, even the simplest fusion of two originally independent units of tradition was in itself already a process of theological interpretation. And, in the course of time, what masses of tradition were welded together to form these blocks!"[15] The historical literature was not the only material for which this could be said; it applied also to prophetic traditions, cultic texts, laws, rituals, and more. As they were retold and reinterpreted, the traditions grew and changed in keeping with the people's theologies.

While these and other studies by Noth and von Rad set the general agenda and method for most subsequent traditio-historical research, another distinctive set of studies deserves note: the approach taken by a number of Scandinavian scholars contemporaneous with the work in Germany we have sketched. Toward the end of the nineteenth and early in the twentieth centuries, several scholars, such as the Danes Vilhelm Grønbech and Edvard Lehmann and the Swedish Nobel Laureate Nathan Söderblom, contributed to the growing interest in the history of religion, which itself forms one of the intellectual contexts for the study of tradition. The Norwegian Sigmund Mowinckel, drawing on his studies with Gunkel, began during this period a life-long study of virtually all parts of the Hebrew Bible in light of the issues of literary forms, traditions, and religious history. The Dane Johannes Pedersen expanded the scope to include psychological and cultural aspects of the ancient Israelites. Also from Denmark, Axel Olrik pursued the study of Old Norse folklore, a specific result of which was a classic article in 1908 on "epic laws" that has been much cited in subsequent traditio-historical work on the Hebrew Bible.[16] But most distinctive for traditio-historical studies is the approach advocated by the Swede Ivan Engnell, professor of Old Testament at Uppsala University from the 1940s until his death in 1964. Through his own work and that of several of his students, he set a course that influenced subsequent traditio-historical research in both positive and negative ways.[17]

While Engnell's studies continue the Scandinavian interest in the history of religion, two specific aspects of his traditio-historical approach stand out. First, he emphasized the role of oral tradition to an extent not previously developed. While others, including Wellhausen, Gunkel, von Rad, and Noth, had acknowledged the presence of oral transmission prior to the written stage of the literature, they had not made orality into a theme of its own. Engnell proposed not only that much if not most of the Hebrew Bible had started with oral traditions, but he also stressed that the creative period of composition occurred during this oral stage, not when the materials were recorded in writing and redacted in that form. Furthermore, for him the oral means of transmission from one generation to the next provided a very reliable manner of preserving the traditions; he did not view this stage as uncontrollable or haphazard. With disdain he dismissed the regnant scholarly focus on the written stage as "*interpretatio europeica moderna*." The reliability of the oral means and transmission in ancient Israel, according to him, was due to the religious significance of these traditions: they were too vital to the tradents and the people as a whole to be subject to the vagaries of folklore. At the same time, though, the tradition process functioned so effectively in fusing together originally separate oral traditions that we should not expect to be able to separate them now.

Engnell's second theme issued from the first. In his view, traditio-historical research should be considered the dominant, if not only, exegetical method for biblical scholars. Not only must it displace what for him was the antiquated approach of source ("literary") criticism, but tradition history in fact embraces all other exegetical methods as well. As he expressed it late in his life, "I would like to state then, that the break with the literary-critical method must be radical; no compromise is possible. The old method must be replaced by a new one. And the only possible alternative is, as far as I can see, what is in Scandinavia called the traditio-historical method."[18] This dogmatic stance has not won the day, despite Engnell's persistent advocacy.

International scholars since the middle of the twentieth century to the present day have produced a wide range of studies that have advanced considerably traditio-historical research. In most cases these analyses have focused on shorter pericopes or portions of biblical books, not on the large expanses of the Pentateuch or the Deuteronomistic or Chronicler's Histories. Reviewing them at this point is perhaps not productive, since the work of von Rad, Noth, and Engnell gives a good sense of the types of questions pursued by tradition historians.[19] We should note, however, that the method has provoked critique on a number of fronts since the outset.[20] These can best be summarized through a series of critical questions: (1) Does traditio-historical analysis of a text yield results that a historian can use? (2) Do not archaeological findings provide more reliable historical evidence than does an internal study of a text? (3) Is oral tradition in antiquity too elusive to be studied with any confidence? (4) Do tradition historians sometimes go too far in detailing the prehistory of a text, resulting in a picture that stretches the limits of plausibility? (5) Does the particular contribution of traditio-historical research become lost if the method is thought to embrace all other exegetical methods, as some practitioners seem to assume? (6) Specifically, do traditio-historical scholars sufficiently take into consideration the range of new research methods and questions that have arisen since the 1960s—feminist criticism, critical race theory, other forms of ideological criticism, the various types of literary criticism, social-scientific approaches, and more?[21] All such questions have produced healthy and at times heated debates over the decades, and the discussions are likely to continue as exegetes explore the possibilities and limits of interpretation.

Methodological Assumptions

As is the case with all other methods, traditio-historical exegesis proceeds on the basis of several assumptions. Of course, unanimity should not be expected on all or even most of these points, and disagreements and divergent positions among tradition historians often yield uneven results. Some of the primary assumptions on which most would agree, even though they are generally not explicitly stated, are as follows.

(1) In ancient Israel, as in other comparable societies, the oral world predominated as the context for expression, recollection, literary creativity, and reception.

(2) The creative composition of traditions, especially narratives, poetry, songs, laws, proverbs, pronouncements (e.g., by prophets), and perhaps even some genealogical lists, was thus possible at the oral level.

(3) Memory in an illiterate or semiliterate social setting must not be underestimated. Substantial bodies of materials can be remembered and recited without written aids.

(4) However, traditions probably began as shorter pieces and became embellished over time.

(5) Traditions also became connected and often fused with other similar or related traditions.

(6) The capacity to write and preserve substantial texts was held in ancient Israel mainly by professionals in the service of the king, the temple, and the elites. Thus, while oral tradition accounts for the origin and initial circulation during the preliterary stages, professional scribes and archivists played the key role in recording these traditions in writing and later redacting them.

(7) The transmission process during the oral and even during much of the precanonical written stages was not static. Traditions and texts could continually be revised, reinterpreted, elaborated, and fused with other materials until they eventually became fairly fixed in written form, which in most cases did not occur until the Persian, Hellenistic, or even Roman periods. Even though canonization did not occur until the Hellenistic and Roman periods depending on the literary block, the materials handed down from generation to generation could still carry some authoritative weight, even if they were still subject to revision.

(8) Identifying an "author" for any part of the Hebrew Bible is unlikely and, actually, of little importance. Normally, groups are the originators and tradents of the various literary materials, and these groups tend to be associated with institutions in ancient Israel: the clans, the cults, the royal house, the priests, the wisdom "school," the prophets, and more.

(9) The tradition history of a text needs to be coordinated with what is known or postulated about the history of the times.

(10) What is true for virtually all exegetical methods is definitely true for traditio-historical research: the results are hypothetical, although they must also be plausible. As is the case with historical hypotheses in general, the traditio-historical results can be considered not "true" but valid or acceptable until more evidence becomes available or another hypothesis is developed that explains the evidence more convincingly.

As is frankly the case also with the other exegetical methods, the traditio-historical approach cannot be reduced to a simple series of steps that, once taken, yield a guaranteed outcome. Biblical texts are too variable, the meaning of a given text is too often elusive and multiple, the interpretive enterprise is more subjective than objective, and too little is known about the social, political, and religious settings in which the traditions were formed. These obstacles notwithstanding, the exegete proceeds in light of leading questions and problems, such as those described above. The various assumptions just mentioned lay out a reasonable field of opportunity. From this starting point, the tradition historian proceeds with flexibility and litheness, open to a wide range of possibilities in reconstructing the prehistory of the text. One must be cautious about speculating without ground or warrant, but one must also not be reluctant to make the effort to penetrate into a text's prehistory. As Martin Noth stated frequently, asking the right questions may outweigh the answers one finds.[22]

Traditio-historical analysis can be and has been conducted on most types of biblical literature, from narratives and historical books to psalms, prophetic texts, and wisdom literature.[23] The example we will now take is from an entirely different corpus: the legal texts found in the Pentateuch. In comparison with other parts of the Hebrew Bible, they are less frequently subjected to traditio-historical study, perhaps because they generally appear as very brief formulations, though often organized loosely according to subject matter or in larger blocks of legal materials. We will focus on one such collection, the Covenant Code in Exod 21:1–23:19 (or, in the view of some, Exod 20:22–23:33).

The Covenant Code

It is now accepted almost as a given in the study of biblical law that the Covenant Code (CC), often called the Book of the Covenant (adopting the phrase in Exod 24:7), is the oldest collection of legal texts in the Hebrew Bible. Several reasons account for this dating: the laws seem to reflect an agricultural setting, such as one might expect in the period before the founding of the Israelite monarchy; in form, many of these laws are casuistic, as is the case for early laws in the ancient Near East—Sumerian, Babylonian, and Middle Assyrian; the CC laws lack the strong sense of political and cultic centralization evident in other biblical laws, which suggests that they stemmed from a prestate period; a strong theological underpinning is also less apparent in this collection than is the case for the Deuteronomic laws, the Priestly laws, or the Holiness Code, and some suppose that theological reflection on the law evolved in later times. All such aspects have caused some scholars to pronounce this early dating of the CC as one of the "assured results" of scholarship. A traditio-historical study of these chapters does not necessarily support this picture, however, just as other types of analyses of this text cast further doubt on it as well. The CC collection deserves new scrutiny and new proposals, and the outcome gives further support to the caveat that one should not assume what needs to be proved.

The first question we face is the delimitation of the text. Both the beginning and the ending of the CC text are, as it turns out, debatable. Exodus 21:1 seems to introduce a new section in the book, employing a distinctive word to designate the following laws, *mišpāṭîm*, the first time it is used among the legal texts. The preceding chapter contains the Ten Commandments, followed by a short section of miscellaneous materials. Its concluding section, Exod 20:22–26, contains some laws, but their form varies in most cases (the exception is in 20:25) from the casuistic form dominating the CC. Their content, however, is quite different from the CC: they start with a prohibition against idolatry (20:23) reminiscent of 20:4, followed then by directions about building altars (20:24–25). While many scholars are inclined to include 20:22–26 with the CC, it is more likely that they were later inserted in this position between the Ten Commandments and the CC because of a loose connection with both collections. A similar assessment can be made about Exod 23:20–33. While some consider these verses to be a part of the CC, they contain quite different kinds of exhortative materials than the CC laws. Thus we are safe to regard the CC collection of laws as being restricted to Exod 21:1–23:19, even though it ends abruptly.

This delimited text is in itself complicated and diverse, containing several sections of laws roughly related to each other. The following is an outline of the CC:

Introduction: 21:1
Slave laws: 21:2–11
Capital offenses: 21:12–17
Personal-injury laws: 21:18–32
Property laws: 21:33–36; 22:1–15 (MT 21:37–22:14)[24]
Social and religious laws: 22:16–31 (MT 22:15–30)
Laws regulating justice: 23:1–12
Cultic laws: 23:13–19

Tradition criticism depends on the prior steps of source criticism and form criticism. The task of source criticism is to determine whether the given pericope is a composite or a unity and then to propose a date and context for its literary source(s). The CC appears to be a collection of laws on several subjects, but there is no strong evidence that it is based on several distinct sources. On the other hand, its mixed arrangement of a wide variety of legal provisions makes it quite difficult to regard it as a unity. Yet it is not composite in the usual sense of having two or more threads of material in it, each with a distinct history. Another explanation will be needed to account for its composition. There is also the question about a possible relationship between the CC and any of the larger sources associated with the Pentateuch. Early source critics, and some in more recent times as well, considered the CC to be a part of the Elohist source. Quite aside from the larger question of the soundness of the pentateuchal source hypothesis, associating the CC with the Elohist is rooted primarily in the presupposition that the CC laws, like the Elohist source, stem from the early part of Israel's history. If this presupposition is discredited, the CC-Elohist linkage becomes much less likely.

Form criticism of legal texts in the Hebrew Bible identifies a variety of forms, chief among which are the casuistic laws, the apodictic laws, and the participial laws. The first part of the CC (Exod 21:2–23:17) combines casuistic with participial laws, while apodictic formulations dominate the last part (22:18 [MT 22:17]–23:19). The casuistic laws, or case laws, begin with "if" or "when" and conclude with a specification of the penalty or punishment. Participial laws, so named because they begin with a participial verb in Hebrew, are usually translated as "whoever" or "the one who" at the start, followed by a statement of the violation and then punishment. In contrast to both of these forms, apodictic laws take the form of a general rule in the second person, such as, "You shall not wrong or oppress a resident alien" (22:21a [MT 22:20a]). Another formal element in some laws is the motivation clause; for example, the apodictic law just cited from 22:21 (MT 22:20) is followed immediately by a statement intended to motivate the people to comply with it: "for you were aliens in the land of Egypt." All of these forms exist also in other legal collections of the Hebrew Bible, so they cannot be considered unique to the CC. Rather, they demonstrate that the CC shares in the language of law and command current in the legal world of the ancient Near East.

On the basis of this source criticism and form criticism, we now proceed with a traditio-historical analysis of the CC. Can we determine or hypothesize that this text underwent a development, including a formative period at a preliterary stage? If so, who was responsible, and what were their special interests in and intentions for the tradition? I will give two illustrations of tradition criticism at work.

The first and most common approach to these questions with regard to legal texts involves a predominantly literary and redactional analysis of the developmental process. A good example is the work of Eckart Otto.[25] In the first sentence of his study he identifies his methods as traditio-historical and redaction-historical, conducted explicitly in light of the history of Israel's society and religion. Otto's thesis incorporates a distinct though not unusual view of the development of Israelite law. The onset is located within the multiple layers of family and tribal or local life, where conflicts were, if possible, negotiated without strict punishments. The state, when founded, added political, economic, and administrative complexities, and the law became institutionalized in juridical structures that could apply sanctions. The poor, once somewhat protected by local customs, became increasingly vulnerable as the state's power expands. Guided by a moral concern for the poor, the law then became theologized as it affirmed the universal rule of YHWH over all of Israel's life, including care for the vulnerable and embracing everyday affairs, a point made clearly by the final Deuteronomistic redaction.

Based on this understanding of the history of Israelite law, Otto identifies several smaller collections of laws, each with distinctive features and its own history:[26]

- Exod 21:33–22:15 (MT 22:14): restitution laws, identifiable by their repeated provision for the recompense due the owner of property that has been damaged or lost. Several different component parts make up this collection, including laws about goods deposited with another person, theft of animals, breaking and entering, damages due to negligence. While some of these laws may derive from premonarchic conditions, most of them reflect the existence of a state and the hierarchical economy it promoted.
- Exod 21:18–32: laws concerning bodily injuries to a free Israelite man/woman/child or a slave, in some cases resulting in death. Mostly in casuistic form, these laws have their traditio-historical kernels in Exod 21:18–19, 22, and 28–29, each of which was developed further with additional laws specifying further conditions. The redactional process placed the

talionic formula (Exod 21:23b–25) at the center of the collection.

- Exod 21:12–17; 22:18–20a (MT 22:17–19a): apodictic laws governing capital cases. The key traditio-historical feature of this collection is that the laws reflect the shift from the context of the family, presumed in the basic law of Exod 21:12, to the jurisdiction of courts for adjudication and punishment of such offenses.
- Exod 21:2–11: slave laws, including regulations pertaining to the release of slaves. With the basic law in Exod 21:2, this collection mirrors the transition from the agriculturalists' protections for their weaker members to their increasing impoverishment during monarchic times. In the process, the concern for the weakest in society becomes theologized, as is evident especially in Exod 21:6.
- Exod 22:21–27 (MT 22:20–26): laws offering social protections for the weak. As with the preceding collection, these laws evince the shift from an agricultural society to a hierarchical setting in which the weak become progressively more victimized by the powerful.
- Exod 22:29–23:12 (MT 22:28–23:12): two collections of laws brought together theologically: Exod 22:29–30 (MT 22:28–29) and 23:10–12 designate crops and firstborn for, respectively, the cult and the poor; and Exod 23:1–3, 6–8 seeks to eliminate acts that pervert the fair administration of justice. Each has its own traditio-historical kernel: Exod 23:10,11aα, 12a for the former; and 23:6 for the latter. Both underwent a long process of additions and adjustments in light of changes in the social and economic spheres.

According to Otto, these smaller collections evolved through traditio-historical and redaction-critical means into two independent compositions: Exod 21:2–22:27 (MT 21:2–22:26) and 22:29–23:12 (MT 22:28–23:12). His detailed analyses of each smaller collection and of the two larger compositions trace the steps whereby the kernels were, over time, interpreted in new ways, with additions and alterations made to the preexisting materials until each collection reached its final form. The laws that arose during this tradition process were eventually combined by redactors into cohesive units. This history of the traditions fits, in his view, the transition from premonarchic, agricultural, family-oriented legal contexts to complicated monarchic settings with hierarchical, institutionalized structures in a heterogeneous, economically asymmetrical society. The CC text becomes theologized in order to give force to the charge for protecting the poor and the powerless in such contexts.[27]

I will now suggest another traditio-historical approach to legal texts in general and the CC in particular. It begins with a marked difference in analytical style, one that shows less confidence in rendering precise distinctions among textual fragments in the effort to align them with separate phases in the text's development. Just as source criticism became preoccupied in the early decades of the twentieth century with dividing between words and phrases and assigning them unhesitatingly to one source or the other, so also traditio-historical criticism has at times proceeded as if it can reconstruct the precise history of the traditions from the wording in the present text. One of the contributions of the method is its effort to identify the preliterary stages in the text's composition, but caution is warranted if that compositional stage predates by perhaps centuries the later redactional and canonical stages. For example, Otto considers the premonarchic period as the source for some of the CC laws, which the monarchy then sought to tailor to its hierarchical preferences. Such an approach assumes that the monarchic period, probably even its early years when the premonarchic social regulations were still remembered, was the period of origin for the CC, yet it does not explain how the compilation would have survived intact until its later redaction by the Deuteronomists or other postexilic groups. A different approach that relies less on written transmission and redactional history may explain some of the text's features more adequately. I will be succinct here, often depending on comments comparing this approach with Otto's.

First, it is hardly warranted to assume that we can recover the premonarchic period and its apprehension by the monarchy. We have no way of knowing that laws governing the early agricultural society were ever recorded and retained; both the monarchic interest in them and the easy means for writing them were probably lacking during Israel's early kingdom. A tension between the state, on the one hand, and the innumerable villages across the landscape, on the other, is very plausible. Yet the tension would have existed not only during the inception of the monarchic state but also throughout the entire period of centralized power and wealth.[28] Thus we can just as well look for the composition of the CC at any time during the monarchy or, for that matter, during the colonial periods after the loss of sovereignty.

The roots of law reach deeply into the soil of the village communities. Law "lived" among the people, most likely emerging in response to real conflicts among people and in turn becoming precedents invoked later for similar conflicts. These laws were remembered orally by the villagers, who generally were not literate enough to have written them even if they had wanted nor to have been able to read what others wrote. Quite naturally, related laws gravitated together, forming some of the nested laws similar to those we see in Exod 21:12–14 or 21:28–36. The notion of a certain law serving as a "kernel" for others related to it may be more conceivable for a literary than for a real-life context, for in the latter new conditions needing to be taken into consideration produced refractions of already-existing laws. A related point must not be overlooked: any village laws that happen to be incorporated into biblical collections can scarcely be considered common to all Israelite villages, which were dispersed throughout the country with no means for a shared voice. Any text thought to be a "kernel" thus does not necessarily represent premonarchic or any other specific period's legal traditions; at most, it may be a law taken arbitrarily from a limited area. Villagers' oral traditions were fluid, diverse, and variable, and most are certainly lost to time. When considered against this social history, the overly precise nature of Otto's analysis stretches credulity.

The laws and the legal texts produced by the state reflect the interests and issues of the powerful and the wealthy. As Otto recognizes, the vulnerability of the poor was not normally taken into consideration by the state; laws and customs benefiting the vulnerable and the powerless were more to be expected in the villages, where these individuals or groups lived. While it plausibly retains traces of laws protecting the poor, the CC is a product of the elite in the cities and state whose interests ran counter to those of the peasants. The tradition historian needs to conduct the textual analysis with this ideological aim in mind.

In my view, it is most likely that the impetus to draft the first version of the CC text occurred in the Persian period. In the context of the kingdoms of Israel or Judah, the rich and powerful already held control and had little interest or need to compile laws that, in part, seemed to benefit the rural poor. In the Persian period, on the other hand, the conditions were ripe for compiling laws: the urban settings had been decimated by the Babylonians, the Persians carried out a ruralization policy in Yehud, indigenous institutions and leadership circles struggled to become established, and the vast majority of the population continued their subsistence economy in the countryside. In these circumstances we can expect that the descendants of the Judean elites—the wealthy, the high officials, and the priestly leadership, all displaced and disenfranchised during the exilic period—sought an opportunity to reestablish themselves through catering to the colonial powers. By compiling a set of laws that suggested order in the country, including a hierarchy of power, they positioned themselves for leadership both over the masses and on behalf of the Persian imperial government. Interspersing protections for the poor in the law collection represented a clever, though probably transparent, means of appealing also to the interests of the poor. It is not unlikely, though, that some village laws practiced for generations became part of the compilation. Situating this collection in the postexilic period can also account for the writers' familiarity with Babylonian and Assyrian laws, which a date in the early Israelite monarchy leaves unexplained. I am not at all suggesting that the final form of the CC was attained in the early Persian period. Rather, some modest collection of laws was drafted in this setting to serve the elites' interests, and thereafter the text underwent a long period of transmission, interpretation, and redaction before reaching a fixed, canonical state. At no stage was it complete or functional enough to have served adequately as an enforceable set of state laws. It existed only as a literary piece and did not represent a majority view of the lived laws.

This traditio-historical picture of the CC thus acquires a different texture than that proposed by Otto. While the traditio-historical method is designed to focus on a textual unit, it must necessarily take into consideration the social, political, economic, religious, and ideological terms of the times. Furthermore, as hypothetical and speculative as traditio-historical study is fundamentally, we are on the best footing by minimizing the number of details in our textual analysis, especially the minute reconstructions of a formative process that the text putatively underwent. So viewed, the monarchic period is a less likely context for the development of the CC than is the Persian period. Also, the formative stage for the initial compilation probably occurred over a relatively brief span of time. The basic aim of any traditio-historical study should be to propose a plausible scenario whereby the given pericope came into existence, keyed to the traditionists and their ideologies and interests. We thereby gain a dimension of depth to the text as an end-product of a process transpiring in the context of real-life circumstances.

For Further Reading

Di Vito, Robert A. "Tradition-Historical Criticism." Pages 90–104 in *To Each Its Own Meaning: An Introduction to Biblical Criticisms and Their Application*. Edited by Steven L. McKenzie and Stephen R. Haynes. Rev. ed. Louisville: Westminster John Knox, 1999.

Fishbane, Michael A. *Biblical Interpretation in Ancient Israel*. Oxford: Clarendon, 1985.

Hayes, John H., and Carl R. Holladay. *Biblical Exegesis: A Beginner's Handbook*. 3rd ed. Louisville: Westminster John Knox, 2007.

Knight, Douglas A. *Rediscovering the Traditions of Israel*. 3rd ed. SBLSBL 16. Atlanta: Society of Biblical Literature, 2006.

———. "Tradition History." *ABD* 6:633–38.

Niditch, Susan. *Oral World and Written Word: Ancient Israelite Literature*. Library of Ancient Israel. Louisville: Westminster John Knox, 1996.

Petersen, David L. "The Ambiguous Role of Moses as Prophet." Pages 311–24 in *Israel's Prophets and Israel's Past: Essays on the Relationship of Prophetic Texts and Israelite History in Honor of John H. Hayes*. Edited by Brad E. Kelle and Megan B. Moore. LHB/OTS 466. London: T&T Clark, 2006.

Rast, Walter E. *Tradition History and the Old Testament*. GBS. Philadelphia: Fortress, 1972.

Steck, Odil Hannes. *Old Testament Exegesis: A Guide to the Methodology*. Translated by James D. Nogalski. 2nd ed. SBLRBS 39. Atlanta: Scholars Press, 1998.

Notes

1. The term for this method varies somewhat according to the scholar: tradition criticism; traditio-historical criticism; tradition-historical criticism; transmission-historical criticism.

2. The highly successful musical, which premiered on Broadway in 1964, was directed by Jerome Robbins (book by Joseph Stein, music by Jerry Bock, and lyrics by Sheldon Harnick). It is based on Sholem Aleichem's Yiddish story, "Tevye's Daughters," from 1894. A film adaptation of the stage production appeared in 1971.

3. For a history of traditio-historical research, especially for the period prior to ca. 1970, see my *Rediscovering the Traditions of Israel* (SBLDS 9; Missoula, Mont.: Society of Biblical Literature, 1973; rev. ed., Missoula, Mont.: Scholars Press, 1975; 3rd ed.; SBLSBL 16; Atlanta: Society of Biblical Literature; Leiden: Brill, 2006). All citations in this essay are to the 3rd ed.

4. Martin Noth, *Das System der zwölf Stämme Israels* (BWANT 4/1; Stuttgart: Kohlhammer, 1930; 2nd ed., Darmstadt: Wissenschaftliche Buchgesellschaft, 1966).

5. Von Rad, "The Form-Critical Problem of the Hexateuch," in idem, *The Problem of the Hexateuch and Other Essays* (trans. E. W. T. Dicken; Edinburgh: Oliver & Boyd, 1966), 1–78.

6. Ibid., 1.

7. Ibid., 2.

8. Ibid., 77–78. Dicken's translation reads "men" instead of "people," but the latter renders von Rad's "Menschen" more clearly. Von Rad italicizes the last sentence in the quotation.

9. The German originals of 1943 have been translated into English as two separate books: Martin Noth, *The Deuteronomistic History* (trans. Jane Doull, John Barton, and Michael D. Rutter; JSOTSup 15; Sheffield: University of Sheffield, 1981; 2nd ed., Sheffield: Sheffield Academic Press, 1991); subsequent citations are from the 1981 edition; and idem, *The Chronicler's History* (trans. H. G. M. Williamson; JSOTSup 50; Sheffield: JSOT Press, 1987). See also the articles in Steven L. McKenzie and M. Patrick Graham, eds., *The History of Israel's Traditions: The Heritage of Martin Noth* (JSOTSup 182; Sheffield: Sheffield Academic Press, 1994).

10. Noth, *The Deuteronomistic History*, 10.

11. Martin Noth, *A History of Pentateuchal Traditions* (trans. Bernard W. Anderson; Englewood Cliffs, N.J.: Prentice-Hall, 1972; repr., Chico, Calif.: Scholars Press, 1981); trans. of *Überlieferungsgeschichte des Pentateuch* (Stuttgart: Kohlhammer, 1948).

12. For some examples, see Knight, *Rediscovering the Traditions of Israel, passim.*

13. Martin Noth, *The History of Israel* (trans. S. Godman; London: Black, 1958); trans. of *Geschichte Israels* (Göttingen: Vandenhoeck & Ruprecht, 1950).

14. Gerhard von Rad, *Old Testament Theology*, vol. 1: *The Theology of Israel's Historical Traditions* (trans. D. M. G. Stalker; Edinburgh: Oliver & Boyd, 1962); trans. of vol. 1 of *Theologie des Alten Testaments* (Munich: Kaiser, 1957); vol. 2: *The Theology of Israel's Prophetic Traditions* (trans. D. M. G. Stalker; Edinburgh: Oliver & Boyd, 1965); trans. of vol. 2 of *Theologie des Alten Testaments* (Munich: Kaiser, 1960); von Rad's approach to biblical theology provoked a wide discussion; see, e.g., the range of articles in *Tradition and Theology in the Old Testament* (ed. Douglas A. Knight; Philadelphia: Fortress; London: SPCK, 1977; repr., Sheffield: JSOT Press, 1990; Atlanta: Society of Biblical Literature, 2007).

15. Von Rad, *Old Testament Theology*, 1:5.

16. Johannes Pedersen, "Epic Laws of Folk Narrative," in *The Study of Folklore* (ed. Alan Dundes; Englewood Cliffs, N.J.: Prentice-Hall, 1965), 129–41; Danish original in 1908; trans. into German in 1909.

17. A detailed analysis is available in Knight, *Rediscovering the Traditions of Israel*, 197–220; see also Knud Jeppesen and Benedikt Otzen, eds., *The Productions of Time: Tradition History in Old Testament Scholarship* (Sheffield: Almond, 1984).

18. Ivan Engnell, "Methodological Aspects of Old Testament Study," *Congress Volume: Oxford, 1959* (VTSup 7; Leiden: Brill, 1960), 21.

19. For a number of specific examples, see Knight, *Rediscovering the Traditions of Israel*, 135–46, 255–86.

20. Ibid., 147–62, 287–317.

21. Ibid., 301–17.

22. Noth, *History of Pentateuch Traditions*, xxxv, 3–4, 147.

23. Knight, "Tradition History," *ABD* 6:633–38.

24. The versification of Exod 22 varies between the Hebrew and the English texts: 22:1–31 in English is the same as 21:37—22:30 in Hebrew. For the convenience of readers, I will cite the English versification first, followed by the Hebrew in parentheses.

25. Eckart Otto, *Wandel der Rechtsbegründungen in der Gesellschaftsgeschichte des antiken Israel: Eine Rechtsgeschichte des "Bundesbuches" Ex XX 22–XXIII 13* (StudBib 3; Leiden: Brill, 1988).

26. Ibid., 12–51.

27. Ibid., 61–75.

28. See my "Village Law and the Book of the Covenant," in *"A Wise and Discerning Mind": Essays in Honor of Burke O. Long* (ed. Saul M. Olyan and Robert C. Culley; BJS 325; Providence, R.I.: Brown University, 2000), 163–79.

Comparative Approaches: History, Theory, and the Image of God*

Brent A. Strawn

Tell all the Truth but tell it slant—
Success in Circuit lies
Too bright for our infirm Delight
The Truth's superb surprise
As Lightning to the Children eased
With explanation kind
The Truth must dazzle gradually
Or every man be blind— (Emily Dickinson[1])

1. Introduction

Put most simply, comparative methodology sets at least two (sometimes more) subjects alongside each other so as to look at them together in order to (1) identify both similarities and differences and (2) reveal aspects of the subjects that may not have been as readily seen if each was looked at in isolation. Despite the simplicity of this explanation, the actual practice of comparison is no easy matter. *How* best to "set subjects alongside" one another, as well as determining *which* subjects are best compared, are just two of the major problems facing comparative methodology.

Somewhat ironically, the question of *why* someone should engage in comparison in the first place (a third major question in the comparative pursuit) may actually be the easiest issue to address. Brain research suggests that the act of comparison is neurologically encoded. Neuro-

---

* I am honored to dedicate this essay to David L. Petersen, whose scholarly erudition, skill in economical presentation, and methodological precision I have long admired. His elegance as a scholar and teacher is matched only by his grace as a friend and colleague.

scientists have documented the fact that when one person sees another person doing something, neurons fire that encourage the first person to act similarly.[2] The subsequent action is, of course, imitation, not comparison, but it is clear, nevertheless, that the imitative activity is based on and facilitated by the initial comparative observation. In short, the process of comparison may be something humans do, neurologically, whether they want to or not. In this light, comparison can be seen, not simply as one more additional or optional method that scholars may choose to employ here or there with this or that text. Rather, comparison seems to be the default disposition, perhaps the most foundational of all methods. While someone may choose to look at sources, forms, literary style, or other aspects of critical biblical study, comparison is evidently not a choice but a *requirement*, a reflex of how human beings are wired.[3]

The present study offers a brief overview of comparative approaches in Hebrew Bible and ancient Near Eastern studies (§2) before comparing insights on comparative method offered by two scholars outside these fields (§3). As an example of comparative method, I then take up once again the notion of the image of God (*imago Dei*), which has been repeatedly discussed in comparative perspective (§4). Finally, I offer some methodological suggestions by way of conclusion (§5).

2. An Overview of Comparative Approaches in Biblical and Ancient Near Eastern Studies

Friedrich Max Müller and Following

The crucial role of comparison in the academic study of religion is usually traced to Friedrich Max Müller's lecture before the prestigious Royal Institution of London in 1870. Among other things, Müller drew upon Johann Wolfgang von Goethe's famous remark about the importance of knowing multiple languages in order to argue that, in the case of religion, "*He who knows one, knows none*."[4] Müller believed that the time had come to investigate religion more generally, not to prove one's own religion true, but instead to seek out "those elements, patterns, and principles that could be found uniformly in the religions of all times and places."[5] Comparison was his tool of choice. As to why this should be, he penned the following:

> People ask, What is gained by comparison?—Why, all higher knowledge is acquired by comparison, and rests on comparison.… [T]he character of scientific research in our age is pre-eminently comparative, this … means that our researches are now based on the widest evidence that can be obtained, on the broadest inductions that can be grasped by the human mind.[6]

By the time Müller spoke, the (Western) rediscovery of ancient Near Eastern civilizations that would transform academic study of the Bible was already well under way. Egyptian hieroglyphs and Babylonian cuneiform had been deciphered for some time, and therefore the comparison of these ancient cultures with that of the Bible could proceed apace. Müller was aware of these advances even if he did not make full use of them, partly because the study of the ancient Near East was still very much in its infancy at that time. Whatever the case, the years following these discoveries, decipherments, and Müller's lecture witnessed three important developments, which were in truth processes of differentiation.

The first process was that biblical and ancient Near Eastern studies moved away from general comparative-religion theory, at least as that was encapsulated in a scholar such as Müller, who was as interested in Buddhism, Islam, and Hinduism as he was in "biblical" religions such as Christianity and Judaism or their ancient antecedents. Biblical and ancient Near Eastern studies drew the comparative circle much more narrowly than Müller and those who followed his lead, and, in many cases, this situation still obtains.[7] To be sure, this development was (and is) not without good reason. On the one hand, the sheer amount of material coming to light from the ancient Near East demanded a scholar's full attention, if not one's entire career. On the other hand, methodological considerations (no doubt related to the problem of massive data and its control) have kept biblical and ancient Near Eastern studies close to home. Shemaryahu Talmon, for example, delineated several principles that he believed should govern comparative work. Paramount among these was "geographical proximity" and "historical propinquity."[8]

The second process of differentiation is directly related to the first. From their beginnings as "handmaids" to biblical study, Assyriology and Egyptology have emerged as self-standing disciplines unrelated to the study of Scripture. Here again this process was at least partially pragmatic: there are simply too many texts, languages, and dialects to master in Assyriology for one to be equally fluent in Egyptology and/or the study of Israelite history and religion. But another part of the differentiation was developmental, if not ideological: some Assyriologists and Egyptologists resented the often limited and utilitarian appropriation of their disciplines and data for biblical study. The coming of age of Assyriology and Egyptology, as well as related cognate fields, has thus not been without its fair share of antagonism.[9] Moreover, while disciplinary specialization inevitably produces more precise and technical results, it also complicates interdisciplinary or cross-disciplinary (including comparative) endeavors, if for no other reason than that these pursuits are often ridiculed as dilettantish by purists. That scenario serves only to reinforce further specialization and the increased separation of fields and their data that might profitably be compared.

The third process of differentiation is that scholars who have continued to engage in comparative analyses have tended to fall into one of two camps: those who (over)emphasize similarity or those who (over)emphasize difference. Presumably and purportedly, comparison always involves *both* similarity and difference, but in actual practice scholars have tended to favor one, sometimes to the total neglect of the other. Those who have (over)stressed difference have sometimes been called, derogatively, "contrastivists."[10] There is no doubt that, to cite a famous example, the differences between "wicked Canaanite" religion and the religion of ancient Israel have often been overdrawn. It is also true that such distinctions were often made for apologetic purposes.[11] It is equally obvious, however, that scholars who (over)emphasize similarity are not above error. They, too, can be guilty of drawing facile similarities; their efforts, too, can reveal traces of ideology and apology.[12] When scholars in the "too-similar" camp are spoken of derisively, they are typically called members of the "pan-X school," where the variable stands for any locus of recent and important discovery (e.g., pan-Babylonianism, pan-Ugariticism).

While the difficulties in balancing similarity and difference are real and pronounced, such balance is an essential priority in comparative method.[13] Problems result when either of the two sides is unjustly or uncritically favored. The concepts of similarity and difference, along with the problem of their appropriate balance, are also found in other discourses, thereby connecting biblical and ancient Near Eastern comparisons to other disciplines that also care about comparing like and unlike—for example, the study of repetition, narrative ethics, even systematic theology and intertextuality. Quite apart from brain science, then, one finds here further proof of the ubiquity of comparison and its significance for the task of hermeneutics.

William W. Hallo and the "Contextual Approach"

In recent years, a major theorist of comparative method in biblical and ancient Near Eastern studies has been William W. Hallo,[14] who has moved from work that stressed contrast between the Bible and the ancient Near East[15] to advocate for what he now calls the "contextual approach."[16] In this newer approach, both contrast and comparison (or what he calls "negative" and "positive" comparison) are at work.[17] In a programmatic essay, Hallo defines his method as follows:

> The goal of the contextual approach is fairly modest. It is not to find the key to every biblical phenomenon in some ancient Near Eastern precedent, but rather to silhouette the biblical text against its wider literary and cultural environment and thus to arrive at a proper assessment of the extent to which the biblical evidence reflects that environment or, on the contrary, is distinctive and innovative over against it.[18]

It should be noted that the environment or "context" of any given text is understood by Hallo in two dimensions: (1) the *horizontal*, which is "the geographical, historical, religious, political and literary setting in which it was created and disseminated"; and (2) the *vertical*, which refers to the "axis between the earlier texts that helped inspire it and the later texts that reacted to it."[19] Both synchronic (literary) and diachronic (historical) aspects of comparison are thus operative in Hallo's theory.

In several ways, Hallo's contextual approach reflects the latest and best in comparative theory in biblical and ancient Near Eastern studies. So, for example, while comparative studies have often been overly enamored with similarity and, correlatively, questions of influence or borrowing, Hallo argues that such issues, while important, are not everything.[20] Yet, despite real advances, Hallo's method reflects positions and problems that have plagued comparative studies from the start. As examples, one might note that Hallo believes there is something scientific or empirical in his approach and that, despite an admirable attempt at balancing similarity ("comparison") and difference ("contrast"), his method is still largely confined to Talmon's criteria of comparable location and date.[21] More importantly, the well-intentioned attention to "context" in Hallo's approach is not foolproof. As Howard Eilberg-Schwartz has remarked about "contextualism" in general: "determining just what is 'the context' is itself always an interpretive act.... The twentieth-century refrain that cultural items have to be interpreted 'in their context' hides more than it reveals."[22]

The Politics of Comparison

Before proceeding further, a crucial observation must be made regarding the history of comparative approaches. Hallo has noted that, among other things, comparative study has revealed the political nature of much ancient literature.[23] But studying the history of scholarly comparison reveals that comparative method *itself* is fraught with politics. We might begin by noting the role of the Mesopotamian discoveries in Friedrich Delitzsch's first "Babel und Bibel" lecture on 13 January 1902.[24] Delitzsch represented (and helped further) "pan-Babylonianism," the perspective in which everything in the Bible found an antecedent of some sort in the cuneiform literature. The ordering evident in the lecture's title—(first) Babylon and (only then) Bible—is therefore telling.

It was a short step from Delitzsch's first lecture to his second (1903), in which he attacked the validity of the Old Testament as authoritative for German Christians. In the published version, Delitzsch went so far as to suggest that German Christians leave aside ancient Israelite literature altogether (given its inferiority) and turn with renewed appreciation to their own German myths. The anti-Semitic sentiment of Delitzsch's lectures, conjoined with their unrestrained nationalism, cannot be missed. This was hardly an "objective" comparison, despite Delitzsch's protestations to the contrary. Indeed, Delitzsch's bias culminated in his two-volume *Die grosse Täuschung*: the "great deception" in question was nothing less than the Hebrew Bible itself.[25]

The proximity of Delitzsch's work to the rise of Nazism in post–World War I Germany and its contribution to (and reflection of) anti-Jewish sentiment in Germany throughout this period are disturbing realities. Further, while it is obvious that Delitzsch's comparisons were colored by a number of additional, noncomparative (and nonobjective) datasets and commitments, it is equally clear that his lectures provoked responses that, when compared to Delitzsch's, are shown to be equally fraught with political significance.

Paramount among such responses was Benno Landsberger's inaugural lecture at Leipzig in 1925.[26] In this essay, Landsberger explicitly denied that the Babylonians and the Egyptians were "our spiritual fathers," a refutation with teeth in it following the work of the pan-Babylonian school; quite to the contrary: "if we are not to deprive ourselves of the most important key to understanding, we [must] seek out the conceptual autonomy [*Eigenbegrifflichkeit*] of a *particular* civilization."[27] Scholars must not operate with fixed, preconceived systems of "conceptual referents"; that can only lead to limited, perspectival results (think Delitzsch). Instead, the only suitable measure with which to judge a civilization and its ideas must be derived from within that selfsame civilization, from its own culture and texts, from its world of ideas. Only then, and only slowly, can one move from the autonomous concepts to larger systems. Landsberger argued that it was only by constructing the larger "system of concepts" that we can "find our way into the nature of a civilization."[28]

Though Delitzsch's Babel und Bibel lectures are not named in Landsberger's essay, the implications of his *Eigenbegrifflichkeit*-program for any pan-Babylonian approach are nevertheless obvious. Civilizations are *autonomous*, conceptually, and must be carefully and painstakingly studied. It is only via detailed philological work that larger systems can be (re)constructed; one gets the impression that the speed of such work will be glacial at best. Broad comparisons that assume "one abstract, formal pattern for all the various objectivizations of the human mind" will simply not do.[29] Landsberger's program can be seen as a direct challenge to Delitzsch's. It comes as no real surprise to learn that Landsberger was Jewish and that he was later dismissed from his Leipzig post under the Nazis.

Landsberger's notion of "conceptual autonomy" has proved enormously influential on subsequent scholarship. Much of the comparative theory discussed above, especially of the kind that places particular emphasis on difference, makes explicit reference to Landsberger: Hallo, for example, in his early work on the "contrastive approach," or Talmon, in his insistence "on the particularity of the Hebrew culture and its dissimilarity from neighbouring cultures."[30] But others could be added: Jacob J. Finkelstein, for example, in an essay entitled "Bible and Babel" (note the reversed order), or, especially, the still seminal work on Mesopotamia by A. Leo Oppenheim.[31]

Two Conclusions to This Point

Two important conclusions can be deduced from this brief overview of comparative approaches in biblical and ancient Near Eastern studies. (1) Comparison is a deeply hermeneutical enterprise. Müller framed his lectures as introducing the "science of religion," but the history of comparison demonstrates that the endeavor is far from objective—it is no exact science, let alone a hard one. Müller himself argued against comparisons that artificially denigrated or exalted Christianity, because "[s]cience wants no partisans." But despite this laudable attempt at objectivity, he immediately went on to write, "I make no secret that true Christianity, I mean the religion of Christ, seems to me to become more and more exalted the more we know and the more we appreciate the treasures of truth hidden in the despised religions of the world."[32] Evidently, while "science" wants no partisans, partisans run amok in "(comparative religious) science." Such partisanship is often ideologically, religiously, and/or theologically problematic, sometimes with profoundly deleterious consequences—political and otherwise.

(2) The pan-Babylonian movement was not the only one to (over)stress "parallels" and similarities. Mark Chavalas has pointed out that virtually every significant archaeological discovery has led to a rash of overstatements regarding cultural parallels, typically replete with arguments about influence or dependence.[33] Similar overstatements regarding rabbinic parallels to the New Testament were the subject of a biting essay by Samuel Sandmel, against what he called "parallelomania."[34] But if Delitzsch and the pan-Babylonian school overstressed similarity and dependence, one can also see that, while that tendency never fully died out, the opposite tendency—overstressing uniqueness or autonomy—also obtained among many scholars, some of whom became "parallelo-noid" about parallelomania.[35] Either way, we see that the crucial dialectic of similarity and difference that is essential to the best comparative inquiry has often been lost.

3. A Further Comparison: Comparing (with) Other Comparativists

Things seem at something of an impasse. It is instructive, then, to take leave of the comparative pursuit within biblical and ancient Near Eastern studies, without forgetting it altogether, to consider wider research on comparison. I begin with Jonathan Z. Smith's work on comparative method.[36]

Jonathan Z. Smith on Method in Comparative Religion

Smith begins one of his earliest pieces on comparison with a bold assertion:

> The process of comparison is a fundamental characteristic of human intelligence. Whether revealed in the logical grouping of classes, in poetic similes, in mimesis, or other like activities—comparison, in the bringing together of two or more objects for the purpose of noting either similarity or dissimilarity, is the omnipresent substructure of human thought. (1971, 67)

Not all comparisons are created equal, however; Smith thus proceeds to delineate four major types of comparison: ethnographic; encyclopedic; morphological; and evolutionary (1971; 2000a, 27–29). Each has strengths as well as significant weaknesses. So, for example, much comparison, especially *ethnographic* comparison, appears "idiosyncratic, depending on intuition, a chance association, or the knowledge one happens to have at the moment of another culture. There is nothing systematic to such comparisons, they lack any basis, and so, in the end, they strike us as uninteresting, petty, and unrevealing" (1971, 75). Further, *encyclopedic* comparison like that found in James George Frazer's *The Golden Bough* typically eventuates in "contextless lists held together by mere surface associations rather than careful, specific, and meaningful comparisons" (1971, 80).

Smith believes that *morphological* comparison is probably the best type, but it, too, has significant problems, especially when erroneously combined with *evolutionary* comparative approaches (see 1971, 82, 86; 2000a, 28–29, 34). Smith seems to conclude in despair: in the face of the profound methodological problems besetting each of the four types of comparison, "[t]he only option appears to be no option at all" (2000a, 29). Without a cogent and compelling method, comparison remains a mostly subjective enterprise, "a sort of déjà vu" (2000a, 26), at least in part because "[w]e have yet to develop the responsible alternative: the integration of a complex notion of pattern and system with an equally complex notion of history" (2000a, 34).

Clearly, Smith is pressing for a more careful method and rationale for the comparative enterprise. He is also at pains to point out that—no doubt for want of a cogent and compelling method—comparison has too often served apologetic ends. The profoundly hermeneutical nature of comparison (see §2), therefore, has been severely underestimated. Comparison must be recognized as an interpretive exercise in which scholars are profoundly and personally involved. If this is not acknowledged and self-consciously engaged, comparisons become unfair and unduly colored by apologetics (often unacknowledged) of whatever sort. Smith also observes that comparative work has been overly fixated on sameness and contiguity (see 1990, 46; 2000a, 25; 2000b, 237–38). In point of fact, "comparison is, at base, never identity. Comparison requires the postulation of difference as the grounds of its being interesting (rather than tautological) and a methodical manipulation of difference, a playing across the 'gap' in the service of some useful end" (2000a, 40; see also 1990, 47).

The issues Smith has identified are interrelated: the lack of careful method, combined with unacknowledged apologetics and an overfocus on contiguity, has created the false impression that the comparative endeavor is objective in some fashion, but that is patently not the case. To the contrary, the unscholarly combination of apologetics with theories of influence makes for comparison that is not scientific at all but little more than "magic" (2000a, 26). Still further, the obsession with limiting comparison to contiguous phenomena (ever more narrowly construed) has been used "as the smug excuse for jettisoning the comparative enterprise [altogether] and for purging scholarship of all but the most limited comparisons" (2000a, 29). What is needed, then, is "a discourse of 'difference,' a complex term which invites negotiation, classification and comparison," which "at the same time, avoids too easy a discourse of the 'same'" (1990, 42).

Toward that end, Smith helpfully introduces the notions of analogy and homology as understood in biology (1990, 47–48 and n. 15). Homologous structures are ones that are genetically related (e.g., a whale fin and a human arm), which go back, genealogically, to a common ancestor. Analogous structures (e.g., a fish fin and a human arm), while similar, do not trace back to a shared predecessor. While most comparative studies have operated as if they trafficked in homology, Smith argues that all comparisons in religious studies are properly analogical; only amateurs think only of homology (1990, 50–51). In truth, "[d]ifference abounds" (1990, 40). More to the point, the apologetics that have dominated so much comparative work demonstrate that genetics in scientific mode is far from the reality in comparative religion.

The deeply interpretive function—if not interested nature—of comparison (see, e.g., 1990, 46, 50, 143) means, correlatively, that it is political and ideological, in large part because it is done by *us*; *we* are the ones doing the comparison. Comparison is, therefore, "by no means an innocent endeavor" but rather "a disciplined exaggeration in the service of knowledge" (1990, 34, 52). But this is no invitation to total subjectivity;

rather, Smith uses the point to urge greater clarity regarding the purposes of our comparisons. Comparison, after all, "provides the means by which *we* 're-envision' phenomena as *our* data in order to solve *our* theoretical problems" (1990, 52; emphasis original). Far from being afterthoughts, it is precisely the purposes motivating our comparative work that make it interesting, not to mention potentially valid and/or invalid, useful and/or unhelpful (see 1990, 53, 115). Indeed, the language of *invention*, rather than discovery, might serve comparative analyses best, since identifying similarities and differences is "the result of mental operations undertaken by scholars in the interest of their intellectual goals" (2000b, 239). Let it be stressed again: *all* comparisons are motivated by some purpose(s). These simply need to be made more transparent; they should also be interesting and important.

Earl Miner on Comparative Poetics

Comparing another comparativist is useful—this one from the field of comparative literature. The title of Earl Miner's book is revealing, as it showcases his major methodological point: *Comparative Poetics: An Intercultural Essay on Theories of Literature.*[37] Miner puts the matter straightforwardly from the very start: "it is an assumption of this study that the phrase 'comparative poetics' is meaningful only if the evidence is intercultural and taken from a reasonably full historical range.... Comparative poetics is, then, by its nature an extensive, complex subject" (3).

Miner states that virtually every poetics "is avowedly partial" but notes that this is in striking tension with the "dream of a pantascopic poetics" and the "transtemporal theories" that otherwise mark the work of comparative literature (4–5). Pragmatically, of course, one often sticks with one's own "partial poetics" because real effort is required to become an authority on a particular author or corpus; but "curiosity is one parent of comparative poetics" (5), so we often end up searching for further, if not greener, pastures. Hence, while in practice literary comparison is too frequently limited in execution, *truly comparative* literature "involves something more than comparing two great German poets, and something different from a Chinese studying French literature or a Russian studying Italian literature" (5). In fact, to consider the poetics

> of but one cultural tradition is to investigate only a single conceptual cosmos, however intricate, subtle, or rich that may be. To consider the

> other varieties of poetics is by definition to inquire into the full hetero-cosmic range, the full argument from design, of literature. And to do so comparatively is to establish the principles and the relations of those many poetic worlds. (7)

In Miner's judgment, most comparativists have failed at precisely this point and in so doing have failed to conduct *real* comparison. Again, there are no doubt reasons that scholars have defined their work rather narrowly. By restricting our foci, "we feel secure, because we sense that we honor, somehow, canons of comparability," in part by the avoidance of serious category errors (21).

All of this sounds familiar from the materials discussed above, especially the works of Talmon and Hallo, but Miner insists that such safety is "illusory" and at best affords "only modest help" because it ensures only the most minimum of bases for the comparison of comparable elements (21). But exceedingly narrow, "intra-only" sorts of comparison are surely not the only way, nor the best, to establish such bases! To be sure, comparison depends on "sufficient resemblance" (21). Part of said sufficiency involves *scale*: differences should not be so large as to preclude reasonable comparison. At the same time, an enlarged scale of reference can alter what appears similar and what appears different, often with quite profound results.

Miner argues that it is exactly such an enlarged scale—the "wider, intercultural context" (10; see also 234, 238)—that makes for good comparison, though he admits that a larger scale also raises the problem of relativism: the problem that cultural data can appear culturally and temporally specific, and, therefore, to some degree at least, noncomparable (214). Understood in this way, "relativism" does pose serious problems for comparison. In Miner's opinion, however, relativism is overcome "by linguistic and historical understanding of divergent literatures"—and, once again, the more divergent the better (215).

Despite Miner's confidence in bridging the gap, various issues remain. Most intractable among these is the "comparable" quality itself. "In literary study, the *tertium comparationis* [the third part of the comparison: the comparable quality] is not only not immediately given. It is not given at all" (232). One fights the specter of relativism here by identifying "formally identical features in the things being compared" (232). However, given the elusiveness of the *tertium comparationis*, such a discipline is hardly foolproof; we might have compared wrongly. That admitted, practical choices must be made if one wishes to proceed with comparative analysis. Like Smith, then, Miner believes that historical and theoretical rigor, while necessary, is heuristic but certainly not infallible. Despite possible risks, "true" comparison is worthwhile: "The great gain from intercultural comparative study is that it avoids taking the local for the universal, the momentary for the constant and, above all, the familiar for the inevitable" (238).

Two (More) Conclusions to This Point

The work of Smith and Miner supports the two conclusions delineated above (§2) and adds at least two more. (3) Ideally, the best comparisons are intercultural, which means they include historically unrelated and/or noncontiguous cultural and/or linguistic traditions. Correlatively, comparison benefits from the triangulation of a third element. This enlarges the scale of the comparison and permits more varied assessments of similarities, differences, (re)semblance, and so forth.

(4) The hermeneutical or constructed nature of comparison means that the purpose(s) or end(s) of the comparative endeavor matter. These motivate, if not justify, the enterprise and make it interesting and significant now. Because *we* are the ones that perform these comparisons, we ought to do them about things that matter; otherwise, the project loses its raison d'être and significance for all but the most committed of antiquarians.

4. The Image of God in Comparative Perspective, Once Again

It remains to look at a biblical issue in comparative perspective, armed with the insights and conclusions derived from §§2–3. A case study drawn from Genesis makes excellent sense, given the fact that it has been a primary locus of comparative work. It was, after all, George Smith's remarkable discoveries regarding the flood story in the Epic of Gilgamesh and its relationship to Gen 6–9 that ignited the public's imagination and inspired the financial backing that undergirded so much of the early energy around and expeditions to Mesopotamia.[38] Ever since then, countless studies have been offered on the opening chapters of Genesis and various ancient Near Eastern epics, despite some Assyriologists' objections that the epic literature is of only limited import for the Mesopotamian canon or "stream of tradition."[39]

Comparative work spread quickly from the first chapters of Genesis to other parts of the Primeval History (Gen 1–11) and from there to the rest of the Bible: from creation and flood to stories like the tower of Babel and even nonnarrative genres such as the genealogies. In addition to these unit-level comparisons, scholars have looked at specific details for possible comparative "pay-off." It is no exaggeration to say that the most famous of these details in Gen 1–11 concerns the creation of humans in "the image/likeness of God" (*ṣelem*/*dĕmût ʾĕlōhîm*), which is mentioned in Gen 1:26–27; 5:1 (see also 5:3); and 9:6.[40]

The literature on the image of God is "limitless."[41] Many helpful studies exist, and it is unnecessary to repeat the main arguments here.[42] It suffices to say that there is widespread agreement that the precise meaning of the image of God in its current biblical context is unclear. That is, the *imago Dei* is not presented with sufficient explication so as to know what it signifies. Some scholars have argued that this ambiguity is intentional, but most assume that the image of God *does* (or did) mean something. The lack of immediate contextual clues as to that meaning, however, has led to all manner of discussion in the secondary literature. At least four broad tendencies can be identified: (1) wide-ranging speculation about the meaning of the image from both biblical scholars and theologians;[43] (2) studies attuned to the syntax of (especially) Gen 1:26–27;[44] (3) inferences from larger literary contexts, whether Gen 1–11 or beyond; and (4) comparative studies of the image. In truth, the comparative approach has been used in conjunction with each of the other three—whether to support or challenge interpretations belonging to categories 2 and 3 or to chasten if not rebut certain interpretations from category 1.

Given their number and scope, these studies and their results have varied widely. For our purposes it is sufficient to note that prior investigations have produced much material from both Egypt and Mesopotamia pertaining to the image of God. The data regarding the image of God from both areas centers on two primary referents: (1) Egyptian materials speak of images of *gods* (i.e., depictions) and also speak of the *pharaoh* as the image of God/gods;[45] (2) Mesopotamian sources, too, know of *divine images* and of the *king* as the image of God/gods; they also speak of the *king's own image* in at least two ways: (a) as a votive object within a temple or worship context; or (b) as a physical representation (statue) of the king, especially in subjugated territories.[46]

Despite the legitimacy of both regions and both referents, recent scholarship favors comparing the *imago Dei* with the Mesopotamian materials and the royal figure, such that there is rather widespread agreement that the image of God is a notion derived from royal ideology. The biblical image, especially in Gen 1, is thus seen as a royal image, designating the human as special and unique, elevated over the rest of creation. Furthermore, the practice of placing depictions of kings in subjugated areas may suggest that humans exercise a similar sort of representative function vis-à-vis creation.

I see no reason to challenge this general consensus but wish to reconsider it in light of the theory discussed above. That theory suggests several things that must be kept in mind during comparison, including, at least: (1) the broader contexts of the comparable items so that one avoids excerption that would skew the comparison; (2) the dialectical interplay of similarity and difference; (3) the hermeneutical (i.e., constructed) nature of comparison, which leads directly to (4) the purposes motivating the comparative inquiry—that is, the larger intellectual questions served by the comparison. In light of these considerations, I want to look again at the image of God in a very specific comparative perspective: that of the Neo-Assyrian Empire.

The Neo-Assyrian kings were fond of setting up images (*ṣalmū/ṣalmāni*) of themselves celebrating their victories. So, as one of many examples, Ashurnasirpal II (883–859 B.C.E.) wrote: "I made an image of myself (and) wrote thereon the praises of my power" to celebrate the military exploits of his first year; he did the same after receiving the tribute of Ḫaiiānu.[47] Later, after describing his defeat of the land of Suḫu, he states:

> fear of my dominion reached as far as Karduniaš [Babylonia], *awe* of my weapons overwhelmed Chaldea; I unleashed my brilliance upon the mountains on the banks of the Euphrates. I made an image of myself (and) wrote thereon (an account of) my victory and strength. I erected (it) in the city Suru. (The inscription reads): "Ashurnasirpal, the king whose strength is constantly praiseworthy, whose face is turned towards the desert, who delights in loosing his javelin."[48]

The function of these images and inscriptions—inscribed, as they are, after military victories—was to declare the might and power that was the Assyrian king. Moreover, the inscriptions' content and the images' location (often within defeated cities) indicate that the king's enemies, whether real or potential, are the proper audience of this royal rhetoric. The *ṣalmu* represents the king—not only his dominance, but also his persona, his body; the *ṣalmu* can even become an independent being of its own. So it is the case that the image was typically a place of obeisance and care by obedient subjects or a locus of destruction and defacement by enemies.

One might take these data back to the biblical *imago Dei*, as many scholars have done, in order to find similar meaning(s) in Gen 1. John T. Strong, for instance, concludes: "Humankind, then, was set up after God's victory and to declare God's dominion in a conquered region."[49] Strong's remark assumes that a combat myth lies behind Gen 1—a position that has been challenged by J. Richard Middleton, Jon D. Levenson, and W. Randall Garr.[50] Regardless, more material should be considered beyond just those instances (excerpts) where *ṣalmu* occurs. The rhetoric of the Neo-Assyrian kings did not end with the extensive and gruesome accounts of their military victories. Or, rather, one should say that more accompanies these military victories than the details of the combat itself. Victories on the field of battle were often preceded by or juxtaposed with victories in another "field": the arena of the royal hunt.[51] The Neo-Assyrian kings loved to brag about their hunting successes, both locally and abroad, whether with domestic species or wild game. Consider Shalmaneser III (858–824 B.C.E.):

> The gods Ninurta and Nergal, who love my priesthood, gave to me the wild beasts and commanded me to hunt. I killed from my … chariot 373 wild bulls (and) 399 lions with my valorous assault. I drove twenty-nine elephants into ambush.[52]

Or, again, Ashurnasirpal II:

> The gods Ninurta (and) Nergal, who love my priesthood, gave to me the wild beasts and commanded me to hunt. I killed 450 strong lions. I killed 390 wild bulls from my … chariot with my lordly assault. I slew 200 ostriches like caged birds. I drove 30 elephants into an ambush. I captured alive 50 wild bulls, 140 ostriches, (and) 20 strong lions from the mountains and forests.[53]

The close relationship between the hunt and war should not be missed. As William P. Brown puts it, "the royal hunt was a military campaign in miniature."[54] Not only are descriptions of hunts found before or after descriptions of battles, the inscriptions (which were in some cases stockly reused) often depict the king's enemies as animals to be vanquished. Foes are likened to domesticated species that are decapitated and butchered, but also to wild animals such as deer, goats, foxes, elephants, and lions. This metaphorical use of animal imagery "serves to stress the flight, fear, and subordinated status of the king's enemies."[55] It also connects the king's hunting prowess to his military prowess. Success on either field relates to and/or implies success on the other. The official seal of the Neo-Assyrian Empire captures the relationship visually, depicting the king in hand-to-hand combat with a raging lion (fig. 1).[56]

How does this information about the hunt relate to the image of God in Genesis? If the biblical *imago Dei* is indeed related to (or derived from) ancient Near Eastern royal rhetoric, it pays to look closely at a *specific exemplar* of such rhetoric to identify the similar and the different. As Sandmel states, "it is in the detailed study rather than in the abstract statement that there can emerge persuasive bases for judgment."[57] In a word, Neo-Assyrian royal rhetoric is *violent*. These kings were dominant and destructive, and their violence extended to both human and animal worlds. Indeed, there were close connections between these two realms: the hunt often led directly to the battle (or took place on the way to battle), and hunts became symbolic or emblematic of war. The king as warrior is related to and dependent on the king as hunter and vice versa. The enemies, often portrayed as animals, are thus sport for the great king, who is either the master hunter or the master predator, "top of both the food chain and the chain of command."[58] Moreover, the king's action—all his killing, as both warrior and huntsman—was sanctioned and supported by the gods.[59] Attention to the larger rhetorical context of the Neo-Assyrian royal image goes far beyond simply noting that Hebrew *ṣelem* is cognate with Akkadian *ṣalmu* and then locating passages where the latter occurs. A more detailed comparison casts more light on the image of the Neo-Assyrian king.

Fig. 1. Clay bulla, Samaria, seventh century B.C.E.; Strawn, *What Is Stronger*, fig. 4.109.

But how does that image compare with the biblical image? Despite the ambiguities surrounding the biblical passages, the *imago Dei*, no less than ancient Near Eastern images, can be looked at contextually from a number of different angles—if for no other reason than that all three passages are typically attributed to the Priestly source(s) and occur within a delimitable unit of Genesis. When these larger literary contexts are considered, it becomes striking, comparatively speaking, that the human creatures made in the image of God are immediately given a vegetarian diet (Gen 1:29). Not until after the flood are humans allowed to eat meat (Gen 9:2–3); even then, the practice is linked to the image of God.

Moving beyond the instances of *ṣelem* in P, the larger literary context of Gen 1–11 casts further light on the nature of the biblical image and, more specifically, its difference from the Neo-Assyrian royal image. So, while the use of the terms "subdue" (*kbš*) and "rule" (*rdh*) with reference to the earth and its creatures in Gen 1:28 may carry overtones that, in some passages, are as violent as Neo-Assyrian royal inscriptions—and that were perhaps derived from ancient Near Eastern royal rhetoric[60]—the next two chapters of Genesis define this rule and dominion in terms of "serving" (*šmr*) and preserving (*ʿbd*) the ground, the earth, or the garden of Eden itself. This second creation account also reasserts a vegetarian diet for the human beings within the garden (Gen 2:16).

In comparing the datasets, one finds that the biblical *ṣelem* evokes much of ancient Near Eastern royal ideology (similarity) but certainly not all of it (difference). The differences revolve particularly around violence. The image in Genesis may well be a royal figure, but it is no warrior like the Neo-Assyrian kings, who kill in battle and in the hunt with the approval and power of the gods. But one might quickly object: Is this not simply due to the literary context? There are, after all, no other humans in Gen 1–3, no monarchs per se, and no enemies with which to wage war. While this is true, there are other *animals*, and the biblical image appears strikingly pacifistic vis-à-vis these other creatures, especially in comparison with the venerable ancient Near Eastern tradition of the royal hunt and the wanton destruction of Neo-Assyrian kings. Here, then, in the Neo-Assyrian royal image, one finds a comparable dataset that manifests profound similarities but also marked contrasts from the biblical *imago Dei*.

The sharp difference between these images concerning violence receives further support from Gen 9:2–5, where, when humans are finally permitted to eat meat, the provision is connected with the image of God: "Whoever sheds human blood, by a human will that person's blood be shed, because in the image of God, God made human beings" (Gen 9:6). While debate continues over the precise relationship of Gen 9:4–5 to other biblical laws about diet and homicide, most agree that 9:6 functions as explanation and motivation for the verses that prohibit humans from eating meat with the blood still in it (9:4) and from killing other humans (9:5).[61] The biblical image is nonviolent toward animals (1:29; 2:16; 9:4) *and* humans (9:5–6). The use of animals as images and metaphors for foes in ancient Near Eastern inscriptions lends further comparative support to the view that the vegetarianism in Gen 1–2 reflects the biblical image's nonviolence more generally—a point confirmed by the fact that the first mention of sin (*ḥaṭṭāʾt*) in the Bible is associated with Cain, who murders his brother Abel (Gen 4:7–8; see also 4:23). Any lingering doubts that remain are removed by Gen 9. The *imago Dei*, widely regarded as a royal figure, is, in biblical garb, stripped of many of the trappings of ancient Near Eastern royalty. The biblical image is essentially nonviolent toward animal and human others, in sharp distinction from the royal ideology of Neo-Assyria, but also from other such ideologies from different periods in both Mesopotamian and Egyptian history.

5. More Conclusions, Environmental and Methodological

Much more could be said about the biblical *imago Dei*, even and especially in Neo-Assyrian perspective, but the above suffices to illustrate several of the methodological points that have been developed in comparative approaches to the Bible. I lift up six by way of conclusion.

1. Looking at the biblical image in Neo-Assyrian contexts showcases the dialectic of similarity and difference: both are important, both must be assessed, both should be held together.

2. This particular comparison reveals that both similarity and difference receive greater nuance when the comparison moves beyond initial observations at the level of related lexemes and proceeds to consider broader literary and rhetorical contexts. That is, one must not only recognize that biblical Hebrew *ṣelem* is cognate with Akkadian *ṣalmu*; one must investigate the larger dataset of royal ideology in Akkadian and other languages.

3. The mention of "other languages" underscores Miner's point that the best comparisons are intercultural. Egyptian has various terms for "image/statue" (*snn, mjtj, šsp, twt, sšmw, sḫm, ẖntj*), but none of these are cognate with Hebrew *ṣelem*. If in comparative work one cares only about the same or closely similar cultural and/or linguistic streams, one might overlook the Egyptian data about the image of God and fail to consider Egyptian royal ideology. While space has precluded discussion of the Egyptian materials here, it should be noted that the themes of violence and the royal hunt are no less pronounced in Egypt (especially among the Ramessides in the New Kingdom), and this reinforces the points made

from the Neo-Assyrian materials, only from a different place and time.[62] But the existence of comparable Egyptian data also raises questions, the most important of which is: Why focus on Neo-Assyria if there are earlier and later materials—including materials from other locales—that seem equally pertinent for comparison?

4. This very valid question leads directly to the fourth methodological point, namely, that comparisons should *not* be restricted to just two entities. Miner and Smith's work would urge that a third, preferably intercultural dataset be included (see §3). Study of the *imago Dei* is just one example demonstrating that biblical scholars would do well to learn (as they once did) to pay close attention to Israel's major neighbor to the south, Egypt. The cultural and linguistic differences between Egypt and Israel are large, making it a suitable, if not ideal, "third party" in comparative analyses.[63] Of course other cultures, too, might be used (e.g., Greece, Hatti), and these could well include those that are not geographically proximate or historically propinquitous.

5. In my judgment, the third dataset may be profitably drawn from nontextual media. Iconographical materials offer alternative ways to construe comparison.[64] Sometimes artistic remains reinforce observations derived from the texts—as in the case of figure 1 above. At other times, the iconography supports a point not (as) clearly articulated via textual comparison or suggests an altogether different one. As examples, figures 2–3 could be interpreted as evoking the kind of interpretation suggested above for the *imago Dei*: the royal image is one that rules, like a monarch or mighty person, but *on behalf of* those who need assistance and help. In these particular depictions, the needy are notably *animals*—the caprids in front of the human figure and directly underneath the lion's paws. These images demonstrate that if killing is required, it is done for the sake of the weak, and it is to protect them from certain death from deadly predators. It is certainly not sport. Including nontextual material stretches the work of comparison beyond the ways it has been traditionally understood and practiced. But, as Smith would remind us, comparison is only interesting if it is done for specific cognitive purposes.

6. The "third thing" in some comparisons may not be additional (non)contiguous cultures or (non)textual datasets but the very (contemporary) reasons we have for considering the issue at hand. After all, "[c]omparison provides the means by which *we* 're-envision' phenomena as *our* data in order to solve *our* theoretical problems."[65] The case study offered above on the *imago Dei* in Neo-Assyrian perspective is a perfect

Fig. 2. Seal, Middle Assyrian Period (1350–1000 B.C.E.); Strawn, *What Is Stronger*, fig. 4.22.

Fig. 3. Seal, Neo-Assyrian Period (ninth–seventh centuries B.C.E.); Strawn, *What Is Stronger*, fig. 4.55.

example of such re-envisioning. It is colored, no doubt, by contemporary concerns with the environment, ecology, and sustainability. That does not invalidate the comparison or the comparative data utilized; to the contrary it makes both *interesting*. The fact that there are other valid comparisons and additional pertinent evidence (mounds, really) is no refutation of the example offered above. It is simply proof of Emily Dickinson's poetic insight. "The Truth," after all, "must dazzle gradually." And it may well be that the only way to "Tell all the Truth" is to "tell it slant"—that is, sideways, obliquely, *comparatively*.[66]

For Further Reading

Chavalas, Mark W., and K. Lawson Younger Jr., eds. *Mesopotamia and the Bible: Comparative Explorations*. JSOTSup 341. Sheffield: Sheffield Academic Press, 2002.

Greenspahn, Frederick E., ed. *Essential Papers on Israel and the Ancient Near East*. New York: New York University Press, 1991.

Hallo, William W., and K. Lawson Younger Jr., eds. *The Context of Scripture: Canonical Compositions, Monumental Inscriptions, and Archival Documents from the Biblical World*. 3 vols. Leiden: Brill, 1997–2002.

Patton, Kimberly C., and Benjamin C. Ray, eds. *A Magic Still Dwells: Comparative Religion in the Postmodern Age*. Berkeley and Los Angeles: University of California Press, 2000.

Oppenheim, A. Leo. *Ancient Mesopotamia: Portrait of a Dead Civilization*. Revised by Erica Reiner. Chicago: University of Chicago Press, 1977.

Roberts, J. J. M. *The Bible and the Ancient Near East*. Winona Lake, Ind.: Eisenbrauns, 2002.

Notes

1. Emily Dickinson, "Tell All the Truth But Tell It Slant (1129)," in *The Complete Poems of Emily Dickinson* (ed. Thomas H. Johnson; Boston: Back Bay Books, 1976), 506.

2. See V. S. Ramachandran, *A Brief Tour of Human Consciousness: From Imposter Poodles to Purple Numbers* (New York: Pi, 2004), esp. 37–39, 106–7. Ramachandran thinks these motor command (or "mirror") neurons were crucial for the development of human culture, which depends on imitation, "and the imitation of complex skills may require the participation of mirror neurons" (38; see also 107). For more on comparison and ocular-cortical functions, see Lawrence E. Sullivan, "The Net of Indra: Comparison and the Contribution of Perception," in *A Magic Still Dwells: Comparative Religion in the Postmodern Age* (ed. Kimberly C. Patton and Benjamin C. Ray; Berkeley and Los Angeles: University of California Press, 2000), 206–34.

3. This receives further support by noting the role comparison plays in many scholarly methods, e.g., source criticism, form criticism, redaction criticism, textual criticism, and so forth.

4. Frederich Max Müller, *Introduction to the Science of Religion: Four Lectures Delivered at the Royal Institution in February and May, 1870* (1872; new ed.; London: Longmans, Green, 1893), esp. 1–51, here 13 (emphasis original).

5. Daniel L. Pals, *Eight Theories of Religion* (2nd ed.; New York: Oxford University Press, 2006), 4.

6. Müller, *Introduction to the Science of Religion*, 9–10.

7. Exceptions are rare and recent, at least in mainstream academic biblical scholarship. See, e.g., Vanessa R. Sasson, *The Birth of Moses and the Buddha: A Paradigm for the Comparative Study of Religions* (Hebrew Bible Monographs 9; Sheffield: Sheffield Phoenix Press, 2007). For an important earlier argument advocating for broader cross-cultural comparisons, see Howard Eilberg-Schwartz, "Beyond Parallel-anoia: Comparative Inquiry and Cultural Interpretation," in idem, *The Savage in Judaism: An Anthropology of Israelite Religion and Ancient Judaism* (Bloomington: Indiana University Press, 1990), 87–102.

8. Shemaryahu Talmon, "The 'Comparative Method' in Biblical Interpretation—Principles and Problems" (orig. 1978), in *Essential Papers on Israel and the Ancient Near East* (ed. Frederick E. Greenspahn; New York: New York University Press, 1991), 381–419, here 386.

9. See, e.g., Mark W. Chavalas, "Assyriology and Biblical Studies: A Century and a Half of Tension," in *Mesopotamia and the Bible: Comparative Explorations* (ed. Mark W. Chavalas and K. Lawson Younger Jr.; JSOTSup 341; Sheffield: Sheffield Academic Press, 2002), 21–67.

10. See Delbert R. Hillers, "Analyzing the Abominable: Our Understanding of Canaanite Religion," *JQR* 75 (1985): 253–69. Further instructive rebuttals of "oversimplified" comparative treatments may be found in J. J. M. Roberts, *The Bible and the Ancient Near East* (Winona Lake, Ind.: Eisenbrauns, 2002), esp. 59–82.

11. See Hillers, "Analyzing the Abominable," esp. 254, who criticizes William F. Albright, Yehezkel Kaufmann, G. Ernest Wright, Frank Moore Cross, and Norman Gottwald on this score. Wright's work, which has become emblematic of the "too-different" approach, is *The Old Testament against Its Environment* (SBT 2; London: SCM, 1968).

12. See Jack M. Sasson, "About 'Mari and the Bible,'" *RA* 92 (1998): 97 and n. 1; also Pals, *Eight Theories of Religion*, 9; and further below.

13. See William W. Hallo, "Compare and Contrast: The Contextual Approach to Biblical Literature," in *The Bible in the Light of Cuneiform Literature: Scripture in Context III* (ed. William W. Hallo, Bruce William Jones, and Gerald L. Mattingly; Ancient Near Eastern Texts and Studies 8; Lewiston, N.Y.: Mellen, 1990), 3.

14. Note the four volumes that emerged under Hallo's supervision: *Scripture in Context: Essays on the Comparative Method* (ed. Carl D. Evans, William W. Hallo, and John B. White; PTMS 34; Pittsburgh: Pickwick, 1980); *Scripture in Context II: More Essays on the Comparative Method* (ed. William W. Hallo, James C. Moyer, and Leo G. Perdue; Winona Lake, Ind.: Eisenbrauns, 1983); Hallo, Jones, and Mattingly, *The Bible in the Light of Cuneiform Literature*; and *The Biblical Canon in Comparative Perspective: Scripture in Context IV* (ed. K. Lawson Younger Jr., William W. Hallo, and Bernard F. Batto; Ancient Near Eastern Texts and Studies 11; Lewiston, N.Y.: Mellen, 1991).

15. See William W. Hallo, "New Moons and Sabbaths: A Case Study in the Contrastive Approach" (orig. 1977), in Greenspahn, *Essential Papers*, 313–32.

16. See Hallo, "Biblical History in Its Near Eastern Setting: The Contextual

Approach," in Evans, Hallo, and White, *Scripture in Context*, 1–26, esp. 2, where he states that the contextual method combines comparative and contrastive approaches.

17. William W. Hallo, "Ancient Near Eastern Texts and Their Relevance for Biblical Exegesis," *COS* 1:xxv; idem, "The Bible and the Monuments," *COS* 2:xiii.

18. Hallo, "Compare and Contrast," 3.

19. Hallo, "Ancient Near Eastern Texts," xxvi.

20. See Hallo, "Compare and Contrast," 5–6.

21. To Hallo's credit, he does make some allowance for other kinds of comparable phenomena; see, e.g., "Compare and Contrast," 4.

22. Eilberg-Schwartz, "Beyond Parallel-anoia," 95.

23. Hallo, "Ancient Near Eastern Texts," xxviii.

24. See Bill T. Arnold and David B. Weisberg, "A Centennial Review of Friedrich Delitzsch's 'Babel und Bibel' Lectures," *JBL* 121 (2002): 441–57. Much of the following is indebted to Arnold and Weisberg, who detail anti-Catholic/Christian aspects of Delitzsch's work along with the anti-Semitic.

25. Friedrich Delitzsch, *Die grosse Täuschung* (1920–1921; new ed.; 2 vols. in 1; Stuttgart: Deutsche Verlags-Anstalt, 1921–1922).

26. The address was published the next year as Benno Landsberger, "Die Eigenbegrifflichkeit der babylonischen Welt," *Islamica* 2 (1926): 355–72; translated into English as *The Conceptual Autonomy of the Babylonian World* (trans. Thorkild Jacobsen, Benjamin Foster, and Heinrich von Siebenthal; MANE 1/4; Malibu: Undena, 1976).

27. Landsberger, *The Conceptual Autonomy*, 6 (emphasis original).

28. Ibid., 7.

29. Ibid.

30. Hallo, "New Moons and Sabbaths," 313; Talmon, "The 'Comparative Method,'" 389.

31. See Jacob J. Finkelstein, "Bible and Babel: A Comparative Study of the Hebrew and Babylonian Religious Spirit" (orig. 1958), in *Essential Papers on Israel and the Ancient Near East*, 355–80, esp. 368; and A. Leo Oppenheim, *Ancient Mesopotamia: Portrait of a Dead Civilization* (1964; rev. ed. Erica Reiner; Chicago: University of Chicago Press, 1977), 334.

32. Müller, *Introduction to the Science of Religion*, 28. He later speaks of Zulu traditions as "the religions of the savages" compared to the "sacred traditions of the Semitic and Aryan nations" (41–42).

33. Chavalas, "Assyriology and Biblical Studies," esp. 43–45. An example would be the excitement over the discoveries at Ugarit. For an excellent overview, see Mark S. Smith, *Untold Stories: The Bible and Ugaritic Studies in the Twentieth Century* (Peabody, Mass.: Hendrickson, 2001).

34. Samuel Sandmel, "Parallelomania," *JBL* 81 (1962): 1–13, esp. 10–11.

35. See Eilberg-Schwartz, "Beyond Parallel-anoia," 87–102; Hallo, "Compare and Contrast," 16.

36. The corpus of Smith's pertinent work is vast. I draw on four representative pieces, cited parenthetically in what follows: (1) "*Adde Parvum Parvo Magnus Acervus Erit*," *HR* 11 (1971): 67–90 (cited as 1971); (2) "In Comparison a Magic Dwells" (orig.

1982), in Patton and Ray, *A Magic Still Dwells*, 23–44 (cited as 2000a); (3) *Drudgery Divine: On the Comparison of Early Christianities and the Religions of Late Antiquity* (Chicago: University of Chicago Press, 1990), esp. 36–53 (cited as 1990); and (4) "The 'End' of Comparison: Redescription and Rectification," in Patton and Ray, *A Magic Still Dwells*, 237–41 (cited as 2000b).

37. Earl Miner, *Comparative Poetics: An Intercultural Essay on Theories of Literature* (Princeton: Princeton University Press, 1990); subsequent citations will be made parenthetically in the text.

38. See George Smith, *The Chaldean Account of Genesis* (New York: Scribner, Armstrong, 1876), esp. 1–18.

39. See, e.g., Oppenheim, *Ancient Mesopotamia*, 177. In my judgment, the yearly recitation of the Enuma Elish as part of the Akitu celebration is significant proof of at least some epics' import in Mesopotamian religious experience.

40. Claus Westermann, *Genesis 1–11: A Continental Commentary* (trans. John J. Scullion; CC; Minneapolis: Fortress, 1993), 604, calls it the "most striking statement of the primeval story."

41. Ibid., 148.

42. Classic studies include Westermann, *Genesis 1–11*, 142–65; Gerhard von Rad, *Genesis: A Commentary* (trans. John Marks; rev. ed.; OTL; Philadelphia: Westminster, 1972), 57–61; Edward M. Curtis, "Image of God (OT)," *ABD* 3:389–91; Gunnlaugur A. Jónsson, *The Image of God: Genesis 1:26–28 in a Century of Old Testament Research* (ConBOT 26; Lund: Almqvist & Wiksell, 1988).

43. For a partial listing, see W. Sibley Towner, "Clones of God: Genesis 1:26–28 and the Image of God in the Hebrew Bible," *Int* 59 (2005): 343.

44. See W. Randall Garr, *In His Own Image and Likeness: Humanity, Divinity, and Monotheism* (CHANE 15; Leiden: Brill, 2003), esp. 95–176.

45. At least one text (*Instruction for Merikare*) speaks of all humankind as the image of god (see *ANET*, 417; *AEL* 1:106). For the Egyptian materials, see J. Richard Middleton, *The Liberating Image: The Imago Dei in Genesis 1* (Grand Rapids: Brazos, 2005), 99–111.

46. For the Mesopotamian materials, see Peter Machinist, "Kingship and Divinity in Imperial Assyria," in *Text, Artifact, and Image: Revealing Ancient Israelite Religion* (ed. Gary Beckman and Theodore J. Lewis; BJS 346; Providence, R.I.: Brown University, 2006), 152–88; also Zainab Bahrani, *The Graven Image: Representation in Babylonia and Assyria* (Philadelphia: University of Pennsylania Press, 2003), 121–48.

47. Ninurta Temple Inscription, column i lines 58b–69a (A. Kirk Grayson, *Assyrian Rulers of the Early First Millennium BC [1114–859 BC]* [RIMA 2; Toronto: University of Toronto Press, 1991], 197–98; hereafter RIMA 2); and column i lines 95–99a (RIMA 2:200), respectively.

48. Ninurta Temple Inscription, column iii lines 23b–26a (RIMA 2:214).

49. John T. Strong, "Shattering the Image of God: A Response to Theodore Hiebert's Interpretation of the Story of the Tower of Babel," *JBL* 127 (2008): 631. Cf. Garr, *In His Own Image and Likeness*, 163, 171.

50. See Middleton, *The Liberating Image*, 235–69; Jon D. Levenson, *Creation and the Persistence of Evil: The Jewish Drama of Divine Omnipotence* (rev. ed.; Princeton:

Princeton University Press, 1994), esp. 122, 127; Garr, *In His Own Image and Likeness*, 191–211.

51. See Chikako E. Watanabe, *Animal Symbolism in Mesopotamia: A Contextual Approach* (WOO 1; Vienna: Institut für Orientalistik der Universität Wien, 2002), 69–88; Brent A. Strawn, *What Is Stronger than a Lion? Leonine Image and Metaphor in the Hebrew Bible and the Ancient Near East* (OBO 212; Fribourg: Academic; Göttingen: Vandenhoeck & Ruprecht, 2005), 161–74.

52. Shalmaneser III Clay Tablets, column iv lines 40–44 (A. Kirk Grayson, *Assyrian Rulers of the Early First Millennium BC II [858–745 BC]* [RIMA 3; Toronto: University of Toronto Press, 1996], 41).

53. Calah Stone Slab, lines 84b–94b (RIMA 2:291).

54. William P. Brown, *The Ethos of the Cosmos: The Genesis of Moral Imagination in the Bible* (Grand Rapids: Eerdmans, 1999), 358.

55. Ibid., 352.

56. The royal seal was used for at least three centuries, from the time of Shalmaneser III (858–824) to Aššur-etel-ilāni (ca. 631–627 B.C.E.). Note that the bulla in fig. 1 was found in Samaria.

57. Sandmel, "Parallelomania," 2.

58. Brown, *Ethos of the Cosmos*, 359.

59. See the texts cited above and note the offering and libations (evidently for Ishtar) that Ashurbanipal (668–627 B.C.E.) pours over the lions he kills in his royal hunt (Strawn, *What Is Stronger*, 167–70 and fig. 4.129). The warlike nature and connotations of patron gods of the royal hunt such as Nergal, Ninurta, and Ishtar are not to be missed.

60. See, e.g., Westermann, *Genesis 1–11*, 158–60; Garr, *In His Own Image and Likeness*, 158.

61. See conveniently, Westermann, *Genesis 1–11*, 461–69.

62. See, e.g., Strawn, *What Is Stronger*, 161–63, 174–78.

63. Erik Hornung's *Conceptions of God in Ancient Egypt: The One and the Many* (trans. John Baines; Ithaca, N.Y.: Cornell University Press, 1982) remains an excellent introduction.

64. See the essay on iconographical approaches by Joel M. LeMon in the present volume.

65. Smith, *Drudgery Divine*, 52 (emphasis original).

66. I thank Bill T. Arnold, Christopher B. Hays, Joel M. LeMon, Peter Machinist, Patrick D. Miller, Kent Harold Richards, and Mark S. Smith for their help with various aspects of this paper.

Iconographic Approaches: The Iconic Structure of Psalm 17

Joel M. LeMon

Exploring the Relationship between Art and Text

Ancient art, or *iconography*, is an important resource for biblical scholars exploring the cultural milieu from which the Bible emerged. Indeed, many scholars consider the images from the ancient world at least as valuable for understanding the historical background of the Bible as ancient textual sources.[1] Methods for appropriating such iconographic material within biblical studies have been developing gradually, with the most important advances coming since the 1970s. Today, while biblical scholars generally affirm the increased attention paid to iconography, there remains a degree of uncertainty about the best methods for interpreting biblical texts in light of ancient art.

The impulse to use ancient art to illuminate biblical texts is not new. Beginning in the nineteenth century, with the rise of the great archaeological collections in Paris, London, Turin, and Berlin, art from the ancient world captivated scholars and laypeople alike. Generally, these interpreters assumed that this ancient pictorial material provided *illustrations* of the Bible or other ancient Near Eastern literature, similar to the ways in which "biblical art" illustrates characters and stories from the Bible (e.g., Rembrandt's *The Prodigal Son*, DaVinci's *The Last Supper*, Michelangelo's paintings in the Sistine Chapel). The subjects in both biblical art and ancient iconography were thought to be based on texts. Or, put more simply, art refers straightforwardly to literature.

The case of the so-called "Adam and Eve" seal (figs. 1–2) illustrates this tendency. In 1876, the British Assyriologist George Smith proposed the existence of a Mesopotamian account of "The Fall of Man" that paralleled

Gen 3:1–24. Smith based his argument on the iconography of a cylinder seal housed in the British Museum. He describes the scene:

> "One striking and important specimen … has two figures sitting one on each side of a tree, holding out their hands to the fruit, while at the back of one is stretched a serpent. We know well that in these early sculptures none of these figures were chance devices, *but all represented events or supposed events, and figures in their legends*; thus it is evident that a form of the story of the Fall, similar to that of Genesis, was known in early times in Babylonia."[2]

The idea of an "Adam and Eve" seal quickly took hold. In his famous *Babel und Bibel* lecture, Friedrich Delitzsch commented: "May I lift the veil, may I point to an Old Babylonian cylinder-seal? … Is it not the very acme of likelihood that there is *some connection* between this old Babylonian picture and the Biblical tale of the Fall of Man?"[3] J. N. Fradenburgh made an even more forceful claim. In a popularizing work (aptly titled) *Witnesses from the Dust, or The Bible: Illustrated from the Monuments* (1886), he writes: "Upon this cylinder is represented a tree with four and five nearly horizontal branches on either side, the two lowest branches bearing each a large bunch of fruit. A man wearing a Babylonian turban sits on one side of the tree and a woman sits on the other side. They stretch out their hands as if to pluck the fruit. Behind the woman a serpent stands upreared." He concludes: "This *illustrates* the story of Genesis, and admits of no other satisfactory explanation."[4]

It comes as no surprise that Fradenburg's conclusion about the illustrative value of the seal has not withstood a century of scholarly scrutiny. In short, Fradenburgh's interpretation of the "Adam and Eve" seal is incorrect because he evaluated the images solely by recourse to the literature of the ancient Near East—and not only that, but a work of literature from a different historical period and geographical region. By contrast, Dominique Collon's more recent analysis of the seal interprets the scene according to the conventions of post-Akkadian art (2192–2004 B.C.E), that is, within its art-historical context.

Fig. 1. Cylinder seal; post-Akkadian; 2192–2004 B.C.E. Line drawing from George Smith, *The Chaldean Account of Genesis*, 91.

Fig. 2. The "Adam and Eve" seal and a modern impression. British Museum, ME 89326 © Trustees of the British Museum.

Collon rightly maintains that this particular seal belongs in the well-established tradition of the Akkadian banquet scene.[5] In order to prove her case, she points to several features in the so-called "Adam and Eve" seal that may be found in contemporary images. First, there is a long tradition in Mesopotamian art of representing figures facing a central plant, here a date palm. Also, the horns of the seated figure on the right indicate divine status, in accordance with long-held iconographic conventions. The identity of the figure on the left is probably a worshiper, and not a woman at all, as Fradenburgh assumed. As for the snake, it may well be a representation of a snake-god (such as Niraḫ) or possibly a more general symbol of regeneration and fertility.[6]

As biblical scholars and art historians discredited the facile claims about the simplistic, illustrative understanding of the relationship between art and texts, a more cautious era emerged in the early and mid-twentieth century. Scholars became increasingly wary of interpreting ancient images as mere illustrations of characters or scenes in ancient Near Eastern texts. Instead, biblical scholars utilized ancient images to provide illustrations of a different sort; they realized that such images could convey information about various aspects of cultures of the ancient Near East.[7] Thus, while the "Adam and Eve" seal does not *illustrate* Gen 3, it could nevertheless help one understand ancient clothing, the significance of various types of headgear, or even the types of trees that grew in ancient Mesopotamia.

However, this approach to ancient art had drawbacks as well, for scholars often discussed the images out of their artistic contexts and in a fragmentary way. Othmar Keel describes the problem as follows:

> Fragmentation … followed by many biblical scholars, is still typically the way in which Egyptian and Assyrian pictures are presented in illustrating biblical civilization. Very seldom is an entire relief or a complete wall painting reproduced. Usually particular kinds of agricultural activity, specific cult utensils, or single musical instruments are selected for illustration. This is legitimate for those interested in material culture in a narrow sense.… Under such fragmentization the sociological aspect of the pictures is not revealed.… For example, when the great relief of the conquest of Lachish by Sennacherib serves to illustrate "battering rams," "women's clothes," and "wagon types" that is indeed useful; but the picture's possibilities for information do not stop there. This method of presenting only fragments, characteristic of all the [Bible] handbooks, pays no respect to the original message of these works, the purpose of which was not the illustration of perceptual material culture, but of concepts like divine rule, world order, kingship and the gods, etc.[8]

Othmar Keel's groundbreaking work, *The Symbolism of the Biblical World* demonstrates this use of art to illustrate these larger cultural constructs.[9] By analyzing the iconography of the ancient Near East, Keel explores ancient cosmologies, notions of kingship, and humanity's ways of approaching deities, among other topics. Overall, Keel shows how ancient Near Eastern images can and do illustrate the ancient conceptions that were the common heritage of the biblical authors. Keel's work has ushered in a new era of iconographical research.

A Typology of Iconographic Studies

As a relatively recent venture within biblical and ancient Near Eastern studies, scholars have liberally applied the rubric "iconographic study" to a variety of pursuits. One could distill these studies into three related subfields, each motivated by a different question: (1) How does one discern the meaning(s)/significance of an ancient Near Eastern image? (2) How does one reconstruct ancient Near Eastern history and religion with the help of these images? (3) How can these images inform readings of particular biblical texts?

The Iconographic-Artistic Approach

The first question spurs the study of iconography *qua* iconography, what might be called the iconographic-artistic approach. At the risk of oversimplifying, those who engage in this approach are principally concerned with interpreting images in their artistic contexts. According to the methodology advanced by Keel and informed by Panofsky especially, each ancient Near Eastern artistic motif can convey different meanings depending on the contexts in which it is found.[10]

Caprids, for example, show the polyvalence of a single artistic motif. A common scene on Palestinian seals from Iron Age IIB depicts caprids flanking a person, widely understood as an image of the "Lord of the Animals" (fig. 3).[11] According to Keel and Uehlinger, in this context, the caprids represent the entire animal world mastered by the human in the center of the scene.[12] Yet when caprids appear flanking a stylized tree, as in the Kuntillet ʿAjrud pithos A (fig. 4), Keel and Uehlinger offer another assessment. Here caprids symbolize blessing and fertility, since they surround and feed on a tree, a classic representation of the mother goddess.[13] Keel and Uehlinger offer yet another interpretation of the animal on a cylinder seal from Beth-shean (fig. 5) in which an archer takes aim at a leaping caprid. Keel and Uehlinger consider the two figures as one of several "star signs" on the seal, possibly representing the astral constellation Sagittarius.[14]

Fig. 3. Seals; Israel/Palestine; Iron Age IIB. After Keel and Uehlinger, *Gods, Goddesses, and Images*, figs. 196a, b, 197a.

As the example of the caprid shows, according to the iconographic-artistic approach, both single motifs and related images should be understood *within their artistic contexts*; as contexts change, the meaning and significance of the image will also change. Keel and Uehlinger designate this relationship between individual images as the "iconographical syntax" or the "constellation" of a scene.

The Iconographic-Historical Approach

The second type of iconographic approach—the iconographic-historical

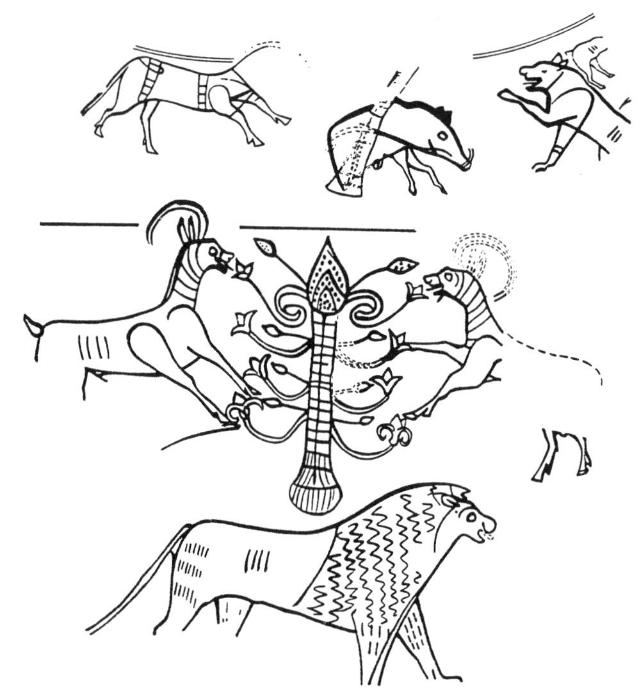

Fig. 4. Pithos A; Kuntillet ʿAjrud; Iron Age IIB.
After Keel and Uehlinger, *Gods, Goddesses, and Images*, fig. 219.

Fig. 5. Cylinder seal; Beth-shean; Iron Age IIC.
After Keel and Uehlinger, *Gods, Goddesses, and Images*, fig. 308.

approach—employs iconography for the reconstruction of ancient Near Eastern history and cultural phenomena. Uehlinger's recent study of the Lachish Reliefs (fig. 6) provides a clear example of this mode of investigation.[15] He treats the famous reliefs as a "pictorial narrative"[16] that must be "read for itself" according to the principles and conventions of Assyrian art. Uehlinger's primary goal is to treat the reliefs as a unique historical voice, standing alongside archaeological, textual, and biblical sources, that can contribute to a better understanding of Sennacherib's campaign against Judah.[17]

A related goal governs Keel and Uehlinger's *Gods, Goddesses, and Images of God in Ancient Israel*.[18] In this prime example of the iconographical-historical approach, the authors' aim is not to enrich the understanding of a particular historical event but rather to track the development (i.e., the history) of religious traditions in Syria-Palestine using iconography as a primary source of data. The authors maintain that iconography reflects

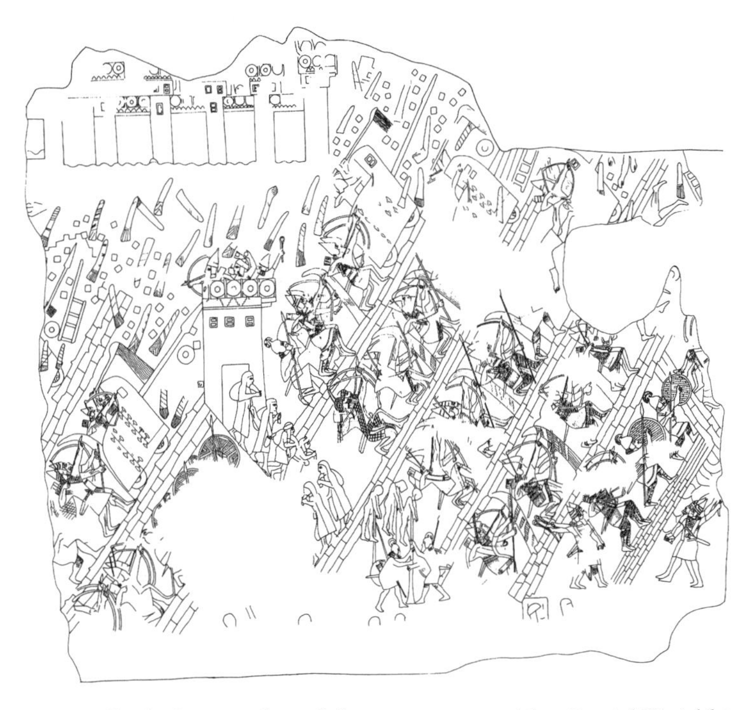

Fig. 6. Wall relief; Nineveh; eighth century B.C.E. After Daniel Ussishkin, *The Conquest of Lachish by Sennacherib* (Tel Aviv University Publications of the Institute of Archaeology 6; 1982), fig. 68. Courtesy of the Institute of Archaeology, Tel Aviv University.

political, social, and especially religious realities of any given period. Thus, iconography can be "read" to determine the discrete symbolic systems that underlie individual periods of Syro-Palestinian history. Further, an analysis of the changes in the artistic record informs an understanding of the development of the religious beliefs and practices. It is notable that the practitioners of the iconographic-historical approach typically treat iconographic sources as the primary mode of inquiry, such that biblical texts become secondary or even tertiary sources of religio-historical data. Silvia Schroer and Keel are carrying out this approach to the fullest extent with the multivolume "history of religion in images," *Die Ikonographie Palästinas/Israels und der Alte Orient: Eine Religionsgeschichte in Bildern*.[19]

The Iconographic-Biblical Approach

The third mode of iconographic study—the iconographic-biblical approach—is closely related to the first two. This approach employs iconography for the express purpose of interpreting the Bible's literary imagery and figurative language, especially metaphors. Numerous works could be cited that fall within this category, but it will suffice to highlight a handful of studies: Keel's commentary on the Song of Songs; Martin Klingbeil's investigation of "warrior" and "god of heaven" imagery in the Psalms; and Brent Strawn's examination of leonine imagery and metaphor.

In his commentary on the Song of Songs, Keel presents the clearest description of his iconographic-biblical method, which might be characterized as the "concentric circles" approach. When faced with a difficult or ambiguous literary image, Keel advocates first exploring the immediate context of the literary image to find clues to its meaning. Second, he advocates searching the Song of Songs (the next concentric circle) for similar imagery for comparison. Third, he suggests that one look to the entire Hebrew Bible, giving special consideration to contexts *similar* to that of the Song. After textual avenues have been exhausted, Keel advocates the engagement of nontextual sources, particularly "pictorial images in seals, amulets, ivories, and other valuables."[20] Keel's approach provides a helpful guide for gathering data and evaluating the relative importance of biblical versus iconographic evidence. However, one is left to wonder: How should one judge between contrasting evidence within the same concentric circle, as data within each concentric circle can and often do conflict?

In Klingbeil's detailed study of "warrior" and "god of heaven" imagery, he identifies a series of metaphors and submetaphors for God in the

Psalms. He has isolated 507 occurrences of metaphorical language for God, which he then groups into seventeen categories (e.g., God of heaven, God as warrior, God as king, God as rock, God as judge).[21] Further, each category contains a series of submetaphors. Klingbeil identifies the iconography that interacts with and illumines the larger "God as warrior" and "God of heaven" metaphors by identifying artistic depictions of the various submetaphors.

In Strawn's exhaustive analysis of leonine imagery in the Hebrew Bible and the ancient Near East, he emphasizes the point that metaphors are "contextually conditioned"; that is, semantic and cultural contexts have an impact on the "construction, reception, and interpretation of a metaphor."[22] If the modern reader and ancient writer do not share a common knowledge of the subject of the metaphor and the set of associations it evokes, then, according to Strawn, "the full significance of the user's metaphor may be lost to (and on) the receiver."[23] Strawn then proceeds to explore how iconography of lions can inform biblical texts describing YHWH as a lion or describing particular actors, such as the enemies within the psalms, as lions or like lions.

Evaluation

The merits of these iconographic studies of metaphors and literary imagery cannot be overstated. Keel has systematically applied iconographic material to rich and evocative text and, in doing so, has blazed the trail for others employing his methods. For their part, Klingbeil and Strawn have provided particularly sophisticated treatments of the intersection of metaphor theory and iconographic study. Yet, as we have seen thus far, these scholars utilizing the iconographic-biblical approach have tended to focus on how iconographic material from the ancient Near East can inform interpretations of discrete metaphors within the biblical text. One consequence of these investigations is that the iconographic studies have tended to treat relatively small literary contexts, namely, the text immediately surrounding the metaphor.

The same could even be said about Keel's programmatically iconographic commentary on the Song of Songs. In his introduction to the commentary, Keel argues that the Song of Songs is a relatively random collection of forty-three discrete literary units, each comprising no more than a few verses.[24] Thus, when he employs iconographic data to interpret metaphors in the Song, his discussion is limited to these small units of text in which each image resides. Evaluating Keel's form-critical conclusions about the Song is not my goal here. I wish only to point out that, in this prominent example of the iconographic-biblical approach, Keel does not assess the larger literary context of each image due to the form-critical decisions he has made about the size of the discrete literary units in which the images are embedded.

In short, as iconographic-biblical approaches have become more prominent and focused on interpreting individual metaphors, the larger *literary* contexts of the biblical images have tended to receive relatively little attention. Thus, while many practitioners of the iconographic-biblical approach have been careful to avoid fragmentary readings of *iconographic* constellations according to Keel's apt admonition cited above, these same interpreters have often tended toward literary "fragmentation." This tendency does not diminish the value of these studies. Instead, the careful work on metaphors done by Keel, Klingbeil, and Strawn (to name but a few) opens up avenues for scholarship to apply iconographic data to ever-larger literary contexts. Said differently, the next potential advancement of the iconographic-biblical approach is for scholars to bring ever-larger constellations of literary imagery into conversation with congruent constellations of iconographic motifs. Moreover, comparing constellations of literary and pictorial imagery may help one determine the background and significance of literary imagery that might otherwise be tremendously difficult to identify. An example will help clarify this point.

Case Study: YHWH's Winged Form in Psalm 17

A compelling image of YHWH in winged form appears in Ps 17:8, "Hide me in the shadow of your wings" (*bĕṣēl kĕnāpêkā tastîrēnî*). It seems clear in the context of the psalm that the wings connote YHWH's protection, as they do in the other five occurrences of this image in the Psalms (36:8; 57:2; 61:5; 63:8; 91:4). Yet scholars have disagreed widely about the background, meaning, and significance of this image. A survey of the rather extensive scholarship on this issue reveals that there are basically three proposals for interpreting YHWH with wings. (1) Some scholars understand the wings to evoke some sort of *divine image*, that is, the iconography of deities such as a winged sun-god or other winged gods or goddesses, such as Aššur or Isis and Nephthys.[25] (2) Others understand the wings in these psalms to refer to the wings of the cherubim in the temple (or on the ark itself). According to this interpretation, the wings function as a *metonym*, referring *pars pro toto* to the protecting presence afforded by the temple.[26] (3) Still others argue that the image of YHWH's wings is best and most simply understood as a conceptual *metaphor*: YHWH IS A BIRD.[27]

The problem is that scholars supporting all three of these proposals can and do appeal to iconographical data in support of their arguments. How, then, should one weigh these various, complex, and potentially contradictory iconographic data? Just one artifact from Syria-Palestine illustrates the difficulties one faces when bringing iconography to bear on the literary image of YHWH in winged form. The famous Megiddo ivory depicts a scene in which many wings appear. The tableau might well support three different ways for interpreting the image of the winged YHWH: divine image; metonym; and metaphor. Wings appear as an aspect of a divine image, namely, the sun disk suspended above the triumphant one in his chariot. Does YHWH's winged form reflect this image? With regard to the metonymic option, one notes that wings also appear on a cherub adorning the throne of the royal figure. Might YHWH's wings refer to a similar representation of YHWH's cherubim throne in the temple? Finally, three (winged) birds appear in this scene around the throne of the royal figure: one under the seat and two in flight. Does the image of YHWH's wings come from such "naturalistic" depictions of birds, making YHWH's wings a metaphor? To which, then, of these iconographic motifs, if any, does the verbal image of YHWH's wings *most closely* relate?

When, as in Ps 17, the iconographic materials provide potentially contradictory evidence, one way forward is to explore more fully the literary context of the biblical image. To borrow and modify slightly William Brown's terminology, one should map the "iconic structure" of a text; as one understands the literary image in its larger context, one can better explore the possible relationships with iconographic materials.[28] This process entails understanding the psalm as a constellation of literary

Fig. 7. Ivory plaque; Megiddo; Late Bronze Age. After Keel and Uehlinger, *Gods, Goddesses, and Images*, fig. 65; cf. Loud, *The Megiddo Ivories*, pl. 4, 2a and 2b.

images—images that come together to create meaning in much the same way as numerous individual artistic motifs constitute an artistic scene. Mapping the iconic structure of a text presumes that the characterization of the actors in the text creates a series of pictures in the mind of the reader.

Psalm 17 pictures three main actors: the psalmist; God; and the enemies. The psalmist portrays himself as the very essence of righteousness and one who is desperately in need of YHWH's help (17:1–5, 15). According to the logic of the psalm, the righteousness of the psalmist merits YHWH's decisive saving action. Armed with this confidence of his own righteousness, the psalmist consistently petitions YHWH to confront and overthrow the psalmist's enemies (17:13–14).

The enemies are diametrically opposed to the psalmist and to YHWH. While YHWH's mouth and lips are righteous (17:1, 4), the mouth of the enemy is rebellious and proud (17:10). While the psalmist's heart has been tested and proven righteous (17:3), the heart of the wicked is fat, that is, dull and unresponsive (17:10). And while the psalmist hides for protection under the wings of YHWH (17:8), the enemies hide in a different place for a different purpose; like lions they seize prey without warning (17:12).

The description of the enemies as lions in 17:12 is pivotal for understanding their characterization. In the mind of the reader/suppliant, the martial imagery of the enemies surrounding (17:9), advancing, and encircling the psalmist (17:11) combines with the leonine imagery to convey a terrifying composite picture of the foes. The psalmist pleads for YHWH to overthrow these enemies / this lion (17:13), in response to their desire to overthrow the psalmist (17:11). In sum, the imagery of the enemies as lurking, slanderous, violent lion-warriors is a grave threat that YHWH must overcome.[29]

YHWH's triumph over the enemies is realized only when the psalmist beholds YHWH's *tĕmûnâ*, the divine "form" (17:15). What, then, is the form of YHWH that the psalmist so desires to see? Anthropomorphisms for YHWH abound in the psalm. God is described as having eyes (17:2, 8), ears (17:1, 6), lips (17:4), hands (17:7, 14), and a face (17:2, 15). Verse 13 further describes YHWH bearing a sword. This anthropomorphic imagery combines with the reference to the wings of YHWH in 17:8 to create a composite picture of YHWH in the mind of the reader (see below).

Moving from God's physical attributes to God's actions, the psalm clearly depicts YHWH as a judge, the God of righteousness who creates and preserves orderly relationships, in part by punishing those who violate the divine order. Three aspects of divine judgeship appear in the psalm: YHWH serves as lawgiver (17:4), examiner (17:1–6), and executer of justice (17:7–15).[30] The imagery of YHWH as warrior and executor of justice culminates in 17:13b–14, which contain a vicious imprecation against the enemies.[31] YHWH's sword brings deliverance to the psalmist and utter destruction to the enemy, to such an extent that the judgment resounds through the generations.

YHWH as Winged Lion-Slayer

When one takes all this vivid imagery together, the entire psalm presents an arresting juxtaposition of images: YHWH in the form of a winged anthropomorphic deity encountering enemies in the form of lions, which YHWH dispatches with his sword in a brutal and efficient manner (17:13). An image of such an encounter appears frequently in the iconography of the ancient Near East, especially in seventh-century B.C.E. Cypro-Phoenician art. In a silver bowl from Kourion, for example, a winged, anthropomorphic deity battles a lion at the center panel.

Fig. 8. Silver bowl; Salamis; seventh century B.C.E.
After Strawn, *What Is Stronger*, fig. 4.214.

Fig. 9a. Silver bowl; early seventh century B.C.E.; Idalion. After Markoe, *Phoenician Bronze and Silver Bowls*, 242.

Fig. 9b. Detail of fig. 9a.

The same scene also appears numerous times on a seventh-century B.C.E. silver bowl from Idalion. In this piece the image appears not in the center but alternating with images of a young hero slaying a griffin (fig. 9a, b).[32]

The Phoenician artisans who created these bowls were borrowing from a well-established Assyrian artistic tradition of winged figures in combat with lions.[33] Neo-Assyrian art provides numerous examples of this motif, though the winged figure is never pictured with a sword, as in the Cypro-Phoenician bowls.

Fig. 10. Detail of wall relief; ninth century B.C.E.; Nimrud. After Strawn, *What Is Stronger*, fig. 4.215.

A ninth-century B.C.E. wall relief from Nimrud illustrates this artistic tradition (fig. 10), on which a winged genius grasps the rear legs of two lions, which in turn are attacking bovines.

The trope of winged figures grasping a lion or lions has a very long tradition in ancient Near Eastern art and appears over a wide geographic range.[34] However, the only direct iconographic parallel to the Cypro-Phoenician bowls is a ninth-century B.C.E. relief from Tell Halaf (fig. 11).

Fig. 11. Relief; Tell Halaf; ninth century B.C.E. After Keel, *Jahwe-Visionen*, fig. 136.

The remarkable similarity between the Tell Halaf relief and the Cypro-Phoenician bowls—some two centuries later—attests that this particular image was stable and well-known throughout Syria-Palestine in the Iron Age and later. Based on the apparent availability and distribution of this imagery, we may conclude that the psalmist redeployed it in literary form in Ps 17 with Yawheh as the sword-wielding, winged lion-slayer and the enemies as lions.

YHWH as a Falcon

More than one iconographic constellation can inform an understanding of the psalm's characterization of God, however. Indeed, when utilizing the iconographic-biblical approach, one must recognize that multiple iconographic constellations can provide background and comparative material by which to understand the Bible's literary imagery. Space does not permit a full exploration of all the congruent iconographic motifs for Ps 17.[35] Let it suffice here to say that, just as one can argue for the Cypro-Phoenician bowls as a congruent constellation of images, so also could one argue that the image of God's wings in Ps 17 derives from the image of the Horus falcon offering protection to the king.

In both its original Egyptian context and in Syro-Palestinian iconography, the falcon frequently appears with wings outspread over or toward an image of the king.[36] Thus the falcon serves as a symbol of divine protection and authorization of the king and, indeed, divine incarnation in the

Fig. 12. Wall relief of Seti I; Chapel of Seti I at Abydos; Nineteenth Dynasty. After Keel, *Studien zu den Stempelsiegeln*, 131, fig. 54.

Fig. 13. Seal, Tell el-Ajjul, tenth–ninth century B.C.E. After Keel, *Studien zu den Stempelsiegeln*, 125, fig. 7.

person of the king.[37] A relief of Seti I provides an example from Egyptian art in which two such falcons appear: one above and behind the king's head with outstretched wings; and another as a part of his throne with its wings wrapped around the lower torso of the king in a clear gesture of protection (fig. 12).

This iconographic nexus migrated from Egypt into Syro-Palestinian miniature art, where images of a king on a throne surrounded by falcons appear frequently, as in this scarab from Tell el-Ajjul (fig. 13).[38] The central figure can be identified as a king in part because of the classic Egyptian throne upon which he sits. The figure is flanked by four schematized pairs of falcon wings; the bodies of the falcons are not distinguishable.

Fig. 14. Seal; Achzib; ninth–seventh century B.C.E. After Keel, *Studien zu den Stempelsiegeln*, 125, fig. 10.

Numerous other Syro-Palestinian seals depict similar scenes. For example, a ninth- to seventh-century B.C.E. seal from Achzib pictures a seated king with a *uraeus* extending from his mouth (fig. 14). Facing him are two large outspread falcon's wings, the body of the falcon being represented only as a slim stalk-like line connected to the upper wing. Two sun disks appear between the king and the wings, along with a *djed*-pillar, a symbol of stability and order. So, while the falcon's body here has been radically schematized, the wings are certainly to be understood as belonging to the falcon because of the constellation of images in the scene.

It is important to note here that in the many depictions of birds in Syro-Palestinian iconography (i.e., vultures, ostriches, roosters, doves), only falcons are depicted with outstretched wings in gestures of protection and authorization in the Iron Age or later. In light of this Syro-Palestinian iconographical tradition, it becomes clear that the protecting wings of YHWH in Ps 17 should not be understood in a solely naturalistic manner. That is to say, the psalmist is not simply employing the conceptual metaphor YAHWEH IS A BIRD. Rather, when the psalmist speaks of YHWH's wings, he seems to be evoking the particular iconography of the falcon, which protects and authorizes the rule of the divinely appointed and, thus, implicitly righteous king (see 17:1, 15). One should note, too, that many interpreters have suggested that the suppliant in Ps 17 is indeed the king.[39]

YHWH AS A WINGED SUN DISK

But the iconography of winged lion-slayers and falcons does not exhaust the possibilities for interpreting the literary image of YHWH with wings in Ps 17. That imagery also finds congruence in the iconography of winged sun disks, one of the most common motifs in ancient Near Eastern—and, specifically, Syro-Palestinian—art from the Late Bronze Age to the Persian period. Tallay Ornan has recently traced the development of the image of the winged sun disk as it moved from its origin in Egyptian iconography

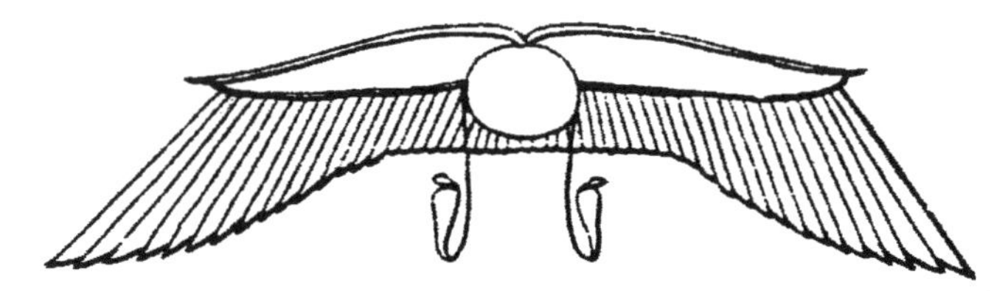

Fig. 15. Winged sun disk from a stela of Ramesses II, Nineteenth Dynasty. After Keel, *Studien zu den Stempelsiegeln*, 133, fig. 73.

throughout the larger ancient Near East.[40] As Mesopotamian and Syrian artists appropriated the image, military and anthropomorphic elements appear in the iconography, features that were absent in its original Egyptian form (fig. 15).

Ornan points to the glazed tile of Tukulti-Ninurta II (890–884 B.C.E.) as an example of the anthropomorphizing and militarizing of the winged disk (fig. 16). A two-winged deity with feathers for lower-parts—or wearing a skirt made from feathers—is incorporated within what appears to be a blazing sun disk. The deity in the disk bears a drawn bow with arrow ready. The slightly dipped forward wing, discernible by reference to the registers of text above, and the face of the deity in profile combine to sug-

Fig. 16. Glazed tile of Tukulti Ninurta II; 888–884 B.C.E. After Keel, *Symbolism of the Biblical World*, fig. 295.

gest that this deity is in motion, on the attack.

The deity pictured in a ninth-century B.C.E. relief from Nimrud provides another example. In this representation, the torso of the figure appears encircled within the disk (fig. 17). This figure is also very clearly on the attack as he draws back his bow and prepares to shoot his arrow.

Fig. 17. Relief; Nimrud; 883–859 B.C.E. After Keel, *Symbolism of the Biblical World*, fig. 296.

Ornan argues that the martial aspect of the figure in these images confirms his identity as Aššur.[41] This argument puts her at odds, however, with Ruth Mayer-Opificus, among others, who argues that Šamaš is represented in the disk.[42] Yet Ornan rightly contends that the winged disk could serve as a symbol for two gods in the same culture, in this case, both Aššur and Šamaš. As a result, the winged disk in Assyrian art bears a "double meaning."[43] The complexity of the symbol is consistent with its history throughout the larger ancient Near East. Since it was originally an Egyptian symbol that was first adopted into Phoenician art and subsequently adopted by Mesopotamian artists, it should come as no surprise that the winged disk could represent two different deities, even at the same time and within the same culture.

The complex symbolism of the winged disk also pertains in the art of Syro-Palestine. An example of a Mesopotamian-style winged disk can be seen in a ninth-century B.C.E. relief from Tell Halaf, in which a winged sun disk is pictured with two bull-men supporting it (fig. 18). The constellation of images suggests that the image represents Šamaš, the Mesopotamian solar-god of order, justice, and law.[44]

Fig. 18. Wall relief; Tell Halaf; ninth century B.C.E. After Ornan, "A Complex System of Religious Symbols," fig. 23.

That the winged disk could serve as an emblem for both

Aššur and Šamaš has implications for the interpretation of the wings of YHWH in Ps 17:8, where YHWH is depicted clearly as a militant deity able and willing to devastate the enemy, like the winged Aššur within the disk, but also as a divine judge who is concerned with creating and maintaining order, like Šamaš.[45] In sum, by describing YHWH in winged form in Ps 17, the psalmist has drawn, at least in part, from the iconography of the winged disk, a rich image that can evoke the ideas of divine military strength and world-ordering justice.

The Multistability of YHWH's Wings in Psalm 17

In light of this analysis of the wings of YHWH in Ps 17, it is wise to reconsider the lessons learned at the dawn of the twentieth century about the relationship between texts and images. Smith, Delitzsch, and Fradenburgh looked at the iconographic "constellation" in the "Adam and Eve" seal in the British Museum and identified what they presumed to be congruent literary images in Gen 3. However, faulty assumptions doomed their analysis, among them that ancient art refers straightforwardly to literature. Modern interpreters must always reckon with the fact that the relationship between the literary images and iconographical ones is remarkably complex; clearly, there are no simple "illustrations" like the "Adam and Eve" seal once seemed to be.

The most important lesson that one can learn from these early iconographic analyses is that the full art-historical context of the images must be taken into account if one wants to say anything worthwhile about the relationship between texts and images. Thus, for those pursuing the iconographic-biblical approach as I have suggested above, the focus must be on thoroughly interdisciplinary work. One must employ consistently nonfragmentary and sophisticated readings of iconographic materials within their art-historical contexts, as Keel, Klingbeil, and Strawn have done, while at the same time utilizing the range of historical-critical and literary-critical approaches within rather large literary pericopes.

As scholars begin to compare larger constellations of iconographic and literary materials, as I am suggesting here, the dangers of facile (and faulty) comparisons may continue. However, through careful attention to context, one can identify striking areas of congruency where pictorial and literary imagery interact. Exploring a text's iconic structure helps one realize the complexity and reality of the numerous interactions between art and text, and, thus, one can begin to understand and honor the richness of the symbolic texture of the Hebrew Bible.

Finally, one important implication of this type of iconographic-biblical approach deserves mention. The case study on Ps 17 reveals that certain biblical images can evoke a number of iconographic motifs at the same time. One may understand these multiple meanings of the image of YHWH's wings by analogy to the phenomenon of "multistability" in certain types of visual imagery. Multistability occurs where an image conveys two different but equally valid interpretations simultaneously.[46] Two classic examples of this phenomenon are the rabbit-duck (fig. 19), and the faces-goblet (fig. 20). In each of these images, two equally valid interpretations toggle back and forth in the observer's perception.

Fig. 19. Rabbit or Duck? Cf. Mitchell, *Picture Theory*, 46, fig. 3.

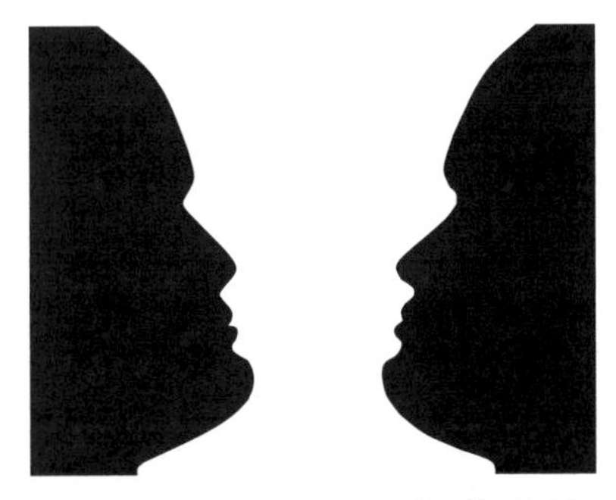

Fig. 20. Two Faces or a Goblet? Cf. Raymond J. Corsini, *The Dictionary of Psychology* (Philadelphia: Brunner/Mazel, 1999), 854.

Analogically, one may thus see the winged YHWH in Ps 17 as a *literary* image exhibiting multistability. Still, the multistable image of the winged YHWH is not "unstable." There is a limit to the possible interpretations of that image based on congruent iconographical constellations. By taking iconographic context, periodization, and geography into account, one can exclude certain interpretations of biblical images; so also with the multistable visual images above. The duck interpretation and the rabbit interpretation are the only viable "readings" of figure 19. A forklift, for example, is not a reasonable interpretation of the image. Further, while one could argue for interpreting figure 20 as two faces or a goblet, or even an inverted candlestick, one cannot interpret it as, say, a rocking chair.

Similarly, the analysis of iconographic congruencies for Ps 17 excludes certain interpretations. An analysis of psalm's iconic structure denies, for example, the possibility that the wings of YHWH in the Psalter refer to the wings of the cherubim of the temple, as many have claimed. In the context of Ps 17, the wings of YHWH belong to YHWH alone, not to any other creature. Furthermore, nowhere in the biblical text nor in Syro-Palestinian iconography do the cherubim appear as substitutes for YHWH or any other chief deity.[47] Moreover, while numerous depictions of winged cherubim appear in Syro-Palestinian art, an examination of the iconographic context of these images reveals no clear examples of such creatures providing protection to humans. The cherubim rather carry and support the deity or king (see fig. 7).

So while the image of YHWH with wings in Ps 17 should not be associated with the cherubim, the portrayal of YHWH in this literary context does indeed seem to be related to three unique iconographic constellations in Syro-Palestinian art: images of winged lion-slayers; the Horus falcon; and winged sun disks. It may well be that this multistability of the image of the winged YHWH in Ps 17 is what makes it so compelling. It can convey divine protection in distinct and striking ways. Describing the allure of visual images that exhibit multistability, W. J. T. Mitchell writes: "the ambiguity of their referentiality produces a kind of secondary effect of auto-reference to the drawing as drawing, an invitation to the spectator to return with fascination to the mysterious object whose identity seems so mutable and yet so absolutely singular and definite."[48]

Mitchell's comments may well describe the phenomenon at work in the literary image as it appears in Ps 17. For the ancient psalmist, evoking YHWH's winged form with its "ambiguity of referentiality" may have produced a "secondary effect of auto-reference" to the image of the deity, for the entire context of Ps 17 attests to the psalmist's preoccupation with beholding YHWH's "image" (*tĕmûnâ*, v. 15). Thus, the employment of the multistable image of YHWH's wings reveals the psalmist's fascination with this mysterious divine image, which at once seems so changeable and yet so absolute.

For Further Reading

Brown, William P. *Seeing the Psalms: A Theology of Metaphor*. Louisville: Westminster John Knox, 2002.

Hulster, Izaak J. de. *Iconographic Exegesis and Third Isaiah*. FAT 2/36 Tübingen: Mohr Siebeck, 2009.

Keel, Othmar. *Song of Songs*. Translated by Frederick J. Gaiser. CC. Minneapolis: Fortress, 1994.

———. *The Symbolism of the Biblical World: Ancient Near Eastern Iconography and the Book of Psalms*. Translated by Timothy J. Hallett. Winona Lake, Ind.: Eisenbrauns, 1997.

Keel, Othmar, and Christoph Uehlinger. *Gods, Goddesses, and Images of God in Ancient Israel*. Minneapolis: Fortress, 1998.

Pritchard, James B. *The Ancient Near East in Pictures Relating to the Old Testament*. 2nd ed. Princeton: Princeton University Press, 1969.

Strawn, Brent A. *What Is Stronger Than a Lion? Leonine Image and Metaphor in the Hebrew Bible and the Ancient Near East*. OBO 212. Fribourg: Universitätsverlag; Göttingen: Vandenhoeck & Ruprecht, 2005.

Uehlinger, Christoph, ed., *Images as Media: Sources for the Cultural History of the Ancient Near East: 1st Millennium BCE*. Fribourg: Universitätsverlag; Göttingen: Vandenhoeck & Ruprecht, 2000.

Notes

1. See, e.g., Othmar Keel and Christoph Uehlinger, Gods, *Goddesses and Images of God in Ancient Israel* (trans. Thomas H. Trapp; Minneapolis: Fortress, 1998), xi.

2. George Smith, *The Chaldean Account of Genesis* (London: Sampson Low, Marston, Searle & Rivington, 1876), 90–91, emphasis added. See also T. C. Mitchell, *The Bible in the British Museum: Interpreting the Evidence* (Mahwah, N.J.: Paulist, 2004), 24. Mitchell refers to this object as the "Temptation Seal."

3. Friedrich Delitzsch, *Babel and Bible: Two Lectures on the Significance of Assyriological Research for Religion, Embodying the Most Important Criticisms and the Author's Replies* (trans. Thomas J. McCormack and W. H. Carruth; Chicago: Open Court, 1903), 48, emphasis added.

4. J. N. Fradenburgh, *Witnesses from the Dust, or The Bible: Illustrated from the Monuments* (Cincinnati: Cranston & Stowe, 1886), 50–51, emphasis added.

5. Dominique Collon, *First Impressions: Cylinder Seals in the Ancient Near East* (Chicago: University of Chicago Press, 1987), 36.

6. Jeremy Black and Anthony Green, *Gods, Demons, and Symbols of Ancient Mesopotamia: An Illustrated Dictionary* (London: British Museum Press, 1992), 166–67.

7. See, e.g., Yigael Yadin, *The Art of Warfare in Biblical Lands in Light of Archaeological Study* (trans. M. Pearlman; 2 vols.; New York: McGraw-Hill, 1963); James Pritchard, *The Ancient Near East in Pictures: Relating to the Old Testament* (2nd ed.; Princeton: Princeton University Press, 1969); Hugo Greßmann, *Altorientalische Texte und Bilder zum Alten Testament* (2nd ed.; 2 vols.; Berlin: de Gruyter, 1926–1927).

8. Othmar Keel, "Iconography and the Bible," *ABD* 3:357–74, here 360–61.

9. Othmar Keel, *The Symbolism of the Biblical World: Ancient Near Eastern Ico-*

nography and the Book of Psalms (German orig., 1972; trans. Timothy J. Hallett; New York: Crossroads, 1985).

10. See Othmar Keel, *Das Recht der Bilder gesehen zu werden: Drei Fallstudien zur Methode der Interpretation altorientalischer Bilder* (OBO 112; Fribourg: Universitätsverlag; Göttingen: Vandenhoeck & Ruprecht, 1992).

11. Keel claims this motif appears textually in Job 38 (*Jahwes Entgegnung an Ijob: Eine Deutung von Ijob 38–41 vor dem Hintergrund der zeitgenössischen Bildkunst* [FRLANT 121; Göttingen: Vandenhoeck & Ruprecht, 1978]).

12. Othmar Keel and Christoph Uehlinger, *Gods, Goddesses, and Images of God in Ancient Israel* (Minneapolis: Fortress, 1998), 182.

13. Ibid., 215.

14. Ibid., 294 n. 6.

15. Christoph Uehlinger, "Clio in a World of Pictures—Another Look at the Lachish Reliefs from Sennacherib's Southwest Palace at Nineveh," in *Like a Bird in a Cage: The Invasion of Sennacherib in 701 BCE* (ed. Lester L. Grabbe; JSOTSup 363; London: Sheffield Academic Press, 2003), 221–305.

16. Ibid., 275.

17. Ibid., 244.

18. Keel and Uehlinger, *Gods, Goddesses, and Images*, 7–9.

19. To date, two of these volumes have been published: Silvia Schroer and Othmar Keel, *Vom ausgehenden Mesolithikum bis zur Frühbronzezeit* (vol. 1 of *Die Ikonographie Palästinas/Israels und der Alte Orient: Eine Religionsgeschichte in Bildern*; Fribourg: Academic Press, 2004); Silvia Schroer, *Die Mittelbronzezeit* (vol. 2 of *Die Ikonographie Palästinas/Israel und der Alte Orient: Eine Religionsgeschichte in Bildern*; Fribourg: Academic Press, 2008).

20. Othmar Keel, *The Song of Songs* (trans. Frederick J. Gaiser; CC; Minneapolis: Fortress, 1994), 27.

21. Martin Klingbeil, *Yahweh Fighting from Heaven: God as Warrior and as God of Heaven in the Hebrew Psalter and Ancient Near Eastern Iconography* (OBO 169; Fribourg: Universitätsverlag; Göttingen: Vandenhoeck & Ruprecht 1999), 28–34.

22. Brent A. Strawn, *What Is Stronger Than a Lion? Leonine Image and Metaphor in the Hebrew Bible and the Ancient Near East* (OBO 212; Fribourg: Academic Press; Göttingen: Vandenhoeck & Ruprecht, 2005), 10.

23. Ibid., 13.

24. Keel, *The Song of Songs*, v–vi.

25. Silvia Schroer, "Im Schatten deiner Flügel: Religionsgeschichtliche und feministische Blicke auf die Metaphorick der Flügel Gottes in den Psalmen, in Ex 19:4; Dtn 32:11 und in Mal 3:20," in *"Ihr Völker alle, klatscht in die Hände!": Festschrift für Erhard S. Gerstenberger zum 65. Gerburtstag* (ed. Rainer Kessler et al.; Exegese in unserer Zeit: Kontextuelle Bibelinterpretationen aus lateinamerikanischer und feminisistischer Sicht 3; Münster: LIT, 1997), 296–316; Louis Alexis Frederic le Mat, *Textual Criticism and Exegesis of Psalm XXXVI: A Contribution to the Study of the Hebrew Book of Psalms* (Studia Theologica Rheno-Traiectina: Disputationes Instituti Theologici in Universitate Rheno-Traiectina conditi 3; Utrecht: Kemink, 1957), 23.

26. Artur Weiser, *The Psalms: A Commentary* (trans. Herbert Hartwell; OTL;

Philadelphia: Westminster, 1962), 181; Hans-Joachim Kraus, *Psalms 1–59* (trans. Hilton Oswalt; CC; Minneapolis: Fortress, 1993), 249; Marvin E. Tate, *Psalms 51–100* (WBC 20; Dallas: Word, 1990), 78. So also, earlier, Charles Augustus Briggs and Emilie Grace Briggs, *A Critical and Exegetical Commentary on the Book of Psalms* (2 vols.; ed., ICC; Edinburgh: T&T Clark, 1906, repr., 1960), 1:130.

27. Following the conventions of cognitive linguistics, conceptual metaphors are often characterized through the formula: CONCEPTUAL DOMAIN (A) IS CONCEPTUAL DOMAIN (B) (so Zoltán Kövecses, *Metaphor: A Practical Introduction* [Oxford: Oxford University Press, 2002], 4). For numerous worked examples of this formula, see George Lakoff and Mark Johnson, *Metaphors We Live By* (Chicago: University of Chicago Press, 1980), 3–6. Several scholars have proposed that some sort of bird metaphor is at work in the image of the winged YHWH in the Psalms. See Hermann Gunkel, *Die Psalmen* (HKAT; Göttingen: Vandenhoeck & Ruprecht, 1926), 57–59; Marjo C. A. Korpel, *A Rift in the Clouds: Ugaritic and Hebrew Descriptions of the Divine* (UBL 8; Münster: Ugarit-Verlag, 1990), 550; Peter C. Craigie, *Psalms 1–50* (WBC 19; Waco, Tex.: Word, 1983), 292; Franz Delitzsch, *Commentary on the Book of Psalms* (trans. David Eaton and James E. Duguid; New York: Funk & Wagnalls, 1883), 298; Richard J. Clifford, *Psalms 73–150* (AOTC; Nashville: Abingdon, 2003), 103.

28. William P. Brown, *Seeing the Psalms: A Theology of Metaphor* (Louisville: Westminster John Knox, 2002), 14.

29. On the use of leonine imagery for enemies in the psalms, see Strawn, *What Is Stronger*, 248–50.

30. See Brown, *Seeing the Psalms*, 31–53.

31. Note, however, that 17:14 contains a host of text-critical problems. The options for translation range widely—from regarding the verse as a ruthless imprecation to understanding it as a statement of generosity toward the enemies.

32. For the dating of this piece, see Glenn Markoe, *Phoenician Bronze and Silver Bowls from Cyprus and the Mediterranean* (Berkeley and Los Angeles: University of California Press, 1985), 6–12, 154.

33. Ibid., 48. For a discussion of the ancient Near Eastern iconographical trope of "The God(s) Fighting/Encountering the Lion," see Strawn, *What Is Stronger*, 187–90.

34. See, e.g., a fifteenth-century B.C.E. seal impression from Nuzi (Othmar Keel, *Jahwe-Visionen und Siegelkunst: Eine neue Deutung der Majestätsschilderungen in Jes 6, Ez 1 und 10 und Sach 4* [SBS 84/85; Stuttgart: Katholisches Bibelwerk, 1977], fig. 11) and the boss of a shield from Luristan dated from the beginning of the first millennium (Strawn, *What Is Stronger*, fig. 4.209.)

35. See Joel M. LeMon, *Yahweh's Winged Form in the Psalms: Exploring Congruent Iconography and Texts* (OBO; Fribourg: Academic Press, forthcoming).

36. See Othmar Keel, "Der Pharao als Sonnengott: Eine Gruppe ägypto-palästinischer Siegelamulette des 10./9. Jarhunderts," in idem, *Studien zu den Stempelsiegeln aus Palästina/Israel*, Band 4 (OBO 130; Göttingen; Vandenhoeck & Ruprecht; Fribourg: Univertätsverlag, 1994), 94–95.

37. Ibid., 95.

38. Ibid.

39. John Eaton, for example, claims that this psalm has "clearly royal content," i.e., that the king is the "I" of the psalm. He bases this conclusion on the military imagery used for the enemies and the intimate tone with which the psalmist addresses God (*Kingship and the Psalms* [SBT 32; Naperville, Ill.: Allenson, 1976], 33–34. See more recently idem, *The Psalms: A Historical and Spiritual Commentary* (London: T&T Clark, 2003), 99.

40. Tallay Ornan, "A Complex System of Religious Symbols: The Case of the Winged Disc in Near Eastern Imagery of the First Millennium BCE," in *Crafts and Images in Contact: Studies on Eastern Mediterranean Art of the First Millennium BCE* (ed. Claudia E. Suter and Christoph Uehlinger; OBO 210; Fribourg: Academic Press; Göttingen: Vandenhoeck & Ruprecht, 2005), 207–41. Throughout, Ornan does not refer to the image as "the winged sun disc," arguing instead that the iconography does not necessarily represent a solar deity, particularly in Mesopotamian incarnations, where it "could signify major gods functioning as heads of pantheons" such as Aššur and Marduk (206).

41. Ibid., 212.

42. Ruth Mayer-Opificius, "Die geflügelte Sonne: Himmels- und Regendarstellungen im alter Vorderasien," *UF* 16 (1984): 189–236.

43. Ornan, "A Complex System," 231. William G. Lambert makes a similar argument, that the winged disk can allude to one or the other deity depending on the iconographic context. When the winged disk appears as a sole emblem of the king, it represents Aššur; in combination with other symbols, the winged disk represents the sun-god Šamaš. See William G. Lambert, "Trees, Snakes and Gods in Ancient Syria and Anatolia," *BSOAS* 48 (1985): 439 n. 27.

44. Ornan, "A Complex System," 231.

45. For textual expression of Šamaš's role as judge and god of righteousness, see "The Shamash Hymn," trans. Benjamin Foster (*COS* 1.117:418–19).

46. W. J. T. Mitchell, *Picture Theory: Essays on Verbal and Visual Representation* (Chicago: University of Chicago Press, 1994), 43.

47. Peter Riede, *Im Netz des Jägers: Studien zur Feindmetaphorik der Individualpsalmen* (WMANT 85; Neukirchen-Vluyn: Neukirchener, 2000), 330.

48. Mitchell, *Picture Theory*, 43.

I would like to thank my colleagues Christopher Hays, Matthew Schlimm, and Brent Strawn for their helpful comments on earlier drafts of this essay. I must also thank David Petersen, my dissertation advisor, for this essay grew out of that larger work.

Religio-historical Approaches: Monotheism, Method, and Mortality*

Christopher B. Hays

The religio-historical study of the Hebrew Bible is inherently interdisciplinary. The reconstruction of ancient Israelite religion depends on data and theories drawn from a number of other methodologies; a partial list would include historiography, sociology, archaeology, comparative religion, and biblical composition theory. A scholar must bring all these subfields together to produce a coherent understanding of Israelite religion.

Many of the critical topics in Israelite religion and its most pressing methodological issues intersect with the conversation about monotheism. Therefore, the first section of this essay will survey, through a methodological lens, shifting currents in the study of monotheism.[1] The second section will be a case study of a specific religio-historical problem, reexamining God's relationship to death and the underworld in Israelite religion, and also the power of God to raise the dead.

More comprehensive surveys of the history of the study of Israelite religion and its critical issues are available elsewhere.[2] What is in view in this first section is an overview of recent scholarship and methodological directions.

Religio-historical Approaches: An Overview of Trends and Methods

Terminology

Generalizing terminology is often inadequate to the task of categoriz-

* It is an honor to dedicate this essay to David L. Petersen, whose broad command of critical issues and preference for the concise and precise served as a model.

ing diverse religious systems. However, a recent synthesis of definitions by Nili Fox seems to make useful distinctions. She defines *monotheism* in part as "a definite denial of the existence of other gods."[3] While agreeing with a scholarly consensus that explicitly monotheistic claims do not emerge clearly until the time of Second Isaiah (e.g., 45:5, "besides me there is no god"), I will suggest that one of the more interesting problems in Israelite religion is the cultural shift from *henotheism* to *monolatry*. Those are two terms that Petersen found "difficult to distinguish,"[4] but Fox has correctly assessed their usage recently: neither term denies the existence of other gods, as is the case with monotheism, but under monolatry, "[t]he exclusive worship of a god within a certain social group is enforced by prohibitions of allegiance to other gods.... Henotheism is sometimes distinguished from monolatry in that allegiance to a specific deity is temporary rather than long-lasting."[5] Thus Israel in book of Judges could be said to be portrayed as henotheistic, whereas Josiah's promulgation of the Deuteronomic code with its assertion that "YHWH is our God" would serve to enforce monolatry. New research has shed light on the likely social and historical processes by which this religious shift took place. Such a project clearly follows in the footsteps of Bernhard Lang, who wrote that "Yahweh-alone worship can be understood as a crisis-cult which is continued beyond the actual crisis situation."[6] In contrast to Lang's emphasis on the exile as the watershed crisis, however, I think one could look somewhat earlier in the history of Israel and Judah, in the period of the Neo-Assyrian conquest of Syria-Palestine.

Religio-historical Approaches, History, and Society

The study of Israelite religion has evolved into its present form for reasons similar to those that are behind the critical study of the history of Israel. Just as the Bible's accounts of Israel's history have been shaped and layered over time to produce a stylized final portrait that obscures many details, so also one may assume that Israelite religion differed from what a casual observer might derive from a prima facie reading of the Hebrew Bible.

The most detailed recent histories of Israelite religion emphasize diachronic change and thus favor a middle way between extremes of credulity and skepticism (or, to use terms familiar from the historical conversation, maximalism and minimalism). Either extreme tends to produce essentially synchronic understandings of Israelite religion. On the one hand, some would make the whole of Israelite religion a gift of God at Sinai,[7] which might be preserved more or less intact and did not change in any essential way. On the other hand, for others the Hebrew Bible and the religion it portrays are nearly whole-cloth inventions of postexilic Judah, before which time "we know nothing about the prehistory of the people of God and its faith."[8] The covenant between Israel and YHWH, which G. E. Wright perceived as a touchstone of Israelite religion from the Late Bronze Age onward, is for J. Alberto Soggin no earlier than Josiah.[9] Between these two extremes lie most of the six centuries of the Iron Age, and many of the conversations about Israelite religion focus on that contested period.

Neither the maximalist nor the minimalist extreme fits best with the available data—the maximalists because there exists so little data about *any* aspect of Israel prior to Iron Age II (1000 B.C.E.), and the minimalists because they tend to dismiss available data about Israel during Iron Age II. A scholarly majority has long perceived a large amount of textual production in Israel and Judah during Iron Age II; if that is an important period for the production of Israel's religious documents, then it is also an important period for Israel's religion. Further, just as Israel's traditions and texts changed and were interwoven and hybridized over time, so also was its religion.

In addition to diachronic change, a second major aspect of the diversity of Israelite religion is along social lines. There can be little doubt that, at any point in the history of Israel and Judah, different segments of the society practiced religion differently. These varieties are variously labeled, but they include "family religion" (sometimes overlapping with "women's religion"), the religion of local and regional cults, and royal (sometimes called "elite") religion. Recent monographs on Israelite religion by Rainer Albertz and Patrick D. Miller lay out those types of religiosity within historical frameworks.[10] These frameworks are useful as long as the reader remembers that they are heuristic and that the varieties overlapped even more extensively than a cursory reading of the Bible might suggest. Furthermore, the distinctions between these categories were under constant negotiation. Popular religion—or "para-religion," to use Karel van der Toorn's preferred term—existed alongside official religion.[11] Yet in the final form of the Bible, the reader gets only glimpses of para-religion (e.g., sorcery, necromancy, Tammuz festivals, and the worship of the Queen of Heaven) and its female practitioners.

Finally, one should not forget in the rush of new information and methods that the theology of the central Jerusalem cult was certainly not monolithic (open conflicts between elite Yahwists such as Jeremiah and Hananiah are only the most obvious examples). The rhetorical force of many biblical texts calls attention to the need to convince. Only in comprehending the sum of these many diversities does one appreciate "the polyvalent nature of ancient Israel."[12] As the titles of recent monographs attest—Ziony Zevit's *The Religions of Ancient Israel* and Richard S. Hess's *Israelite Religions*[13]—one can no longer speak of a single religion while claiming to treat the data comprehensively.

Religio-historical Approaches and Theories of Composition

Although the general portrait of Israelite religion in the Bible has met with forceful skepticism on the part of archaeologists (see below), the Bible remains the primary and the fullest source of data in the conversation. It is rare for a scholar to put forward a theory about Israelite religion that has no grounding in the biblical text. However, employing it in historical reconstruction presupposes prior conclusions about the periods and backgrounds of its composition.

Nearly all of the Hebrew Bible can be considered a religious document (and thus significant to religio-historical study), but four sections have received particular focus: (1) the family stories of Genesis, which have often been thought to preserve memories of Israel's premonarchic religious practices; (2) the cultic legal materials in the rest of the Torah, including the covenantal frames; (3) the accounts of religious transgressions and reforms in the Deuteronomistic History; and (4) the Psalms, which have been mined for information about Israelite worship, prayer, and for hints of early beliefs that may been preserved by being frozen in poetic tradition.

The most meaningful change in recent years has been in the second category. The significance of the Priestly literature to Israelite religion has always been recognized as paramount. However, the traditional scholarly assignation of the Priestly law to the Persian period had made that period less interesting, in that scholars from Julius Wellhausen onward were comfortable assuming that the religion of the Priestly source was apparent from the surface of the text, as the product of the last major hand to edit the Pentateuch. In the wake of that assumption, many scholars have felt that the challenge was to excavate the religious strata *prior* to P. Priestly theology itself posed less of a challenge, from a religio-historical perspective. Source critics differentiated Priestly and Deuteronomistic redactions of the Pentateuch (and beyond), which could be untangled and removed, leaving the (admittedly tattered) remnants of pre-Deuteronomistic Israelite religion. As van der Toorn writes, "What is beginning to emerge from the new scholarship on Israelite religion is the hitherto unwritten history of the beliefs and religious practices of ordinary men and women before the Deuteronomistic revision. It is the story of the other side of Israelite religion."[14]

In recent years, however, the old consensus about the date of the Priestly legal material has come under scrutiny. It has become increasingly clear that Wellhausen's formulation of the Documentary Hypothesis depended on a particular idea of religious devolution that could no longer be defended, especially in light of comparative ancient Near Eastern data showing that legal codification was not by nature a late development within a religion.[15] At the same time, Avi Hurvitz's linguistic arguments for the relative antiquity of P might be said to have opened the way for a broader reconsideration.[16] Therefore, a new model of the formation of the Priestly material has been advanced by Israel Knohl and Jacob Milgrom, in which the Priestly Torah dates no later than the mid-eighth century and was redacted by the Holiness School (HS, who authored Lev 17–26) at the end of the eighth century.[17] This would mean that aspects of Israelite religion once thought to be late were in fact codified earlier on; as long as one bears in mind that codification is not equal to promulgation—let alone popular adoption—many of the critical objections to this theory can be quelled.

Wellhausen famously argued that what Deuteronomy commands, the Priestly Code presupposes;[18] for example, P does not speak of the centralization of the cult because it was already achieved. Wellhausen was aware of the alternative view that P is simply "indifferent" on the issue,[19] and Knohl revives precisely that view: "PT [Priestly Torah] concentrates on its own inner world and has little interest in what takes place outside the Temple and the cult."[20] In fact, Wellhausen does not seem to have grappled with the fact that it was absolutely the norm throughout the ancient world to have sanctuaries to prominent gods in multiple cities. The Kuntillet ʿAjrud inscriptions refer to a "YHWH of Samaria" and a "YHWH of Teman," strongly suggesting that there were also local cults of YHWH at those places around the turn of the eighth century B.C.E. To expect a polemic against that reality in the Priestly law is to cast the priests as reformers, a shoe that does not fit. Centralization might have been a welcome event to the Jerusalem priesthood, but one that probably was not even envisaged earlier. In fact, Hezekiah probably supported centralization for *practical* reasons; since Sennacherib's invasion of Judah in 701 overwhelmed many Judean cities, many outlying Judean cult centers would have ceased functioning anyway (2 Kgs 18:4 does not give the date of the removal of the high places). The concurrent rise in the population of Jerusalem surely would have enriched the Jerusalem temple in the long run and empowered its priests by making theirs the unrivaled house of YHWH. There is no indication, however, that they advocated for this policy in advance.

Although this new model is being interrogated in scholarly circles and appearing in more popular literature,[21] the issue should not be taken as settled. In particular, it remains to be analyzed how an earlier date for P and HS would affect the long-standing perception that it was Priestly tradents who had the final hand in editing the Pentateuch's narrative traditions.[22] From a comparative perspective, however, the assertion that cultic law should have existed under the preexilic monarchs is eminently sensible.

Turning from pentateuchal law to the historical books, a spate of monographs on various non-Yahwistic (or at least "heterodox")[23] religious practices in the Hebrew Bible has gone a long way toward demonstrating that religious and theological diversity did not disappear in the literary tradition of the Hebrew Bible, as is too commonly stated.[24] Despite the commands in certain biblical texts to keep the nation pure and free of foreign religious influence (e.g., Deut 4:1–40), there is almost nothing in the Scriptures to make one think that a uniform orthodoxy in Israelite religion was ever achieved in practice. The people are depicted as swearing exclusive allegiance to YHWH in Josh 24 and its echo in Ezra 10:9–12, but regardless of the historical veracity of those accounts, there is no question that the people failed to maintain any such faithfulness—on this the most pious theologian and the staunchest minimalist must agree. If the Hebrew Bible is a history of anything, it is a history of apostasy from YHWH, from the wilderness to the tribal league to the monarchy. Without laying historical weight on particular stories, it seems clear that the authors of the Bible were not impressed with the nation's singular devotion to YHWH. It is possible, of course, that this portrait is the result of a disappointed Yahwist rewriting history to explain the Babylonian exile, but since biblical and archaeological evidence seem to agree that Israelite religion was a rather diverse *mélange*, it seems unnecessary to seek another answer.

Religio-historical Approaches and Archaeology

The growing number of early Hebrew inscriptions (e.g., the Tel Zayit abecedary and the Khirbet Qeiyafa ostracon) have encouraged scholars to perceive the existence of an Israelite scribal culture at an ever earlier date.[25] Earlier dates for the composition of biblical texts are thus slightly more likely. Apart from such inscriptions, however, archaeology has not offered any new discoveries in the past decade or two to revolutionize the discussion of Israelite religion. The challenging data that are still most often discussed include the Taanach cult stands, in which some perceive a portrait of Asherah; the Kuntillet ʿAjrud and Khirbet el-Qôm inscriptions that proffer blessing from "Yahweh and his A/asherah"; the multiple Arad *maṣṣebôt* that might indicate Asherah-worship alongside YHWH; female clay figurines found widely and consistently in Iron Age burials; the "Bull Site" near Ibleam, named for the bronze statue of a Zebu bull found there; and, of course, the *bamôt*—the stone shrines at "high places" that Albright long ago linked to an ancestor cult.[26] There is a perceived tension between these archaeological finds and the portrait of YHWH as a jealous god in the Bible, a characteristic that recurs in confessional formulae that are taken to be ancient, such as Exod 20:5.[27] If YHWH is a god who jealously demanded devotion, goes the logic, why were the Israelites not more devoted?

Then again, before concluding that ancient Israel and Judah were seething with polytheism, one must acknowledge the chastening effect of Jeffrey H. Tigay's study of Hebrew inscriptions, and particularly the Israelite and Judean onomastica.[28] Out of more than twelve hundred names attested from the preexilic period, Tigay found that only between 5 and 11 percent were plausibly "pagan," the vast majority being Yahwistic. Nor were there statistically significant changes over time, although one might have expected more uniformity in periods of reform, such as the reign of Josiah. It is likely that to some extent this phenomenon reflects a preference for naming children after the national deity; it does not necessarily indicate that 90–95 percent of the population scrupulously avoided non-Yahwistic practices.

Rather than an influx of new data, recent decades have seen new methodological trends. William G. Dever has gradually become the dominant archaeological voice in the conversation about Israelite religion, and he has repeatedly argued that the aforementioned finds and others should be taken as the field's primary source of data. He presents his project as an attempt to get at "popular religion" as common people actually practiced it. In his view, archaeology liberates the study of Israelite religion from reliance on the Hebrew Bible and its portrait of Yahwism. Dever champions the category of "cult," a term that seeks to locate the conversation within comparative religious studies, as against the theological and philological interests that many scholars bring to Israelite religion.

For the purposes of religio-historical study, there is much to be said for treating "uncurated" archaeological artifacts as a counterpoint to the "curated" biblical text. Indeed, such artifacts would surely be taken more account of if their significance were more clear. To expand on just one of the aforementioned examples, the female pillar figurines that have been discovered so widely at Judean sites have no apparent place in the Yahwistic cult as it is reflected in the Bible. Since they are female, they are unlikely to represent deified ancestors. Instead, they are regularly identified with various goddesses, especially Asherah.[29] If that is correct, then it is significant that even though Josiah is said to have banned Asherah worship (2 Kgs 23:4–7), there is no reduction in the appearance of the figurines during or after his time. But no one to date has been able to prove their identity; we have only assertions.

Because of the difficulty of assessing the religious meaning of archaeological data, the "Fribourg school" led by Othmar Keel, Christoph Uehlinger, and Silvia Schroer has special significance, since it has begun to make the study of ancient Near Eastern iconography systematic enough to offer more persuasive interpretations of uninscribed artifacts.[30] Crucial to this process has been the comparably large quantity of stamp seals available, which have allowed scholars to trace the spread and change of iconographic motifs, even in the absence of a consistent tradition of monumental art in Iron Age Palestine. If not quite in a nascent phase, the iconographic method is at least still gathering steam,[31] and the extent to which it will revolutionize Israelite religion remains to be seen. Already, however, it has been of great help in identifying foreign cultural influences on ancient Israel and Judah throughout their histories, which may empower historians of religion to posit influence as well.

As I have already hinted, Dever raises important concerns akin to those of the "social history" movement, championing the stories of those who are not well represented in monuments and contemporary historical texts. He is correct that a religio-historical approach to Israelite religion might be expected to discuss the religion of *all* Israelites, not only those who helped to produce the Bible. Furthermore, maintaining clarity about whose beliefs are and are not reflected in the Bible goes a long way toward resolving the perceived dissonance between the Bible and archaeology in religio-historical matters. We assume that the biblical text records the religious currents primarily of the royal court at Jerusalem, since that would have been the largest center of scribal activity, and that at Jerusalem the reforms for centralizing and homogenizing the religion had their greatest impact. Unfortunately, with the remains of the central shrine (Solomon's temple) inaccessible to archaeological research beneath the Dome of the Rock, there is no way at present to see whether the material remains would indeed indicate a distinct religious subculture.

There are reasons to think that textual and archaeological approaches may find a new equilibrium. Elizabeth Bloch-Smith's *Judahite Burial Practices and Beliefs about the Dead* is often mentioned as a model for the integration of archaeology and textual scholarship. Although the book actually explores the archaeological data more richly, Bloch-Smith's interest in making sense of the text in light of archaeology helps her to raise important questions. Another example is Ziony Zevit's *The Religions of Ancient Israel*, which aims for "a synthesis of parallactic approaches"; in practice, this means consistent attention to both text and archaeology. He also patiently explores the philosophical and methodological ramifications of his work and has called for the fields of Israelite religion and history to move beyond stubborn allegiance to a single method and set of data. He recently expressed frustration with the "methodological numbskullery" of doctrinaire approaches to history in which one assumes that either text or archaeology must contain the whole truth.[32] Instead, he says, "If the archaeological data do not jibe well with what analyzed texts contain, then we must understand that there is meaning in the nonconfirmatory dialectics of the archaeological and the textual."[33] This formulation is potentially helpful, in that it calls not simply for compromise but for creative reasoning about the differences between archaeological data and biblical texts.

One might take Asherah as an example. Although all the data are surely not in, we might make sense of the nonconfirmatory nature of the data by thinking beyond binary logic ("Asherah is deity/not a deity") to attempt to enter into that logic of ancient Israel. Analogies may be supplied by other theological systems. For example, instead of Asherah being a "hypostasis" of YHWH (a term too heavily freighted with Christian/

Trinitarian theological overtones), one might describe YHWH's relationship to Asherah with an etic category derived from African religions: "diffused monotheism," in which one god is supreme and all-powerful but "delegates certain portions of his authority to particular divine functionaries who work as they are commissioned by him."[34]

Religio-historical Approaches and the Comparative Method

The study of Israelite religion has moved beyond one-sided claims about its relationship to its ancient Near Eastern religious context, such as Morton Smith's argument for a "common theology" and G. E. Wright's portrait of the Old Testament as being consistently opposed to its environment. It is clear that the biblical authors worked in various ways with the materials supplied by their cultural context—sometimes polemicizing, sometimes adopting, but most often spinning or transposing them in new and creative ways. Therefore, more nuanced formulations now rule the day.

In his magisterial works *The Origins of Biblical Monotheism* and *The Early History of God*, Mark S. Smith conceptualized as *convergence and differentiation* the processes by which Israelites claimed for YHWH the attributes of other gods, then ultimately rejected the other gods.[35] In so doing, he has adapted and systematized the work of a whole generation of scholars, most notably Frank Moore Cross.[36] The work of Cross and his earlier students (including Miller) on the continuities between "Canaanite" and Israelite religion have become foundational.

Smith's emphasis on monotheizing as a rhetorical phenomenon is particularly important;[37] in a world in which monotheism was unusual, most early biblical passages that express monotheistic ideas must be understood as hortatory. So also YHWH's adoption of the roles, characteristics, and even epithets of other gods are best understood as a form of rhetorical competition among competing cults.

There are, however, certain attributes common to other ancient Near Eastern divinities that are conspicuous by their absence in the biblical portrait of YHWH. Smith indentifies sex and death as two realms in which YHWH does not take part. In addition, he observes that there is much evidence for assimilation of other gods traditional to the Syro-Palestinian context, such as Baal, El, and Asherah.

A most exciting and rich application of the comparative method to the study of Israelite religion has come in the work of Baruch Levine, who argues that monotheism has its roots in a reaction against the universalizing claims of the Neo-Assyrian Empire.[38] Against the claims of the Assyrian emperor, who took titles such as "king of the universe" and "ruler of the four corners (of the earth)," Isaiah in particular responds with the opposing claim, that YHWH was king of the universe. Thus, already in eighth-century texts such as Isa 10:5–15 and 14:24–27, Levine quite rightly perceives the assertion that YHWH controls the workings of the universe as "an explicit statement of Isaiah's monotheism."[39]

Another debate significant to the comparative study of Israelite religion that has continued to percolate surrounds Assyrian religious imposition. The opinion of Mordechai Cogan and John McKay[40] that the Neo-Assyrian Empire did not impose its religion on Judah has generally been affirmed,[41] but here again a binary approach is not ideal. In ancient times as well as modern, it is the nature of colonial hegemony that it functions not only by force but by prestige, an insight that has been advanced by postcolonial critics, among others.[42] As Richard Harlin Lowery writes, "In lopsided social-political relationships, the line between force and persuasion is very thin. In such cases, 'imitation' is very difficult to distinguish from 'imposition.'"[43] J. Nicholas Postgate notes that Assyrian cultural influence is "plainly visible" in the material culture even in client states where it was not imposed, and he perceives the process as "one of active emulation: we should not see the client rulers as cowering in their citadels waiting to be irradiated with Assyrian influence, but absorbing the scene in Nineveh, fingering the tapestries and envying the silverware."[44] In sum, Assyrians do not seem to have been overly concerned about religion as such; the hallmark of their *imperium* was the concern for political control and stability—by any means necessary—in order to enrich the homeland. Nevertheless, Judeans (especially elites with Assyrian contacts through trade and/or diplomacy) may have absorbed Assyrian ways almost by osmosis.

This interest in the details of Neo-Assyrian imperial practice may seem excessive, but I am arguing for increased attention to *mechanisms of influence*; although certainty usually eludes us, we are well advised to weigh the historical plausibility of cultural connections. Elsewhere I have also suggested the usefulness of the concept of *transposition*, a term borrowed from the literary theory of Julia Kristeva, which calls attention to the reality that authors almost never simply "borrow" an idea or a motif. Even in a case of direct quotation, the old idea is transposed into a new cultural register; transference from one text and context to another text and context creates new meaning.[45]

Summary: Monotheism and Method

Above all, monotheizing texts must be understood rhetorically, as persuasive speech in their historical context. One can only agree with the comment of James Sanders that Petersen quoted two decades ago: "To monotheize is not to progress or evolve toward monotheism, but rather to struggle within and against polytheistic contexts to affirm God's oneness, both in antiquity and today."[46] Although the nature of this process as struggle robs the scholar of neat historical phases, our ability to describe the complex rhetorical situation of ancient Israelites continues to be enriched.

"YHWH alone" is, in the first instance, the rhetoric of early Yahwists in a time when Israel and Judah had multiple gods and multiple divinatory options. One should envision mono-Yahwism as only one voice among many, though perhaps it was the theology of the central royal shrine throughout most of the monarchy. It was only later, however, seemingly in the encounter with the Neo-Assyrian Empire, that that theology became more forceful in its exclusion of other deities. Coincidentally, it was simultaneously allied with enough political power to effect broader changes in Judean society. YHWH may always have been a jealous god, but it was particularly in the face of a threat from the Neo-Assyrians (and later the Neo-Babylonians) that this tendency was wedded to political power willing to enforce it.

As is well known, there are partial analogies to the Hezekian and Josianic religious reforms in the ancient Near East; they include Akhenaten in Egypt and Nabonidus in Babylon. Unlike those failed efforts, however, mono-Yahwism, shockingly, became normative. Certainly the Babylonian exile was the final historical shock ensuring that mono-Yahwism endured rather than being reversed like those earlier religious reforms. Not only was the exile interpreted as validating the condemnations of the prophets; it also broke ties with the land, meaning both with the regional shrines and with local ancestor cults.[47] Nevertheless, it may be possible to see the roots of monotheism already in the reign of Hezekiah, when Sennacherib's overthrow of dozens of minor cities around Jerusalem may have had the effect of breaking the people's ties with the land and its cults almost as profoundly as exile would have done, and when Isaiah pictured YHWH as the only true Lord of history. It was a rare confluence of historical and social events that created the conditions for the rooting of this unusual religious revolution.

A rhetorical approach to the development of monotheism not only calls into question the extent of Yahwistic fidelity in ancient Israel but also casts doubt on descriptions of polytheism. In light of Tigay's onomastic analysis, it seems likely that some of the non-Yahwistic practices described in the Bible were amplified in the rhetoric of the prophets and the historians. It does not seem wise, for example, to draw historical conclusions from Elijah's repeated appeals that he was the lone Yahwistic representative remaining in Israel (1 Kgs 19:10, 14) facing 450 prophets of Baal (1 Kgs 18:19). The conclusion that *does* make sense from the stories of Elijah's contest with the prophets of Baal is that Yahwism and its proponents were in a situation of competition throughout most of the monarchic period.

The subfield of Israelite religion is fiercely contested and ideologically freighted. Nevertheless, in the discussion of monotheism, I suspect we will see a growing emphasis on the late-tenth through eighth centuries as the locus for the social normalization of Yahwistic monoltary, although there will remain room to disagree about the status of Asherah vis-à-vis YHWH. The reasons for this, laid out briefly above, include the evidence for earlier literacy and scribal culture, as well as the strong arguments for Neo-Assyrian influence on Yahwistic theology. The polyvalence of Israelite religion might answer the objections of those who are troubled by the inconsistencies of the archaeological record. Again, this would signal a return to fields already worked by Morton Smith and especially Lang, both of whom identified the emergence of a YHWH-alone faction in precisely the period I am suggesting.[48] Lang's emphasis on political and social forces and effects seem particularly well-suited to the new comparative and archaeological data described above.

The monotheism agenda remains unfinished, but one can hope that the gradual accretion of data will eventually narrow the extremes, so that more scholars (in Hallo's charming phrase) "stake out a place on the middle ground of sweet reasonableness."[49]

Case Study: YHWH and the Dead

The debate about YHWH's contact with the realm of the dead has been somewhat analogous to that about monotheism, if less widely and hotly contested. That is to say, it has been subject to preconceived notions, a lack of definitional clarity, a tendency to oversimplify, and inattention to certain important biblical texts. It needs to be clarified that YHWH was by no means perceived as being separate and aloof from contact with death, nor is a belief in his power to raise the dead a late development in Israelite religion, as is sometimes thought.

Historians of religion have often proceeded as if YHWH had been thought to have no commerce with death and the underworld in mainstream preexilic Yahwism. According to Mark Smith, YHWH was "unrelated to the realm of death."[50] Sigmund Mowinckel expressed this idea with great force: "Yahweh was kept as far away from death and the realm of the dead as possible. Yahweh has nothing to do with the realm of the dead, where he makes no 'wonders'; the dead 'are torn out of his hand,' a thought which is emphasized so strongly that logically it enters into opposition to the belief in the omnipotence of Yahweh."[51] Nicholas Tromp produced a compendium of similar comments by prominent scholars, and this perspective is still widespread among scholars of the ancient world whose specialties lie outside the Hebrew Bible.[52] One prominent recent exponent of this view is Ziony Zevit, who wrote, "Yahwism as presented in extant biblical texts conceived of YHWH as lord of the living. Death was the ultimate contamination of all that was particularly sacred to him."[53]

From a comparative perspective, it would be passing strange if YHWH had no commerce with the realm of death, since data come to us from numerous ancient Near Eastern cultures showing that contact with that realm was considered quite normal, in some cases central to major gods' functioning. Furthermore, numerous Mesopotamian gods are said to heal or save (*balāṭu*, D stem) from death. Often these are given the Akkadian title *muballiṭ mīti* "the one who heals/raises the dead," and they include Nabu, Ninlil, and Marduk, with attestations continuing into the Neo-Assyrian and Neo-Babylonian periods.[54] It is clear that this claim intended more than just healing, as one can see from the fourth tablet of *Ludlul bel nemeqi*, which dates to the Kassite period (ca. 1600–1200 B.C.E.):

> The Lord gave me life. …
> Who but Marduk restores his dead to life? …
> Marduk can restore to life *from the grave*. (*Ludlul* IV.4, 33, 35)[55]

Revivification imagery was operative in Babylonian texts before the biblical period, and it continued throughout the history of Babylon and Assyria. Furthermore, myths frequently portrayed contact between high gods and the underworld.

In Ugaritic myth, Baal, defeated by Mot, dies and rises again. Furthermore, it appears that Baal was portrayed as having the power to grant eternal life and raise the dead. The best support for it comes from the Aqhat Epic; when Anat tries to acquire Aqhat's bow, she famously says, "Ask for life, and I will give it to you / For immortality, and I will make it yours" (*CAT* 1.17 vi:26–28).[56] She continues: "I will make you count the years with Baal / With the sons of the El will you count months" (lines 28–29). She seems to compare this offer of life to one made by Baal:

> As Baal, when he revives, invites to a feast
> He invites the living one to a feast and offers him drink…
> So I will give life to noble Aqhat. (vi:30–33)

Thus, Ugaritic deities could be said to give or restore life. A recently published seal from Tell Afis may attest a similar conviction, since it bears the name *bʿl ḥww*, arguably to be translated "Baal gives life."[57]

It is possible to see a later manifestation of this same belief in the inscription of Pannamuwa, king of the Aramean state of Samal in the eighth century. In the text written on his sarcophagus, he instructs whichever of his sons inherits the throne to make sacrifices and say to Hadad: "May the soul [*nbš*] of Panammuwa eat with you, and may the soul [*nbš*] of Panammuwa drink with you."[58] In context, this looks very much an appeal to Hadad to raise the king, not to revivify him but to assure him a happy afterlife. In any case, it is quite clear that Hadad has contact with the dead.

The Egyptian idea that the gods help protect the dead in the afterlife and raise them into the second life in the Blessed West is so well-attested and so well-known that a full discussion is unnecessary. The mythic drama of the journey to the afterlife is recounted in many forms, all of them presuming the grace and favor of the gods. As a further example of the gods' power over the underworld and contact with it, one might mention the genre of the Amun decrees, which the deceased persons carried with them. In one, Amun says, "I shall deify PN in the West; I shall deify her in the realm of the dead. … I shall command that PN eat and drink in the same way as every god and every goddess in the realm of the dead."[59]

Is YHWH, then, truly *sui generis* when it comes to his relationship with death and the dead? The archaeological data from Judah might suggest otherwise. Bloch-Smith notes consistent provisioning of graves throughout the biblical period, including items such as household goods and food, which might be taken to reflect an expectation of afterlife.[60] Furthermore, Emile Puech, in a discussion of Palestinian funerary inscriptions, perceived that they reflect "a certain concept of life after death."[61] Although this is perhaps a stretch based on the few, laconic, and difficult tomb inscriptions, the archaeological context of the Ketef Hinnom silver scroll with part of the Aaronic blessing (Num 6:24–26) might indicate precisely a hope for YHWH's protection and blessing in the afterlife, since it was discovered in a grave. Then again, it might not, so one is ushered back to the biblical texts.

On a fresh reading, the claim that YHWH has no contact with the underworld is much too simple, as are models in which there is a sudden shift in the postexilic period to belief in afterlife and YHWH's authority over the underworld. It is possible to see diachronic change, but the roots of YHWH's contact with the realm of the dead are much deeper than is usually thought.[62] The extension of God's power into Sheol is expressed already in Amos 9:1–2 (see also Ps 139:8):

> Not one of them shall flee away;
> not one of them shall escape.
> Though they dig into Sheol,
> from there shall my hand take them;
> though they climb up to heaven,
> from there I will bring them down.

This eighth-century text is among the earliest in the Hebrew Bible that shows YHWH's full access to the underworld.[63] This may be part of a larger tradition; Alan Cooper has argued that Ps 24:7–10 is "a fragment or remnant of a descent myth—a myth in which a high god, forsaking his ordinary domain, descends to the netherworld, where he must confront the demonic forces of the infernal realm."[64] The phrase "doors of eternity" (Ps 24:9) and the command that they be opened have particular resonance with Egyptian mythology, but they are reused in the psalm to assert YHWH's power as a warrior.

Further texts likely to be preexilic that affirm God's power over death include 1 Sam 2:6, which affirms that he "kills and brings to life … brings down to Sheol and raises up" (see also Deut 32:39). As John T. Willis has remarked, this claim "is similar to a number of statements in *early Hebrew poems*."[65] Although proverbs are difficult to date with certainty, one might also mention Prov 15:11: "Sheol and Abaddon lie open before YHWH;

how much more human hearts!" In a comparison of this sort (reminiscent of the rabbinic *qal wa-homer*), the first term must seem obvious to the hearer in order to elucidate the second.

Already in the preexilic period, therefore, YHWH was a God who saved from death. In light of the parallels between biblical prayer and the prayer of other ancient Near Eastern civilizations (particularly Mesopotamia), this conclusion might have been predicted. In these cultures, prayer was first and foremost a response to suffering, whether on account of sickness, mistreatment, or other causes. In such a condition, the supplicant commonly portrayed himself or herself as approaching death. YHWH, like other gods, was perceived to have the power to save from this near-death condition. Bernd Janowski has framed his study of the Psalter in two parts: "*Von Leben zum Tod*" (from life to death) and "*Vom Tod zum Leben*" (from death to life)—and indeed the Psalter manifests clearly the Israelite affirmation that YHWH has power over *both* life and death.[66] In some cases, it would seem that God's salvation was needed *prior* to death (e.g., Pss 13:3; 28:1; 143:7). At other times, the psalmist states quite nakedly that God redeems from death (e.g., Pss 9:14; 49:15; 56:14; 68:21; 103:4; Hos 13:14; Lam 3:55–58) and brings people up from Sheol (Pss 30:3; 86:13; Jonah 2:2). Gary A. Anderson has suggested that this progression from Sheol to salvation in the Psalms was somehow enacted ritually.[67] In more poetic terms, God is frequently said to have the power to turn darkness into light (Amos 5:8; Job 12:22; see also Job 10:22), probably also evocative of salvation from death, since the tomb was characterized by darkness.[68]

YHWH's authority over death is also enacted by Elisha in the (admittedly exceptional) story of the Shunammite woman (2 Kgs 4:32–37; see also 8:5). The man of God "personifies the deity,"[69] in this case channeling YHWH's power to raise the dead. In the same general context, Jehoram's question, "Am I God, to give death or life?" (2 Kgs 5:7), reflects the same assumption about YHWH's power.

In early strata of the book of Hosea, the assertion that YHWH raises the dead becomes the basis for images of his salvation of the nation:

> Come, let us return to the Lord,
> for it is he who has torn, and he will heal us [*yirpāʾēnû*];
> he has struck down, and he will bind us up.
> After two days he will revive us [*yĕḥayyēnû*];
> on the third day he will raise us up [*yĕqimēnû*],
> that we may live before him. (6:1–2; see also 13:14)[70]

As with similar Mesopotamian imagery, some scholars have objected that this is not a description of resurrection, only of healing,[71] but this objection introduces a modern distinction that was much less clear to the ancient authors. Death was not different from sickness but was simply the most serious kind of sickness; the two phenomena existed on the same continuum.[72] In any case, the use of the verbs *qwm* and *yḥḥ* mark lexical connections both with later biblical references to resurrection (e.g., Isa 26:14, 19; Job 14:12, 14)[73] and with much older ancient Near Eastern texts such as the Aqhat Epic (*CAT* 1.17 vi 30–33). Indeed, the idea of rising from the dead on the third day has precedents as ancient as the Sumerian Inanna traditions and Egyptian Osiris traditions.[74] John Day cleverly suggests that the Hosea account is part of the polemic against the cult of Baal. He argues that Hosea's message was that "it is not Baal who dies and rises but Israel that dies for worshipping Baal, followed, if repentant, by resurrection."[75]

To comprehend the extent of these traditions regarding revivification is to recognize that the biblical texts cannot be fitted into a simple evolutionary model. It is no doubt true that Israelite thought about the restoration from death became more elaborate and central over time, but it is also true that, from the early stages of biblical literature, YHWH was always portrayed as a god who had the power to save from death and who was quite able to access and control the underworld, even if such actions were seen as exceptional. Surely expressions of belief in the raising of the dead have always been extravagant expressions of faith. Andersen and Freedman formulated the matter carefully, and in my view correctly, in their comments on Hos 6:

> The language of resurrection can be used dramatically to describe the recovery of a sick person from illness … but it does not follow that such language was exclusively metaphorical, and even if so, it must have been grounded in a certain type of expectation about the future life. Its currency testifies to the fact that the idea of resurrection after death was entertained.[76]

Hence, it is difficult to comprehend the comments of an author such as Robert Martin-Achard: "The writers of these hymns [that speak of resurrection] did not envisage the resurrection of the dead, they are simply asserting that the Living God is able to intervene, effectively, everywhere and at all times, even in the darkest hour."[77] It is invalid to claim that the writers were trying to find a way to express an abstract thought and had no other way of doing so. Rather, the extension of YHWH's power to save from death to the entire community would have been a fresh and perhaps surprising twist on a familiar theological theme. Certainly the Israelites had no systematized "doctrine of resurrection" in the preexilic period, but just as certainly they *did* claim that their God raised the dead. Especially since the medical boundaries between life and death were less clearly formulated in ancient times, it seems unfruitful to ask whether they meant those claims in a literal way. Nicolas Wyatt's comment about certain aspects of Ugaritic theology applies well to the Israelite rhetoric of resurrection: "The language … was of course symbolic—when is language *not* symbolic?—but all the more real for so being."[78]

Some caveats are in order. First, there are certainly conflicting, negative traditions about hope for YHWH's salvation after death. Job 7:9 says, "As a cloud vanishes and is gone, so the one who goes down to the grave does not return." Further, even a king such as David is portrayed as despairing of the return of his son: "Now he is dead; why should I fast? Can I bring him back again? I shall go to him, but he will not return to me" (1 Sam 12:23). Second, salvation from death is an exceptional and individual matter in the early periods of Israelite religion: one may pray for it, but it is not a general expectation, much less a dogma.[79]

In sum, however, this synthesis of historical, textual, comparative, and archaeological data strongly suggests that YHWH was believed to save from death and have power over Sheol even in very early periods. That the gods had the power to revive the dead in some way was a normative belief much earlier in Ugarit and Mesopotamia and was a central point of Egyptian religion. In this case, the conflicting data come not from archaeology but from the text itself. We may make recourse, however, to two principles introduced earlier. First, there is in the Hebrew Bible the phenomenon of theological diversity. For example, Job 7 reflects a pessimistic viewpoint about Yahweh's power over death that is clearly not representative of the mainstream theological view in the Israelite tradition. Second, the rhetorical context shapes our interpretation of the claims about Yahweh and the dead. For example, the psalmists frequently assert that "the dead do not praise," and while this may reflect a genuine theological tradition as well, it is also intended to motivate YHWH to save.

One might object on the basis of cultic law. Leviticus 19:2 commands: "You shall be holy, for I, YHWH, your God, am holy." The same code goes on to say that corpses contaminate that purity. By analogy to the priests, should YHWH not kept himself separate from the dead? But criminal law in the Torah does not hold God and humankind to the same standards[80]—why should it be different for purity laws? Why should YHWH have had to abide by priestly standards of cultic purity? As Isaiah says, YHWH's ways are different from human ways (55:8). Cultic purity, after all, is instituted partly to protect the people *from YHWH*! What need, then, does YHWH have of it? He was no more made impure by contact with death and the dead than light is made impure by contact with darkness.

For Further Reading

Albertz, Rainer. *A History of Israelite Religion in the Old Testament Period.* Translated by John Bowden. Louisville: Westminster John Knox, 1994.

Beckman, Gary, and Theodore J. Lewis, eds. *Text, Artifact and Image: Revealing Ancient Israelite Religion.* BJS 346. Providence, R.I.: Brown University, 2006.

Gittlen, Barry M. ed., *Sacred Time, Sacred Place: Archaeology and the Religion of Israel.* Winona Lake, Ind.: Eisenbrauns, 2002.

Miller, Patrick D. *The Religion of Ancient Israel.* Louisville: Westminster John Knox, 2000.

Cross, Frank Moore. *Canaanite Myth and Hebrew Epic: Essays in the History of the Religion of Israel.* Cambridge: Harvard University Press, 1973.

Smith, Mark S. *The Early History of God: Yahweh and the Other Deities in Ancient Israel.* 2nd ed. Biblical Resource Series. Grand Rapids: Eerdmans, 2002.

Strawn, Brent A. "The History of Israelite Religion," in *The Cambridge Companion to the Hebrew Bible/Old Testament.* Edited by Stephen B. Chapman and Marvin A. Sweeney. Cambridge: Cambridge University Press, forthcoming.

Toorn, Karel van der. *From Her Cradle to Her Grave: The Role of Religion in the Life of the Israelite and the Babylonian Woman.* Sheffield: Sheffield Academic Press, 1994.

Zevit, Ziony. *The Religions of Ancient Israel: A Synthesis of Parallactic Approaches.* London: Continuum, 2001.

Notes

1. This point of emphasis is only fitting, since David Petersen has made significant contributions to the study of monotheism. See especially "Israel and Monotheism: The Unfinished Agenda," in *Canon, Theology, and Old Testament Interpretation: Essays in Honor of Brevard S. Childs* (ed. Gene M. Tucker, David L. Petersen, and Robert R. Wilson; Philadelphia: Fortress, 1988), 92–107.

2. In addition to the monographs cited below, see recently Brent A. Strawn, "The History of Israelite Religion," in *The Cambridge Companion to the Hebrew Bible/Old Testament* (ed. Stephen B. Chapman and Marvin A. Sweeney; Cambridge: Cambridge University Press, forthcoming); Karel van der Toorn, "Currents in the Study of Israelite Religion," *CurBS* 6 (1998): 9–30; and Bill T. Arnold, "Religion in Ancient Israel," in *The Face of Old Testament Studies: A Survey of Contemporary Approaches* (ed. David W. Baker and Bill T. Arnold; Grand Rapids: Baker, 1999), 391–420.

3 Nili Fox, "Concepts of God in Israel and the Question of Monotheism" in *Text, Artifact and Image: Revealing Ancient Israelite Religion* (ed. Gary Beckman and Theodore J. Lewis; BJS 346; Providence, R.I.: Brown University, 2006), 326 n. 1.

4. Petersen, "Israel and Monotheism," 97–98.

5. Fox, "Concepts of God," 326 n. 1.

6. Bernhard Lang, *Monotheism and the Prophetic Minority: An Essay in Biblical History and Sociology* (Sheffield: Almond, 1983), 35.

7. See, e.g., William F. Albright, *From the Stone Age to Christianity: Monotheism and the Historical Process* (Garden City, N.Y.: Doubleday: 1957), 257–72; and Yehezkel Kaufmann, *The Religion of Israel, from Its Beginnings to the Babylonian Exile* (trans. Moshe Greenberg; Chicago: University of Chicago Press, 1960), 133–48. The comments of George Ernest Wright are illustrative of this viewpoint: "The development of ideas is not a theme in which the Biblical writers show much interest, nor is it one which can create a community of faith, a people of God." He inveighs against "the inability of the developmental hypothesis to take seriously the story of God's revelation and covenant on Mt. Sinai" (*The Old Testament against Its Environment* [London: SCM, 1968], 13, 15). For further bibliography, see Mark S. Smith, *The Early History of God: Yahweh and the Other Deities in Ancient Israel* (2nd ed.; Biblical Resources Series; Grand Rapids: Eerdmans, 2002).

8. J. Alberto Soggin, *Israel in the Biblical Period: Institutions, Festivals, Ceremonies, Rituals* (Edinburgh: T&T Clark, 2001), 10.

9. Ibid., 56.

10. Rainer Albertz, *A History of Israelite Religion in the Old Testament Period* (trans. John Bowden; Louisville: Westminster John Knox, 1994); Patrick D. Miller, *The Religion of Ancient Israel* (Louisville: Westminster John Knox, 2000). Note also Erhard S. Gerstenberger's *Theologies in the Old Testament* (trans. John Bowden; Minneapolis: Fortress, 2002), which discusses a similar diversity of religious contexts from a theological perspective.

11. Karel van der Toorn, *From Her Cradle to Her Grave: The Role of Religion in the Life of the Israelite and the Babylonian Woman* (Sheffield: Sheffield Academic Press, 1994), 111.

12. Theodore J. Lewis, "How Far Can Texts Take Us? Evaluating Textual Sources for Reconstructing Ancient Israelite Beliefs about the Dead," in *Sacred Time, Sacred Place: Archaeology and the Religion of Israel* (ed. Barry M. Gittlen; Winona Lake, Ind.: Eisenbrauns, 2002), 206–7.

13. Richard S. Hess, *Israelite Religions: An Archaeological and Biblical Survey* (Grand Rapids: Baker, 2007).

14. Van der Toorn, "Currents in the Study of Israelite Religion," 24.

15. Moshe Weinfeld offers both a critique of Wellhausen's anti-Semitic ideology and a comparative study of Priestly law in *The Place of the Law in the Religion of Ancient Israel* (VTSup 100; Leiden: Brill, 2004).

16. See Avi Hurvitz, "The Evidence of Language in Dating the Priestly Code," *RB* 81 (1974): 24–56; idem, *A Linguistic Study of the Relationship between the Priestly Source and the Book of Ezekiel: A New Approach to an Old Problem* (Paris: Gabalda, 1982).

17. See Knohl, "The Priestly Torah versus the Holiness School: Sabbath and the Festivals," *HUCA* 58 (1987): 65–117; idem, "The Conception of God and Cult in the Priestly Torah and in the Holiness School," (Ph.D. diss., Hebrew University, 1988); idem, *The Sanctuary of Silence: The Priestly Torah and the Holiness School* (Minneapolis: Fortress, 1994).

18. E.g., Julius Wellhausen, *Prolegomena to the History of Ancient Israel* (German orig., 1882; New York: Meridian Books, 1957).

19. Ibid., 34.

20. Knohl, *Sanctuary of Silence*, 202.

21. William M. Schniedewind, *How the Bible Became a Book* (Cambridge: Cambridge University Press, 2004), 84.

22. See, e.g., Frank Moore Cross, "The Priestly Work," in idem, *Canaanite Myth and Hebrew Epic: Essays in the History of the Religion of Israel* (Cambridge: Harvard University Press, 1973), 293–325.

23. On the idea of "heterodox Yahwism," see Miller, *The Religion of Ancient Israel*, 51–56. His list of characteristics of heterodox Yahwism includes the use of certain cult objects and banned forms of divination, especially necromancy.

24. William G. Dever, "'Will the Real Israel Please Stand Up?' Archaeology and Israelite Historiography: Part I," *BASOR* 297 (1995): 61–80.

25. See, e.g., the essays of David M. Carr and Seth L. Sanders in *Literate Culture and Tenth-Century Canaan: The Tel Zayit Abecedary in Context* (ed. Ron E. Tappy and P. Kyle McCarter Jr.; Winona Lake, Ind.: Eisenbrauns, 2008).

26. William F. Albright, "The High Place in Ancient Palestine," in *Volume du Congrès: Strasbourg, 1956* (VTSup 4; Leiden: Brill, 1957), 242–58.

27. Miller, *The Religion of Ancient Israel*, 14.

28. Jeffrey H. Tigay, *You Shall Have No Other Gods* (Atlanta: Scholars Press, 1986).

29. Elizabeth Bloch-Smith, *Judahite Burial Practices and Beliefs about the Dead* (JSOTSup 123; Sheffield: JSOT Press, 1992), 94–100.

30. See Othmar Keel and Christoph Uehlinger, *Gods, Goddesses and Images of God in Ancient Israel* (trans. Thomas H. Trapp; Minneapolis: Fortress, 1998).

31. The forthcoming *Iconography of Deities and Demons in the Ancient Near*

East: An Iconographic Dictionary with a Special Emphasis on First-Millennium BCE Palestine/Israel promises to be a major advancement in the subfield and is partially available in prepublication form at www.religionswissenschaft.uzh.ch/idd/index.php. In paper format, it is forthcoming from Brill. Note also the new Iconography and the Hebrew Bible Consultation of the Society of Biblical Literature, which is chaired by Joel M. LeMon and Izaak J. de Hulster.

32. Ziony Zevit, "Implicit Population Figures and Historical Sense: What Happened to 200,150 Judahites in 701 BCE?" in *Confronting the Past: Archaeological and Historical Essays on Ancient Israel in Honor of William G. Dever* (ed. Seymour Gitin, J. Edward Wright, and J. P. Dessel; Winona Lake, Ind.: Eisenbrauns, 2006), 365.

33. Ziony Zevit, "Philology and Archaeology: Imagining New Questions, Begetting New Ideas," in Gittlen, *Sacred Time, Sacred Place*, 35–42.

34. Fox, "Concepts of God," 329–31.

35. Smith, *The Early History of God*; idem, *The Origins of Biblical Monotheism: Israel's Polytheistic Background and the Ugaritic Texts* (Oxford: Oxford University Press, 2001).

36. Frank Moore Cross, *Canaanite Myth and Hebrew Epic: Essays in the History of the Religion of Israel* (Cambridge: Harvard University Press, 1973).

37. See Smith, *The Origins of Biblical Monotheism*, 155.

38. Baruch Levine, "Assyrian Ideology and Biblical Monotheism," *Iraq* 67 (2005): 411–27.

39. Levine, "Assyrian Ideology and Biblical Monotheism," 423.

40. Mordechai Cogan, *Imperialism and Religion: Assyria, Judah and Israel in the Eighth and Seventh Centuries B.C.E.* (SBLMS 19; Missoula, Mont.: Scholars Press, 1974); John W. McKay, *Religion in Judah Under the Assyrians, 732–609 BC* (SBT 2/26; Naperville, Ill.: Allenson, 1973).

41. Contra Hermann Spieckermann, *Juda unter Assur in der Sargonidenzeit* (FRLANT 129; Göttingen: Vandenhoeck & Ruprecht, 1982). See Mordechai Cogan, "Judah under Assyrian Hegemony: A Re-examination of *Imperialism and Religion*," *JBL* 112 (1993): 403–14; also Steven W. Holloway, *Aššur is King! Aššur is King! Religion in the Exercise of Power in the Neo-Assyrian Empire* (CHANE 10; Leiden: Brill, 2002).

42. See, e.g., Ngugi wa Thiong'o: "The economic and political dependence of this African neo-colonial bourgeoisie is reflected in its culture of apemanship and parrotry enforced on a restive population through police boots, barbed wire, a gowned clergy and judiciary; their ideas are spread by a corpus of state intellectuals, the academic and journalistic laureates of the neo-colonial establishment" (*Decolonizing the Mind: The Politics of Language in African Literature* [London: Currey, 1986], 2).

43. Richard Harlin Lowery, *The Reforming Kings: Cults and Society in First Temple Judah* (JSOTSup 120; Sheffield: JSOT Press, 1991), 140.

44. J. Nicholas Postgate, "The Land of Assur and the Yoke of Assur," *World Archaeology* 23 (1992): 259–60.

45. Christopher B. Hays, "Echoes of the Ancient Near East? Intertextuality and the Comparative Study of the Old Testament," in *The Word Leaps the Gap: Essays on Scripture and Theology in Honor of Richard B. Hays* (ed. J. Ross Wagner, C. Kavin Rowe, and A. Katherine Grieb; Winona Lake, Ind.: Eerdmans, 2009), 20–43.

46. James A. Sanders, *Canon and Community* (Philadelphia: Fortress, 1984), 52; cited in Petersen, "Israel and Monotheism," 103.

47. On the social impact of the Mesopotamian onslaught on Judah, see Mary Douglas, "One God, No Ancestors, in a World Renewed," in *Jacob's Tears: The Priestly Work of Reconciliation* (ed. Mary Douglas; Oxford: Oxford University Press, 2004), 176–95.

48. Morton Smith, *Palestinian Parties and Politics that Shaped the Old Testament* (2nd ed.; London: SCM, 1987).

49. William W. Hallo, "The Limits of Skepticism," *JAOS* 110 (1990): 187.

50. Smith, *The Early History of God*, 205.

51. Sigmund Mowinckel, *The Psalms in Israel's Worship* (Sheffield: JSOT Press, 1992), 138.

52. Nicholas J. Tromp, *Primitive Conceptions of Death and the Nether World in the Old Testament* (BibOr 21; Rome: Pontifical Biblical Institute, 1969), 197–202. As a recent example, Jan Assmann comments: "[I]n the Old Testament world ... the divine and death were kept as far apart as possible" (*Death and Salvation in Ancient Egypt* [Ithaca, N.Y.: Cornell University Press, 2005], 11).

53. Ziony Zevit, *Religions of Ancient Israel*, 664.

54. For a fuller accounting, see "*balāṭu*" in *CAD*.

55. Lambert, *Babylonian Wisdom Literature* (Oxford: Clarendon, 1960), 58–59.

56. All Ugaritic translations are mine.

57. See M. G. Amadasi Guzzo, "Une Empreinte de sceau de Tell Afis," *Or* 70 (2003): 318–24; K. Lawson Younger Jr., "Some of What's New in Old Aramaic Epigraphy," *NEA* 70 (2007): 140.

58. H. Donner and W. Röllig, eds., *Kanaanäische und Aramäische Inschriften* (3 vols.; Wiesbaden: Harrassowitz, 1966), 1:39 (214:17); "The Hadad Inscription," translated by K. Lawson Younger Jr. (*COS* 2.36:156–58).

59. Jan Assmann, *Ägyptische Hymnen und Gebete* (ed. Erik Hornung; Zürich: Artemis-Verlag, 1975), hymn no. 131.

60. Bloch-Smith, *Judahite Burial Practices*, 63–108.

61. Emile Puech, "Palestinian Funerary Inscriptions," *ABD* 5:129.

62. Gönke Eberhardt refers to an expansion of YHWH's authority over the underworld in *JHWH und die Unterwelt: Spuren einer Kompetenzausweitung JHWHs im Alten Testament* (Tübingen: Mohr Siebeck, 2007), 393.

63. On dating, see Hans Walter Wolff, *Joel and Amos* (Philadelphia: Fortress, 1977), 107.

64. Alan Cooper, "Ps 24:7–10: Mythology and Exegesis," *JBL* 102 (1983): 43.

65. John T. Willis, "Song of Hannah and Psalm 113," *CBQ* 35 (1973): 147, emphasis added.

66. Bernd Janowski, *Konfliktgespräche mit Gott: Eine Anthropologie der Psalmen* (Neukirchen-Vluyn: Neukirchener, 2003). See also esp. part 3 of Christoph Barth, *Die Errettung vom Tode: Leben und Tod in den Klage- und Dankliedern des Alten Testaments* (Stuttgart: Kohlhammer, 1997).

67. Anderson's foremost piece of evidence is Ps 30:9–13, which he believes reflects a "ritual descent to Sheol" followed by an inverse movement to deliverance (*A*

Time to Mourn, a Time to Dance: The Expression of Grief and Joy in Israelite Religion [University Park: Pennsylvania State University Press, 1991], 87–97).

68. So already Heidel, *Gilgamesh Epic*, 219 n. 250: "'light' and 'life' are sometimes used as interchangeable terms."

69. David L. Petersen, *The Prophetic Literature: An Introduction* (Louisville: Westminster John Knox, 2002), 6. See also Levenson, who suggests that the eighth-century prophets' (esp. Hosea's) convictions about resurrection stemmed from folkloristic traditions such as these about Elisha (*Resurrection and the Restoration of Israel*, 206).

70. It is notoriously difficult to place texts from Hosea in historical context, but 6:1–2 is located in what is usually taken to be one of the most securely authentic sections. See John Day, "Development of the Belief in Life after Death," in idem, *Yahweh and the Gods and Goddesses of Canaan* [JSOTSup 265; New York: Continuum, 2002], 242).

71. E.g., James L. Mays, *Hosea* (OTL; London: SCM, 1969), 95; Hans Walter Wolff, *Hosea* (Hermeneia; Philadelphia: Fortress, 1974), 117; Wilhelm Rudolph, *Hosea* (KAT 13/1; Gütersloh: Mohn, 1966), 135; Graham I. Davies, *Hosea* (NCBC; Grand Rapids: Eerdmans, 1992), 161.

72. Jon D. Levenson, *Resurrection and the Restoration of Israel: The Ultimate Victory of the God of Life* (New Haven: Yale University Press, 2006), 205.

73. Day, *Yahweh and the Gods*, 119.

74. For references, see Wolff, *Hosea*, 117–18.

75. Day, "Development of the Belief in Life after Death," 245.

76. Andersen and Freedman, *Hosea*, 421.

77. Robert Martin-Achard, *From Death to Life: A Study of the Development of the Doctrine of the Resurrection in the Old Testament* (trans. J. P. Smith; Edinburgh: Oliver & Boyd, 1960), 57.

78. Nicolas Wyatt, "The Religion of Ugarit: An Overview," in *Handbook of Ugaritic Studies* (ed. Wilfred G. E. Watson and Nicholas Wyatt; Leiden: Brill, 1999), 561.

79. So also Eberhardt, *JHWH und die Unterwelt*, 394.

80. Moshe Greenberg, "Some Postulates of Biblical Criminal Law," in *Yehezkel Kaufmann Jubilee Volume* (ed. Menachem Haran; Jerusalem: Magnes, 1960), 25.

Historiographical Approaches: Survey and Principles

John H. Hayes

"Whoever sets out to write history is a liar from the start."
(Anonymous)

A Survey of Approaches

The first volume of *An Universal History* appeared in 1736.[1] The first 110 pages of this learned and heavily annotated work defended the facticity of the events described in Gen 1–9 and the historicity of the narrative accounts presented. The authors drew heavily upon and dialogued with the so-called physico-theologians, a number of scientists who sought to defend the biblical accounts against their recent detractors and reinterpreters.[2] Like their latter-day successors, the creationists, they found a large following.

The physico-theologians could resort to rather incredulous theories about the earth's history—such as earth-circling comets—in order to argue for the credibility of the biblical materials. Certain fanciful freedoms were taken with the biblical texts, and the external evidence offered was sometimes extremely hypothetical. Many, such as Thomas Burnett (1635–1715), reasoned that Gen 1–9 was "a narration suited to the capacity of the people, and not to the strict and physical nature of things," and was to be interpreted so as not "to be repugnant to clear and uncontested Science."[3]

Although the clash between scientific perspectives and biblical materials had its roots in the seventeenth century,[4] biblical interpreters for centuries were already well aware of diversity and even contradictions in the Bible and sought to overcome these in various ways. The greatest and most obvious problems were related to the differences among the four Gospels. One way of handling this issue was with Gospel harmonies, over forty of which were published in the sixteenth century.[5] More comprehensive treatments of biblical problems were dealt with in what were called "reconcilers" or "conciliators."[6]

Radical skepticism, within the mainline academic and ecclesiastical communities, about the biblical portrayals of the history of Israel and whether Old Testament materials could be used to reconstruct that history first made an appearance early in the nineteenth century.[7] After writing a sixteen-page dissertation on Deuteronomy,[8] Wilhelm de Wette (1780–1849) published two volumes[9] of Old Testament introduction in 1806–1807.[10] He was heavily influenced by what came to be called "the mythic school,"[11] strongly opposing those who thought the biblical materials could be used for historical reconstruction: "A complete and thoroughgoing criticism will show that not one of the historical books of the Old Testament has any historical value, and that they all more or less contain myths and traditions, and that we do not have from among any of the books of the Old Testament any real historical witnesses."[12] These same ideas are expressed in his Old Testament introduction.[13] In particular, he had serious qualms about the historical reliability of texts filled with accounts of miraculous events:

> The miraculous in the historical books diminishes just in proportion as they approach historical times, and then it entirely ceases in that period from which we have contemporary accounts. In the earliest times, men have intercourse with God; later, angels appear; still later, the prophets perform the miraculous; but in the times after the exile, from which we have contemporary history, the miraculous ceases altogether.[14]

For him, the Pentateuch was, therefore, "an epic poem, and the poet wishes to be nothing other than a poet, and certainly not a historian."[15]

Rudolf Smend has ably summarized de Wette's general position:

> The young de Wette radicalized the use of the term myth, which was thus offered him. He turned against attempts of Eichhorn and others to reconstruct a history of earliest Israel from the biblical material. In his judgment, we cannot as a rule by eliminating the mythical elements arrive at historical nuclei which can be put together with the help of various hypotheses to build up an overall picture. The aim of the Old Testament is to offer religion, not history. We act contrary to its intention if, in spite of that, we try to abstract from it a history which cannot be abstracted at all, because of the nature of the material. So de Wette sees for the historian only one possibility: to abandon this field and let the Old Testament be what it is—the testimony of a religion which

> intends to awaken religion in its readers. De Wette did not stop short at this general thesis. On the contrary, he himself turned to attack literary-historical criticism, which would now show in detail that the books of the Old Testament hardly ever have any historical value at all. From the outset, therefore, this is a "negative" destructive criticism, which dispenses with a "positive" counterpart, the construction of a coherent whole which will accord with our own way of thinking.[16]

Elsewhere, Smend writes further:

> The fact that the biblical writers offer us no history is not only because they cannot do so, but—and for de Wette this is the more essential point—that they have no wish to. Their desire is to present divine action in the world, and to awaken faith in the reader. As de Wette says, they are not after history, but after religion, and it is as religious utterances that what they say should be understood, and in no other way—even leaving aside the general point that the significance of Israel for us does not lie in its history but in its religion.[17]

In the end, it may be that Smend overemphasizes de Wette's stringent ahistoricism. After all, he published a book with "archaeology" and "history" in its title[18] and also produced "the first work of Old Testament scholarship to present a view of the history of Israelite religion that is radically at variance with the view implied in the Old Testament itself."[19]

The nineteenth century witnessed the encounter of biblical studies with modern critical historiography, a movement that has come to be known as "historicism,"[20] and Ernst Troeltsch (1865–1923) was one of its most learned and influential interpreters and practitioners.[21] In his 1914 article, "Historiography," he summarized the basic principles of modern historiography:

> The history of mankind emerges in the evolutionary history of the earth's surface; it takes its rise in the prehistoric life of primitive peoples; it is determined throughout by the general laws of geographical conditions, and by the various phases of social life, and forms an unspeakable complex, yet altogether coherent, whole of immeasurable duration both in the past and in the future. It is as a part of this array and system that we must survey and estimate our own existence, and find its rationale and origin. On the analogy of the events known to us we seek by conjecture and sympathetic understanding to explain and reconstruct the past. From this point, again, we advance to the criticism of extant traditions and to the correction of generally accepted histori-

> cal representations. Since we discern the same process of phenomena in operation in the past as in the present, and see, there as here, the various historical cycles of human life influencing and intersecting one another, we gain at length the idea of an integral continuity, balanced in its changes, never at rest, and ever moving towards incalculable issues. The causal explanation of all that happens, the setting of the individual life in its true relations, the interpretation of events in their most intricate interaction, the placing of mankind in a rounded system of ceaseless change—these constitute the essential function and result of modern historical reflexion. The latter, viewed as a whole, forms a new scientific mode of representing man and his development, and, as such, shows at all points an absolute contrast to the Biblico-theological views of later antiquity.[22]

Van Harvey has helpfully transposed Troeltsch's rather convoluted language into a more understandable formulation of three principles:

> (1) The principle of criticism, by which he meant that our judgments about the past cannot simply be classified as true or false but must be seen as claiming only a greater or lesser degree of probability and as always open to revision; (2) the principle of analogy, by which he meant that we are able to make such judgments of probability only if we presuppose that our own present experience is not radically dissimilar to the experience of past persons; and (3) the principle of correlation, by which he meant that the phenomena of man's historical life are so related and interdependent that no radical change can take place at any one point in the historical nexus without effecting a change in all that immediately surrounds it. Historical explanation, therefore, necessarily takes the form of understanding an event in terms of its antecedents and consequences, and no event can be isolated from its historically conditioned time and space.[23]

Behind both Troeltsch's description and Harvey's restatement are a number of important conclusions about the writing of history. First, textual and other traditions from the past must be analyzed with a hermeneutic of suspicion; that is, the burden of proof rests upon anyone who would utilize material to reconstruct any version of the past. Thus, one cannot automatically assume the historical trustworthiness of material simply because there is no overwhelming and obvious evidence to the contrary. Second, the historian must operate on the assumption that what was possible in the past is possible today and vice versa. Just as iron axe heads do not float in water today, neither did they at any time in the past. Thus interpretations based on the assumption of miraculous events or divine intervention, so common in the Bible, are automatically ruled out of court. Third, events in the past, like those in the present, must be understood contextually and explained in terms of cause and effect.

Much of nineteenth-century scholarship focused on the first of these, namely, literary and documentary studies.[24] Always in the background, however, were the interests in producing critical and academically respected histories of Israel, Judaism, Jesus, and the early church. For example, on 10 February 1835 the classicist Thomas Arnold (1795–1842) wrote the diplomat-theologian Christian Carl Josias von Bunsen (1791–1860) that "what [Friedrich August] Wolf [1759–1824] and [Barthold Georg] Niebuhr [1776–1831] have done for Greece and Rome seems sadly wanted for Judaea."[25] As late as 1863, Arthur Stanley [1815–81] could write,

> The Jewish History has suffered from causes similar to those which still, within our own memory, obscured the history of Greece and Rome. Till within the present century, the characters and institutions of those two great countries were so veiled from view in the conventional haze with which the enchantment of distance had invested them, that when the more graphic and critical historians of our time broke through this reserve, a kind of shock was felt through all the educated classes of the country. The same change was in a still higher degree needed with regard to the history of the Jews. Its sacred character had deepened the difficulty already occasioned by its extreme antiquity.[26]

In 1878, Julius Wellhausen (1844–1918)[27] artfully and entertainingly summed up and augmented the previous half-century of research with his own analysis of the Old Testament historiographical literature.[28] He had earlier published analyses of the Hexateuch and the historical books in a series of journal articles.[29] These detailed and critical examinations of the biblical documents were executed with an eye on writing a history of Israel and its religion along modern historiographical lines.[30] Ultimately, however, these presentations of the history of Israel had less impact than his *Prolegomena*.[31] Wellhausen was a towering figure, and his literary-critical work cast its shadow over all subsequent biblical study for decades. Most challenging, and to others threatening, were his arguments for the four-source theory of the Pentateuch/Hexateuch, for the temporal priority of the prophets before the law, and for the association of the Mosaic/cultic law with postexilic Judaism.[32] All of these are hypotheses, issues, and conclusions with which historians of Israel still must concern themselves.

New horizons and new sources of knowledge began to confront nineteenth-century historians as a consequence of the decipherment of ancient languages and the beginnings of Palestinian archaeology. The capacity to read and translate ancient texts—Egyptian hieroglyphic (from 1822) and Mesopotamian cuneiform (from 1847) writings—provided a vast storehouse of epigraphic material with relevance for the understanding of biblical traditions. In addition, artifactual material derived from archaeological excavations and accidental finds began to provide scholars with material remains that required interpretation.[33]

Even into the twentieth century, many felt that this "external evidence" would substantiate the historicity of biblical descriptions.[34] Both epigraphic and archaeological data, however, presented a two-edged sword for historical study. Parallels to Gen 1–11 turned up in cuneiform sources,[35] eventually leading to the *Babel-Bibel* controversy.[36] At the same time, George Smith (1840–1876) published part of the *limmu* lists where a reference to an eclipse of the sun (dated to 15 June 763 B.C.E.) provided the base date for first-millennium Near Eastern chronology.[37] While it should be granted that archaeology has helped illuminate aspects of ancient cultures[38] and "confirmed" the historicity of some events reported in the Bible, excavations have also raised serious questions about others, for example, those reported in the book of Joshua.[39]

In the twentieth-century, historians were able to draw upon three sources of information in their efforts to provide a narrative account of ancient Israelite/Judean history: the biblical traditions; greatly expanded nonbiblical epigraphic material; and archaeological data. It has become fashionable, and is not altogether misleading, to divide twentieth-century Israelite historical studies into two heuristic categories associated with the figures of Georg Albrecht Alt (1883–1956)[40] and William Foxwell Albright (1891–1971),[41] though neither scholar produced a comprehensive history, a task that was left to their students. From the vantage point of the present, however, the disagreements between these two groups appear to have focused on premonarchic times and not to have been as extreme as at first appeared.[42] The Altians tended to highlight close and critical analysis of the biblical sources, whereas this was never the case with the Albrightians.[43] Rather, they sought to use archaeological or "external evidence" to "confirm" biblical depictions. In a 1938 article, Albright wrote, "Archaeological and inscriptional data have established the historicity of innumerable passages and statements of the Old Testament; the number of such cases is many times greater than those where the reverse has been proved or has been made probable."[44] Somewhat like the physico-theologians, Albright and his followers often hypothesized scenarios large enough to incorporate contradictory evidence when this could lead to conservative conclusions.[45] The Albrightians tended to be much more theologically and even philosophically concerned than the Altians,[46] though many of Alt's studies were infused with religious concerns.

Martin Noth (1902–1968)[47] was clearly the most influential of Alt's students.[48] His *History of Israel* picked up and built on his earlier literary analysis of the material in Genesis–2 Kings and the books of Chronicles, which he had investigated on the basis of a traditio-historical perspective.[49] His basic positions on early Israelite history were: (1) Israel originated within the land of Palestine; (2) they did so without any military conquest but after groups that would become Israel had settled in the region; (3) their structure showed parallels to Greek amphictyonies; and (4) the biblical materials about the patriarchs and Moses (Genesis–Numbers) do not reflect the course of historical events but reflect traditions organized around certain themes at home in the amphictyony.

In the 1970s, both Albrightian and Altian schools came under serious challenge, and the linchpins of their historical reconstructions loosened.[50] For example, the view of early Israel as an amphictyonic society with a mobile central sanctuary underwent rigorous criticism.[51] Already in the 1960s, George Mendenhall had proposed a new paradigm for the origins of early Israel, proposing a radical restructuring of indigenous peoples in the land.[52] In addition, Thomas L. Thompson and John Van Seters both produced important works that challenged the use of external evidence among the Albrightians.[53] Finally, William Dever undertook an incisive critique of what had come to be called "biblical archaeology."[54] In light of these new developments, a collection of essays entitled *Israelite and Judaean History* aimed to summarize where scholarship stood and in what directions it might move.[55]

In the decades that followed, more books and articles on the history of Israel—both descriptive and methodological—have been published than at any other period in the history of scholarship. Enough has been written to constitute a veritable library of self-help books for the actual or would-be historian of Israel.[56] Two of the most adventurous and praiseworthy initiatives are the twelve-volume series Biblische Enzyklopädie (beginning in 1996 and published by Kohlhammer[57])and the, thus far, nine-volume series of the European Seminar in Historical Methodology under the editorship of Lester Grabbe (beginning in 1998 and published by T&T Clark).

Presently, there is a smorgasbord of approaches to Israelite history reflecting all of the alternatives seen in the above short survey.[58] The old approach of the physico-theologians is still alive and well among the creationist/intelligent-design/antievolutionist advocates who exist on the fringes of academia but flourish in multitudes of churches and synagogues.[59] Some histories are written as if critical historiography had never developed or was a completely illegitimate enterprise.[60] Others are written as if the first rule of historiography were a "hermeneutic of trust."[61] At the same time, de Wettian skepticism about whether the Bible contains or reflects the type of evidence that can be used to write a history of ancient Israel has been a major component in the discussion for the last two decades.[62] This view, which represents a thoroughly legitimate position, has unnecessarily been the object of name-calling, especially in the popular press and at the sideshows held at the national meetings of The Society of Biblical Literature.[63] Another tack has recently been taken by Israel Finkelstein and Neil Silberman, who sought to produce a history of ancient Israel that would be based fundamentally on archaeological data and free of the Bible's dominance in historical reconstruction.[64] Their work, however, turned out to be overly dependent on the biblical account of Josiah's reign (2 Kgs 22–23), understood as an effort to restore a "greater" or "Davidic" Israel that the archaeological evidence fails to support.[65]

Some Guiding Principles

Amid this smorgasbord—or perhaps better, morass—of historiographical approaches and products, how do students find their way, and how does one evaluate between better and worse? Unfortunately, there are no absolute criteria by which to distinguish the various efforts. It does seem, however, that certain principles can assist in determining which works fall within the category of classical, critical historiography.

First, the history of Israel should be investigated and written about in the same manner that one would explore the past of any other nation. No special exceptions should be introduced or involved because of the biblical subject matter.[66]

Second, writing a history of Israel without some reliance on the Bible is an impossibility[67] and at best would produce a kind of imaginative chimera.[68] Using the Bible in historiography, however, should not involve extending to it any unusual privilege. The biblical material must be subjected to critical analysis and interrogated as any other ancient text with regard to genre, ideology, and so on.

Third, ancient inscriptions, ever increasing in number and importance, must be subjected to literary-critical analysis before being related to Israelite history. Epigraphic material should be studied initially in its own right, as is done in works like RIMA, RIMB, SAA, and *SAAB*, rather than simply relying upon anthologies like *COS* and *TUAT*.[69] After such study, inscriptional evidence can and should be related to the history of Israel.[70]

Fourth, it should be noted that archaeological and artifactual evidence is in some ways extremely difficult to interpret. Archaeology, in spite of the adamant claims of some archaeologists, is not a scientific discipline.[71] No artifact ever emerges from the ground with a tag attached that stipulates its age and describes its original function. All of these have to be determined through critical judgment—and so often we find simply what we are looking for.[72] The value of most archaeological data lies in their usage to support and illustrate sociocultural factors and background.[73]

Fifth, when external evidence derived from archaeological and/or epigraphic data clashes with evidence derived from the Bible, priority must be given to the nonbiblical data.[74]

Sixth and finally, authors and readers of histories must realize that history-writing is a humanistic and not a scientific enterprise. At best, one's reconstruction of the past in narrative form falls into the category of probability rather than certainty, is more akin to fiction than scientific writing, and is influenced by numerous conscious and unconscious factors.[75] Much of the time, historians simply do their best to immerse themselves in the issues and evidence and then feel their way forward on the basis of intuition.[76]

For Further Reading

Banks, Diane. *Writing the History of Israel*. LHBOTS 438. New York: T&T Clark, 2006.

Barstad, Hans M. *History and the Hebrew Bible*. Tübingen: Mohr Siebeck, 2008.

Davies, Philip. R. *The Origins of Biblical Israel*. LHBOTS 485. London: T&T Clark, 2007.

Finkelstein, Israel, and Amihai Mazar. *The Quest for the Historical Israel: Debating Archaeology and the History of Early Israel: Invited Lectures Delivered at the Sixth Biennial Colloquium of the International Institute for Secular Humanistic Judaism, Detroit, October 2005*. Edited by Brian B. Schmidt. SBLABS 17. Atlanta: Society of Biblical Literature, 2007.

Grabbe, Lester L. *Ancient Israel: What Do We Know and How Do We Know It?* London: T&T Clark, 2007.

Hayes, John H., and J. Maxwell Miller, eds. *Israelite and Judaean History*. OTL. Philadelphia: Westminster, 1977.

Kofoed, Jens. B. *Text and History: Historiography and the Study of The Biblical Text*. Winona Lake, Ind.: Eisenbrauns, 2005.

Lemche, Niels P. *The Old Testament between Theology and History: A Critical Survey*. Louisville: Westminster John Knox, 2008.

Liverani, Mario. *Israel's History and the History of Israel*. London: Equinox, 2005.

Miller, J. Maxwell. "Israel's Past: Our 'Best Guess Scenario.'" Pages 9–22 in *Israel's Prophets and Israel's Past: Essays on the Relationship of Prophetic Texts and Israelite History in Honor of John H. Hayes*. Edited by Brad E. Kelle and Megan B. Moore. LHBOTS 446. London: T&T Clark, 2006.

Miller, J. Maxwell, and John H. Hayes. *A History of Ancient Israel and Judah*. 2nd. ed. Louisville: Westminster John Knox, 2006.

Moore, Megan B. *Philosophy and Practice in Writing a History of Ancient Israel*. LHBOTS 435. London: T&T Clark, 2006.

Rogerson, John W. "Writing the History of Israel in the 17th and 18th Centuries." Pages 217–27 in *The Scriptures and the Scrolls: Studies in Honour of A. S. van der Woude on the Occasion of His 65th Birthday*. Edited by F. García Martínez, A. Hilhorst, and C. J. Labuschagne. Leiden: Brill, 1992.

Williamson, H. G. M., ed. *Understanding the History of Ancient Israel*. Proceedings of the British Academy 143. Oxford: Oxford University Press, 2007.

Notes

1. George Sale et al., *An Universal History: From the Earliest Account of Time to the Present* (23 vols.; London: Batley, 1736–1765). The publishing history of the volumes is discussed in Guido Abbattista, "The Business of Paternoster Row: Towards a

Publishing History of the *Universal History* (1736–65)," *Publishing History* 17 (1985): 5–50. The work was translated into French and German. For a general background to the period from which this work derives, in terms of biblical history, see John W. Rogerson, "Writing the History of Israel in the 17th and 18th Centuries," in *The Scriptures and the Scrolls: Studies in Honour of A. S. van der Woude on the Occasion of His 65th Birthday* (ed. F. García Martínez, A. Hilhorst, and C. J. Labuschagne; Leiden: Brill, 1992), 217–27.

2. The movement had its beginnings in the 1670s. See Basil Willey, *The Eighteenth Century Background: Studies on the Idea of Nature in the Thought of the Period* (London: Chatto & Windus, 1940), 1–56; idem, introduction to *The Sacred Theory of the Earth*, by Thomas Burnett (Carbondale: University of Southern Illinois Press, 1965), 5–9; Don C. Allen, *The Legend of Noah: Renaissance Rationalism in Art, Science, and Letters* (Illinois Studies in Language and Literature 33; Urbana: University of Illinois Press, 1949); and Jonathan I. Israel, *Radical Enlightenment: Philosophy and the Making of Modernity 1650–1750* (Oxford: Oxford University Press, 2001), 456–64. See also Nigel M. de S. Cameron, "Interpreting Genesis in Light of Science," in idem, *Biblical Higher Criticism and the Defense of Infallibilism in 19th Century Britain* (Lewiston, N.Y.; Mellen, 1987), 290–318.

3. Burnett, *Sacred Theory*, 408. Divine and/or authorial accommodation to the level of human understanding had long been a useful hermeneutical device. See Stephen D. Benin, *The Footprints of God: Divine Accommodation in Jewish and Christian Thought* (Albany: State University of New York Press, 1993).

4. See Kenneth J. Howell, *God's Two Books: Copernican Cosmology and Biblical Interpretation in Early Modern Science* (Notre Dame, Ind.: University of Notre Dame Press, 2002).

5. See Marijke H. de Lang, "De opkomst van de historische en literaire kritiek in de synoptische beschouwing van de evangeliën van Calvijn (1555) tot Griesbach (1774)" (Ph.D. diss., Leiden University, 1993), with English summary (293–97); idem, "Gospel Synopses from the 16th to the 18th Centuries and the Rise of Literary Criticism of the *Gospels*," in *The Synoptic Gospels: Source Criticism and the New Literary Criticism* (ed. C. Focant and F. Neirynck; BETL 110; Leuven: Leuven University Press, 1993), 599–607. Earlier harmonies are discussed in Christoph Burger, A. A. den Hollander, and Ulrich Schmid, *Evangelienharmonien des Mittelalters* (Assen: Van Gorcum, 2004). See also Dieter Wünsch, "Evangelienharmonie," *TRE* 10:626–36.

6. For a list of these, see John Wilkins, *Ecclesiastes: Or, a Discourse Concerning the Gift of Preaching as It Falls Under the Rules of Art* (9th ed.; 1646; repr., London: Churchill & Lawrence, 1718), 92–94. For an example of the latter in English translation, published in 1633–1641 and written by a Dutch Jew, see Manasseh ben Israel, *The Conciliator of R. Manasseh ben Israel: A Reconcilement of the Apparent Contradictions in Holy Scripture, to Which Are Added Explanatory Notes and Biographical Notices of the Quoted Authorities* (ed. and trans. E. H. Lindo; 2 vols.; 1842; repr., New York: Hermon, 1972).

7. Much of the biblical material and its traditional interpretation had been challenged, questioned, and even ridiculed in the seventeenth and eighteenth centuries by what were considered holders of radical views. Among these were La Peyrère

(1592–1676), Hobbes (1586–1679), Spinoza (1632–1677), Bayle (1647–1706), Voltaire (1694–1778), and a host of their less-illustrious co- travelers among the deists, such as Toland (1670–1722), Morgan (d. 1743), Annet (1693–1769), and Reimarus (1694–1768).

8. Wilhelm M. L. de Wette, *Dissertatio critico-exegetica qua Deuteronomium a prioribus Pentateuchi libris diversiem alius cuiusdam recentioris auctoris opus esse monstratur* (Jena: Etzdorf, 1805). In this work, he argued that Deuteronomy was written after the other pentateuchal materials. In a footnote, he suggested that Deuteronomy was probably the law book discovered in the temple in conjunction with Josiah's reform. For earlier persons who had already made the latter point, see M. J. Paul, "Hilkiah and the Law (2 Kings 22) in the 17th and 18th Centuries: Some Influences on W. M. L. de Wette," in *Das Deuteronomium: Enstehung, Gestalt und Botschaft* (ed. N. Lohfink; BETL 68; Leuven: Leuven University Press, 1985), 9–12.

9. Wilhelm M. L. de Wette, *Beiträge zur Einleitung in das Alte Testament* (2 vols.; Halle: Schimmelpfenning, 1806–1807). The first volume bore the subtitle *Kritischer Versuch über die Glaubwürdigkeit der Bücher Chronik mit Hinsicht auf die Geschichte der mosaischen Bücher und Gesetzgebung: Ein Nachtrag zu den vaterschen Untersuchungen über den Pentateuch.* In this work, he concluded that the books of 1–2 Chronicles were basically worthless in any attempt to reconstruct the history of Israel and Israelite religion. The second of these contributions bore the subtitle *Kritik der israelitischen Geschichte: Erster Theil, Kritik der mosaischen Geschichte.* Some of the same issues discussed in this volume were also treated in his *Auffoderung zum Studium der hebräischen Sprache und Litteratur: Zur Eröffnung seiner Vorlesungen* (Jena: Gabler, 1805).

10. On de Wette and the reconstruction of Israelite history, see M. Patrick Graham, *The Utilization of 1 and 2 Chronicles in the Reconstruction of Israelite History in the Nineteenth Century* (SBLDS 116; Atlanta: Scholars Press, 1990), 1–34; Thomas A. Howard, *Religion and the Rise of Historicism: W. M. L. de Wette, Jacob Burckhardt, and the Theological Origins of Nineteenth-Century Historical Consciousness* (Cambridge: Cambridge University Press, 2000); and David S. Katz, *God's Last Words: Reading the English Bible from the Reformation to Fundamentalism* (New Haven: Yale University Press, 2004), 221–28. For recent treatments of de Wette, see Hans-Peter Mathys and Klaus Seybold, eds., *Wilhelm Martin Leberecht de Wette: Ein Universaltheologe des 19. Jahrhunderts* (Studien zur Geschichte der Wissenschaften in Basel 1; Basil: Schwabe, 2001); John W. Rogerson, *DMBI*, 355–58; Rudolf Smend, *From Astruc to Zimmerli: Old Testament Scholarship in Three Centuries* (Tübingen: Mohr Siebeck, 2007), 43–56.

11. See Christian Hartlich and Walter Sachs, *Der Ursprung des Mythosbegriffes in der modernen Bibelwissenschaft* (Schriften der Studiengemeinschaft der evangelischen Akademien 2; Tübingen: Mohr Siebeck, 1952), which offers a survey from Robert Lowth to David F. Strauss.

12. Quoted from John W. Rogerson, *W. M. L. de Wette, Founder of Modern Biblical Criticism: An Intellectual Biography* (JSOTSup 126; Sheffield: Sheffield Academic Press, 1992), 47.

13. See Katz, *God's Last Words*, 221–23. Several of de Wette's works were trans-

lated into English by New England divines. Theodore Parker's (1810–1860) expansion and translation of de Wette's Old Testament introduction (*A Critical and Historical Introduction to the Canonical Scriptures of the Old Testament* [2 vols.; Boston: Little & Brown, 1843]) went through four editions by 1867. De Wette's influence can be seen in the articles contained in the New England *Scriptural Interpreter* published between 1831 and 1836. His stepson, Karl Beck, even taught at Harvard. See Siegfried B. Puknat, "De Wette in New England," *Proceedings of the American Philosophical Society* 102 (1958): 376–95. For contemporary assessments of de Wette, as well as other European scholars, see the articles by Samuel Osgood in *Christian Examiner and General Review* 24 (1838): 137–71; 25 (1838): 1–23; 29 (1840): 153–74; 30 (1841): 145–73; and 35 (1842): 303–11. Thus, for a time at least, New England was more open to continental influence than was Old England.

14. De Wette, *Critical and Historical Introduction*, 2:36–37.

15. De Wette, *Beiträge zur Einleitung*, 2:52; quoted from Rogerson, *W. M. L. de Wette*, 54.

16. Smend, *From Astruc to Zimmerli*, 47.

17. Rudolf Smend, "Nachkritische Schriftauslegung," in *Parrhesia: Karl Barth zum achtzigsten Geburtstag, am 10. Mai 1966* (ed. Eberhard Busch, Jürgen Fangmeier und Max Geiger; Zürich: EVZ, 1966), 215–37, quotation from 237; most recently reprinted in Smend's *Bibel und Wissenschaft: Historische Aufsätze* (Tübingen: Mohr Siebeck, 2004), 230–50. English translation of this section is from John Barton, *The Nature of Biblical Criticism* (Louisville: Westminster John Knox, 2007), 91.

18. Wilhelm M. L. de Wette, *Lehrbuch der hebräisch-jüdischen Archäologie nebst einem Grundrisse der hebräisch-jüdischen Geschichte* (Leipzig: Vogel, 1814).

19. John W. Rogerson, *Old Testament Criticism in the Nineteenth Century: England and Germany* (Philadelphia: Fortress, 1984), 29.

20. Georg Iggers, "Historicism: The History and Meaning of the Term," *Journal of the History of Ideas* 56 (1995): 129–52. See also Friedrich Meinecke, *Historicism: The Rise of a New Historical Outlook* (New York: Herder & Herder, 1972).

21. On Troeltsch, see most recently Roy A. Harrisville and Walter Sundberg, "Ernst Troeltsch: The Power of Historical Consciousness," in their *The Bible in Modern Culture: Theology and Historical-Critical Method from Spinoza to Käsemann* (Grand Rapids: Eerdmans, 1995), 155–79; and Mark D. Chapman, *Ernst Troeltsch and Liberal Theology: Religion and Cultural Synthesis in Wilhelmine Germany* (Oxford: Oxford University Press, 2001).

22. *ERE* 6:718, reprinted in John Macquarrie, *Contemporary Religious Thinkers from Idealist Metaphysicians to Existential Theologians* (New York: Harper & Row, 1968), 76–97.

23. Van A. Harvey, *The Historian and the Believer: The Morality of Historical Knowledge and Christian Belief* (New York: Macmillan, 1966), 14–15.

24. For the Old Testament, see Rogerson, *Old Testament Criticism in the Nineteenth Century*; for the New Testament, see William Baird, *History of New Testament Research* (2 vols.; vol. 1: *From Deism to Tübingen*; vol. 2: *From Jonathan Edwards to Rudolf Bultmann*; Minneapolis: Fortress, 1992, 2003).

25. Quoted in Arthur P. Stanley, ed., *The Life and Correspondence of Thomas*

Arnold, D.D., Late Headmaster of Rugby School and Regius Professor of Modern History in the University of Oxford (2 vols.; New York: Scribner's, 1844), 1:355.

26. Arthur P. Stanley, *Lectures on the History of the Jewish Church, Part One: Abraham to Samuel* (New York: Scribner's, 1863), viii–ix.

27. See Rudolf Smend, *Julius Wellhausen: Ein Bahnbrecher in drei Disziplinen* (Munich: Siemens, 2006); idem, *From Astruc to Zimmerli*, 91–102; John C. O'Neill, *The Bible's Authority: A Portrait Gallery of Thinkers from Lessing to Bultmann* (Edinburgh: T&T Clark, 1991), 198–213; Ronald E. Clements, *DMBI*, 130–34; and John H. Hayes, "Wellhausen as a Historian of Israel," *Semeia* 25 (1983): 37–60.

28. Julius Wellhausen, *Geschichte Israels in zwei Bänden: Erster Band* (Berlin: Reimer, 1878). The slightly revised second edition of this first volume (the second volume never appeared) was later published as *Prolegomena zur Geschichte Israels* (Berlin: Reimer, 1883) and was translated into English with a preface by W. Robertson Smith as *Prolegomena to the History of Israel* (Edinburgh: A&C Black, 1885). For Wellhausen's summation of earlier research, see his "Pentateuch and Joshua," *Encyclopedia Britannica* (9th ed.) 18:505–14, one of the finest of his essays but one seldom noted in English-language research.

29. *JDT* 21 (1876): 392–450, 531–602; 22 (1877): 407–79. These were later published together in Julius Wellhausen, *Die Composition des Hexateuchs und der historischen Bücher des Alten Testaments* (Berlin: Reimer, 1885). See also his *Der Text der Bücher Samuelis* (Göttingen: Vandenhoeck & Ruprecht, 1871).

30. In a letter to Abraham Kuenen (1828–1891), dated 5 August 1878, Wellhausen wrote: "Mein Ideal in allen Stücken ist Theodor Mommsen [1817–1903]" [My ideal in every detail is Theodor Mommsen].

31. See his "Israel," *Encyclopedia Britannica* (9th ed.) 13:396–431; reprinted in the English version of his *Prolegomena*, 427–548; and his later *Geschichte der christlichen Religion, mit Einleitung: Die israelitisch-jüdische Religion* (Berlin: Reimer, 1894).

32. See R. J. Thompson, *Moses and the Law in a Century of Criticism since Graf* (VTSup 19; Leiden: Brill, 1970).

33. See Thomas W. Davis, *Shifting Sands: The Rise and Fall of Biblical Archaeology* (Oxford: Oxford University Press, 2004); and Peter R. S. Moorey, *A Century of Biblical Archaeology* (Louisville: Westminster John Knox, 1991).

34. See the works of Archibald H. Sayce (1845–1933), especially *Fresh Light from the Ancient Monuments: A Sketch of the Most Striking Confirmations of the Bible from Recent Discoveries in Egypt, Palestine, Assyria, Babylonia, Asia Minor* (By-Paths of Bible Knowledge 2; London: Religious Tract Society, 1883); and William F. Albright, "Biblical Archaeology Confronts Biblical Criticism," *American Scholar* 7 (1938): 176–88.

35. See George Smith, *The Chaldean Account of Genesis* (London: Thomas Scott, 1875).

36. See most recently, with bibliography, Hermann Gunkel, *Israel and Babylon: The Babylonian Influence on Israelite Religion* (ed. and trans. K. C. Hanson; Eugene, Ore.: Cascade, 2009).

37. George Smith, *The Assyrian Eponym Canon* (London: Bagster, 1875).

38. See Philip J. King and Lawrence E. Stager, *Life in Biblical Israel* (Library of Ancient Israel; Louisville: Westminster John Knox, 2001).

39. See J. Maxwell Miller, "The Israelite Occupation of Canaan," in *Israelite and Judaean History* (ed. John H. Hayes and J. Maxwell Miller; OTL; Philadelphia: Westminster, 1977), 213–84; and William G. Dever, "Israel, History of (Archaeology and the Israelite 'Conquest')," *ABD* 3:454–58.

40. On Alt, see Rudolf Smend, "Albrecht Alt, 1883–1956," *ZTK* 81 (1984): 286–321; idem, *From Astruc to Zimmerli*, 132–56; and Roy L. Heller, *DMBI*, 114–18.

41. On Albright, see Gus W. Van Beek, ed., *The Scholarship of William Foxwell Albright: An Appraisal* (Atlanta: Scholars Press, 1989); *Celebrating and Examining W. F. Albright*, *BA* special issue 56 (1993); *The House That Albright Built*, *NEA* special issue 65 (2002); and Peter D. Feinman, *William Foxwell Albright and the Origins of Biblical Archaeology* (Berrien Springs, Mich.: Andrews University Press, 2004).

42. John Bright sought to distinguish the differences in approach in his *Early Israel in Recent History Writing: A Study in Method* (SBT 19; London: SCM, 1956).

43. See John Van Seters, *The Pentateuch: A Social-Science Commentary* (Sheffield: Sheffield Academic Press, 1999) 50–57.

44. Albright, "Biblical Archaeology Confronts Biblical Criticism," 181.

45. See J. Maxwell Miller, "W. F. Albright and Historical Reconstruction," *BA* 42 (1979): 37–47; and Burke O. Long, *Planting and Reaping Albright: Politics, Ideology, and Interpreting the Bible* (University Park: Pennsylvania State University Press, 1997).

46. For Martin Noth's review of John Bright's history, see his "As One Historian to Another," *Int* 15 (1961): 61–66.

47. On Noth, see Steven L. McKenzie and M. Patrick Graham, eds., *The History of Israel's Traditions: The Heritage of Martin Noth* (JSOTSup 182; Sheffield: Sheffield Academic Press, 1994); David W. McCreery, *DMBI*, 776–80; and Smend, *From Astruc to Zimmerli*, 198–211.

48. Two other of Alt's students also wrote comprehensive histories of Israel: Siegfried Herrmann, *Geschichte Israels in alttestamentlicher Zeit* (Munich: Kaiser, 1973); and Herbert Donner, *Geschichte des Volkes Israel und seiner Nachbarn in Grundzügen* (ATD 4; Göttingen: Vandenhoeck & Ruprecht, 1984). Someone once quipped that it would be interesting to know which of the three had the best set of Alt's classroom lecture notes.

49. Martin Noth, *Geschichte Israels* (2nd ed.; Göttingen: Vandenhoeck & Ruprecht, 1954), translated into English as *The History of Israel* (2nd ed.; New York: Harper & Row, 1960).

50. Someone once quipped that Martin Noth was "the Heinrich Ewald (1803–75) of the twentieth century." The allusion was to Wellhausen's remark that, because of the dominance of his questionable theories, Ewald had retarded biblical scholarship by a generation. For Wellhausen on Ewald, see Wellhausen's *Grundrisse zum Alten Testament* (ed. Rudolf Smend; TB 27; Munich: Kaiser, 1965), 120–38.

51. See John H. Hayes, "The Twelve-Tribe Israelite Amphictyony: An Appraisal," *Trinity University Studies in Religion* 10 (1975): 22–36; and, on the history of the issue, A. Graeme Auld, "Amphictyony, Question of," *DOTHB*, 26–32.

52. George Mendenhall, "The Hebrew Conquest of Palestine," *BA* 25 (1962): 66–87.

53. Thomas L. Thompson, *The Historicity of the Patriarchal Narratives: The Quest for the Historical Abraham* (BZAW 113; Berlin: de Gruyter, 1974); and John Van Seters, *Abraham in History and Tradition* (New Haven: Yale University Press, 1975). The impact of these new perspectives can be seen as having some, but mostly marginal, impact on the various editions of Bright's history. See William P. Brown, "Introduction to John Bright's *A History of Israel*" and "An Update in the Search of Israel's History" in John Bright, *A History of Israel* (4th ed.; Louisville: Westminster John Knox, 2000), 1–22, 465–85.

54. William G. Dever, *Archaeology and Biblical Studies: Retrospects and Prospects* (Evanston, Ill.: Seabury-Western Seminary Press, 1974).

55. Hayes and Miller, *Israelite and Judaean History*.

56. The following books published just during the last five years on methodological issues are noteworthy (in alphabetical order): Diane Banks, *Writing the History of Israel* (LHBOTS 438; London: T&T Clark, 2006); Hans M. Barstad, *History and the Hebrew Bible: Studies in Ancient Israelite and Ancient Near Eastern Historiography* (FAT; Tübingen: Mohr Siebeck, 2008); Philip R. Davies, *The Origins of Biblical Israel* (LHBOTS 485; London: T&T Clark, 2007); idem, *Memories of Ancient Israel: An Introduction to Biblical History—Ancient and Modern* (Louisville: Westminster John Knox, 2008); Israel Finkelstein and Amihai Mazar, *The Quest for the Historical Israel: Debating Archaeology and the History of Early Israel* (ed. Brian B. Schmidt; SBLABS 17; Atlanta: Society of Biblical Literature, 2007); Lester L. Grabbe, *Ancient Israel: What Do We Know and How Do We Know It?* (London: T&T Clark, 2007); Richard S. Hess, Gerald A. Klingbeil, and Paul J. Ray, Jr., eds., *Critical Issues in Early Israelite History* (Winona Lake, Ind.: Eisenbrauns, 2008); Jens B. Kofoed, *Text and History: Historiography and the Study of the Biblical Text* (Winona Lake, Ind.: Eisenbrauns, 2005); Niels P. Lemche, *The Old Testament between Theology and History: A Critical Survey* (Louisville: Westminster John Knox, 2008); Mario Liverani, *Israel's History and the History of Israel* (London: Equinox, 2005); idem, ed., *Recenti tendenze nella ricostruzione della storia antica d'Israele* (Contributi del Centro Linceo Interdisciplinare 'Beniamino Segre' 110; Rome: Accademia Nationale dei Lincei, 2005); Megan B. Moore, *Philosophy and Practice in Writing a History of Ancient Israel* (LHBOTS 435; London: T&T Clark, 2006); and H. G. M. Williamson, ed., *Understanding the History of Ancient Israel* (Proceedings of the British Academy 143; Oxford: Oxford University Press, 2007).

57. The Society of Biblical Literature will publish English translations of all of the Biblische Enzyklopädie volumes.

58. See Robert D. Miller, "Quest of the Historical Israel," *DOTHB*, 830–37; and Ziony Zevit, *The Religions of Ancient Israel: A Synthesis of Parallactic Approaches* (London: Continuum, 2000), 1–80. Here we bypass the important arguments of postmodernism, some of whose advocates claim that we should forgo the attempt to produce comprehensive narratives about past events. For a brief discussion, see the essay by Martti Nissinen in this volume.

59. It is not by accident that one of the biggest best-sellers on the Bible of all times is Werner Keller, *The Bible as History: A Confirmation of the Book of Books* (New York: Morrow, 1956).

60. Walter C. Kaiser Jr., *A History of Israel: From the Bronze Age through the*

Jewish Wars (Nashville: Broadman & Holman, 1998).

61. Iain W. Provan, V. Philips Long, and Tremper Longman III, *A Biblical History of Israel* (Louisville: Westminster John Knox, 2003).

62. Significant works in initiating this discussion were Giovanni Garbini, *History and Ideology in Ancient Israel* (trans. J. Bowden; London: SCM, 1988); and Philip R. Davies, *In Search of "Ancient Israel"* (JSOTSup 148; Sheffield: JSOT Press, 1992).

63. Whether or not the case has been made that biblical historiographic material is very late and largely unreliable is another matter. Those like Niels Lemche who assert that the Hebrew Bible is a Hellenistic or Roman-age document ("The Old Testament: A Hellenistic Book?" *JSOT* 7 [1993]: 163–93) should read the writings of Lorenzo Valla (1407–1457) (*The Treatise of Lorenzo Valla on the Donation of Constantine* [ed. and trans. C. B. Coleman; Toronto: University of Toronto Press, 1993]) and Richard Bentley (1662–1742) (*A Dissertation upon the Epistles of Phalaris* [London: Mortlock, 1699]) to see how historical philology is used to date documents.

64. Israel Finkelstein and Neil Asher Silberman, *The Bible Unearthed: Archaeology's New Vision of Ancient Israel and the Origin of Its Sacred Texts* (New York: Free Press, 2001).

65. For the most recent critique of this exaggerated view of King Josiah, see Davies, *The Origins of Biblical Israel*, 151–55.

66. "Historically speaking, there is no such thing as a chosen people, only people who believe and claim themselves to be chosen" (Anonymous).

67. See J. Maxwell Miller, "Is It Possible to Write a History of Israel without Relying on the Hebrew Bible?" in *The Fabric of History: Text, Artifact and Israel's Past* (ed. Diana V. Edelman; JSOTSup 127; Sheffield: JSOT Press, 1991), 93–102; and H. G. M. Williamson, "The Origins of Israel: Can We Safely Ignore the Bible?" in *The Origin of Early Israel—Current Debate: Biblical, Historical and Archaeological Perspectives* (ed. Shmuel Ahituv and Eliezar D. Oren; Beer-Sheva 12; Beer-Sheva: Ben Gurion University of Negev Press, 1998), 141–51.

68. Keith Whitelam's goal of writing a history of Palestine is to be commended, but "Palestine" is as, if not more, ambivalent and anachronistic a concept than "Israel." Most recently, see his "Setting the Scene: A Response to John Rogerson," in Williamson, *Understanding the History of Ancient Israel*, 15–23. The same goes for any attempt to write a history of Israel along the lines of some controlling anthropological or sociological paradigm. The statement and restatement of a particular theory or method do not in themselves constitute historical evidence. This has often been a criticism of Norman K. Gottwald's *The Tribes of Yahweh: A Sociology of the Religion of Liberated Israel, 1250–1050 B.C.E.* (Maryknoll, N.Y.: Orbis, 1979).

69. Assyriologists are fallible and occasionally misread and sometimes misinterpret texts.

70. Two fine examples of such work are Jeffrey K. Kuan, *Neo-Assyrian Historical Inscriptions and Syria-Palestine: Israelite/Judean-Tyrian-Damascene Political and Commercial Relations in the Ninth-Eighth Centuries B.C.E.* (Hong Kong: Alliance Bible Seminary, 1995); and Mordechai Cogan, *The Raging Torrent: Historical Inscriptions from Assyria and Babylonia Relating to Ancient Israel* (Jerusalem: Carta, 2008). Oddly,

in spite of their excellence in other respects, neither Kenton Sparks (*Ancient Texts for the Study of the Hebrew Bible: A Guide to the Background Literature* [Peabody, Mass.: Hendrickson, 2005]) nor Lester Grabbe (*Ancient Israel*) makes any reference to the Assyrian *limmu* lists, which are the most reliable of all the Assyrian historical sources. On these, see Kuan, *Neo-Assyrian Historical Inscriptions*, 7–22.

71. "Nothing can destroy your confidence in archaeological research like participation in an excavation" (Anonymous). On some of the problems involved in interpreting archaeological finds, see Anson F. Rainey, "Stones for Bread: Archaeology Versus History," *NEA* 64 (2001): 140–49.

72. See Edward L. Greenstein, "Theory and Argument in Biblical Criticism," *HAR* 10 (1986): 77–93.

73. So already Robert A. S. MacAlister, *A Century of Excavation in Palestine* (London: Religious Tract Society, 1925), 266–67.

74. So already George Mendenhall: "Unless biblical history is to be relegated to the domain of unreality and myth, the biblical and the archaeological must be correlated. Methodologically, the archaeological documents, especially the written ones, must be given priority and considered seriously" (*The Tenth Generation: The Origins of the Biblical Tradition* [Baltimore: Johns Hopkins University Press, 1973], 142). An example of this type of clash can be seen in the differences between 2 Kings and the Tel Dan inscription over who killed Kings Jehoram and Ahaziah. On this topic, see J. Maxwell Miller and John H. Hayes, *A History of Ancient Israel and Judah* (2nd ed.; Louisville: Westminster John Knox, 2006), 324–25, nn. 29–30.

75. See, for example, Hayden V. White, *Metahistory: The Historical Imagination in Nineteenth-Century Europe* (Baltimore, Md.: Johns Hopkins University Press, 1973); and Jack M. Sasson, "On Choosing Models for Recreating Israelite Pre-Monarchical History," *JSOT* 21 (1981): 3–24.

76. See J. Maxwell Miller, "Israel's Past: Our 'Best Guess Scenario,'" in *Israel's Prophets and Israel's Past: Essays on the Relationship of Prophetic Texts and Israelite History in Honor of John H. Hayes* (ed. Brad E. Kelle and Megan B. Moore; LHBOTS 446; London: T&T Clark, 2006), 9–22.

Many thanks go to Travis Bott for his assistance in preparing this manuscript for publication.

Psychological Criticism: Exploring the Self in the Text*

Walter Brueggemann

Introduction

From the beginning, the human self has been a compelling enigma for the community that produced the Bible. Ancient Israel regularly asked, in narrative and liturgical texts, "What are human beings?" (Ps 8:4). Of equal importance, they asked the question with the accompanying phrase, "that you are mindful of them?"[1] The question—as well as the answer—is a theological one: the community addresses the question of the self by means of the defining reality of God. While they gave many answers to that question, Ps 139 seems the most appropriate response to the question "What is a human?"

> For it was you who formed my inward parts;
>   you knit me together in my mother's womb.
> I praise you, for I am fearfully and wonderfully made.
>   Wonderful are your works;
> that I know very well.
>   My frame was not hidden from you,
> when I was being made in secret,
>   intricately woven in the depths of the earth.
> Your eyes beheld my unformed substance.
> In your book were written
>   all the days that were formed for me,
>   when none of them as yet existed. (Ps 139:13–16)

* I am glad to join in salute to a valued colleague, David Petersen, from whom I have learned much and by whom I am always instructed.

Verse 14 exhibits a two-fold response to the question, What is the self? On the one hand, it is a response about the self: "I am fearfully and wonderfully made." But on the other hand, the lead-in phrase is indispensable: "I praise you." The self, in the horizon of this community, is always, everywhere referred to the defining reality of God, and the self cannot be pondered apart from God. Thus the question of Ps 8:4 and the affirmative response of Ps 139:13–16 situate the discussion of the self in the presence of God in a way that makes the question of the self an inescapably theological one.

From that theological beginning point, scholarship has been able to discern that in the Bible the human self is presented as unitary, communal, and situated in worldly vulnerability and contingency in the presence of God.[2] Thus the following obtain. (1) The self is a single unitary agent; there is no notion of mind-body dualism. (2) The self is a member of a community and never an isolated or self-sufficient entity. (3) As both vulnerable and powerful, the human self lives in a drama set between life and death, strength and weakness. The human self waxes and wanes as the gifts of life are given or withheld, received or resisted. (4) The self is mortal and finite and subject to the vagaries of the historical process. Death is the edge of human existence, and all the rest is left to the rule of God. This "history-situated self" is thus called to freedom and responsibility in the finite zone where God has placed the self in community.

Models of Psychological Criticism

Given the centrality of "the self" in the imagination of the community that produced the biblical text, it is quite remarkable that critical study of the self in the text, that is, "psychological criticism," has not, in the modern critical era, been able to arrive at a consensus with regard to its method of study nor even a consensus of perspective on the question.[3] In this regard, psychological approaches to critical study of the biblical text are unlike other critical approaches. The characteristic way of critical study of the Bible is to appropriate a working method from critical scholarship in another field, then to apply that method, with necessary adjustments, to the biblical text. Such appropriation and adjustment enable critics to read the Bible "like any other book." Thus historical criticism has taken over the methods of positivistic history. Social-scientific criticism has in recent time utilized the methods of sociology and anthropological scholarship, and rhetorical criticism has followed the broad outlines of classical reading.

Perhaps psychological criticism of the Bible has not been able to agree on method or perspective precisely because the available methods from the field of psychology are quite varied, each approach following the daring work of a leading theorist. Thus the formation of "schools" of interpretation (e.g., Freudianism, Jungianism, ego psychology, object relations theory) is much more varied than we would find in historical, social-scientific, or rhetorical studies, and that difference is reflected in the interpretive practices of biblical scholars.[4] A review of the rich literature of recent decades, led most notably by Wayne Rollins, exhibits an immense plurality of practices in which numerous studies appeal to a wide variety of models and authorities in the field.[5]

In what follows, I will reflect briefly on the founding models of Sigmund Freud and Carl Jung. Then, as others have done, I will appeal to the theoretical basis that seems most congruent with the texts themselves. In moving from theory to textual specificity, we do well to remember David Jobling's caution that scholars are often tempted to let the power of the theory override the concreteness of the text itself. Jobling comments on David J. Halperin's *Seeing Ezekiel: Text and Psychology* (1993):[6]

> I must go on to say that this book is out of touch with recent work on the psychological reading of texts, including biblical ones, and was so even at the time he published it. His aim, it seems, is to put on the couch and diagnose a real human being, Ezekiel. He simply assumes that the text of the book of Ezekiel will provide everything necessary to accomplish this task. But a great deal of history and, even more importantly, a great deal of *textuality* lie between us and "Ezekiel," a hypothetical person whose very existence has often been called into question. What is available for our analysis is a text, and texts are anything but transparent windows on their subject matter. In this case, moreover, we are dealing with an *ancient* text and a religiously *canonized* text. None of this need ultimately invalidate Halperin's findings, but it necessitates at least a significant reframing of them.[7]

Jobling's stricture is more broadly pertinent. There is a danger, in the eclectic enterprise of psychological criticism, to impose a psychological theory on the text in a way that overrides the specificity of the text itself and that distorts the text in order to serve the theory that an interpreter may advocate. Such a problem may be a temptation for every critical method—including imposing questions of historicity on texts!—but it is a temptation that seems peculiarly pertinent to psychological approaches.

Thus while theoretical reference points are important, in the end such criticism serves well only if it permits us to read and hear the text more discerningly. My judgment is that, while biblical scholars have a wide array of resources available from this perspective, psychological criticism is still very much in its formative period and has reached neither a maturity nor a sophistication that can claim the wide engagement of scholars. We may be grateful for the bold scholars who have made these fresh beginnings in methodological exploration, but much more disciplined work remains to be done before wide assent to method can be achieved. Perhaps such an eclectic practice is inevitable, given the quite eclectic and disputatious field of personality theory in general. In the next section, I will consider the contributions of the towering figures of Freud and Jung, reflect on what I take as the most helpful interface in method among current options, and offer a textual exemplar from that perspective.

A New Era of Psychological Theory: Sigmund Freud and Carl Jung

Any proper understanding of psychological theory that may be appropriated for critical biblical study must, of course, begin where the modern study of the self begins, with Sigmund Freud and his ally and then rival, Carl Jung.

Sigmund Freud dramatically begins a new era of "the psychological." To be sure, he had antecedents, but his work is a breakthrough of stunning proportion that has become the source of all that follows, even among those who depart from him or who repudiate his categories. He sought to situate the study of the self in scientific modes. For all his effort at the scientific, however, we may notice two dimensions of his work that defy the scientific. First, his shaping categories derive from foundational cultural myths that he handles imaginatively and artistically. Second, he makes clear that, for all of the objective data he offers, his own continued struggle for identity and his negotiation between Jewish legacy and Viennese culture are quite personal, defining issues for him. Freud's understanding of the psychological in modern culture is a larger-than-life personal assertion that refuses any surface reading of reality—either social or personal reality or *textual* reality. We may identify four dimensions of his work that pertain to our study.

First, Freud recognized and articulated the multifaceted reality of the human self, its thickness, complexity, and conflictedness that needs to be processed but could not even be fully resolved. His particular naming of that thick complexity as *super-ego*, *ego*, and *id* has, of course, become the assumed vocabulary of subsequent culture, both critical and popular. Freud saw, moreover, that the conflictedness remained largely hidden, because a surface equanimity is essential to managing membership in a stable (Viennese!) society. What Freud saw of selves in their thickness he also knew about texts.

Second, Freud understood the complexity and conflictedness of the self in a powerful, defining intrapersonal reality. But he also knew very well that the conflicted self does not exist in a vacuum. In fact, it has its conflictedness imposed and insisted upon by a demanding and enforcing civilization. Thus Freud's work, while particularly concerned with the personal, actually constitutes a mapping of social conformity and social dissent in a society that cannot tolerate resistance or dissent.[8] Therefore the health and emancipation of the conflicted self poses a threat to an ordered society and perhaps provides an antidote as well to a society ordered in repressive and unhealthy ways. It is on this count that Freud can appeal to the great cultural myths (e.g., Oedipus), because those myths are narrative accounts of power arrangements between society and persons in society.

Third, Freud could not have done without religion. To be sure, at a formal level he is dismissive of religion as an "illusion."[9] Given that declaration, however, both the religious dimension of his nineteenth-century context and his own legacy as a Jew made it inevitable that he would regard the human self in religious categories. While the reduction of super-ego to social coercion dismissed the reality of God from the equation (a reduction Freud himself urged), nevertheless Freud could not escape the force of hiddenness and otherness that required symbolic articulation. As a nineteenth-century "scientist," he could not go further; however, in not going further, Freud allowed for the surging of mystery beyond human control that he located in the "unconscious." As Wayne Rollins reports, Freud himself attests to a remarkable sensation upon entering Notre Dame Cathedral and seeing Michelangelo's Moses, a sensation that surely moves into the direction of the religious.[10] It is clear that Freud was dismissive of any conventional, institutional practice or formulation of religion; he was not, however, dismissive of the reality of "other" that was beyond explanatory category.[11] Thus alongside his "scientific" commitments, the reality of "thickness" was available to him, even if in his own odd categories.

Fourth, the conflicted self, the dissent from conventional civilization, and the sensation of the holy all move to a final accent, namely, that Freud stands in the interpretive tradition of rabbinic Judaism. Freud is, in the end, an interpreter of the depth of the self, even as he probed into the depth of the text.

I am indebted to a remarkable study by Susan Handelman that makes a compelling case that Freud stands in continuity with the exegetical methods and interpretive assumptions of rabbinic Judaism.[12] Freud's work, like that of the rabbis, is to read and interpret texts, to find new meanings that displace old meanings, and to assert that the new meanings are not imposed but have been there in the texts all along.

The work of displacement in interpretation was no doubt a way of negotiating between his two cultures, Jewish and Viennese. He was, moreover, at work on rewriting the identity of his father. The mode of interpretation that served these immediate matters was the work of displacing old interpretation through a process of recovery, reconstruction, and reappropriation. Thus *Moses and Monotheism* (which reads like wild, undisciplined speculation) is in fact an exercise in rabbinic interpretation whereby the interpretive act of patricide concerns old father and old interpretation, and the second Moses who displaces the first Egyptian Moses.[13]

Once one recognizes that *Moses and Monotheism* is not and was not intended to be a historical study but an interpretive venture, it is plain to see what Freud is doing. Handelman writes,

> And like the Rabbis, Freud insisted that he was not creating new meanings, only uncovering, like an archaeologist, what lay buried beneath. Everything is connected under the surface; the interpreter's job is to reveal, elucidate, and construct for conscious awareness those hidden unities that contain a core of definite historical truth.
>
> Interpretation is not, in the Aristotelian sense, the distinguishing of truth from falsehood, but the relationship of hidden to shown: not appearance to reality, but manifest to latent. The idiom is disguise, displacement, censorship of the superego. A dream cannot be true or false, but can only have a more or less deep meaning. Everything that logical consciousness rejects as nonsensical, useless, disconnected, contradictory, and impossible has, in fact, a meaning; and to say that dreams indeed have a meaning, Freud recognized, put him in opposition to every ruling theory. As Ricoeur puts it, Freud was the "exegete who rediscovers the logic of the illogical kingdom."[14]

The outcome of such work is the undoing of what was: "With *Moses and Monotheism*, however, the Jewish science reaches both its culmination and its undoing; it undid the Jews as the murderers of Moses; it undid Moses as an Egyptian, and it undid Freud's whole careful scientific façade."[15]

The undoing offers space for new readings and invites a proliferation of meanings; thus texts—like selves, like dreams—have many layered meanings. Freud's interpretation is an act against closed meanings of texts, just as his psychology is an act against closed selves that are so highly valued in conventional society. It is for that reason not a surprise that, Handelman, after her discussion of Freud, goes on to consider Jacques Lacan, Jacques Derrida, and Harold Bloom as practitioners in the Jewish tradition of deconstruction. Old interpretation must be deconstructed in order to find new readings; old selves must be deconstructed to find new selves; old Moses must be deconstructed for the sake of the new Moses. The line from Freud runs straight toward Harold Bloom and the oedipal need to displace the previous articulation by a sequence of "strong readings." Thus Freud's "Jewish method" is an invitation to readers of texts to go beyond the reductionism of closure too often proposed by conventional historical criticism.

Carl Jung is the second great founder of modern psychology and stands alongside Freud, but also over against Freud in important ways. Freud and Jung share a continual engagement with religious questions, both are attentive to the complexity of a conflicted self, and both are laboring in their scholarship to work out their own unresolved relationships with their fathers. Given the commonalities, however, Freud and Jung work very differently about the issues before them. Whereas Freud is inclined to accent disjunctive and pluralistic reality that appeals to Jewish rhetoric of confrontation, Jung reflects his Christian, Protestant nurture in a way that looks for systemic connectedness and accents the big narrative of salvation. Jung's accent is on the revelatory power of imagination, which he utilizes to identify and appropriate "archetypes" that operate in the unconscious, so that we may detect patterns of discernment and order that are reiterated form person to person. It is therefore not surprising that Jung finds evidence in the Bible for archetypes to which the text bears witness. As a result, it is the archetype, not the text, that is decisive for Jung.

I will rely on Wayne Rollins to indicate the key points in Jung's work.[16] (1) Symbols, archetypal images, and myths provide the primary points of inquiry for Jung. (2) Dreams are a primal venue for disclosures about the self. (3) Biblical personalities are studied as models and examples of the struggle for selfhood. (4) Religious phenomena in the biblical texts, mystical, sacramental, and ritual performances provide primary points of interest. (5) Jung paid attention to what he identified as the pathological dimensions of faith that concerned the "dark side" of human reality; this was matched by his interest in the therapeutic dimension of the biblical text. (6) Biblical ethics have a conflicted character. (7) Jung was attentive to the role of the reader and interpreter in rendering the biblical text. (8) Jung focused upon the origin, nature, and destiny of the human soul, so that his work is intrinsically and inescapably religious.

In sum, while Jung is enormously elusive, it is fair to say that he did not share Freud's deepest sense of human pathology. Rather, he understood that the God of the dark side is a heavy force from which the human soul can be freed for its own actualization. However, he also saw religion as a mode of nurture for the soul.[17] It is not difficult to see why Jung, in all of his elusiveness, is an attraction for religious engagement among those who prefer a "softer" sense of the psyche as a religious reality.

Special reference should be made to Jung's *Answer to Job* (1952). The book exhibits Jung's capacity to read the text carefully, but also his readiness to range widely, take in a great deal of territory, and make connections upon which critical scholarship would look askance. Before he finishes the book, Jung probes the role of Mary, the meaning of the incarnation, the importance of Sophia (that tilts toward Gnosticism), and the sweep of apocalyptic vision. For our purposes it is sufficient to see that God, in the book of Job, is presented as contradiction, as divine darkness, as an antinomy, as "total justice and also its total opposite."[18] In his articulation of original sin and salvation through incarnation, Jung clearly thinks in the broad terms of Christian theology, even if he gives that narrative his own idiosyncratic twist. But it is his particular rendering of God and the human psyche that is of note for us. First, against a common view of redemption, he proposes "reparation for a wrong done by God to man."[19] Second, about God's nature, Jung claims, "the paradoxical nature of God … tears him asunder into opposites and delivers him over to a seemingly insoluble conflict."[20] Third, for Jung, the self is by definition always a *complexio oppositorum*, and the more consciousness insists on its light nature and lays claim to moral authority, the more the self will appear as something dark and menacing.[21] The burden of religion constitutes this human predicament of a psyche rent asunder. Jung's response to this predicament is an offer of the "healing of the soul" from the wounding caused by the God of Job.

D. W. Winnicott and Object Relations Theory

After these comments on Freud and Jung concerning our topic of psychological criticism, I move directly to a third theorist, Donald Woods Winnicott. I do so because Winnicott, along with others who have developed object relations theory, seems to me the theorist whose field of perception and practice is most closely aligned with biblical rhetoric and the practice of covenantal living. Winnicott stands in the tradition of Freud, but Freud had understood the complexity of the human self to be an intrapersonal unresolve. Under the influence of Harry Stack Sullivan and Melanie Klein, Winnicott began to see that the unresolved transactions that constitute the self are not within *the person* but are genuine *interactions between persons.*[22] This move, it seems to me, is fundamental for an interface of psychology with the Bible, for the Bible is relentless in its insistence upon genuine interpersonal interaction, most especially interaction with the personal agency of God.[23] In stressing the interpersonal, we are a long way from Freud's internal sense of conflict and from Jung's archetypal analysis that lacks the dynamism of the interpersonal. While Winnicott is dependent upon his antecedents, he, along with other object relations theorists, has moved well beyond them.[24]

Specifically, Winnicott focuses on the earliest interaction between mother and child.[25] He believes that this dyadic interaction is the make-or-break relationship for the health or unhealth of the child. Health for the child (and the adult to come) depends upon a "good enough mother" who is able to give herself over freely and fully to the child, so that the earliest experience of the child is one of omnipotence, the sense that mother (and world) exist for the child at the behest of the child,

> The good-enough mother meets the omnipotence of the infant and to some extent makes sense of it. She does this repeatedly. A True Self begins to have life, through the strength given to the infant's weak ego by the mother's implementation of the infant's omnipotent expressions.… It is an essential part of my theory that the True Self does not become a living reality except as a result of the mother's repeated success in meeting the infant's spontaneous gesture or sensory hallucination.[26]

As the child ages, the mother must withdraw that unconditional attentiveness so that the child can become aware that the mother has a life of her own and does not exist only for the child.

By contrast, an unhealthy child (and adult to come) will result, so concludes Winnicott, if the mother is not "good enough," that is, cannot give her full attentiveness over to the child. There may be many reasons for which the mother may be distracted or inadequate to this role. Whatever the reason, if the mother does not permit and authorize an early sense of omnipotence, the child very soon learns to hide the genuine self and to present a false self to the mother in order to receive the hoped-for responses from the mother:

> The mother who is not good enough is not able to implement the infant's omnipotence, and so she repeatedly fails to meet the infant's gesture; instead she substitutes her own gesture which is to be given sense by the compliance of the infant. Thus compliance on the part of the infant is the earliest stage of the False Self, and belongs to the mother's inability to sense her infant's needs.[27]

When this early transaction fails, the child is set on a course of false self-presentation that is practiced as dishonesty and hiding, so that the True Self is not permitted to become visible. The outcome is a compliant self who lacks "the essential critical element of creative originality."[28]

While Winnicott himself was a man of deep faith, he does not, as with Freud and Jung, deal directly or explicitly with biblical material. That is, with Winnicot we do not have to contend with anything like *Moses and Monotheism* or *Answer to Job*. What we have, rather, is a practitioner who does not impose large mythic themes (as with Freud and Jung) but who pays attention to the concreteness of interaction; he offers the best interface to the biblical characterization of life and self, because the dynamic interaction of mother and child is a close analogue of the dynamic relationship of God and Israel, God and church, God and individual person under the general rubric *covenant*.[29] I am not aware that Winnicott employs such terminology, but clearly he is concerned with a long-term relationship of *fidelity* that is marked by *obligation* and that has *transformative power*. These defining ingredients of covenant—fidelity, obligation, and transformative power—are at the heart of Winnicott's theory.

In the wake of biblical testimony, Winnicott sees that the human person is constituted by a relationship. That relationship is one of mutual self-giving by the mother and eventually by the child, but it is, at the same time, an incommensurate relationship in which the mother is the defining party.[30] *Mutatis mutandis*, the God-other (I-Thou) relationship is, in the same way, mutual and incommensurate, a mutuality that insists on a two-way interaction, an incommensurability that requires the interaction of mutuality to be bold and courageous. It is clear that Winnicott derives his theories from Freud, but his derivative moves are in the direction of an actual relationship, so that not much energy is used on the intrapersonal and almost none at all on large mythic speculation. It all comes down to mother-child, to a relationship in which everything is at stake. The elemental question of Winnicott about the mother in relation to child is closely paralleled to the God of Israel who is "father of orphans" (Ps 68:5) and to the Christian Messiah who "will not leave you orphaned" (John 14:18).[31]

A Test-Case: Psychological Criticism and Psalm 35

From this quick consideration of three theorists, I now approach a specific text as an exercise in "psychological criticism." I will bring to the study of the text from the foregoing an awareness of a conflicted, complex self, a God who functions as complex other (dark and merciful), and the urgency of a noncompliant dialogic exchange with a dialectic of omnipotence and submissiveness. I consider Ps 35, a lament psalm that is a venue for the sounding of many voices.[32]

I focus on a lament psalm because it is clear, given Winnicott's notion of "good enough mother" and the True Self, that Israel in its complaining, protesting addresses to YHWH speaks the voice of a True Self, with nothing to hide or fake or hold back. Lament is an address of honesty by a courageous voice that is free enough even in the face of YHWH. I propose that the lament is an act of omnipotence wherein the speaker assumes an initiative over against God and summons God to action and to accountability.[33] Such lament in Israel precludes excessive self-indulgence by the counterpoint of praise in which Israel repeatedly cedes initiative over to YHWH. It is Israel's capacity for both lament and praise, for claiming and ceding, that makes possible a full, healthy interaction between a True Self and a sovereign God.[34]

Psalm 35 bears all the marks of lament, according to conventional form-critical analysis. First, it features a series of petitions that reflect urgency, addressing YHWH in the imperative mood. Verses 1–3a articulate that urgency in military figures, though the initial verb ("contend," 35:1) might suggest judicial confrontation. The second set of imperative petition is even more insistent (35:22–25). Second, the imperative petitions are matched by imprecations. The hope of the psalmist is that YHWH will not only do good for the speaker but will retaliate against the enemy (35:4–6, 8, 26). Third, the complaint properly characterizes for YHWH the acute jeopardy of the psalmist and the urgency of divine intervention (35:7, 11–12, 19–20). Fourth, the petition, imprecation, and complaint are supported by motivations that declare the innocence and merit of the speaker, reason enough that YHWH should act (35:13–16). The ground for divine help is the entitlement of the speaker who has been faithful and has contributed to the well-being of the community.

This entire sequence of petition, imprecation, motivation, and complaint constitutes a speech addressed to the God of the covenant who has made promises to this Israelite and who has offered sanctions that guarantee succor to those who remain faithfully in the covenant. These several components are characteristic of Israel's speech in its truth-telling mode.

The psalmist is able to articulate—that is, construct and imagine—the ongoing conversation of faith. In this rendition, the psalmist boldly speaks all of the parts to the conversation that is constitutive of faith. The capacity to line out the several elements of the conversation into a narrative whole indicates a healthy, complex self that is in touch with the many voices of the self, each of which is honored and given airtime. The psalm makes overt the ongoing multivoiced conversation of the self and, further, demonstrates that playful imagination is crucial to health and to faith. This is a daring project because the speaker ventures to anticipate what each party in the conversation may say. In the first instant, we may judge that this is an *internal* dialogue; that internal exchange, however, has profound implications for the *external* conversation that is subsequently to be enacted. We may identify five parties to the conversation that make the exchange of faith fruitfully complex. What is remarkable in this psalm is that each voice among the contesting parties is given explicit rendition.

1. The psalm itself is, in the first place, *the voice of the suppliant*. That voice is, of course, the pervasive one, because the entire psalm is on the psalmist's lips. This is faith "from below" in which, for an instant, the petitioner has the upper hand and addresses YHWH in an imperative. In such utterance there is a provisional reversal of roles: the petitioner assumes the role of senior partner in the exchange, and YHWH is summoned to respond. The petitioner dares to instruct and command YHWH.

2. *The second voice to this exchange is that of YHWH*, who is given one line in the psalm. It is not, however, YHWH who speaks. Rather it is the psalmist who proposes what YHWH should say, thus assigning to

God lines in the exchange. After the series of imperatives in 35:1–3a, the psalmist follows with yet one more, the verb "say":

> Say to my soul,
> "I am your salvation." (35:3)

The words assigned to YHWH are, of course, a standard salvation oracle, only not introduced by the customary "fear not." The proposed utterance is an assurance of YHWH's attentiveness and YHWH's presence, YHWH's readiness and capacity to intervene transformatively in the vexed life of the speaker. It is the voice of faith that evokes the divine voice of rescue.[35] The divine response is, of course, not automatic, as is made evident in the poem of Job. It is, however, regularized enough that the psalmist dared count on it and assumed YHWH's readiness to answer petitions. It is also possible to think that the psalm intends to head off and preclude other, less-affirmative divine responses such as those eventually offered by YHWH to Jeremiah and to Job. The psalmist knows the utterance from YHWH that is needed and desired and takes the initiative to assure that YHWH speaks what is needed and not some other word that YHWH could in freedom have uttered. The psalmist prays in uncommon confidence and with daring freedom, with a sense of entitlement that belongs to a covenantal, dialogic life.

3. In 35:9–10, the speaker quotes himself in anticipation of what he will say in the future, after deliverance by YHWH:

> All my bones shall say,
> "O Lord, who is like you?
> You deliver the weak from those too strong for them,
> the weak and needy from those who despoil them." (Ps 35:10)

The anticipated declaration of praise to YHWH is not only to be given in words, not only by mouth, but by "all my bones," his whole being, every part of his delivered life that is now to be postured in doxology. It is, of course, obvious that his anticipated doxology is in total contrast to his present circumstance and present utterance of complaint. The speaker exhibits sufficient self-control and critical distance to imagine a situation and therefore an utterance other than his current one.

4. Claus Westermann has shown that in the psalms of complaint the relationships always form a triangle that includes, along with YHWH and

Israel, the enemy.[36] Of course, it is possible that the psalmist is simply paranoid. But such paranoia is grounded in the awareness that social life is deeply and always contested. The petitioner is at risk and without resources; therefore, everything depends upon the intervention of YHWH that is anticipated but not certain.

Because of that vigorous and threatening contestation in which the petitioner always finds himself, the adversary is given full play in the text. Thus, the psalm itself serves as an arena of contestation. In order to dramatize and underscore the contestation, the adversary is given full voice in the exchange of the psalm.[37] The speaker can imagine what YHWH ought to say and will say in the future. Further, the psalmist can anticipate what he himself will say upon deliverance. So, too, the speaker is also able to imagine what the adversary might say if he were to triumph over the psalmist—a possibility that is only possible if YHWH fails to intervene. The psalmist anticipates that in such triumph the adversary will gloat:

> They open wide their mouths against me;
> they say, "Aha, Aha, our eyes have seen it." (Ps 35:21)

If YHWH does not act to vindicate the psalmist, moreover, the adversaries are sure to gloat even more,

> Do not let them say to themselves,
> "Aha, we have our heart's desire."[38]
> Do not let them say, "We have swallowed you up." (Ps 35:25)

The adversary is given a full say. But it is not the final say!

5. That imagined defeat of the speaker and of YHWH by the adversary, however, is not the anticipated outcome of the dispute that the psalmist commends. Rather, it is anticipated that YHWH will indeed say, "I am your salvation," and will act to make it so. Thus the psalm ends, as do many of the psalms of complaint, with an immense celebration of YHWH's deliverance of the psalmist and the defeat of the adversary. That celebration is enacted by the psalmist in the "formula of incomparability" (35:10). Such deliverance, however, requires more than one voice of praise. The psalmist mobilizes the entire community of those who stand in solidarity with him and who hope for his acquittal (*ṣedeq*, 35:27). All in that company are to exult in the vindication of their friend and so are summoned to praise. The community recognizes, in its doxology, that

YHWH is great, greater than the adversary, greater than any threat or any other deliverer. What constitutes that divine greatness, as already anticipated in the speaker's doxology in 35:10, is that YHWH delights in the *shalom* ("well-being," 35:27) of the speaker, who is reckoned to be among the weak and needy. YHWH not only delights in such *shalom* but also, in fact, effects *shalom* in a circumstance where no such well-being could have been imagined. The end result of the psalm is that the psalmist is restored to *shalom* that only YHWH can give. By entertaining this final voice of doxological celebration, the speaker has spoken (i.e., imagined) the self upon arrival at a new condition of well-being. To be sure, that arrival is an anticipation, but the arrival is nonetheless palpable, made so by allowing yet another voice to speak.

The Self, Faith, and Dialogic Exchange

The psalmist is permitted, since it is his psalm, to manage the dialogue and place the accents where he will. The controlling capacity of the psalmist is evident in three anticipations of praise and thanks to YHWH for saving intervention.

In verse 9, the anticipated formula of incomparability on the lips of the psalmist is stated.

> *Then* my soul shall rejoice in the Lord,
> exulting in his deliverance.

The "then" of the NRSV is only a *waw* conjunction in Hebrew, but it is enough to indicate that praise is withheld from YHWH until rescue and depends upon that rescue.

In verse 18, a parallel statement again withholds thanks until rescue:

> *Then* I will thank you in the great congregation;
> in the mighty throng I will praise you.

Here there is no indication in Hebrew at all of the "then" of the NRSV. Rather, the context justifies the usage of this coordinating adverb. The speaker is the one who will give thanks, even though the thanks in 35:18 is in the midst of the "great congregation." This anticipated thanks is the connecting point between the psalmist's praise in 35:10 and the congregation's praise in 35:27. The psalmist anticipates standing in the midst of the congregation, uttering both thanks and praise: thanks for YHWH's deliverance from this particular threat; and generic praise of YHWH's power to deliver.

In verse 28, the "then" is again a *waw* conjunction in Hebrew.

> *Then* my tongue shall tell you of your righteousness [*ṣedeq*]
> and of your praise all day long. (Ps 35:28)

Praise concerns YHWH's *ṣedeq*, YHWH's capacity to make things right for the speaker.

All three uses of "then" as rendered in NRSV (and I believe rightly informed by the Hebrew) withhold praise and thanks to YHWH until deliverance is granted. In this way, assuming that YHWH desires praise and thanks, YHWH is at the behest of the speaker who is no easy touch but who bargains hard and holds the upper hand in the process. The psalm offers a dialogic exchange in four voices: YHWH, the psalmist, the enemy, and the congregation—or five, if we distinguish between the *present complaining voice* of the psalmist and the *anticipated doxological voice* of the psalmist in time to come. The strategic articulation of the psalm situates the speaker and the faith of the speaker in the midst of a vigorous dialogic contestation, the place where faith is characteristically at risk and at work, the place where dialogic self-hood can arrive at an exercise of omnipotence and responsiveness.

Recovering the Complex, Dialogic Self

The capacity of biblical scholars to practice "psychological criticism" largely depends on appropriation of available personality theory. It is clear that personality theory has come a very long way from the imposition of huge mythic assumptions (that are mostly alien to the texts) toward a more modest attentiveness to the interactions that take place within the text. Psychological study of texts has often appealed to the more fantastic notions of Freud and the more speculative ideas of Jung. These studies make for interesting reading, but seldom, so it seems to me, do they illuminate the text. Thus an attempt to practice psychological criticism has produced much that strikes me as self-indulgent and misleading.

I have proposed that attention be paid in particular to object relations theory because it focuses upon real human transactions marked by fidelity (and infidelity). These transactions are the nature of real life in the world, which in the Bible is broadly lined out as "covenantal fidelity" (*ḥesed*). Israel's struggle for the self is to come to terms with God and with neighbor, both "others" who are demanding and problematic as well as potentially life-giving. It is coming to terms with the other—a genuine other—that constitutes the hard work and the rich potential of the human self.

I believe that Ps 35 permits a self that is underway in the hard negotiation with Holy Otherness that makes a True Self possible. Such a self never arrives but attends to many voices—many dimensions of self and many acknowledgements of otherness—that must be engaged in an ongoing conversation. In this case study of Ps 35, I have not made any heavy-handed use of Winnicott, but my awareness of Winnicott has been of great heuristic value, and I would not have read the text as I have done without access to his work.

But then, as I reflected on this reading, it occurred to me that Winnicott and his many colleagues have, with varying degrees of success, only belatedly discerned what this ancient community had already recognized in full ways, that the self is complex and problematic and that the fullness of self depends upon an honored, summoned other. This biblical claim radically confronts a modern society that chooses mostly to solve its conflicts in technological ways with various forms of violence. Contemporary evidence might suggest that what is absent among us is an Other who is "good enough." For this absence, the church has much for which to answer, having denied the script of the complex, dialogic self from concrete practice. Perhaps the main work of psychological criticism is precisely to recover the wonder of this interactive practice that is so odd and so urgent in contemporary "modern" society.

For Further Reading

Ellens, J. Harold, and Wayne G. Rollins, eds. *Psychology and the Bible: A New Way to Read the Scriptures*. 4 vols. London: Praeger, 2004.

Johnson, Aubrey R. *The Vitality of the Individual in the Thought of Ancient Israel*. Cardiff: University of Wales Press, 1949.

Kille, D. Andrew. *Psychological Biblical Criticism*. Minneapolis: Fortress, 2001.

Rollins, Wayne G. *Soul and Psyche: The Bible in Psychological Perspective*. Minneapolis: Fortress, 1999.

Rollins, Wayne G., and D. Andrew Kille, eds. *Psychological Insight into the Bible: Texts and Readings*. Grand Rapids: Eerdmans, 2007.

Wolff, Hans Walter. *Anthropology of the Old Testament*. Mifflintown, Pa.: Sigler, 1996.

Notes

1. The ancient Israelites likely asked the question with reference to males. Thus, a wooden translation of Ps 8:4 is "what is man [*ĕnoš*] that you are mindful of him." In our readings, however, the term "man" must always be transposed for the sake of gender inclusion.

2. Among the more important and helpful studies on the dynamism of personality in the Old Testament are Aubrey R. Johnson, *The Vitality of the Individual in the Thought of Ancient Israel* (Cardiff: University of Wales Press, 1949); and Hans Walter Wolff, *Anthropology of the Old Testament* (Mifflintown, Pa.: Sigler, 1996).

3. For a comprehensive review of the history of such study, see Wayne G. Rollins, *Soul and Psyche: The Bible in Psychological Perspective* (Minneapolis: Fortress, 1999); and D. Andrew Kille, *Psychological Biblical Criticism* (Minneapolis: Fortress, 2001).

4. On the various theories and schools of personality development, see Stephen A. Mitchell and Margaret J. Black, *Freud and Beyond: A History of Modern Psychoanalytic Thought* (New York: Basic Books, 1995).

5. J. Harold Ellens and Wayne G. Rollins, eds., *Psychology and the Bible: A New Way to Read the Scriptures* (4 vols.; London: Praeger, 2004). Vol. 1, *From Freud to Kohut*; vol. 2, *From Genesis to Apocalyptic Vision*; vol. 3, *From Gospel to Gnostics*; vol. 4, *From Christ to Jesus*.

6. David J. Halperin, *Seeing Ezekiel: Text and Psychology* (University Park: Pennsylvania State University Press, 1993).

7. David Jobling, "An Adequate Psychological Approach to the Book of Ezekiel," in Ellens and Rollins, *From Genesis to Apocalyptic Vision*, 204.

8. Sigmund Freud, *Civilization and Its Discontents* (trans. Joan Riviere; London: Hogarth, 1951).

9. See Sigmund Freud, *The Future of an Illusion* (trans. W. D. Robson-Scott; The International Psycho-analytical Library 15; New York: Liveright, 1949). In fact, Freud's view of religion is much more complex than this title might suggest.

10. Rollins, *Soul and Psyche*, 37–42.

11. It is possible that Freud might be understood according to the now popular mantra, "I am spiritual but I am not religious." The statement generally refers to a rejection of the institutional aspects of "organized" religion with its legacy of repression and authoritarianism.

12. Susan A. Handelman, *The Slayers of Moses: The Emergence of Rabbinic Interpretation in Modern Literary Theory* (Albany: State University of New York Press, 1982).

13. Sigmund Freud, *Moses and Monotheism* (trans. Katherine Jones; New York: Knopf, 1949).

14. Handelman, *The Slayers of Moses*, 148.

15. Ibid., 145.

16. Wayne G. Rollins, "Jung, Analytical Psychology, and the Bible," in Ellens and Rollins, *From Freud to Kohut*, 89–95.

17. While Jung and Marx may make strange companions, it is worth noting that, in addition to his much quoted statement that religion is an "opiate," Marx also saw that religion is a powerful consolation. It is possible that his "consolation" is not so far from the "healing" that Jung attributes to religion at its best.

18. Carl Jung, *Answer to Job* (trans. R. F. C. Hull; London: Routledge & Kegan Paul, 1979), 3, 4, 10, 15, 23.

19. Ibid., 91.

20. Ibid., 151.

21. Ibid., 133.

22. On the connection from Freud to Winnicott through Sullivan and Klein, see Stephen A. Mitchell and Margaret J. Black, *Freud and Beyond* (New York: Basic Books, 1995), 124–34. See also Ralph L. Underwood, "Winnicott's Squiggle Game and Biblical Interpretation," in Ellens and Rollins, *From Freud to Kohut*, 139–51.

23. In Christian tradition, this interpersonal interaction comes to its remarkable culmination in the incarnation, wherein God comes "bodied" in Nazareth form. The Christian affirmation of incarnation is not to be reduced to philosophical categories but has its roots in the long history of Jewish interactionism.

24. Special attention may be given to the work of Heinz Kohut. More generally, see the discussion in Mitchell and Black, *Freud and Beyond*.

25. Winnicott characteristically speaks of "mother," but of course by such usage he refers to whoever is the primal caregiver, which in some cases may be "father." He understands, however, that the originary physical bond of mother and child has no counterpart with any other caregiver, so the usage of "mother" is surely correct for what he wants to say, even if we might wish for more gender equity.

26. Donald Woods Winnicott, *The Maturational Processes and the Facilitating Environment: Studies in the Theory of Emotional Development* (Madison, Conn.: International Universities Press, 1965), 145.

27. Ibid.

28. Ibid., 152.

29. A great deal of important work remains to be done concerning the interface between the work of Winnicott and the defining categories of biblical faith. Attention may be paid, as a starting point, to Marjorie Parsons, "Winnicott's Model of True and False Self Systems and Barth's Model of Sin with Application to Clinical Material" (Ph. D. diss., Union Theological Seminary, New York, 1987).

30. Fruitful investigation may be undertaken with an interface between Winnicott's interactionism and the dialogic tradition of Jewish thought with reference to Martin Buber, Franz Rosenzweig, and, most especially, Emmanuel Levinas. Such an interface would bring the discussion to serious textual attention rather than to the wild impositions both Freud and Jung have made upon the Bible.

31. On this defining propensity in the God of biblical attestation, see Walter Brueggemann, "Vulnerable Children, Divine Passion, and Human Obligation," in *The Child in the Bible* (ed. Marcia J. Bunge et al.; Grand Rapids: Eerdmans, 2008), 399–422.

32. The material that follows concerning Ps 35 is reiterated from Walter Brueggemann, "Dialogic Thickness in a Monologic Culture," *Theology Today* 64 (2007): 322–39.

33. The study of the lament psalms by Fredrik Lindström, *Suffering and Sin: Interpretations of Illness in the Individual Complaint Psalms* (ConBOT 37; Stockholm: Almqvist & Wiksell International, 1994), suggests that the speaker of these psalms speaks complaint and petition from a position of strength, as if the speaker had a sense of entitlement before YHWH. Lindstrom does not speak of "entitlement" but notices that there is no confession of sin. Rather, the insistence is that God is obligated to respond to such a petition voiced in urgency.

34. The capacity to practice both lament and praise, claiming and ceding, is well characterized by Roy Schafer, *Retelling a Life: Narration and Dialogue in Psychoanalysis* (New York: Basic Books, 1992), 94–95: "A whole person is the one who acts, the agent. A whole person acts knowingly without profound reservations about the fact of acting, and so acts with presence and personal authority and without anxiously introducing serious disclaimers.… In sexual relations, as elsewhere, a whole person acts the role of agent while refusing to deny personhood to the sexual partner, and accepts it as a psychological fact of life that *there cannot be only one whole person in the relationship*.… Guaranteeing the personal wholeness of others entails a readiness on a person's own part to serve on numerous occasions as object, ground, or milieu in relation to them, for they, too, must be given scope to exercise and confirm *their* personal agency and wholeness.… A whole person allows the reversibility, in a relatively conflict-free fashion. He or she refrains from insisting on being only agent or object, only figure or ground, only active or passive, or only masculine or feminine, as conventionally defined. The reversibility is itself a form of action in that both refraining and allowing are actions. A whole person is neither threatened by reversibility nor incapable of enjoying either position in a relationship." Such reversibility is evident in Israel's way with YHWH.

35. On the salvation oracle as divine answer to lament, see Patrick D. Miller, *They Cried to the Lord: The Form and Theology of Biblical Prayer* (Minneapolis: Fortress, 1994), 135–77.

36. Claus Westermann, *Praise and Lament in the Psalms* (trans. Keith R. Crim and Richard N. Soulen; Atlanta: John Knox, 1981), 165–213.

37. Hans Walter Wolff, *Das Zitat im Prophetenspruch: Eine Studie zur prophetische Verkuendigungsweise* (Munich: Kaiser, 1937), has surveyed the way in which prophets in Israel can place alleged statements in the mouths of their opponents. The same rhetorical strategy recurs in the Psalter. What the adversary allegedly says is more often enacted rather than spoken.

38. This psalm evidences the thickness and dynamism of the human *nepeš*. The Hebrew term rendered in NRSV as "heart's desire" is *nepeš*. Before this verse the term is used three times in the psalm: "say to my *nepeš*" (35:3); "my *nepeš* will rejoice" (35:9); "rescue my *nepeš*" (35:17). The *nepeš* (i.e., the "desire") of the adversary in 35:25 is precisely to overcome the *nepeš* of the speaker, who wants to be reassured (35:3), who anticipates praise (35:9), and who petitions for rescue (35:17). On the dynamism of the *nepeš*, see Johnson, *The Vitality of the Individual*; and especially Wolff, *Anthropology of the Old Testament*, 10–25.

Anthropological Approaches: Ritual in Leviticus 8, Real or Rhetorical?

William K. Gilders

Anthropology and the Hebrew Bible: Methodological Potential and Challenges

"Anyone interested in belief, religion, and symbols looks to anthropology for insight."[1] So wrote the anthropologist Mary Douglas in the preface to the second edition of her selected essays, *Implicit Meanings*. In strong agreement with Douglas's assertion of the value of anthropology, I will discuss in this essay how those interested in the ancient Israelite texts preserved in the Hebrew Bible may look to anthropology for insight. My goal is to identify some of the most significant methodological issues at stake in this mode of investigation, exploring both the potential and the challenges involved in applying anthropological ideas to the Hebrew Bible.

For our present purpose, anthropology may be defined simply as the study of human life in social groups (societies) and of the cultural expressions of these societies. Anthropology emerged in the nineteenth century, initially as a project directed at understanding how human culture had developed or evolved through various stages, from "savage" to "civilized." An interest in religious beliefs and practices was at the heart of the emergent discipline. Early anthropologists worked largely with textual materials as their sources of data and evidence. Thus, they have come to be known as "armchair anthropologists" in distinction to later anthropologists, whose data and evidence was derived from direct engagement with living societies. Such fieldwork-based anthropology is now the absolute norm, which poses a significant challenge for the appropriation of anthropological methods by biblical scholars—an issue I will discuss in further detail below.

One way of thinking about the application of anthropology to the Hebrew Bible is in terms of the questions asked, for the questions that are asked determine the sorts of answers that are produced. Thus, in an anthropological approach to the Hebrew Bible, the types of questions that, for example, Mary Douglas asked about the social world and culture of the Lele people of the Congo can be asked about the ancient Israelites. Application of an anthropological approach to the Hebrew Bible means allowing that ancient Israelite society and culture can be studied like any other society or culture. Furthermore, it means that ancient Israel can be studied by asking questions formulated through the comparative study of societies and cultures and in the light of general theories and hypotheses emerging from such comparative work.[2]

For example, questions may be asked about social organization, family structures, and gender roles. What kind of society was ancient Israel? What light can be shed on Israelite social organization by comparative ethnographic data and general theoretical categories employed by anthropologists? Carol Meyers, for example, pursued such questions, focusing on developing insights about the roles and status of women in ancient Israelite society.[3]

It should be noted at this juncture that it is not simply the case that biblical scholars draw on ideas and approaches from anthropology. Rather, anthropology and biblical studies have been closely connected since the emergence of the comparative study of human culture in the nineteenth century.[4] For example, William Robertson Smith figures in the history of anthropology as well as of biblical studies, and the still-influential work on sacrifice by Henri Hubert and Marcel Mauss dealt extensively with biblical data.[5] More recently, notable anthropologists have engaged with the Hebrew Bible in their work, Edmund Leach and Mary Douglas being prime examples. Leach published two collections of essays on the Bible, and in his frequently reprinted introductory textbook on structuralist analysis in anthropology, *Culture and Communication*, the final chapter ("The Logic of Sacrifice") uses the biblical account of the ordination of Aaron and his sons as its case example on sacrificial ritual.[6] Mary Douglas is well-known for her influential study of the structuring principles behind the dietary laws of Lev 11 and Deut 14:3–20.[7] She developed her engagement with the Hebrew Bible throughout her career, culminating in three monographs devoted to setting out her views on Israelite ideology, literature, and ritual.[8]

This essay will focus on the area of my own engagement with anthropological approaches, the study of ritual.[9] Ritual theory or ritual studies is an interdisciplinary field, and in this essay I will refer to the work of students of ritual who are not members of the anthropological guild. Thus, this piece might easily have been titled "Ritual Studies Approaches." However, ritual studies is strongly rooted in and continues to be nourished by anthropology, as is clear from any examination of the bibliographies of works by ritual theorists who are not anthropologists.[10]

While an anthropologically informed study of the Hebrew Bible need not focus on ritual, any serious attempt to deal with ritual in the Hebrew Bible must engage with the work of anthropologists, who have contributed much to the understanding of ritual and who have also problematized this understanding in various ways. Although my focus here will be on ritual, much of what I discuss will be generally relevant to identifying the potential and the challenges in applying anthropological approaches to biblical texts.

The first key methodological issues to address concern the nature of the data. Edmund Leach encouraged readers of *Culture and Communication* to treat biblical texts as if they were ethnographic field notes, an approach that I find quite problematic. Biblical texts are not ethnographic writings, that is, records of what a "participant-observer" has experienced. Rather, the texts are cultural products, best regarded as equivalent to the information provided by "native informants" whose statements about their society and its culture must be recorded, organized, compared, collated, and interpreted.

The fact that our "native informants" speak to us through texts points up another issue. Unlike ethnographers, biblical scholars have no access to lived practice. Thus, every biblical scholar must of necessity be an "armchair anthropologist" and runs the risks that the early armchair anthropologists did: depending on data that is variously incomplete or unreliable or making too much of the data that is available. The issue of the unreliability of the text is particularly significant. In this regard, despite my reservations about his characterization of biblical texts as field notes, it is worth quoting Leach's advice to anthropologists, as his advice about dealing with native information is helpful when thinking about the nature of the biblical texts:

> The observer must distinguish between what people actually do and what people say that they do; that is between normal custom as individually interpreted on the one hand and normative rule on the other. When they come to write up the results of their research different

> anthropologists will, for doctrinal reasons, give very different weight to those two major aspects of the data, but in the field, the anthropologist must always pay attention to both sides. He … must distinguish behavior from ideology.[11]

Commenting on the relevance of Leach's warning for biblical scholars, Meyers writes: "The biblical scholar does not have the methodological option of observing behavior. Only the ideology is available. Hence there is danger in equating ideology with daily reality, which can diverge from the normative expression contained in the biblical text."[12] As applied to the study of biblical texts about ritual, this warning requires biblical scholars to take seriously the possibility that a text is not simply describing practice as it really was but is shaping a picture to serve some ideological purpose. Biblical scholars must also face the fact that we have no way of comparing a textual claim with observed reality. Thus, some form of a hermeneutic of suspicion is always necessary.

Another key methodological question concerns the object of study within the textual corpus: ritual. What is "ritual"? What counts as such? These are not easy questions, as Bruce Kapferer explains: "Even though, it seems, that anthropologists can recognize a ritual when they see one, they have very diverse criteria for labeling what they see as ritual."[13] In many of the classic definitions of ritual, communication is a key component. Mary Douglas, for example, describes ritual as "pre-eminently a form of communication."[14] In particular, ritual is said to communicate *symbolically*, and the presence of symbolism is made definitional of ritual. David I. Kertzer, for example, defines ritual as "symbolic behavior that is socially standardized and repetitive" and as "action wrapped in a web of symbolism," adding that "[s]ymbols provide the content of ritual."[15]

What, then, are *symbols*, and what are their characteristics? According to Clifford Geertz, a symbol is "any object, act, event, quality, or relation which serves as a vehicle for a conception—the conception is the symbol's meaning." He elaborates that symbols are "tangible formulations of notions, abstractions from experience fixed in perceptible forms, concrete embodiments of ideas, attitudes, judgments, longings, or beliefs." Moreover, cultural activity is "activity in which symbolism forms the positive content."[16] It should be noted that Geertz's category of the symbolic is clearly very large, taking in most social activities of any significance.

According to Kertzer, who builds on ideas developed by Victor Turner, symbols have three properties that are fundamental to their role within ritual: "condensation of meaning, multivocality, and ambiguity." *Condensation of meaning* "refers to the way in which individual symbols represent and unify a rich diversity of meanings. The symbol … somehow embodies and brings together diverse ideas." *Multivocality* refers to "the variety of different meanings attached to the same symbol. While condensation refers to the interaction of these different meanings and their synthesis into a new meaning for an individual, multivocality suggests another aspect, the fact that the same symbol may be understood by different people in different ways." *Ambiguity* means that "the symbol has no single precise meaning. Put in more positive terms, this means that symbols are not arcane ways of saying something that could be more precisely expressed in simple declarative form. The complexity and uncertainty of meaning of symbols are sources of their strength."[17]

In the 1970s and 1980s, the anthropological study of ritual and other social practices was dominated by symbolic-communicative approaches, and biblical scholars have drawn on these approaches to produce some insightful studies of ritual in the Hebrew Bible. For example, Ronald S. Hendel has offered a sophisticated and productive study of the covenant ritual narrated in Exod 24:3–8. Drawing on insights from Geertz and Turner, he treats Israelite sacrifice as "a coherent symbolic act, a central expression of the social and religious self-consciousness of ancient Israel."[18] Also worthy of note is Frank Gorman's study of Priestly ritual texts, which draws on the work of major exponents of a symbolic-communicative approach to ritual, offers careful reflection on major theoretical presuppositions, and provides a clear statement of his understanding of ritual.[19] Finally, mention must be made of Saul M. Olyan's two monographs that draw on and develop classic anthropological models of the expressive and constructive work of ritual.[20] Olyan's work differs from that of Hendel and Gorman in giving relatively little explicit attention to symbolism; instead, Olyan treats the category of "communication" much more broadly to address how ritual acts express and enact status identity and changes of condition. In addition, Olyan makes a special point of emphasizing that his focus is on textual representations of ritual rather than on ritual actions themselves, recognizing that the biblical scholar is working with texts, not living cultural practices.

Having identified some examples of anthropologically informed work on ritual in the Hebrew Bible, I must now take a step back and ask further methodological questions. If one identifies an Israelite practice as "ritual," what is one doing? What consequences follow from such identification?

If one begins with a general definition of a universal phenomenon, then one is attempting to identify particular Israelite performances as culturally specific manifestations of this universal phenomenon. Moreover, one is assuming that this practice fits the definition of the universal phenomenon. Thus, if symbolic communication is understood to be an essential element of ritual, one will treat Israelite practices identified as ritual as symbolic and communicative. This is the approach taken recently by Jonathan Klawans in his study of ancient Israelite and Jewish sacrifice.[21] Klawans affirms, as a general principle, that sacrificial ritual has an "inherent symbolic meaning"[22] and argues specifically that ancient Israelites thought of their sacrificial practices in symbolic terms in relation to two large conceptual organizing principles: *imitatio Dei* (sacrifice as a practice by which human beings follow divine, heavenly models); and attraction and maintenance of the divine presence.

However, not all theories of ritual affirm that the communication of coherent and systematic conceptual meaning is in fact an inherent aspect of ritual. Frits Staal, for example, bluntly declares that ritual is "meaningless." Rather than communicating anything, ritual is simply rule-governed action for its own sake.[23] It would be a mistake, distorting the nature of the debates, to take Staal as representative of all theories that challenge communication-oriented approaches to ritual. Staal simply advocates in an extreme and not terribly nuanced form a widening and deepening critique of theories of ritual that treat symbolic communication as an essential element of ritual.[24] Even Staal accepts that practitioners of ritual interpret and identify meanings of rituals. What Staal and others challenge is the notion that meaningfulness, in a conceptual sense, is *inherent* to ritual. This critique of the dominant symbolic-communicative approach to ritual has recently been adopted, in various ways, by several biblical scholars working on ritual, including myself.[25]

Anthropology provides biblical scholars a variety of ways of treating ancient Israel as a society like any other and of approaching the texts of the Hebrew Bible as cultural products. It offers questions to be asked, which can be productive of new types of answers to old problems. However, as I have noted, the application of anthropological approaches to ritual to biblical textual material raises and faces several complex challenges. To address the potential and some of the challenges, I will now engage in a concrete case study to look at ritual in the Hebrew Bible through anthropological lenses.

A Rite of Passage: Anthropology and Leviticus 8

Leviticus 8 is a narrative account of ritual performance, specifically of the rituals Moses performed to initiate Aaron and his sons as priests of the tabernacle. I will treat the text as a piece of "native" information and will discuss the cultural significance of this narrative of a past ritual. Thus, my approach differs from the one taken by Leach, who suggested treating Lev 8 as if it were ethnographic field notes. Clearly, this is not what the text is. It is not ethnography, the record made by an ethnographer interested in recording the facts of a cultural practice. Rather, the text is itself a product of cultural practice. I will treat brief selected portions of the narrative, with special attention to the beginning of the chapter, considering how insights drawn from anthropologically informed ritual theory may help to illuminate the material. I will also highlight the ways in which such insights call for sensitivity to the text as a cultural product. I have chosen this text for discussion because it has already been the focus of anthropologically informed analysis. As I noted above, Leach used Lev 8 as a test case for structuralist analysis of sacrificial ritual. The text has also been discussed from an anthropologically informed perspective by several biblical scholars.[26]

I begin with a basic identification of the author, that is, the native informant, drawing on the strong consensus of biblical scholarship. This story of a founding ritual comes to us from an heir to that foundation, an Israelite priest who claimed descent from Aaron. Our informant was not "neutral"; he (and his male gender is also significant) had a strong vested interest in this narrative. Thus, we may speak of this story as expressive of the values and convictions of this informant and his group. This is the primary reason why it cannot be treated simply as an ethnographic report.

As Leach notes, Lev 8 presents what anthropologists, following the groundbreaking work of Arnold van Gennep, refer to as a "rite of passage," a rite that marks and effects a change of status or identity.[27] "Rite of passage" is one of the master theoretical categories in anthropology, developed in the twentieth century through the comparative method and used to structure understanding of a culturally specific phenomenon. Of course, nothing in the Hebrew text strictly equivalent to the designation "rite of passage" appears in Lev 8, and the ritual performance is not presented there in accordance with the structuring terms developed by van Gennep.[28] However, through an anthropologically informed analysis, one can test whether van Gennep's distinctive pattern of a rite of passage is in this text. In the case of Lev 8, I believe that van Gennep's model can indeed be generative of productive insights into what the text portrays taking place.

The story of the ritual performance begins with a notice of divine speech (8:1–3): "Then YHWH spoke to Moses as follows: 'Take Aaron, and his sons with him, and the garments, the anointing oil, the sin-offering bull, the two rams, and the basket of unleavened bread, and assemble the whole congregation to the entrance of the tent of meeting.' "[29] Here YHWH commands Moses to prepare for the ritual. The divine statement clearly assumes prior instruction, which in the present form of the Pentateuch appears in Exod 29. YHWH now tells Moses to prepare to enact that prior instruction. This is not, therefore, a narrative about normal human activity but about actions carried out in response to divine decree. Our source claims that this foundational performance was directly and explicitly encoded by YHWH. Here we may note a key element of Roy A. Rappaport's characterization of ritual, that it consists of "acts … not entirely encoded by the performers."[30] This is certainly true of the action to be presented here.

The narrative reports that Moses obeyed the divine instructions and that "the congregation was assembled to the entrance of the tent of meeting" (8:4). This action marks the beginning of the ritual process. The congregation having been assembled, the first public act of the rite is Moses' brief but significant statement to the assembly telling them that what is about to happen was commanded by YHWH (8:5): "This is the thing that YHWH commanded to do!" This statement indicates the meaning of the coming actions in the most fundamental way: they are divinely mandated. Thus, their correct performance will *express* obedience to YHWH. The correspondence of what Moses did with the divine command is the major emphasis of this text and its dominant theme, as is indicated by the number of times the text specifies that the actions corresponded to divine instruction (see, e.g., 8:9, 13, 17, 21, 29, 36). A further fact to note is that Moses refers to the coming ritual as "the thing … to *do*." Moses offers no other words of explanation about the coming actions except that they *are* actions, a thing to be done in response to divine command. To reiterate, the key element of meaning in this ritual is its faithful performance in response to the divine mandate.

Having announced the fundamental meaning of the actions he will perform, Moses then began to carry them out. The first act, according to the narrative, was the bathing of Aaron and his sons: "Moses brought forward Aaron and his sons, and he bathed them with water" (8:6). We should note how sparse the descriptive information is. We are given only a basic report of what was done. We are not told where Moses "brought forward" Aaron and his sons, nor where or how exactly they were washed. For our textual informant, only two facts seem to matter: Aaron and his sons were washed with water; Moses was the actor in this process. Moses is the subject of the active verb, while Aaron and his sons are objects. They are made dependent on Moses, objects of his ritual attention, acted-upon rather than acting. Thus, Moses enacts his special status within the ritual, and we can note that whatever else it achieves, one of its effects is to enhance Moses' authority.

Completely absent here is any explanation of what the washing accomplished. Since washing with water is practiced by most people and its purpose is well-known, it is easy enough to conclude that *cleansing* is the purpose of the act. This very basic cross-cultural understanding can be enhanced by referring to cultural evidence from the same textual corpus, which makes it clear that washing deals with various forms of cultic impurity (see, e.g., Lev 14:8–9). Given the context of this act of washing, it is appropriate, therefore, to conclude that it deals in some way with cultic impurity. Additionally, what happens immediately after the washing may be noted. Aaron is dressed in special cultic vestments. Thus, it appears that the washing is a precondition for putting on such vestments. To make sense of this specific act, one must situate it within the framework of a full cultural system, or, as Mary Douglas puts it, a "world."[31] Our only access to this particular cultural world is through its textual record, beginning with Lev 8 itself and then moving out to other texts of the Priestly (P) tradition, and from there to other Israelite texts that *may* reflect the same values and beliefs—although care is required in making this move, given the evidence for diversity of beliefs and values in ancient Israel in various historical periods and in various groups.

The narrative continues by listing the vestments Moses put on Aaron, giving what appears to be a logical sequence, and emphasizes that the act of vesting Aaron fulfilled divine commandment (8:7–9). The next act in the ritual process, according to the narrative, was anointing with oil (8:10–12):

> Then Moses took the anointing oil and anointed the tabernacle and all that was in it and consecrated them. Then he sprinkled some of it on the altar seven times, and anointed the altar and all its implements, and the

> laver and its stand, to consecrate them. Then he poured out some of the anointing oil upon Aaron's head and anointed him to consecrate him.

Having completed the anointing of the tabernacle, its appurtenances, and Aaron, "Moses brought forward Aaron's sons and dressed them with tunics and girded them with sashes and tied caps on them, as YHWH commanded Moses" (8:13).

The text portrays a process of transition. This process begins with actions van Gennep termed "rites of separation" (undressing and washing). Next come actions that mark and effect the creation of new identity and changed status (new clothing and anointing). However, these actions do not complete the transformation, as is made clear by the need for further transformative acts to be performed (described in 8:14–31) and for the entire ritual process to be repeated each day for seven days (8:33–35). These seven days are the "liminal" (i.e., "threshold") period for Aaron and his sons, when they are no longer ordinary Israelites but still not yet priests. As the text emphasizes, this is a period of danger, when death is a serious risk, and the initiates must remain within the consecrated precinct (8:35). This brief and basic discussion illustrates how theoretical constructs such as those offered by van Gennep can provide a framework for making sense of specific cultural realities and language with which to describe them.

Aaron and his sons have been brought from within the community, outside the tent of meeting, to the tent of meeting. They have shed their normal clothing. They have been washed. Now new clothing is given to them, clothing designated explicitly as being for the service of the cult (8:6–13). They are literally putting on their new identity. It is appropriate in this context to speak of the vestments as *symbols*, not by assigning specific allegorical significance to each item, but in a more general way. The vestments indicate a change of status and identity being given to Aaron and his sons. Like any uniform, the vestments are symbolic of status and identity. Of course, as Rappaport has noted, symbolic communication, like any other type of communication, risks misunderstanding or outright deception ("the lie").[32] A police uniform itself does not make an individual a police officer; it may simply be a Halloween costume worn by a college professor. Likewise, priestly vestments could be put on by a nonpriest but would not make this individual a priest. However, in this controlled textual context, the risk of miscommunication is eliminated. Moses, acting as YHWH's agent, controls access to the vestments, and the narrator has made it clear that the right individuals actually have been vested. Thus, the vestments, as symbols, correctly communicate their message about the changing status of Aaron and his sons.

The actions of washing, dressing, and anointing, quite simple in their basic execution (as represented by the text), enact and effect the partial transition into a new status. They also communicate to the textual "audience," the congregation, and to the readers of the textual representation, signaling the transition. Rather than the change being announced verbally, it is demonstrated. The vesting of Aaron specifically marks his identification as the leading priest, his special vestments having been encoded elsewhere in the larger textual context (see Exod 28) as marking this status, and the fact that the sons are vested in different garments, encoded as belonging to ordinary priests, enacts their distinct status. We may go a step further and note that besides the explicit encoding of distinction, the difference in elaboration and ornamentation itself signals difference.

In 8:10–12 we encounter the first of a small handful of explanatory statements in the narrative indicating the effect of a ritual act. In this case, we are told that the act of anointing the tabernacle and its appurtenances "consecrated" them; it effected a change in their status. Anointing had the same effect on Aaron, changing his status. This is "native" interpretation of ritual and should be recorded and considered as such, in its own terms. Our narrator does not speak in terms of symbolic meaning but of instrumental effect. While we may refer to what the anointing signals symbolically—that it indicates Aaron's change of identity and status—this is not the concern of the narrator; he specifies what the anointing *does*: it gives Aaron a quality he did not previously have.

Leviticus 8:7–12 tells us how Moses dressed Aaron in his liturgical robes, then anointed the tent of meeting and its appurtenances, and finally anointed Aaron. Only in 8:13 are we told that Moses dressed Aaron's sons. Jacob Milgrom, along with other scholars, notes the problem here: as it stands, the text seems to indicate that Aaron's sons were bathed and then left standing around naked for quite some time while Moses dealt with the tent and their father.[33] Milgrom suggests that what is represented in the text does not make sense if taken literally and argues that we should not read the text as providing a sequential representation of activity. Rather, we should construe the activity as being presented thematically: we should envisage the dressing of Aaron and his sons as taking place at approximately the same time, with the anointing of Aaron following this, and the anointing of the tent and it appurtenances taking place after the first sacrificial offering had been made. If Milgrom is correct, we have a good example of a representation of a ritual that does not correspond to actual activity. Whether Milgrom is correct or not, we are nevertheless cautioned about assuming that a literary representation of activity corresponds to actual practice. This is true even when what is represented "makes sense" to us. Verisimilitude does not guarantee that we have access to actual practice.

Whether or not we accept Milgrom's argument, we must consider the significance of the narrative representation as it stands. To what effect is the ritual represented as it is by our source? A number of interpreters have noted that the representation directly links Aaron's anointing with the anointing of the tent and its appurtenances. Interpreting the text as if it presented an actual ritual, Gorman writes:

> The anointing rite functions primarily to place Aaron and the anointed objects in a common ritual state. The common anointing also serves to emphasize that these are the primary "spaces" of Aaron's cultic officiating as high priest.... In this way, the area and its functionary share common boundaries and status; cultic space and correct cultic activity are coordinated through this dual anointing with the holy anointing oil.[34]

In agreement with Gorman's observation, but using different theoretical terminology, I would identify the shared anointing as an *indexical sign*. According the semiotic theory of Charles Sanders Peirce, when dealing with signs, we must distinguish between three types: symbol, icon, and index.[35] It is particularly important to note that signs are not always primarily symbolic in character or quality. A symbol, Peirce emphasizes, "is a sign which refers to the Object that it denotes by virtue of a law, usually an association of general ideas, which operates to cause the Symbol to be interpreted as referring to that object."[36] To put it more simply, as Nancy Jay does, a symbol "is related to its object by convention."[37] The meaning of a symbol, then, is assigned to it and is not inherent in the thing itself. An index, however, "is a sign which refers to the Object that it denotes by virtue of being really affected by that Object."[38] An indexical sign "is in dynamical (including spatial) connection both with the individual object, on the one hand, and with the senses or memory of the person for whom it serves as a sign, on the other hand."[39] While discussing examples of indices, Peirce provides perhaps his simplest definition of an index:

"A rap on the door is an index. Anything which focusses the attention is an index. Anything which startles us is an index, in so far as it marks the junction between two portions of experience."[40] This explanation clarifies that Peirce's category of the index integrally includes deliberate human actions that indicate something. Thus, in his refinement of Peirce's theory, Rappaport refers to "constructed indices," which "are deliberately constructed and employed by humans to indicate whatever they do indicate."[41] Such constructed indices, while dependent on human action and thus conventional, do not depend on convention for their significance. Rather, as Jay helpfully explains, "Because the relation of sign to signified is not conventional, indices can be understood across cultural and linguistic boundaries. They *indicate* their object rather than represent it."[42]

When viewed in the light of Peirce's semiotics, it is clear that the anointing acts have an indexical dimension. Whatever we might say about their conventional symbolic or instrumental significance, when we imagine the performance of the anointing acts as narrated in the biblical text, we can speak of them as indices that point to a relationship between Aaron and the shrine and its appurtenances. When the oil is placed on the shrine and its furnishings, a relationship is created. The oil is existentially *on* the objects in question. When the oil is placed on Aaron, the same kind of relationship is created. Furthermore, the fact that Aaron bears the oil as the shrine and its appurtenances bear the oil places Aaron and these objects into a relationship. These are points that can be made about the effect of the textually represented ritual in addition to taking note of the specific instrumental claims made by the text and apart from any additional symbolic-communicative meaning one might identify in the act.

Having given some attention to the specific rituals with which the ordination rites began, I turn now to some reflection on the rite as a whole and how its textual form may itself be a focus of anthropological analysis. Jonathan Z. Smith, in his article "The Bare Facts of Ritual," proposes that one of the functions of ritual is to enact perfect, controlled activity, in conscious tension with imperfect, uncontrolled activity. In offering this theoretical suggestion, he looks at the case of Arctic Siberian bear hunters. These hunters make surprising claims about their hunting activity that both defy credulity and contradict observed behavior. Smith correctly observes that these hunters are quite aware that what they say they do is not what they actually do. They are not deceiving themselves, and they do not intend to deceive ethnographers, although Smith notes that some ethnographers managed to deceive themselves! For the hunters, there is an acknowledged tension between what they wish to do when they hunt and what they actually do. This tension is resolved in a ritual hunt carried out in the village. In this ritual hunt, a bear cub is raised to be tame and gentle with humans. It is then constrained to participate in a hunt structured according to the ideal: it walks happily to its death; it waits while the hunters sing hymns to it; it is held in the required posture; it is killed virtually bloodlessly; the meat is carefully distributed according to established rules.

If a ritual is perfect activity, which may be contrasted with normal, imperfect activity, and if reflection on ritual action in the course of normal action helps to give meaning and structure to life, might not represented ritual play a similar function in relation to actual ritual? Real rituals, after all, are always carried out by imperfect human beings in imperfect settings. Sacrificial animals bleat and struggle, jugs get knocked over, knives are dropped, ceremonial words are forgotten, disagreements surface over proper procedure. If ritual is supposed to be perfected activity, it often falls short of that goal. Textually represented ritual, however, avoids all the difficulties faced by real ritual; it escapes all the accidents that can corrupt the perfection for which ritual may strive.

Leviticus 8 is an excellent example of a representative text that functions this way. The narrator constantly reiterates in various ways that what was done was the perfect fulfillment of YHWH's will. The rituals enacted are prescribed by YHWH and executed by Moses in conformity with YHWH's instructions. The text begins with the notice that YHWH spoke to Moses and that Moses obeyed what YHWH told him (8:1–2), and it ends with the declaration that Aaron and his sons did everything that YHWH commanded through Moses (8:36). In between, the formula is repeated several times that the actions carried out by Moses were "as YHWH commanded Moses." If we reflect on the experience and effect of reading this narrative of a ritual, what might we suggest about its cultural purpose? I would suggest that Lev 8 functions as the perfect paradigm for all subsequent priestly ritual activity in the world in which it is preserved and read. It establishes that the reality of the priesthood as a body of ritual specialists is rooted in a perfect ritual commanded by YHWH and executed by Moses. While it is impossible to know if the ritual described in Lev 8 was ever performed as represented, we do know that the narrative was read and that its representation conveyed an image of a perfect ritual lying behind the living reality of a priesthood that traced its lineage to Aaron. Reading the text through anthropological lenses, we can see how a specialized group within a society expressed and sought to advance its ideology. Thus, the study of textual rhetoric about ritual is as much an exercise in anthropological analysis as is the study of the ritual actions themselves.

For Further Reading

Douglas, Mary. *Implicit Meanings: Selected Essays in Anthropology*. 2nd ed. London: Routledge, 1999.

Eilberg-Schwartz, Howard. *The Savage in Judaism: An Anthropology of Israelite Religion and Ancient Judaism*. Bloomington: Indiana University Press, 1990.

Meyers, Carol. *Discovering Eve: Ancient Israelite Women in Context*. New York: Oxford University Press, 1988.

Gilders, William K. *Blood Ritual in the Hebrew Bible: Meaning and Power*. Baltimore: Johns Hopkins University Press, 2004.

Hendel, Ronald S. "Sacrifice as a Cultural System: The Ritual Symbolism of Exodus 24,3–8." *ZAW* 101 (1989): 366–90.

James, Wendy. *The Ceremonial Animal: A New Portrait of Anthropology*. New York: Oxford University Press, 2003.

Olyan, Saul M. *Rites and Rank: Hierarchy in Biblical Representations of Cult*. Princeton: Princeton University Press, 2000.

Overholt, Thomas W. *Cultural Anthropology and the Old Testament*. Minneapolis: Fortress, 1996.

Rappaport, Roy A. *Ritual and Religion in the Making of Humanity*. Cambridge Studies in Social and Cultural Anthropology 110. Cambridge: Cambridge University Press, 1999.

Notes

1. Mary Douglas, *Implicit Meanings: Selected Essays in Anthropology* (2nd ed.; London: Routledge, 1999), vii.

2. For a discussion of these points, see Howard Eilberg-Schwartz, *The Savage in Judaism: An Anthropology of Israelite Religion and Ancient Judaism* (Bloomington: Indiana University Press, 1990), esp. 31–102.

3. Carol Meyers, *Discovering Eve: Ancient Israelite Women in Context* (New York: Oxford University Press, 1988).

4. Wendy James, *The Ceremonial Animal: A New Portrait of Anthropology* (New York: Oxford University Press, 2003), 122–25.

5. Henri Hubert and Marcel Mauss, *Sacrifice: Its Nature and Function* (trans. W.

D. Hall; Chicago: University of Chicago Press, 1964); trans. of "Essai sur la nature et la fonction du sacrifice," *L'Anée Sociologique* (1898).

6. Edmund Leach, *Genesis as Myth, and Other Essays* (London: Cape, 1969); Edmund Leach and D. Alan Aycock, *Structuralist Interpretations of Biblical Myth* (Cambridge: Cambridge University Press, 1983); Edmund Leach, *Culture and Communication: The Logic by Which Symbols Are Connected: An Introduction to the Use of Structuralist Analysis in Social Anthropology* (Themes in the Social Sciences; Cambridge: Cambridge University Press, 1976). The copyright page of the volume indicates that it was reprinted fifteen times between 1976 and 1995. In a slightly modified form, the chapter "The Logic of Sacrifice" is reproduced in *Anthropological Approaches to the Old Testament* (ed. Bernhard Lang; IRT 8; Philadelphia: Fortress, 1985), 136–50.

7. Mary Douglas, *Purity and Danger: An Analysis of Concepts of Pollution and Taboo* (London: Routledge, 1966); see also idem, "Deciphering a Meal," in *Implicit Meanings*, 240–49; repr. from *Daedalus* 101 (1972).

8. Mary Douglas, *In the Wilderness: The Doctrine of Defilement in the Book of Numbers* (JSOTSup 158; Sheffield: Sheffield Academic Press, 1993); idem, *Leviticus as Literature* (New York: Oxford University Press, 1999); idem, *Jacob's Tears: The Priestly Work of Reconciliation* (New York: Oxford University Press, 2004).

9. William K. Gilders, *Blood Ritual in the Hebrew Bible: Meaning and Power* (Baltimore: Johns Hopkins University Press, 2004); idem, "Why Does Eleazar Sprinkle the Red Cow Blood? Making Sense of a Biblical Ritual," *JHS* 6 (2006); online: http://www.arts.ualberta.ca/JHS/Articles/article_59.pdf.

10. See, e.g., Catherine Bell, *Ritual Theory, Ritual Practice* (New York: Oxford University Press, 1992); idem, *Ritual: Perspectives and Dimensions* (New York: Oxford University Press, 1997); Philippe Buc, *The Dangers of Ritual: Between Early Medieval Texts and Social Scientific Theory* (Princeton: Princeton University Press, 2001); Jonathan Z. Smith, "The Bare Facts of Ritual," in idem, *Imagining Religion: From Babylon to Jonestown* (Chicago: University of Chicago Press), 53–65; idem, *To Take Place: Toward Theory in Ritual* (Chicago: University of Chicago Press, 1987).

11. Edmund Leach, *Social Anthropology* (Glasgow: Fontana, 1982), 130, quoted in Meyers, *Discovering Eve*, 13.

12. Meyers, *Discovering Eve*, 13.

13. Bruce Kapferer, "Ritual Dynamics and Virtual Practice: Beyond Representation and Meaning," *Social Analysis* 48 (2004): 36.

14. Mary Douglas, *Natural Symbols: Explorations in Cosmology* (New York: Random House, 1970), 20.

15. David I. Kertzer, *Ritual, Politics, and Power* (New Haven: Yale University Press, 1988), 9, 11.

16. Clifford Geertz, "Religion as a Cultural System," in idem, *The Interpretation of Cultures: Selected Essays* (New York: Basic Books, 1973), 91.

17. Kertzer, *Ritual, Politics, and Power*, 11; see also Victor Turner, *The Ritual Process: Structure and Anti-structure* (Chicago: Aldine, 1969), 52.

18. Ronald S. Hendel, "Sacrifice as a Cultural System: The Ritual Symbolism of Exodus 24,3–8," *ZAW* 101 (1989): 366–90, here 366.

19. Frank Gorman, *The Ideology of Ritual: Space, Time and Status in the Priestly Theology* (JSOTSup 91; Sheffield: JSOT Press, 1990).

20. Saul M. Olyan, *Rites and Rank: Hierarchy in Biblical Representations of Cult* (Princeton: Princeton University Press, 2000); idem, *Biblical Mourning: Ritual and Social Dimensions* (New York: Oxford University Press, 2004); see also Olyan's "What Do Shaving Rites Accomplish and What Do They Signal in Biblical Ritual Contexts?" *JBL* 117 (1998): 611–22.

21. Jonathan Klawans, *Purity, Sacrifice, and the Temple: Symbolism and Supersessionism in the Study of Ancient Judaism* (New York: Oxford University Press, 2006), esp. 49–73; see also idem, "Methodology and Ideology in the Study of Priestly Ritual," in *Perspectives on Purity and Purification in the Bible* (ed. Baruch J. Schwartz et al.; LHBOTS 474; New York: T&T Clark, 2008), 84–95.

22. Klawans, *Purity, Sacrifice, and the Temple*, 67.

23. Frits Staal, "The Meaninglessness of Ritual," *Numen* 26 (1979): 2–22.

24. See, e.g., Talal Asad, "Toward a Genealogy of the Concept of Ritual," in idem, *Genealogies of Religion: Discipline and Reasons of Power in Christianity and Islam* (Baltimore: Johns Hopkins University Press, 1993), 55–79; idem, "On Discipline and Humility in Medieval Christian Monasticism," in *Genealogies of Religion*, 126–31; Bell, *Ritual Theory, Ritual Practice*, esp. 69–74; Buc, *The Dangers of Ritual*, esp. vii–viii, 1–12; Caroline Humphrey and James Laidlaw, *The Archetypal Actions of Ritual: A Theory of Ritual Illustrated by the Jain Rite of Worship* (Oxford Studies in Social and Cultural Anthropology; Oxford: Clarendon, 1994); Nancy Jay, *Throughout Your Generations Forever: Sacrifice, Religion, and Paternity* (Chicago: University of Chicago Press, 1992), esp. 6–7; Smith, "Bare Facts of Ritual," esp. 63.

25. Wesley J. Bergen, *Reading Ritual: Leviticus in Post-modern Culture* (JSOTSup 417; New York: T&T Clark, 2005); Roy Gane, *Cult and Character: Purification Offerings, Day of Atonement, and Theodicy* (Winona Lake, Ind.: Eisenbrauns, 2005), esp. 3–24; Gilders, *Blood Ritual in the Hebrew Bible*, esp. 2–8; Ithamar Gruenwald, *Ritual and Ritual Theory in Ancient Israel* (Brill Reference Library of Ancient Judaism 10; Leiden: Brill, 2003); James W. Watts, *Ritual and Rhetoric in Leviticus: From Sacrifice to Scripture* (Cambridge: Cambridge University Press, 2007), esp. 1–36.

26. See, e.g., Gorman, *Ideology of Ritual*; Gilders, *Blood Ritual in the Hebrew Bible*; Gerald A. Klingbeil, *Bridging the Gap: Ritual and Ritual Texts in the Bible* (Bulletin for Biblical Research Supplements 1; Winona Lake, Ind.: Eisenbrauns, 2007), 147–54, 163–64; idem, "Syntactic Structure of the Ritual of Ordination (Lev 8)," *Bib* 77 (1996): 509–19; Jacob Milgrom, *Leviticus 1–16: A New Translation with Introduction and Commentary* (AB 3; New York: Doubleday, 1991).

27. Leach, *Culture and Communication*; Arnold van Gennep, *The Rites of Passage* (trans. M. B. Vizedom and G. L. Caffee; Chicago: University of Chicago Press, 1960); trans. of *Les rites de passage* (Paris: Émile Nourry, 1909).

28. As Edith Turner notes, "the idea of a rite of passage is comparatively new, sprung by van Gennep upon our twentieth century as a surprise (1909/1960). The rites have been occurring for millennia, but no one could see or was conscious of the distinct form in them. People just performed them, and they worked" (Edith Turner, preface to *The Nature and Function of Rituals* [ed. Ruth-Inge Heinze; Westport, Conn.:

Bergin & Garvey, 2000], x.)

29. All translations my own unless otherwise noted.

30. Roy A. Rappaport, *Ritual and Religion in the Making of Humanity* (Cambridge Studies in Social and Cultural Anthropology 110; Cambridge: Cambridge University Press, 1999), 24, 32–33.

31. Douglas, *Implicit Meanings*, vii.

32. Rappaport, *Ritual and Religion*, 11–17.

33. Milgrom, *Leviticus 1–16*, 501.

34. Gorman, *Ideology of Ritual*, 118–19.

35. For a helpful entry to Peirce's theory of signs, see Justus Buchler, ed., *Philosophical Writings of Peirce* (New York: Dover, 1955), 98–119. On the relevance of Peirce's ideas for the understanding of sacrificial ritual, see Jay, *Throughout Your Generations Forever*, 6–7. See also Rappaport's subtle elucidation and critique of Peirce's theory (*Ritual and Religion*, 54–68). For a lucid discussion of Peircian semiotics from the perspective of a different tradition of semiotics, see Gerard Lukken, *Rituals in Abundance: Critical Reflections on the Place, Form and Identity of Christian Ritual in Our Culture* (Liturgia condenda 17; Leuven: Peeters, 2005), 75–83.

36. Cited in Buchler, *Philosophical Writings of Peirce*, 102.

37. Jay, *Throughout Your Generations Forever*, 6; see also Rappaport, *Ritual and Religion*, 54, 67.

38. Cited in Buchler, *Philosophical Writings of Peirce*, 102.

39. Ibid., 107.

40. Ibid., 108–9.

41. Rappaport, *Ritual and Religion*, 63.

42. Jay, *Throughout Your Generations Forever*, 6.

Sociological Approaches: Toward a Sociology of Childhood in the Hebrew Bible

Naomi Steinberg

Introduction

Sociology is a discipline that develops theories, methods, and models that allow for the interpretation of social phenomenon. Sociological research explains patterns of individual and group behavior as reflections of their social context. In general, sociology recognizes that "society" is not one thing but that it consists of interconnections between different levels and processes of individual and group interaction. What separates sociology from its closest branch of the social sciences, anthropology, is sociology's emphasis on how societies conceptualize and organize patterns of social behavior rather than anthropology's emphasis on comparative cultural phenomena.

Sociological studies of the Hebrew Bible are based on patterns of social behavior described in the biblical text and other ancient sources and the behavior that can be gleaned from archaeological finds such as burial sites. These patterns reflect both the social world described in the biblical text and the social world behind the text, that is, the world that created the text. Sociological methods and theories were initially employed to understand the religion of ancient Israel. This initial sociological research on the Hebrew Bible maintained that religion was the key to recovering the social origins of the Hebrew Bible and that the religion of earliest Israel described in the Hebrew Bible was an expression of the character of its social structure. In addition, these studies also considered the economic motivations that might account for the development of biblical Israel. As time passed, the foci of sociological approaches to the Hebrew Bible have expanded beyond an interest in the origins of Israel. In the space of one short chapter, it is impossible to provide an exhaustive history of the application of social-scientific approaches to the Hebrew Bible. The following discussion will trace, in broad strokes, the development of sociological theory and methods with respect to the interpretive study of the Hebrew Bible.

A Survey of Social-Scientific Research on the Hebrew Bible

Israel's Origins

The study of Israel's origins is a good example of where sociological theory has been used to expose the history behind the Hebrew Bible. Prior to the 1960s, most scholars understood the Israel that existed before the rise of the monarchy as a pastoral nomadic society that rejected the hierarchical model of Canaanite government. It was not until the rise of its own monarchic system that Israel became a stratified state.

On the American scholarly scene, Louis Wallis (1912) at the University of Chicago wrote a sociological analysis of the origins of ancient Israel. Wallis drew the lines for early Israel based on a rural-urban split (e.g., Gen 4:2 and the antagonism between Cain and Abel). In this view, the rural represented the origins of the ideals of Yahwism, while the urban served as the setting for the stratified elite from which early Israel separated itself. Wallis's emphasis on the tension between rural and urban lifestyles in early Israel led him to conclude, "monotheism is a byproduct of a utopian struggle to impose migratory clan ethics upon a territorial state."[1] In Wallis's view, biblical religion is not the *cause* of the class struggle between the rural and urban populations; rather, it was the *result*. Thus, Wallis may be classified as a conflict theorist in that he understands society as the product of the balancing of the ideals and material interests of differing groups living together.

Systematic analysis of the connection between religion and society in the formation of the world of the Hebrew Bible finds its fullest expression in *Ancient Israel*, Max Weber's pioneering sociological work.[2] His interest in ancient Israel derived from his studies on the origins of capitalism, the rise of Calvinism, the Protestant ethic, and a value system that emphasized hard work and the importance of saving wealth. Weber understood society as being composed of groups with opposing ideas and material bases. In the case of ancient Israel, Weber distinguished four social groups: nomads; seminomadic herders; settled agriculturalists; and city dwellers. Despite the clashes between the their lifestyles and their ideals, these groups came together in a common religious commitment expressed as a special relationship to their God YHWH, stipulated in a covenant.

According to Weber's reconstruction, in its early history Israel was nonhierarchical in political organization and embraced notions of social equality grounded in the covenant tradition. In the period preceding the rise of the monarchy, the interrelationship between religion and society was in balance. Authority was located in the family unit. This local authority was eroded, argued Weber, when sociopolitical stratification separated landholders from the landless. With this, authority was taken out of the hands of the family and shifted to those with no economic or social-justice investment on the local level. Consequently, prophets arose to critique this shift from a society committed to covenant equality to one that permitted social injustice and economic disenfranchisement. For Weber, the changing nature of ancient Israelite society lay in the political and economic institutions that marked its development from one system of organization to the next. Weber saw the development of Israel as being based in socioeconomic crises that undermined the importance of the covenant between tribes and God.

The prophets who arose in response to these crises critiqued Israelite society based on religiously grounded economic policy as expressed in the ethical principles of the covenant initiated by God. Israel needed rulers that would govern through policies of socioeconomic justice. Thus, the spirit of the Protestant ethic, according to Weber, was rooted in the covenant notion that working for the sake of work, not profits, was part of God's will. Weber's sociological theory located religious principles at the center of economic policies. This understanding grew out of the similarities Weber found between the Protestant work ethic (i.e., the spirit of capitalism) and the socioeconomic conditions that were integral to the development of the religious traditions of the Hebrew Bible from Israel's earliest ancestors to its experiences in the Babylonian exile.

French biblical scholar Antonin Causse, whose work is indebted to that of sociologist Emile Durkheim (1858–1917), argued, like Weber, that social organization and religion were originally tied together in early Israel.[3] Causse explains the shift in ideology in biblical Israel as resulting from Israel's establishment in Canaan and the move away from collective interests to individual concerns. The former ideology represented a kind of "nomadic ideal" that, ironically, was lost in the so-called promised land. Like Weber, Causse interpreted the prophets of the Hebrew Bible as the standard-bearers of the ethic expressed in the older collective-responsibility ideology. In the end, the prophetic movement brought about a shift in the religion of ancient Israel, resulting in individual piety. Like Weber and Wallis, Causse presupposed that Israel's political and religious origins stemmed from the competitive interaction of groups living side by side.

In their times, the works of twentieth-century biblical scholars Johannes Pedersen and Roland de Vaux were considered significant sociological analyses into questions relating to social life in ancient Israel.[4] Both Pedersen and de Vaux used approaches to the biblical tradition that were considered to be sociological at the time but now are recognized to be weak in sociological theory and lacking a clear-cut methodology. These scholars, like those discussed above, relied on the prevailing theory that early Israel was a pastoral nomadic society and subsequently offered sociological explanations for a variety of Israelite social and religious institutions.

Despite the insights of all these scholars, the basic theory on which their research was grounded is no longer tenable. Recent social-scientific studies on pastoral nomadism seriously challenge the theory that this mode of existence was characteristic of early Israel. The nomadic model assumes a group of people who wander freely with their flocks looking for water and pastures to sustain their animals and their family. However, the biblical evidence does not support such features for early Israel. With the possible exception of the ancestors of Genesis—and here the evidence is too slight to draw firm conclusions—earlier Israelites appeared to have led a more settled existence than previously thought.

German biblical scholar Martin Noth also attempted to relate the literature of ancient Israel to its social structure.[5] Based on the analogy of a Greek amphictyony, a tribal confederation centered on a common religious shrine, Noth believed he had recovered the origins of early Israel. Noth's amphictyony model, though initially thought plausible, is not well supported by the biblical record, which points to a lack of unity in Israel prior to the introduction of a centralized monarchy. However, Noth's work is distinguished from the authors above by virtue of its detailed analysis of the literary traditions of the Hebrew Bible and its reliance on the archaeological data.

Since the beginning of the 1960s, the focus of sociological research into the origins of Israel shifted, most notably through the contributions of George Mendenhall and Norman Gottwald. Both scholars came to reject the model of seminomadic society as the basis for ancient Israelite life and, instead, turned to models of peasant society to understand Israel's beginnings in Canaan. Thus, these two scholars also bring an economic perspective to their initial model for the origins of Israel, albeit a different one than their predecessors.

In work that gave rise to the contemporary wave of sociological study of the Hebrew Bible, Mendenhall used a model of peasant revolt to understand the origins of ancient Israel.[6] According to this theory, early Israel was originally founded as a peasant-based union of subsistence farmers that ultimately revolted against its oppressive hierarchical Canaanite overlords and became united around its covenant with God. While his approach is rooted in social-scientific analysis, Mendenhall ultimately sees the ethical dimensions of Israelite religion, not socioeconomic factors, as the primary factor explaining Israel's development.

Gottwald, on the other hand, utilized a sustained socioeconomic perspective to explain Israel's social origins. His study of premonarchical Israel led Gottwald to reject Weber's pastoral, nomadic societal model and to embrace instead theories associated with sociologist Karl Marx (1818–1883), who analyzed historical change in light of socioeconomic issues. Based not only on the biblical text but also on texts of the ancient Near East and emerging archaeological data, Gottwald broke with past biblical scholarship and argued that the roots of ancient Israel go back to a retribalization phenomenon that resulted from an internal peasant revolt against Canaanite overlords.

Both Mendenhall and Gottwald expose the romantic notions of nomadism that lay behind earlier social histories of early Israel. While Mendenhall reintroduced social-scientific study of the Hebrew Bible to biblical scholarship, Gottwald offers a more systematic attempt at laying out both a method and theory for interpretation of the biblical data on Israelite origins. The theories of both scholars are still being debated. What unites the work of Mendenhall and Gottwald—and separates them from the work of the classical theorists above—is the central role of socioeconomic revolution in each model. Rather than simply describing social developments in ancient Israel, Mendenhall and Gottwald see in ancient Israelite economic developments the basis for and the continuing relevance of the ethical dimensions of Israelite religion.

Israel's Institutions

In recent years, biblical scholars have gained a better understanding of many of Israel's social institutions because of the application of microsociology, the study of small groups. Prophecy, for example, has been the subject of much sociological investigation. Already in the early twentieth century, Weber had drawn attention to the centrality of the charismatic figure of the prophet in the changing nature of Israelite society. Yet fleshing out of the workings of prophecy came later, especially with the work of Robert R. Wilson and David L. Petersen, who carefully applied sociological theory to understanding the institution of prophecy.[7] Their interests lay in both the social function and social location of the prophet. In sum, social-scientific approaches suggest that those prophets who operated within the established social institutions of ancient Israel, such as the royal court or temple, worked to maintain the status quo, while those who were outside the boundaries of the established social institutions aimed to bring about change.

The subject of apocalypticism has also been illuminated through the application of sociological theory and methods, often returning to ideas first proposed by Weber. On the theoretical level, research on group alienation suggests that marginalized groups in ancient Israel channeled their feelings into apocalyptic ideologies. Such ideologies gave rise to alternative viewpoints on reality in which the alienated groups are championed and are no longer at the margins. The conflict between the haves and the have-nots, building on sociological theories of social upheaval, is often the subtext of apocalyptic literature.

The institutions of family and kinship are other subjects about which we know more because of the application of sociological models to the biblical text. Scholars have explored kinship as a means of organizing social structure that is based on an emphasis on a particular relationship between individuals, especially in contexts where there is economic gain or property involved. Sociological study constructs family life in the Hebrew Bible on three levels: the *bêt ʾāb*, the family household; the *mišpāḥâ*, the neighborhood or residential kinship group; and the *šēbeṭ*, the tribe. Different levels of social organization predominated at different periods in the history of ancient Israel. Early Israel's move from a locally based social structure to a hierarchically organized, centralized, state-level government had repercussions for the family. Family-organized life shifted from an emphasis on the importance of the *mišpāḥâ* to the *bêt ʾāb* as the basic unit of social organization. Sociological theory explains this shift in emphasis as an attempt by a newly formed centralized government to subvert the power of local extended family units. The theory is that, if the dominant social structure is the nuclear family of the *bêt ʾāb*, it would be more difficult for large numbers of individuals to come together in rebellion against the state-level monarchy. It is important to note that in early Israel the *bêt ʾāb* referred to a residential unit composed of related individuals and servants, while in the postexilic period, the *bêt ʾāb* was defined as those who could trace their ancestry back to individuals who were part of the Babylonian Diaspora.

Finally, research on family life in ancient Israel and the changes brought about by the introduction of the monarchy has resulted in sociological analysis on the change in women's roles over the course of biblical history. The consensus is that women lost power and status in the family, relative to conditions in early Israel, when the monarchy began. Sociologically oriented approaches to gender issues in the Hebrew Bible shed light on women's roles within the larger context of the changing social world of ancient Israel.

Critique

Social-scientific methods have done much to nuance contemporary understandings of the origins, development, and function of some of the institutions and structures that are integral to the ancient Israel. However, the application of such approaches to the Hebrew Bible has met with criticism. Some critics argue that the models used to study ancient Israel are ahistorical and universal, rather than culture-specific, and that the data for constructing such models is often outmoded. Others are more focused on critical approaches that principally concentrate on the (e.g., literary) dynamics within the text rather than on dynamics behind the text. Moreover, many critics maintain that the inherent difficulties in interdisciplinary studies—when scholars from one academic discipline embrace the theories and methods of another academic discipline—are magnified when biblical scholars uncritically draw upon the work of sociologists who study industrialized societies and apply it to ancient Israel.

Even those who engage in sociological study of the Hebrew Bible recognize potential problems in its application. Sociology has many theorists and many subfields, and the choice of one sociological perspective over against another dramatically influences the interpretation of biblical data. For example, Gottwald's Marxist reading of the origins of early Israel yields a very different understanding of this time in Israelite history than does Weber's economic analysis. Given different theoretical starting points, the application of social-scientific approaches might still yield significantly different conclusions. Thus, it might be said that the greatest contribution of social-scientific approaches to the study of the Hebrew Bible is found in the new set of presuppositions, perspectives, and questions that this methodology introduces. Far from supplanting other methodological approaches, the social-scientific approach provides a distinctive lens through which scholars can examine biblical Israel. Consequently, social-scientific methods typically are not applied to the Hebrew Bible in isolation from other methodologies. Study of the social construction of ancient Israelite life is an interdisciplinary approach that allows alternative models and theories about biblical Israel to complement more traditional biblical scholarship.

Application: The Sociology of Children in the Hebrew Bible

> "We know nothing of childhood: and with our mistaken notions the further we advance the further we go astray." (Jean Jacques Rousseau[8])

Nearly 250 years after Rousseau's observation, the sociology of childhood has reemerged as an area of study within the social sciences. The comments of Alan Prout and Allison James exemplify how modern social-scientific research investigates how societies conceptualize and organize childhood: "The immaturity of children is a biological fact of life but the ways in which this immaturity is understood and made meaningful is a fact of culture. It is these 'facts of culture' which may vary and which can be said to make childhood a social institution. It is in this sense, therefore, that one can talk of the social construction of childhood and also of its re- and deconstruction."[9] The sociology of childhood centers on the child and conceptions of childhood as central to membership in society, rather than viewing children as marginal or outsiders to the society maintained by adults.[10]

In this section I will explore how past sociological study of the Hebrew Bible and the interest in economic variables can be applied to the development of a new area of biblical study, a sociology of childhood. I shall attempt to develop the sociological interest in the economic core motivations for social organization in the Hebrew Bible as this pertains to the concept of childhood. What follows is a suggestion for how to begin to do research on the topic of childhood in the Hebrew Bible, rather than a discussion of any particular biblical text. My aim is to lay out a programmatic agenda for the child as a category for future sociological analysis by biblical scholars.

Answering the simple question, What is a child? may appear obvious. We all assume we know what a child is. But do we really? The answer is clear in the United States, where an individual legally moves out of childhood at the age of sixteen for driving, at age eighteen for voting, and at age twenty-one for drinking, all of which indicate differing legal definitions of adulthood based on activity. Separate from legal issues, in American culture we distinguish the developmental stages of infancy, childhood, adolescence, and adulthood with no hard and fast markers to indicate passage from one social stage to another. If we realize that in our own time and place it is difficult to find an answer to the question of what is a child, we begin to appreciate how difficult it is to answer this question for other times and places. Given this contradictory data about the definition of "the child" in contemporary America, how can we begin to understand another culture's ideas about childhood, particularly when that culture is an ancient one? Obviously, we must avoid unjustifiably transposing our views of childhood to ancient Israel. Steven Mintz comments on several typical misunderstandings (or myths) about childhood:

> One is the myth of carefree childhood ... [in which] we cling to a fantasy that once upon a time childhood and youth were years of free adventure, despite the fact that for most young people in the past, growing up was anything but easy.... [Another] myth is that childhood is the same for all children, a status transcending class, ethnicity, and gender. In fact, every aspect of childhood is shaped by class—as well as ethnicity, gender, geography, religion, and historical context. We may think of childhood as a biological phenomenon, but it is better understood as a life stage whose contours are shaped by a particular place and time.... [Another] myth is that the United States is a peculiarly child-friendly society, when in actuality Americans are deeply ambivalent about children.[11]

This ambivalence about children in American society is reflected in the development of the sociology of childhood. This ambivalence stems partly from the difficulty in separating historical research on the social construction of childhood from studies promoting social policies on the social good and rights of children today. Although both objects of inquiry have legitimate objectives, these objectives have often been blurred due to a failure to separate the study of cultural/societal notions about childhood from the study of children. Topics such as when life begins and babies' human rights, as important as they are for contemporary law and morality, are different from questions about the social construction of childhood and, for example, the phenomenon of children's play or the economic growth of the toy industry in the United States.

Pioneering work in the study of childhood began with Phillipe Ariès. He broke new ground in the study of child in his classic work, *Centuries of Childhood*.[12] He argued that childhood as a distinct and innocent period of life first began in Europe in the Middle Ages. Although this position has since been challenged, he deserves credit for recognizing the social construction of childhood. His characterization of childhood as an "innocent period" has had more impact on subsequent study of childhood than any other argument in his writing. Ariès's work leads the present generation of sociologists of childhood to ask the fundamental question, What is a child? The question is ultimately an interdisciplinary one and recognizes that childhood is a sociological variable that must be analyzed not only with attention to time and place but must be added to other variables such as gender, socioeconomic class, ethnicity, and so on, in order to understand society. Recent studies of "the child" advance the insights of Ariès—without the Eurocentrism of his analysis.

The paradigms for the sociology of childhood are often broken down into three historically separate concepts of childhood: (1) children as chattel in preindustrialized settings, the property paradigm; (2) children as objects to be protected, the protection paradigm; and (3) children as independent beings with rights to independence, the personal paradigm. These three concepts of childhood may be oversimplistic, but they are helpful as a means to refocus our attention on children because they swim against the stream of romanticized conceptions of childhood and instead highlight the social construction of childhood in the past.

One of the methodological challenges facing biblical scholars who apply sociological paradigms—whether they are about children or anything else—is the need to be certain that the models imported from the social sciences are relevant to the Hebrew Bible. If one distorts the biblical material by interpreting it in ways that do not adequately address the original setting of ancient Israel, the value of sociological approaches is greatly diminished. For example, ancient Israel provides no evidence that childhood was understood as a carefree and innocent stage of life, unless one understands Abraham's comment to Isaac before his near sacrifice in Gen 22—"God will provide"—as an expression of such innocence. The text does not make it clear whether Isaac is perceived as innocent and carefree or nothing more than a mini-adult.

With these caveats in mind, useful hypotheses for beginning a sociological study of childhood in biblical Israel might include the following.

Hypothesis 1: There is enough data in the Hebrew Bible and related literature and archaeological studies to apply sociological methods in order to draw useful and important conclusions concerning the definition of "the child" in biblical Israel.

Hypothesis 2: Models of preindustrialized societies—where the emphasis is on economics—fit the biblical evidence. In such societies, the family was an economic unit. According to Ariès, "This did not mean that parents did not love their children, but they cared about them less for themselves ... than for the contribution those children could make to the common task."[13] In contrast to the present, where one typically thinks about what a parent owes a child, in preindustrialized societies, as in ancient Israel, the emphasis is on what a child owes a parent.

Hypothesis 3: Understanding childhood in the Israelite family depends on the place of the child in the developmental cycle of family life.

Hypothesis 4: The family ideology and concern for patrilineal family preservation from one generation to the next must be considered in an investigation of the meaning and content of childhood in the Israel of the Hebrew Bible.

Hypothesis 5: The more economically valuable a child is for the survival of the family unit, the less social value the child has. Social circumstances and changing historical conditions are variables in the economic value of a child and affect the meaning of being a child.

Hypothesis 6: Child abandonment is a social mechanism to control family structure and limit inheritance to the primary heir to the patrilineage.

Hypothesis 7: Gender is a variable in determining the economic value of a child.

With regard to hypothesis 1, we note that there is data from the ancient Near East that can inform a sociology of children, though biblical scholarship has, up until now, paid little attention to it.[14] Only the broadest generalizations have been stated regarding the meaning of childhood in the Bible, and what is available in past research appears to be clouded by sentimental interpretations grounded in views of childhood as a time of carefree innocence. Despite this reality, the discussion in the first part of this essay suggests new research possibilities for using sociological approaches to address this topic and to begin to fill in the gaps in our knowledge about children in the biblical world. One could begin with a careful consideration of the Hebrew word *yeled* "child," to determine whether it has the same range in Hebrew and cognate languages as the English word "child," which, as explained above, is ambiguous in both legal and social terms in American society.

Hypothesis 2 would build on the perspective that economic factors are the foundation of marriage and the family in ancient Israel. Family values include production and reproduction from one generation to the next, that is, carrying on the patrilineal estate. Such an understanding of the economic interests of the family requires that protection of family wealth—rather than protection of children—is the primary family value. A child, whether related by birth or adoption, is someone who guarantees the survival of family wealth through the patrilineage. Thus, the economic circumstances of the family shape the contours of a child's life. Given the changing economic circumstances from earliest Israel to the time of the exile, the definition of "the child" likely shifted over the course of the more than one thousand years of biblical history.

For hypothesis 3, our understanding of "the child" in the Hebrew Bible must explore the linguistic possibilities for distinctive Hebrew terminology that refers to categories in the sociology of children in ancient Israel that might not be obvious based on modern definitions. For example, biblical scholars recognize that the Hebrew word *na'ar*, typically translated "youth," is not an age category but refers to an unmarried son who has yet to receive family land through inheritance, that is, a son who has yet to assume the role of head of the household. The word refers more to a social status than to a precise age category. Similarly, *zāqēn* does not simply mean "old" as an age designation but instead is a term indicating the status of a male who has become head of a household. Thus, a *na'ar* can be older than a *zāqēn*, if the latter has become head of the household and the former has not. Further research is needed to explore what other phases of the developmental cycle of the family unit is reflected in the terminology and ideology of the Hebrew Bible.

An exploration of hypothesis 4 could begin with the legislation against adultery. Although laws such as Exod 20:14, Deut 5:18, and Lev 18:20 focus on the fate of the couple who had illicit sexual intercourse, nothing is mentioned about the children born from such a union. The understanding of a child as one who continues the patrilineage of his father has direct bearing on understanding childhood as including only those who have been born of a "legitimate" union of a man and woman. A so-called illegitimate child is by this definition a nonperson. The repeated instructions from father to son that a married man should not go after loose women (e.g., Prov 5:15–20) draw our attention to the link between adultery and definitions of a child. Thus we must inquire about the fate of a child born outside the protection of the patrilineal family unit. Similarly, texts about prostitution (e.g., Judg 11:1) suggest that there were children who did not fall under the family protection of the ancient Israelite patrilineage system. With no links to their father's patrilineage because of the indeterminate nature of their parentage, such offspring might be abandoned due to shame or lack of resources of the mother and father or, simply, the lack of interest in such a child.

As for hypothesis 5, we can explore the *social value of children* in a society and compare that to the data in the Hebrew Bible and related ancient Near Eastern material. In the modern era, as value of the child was separated from the economic market, the social value of the child sky-rocketed. By contrast, we should think of the story of Sarah's barrenness in Gen 16. Her need for a child appears to be based on the child's social value and its ability to give her status as a person, and thereby provide her husband Abraham with the preferred heir he needs to continue his lineage after his death. Further, her need for a child underscores the economic value of a child to his father and as a protector of his mother in her old age after the death of her husband.

Other regulations support hypothesis 5: if a son was ill-behaved, his father could discipline him; if he was totally out of line, he could be killed (Deut 21:18–20). Positively, if he was the firstborn, the son was entitled to a double portion of his father's inheritance (Deut 21:17). Additionally, a son could be taken by a creditor to pay off a debt (2 Kgs 4:1).

Furthermore, we must consider the possibility that the eunuchs of ancient Israel may have been abandoned males whose parents had no economic options for them later in life or that their fate was a result of biblical legislation against bodily deformity (Lev 21:16–24). In the latter case, ironically, bodily deformity contributes to their economic value—but only removed from the family of birth.

In light of our limited knowledge of the world of ancient Israel, consideration should also be given to the data from the ancient Near East on the social value of a child as relates to its economic value. For example, in the Babylonian Code of Hammurabi (ca. 1792–1750 B.C.E.), law 117 recognizes the right of a father to sell his child to cover a debt or an obligation, suggesting that the sale of a child was an accepted form of abandonment in the cultural and legal context of the ancient Near East.

The greater the economic ability of a child to meet a parent's debt, the less social value such a child would have.

As for hypothesis 6, despite the repeated concern in the Hebrew Bible to "be fruitful and multiply," child abandonment was a reality in ancient Israel. There is, for example, the double abandonment of Ishmael, the firstborn son of Abraham: first Abraham abandons Ishmael and Hagar (Gen 21:14), then Hagar abandons Ishmael (Gen 21:15; see also Exod 1:22; Ezek 16:5). However, despite the fact that the term, *yātôm* "orphan" occurs forty-two times in the Hebrew Bible, critical biblical scholarship has rarely considered the possibility of orphans caused by child abandonment in ancient Israel. The conceptual framework for interpreting the term *yātôm* in biblical scholarship has focused on whether the term *yātôm* refers to one who is simply bereft of a father or is completely parentless, the literal sense in English of an orphan. Yet scholars have not addressed the evidence for the figurative meaning of an abandoned child, someone lacking the protection of a parent or guardian—either by death or by abandonment.

The variability of meaning for a number of Hebrew and English terms relevant for this study requires that terminological precision be a starting point in the analysis. Without this clarity, serious problems of interpretation will result. For example, one must be careful to make distinctions between the terms *child abandonment* and *infanticide*. According to John Boswell, abandonment "refers to the voluntary relinquishing of control over their children by their natal parents or guardians, whether by leaving them somewhere, selling them, or legally consigning them to some other person or institution."[15] Infanticide, on the other hand, refers to exposure intended to result in the death of the child—although one certainly recognizes that abandonment might unintentionally result in death. In ancient sources, including the Hebrew Bible, it may not always be possible to discern between the intention of abandonment and infanticide on the part of the parent. However, according to these definitions, Hannah's decision in 1 Sam 2 to turn her newborn son Samuel over to the priest Eli presents a possible case of child abandonment.

In addition to references to the *yātôm*, and to literary depictions of child abandonment, research must explore additional less-obvious references to child abandonment that often have gone unnoticed. In particular, data to be examined can be found in the Hebrew roots *ʾsp* "to gather" and *ʾmn* "to support," all of which in certain verbal inflections may be translated respectively as "foundling" and "foster parent." Additionally, one should consider the semantic fields of the roots *ʿzb*, *ntš*, and *šlk* (in the *hipʿil*),[16] all of which can be translated within the range of "forsake, abandon, expel, send out." Using these less-obvious references, it is possible to explore reasons for child abandonment as well as the fate of children without family or social network to maintain them. The results of such study will contribute to the larger scholarly project of Hebrew Bible scholars reconstructing the social world of ancient Israel.

Establishing the sociology of children would also include exploring the possibility that the abandoned/orphaned child in ancient Israel was the object of social-welfare legislation (e.g., Exod 22:21–22; Deut 14:28–29; 24:19–21), because such children were the equivalent of today's "street child." Although social policies in many countries toward street children appear to be built on social concerns, the reality is that the concept of a street child also builds on the reality that such children are a social problem. They violate whatever notions a culture may have for how the family should operate and can also be a physical threat to others, if they are violent. By disrupting such ideas, the street child raises question of what childhood should be. For example, today's "problem" of street children refers to individuals who fall outside the family norm of children in a family setting cared for by a responsible adult. Does such a class of children exist in ancient Israel, and if so, are they referred to by particular Hebrew terms?

Abandonment was not the only option for a child who did not inherit family land. The archaeological reconstructions of the closing of the highland frontier at the time of the transition from the premonarchic to the monarchical period and the limits on family land available as a resource for family livelihood suggest that there were other institutions to which children could turn for economic stability if they were not the beneficiaries of landed inheritance.[17] According to some scholars, sons could be dedicated to the temple or trained for a future profession as an alternative to inheriting and farming family land. Sons also might become priests or soldiers (although professional soldiering requires a stage of development beyond childhood in most societies). These professions oriented the son not only to the continuation of the family line but to the perpetuation of Israelite society.

With regard to hypothesis 7, we recognize that the Hebrew Bible provides less data on daughters than on sons. We do know that unmarried girls had a certain economic value in their families; they did chores, such as watering their father's animals (Exod 2:16). We also know that a father could sell his daughter (and sons) into slavery to pay off his debt (Exod 21:7). Moreover, the text attests that negotiations between families on the economic terms of an impending marriage took place (Gen 24). Although we know little about how a daughter constructed her life, the story of Jephthah's daughter would suggest that daughters were also socialized into a world where reproduction was the ultimate family value (Judg 12). A daughter's virginity was probably her highest economic value, and stoning was the fate of a bride whom her new husband did not believe to be a virgin (Deut 21:13–21). Based on the evidence from the sources available to us, it is impossible to determine whether female infanticide was what social scientist Jack Goody calls "a hidden economy of kinship"[18] in a society that needed sons to continue the patrilineage; the dowry due a daughter for her marriage diminished the wealth of the family and might account for the abandonment and death of baby girls.

In ancient Israel, childhood was apparently a time to be educated into family values, so that one could take over in the next generation of the patrilineage. The instructional literature of Proverbs provides information for both boys and girls about how to maintain the family. Proverbs 31 functions as an instruction manual on how girls should act—and what a man should expect from his wife. The emphasis on remaining faithful to the bride of one's youth and on avoiding the snares of the loose woman educate a young boy into how to maintain the patrilineage and uphold the ideology of heirship from the union of a male and his appropriate wife.

Proverbs 31 is thought to come from the court circles of monarchy and seems to address the sociohistorical circumstances of an elite population—although Proverbs undoubtedly reflects folk wisdom from an earlier time. This literature, as well as the stories of Zelophehad's daughters (Num 27:1–11; 36:1–12), alerts us to the economic value of daughters as recipients of land from their fathers in certain circumstances, namely, inheritance, betrothal, and marriage.

Conclusion

The future of sociological study of the Hebrew Bible holds much promise. Such study will not provide *the* answer to questions in biblical scholarship that have eluded researchers until now, but it does offer new possibilities for understanding old questions and for shedding light on new issues. The sociology of childhood is one area of research that can benefit from the application of sociological approaches to the Hebrew Bible, but hardly the only one. The possibilities for understanding childhood in ancient Israel from a sociological perspective will allow us to move beyond romanticized notions of the child based on biological immaturity alone. The cultural, historical, political, and economic context relevant to childhood sociology should be central topics for future research, just as these topics issues have been linked to family reality in ancient Israel.

I conclude this programmatic introduction to the sociology of the child in the Hebrew Bible by noting that the meaning of childhood in biblical Israel cannot be separated from an accounting of the family in ancient Israel and the place of humanity in the cosmos. Humans are part of creation, and humans are to work with creation. This ideology serves the larger Israelite value of production and reproduction to guarantee the continuation of the Israelite family. With such a backdrop to our research, the child may better come into view in the world of the Hebrew Bible, and we may better understand childhood as a social institution that changes over time and space.

For Further Reading

Carter, Charles E., and Carol L. Meyers, eds. *Community, Identity, and Ideology: Social Science Approaches to the Hebrew Bible*. Sources for Biblical and Theological Study 6. Winona Lake, Ind.: Eisenbrauns, 1996.

Gottwald, Norman K. *The Tribes of Yahweh: A Sociology of the Religion of Liberated Israel, 1250–1050 B.C.E.* Maryknoll, N.Y.: Orbis, 1979.

Mendenhall, George. E. *The Tenth Generation: The Origins of the Biblical Tradition*. Baltimore: Johns Hopkins University Press, 1973.

Noth, Martin. *The History of Israel*. Translated by Stanley Godman. New York: Harper & Brothers, 1958.

Pedersen, Johannes. *Israel: Its Life and Culture*. Translated by A. Moller and A. I. Fausbell. 2 vols. London: Oxford University, 1926–1940.

Petersen, David L. *The Roles of Israel's Prophets*. Journal for the Study of the Old Testament: Supplement Series 17. Sheffield: JSOT Press, 1981.

Vaux, Roland de. *Ancient Israel: Its Life and Institutions*. Translated by John McHugh. 2 vols. New York: McGraw-Hill, 1961.

Wilson, Robert R. *Prophecy and Society in Ancient Israel*. Philadelphia: Fortress, 1980.

Notes

1. Louis Wallis, *God and the Social Process* (Chicago: University of Chicago Press, 1935), 7.

2. Max Weber, *Ancient Judaism* (trans. and ed. Hans H. Gerth and Don Martindale; New York: Free Press, 1952).

3. Antonin Causse, *Du groupe ethnique à communauté religieuse: Le problème sociologique de la religion d'Israël* (Études d'histoire et de philosophie religieuses 33; Paris: Alcan, 1937).

4. Johannes Pedersen, *Israel: Its Life and Culture* (trans. A. Moller and A. I. Fausbell; 2 vols.; London: Oxford University, 1926–1940); Roland de Vaux, *Ancient Israel: Its Life and Institutions* (trans. John McHugh; 2 vols.; New York: McGraw-Hill, 1961).

5. Martin Noth, *Das System der zwölf Stämme Israels* (Stuttgart: Kohlhammer, 1930).

6. George E. Mendenhall, *The Tenth Generation: The Origins of the Biblical Tradition* (Baltimore: Johns Hopkins University Press, 1973).

7. Robert R. Wilson, *Prophecy and Society in Ancient Israel* (Philadelphia: Fortress, 1980); David L. Petersen, *The Roles of Israel's Prophets* (JSOTSup 17; Sheffield: JSOT Press, 1981).

8. Jean Jacques Rousseau, *Emile* (1762; trans. B. Foxley; New York: Dent, 1957), 1.

9. Alan Prout and Allison James, "A New Paradigm for the Sociology of Childhood? Provenance, Promise and Problems," in *Constructing and Reconstructing Childhood: Contemporary Issues in the Sociological Study of Childhood* (ed. Alan James and Allison Prout; London: Falmer, 1997), 7.

10. The importance of the sociology of childhood as a topic worthy of study parallels the emergence of feminist studies. Just as feminist studies began as a critique of the male-centered scholarship of the past, childhood studies critique the adult-centered scholarship of earlier investigations. Moreover, just as much recent feminist criticism—both in biblical studies and in other areas of feminism—aims to bring about changes for the social good of women, much of the recent scholarship in the sociology of childhood targets the social welfare of children today. Furthermore, just as feminist criticism distinguishes sex roles—i.e., biological roles from gender roles—as a social construct, the sociology of childhood distinguishes "the child" as a biologically immature being from "childhood," a social construct. New paradigms for feminism and the sociology of childhood move beyond the essentializing models that attempt to find the essence of the categories of individuals to which they refer. However, the sociology of childhood comes late to the scene of critical scholarship because children are obviously unable to write articles about themselves, whereas women have found their places with academic discourse.

11. Steven Mintz, *Huck's Raft: A History of American Childhood* (Cambridge: Harvard University Press, 2004), 2.

12. Philippe Ariès, *Centuries of Childhood* (New York: Vintage, 1962).

13. Ariès, *Centuries of Childhood*, 368.

14. However, see now the recently published *The Child in the Bible* (ed. Marcia J. Bunge et al.; Grand Rapids: Eerdmans, 2008).

15. John Boswell, *The Kindness of Strangers: The Abandonment of Children in Western Europe from Late Antiquity to the Renaissance* (New York: Vintage, 1990), 24.

16. For more on this root, see Meir Malul, "Adoption and Foundlings in the Bible and Mesopotamian Documents: A Study of Some Legal Metaphors in Ezekiel 16. 1–7," *JSOT* 46 (1990): 97–126.

17. Lawrence E. Stager, "The Archaeology of the Family in Ancient Israel," *BASOR* 260 (1985): 24–28.

18. Jack Goody, *The Development of Marriage and Family in Europe* (Cambridge: Cambridge University Press, 1983).

Narrative Analysis: Meaning, Context, and Origins of Genesis 38

Yairah Amit

Scholars have long argued whether the story of Judah and Tamar in Gen 38 is an integral part of the story of Joseph or a late interpolation. Scholars also disagree as to whether this text shows Judah in a favorable or unfavorable light. Given the lively debate about the composition, redaction, and literary features of Gen 38, the story of Judah and Tamar presents a particularly appropriate case study for narrative analysis. The following interpretation utilizes literary criticism to reveal the design and poetics of the story. It also examines the text so as to discern matters of composition and editing. Thus, the essay seeks to address the following questions: To what extent is the narrative internally consistent? What does the story contribute to its larger literary context(s)? When was it written and by whom? This combination of literary-critical and historical-critical concerns enables one to address questions about the textual infrastructure while also evaluating the artistic features of the text.

Presenting the Approach

The extensive and methodical analysis of biblical narrative—with particular emphasis on the poetics of biblical stories—began to develop only in the mid-twentieth century, yet a general awareness of the literary features of biblical narratives had long been present: in the writings of the sages, in medieval Jewish commentaries, and subsequently in the work of modern philological-historical scholars. In fact, these modern scholars paid particularly close attention to such elements as plot, characters, and style in order to identify and categorize the various sources within the text and the interventions of later redactors. But for most historical-critical Bible scholarship, identifying the literary aspects of texts had been a means to an end rather than an end in itself, with the result that commentary on the literary-artistic aspects of the texts was usually confined to side comments and specific illustrations.[1]

Since the 1960s, however, narrative criticism has become a major mode of analysis in its own right. Narrative criticism is based on the assumption that content and form are interlinked; observing the form of a narrative necessarily deepens one's understanding of its content. While this assumption is generally shared by narrative critics, the study of biblical narrative has nevertheless diverged with regard to synchronic or diachronic perspectives. Those who take the synchronic course presuppose the essential unity of the story by analyzing the final form of the text and mostly eschew redaction- and source-critical issues. These scholars do so for any number of reasons, including their religious commitments, disciplinary ideology, and (to put it bluntly) their unfamiliarity with the broad scope of redaction- and source-critical research.

The diachronic course of analysis, which I advocate, is preferred by scholars who assume that biblical texts have a complex history that requires careful consideration. These scholars do not ignore the existence of different versions and variant readings. They also consider the possibility of secondary additions to the text or even a different original literary context.[2] In such a case, it is necessary to consider the manner of the interpolation, as well as the reasons for it in relation to the immediate and wider contexts. These broader circles of context include the biblical book in which it has been inserted and even the rest of the biblical canon.

Since hundreds of years may have passed between the composition of biblical material and its canonization, the question of the editing of a text is of paramount importance. This editorial work was an ongoing, dynamic process, collective and prolonged, rather than a single event. Despite the repeated editorial interventions and the various motivations of the editors, the text that has come down to us is readable. To understand how this is possible, one must understand the editor as a kind of author, one who undertakes the rhetorical responsibility of producing a text that is easily understood—and, more important, gives rise to moral lessons. With these primary goals of readability and moral exhortation in mind, the editors of the biblical text observed a coherent editorial policy that gave the work the appearance of consistency. I call this continuous editing that sustained the text's rhetorical function "implicit editing" and consider it one of the distinguishing characteristics of the biblical text.[3] Further, since these author-editors appreciated the value of the rhetorical function—namely, the ability of an interesting story to convey messages—they took pains to design the stories so as to direct and influence their intended audiences.

These assumptions about the processes of composition and editing guide my analysis of biblical narratives. Thus the goal of this inquiry is to discover the social and intellectual world of the authors-editors through the texts and, in doing so, to elucidate the meaning of the text. Rarely does this meaning appear openly; most of the time it is elicited indirectly, and the reader can follow it by examining the elements of the story and their interaction.[4] Thus, the following study begins with an analysis of the literary features of the story of Judah and Tamar and only then moves to associate the narrative with a particular ideological trend.

Studying the Story and Its Parts

The First Reflective Reading

Diverting from the main storyline of Joseph (Gen 37–50), the story of Judah and Tamar (Gen 38) is a closed, demarcated literary unit that provides a subsidiary story about Judah and his family: from his marriage to the daughter of Shua the Canaanite to the birth of his sons, Zerah and Perez, by his daughter-in-law Tamar.[5] Its unusually lengthy introduction (vv. 1–12, out of thirty verses in the chapter) provides a background for the ensuing interaction between Judah and Tamar. This part of the narrative summarizes a long period of time: beginning with Judah's marriage, continuing through the death of two of his three sons and the expulsion of his daughter-in-law, and ending after Judah's recovery from the loss of his wife. But it is doubtful if all this accounts for the length of the exposition.

In contrast to most biblical narratives, Gen 38 is replete with information about the causes of events and motivations of characters. Some explanations are offered by the narrator as his own interpretation. Others appear indirectly, as a statement by the narrator representing the mind of the character. Still others are offered by the characters themselves. All told, the reader finds eleven different explanations about the characters' actions: In 38:7 the narrator explains the deity's decision to end Er's life: "But Er, Judah's first-born, was displeasing to the LORD, and the LORD took his life."[6] Verses 9–10 account for the death of Onan and present Onan's thoughts in the narrator's words: "But Onan, knowing that the seed would not count as his, let it go to waste." In 38:11 the narrator reaches into

Judah's mind to explain why Shelah was not given to Tamar and why she was sent to her father's house: "For he thought, 'He too might die like his brothers.'" The second part of 38:14 explains Tamar's decision to pretend to be a harlot on the roadside: "for she saw that Shelah was grown up, yet she had not been given to him as wife." Verse 15 clarifies why Judah did not recognize Tamar: "for she had covered her face." Verse 16 reiterates that Judah addressed the supposed harlot because he did not recognize Tamar: "for he did not know that she was his daughter-in-law." In 38:23 Judah explains to his Adullamite friend why there was no point in searching for the harlot: "Let her keep them, lest we become a laughingstock." In 38:26 Judah justifies Tamar, saying: "inasmuch as I did not give her to my son Shelah." The conclusion of the story presents two further interlinked explanations: the first is an explanation for tying a thread onto the wrist of one baby: "the midwife tied a crimson thread on that hand, to signify: This one came out first" (38:28); the second explanation has to do with the thread, which may account for the name Zerah, meaning "shine" (38:30).[7] Verse 29 offers an explanation in the form of an etiology for the name Perez: "and she said, 'What a breach [*pāreṣ*] you have made for yourself!' So he was named Perez [*pāreṣ*]." In sum, this long exposition and these many different explanations are highly unusual for biblical narrative and must be seen as a guide for understanding the story's significance.

Reading the Narrative Units

The story comprises four tightly linked units that represent the stages in the development of the plot. The exposition (unit 1, 38:1–12), which focuses on the unsolved issue of the levirate marriage, is followed by a detailed description of Tamar's act, which is intended to solve the problem (unit 2, 38:13–23). Unit 3 (38:24–26) deals with Judah's response to Tamar's act, acknowledging his sin in the matter of the levirate marriage (cf. unit 1), and the justification of Tamar (cf. unit 2). Unit 4 (38:27–30), the conclusion, reveals the successful solution to the problem presented in the exposition.

Unit 1: The Exposition (38:1–12). The opening of the story, "A long time afterward" (38:1aα), has intrigued commentators from the sages to the present time. All are aware of the chronological problem this introduction creates, because it links up events that must have occurred over twenty-two years—the implied length of time from the sale of Joseph into slavery to the migration of the entire family to Egypt.[8] The opening formula serves the editorial purpose of both connecting the story to the preceding one and locating the story in the period from the sale of Joseph to his advancement in the Egyptian king's court.[9]

The text also reports Judah leaving his brothers, associating with his Adullamite friend Hirah, marrying a Canaanite woman (see 1 Chr 2:3), her bearing him three sons, and the marriage of his firstborn Er to Tamar, whose origin is not given. Thus Judah is completely surrounded by Canaanites. They are his friends and family; the text describes Hirah and Tamar—Er's wife, who lived near Timnath in the Judean lowland—as local inhabitants who were mostly Canaanites during the period in question.[10]

This tranquil picture is shattered when Judah's two eldest sons are killed by God, one after the other, because of their wickedness. What made them wicked in the sight of the Lord? The explanation specifying Onan's sin—his refusal to impregnate Tamar, his eldest brother's widow—shows that God's judicial standard applied to the behavior of the sons, not their Canaanite mother, and that the duty of levirate marriage was more important than the question of ethnic origin.[11]

Judah himself sinned in preventing his third son, Shelah, from marrying Tamar, the widow of his two older sons. However, the narrator does not criticize Judah. Rather, he intervenes to explain that Judah had acted this way out of fear that his youngest son might die as well (38:11). Judah, then, has the narrator's support, even though he did not fulfill the duty of levirate marriage. Instead, he ordered Tamar to wear a widow's garments and sent her to her father's house. As a result, Tamar lost status after being removed from her husband's family, and she became an indigent at the mercy of her father's house.[12]

The detailed events and explanations regarding Judah's family up to this stage indicate the vital importance of levirate marriage. As the head of the family, Judah was responsible for its implementation. Onan's evasion of this law was explained as wicked, while Judah's failure to impose its observation, as in the case of Shelah, is given a mitigating explanation. Moreover, the levirate marriage was a duty required in any situation, regardless of the woman's origin—even if she was a stranger.

The short second part of the exposition (38:12) proceeds to the concrete setting of the events. It reveals that sometime after the death of Judah's wife (the daughter of Shua), when Judah was comforted and ended the mourning period, he resumed his usual life and went to shear his sheep in Timnath, in the Judean lowland—presumably near the place where Tamar resided.

The exposition in 38:1–12 summarizes a period of decades, but that is not a sufficient reason for its length; after all, it is possible to summarize centuries in a single verse.[13] Rather, the length of the exposition is due to the detailed discussion of the levirate marriage predicament in Judah's family, especially as it pertained to Judah's connections with the local population. With its numerous explanations, this first unit prepares the background for a discussion of the relations with the local inhabitants.

The exposition tells us that the problem of the levirate marriage has not yet been resolved and that even at this stage Shelah is still immature but is the next in line, meaning that the levirate marriage remains central to the continuing development of the narrative. Although Tamar has been sent to her father's house, she has been ordered to maintain her widowed status, which implies her continuing connection with Judah's family. We may ask if a foreign woman who has been sent to her father's house must remain faithful to the laws of Judah's family, or, alternatively, whether a foreign woman who followed the laws of Judah's family and was sent to her father's house remains a member of the house of Judah at all.

Unit 2: The Act of Tamar (38:13–23). Tamar's act is described in detail and explained from its planning stage to its conclusion. Thus her actions cannot be ascribed to whim or to her Canaanite upbringing, which was sometimes depicted as one of lechery and uncleanness (see Lev 18). To convince the reader that it was a single, intentional act, the encounter between Tamar and Judah opens and closes with Tamar putting on and taking off her widow's garb (38:14, 19). The mention of the widow's garments shows that Tamar continued to assert her membership within Judah's family. Tamar is therefore shown as acting the way she did only in the encounter with Judah and doing so only in order to break out of the social isolation into which Judah has driven her when he sent her away and did not fulfill the requirements of levirate law (see Deut 25:5–10). In this way, the narrative ensures that Tamar would not be depicted as representing "the practices of the land of Canaan" (Lev 18:3). Instead, Tamar represents an example of a woman of the local population who was attached by marriage to the house of Judah and who identified wholly with the laws of the community she joined. She feels committed to abide by the laws and customs of her new family, even after she was returned to her father's house. Her loyalty to the laws of Judah's family helps present her as a positive figure who, although a victim of circumstances, has the force of character to withstand them.

Judah is also seen as a positive figure. He is not projected as a compulsive womanizer nor as one who trawls for whores in his leisure hours. The connection with the supposed harlot happens only when he has recovered from mourning for his wife. The narrator makes sure to eliminate any possibility that he might knowingly have committed incest, with combined explanations why he could not recognize Tamar. Judah's gentle, hesitant approach to Tamar—"Here, let me sleep with you" (38:16)—requesting and asking permission, also seems to indicate that he was not in the habit of associating with harlots. This contrasts with the direct, matter-of-fact, and, indeed, somewhat vulgar speech that Tamar uses as part of her disguise (38:16b, 17b, 18a). She goes straight to the point, namely, the payment or forfeit. Judah is portrayed as a tragic hero punished for his fateful error in not giving Shelah to Tamar, out of fear for his life, thus breaking the levirate law.[14] Seeing Judah as a tragic hero helps us to understand his conduct, feel compassion for him, and accept his characterization as a positive figure.

The narrator defends the two leading figures, Tamar and Judah, by means of three consecutive justifications (38:14, 15, 16). The repetition ensures that the reader is aware of the effort to justify the protagonists.

Unit 3: Judah's Reaction (38:24–26). This part of the story also conveys the narrator's desire to defend the protagonists. Judah's statement, "She is more in the right than I," shows that he feels they are both in the right, but one of them more than the other. Evidently Judah is aware of his guilt but finds justification in the emotional motive for his actions: his anxiety for his youngest son, having lost the two older sons. Yet he has no doubt, and admits openly, that Tamar had a greater right.[15] The narrator does not tell us where the statement was made, but it is reasonable to assume that Judah said it in public, either at the city gate or in front of the people whom he sent to take Tamar to be burned and with whom she returned the forfeited items.[16] Thus, justice was both heard and done. This part of the story ends with the statement that Judah "was not intimate with her again" (38:26).[17] The inclusion of this important detail further enhances the tragic quality of the story, indicating that neither Judah nor Tamar would enjoy normal family life, while at the same time underscoring the perspective that the sin was unintentional.

The fact that Tamar became pregnant shows that her act was God's will, since an occasional, single intercourse between a man and a woman does not guarantee conception. It must also be kept in mind that biblical literature portrays every conception as a sign of divine intervention, as shown in the case of Hannah's impregnation: "Elkanah knew his wife

Hannah, and the LORD remembered her. Hannah conceived, and at the turn of the year bore a son" (1 Sam 1:19b–20).[18] That Tamar conceives reiterates that the relations between her and Judah occurred at God's will and under divine providence and therefore received the divine blessing. This implies that the explanations offered to the readers had been accepted by the divine court and neither side was to be censured. Both Judah and Tamar were in the right.

Unit 4, The Conclusion: The Birth of Twins (38:27–30). Concluding the story with the birth of twins suggests a double blessing. The positive perception of the story is further enhanced by the implied compensation: Judah, who had lost two sons, was given two others.[19]

The birth of Perez and Zerah provides a happy ending to the tangled sequence that preceded it. The favorable finale obliges the reader to reevaluate Judah's conduct and acknowledge that if Judah was thus blessed, he cannot be regarded as a negative character; though he sinned, it was understandable given the circumstances. Some readers view this sequence of events and hold a negative view of Judah's actions, censuring him for ignoring his father's grief, preferring the company of strangers, marrying a Canaanite wife, preventing the fulfillment of the levirate law, and, in effect, deceiving and abandoning Tamar. To this list of despicable behavior they add associating with a harlot and engaging in an incestuous act. Moreover, even though Judah did not intend to marry Tamar to his son, no sooner does he hear of her pregnancy than he condemns her to be burned.[20] Such a series of accusations does not correspond with the story's favorable conclusion, leaving the reader to wonder, Where was the punishment? What about the principle of "measure for measure"?

It appears, therefore, that the ending that says "All's well that ends well" is intended to repel any interpretation that would condemn or vilify Judah. I call such a conclusion designed to reverse or alter other potential interpretations a "reversal ending."[21] The goal of the reversal ending in this particular story is to convince the reader that God had a hand in the developments of the plot. Therefore, readers should abandon any attempt to condemn Judah and understand the story in the light of its conclusion, namely, in the positive meaning of a blessing. In view of the reversal ending, the reader becomes all the more conscious of the narrator's effort to defend Judah and will inevitably praise him for being brave enough to justify Tamar and bring the truth to light.

Thus the ending of the story decisively affects its interpretation. The story does not condemn Judah but shows him in a positive light.[22] Had the story ended in 38:26, it would have meant that Judah admitted his error and repented of the consequences.[23] But the birth of the twins, the added motif of the younger taking precedence over the firstborn, and the allusion to the future dynasty of the house of David, hinted at in the name Perez—all of these taken together direct the reader to examine the events not in a stigmatizing manner but as a revelation of God's intricate, complex, and unexpected ways.

The Meaning of the Story

What does the story mean to convey to the readers? To find out what a story signifies, it is necessary to connect its components in the most thorough and logical way, while observing the various hues and subtleties of the narrative. The preceding analysis has connected the story's component parts in light of its narrative subtleties and has concluded that the story's main concern was to sharpen the debate about marrying women from the local populace, with the levirate law as a test. The critical message in the story is devotion to the law, here represented by the obligation of levirate marriage. In this story, the observation of the law prevails over the question of origin. Judah's trespass was his attempt to postpone and evade the levirate law, and Tamar's righteousness lies in her demand to fulfill it. Tamar's loyalty to the laws of Judah's family is the reason for her return and acceptance by that family, and as a result there is not the slightest objection to her ethnic origin. Not only is her loyalty rewarded with the divine blessing of twin sons; it is also expressed, as we shall see, by the indication that the young Perez, one of whose descendants would be King David, was a subject of divine favor. Thus the story teaches the reader that loyalty to the law, not ethnic origin, is the leading and decisive criterion for belonging to the people.[24]

The Story's Contexts

The Proximate Context

Commentators ancient and modern have noted the problem of the story's location in the text. Some are persuaded that Gen 38 is an integral element in the larger narrative in which it is set, while others are convinced that the story is a late insertion. The commentators in the former category highlight linguistic and motivic links between the story and its proximate setting. For example, they point to the recurrence of the expression *hakker-nā'* "take note, please!" (Gen 37:32–33; 38:25–26), the verb *šlḥ* "to send" (37:32; 38:17, 20, 25), the use of a goat (37:31; 38:17, 20), and the central motif of a garment in the adjoining stories: Joseph coat (Gen 37), the widow's and harlot's garments (Gen 38), as well as the garment left by Joseph in the hands of Potiphar's wife (Gen 39). The motif of deception also runs through all three stories: Joseph's brothers deceive their father (Gen 37); Tamar deceives Judah (Gen 38); and Potiphar's wife deceives her husband and her household (Gen 39). The motif of the pit appears in the story of the sale (37:24–30) as well as when Joseph is brought out of the "pit" in which he was imprisoned following the affair of Potiphar's wife (41:14). There is also the motif of guilt acknowledgement in the case of Judah, later in that of Joseph's brothers (38:26; 42:21–22), and others.[25]

Those who consider Gen 38 a late insertion base their arguments on the narrative sequence, the chronological problems, and the way the story fits—or in this case, does not fit—within its context.[26] There is no doubt that the story breaks the sequence of the Joseph story and attempts to enclose the Judah and Tamar story into a short chronological span. This is why commentators who seek to present it as realistic have to come up with forced and tortuous solutions. Cassuto, for example, proposes that when Perez and Zerah moved to Egypt they were only a few months old and that Perez's sons Hezron and Hamul, who appear in the list of the family members who went to Egypt (46:11), were in fact born there.[27] Moreover, those doubting the current position of Gen 38 point out that the use of a "resumptive repetition," which takes the reader back to the story of the sale of Joseph (Gen 39:1; cf. 37:36), indicates a deliberate break and is a common editorial technique for handling inserted passages.[28] Finally, from a structural viewpoint, it is possible to remove the story from its setting without damaging the chain of events in the story of Joseph, where every link is necessary to the one that follows. Thus, another indication that the text is a late insertion is the fact that the story of Judah and Tamar could have been fitted within the Joseph story without altering its effect (e.g., after the encounter with Potiphar's wife in Gen 39).

Elsewhere I have discussed the methods of editor-authors who took pains in their redactional work to adapt their insertions to the settings in which they embedded them.[29] Such redactors not only seek out a suitable context for their insertions; they also edit the text so that the insertion harmonizes with its setting. Thus the editorial statement at the start of the so-called Joseph novella in 37:1–2, "This, then, is the line of Jacob," implies an introduction to matters involving the family of Jacob; that is, not all of what follows is necessarily a direct part of Joseph's story but broadly associated with Jacob.[30] In sum, all these considerations lead me to agree with the scholars who regard this story as a tendentious insertion, and it remains to be asked: Who did the insertion and why?

The story's existing location in the narrative tells the reader that, after Joseph was sold away, family life proceeded with relative normalcy. After the sale of Joseph, Judah's moral image was equivocal. On the one hand, he, unlike Reuben, showed some responsibility; amid the murderous clamor, he did not leave the place where Joseph was abandoned. Indeed, it is said that Judah did not join his brothers' plan to kill Joseph but succeeded in persuading them to sell him instead. On the other hand, the very idea of selling Joseph into slavery amounted to criminal abandonment (see Exod 21:16; Deut 24:7). Moreover, Judah was complicit in the brothers' deception of their father, suggesting that he acquiesced in the sale. The reader notices that Judah has special prominence in the collective image of the brothers. This prominence strengthens the impression that Judah's actions and discourse merit particular attention.

Genesis 38 goes on to heighten the positive view of Judah by describing his tragic situation, his repentance, his just decision regarding Tamar, and his concern for those in his care. Nevertheless, the setting of the story gives rise to other questions: Did Judah act as he did because he had learned his lesson from the sale of Joseph? Did he perhaps regret not having persuaded his brothers to act otherwise? Did his feelings of guilt sharpen his sense of justice and his responsibility for his dependents? Did he repent of his part in the sale of Joseph and therefore move apart from his brothers? We can only speculate about these questions, but it is certain that the qualities of responsibility, concern for the family, and a first-rate persuasive ability continue to characterize Judah further on in the Joseph account (43:8–10; 44:16–34; 46:8–12) with or without the present story in this place.

Readers juxtapose Joseph and Judah and discover that, without Judah as an unwitting tool of Providence, Joseph would not have reached his eminence in Egypt and his role in the future of the Israelites.[31] Examining the affair of the sale of Joseph in relation to the Tamar story (wherever it is situated) and seeing Judah's pivotal role in the fulfillment of the divine plan have the effect of shining a new and different light on Judah's character and of mitigating criticism of his behavior.[32]

The Wider Context

The story of Judah and Tamar exhibits a style and motif that resonant with similar features found in Genesis and, more broadly, biblical literature as a whole. First, in the book of Genesis, one finds similarities between Judah and Israel's patriarchs. The transfer of birthright to the younger brother links Judah with Isaac in that they both fathered twin sons, the younger of whom won the birthright. In other words, even a reader who does not associate Perez with (his heir) David understands that Perez is the chosen one who represents a future promise.[33]

Another point of connection is found in the theme of an Israelite who marries a woman from the local population, rather than one brought from another land (see Gen 24:5, 7). This leads many readers to criticize Judah for his connection with the Canaanites, though the text itself does not condemn the marriage with a local woman, unlike Gen 24; 26:34–35; 27:46–28:8. Yet a broad view of Genesis reveals its ambivalence about the ethnic origin of wives, which is why, for example, it does not condemn Abraham for taking an Egyptian woman (Hagar, 16:1). Likewise, Abraham is not censured for his connection with Keturah (25:1), whose origin, like Tamar's, is not mentioned.[34] The specified Canaanite origin of Judah and Simeon's wives (46:10) also remains uncensored, raising the possibility that such ethnically mixed marriages were not isolated cases.

Seen from even a broader vantage point, the midrashic derivation on the name Perez ("What a breach [*pāreṣ*] you have made for yourself!" Gen 38:30) recalls David's statement, "The Lord has broken through my enemies before me as waters break through [*pāreṣ*] " (2 Sam 5:20), hinting at the connection between Perez and David.[35] Thus the wider context supports the interpretation that the birth of Perez is a blessing, similar to the blessing in the book of Ruth: "And may your house be like the house of Perez whom Tamar bore to Judah, through the offspring which the Lord will give you by this young woman" (Ruth 4:12).

In the wider context of the Bible, this story makes an important contribution to the dispute about intermarriage. As we have seen, the story adopts a positive appraisal of intermarriage while standing at odds with the Deuteronomistic texts, or those that were influenced by the Deuteronomistic literature, namely, Ezra and Nehemiah, which support the expulsion of strange women (Ezra 9–10; Neh 9:1; 13:1, 23–30; see also Mal 2:11–12). The broader context reminds the reader that the issue of marriage with foreign women was not unequivocal. The book of Genesis, as indeed the entire Bible, reveals two distinct tendencies with regard to foreign wives: one is isolationist and exclusive, while the other is open, accepting, and adopting. This latter attitude is evinced by both the story of Joseph, which highlights his marriage with the Egyptian Asenath, the daughter of the priest of On (41:45; 46:20), and the story of Judah and Tamar.[36]

The Author of the Judah and Tamar Story: A Proposal

In light of all the above, it appears that the story was written by a Judahite author who wanted to interpolate it into the story of Joseph both because in his day the Judahites had lost their predominance and the issue of mixed marriages was hotly disputed. The author of this story felt that it was necessary to reinforce the status of the Judahites vis-à-vis other groups, while presenting a position that did not rule out mixed marriage. It seems to me that the period that best matches this description is the early Persian period, a time of growing tensions in the country with the return of the Babylonian exiles and the establishment of the province of Yehud.[37] The Babylonian exile had undermined the superiority of the Judahite community with respect to the Benjamites (centered in Mizpeh)[38] and the dominant Israelite community inhabiting the province of Samaria after the Assyrian conquest (cf. Ezra 4:1: "the adversaries of Judah and Benjamin").[39]

At the same time, issues emerged in the early Persian period with regard to the marriage of a woman who was not of pure Israelite descent—meaning that her origins, unlike those of the ancient matriarchs, was not traced back to Mesopotamia and had not been forged in the furnace of the Babylonian exile. According to Ezra and Nehemiah, these women had various ethnicities: Canaanite, Hittite, Perizite, Jebusite, Ammonite, Moabite, Egyptian, Amorite, Tyrian, Ashdodian, and, quite possibly, Israelites and Judahites who had not been exiled.[40] On the issue of foreign wives, the author of the Judah and Tamar story adopts the stricter position by assigning the daughter of Shua to the Canaanites. However, adopting the stricter position indirectly permits marriage with the other different groups, such as the term "peoples of the lands" (Ezek 9:11; 2 Chr 32:13) or "the people who were left in the land" (Jer 40:6). Acceptance or rejection of these women was part of the power struggle between different groups in the consolidating population of the province of Yehud.[41]

Israel Knohl argues that "the principle of the equality of stranger and citizen is widespread throughout the Holiness code."[42] He regards this principle as indicating the authorship of the Holiness school and deduces from it the idea of the equality of the stranger in justice, in the law, and in the constitution. In Gen 38, Tamar is defined as a stranger living among the family of Judah. The laws of the family, including that of levirate marriage, apply to her, as it is written: "There shall be one law for you, whether stranger or citizen of the country" (Num 9:14). All of these factors lead me to conclude that an author-editor of the Holiness school was responsible for inserting this story in its location. Tamar is defined as a sojourning stranger who was integrated into the family of Judah. Her original identity became irrelevant, which may be the reason that it is never specified in the story.

The reference to Perez and the absence of the list of generations leading to David—that is, the lack of any explicit mention of David—seem to me also appropriate to this period. The Persian overlords undermined political aspirations with their reluctance to appoint a descendant of the House of David as governor—the last one was Zerubbabel. The prophecies of Second Isaiah also mention David only once (Isa 55:3). In fact, if we depended on the books of Haggai, Zechariah, and Ezra alone, we would not have known that Sheshbazar and Zerubbabel were descendants of David at all, and Second Isaiah would have led us to expect the liberation to come from Cyrus, king of Persia, rather than from the house of David.[43]

The story of Judah and Tamar, then, presents a pro-Judahite position, favoring an open attitude toward the integration of the local populace as a way of strengthening and consolidating the people, while depicting the superiority of Judah as a source of future political hope. We may also infer that the story was composed by a member of the "universalist" movement that sought to bring in the strangers and opposed the isolationism that characterized the Deuteronomistic movement or, subsequently, Ezra and Nehemiah.[44] In addition to promoting the expansion of the Judean populace, the Judah and Tamar narrative was inserted into the story of Joseph because it served the aim of promoting the figure of Judah vis-à-vis the northerners (the people of Samaria), who regarded themselves as the descendants of Joseph, and vis-à-vis the Benjamites, who are portrayed in the narrative as the descendants of Joseph's youngest and beloved brother. These aims correspond with the early years of the Second Temple and also express the worldview of the Holiness school.[45]

The book of Ruth echoes the story of Judah and Tamar in its affirmation of a non-Israelite wife (Ruth's Moabite identity is continually emphasized; see Ruth 1:4, 22; 2:2, 6, 10, 21; 4:5) and in its focus on the levirate marriage law. Specifically, in the book of Ruth the law of redemption in Lev 25 is further extended by the levirate law, whereby the redeemer of the land becomes the redeemer of the widow, and the plucking off of the shoe becomes part of the ritual. Another issue that is brought out more explicitly in the book of Ruth is the reference to the house of David. It not only names David as a descendant of Boaz (Ruth 4:17) but includes the entire genealogy from Perez to David (4:18–22). The book of Ruth also refers by name to the story of Judah and Tamar (4:12). We may therefore assume that the story of Judah and Tamar was the ideological and poetical basis for the book of Ruth.

In conclusion, the story of Judah and Tamar served as an anti-isolationist polemical position on the crucial issue of marriage with foreign women. These women came from the local population, encountered by the returnees from Babylonian exile, when the term "the peoples of the lands" had not yet been coined.[46] The story upholds a moral principle: the integration of the stranger on the basis of loyalty to the host society. Tamar, the local and therefore "foreign" woman, who insists on the levirate law, despite the difficulties and risks that she undertakes, is a model of positive integration that wins divine support and blessing. In this way, the story expressed the author's positive view on the issue of foreign women and paved the way to the possibility of proselytizing in later periods.

For Further Reading

Alter, Robert. *The Art of Biblical Narrative*. New York: Basic Books, 1981.

Amit, Yairah. *Reading Biblical Narratives: Literary Criticism and the Hebrew Bible*. Minneapolis: Fortress, 2001.

Berlin, Adele. *Poetics and Interpretation of Biblical Narrative*. Winona Lake, Ind.: Eisenbrauns, 1994.

Fokkelman, J. P. *Reading Biblical Narrative: An Introductory Guide*. Louisville: Westminster John Knox, 1999.

Gunn, David M., and Danna Nolan Fewell. *Narrative in the Hebrew Bible*. Oxford Bible Series. Oxford: Oxford University Press, 1993.

Miscall, Peter D. *The Workings of Old Testament Narrative*. SemeiaSt. Philadelphia: Fortress, 1983.

Powell, Mark Allan. *What Is Narrative Criticism?* Minneapolis: Fortress, 1990.

Sternberg, Meir. *The Poetics of Biblical Narrative: Ideological Literature and the Drama of Reading*. Indiana Studies in Biblical Literature. Bloomington: Indiana University Press, 1987.

Notes

1. Hermann Gunkel, whose influence on the development of narrative criticism is beyond doubt, used his literary sensibilities mainly to define literary forms. For example, his literary insights appear in the introduction to his commentary on the book of Genesis, not throughout the body of the commentary. See Hermann Gunkel, *Genesis* (German orig. 1901; trans. Mark E. Biddle; Mercer Library of Biblical Studies; Macon, Ga.: Mercer University Press, 1997), vii–xlviii.

2. For an exhaustive treatment of the history of research on biblical narrative, see Frank Polak, *Biblical Narrative: Aspects of Art and Design* (The Biblical Encyclopedia Library 11; Jerusalem: Mosad Bialik, 1994), 421–40. See also Yairah Amit, *Reading Biblical Narratives: Literary Criticism and the Hebrew Bible* (trans. Yael Lotan; Minneapolis: Augsburg Fortress, 2001), 22–32.

3. For a detailed statement of my approach, see the first chapter of my book on the art of editing in the book of Judges, including attention to the ideological and rhetorical aspects of texts, the general editorial process, and the use of the terms "author-editor," "implied editing," "immediate or proximate context," and "distant or wider context" (Yairah Amit, *The Book of Judges: The Art of Editing* [trans. Jonathan Chipman; BibInt 38; Leiden: Brill, 1999], 1–24).

4. On the polemical character of biblical literature and the search for the meaning therein, see Yairah Amit, *Hidden Polemics in Biblical Narrative* (trans. Jonathan Chipman; BibInt 25; Leiden: Brill, 2000).

5. On the expositions of biblical narratives, their character and function, and on a special case of a very long exposition, see Amit, *Reading Biblical Narratives*, 33–45.

6. Translation from NJPS throughout with only minor variations.

7. See Rashi's comments: "On the name of the red-shining appearance, as it is written: 'The sun was shining over the water, and from the distance the water appeared to the Moabites as red as blood' (2 Kgs 3:22)."

8. This calculation is based on details from the story: twenty-two years elapsed between the sale of seventeen-year-old Joseph (Gen 37:1) and his reunion with his brothers. He arrived at Pharaoh's court at age thirty, thirteen years after the sale (41:46). To this one must add seven years of plenty and two more years of famine until he met the brothers (44:11). It simply cannot be that during that twenty-two-year interval Judah married and had three sons, married off two of them, and fathered Tamar's two children (Perez and Zerah), for when they went to Egypt, Perez already had two children of his own, Hezron and Hamul (46:12).

9. On the editor's combining technique, see Isac Leo Seeligmann, "Hebrew Narrative and Biblical Historiography," in *Studies in Biblical Literature* [Hebrew] (ed. Avi Hurvitz, Sara Japhet, and Emanuel Tov; Jerusalem: Magnes, 1992), 50–53; trans. of "Hebräische Erzahlung und biblische Geschichtsschreibung," *TZ* (1965): 305–25.

10. On Tamar's Canaanite origin and Judah's Canaanite environment, see Gerhard von Rad, *Genesis: A Commentary* (trans. John H. Marks; OTL; Philadelphia: Westminster, 1961), 352–53. John A. Emerton ("An Examination of a Recent Structuralist Interpretation of Genesis xxxviii," *VT* 26 [1976]: 90) argues for the Canaanite origin of Tamar: he completely rejects Edmund Leach's suggestion that Tamar was an Israelite; and he even suggests that Judah's friendly relations with the Canaanites imply the Canaanite origin of the story before it was reworked (idem, "Judah and Tamar," *VT* 29 [1979]: 405, 412). Claus Westermann objects, suggesting that the story is Israelite, and, even if Tamar is a Canaanite, she becomes an integral part of Judah's family (*Genesis 37–50: A Commentary* [trans. John J. Scullion; CC; Minneapolis: Augsburg Fortress, 1987], 50).

11. The sages also did not explain the sin on account of Tamar's Canaanite origin but deduced Er's sin from that of Onan, namely, because he did not want her to become pregnant and lose her beauty. On other solutions of the early interpreters, see Emerton, "An Examination"; and Avigdor Shinan and Yair Zakovitch, *The Story of Judah and Tamar: Genesis 38 in the Bible, The Old Versions and the Ancient Jewish Literature* [Hebrew] (Research Projects of the Institute of Jewish Studies, Monograph Series 15; Jerusalem: The Hebrew University Press, 1992).

12. Susan Niditch examines the social structures that supported this situation ("The Wronged Woman Righted: An Analysis of Genesis 38" *HTR* 72 [1979]: 169–76). See also Phyllis Bird's statement: "I am convinced that literary art and social presuppositions are so interrelated in any literary work that adequate interpretation requires the employment of both literary criticism and social analysis" ("Three Old Testament Texts," *Semeia* 46 [1989]: 119–39, here 119).

13. For example, the time spent in Egypt from Joseph's death to the exodus was, according to Gen 15:13, four hundred years, but it is told in Exod 1:7 in a single verse.

14. On Judah as a tragic hero, see my student's M.A. thesis: Dalia Ravid, "'She Hath Been More Righteous Than I': Circles of Interpretation in Gen 38" [Hebrew] (M.A. thesis, University of Tel Aviv, 1993), 38–45. For the application of the Aristotelian tragic model of five stages to Saul's kingship (fateful error, terrible act, change, recognition, and suffering) and the portrayal of Saul as a tragic hero, see Amit, "The Incident of the Concubine in Gibeah as a Hidden Polemic against Saul's Kingship and Its Supporters" [Hebrew], *Beit Mikra* 129 (1992): 109–18, esp. 114–16; and idem, *Hidden Polemics in Biblical Narrative*, 173–76. In the case of Judah, the stage of the terrible act is the encounter with Tamar disguised as a harlot; the change occurs when her pregnancy becomes known; the recognition, when she presents the forfeit; and the suffering occurs because he was not intimate with her again.

15. Another interpretation of the Hebrew text that does not match the cantillation marks is: "She is right, [the pregnancy is] from me." For other renderings, see Richard J. Clifford, "Genesis 38: Its Contribution to the Jacob Story," *CBQ* 66 (2004): 519–32, esp. 530–31.

16. Yehuda Kiel emphasizes that "his acknowledgement was not in secret but in public; it could have taken place in the presence of those who came to the city gate, or in court, or both, similarly to what is told about Boaz and Ruth in the gate of Bethlehem" (*The Book of Genesis* [Hebrew] [Tanach Da'at Miqra; Jerusalem: Mossad Harav

Kook, 2003], 91).

17. Kiel, following Rashi—who commented "some say 'no more' and others say 'did not cease'"—interprets this verse to mean that Judah did not have intercourse with her while she was pregnant but did not refrain from it after the birth. Niditch thinks that this phrase is an addition of a late Priestly editor. See Niditch, "The Wronged Woman Righted," 143–49.

18. This translation (NJPS) follows LXX, which reflects an inversion of parts in the sentence. In the MT the words "and at the turn of the year" appear before "Hannah conceived."

19. For similar compensations, compare Gen 4:24; 2 Sam 12:14–25; and Job 42:12–16 (esp. v. 13). See, too, Judah Goldin, "The Youngest Son or Where Does Genesis 38 Belong?" *JBL* 96 (1977): 27–44, esp. 30.

20. For such a negative view of Judah's every action, see Shinan and Zakovitch, *The Story of Judah and Tamar*; David M. Gunn and Danna Nolan Fewell, "Tamar and Judah: Genesis 38," in their *Narrative in the Hebrew Bible* (New York: Oxford University Press, 1993): 34–45; and Clifford and Richard, *Genesis 38: Its Contribution*, 519–32. Shinan and Zakovitch present the narrative as "anti-Judaic story, which mocks the father of the tribe of Judah, the father of the house of David.... The one who planted ch. 38 in the midst of Joseph's stories, after ch. 37, seeks to reduce Judah's figure.... And it is not impossible that this chapter is also against Perez, to whom king David is related" (220). A similar approach is found in Gary A. Rendsgurg, "David and His Circle in Genesis xxxviii," *VT* 36 (1986): 438–46, here 444–45. Gunn and Fewell present the story from a feminist perspective, which sees in Judah's every act clear signs of (typically) male, patriarchal, and inconsiderate behavior. Clifford, however, is impressed by the transformation of Judah, who was shocked by Tamar's deed and is transformed into a better example for his brothers.

21. See Yairah Amit, "Endings—Especially Reversal Endings," *Scripura* 87 (2004): 213–26.

22. The purpose of Ravid's research is to prove that "the original intention of the implied author-editor was precisely to explain Judah's deeds, which show his greatness, and to hint at his similarity to the Almighty" ("She Hath Been More Righteous Than I," vii). For a positive view of Judah, see also Amit, *Hidden Polemics in Biblical Narrative*, 96–97. Petersen analyzes the different readings, while paying attention to the changes Judah goes through, which appear in order to cast him in a favorable light. See John Petersen, *Reading Women's Stories: Female Characters in the Hebrew Bible* (Minneapolis: Fortress, 2004), 119–64.

23. In Bird's analysis, v. 26 is the ending of the story ("Three Old Testament Texts," 122–26).

24. John Skinner (*A Critical and Exegetical Commentary on Genesis* [ICC; Edinburgh: T&T Clark, 1930], 449–50) considers that the function of this story is to present the structure of the tribe of Judah, its components, and its settlement in the region. Similarly, Emerton also looks at the affinity with the Canaanites ("Judah and Tamar"). Von Rad emphasizes the ethnological aspect but is aware that the story has something more to say (*Genesis*, 356–57), while Westemann highlights the family aspect and pays attention to the shaping of the characters (*Genesis 37–50*, 49–50,

56). According to Judah Goldin, who focuses on the story's ending, the tale is about the election of the younger son in preference to the elder ("The Youngest Son," 44). Others emphasize the story's contribution to the appreciation of Judah and his development in a positive way. But Shinan and Zakovitch think that the purpose of the story is to diminish the character of Judah, who must ultimately realize that both God and Tamar are more clever than he; Tamar made him the father of her children, and God replaced the elder with the younger by advancing Perez over Zerah (*Story of Judah and Tamar*, 220). See David W. Cotter, *Genesis* (Berit Olam; Collegeville, Minn.: Liturgical Press, 2003).

25. Already the sages saw the connection between Gen 38:25–26 in our story and Gen 37:32–33 (Gen. Rab. 85:11). Many scholars have followed them: e.g., Umberto Cassuto "The Story of Tamar and Judah" [Hebrew] in idem, *Biblical and Canaanite Literatures* (vol. 1 of *Studies on the Bible and Ancient Orient*; Jerusalem: Magnes, 1972), 108–10. Robert Alter concluded from these connections the advantage of the literary approach as in *The Art of Biblical Narrative* (New York: Basic Books, 1981), 3–12. Gordon J. Wenham points to the importance of the story to understanding the characters' later development in *Genesis 16–50* (WBC 2; Dallas: Word, 1994), 363–65. Cotter also thinks that the story is an integral part of its context (*Genesis*, 277–79).

26. See Goldin's survey of these interpretations ("The Youngest Son," 27–29). According to Westermann, it is an individual story about one of Jacob's sons, and he stresses that it is a supplement to Jacob's stories (*Genesis 37–50*, 49). Shinan and Zakovitch also decide that it is an addition and highlight the resumptive-repetition technique (*Story of Judah and Tamar*, 207); see also Amit, *Reading Biblical Narratives*, 143–47.

27. Cassuto, "The Story of Tamar and Judah."

28. The first to discover the phenomenon of "resumptive repetition" was C. Kuhl, "Die 'Wiederaufnahme'—ein literar-kritisches Prinzip?" *ZAW* 64 (1952): 1–11.

29. See my discussion on the inclusion of the story of the concubine in Gibeah within the book of Judges (Amit, *The Book of Judges*, 351–57). See also Goldin's praise for the editor who placed Gen 38 in its setting: "Whoever put the story as we have it in its present position, must have been guided by what seemed to him a sound literary principle: either a thematic or idiomatic connection or association must present between the story of the sale of Joseph into bondage and the account of Judah's encounter with Tamar" ("The Youngest Son," 29). Shinan and Zakovitch assume that "the one who wrote the story of Judah and Tamar and gave it its present form did so in order to interpolate it in this place and to shape its meaning in the background of its present context" (*The Story of Judah and Tamar*, 207).

30. Wenham concluded from this that one must accept that the larger narrative context of Gen 38 is the story of Jacob's family. Thus, one need not wonder about the appearance of narrative units that deal with sons other than Joseph (*Genesis 16–50*, 364–65). But Wenham ignores the fact that only Gen 38 is devoted to a particular son. It seems to me this statement in 37:1–2 is an editorial device that legitimizes other editorial interpolations. Further, it is intended to reduce Joseph's status and to prevent his appearance as one of the fathers of the nation.

31. By scrutinizing terminological patterns, Wilfried Warning ("Terminological Patterns and Genesis 38," *AUSS* 38 [2000]: 293–305) shows that the story in its present form is intended to highlight the place of Judah alongside Joseph.

32. There is no doubt that, in order to see this, one must reread the story from beginning to end. On the importance of second and third readings in the dynamic of the reading process, see Menakhem Perry, "Literary Dynamics: How the Order of a Text Creates Its Meaning," *Poetics Today* 1 (1979): 35–64.

33. Goldin, "The Youngest Son," 30.

34. Wenham even emphasizes that the behavior of the Canaanite Tamar, the story's protagonist, resembles that of Melchizedek (Gen 14:18–28) and Abimelech (Gen 20), two kings who acknowledged God's active involvement in Abraham's family (*Genesis 16–50*, 365).

35. Compare also with Micah's prophecy: "One who makes a breach goes before them; they enlarge it to a gate and leave by it; their king marches before them, the LORD at their head" (2:13). While Emerton argues against exaggerating the importance of the house of David in this story ("Judah and Tamar"), Rendsburg is convinced this story is primarily built on the affinities with the family of David and lists seven issues common to Gen 38 and the book of Samuel ("David and His Circle"). It is worth noting that the genealogical line from Perez to David is not mentioned in the book of Samuel, only in later literature: the ending of Ruth (4:18–22) and the genealogies of Chronicles (1 Chr 2:3–15). Westermann stresses the fact that David is not mentioned by name in the story (*Genesis 37–50*, 57). Wenham extends the connection with David as far as Jesus (Matt 1:6, 16) (*Genesis 16–50*, 370). According to him, the importance of the story lies in creating the connection with the salvation history of the world.

36. On the different approaches to foreigners and aliens in the book of Chronicles and other writings, see Sara Japhet, *The Ideology of the Book of Chronicles and Its Place in Biblical Thought* (Frankfurt am Main: Lang, 1989), 334–51; Yonina Dor, *Have the "Foreign Women" Really Been Expelled? Separation and Exclusion in the Restoration Period* [Hebrew] (Jerusalem: Magnes, 2006), 123–50 and the bibliography there.

37. Emerton's ("Judah and Tamar," 338–61) view is that the story was told among the Canaanites in the area of Adulam from the end of the eleventh century B.C.E. and was reworked by J, but not later than the eighth century B.C.E. He even proposes that the author was of Calebite origin. Rendsburg ("David and His Circle," 438–46) thinks that the story was written around 900 B.C.E. as a satire intended to mock the royal family.

38. On the strengthening of the area of Benjamin and the center of Mitzpeh, see Oded Lipschitz, *The Fall and Rise of Jerusalem: Judah under Babylonian Rule* (Winona Lake, Ind.: Eisenbrauns, 2005), 92–97, 102–22, 149–54.

39. See, for example, Haim Tadmor, "The Relation of the Jewish People to the Land of Israel in the Light of the Babylonian Exile and the Return to Zion," in *Exile and Diaspora: Studies in the History of the Jewish People Presented to Professor Haim Beinart on the Occasion of His Seventieth Birthday* [Hebrew] (ed. A. Mirsky, A. Grossman, and Y. Kaplan; Jerusalem: Ben Zvi Institute and the Hebrew University of Jerusalem, 1988), 50–56; Israel Finkelstein and David Silbermanm, *The Bible*

Unearthed: Archaeology's New Vision of Ancient Israel and the Origin of Its Sacred Texts (New York: Free Press, 2001), 221–22.

40. Following Kaufman, Milgrom declares: "Let me state my conclusion in advance: religious conversion is neither attested nor possible in ancient Israel before the Second Temple period." See Jacob Milgrom, "Religious Conversion and the Revolt Model for the Formation of Israel," *JBL* 101 (1982): 169–76.

41. According to Yonina Dor, the convincing identification of the foreign women is with the inhabitants of Judah and Israel who had not gone into exile (*Have the "Foreign Women,"* 127–54).

42. So Israel Knohl, *The Sanctuary of Silence: The Priestly Torah and the Holiness School* (Minneapolis: Fortress, 1995), 21; see also Lev 17:8, 10, 12, 13, 15; 18:26; 19:33, 34; 20:2; 22:18; 24:22.

43. Dor, *Have the "Foreign Women,"* 146. In a forthcoming article I argue that the absence of the name of David is a sign of hidden polemic. For the meaning of "hidden polemic," see Amit, *Hidden Polemics in Biblical Narrative.*

44. Second Isaiah is another prominent representative of this current. See, for example, Isa 43:9–10; 45:20–23; and especially 56:1–9. See also Moshe Weinfeld, "Universalism and Particularism in the Period of Exile and Restoration" [Hebrew], *Tarbiz* 33 (1964): 228–42. It is worth noting that the Holiness school emphasized the rights of foreigners. See, e.g., Lev 19:33–34. According to Knohl (*The Sanctuary of Silence*, 219–20): "The application of this law to the resident aliens as well (Lev 17:8), along with the granting of equal cultic and judicial status (Num 15:14–16), is an additional defense measure against the incursion of idolatrous practices into the land." Knohl classifies Exod 12:43–49 with the Holiness school (28 including n. 35, 62). See also Ezek 47:22–23, which gives to the foreigners rights on the land. However, I am aware of the absence of proof from the linguistic aspect.

45. Contra Knohl, who thinks that the background of the emergence of the Holiness school is the time of Ahaz and Hezekiah (*The Sanctuary of Silence*, 199–224).

46. On the term "the peoples of the land" in a derogatory sense, and its positive origin meaning ownership, see Tadmor, "The Relation of the Jewish People," 54.

Poetic Analysis: Psalm 121*

Kirsten Nielsen

In 1968 James Muilenburg gave his famous lecture "Form Criticism and Beyond."[1] His purpose was not to abandon form criticism but to argue that it required a supplement. The strength of form criticism was to be found in its division of poetic texts into specific genres (*Gattungen*) and in its insistence on the link between the genre and the situation in which the particular genre was used (*Sitz im Leben*). Using this method, it had become possible to show the common factors in, for example, a group of psalms and to reconstruct their *Sitz im Leben*. However, this interest in common factors had led interpreters to ignore the specific character of an individual text. Muilenburg therefore formulated his particular interest as follows:

> What I am interested in, above all, is in understanding the nature of Hebrew literary composition, in exhibiting the structural patterns that are employed for the fashioning of a literary unit, whether in poetry or in prose, and in discerning the many and various devices by which the predications are formulated and ordered into a unified whole. Such an enterprise I should describe as rhetoric and the methodology as rhetorical criticism.[2]

Muilenburg's call for an increased interest in the rhetorical devices of a text in both prose and poetry pointed the way forward but simultaneously meant a return to the interest of previous scholarship in the specific characteristics of Hebrew poetry.[3]

---

* In 1977–1978, David Petersen was Visiting Professor at the Institute for Old and New Testament at the Faculty of Theology, University of Aarhus. It is therefore a particular pleasure to be able to bring a Danish greeting now as we celebrate his career.

Characteristics of Hebrew Poetry

An analysis of Hebrew poetry must of necessity concern itself with a number of different factors. In the following overview, I shall deal with four important aspects: rhythm and phonology; grammatical features; structural elements; and the use of imagery and the many opportunities it affords for intertextual links. To begin, language consists of sounds that have become visual signs in written form. We shall therefore examine the features of sound in poetic language.

Features Associated with Rhythm and Phonology

The fact that poetry and sound are closely associated is of course not specific to Hebrew poetry, but it is nevertheless an aspect of Hebrew poetry that raises a number of difficulties. We cannot know, for instance, how the psalms of David sounded when they were composed and orally presented. We have no direct access to the pronunciation of the time, so we are forced to build on the Masoretic Text and the information we can gain from accents that were added later. From this it becomes clear that Hebrew poetry is rhythmic, though, unlike much other poetry, such as Greek poetry, there is no evidence of a specific meter. In Hebrew, the rhythm of the text is created by the use of stressed syllables, whereas unstressed syllables are not counted. It is thus not the actual number of syllables that determines the rhythm but only the number of *stressed* syllables that creates the rhythm.

In *Interpreting Hebrew Poetry* David Petersen and Kent Richards quote T. Brogan's description of rhythm as "a cadence, a contour, a figure of periodicity, any sequence perceptible as a distinct pattern capable of repetition and variation."[4] From this they conclude that "Hebrew poetry is marked by a delicate balance between regularity and variation," and they argue that this allows considerable room for variation.[5] There is thus much skepticism today toward the textual corrections of earlier times, when scholars proposed emendations to otherwise completely comprehensible texts on the grounds that the correction would better suit the rhythm of the text (*metri causa*). Our knowledge of the aesthetic ideals of the past is simply too flimsy to make such textual "improvements."

Even though we do not know the exact pronunciation of Hebrew, it is of course possible to note phenomena in the written text such as *assonance* (repetition of vowels) and *alliteration* (repetition of consonants).[6]

Repetition of this sort increases the cohesion of the poem; similarity of sound creates not only sound but also cohesion of content. However, the actual *sound* of the poetry cannot be rendered into another language. In Danish, "heart" (*hjerte*) rhymes with "pain" (*smerte*), so Danes grow up with the idea that love can also be linked to pain. But such a connection between sound and content cannot be re-created in English, where "love" rhymes with "above." Likewise, it can be difficult with either a Danish or an English translation to understand why "name" is linked to "oil" in Song 1:3. The literal translation is: "Your name is an oil poured out." This is a somewhat surprising expression unless one is familiar with Hebrew, where the word "name" (*šēm*) resembles the word "oil" (*šemen*), creating a word-play that links the two. Thus, listening to the beloved's name is similar to the pleasure of being anointed with fragrant oil. What we as readers must consider is whether the reference is to the fragrance of oil or to another aspect of oil that describes what young girls feel when they hear the name of their beloved.

Grammatical Features

Form plays a major role in Hebrew poetry. This is apparent from its general freedom of syntax. To take but one example, normal word order can be reversed in the second part of a phrase to create a chiasmus (AB // B'A'): "For the Lord knows the way of the righteous, but the way of the wicked will perish" (Ps 1:6). Besides the freedom of syntax, one may also find the phenomenon that particles, which are an important part of ordinary prose (the definite article, the direct object marker, and relative pronouns), can be omitted in Hebrew poetry as a matter of course. Similarly, the verb in the second part of a parallelism can be omitted because it is inferred, as in 1 Sam 18:7. This feature does not occur in prose texts. Nor does the use of the perfect and imperfect tenses (*qātal* and *yiqtōl*) in poetry correspond to what we know from Hebrew prose. So far it has proved impossible to put forward a convincing theory explaining the use of these verbal forms in Hebrew poetry.

Structural Elements

If we ask what is most characteristic of Hebrew poetry, the answer is likely to be *parallelism*. In 1753 Robert Lowth lectured on Hebrew poetry at Oxford and pointed to parallelism, *parallelismus membrorum*, as an important element. Lowth distinguished between three types of parallelism: *synonymous parallelism*, where two parallel statements express the same thought using different words (e.g., Ps 1:1); *antithetical parallelism*, where two statements indicate a contrasting parallel (e.g., Ps 1:6); and *synthetical parallelism*, in which the line of thought from the first statement is continued in the parallel statement (e.g., Ps 1:3). In practice, however, this third category has been difficult to define, as Lowth himself was well aware.[7]

This division into three types has been criticized by James Kugel, who argues that there is either one type of parallelism or there are hundreds—but there are certainly not three.[8] Kugel's point is that, in all forms of parallelism, each example should be read as a complete unit. The interpreter must therefore be aware of the *difference* between the two parallel statements. The second element in a parallelism is not merely a repetition but an amplifier that qualifies the first element. To illustrate this, Kugel coined the phrase: "A, and what is more, B."[9] The second element adds meaning to the first. Parallelism has thus not only an aesthetic function but also a semantic one.

While parallelism plays a significant role in Hebrew poetry, we might also consider, along with C. S. Lewis in his *Reflections on the Psalms*, whether one of the reasons why scholars focus precisely on this phenomenon is that it is possible to reproduce it when translating from Hebrew into another language: "It is (according to one's point of view) either a wonderful piece of luck or a wise provision of God's, that poetry which has to be turned into all languages should have as its chief formal characteristic one that does not disappear (as mere metre does) in translation."[10]

Parallelism can indeed be rendered into other languages, provided we think of it solely as a "thought-rhyme," a way of expressing a particular thought. But from a linguistic point of view, parallelism is not just a semantic phenomenon.[11] Parallelism consists of a combination of correspondence and contrast, but these find expression on different levels.

At the sound level (the *phonological*), parallelism occurs as assonance and alliteration. There is a certain sound correspondence between the two statements in question (e.g., Isa 5:7). At the *morphological* level, a correspondence is created when, for example, two verbs are used in the same conjugation, person, number, and gender (e.g., Ps 6:2), while contrast can be created by alternating between masculine and feminine or singular and plural. *Syntactical* correspondence and contrast occur when the word order is, respectively, identical (e.g., Ps 6:2) and chiastic (e.g., Ps 2:1–2). Finally, this is also true at the *semantic* level, where the use of contrasts is widespread in the stock forms, such as *anger // grace* or a *moment //* a *lifetime* (e.g., Ps 30:6). Thus, when two statements are regarded as parallel and understood as a whole, it is not just the thought content but also the formal features that serve to create cohesion.

In *The Art of Biblical Poetry*, Robert Alter makes a detailed analysis of "the dynamics of parallelism" and offers many examples of how the second element in parallelism strengthens and amplifies the first. For Alter, it is therefore important that within parallelism a certain disharmony is created in the midst of harmony, so that "semantic modifications" can occur.[12] Such modifications remind us of the way a metaphor works, inasmuch as it is precisely the compounding of two different statements that creates new meaning.

When we turn to the psalms of David as poetry, we have the great advantage that there is no problem in delineating the text, as is often the case with prophetic texts. Nevertheless, a text can be more or less "well-structured," and scholars disagree as to what extent the concepts of *stanza* and *strophe* are relevant for Hebrew poetry. Whatever the case may be, when employing these terms, we must not expect fixed rules for the size and length of such brief pieces.[13] It is more important to be aware of the poetic devices that are employed to structure a *lengthy* piece of text. Such structuring can occur, for instance, through the repetition of the same introduction, as is the case with the woe oracles in Isa 5:8, 11, 18, and 20–22. The phenomenon of repetition itself, possibly with variations, can thus help to build the structure of a poem while simultaneously intensifying its message. Through the use of a *refrain*, the poet can round off the poem in a convincing way, as is the case with Ps 8, which begins and ends in the same way, or Isa 5:25; 9:11, 16, 20; and 10:4, where the refrain describes YHWH's persistent anger. By various means the poet can also form the text into a ring, where the beginning and the ending correspond. Here not only the refrain, but also the chiastic structure, serves to round off the text (e.g., Jer 2:5–9).

A very special way of creating unity occurs in the *alphabetical psalms*, in which the first verse begins with the first letter of the Hebrew alphabet, *aleph*, after which each subsequent line starts with the next letter, all the way down to the final letter, *taw*. This creates a rounded text of twenty-two lines, corresponding to the twenty-two letters of the Hebrew alphabet. A good example of this is Ps 111 or the highly refined

Ps 119, where each of the twenty-two stanzas contains eight lines, all of which begin with the same letter, thus covering the whole alphabet with its 176 verses.

Imagery and Intertextuality

The final feature of Hebrew poetry is its extensive use of imagery, that is, of similes and metaphors. *Imagery* as such is not reserved for poetry, of course. However, what is characteristic of Hebrew poetry is the *choice* and *number* of similes and metaphors that help to give the poetry its special style. Poetry dealing with the relationship between God and humans demands a language that can say what cannot be said. All attempts to talk about God face the difficulty that, unlike humans and everything else in this world, God is not immediately present. That the Old Testament poets were aware of this is clear from their way of speaking about God. In their experience, God is paradoxically both strange and familiar, and the poets use imagery to express this double identity. What characterizes both metaphor and simile is that they connect two contexts that are normally unconnected.[14] The result is a statement that demands that the audience actively sort through the potential meanings of the expression in order to decide which of them are relevant. When the psalmist calls God "my rock" (Ps 18:3), the word "rock" also contains a number of potential meanings that are *not* relevant in this case. God does not consist of flint, for example, nor is God dimensioned like a rock. But among the likely candidates for a meaningful resonance is this: as a rock, God can offer protection from the enemy, or God is immovable and thus reliable. In a metaphorical statement, therefore, likeness and unlikeness are equally necessary. On the one hand, if the two statements were completely alike, they would no longer be figurative but *literal* language. On the other hand, if they were completely different, they would be unable to create any kind of cohesion and would consequently be meaningless.

Such imagery thus maintains both God's "otherness" (i.e., there is a difference between the image and God) and the possibility of saying something intelligible about God (i.e., there is, after all, a similarity between the image and God). When we add to this the fact that the Old Testament poets employ a multitude of images about God rather than merely one or two, it becomes clear that imagery consists of what T. S. Eliot calls a "raid on the inarticulate." Imagery simultaneously reveals yet obscures God's reality; ultimately, God is made familiar despite unfamiliarity.

It is often fruitful to look for links between metaphors. They can therefore also function as referential markers that point us to other texts where the same or similar metaphors are used.[15] These *intertexts* can then act as keys to interpreting the text in question. In this, poetry is similar to prose, but the frequency of metaphors gives rise to the need to compare several different intertexts to throw light on a particular text, as is the case with Ps 121 (see further below). The poets' way of speaking about God is thus characterized by its openness to *other* ways of speaking about God. This is not quite the same as with parallelism: "A, and what is more, B." In God's case it is rather: "A, and what is more, B; and what is more, C; and what is more…." What is said about God is never finally complete. There is always room for yet another association, yet another parallelism, yet another metaphor, which is why there is always room and a need for an active audience who participates in the analysis and interpretation of the poetry. The many literary devices available to poets thus serve to emphasize that when we speak of the ultimate questions of existence—be it the relationship between two people as we know it from love poetry or between God and humanity as we know it from the Bible—the poet must choose a language that does not define the beloved to such a degree that limits are set on further insights.

Analysis of the Poetry of Psalm 121

As we have seen, there are four specific features of Hebrew poetry: features associated with rhythm and phonology; grammatical features; structural elements; and imagery and intertextuality. As an example of a poetic text, we turn now to Ps 121, beginning with its rhythmic formation. There are a number of stressed syllables in the individual verses that create the following *rhythm*:

vv. 1–2:	3 + 3
v. 3:	3 + 2
vv. 4–5:	2 + 2 + 2
vv. 6–7:	3 + 2
v. 8:	2 + 2 + 2

Of these eight verses, two have the rhythm 3 + 3, while three have the rhythm 3 + 2, and three others have 2 + 2 + 2. There is thus no fixed meter. The rhythm does help, though, to create cohesion between the individual verses. Giving the same rhythm to the first two verses (3 + 3) creates a unity that corresponds to the whole structure of the psalm. The psalmist raises a question in verse 1 that he answers in verse 2. In correspondence with the new rhythm in verse 3 (3 + 2), there is also a change in content: a new person is introduced who addresses the psalmist. In the following two verses (vv. 4–5) the content of verse 3 is amplified in the form of a negative and a positive definition of YHWH's care. In verses 6–7, the rhythm of verse 3 (3 + 2) is resumed, and, just as in verses 4–5, the message is formulated as a negative and then a positive definition of YHWH's care. The last verse ends with 2 + 2 + 2, linking it rhythmically to the middle two verses (vv. 4–5). So, in this psalm both repetition and variation are features of the rhythm and as such serve to create unity and cohesion.

Other sonic phenomena such as *assonance* and *alliteration* also serve to create cohesion. In verse 3 there is an example of rhyme in which both the first and the second part of the verse end on the same two vowels (*e-ā*), linked by the same consonant, *k* (the suffix for the second-person masculine singular). Again, in verse 5 the same suffix is repeated three times, corresponding to the rhythm (2 + 2 + 2). In addition, the verb *šmr* is used six times to create a sound link between verses 3 (once), 4 (once), 5 (once), 7 (twice), and 8 (once). It is difficult to say more about the effect of these phenomena than that they help to give an impression of cohesion and unity.

This impression is further supported by a number of *grammatical phenomena* that are closely connected to the sound and structure of the psalm. As mentioned, the suffix for the second-person singular masculine form is frequently used, providing not only rhyme but also a grammatical unity that holds the statement together. Furthermore, other grammatical parallels, such as the prohibition *ʾal* twice in verse 3 and the prohibition *lôʾ* twice in verse 4, reveal a unity of word order (negation + verb) with variation.

A structural effect that may also be found in the psalm is *chiasmus*, which serves to create a close connection between the question and answer in verses 1–2. The question is formulated, "From where comes my help [*ʿezrî*]?" and answered, "My help [*ʿezrî*] [comes] from YHWH." It is characteristic of poetry, in contrast to prose, that the verb can be omitted in the parallel statement. In verse 6 a chiasmus is created by the expression "by day" (*yômām*) opening the verse and the expression "by night" (*ballāylâ*) closing it. Similarly, the sun (*šemeš*) is contrasted with the moon (*yārēaḥ*), while the negated verb takes the middle position in order to convey the central point: the psalmist is not in danger. Here, too, the verb is omitted in the second round.

Parallelism is often regarded as the most characteristic feature of Hebrew poetry, and Ps 121 is no exception. Many parallel expressions are used to develop the way in which YHWH protects the psalmist and Israel in verses 3–5. Again, in verse 7 YHWH's care is praised through two parallel expressions, where the first signifies protection against evil and the other the consequence of this protection in the psalmist's life. The many parallels throughout the psalm serve to amplify what it means that YHWH is the creator, helper, and protector. Another feature of parallelism is the use of contrasting *stock phrases* such as "heaven and earth" (v. 2), "day and night" (v. 6), and "exit and entrance" (v. 8).

The *imagery* of the psalm is dominated by the protector image, which must be seen as a continuation of the introductory description of YHWH as creator and helper.[16] The repeated use of the verb *šmr* is so typical that even the genre of the psalm is determined by it. On the basis of the superscription, "song of ascents," the psalm must be regarded as a pilgrim song, but its content and tone are similar to a psalm of trust (cf. "the pastoral psalm," Ps 23). The verb *šmr* is used in two different contexts: with regard to the shepherd who tends his flock (Jer 31:10) and with regard to guarding a city (Ps 127:1), a garden (Gen 2:15; 3:24), or a sacred object (1 Sam 7:1). In every case what is demanded of those who watch or guard is that they should be vigilant. The image of YHWH as the guard is found in a number of confessions about God as the faithful one who preserves covenant loyalty, as in Deut 7:9; 1 Kgs 8:23; and Ps 89:29. But it can also be used to describe how God watches and guards a person against evil (Pss 16:1; 25:20; 86:2; 145:20).

The many potential meanings of this verb are activated depending on which other Old Testament texts are introduced as intertexts in order to interpret Ps 121. If we choose a pastoral text as an intertext, our ideas of the shepherd who wanders with his flock and leads them to their goal will help determine the verb's connotation. Thus, it is not surprising that such an interpretation makes good sense together with the pilgrim motif: on the way to and from the holy place, the pilgrim is under the guidance of the divine shepherd. He or she is therefore not only protected from danger but is also on the right path. If, on the other hand, we choose a depiction of the watchman's task as the intertext, we would look more toward protection from outward danger as being the focus. In this case, the verb does not so much connote wandering toward a goal, but rather it makes us think of something valuable that must be protected from the enemy. Of these two, however, the shepherd metaphor has the widest spectrum of meaning, since it contains both the wandering motif and the idea of protecting the valuable object, the flock or the individual animal.

It is debatable how many of the expressions used in the psalm are to be understood metaphorically. What is said about YHWH is, of course, said by means of imagery, such as the word "shade" in verse 5. There are various potential meanings here. The placing of the shade on the right side may create associations with the idea of a helper at the right hand (Pss 16:8; 110:5). The shade image could also be linked to that of the protecting bird under the shade of whose wings one can seek shelter (Pss 17:8; 63:8; 91:1). The threatening powers described here are the sun and the moon. These can be taken literally, and the shade would thus be intended as literal shade, through which YHWH cares for the psalmist in the climate of Palestine. But if we maintain the metaphorical use, the sun and moon can also represent the forces of evil (note that, in contrast to the Old Testament, the sun and moon in the Middle East were regarded as divine beings). Similarly, the hills in verse 1 may not only be the physical hills to which the psalmist turns his gaze. They may also represent the highest points on earth and thus the place that comes closest to the divine world. In this context, we must decide whether the psalmist means that YHWH dwells in the high hills (see Ps 125:2) or that the hills, as the place of idols, are contrasted with YHWH and cannot be turned to for care or help.

Interpretation of Psalm 121

Our analysis of the poetic features of Ps 121 has shown that the psalm contains examples of all the elements that are characteristic of Hebrew poetry, including imagery rich in interpretative possibilities. We shall therefore now attempt a general interpretation of the psalm.

Psalm 121 bears the superscription "song of ascent," but it is, in form, a psalm of trust. The superscription reflects the redactional understanding of the psalm as one for use on the *pilgrimage* up to the temple in Jerusalem. This interpretation is supported in the first place by the structure of the psalm. The psalmist begins with his teaching about who YHWH is and why the psalmist can feel safe on his pilgrimage. It is therefore reasonable to see the psalm as a liturgy, either for leaving home or for leaving Jerusalem—in the style of the gate liturgy of Ps 24. The hills mentioned in verse 1 could then be interpreted as Zion, the place where YHWH lives. The shepherd metaphor (the verb *šmr*) also suits the pilgrim motif, while mention of the foot that will not stumble (v. 3) could be understood literally to refer to the pilgrim's foot. If so, it corresponds to Ps 122:2, where the psalmist rejoices that the pilgrimage has been brought to a happy close and shouts, "Our feet are standing in your gates, Jerusalem." Also, the shade in verse 5 could be understood as the pilgrim's elementary need to be protected from the sun. The moon's influence on illness was a widespread belief at the time and can therefore also be taken literally (v. 6). The closing prayer for protection, both on leaving and returning, would then encompass the pilgrimage from start to finish in verse 8.

Another way of reading the psalm is to ignore the superscription as a redactional addition and to take it as a psalm of trust that only later was included in the songs of ascents (Pss 120–134). It is characteristic of these psalms that they do not constitute a specific *Gattung*. There are psalms that were clearly used in connection with a pilgrimage (Ps 122), but many other types of psalms are also to be found among them. There are examples of individual psalms of lamentation, such as Pss 120 and 130. On the other hand, Ps 124 is a psalm of thanksgiving, and Ps 134 is a hymn. There are psalms of trust, such as Pss 121 and 125, and at least one wisdom psalm (Ps 128). Some of the psalms are very difficult to identify based on the classic *Gattungen*, while others can barely be called psalms, being rather brief songs for use on festival occasions in everyday life (see Ps 133).

Read solely as a *psalm of trust*, Ps 121 deals with daily life under YHWH's protection. In this case, it depicts life as a path on which the psalmist has YHWH to guide and protect him. The "foot that does not stumble" (v. 3) can be understood metaphorically as an expression for avoiding various forms of error. Shade is the image of YHWH's constant protection (see the mention of the wings of God's shade in Pss 17:8; 63:8), just as the sun and the moon can be read as expressions for day and night, meaning the whole twenty-four-hour cycle. Finally, the expression "your entrance and your exit" (v. 8) can be taken to refer to the period from leaving home to go to work until the return home again.

Ps 121 ends with a wish for blessing (vv. 7–8), and the verb *šmr* is employed three times to describe the content of this blessing. A reasonable intertext for this wish is the Aaronic blessing (Num 6:24–26), the first element of which contains this verb: "The LORD bless you and *keep* you." The actual meaning of this blessing is explained further in the following two elements of the prayer: "The LORD make his face shine upon you and be gracious to you"; and "The LORD raise his face toward you and give you peace." In Ps 44:24, where God is accused of falling asleep, sleeping is equated with hiding one's face and forgetting. If YHWH hides the divine face and forgets, one is helpless (see also Ps 27:8–9). Conversely, the light of the face expresses presence and grace, while the face raised toward the people creates peace (*šālôm*) in the sense of a good life. These intertexts amplify what in Ps 121 is summarized in the wish for YHWH to protect the people from all evil and preserve life, not just from morning until night but "from now till eternity." The God of the psalm is a personal God, a blessing God, who looks after the individual. God is like a shepherd or a guard who never sleeps.

As we have seen, there are two speakers in Ps 121. The psalmist opens with a question and answer, after which the content of YHWH's help is revealed. But whose voice is it we hear in verses 3–8? If we are dealing with a ritual act linked to the start of a pilgrimage, it is reasonable to imagine verses 3–8 being spoken by a priest to inspire the pilgrims, followed by the pronunciation of a blessing upon them. But as a psalm for use wherever God's people need to be reminded of God's presence and blessing, it is perhaps not quite so clear why there are two different voices in the psalm.

Indirectly, it appears from the psalm that there must be some doubt in the psalmist's mind as to YHWH's ability to live up to expectations, since it has to be emphasized to such an extent that YHWH does not sleep (cf. the accusation against God of sleeping in Ps 44:24). The psalmist may have expressed his confidence in the creator of heaven and earth in verse 2, but faith and doubt often go hand in hand. We hear in Gen 15:1–6 how Abram was losing confidence in YHWH's promise of a great family, but when YHWH repeats his promise, "Abram believed the LORD, and he credited it to him as righteousness." When Abram immediately afterward is again told that he will take possession of the land, we might imagine that faith had overcome doubt. But with great human insight, the narrator has Abram ask the skeptical question: "Lord GOD, how can I *know* that I shall take possession of it?" (Gen 15:8).

In Ps 121, however, the skeptical question is not asked. Rather, verses 3–6 serve to calm the unvoiced doubt, and the answer provides the basis for the closing blessing. If doubt is to be overcome, another voice must be heard speaking against doubt. It may be God himself, as in Gen 15, or it may be the tradition, that is, the childhood teaching, that breaks in as the necessary response "from without." The division into two separate voices thus gives not only meaning in a ritual situation but makes sense in everyday life when doubt is to be overcome and trust in God restored.

So the fact that, in their edited form, these psalms are to be read as songs of ascents does not prevent Ps 121 from also being a psalm of trust dealing with the everyday path of people under God's blessing. In fact, the divine imagery in Ps 121 plays a significant role, for what humanity needs, whether on a pilgrimage or on life's path, is a God who is like a shepherd, watching and protecting.

Ps 121 first came into being as a psalm of trust. Not least because of its imagery, it has since been possible to read it as a song of ascents. But why have the redactors chosen to interpret it in this way? What was their purpose?

Psalm 121 as Part of the Fifth Book

The Psalter actually consists of five books: Pss 1–41; 42–72; 73–89; 90–106; and 107–150. Psalm 121 thus belongs to the fifth and final book of Psalms, the composition of which has presented scholars with a number of problems. Many have regarded Ps 119 as the center of the fifth book. Others have stressed the close link between the two psalms of wisdom, Pss 1 and 119. Both psalms call the person "happy" who keeps the Torah, and they may very well have formed the framework of an earlier and shorter book of Psalms. The identification of such a ring composition has probably convinced scholars not to expect any particular link between Pss 119 and 120–134. Norman Whybray also settles for noting that Ps 119 comes before the songs of ascents, but it is difficult to determine why the fifth book is structured in precisely this way.[17] In my opinion, however, an analysis of the poetry of Ps 121 can help form an understanding of why the redactors chose to place the songs of ascents after Ps 119, for there is indeed an element that links the two parts: Ps 119, which deals with the law and expresses *torah* reverence, and Pss 120–134, the songs of ascents.

In terms of imagery, abiding by the *torah* in Ps 119 is the same as following a *way* or *path*.[18] Words such as "foot" and "step" (119:59, 101, 105) also point to a path motif, and the same goes for the expression "straying" (119:10), "losing one's way" (119:67), and "getting lost" (119:110). The psalm can therefore close with the prayer: "If I have strayed like a lost sheep, search out your servant, for I shall not forget your commandments" (119:176). Life is like walking a path, and the psalmist is like a sheep in need of a shepherd.[19] So we are back with the same line of thought as in Ps 121, whether or not in this psalm we think solely of the road as a pilgrim's path or include the idea of a life-path.

The placing of Ps 119 together with the songs of ascents offers the reader the opportunity to reflect on the two paths that have been of decisive importance for Judaism: the path to the temple with its cult of sacrifice and the path of the law. The redactors have thus underlined that there is more than one path to God. On the one hand, the path to the temple provided an opportunity for those who lived close to the sanctuary to travel there as pilgrims for the three great festivals. The path of dedication to the *torah*, on the other hand, was open to everybody wherever they lived, and it treated the whole of life as walking a path with God.

One of the Jewish groups that stressed the importance of the daily walk in obedience to God was the Qumran sect. Admittedly, they did not live so far away from the temple in Jerusalem, but their break with the priesthood and the temple cult meant that they never *went* on pilgrimage to Jerusalem. This rejection of pilgrimage has also had consequences for their use of the book of Psalms. If we look at the position of Ps119 in 11QPs[a], we note that this psalm is not placed between Ps 118 and the songs of ascents, as is the case in the MT version, but directly after Ps 132.[20] Matthias Millard understands the difference between the Qumran version and the MT version to mean that the Qumran version hears only the *call* to go to YHWH's dwelling-place (Ps 132:7). But the Qumran sect has moved the description of how the pilgrims stand in the temple, rejoicing and praising (Ps 134), to a different context in order to keep their distance from the temple and the idea of a pilgrimage to Jerusalem.[21] What they wished to emphasize was the other way of walking with God: the path of dedication to *torah*. They achieved this by placing Ps 119 immediately after Ps 132. For them, the real pilgrimage was to follow the *torah*.[22]

Psalms 120–134 is a collection of psalms that have only become songs of ascents as a secondary usage. They have come into being in an environment of peasants and the lower middle-class citizens, where individuals turn to YHWH as a personal God with a prayer for help and care. They pray to YHWH, trusting that he will protect them from all evil, both when they leave their home in the morning and when they return in the evening (Ps 121:8). In his book on the songs of ascents, Loren Crow has argued convincingly that these folk psalms were most likely edited in the postexilic period, when the restoration of the temple had created a need for psalms that could legitimize Zion as a shrine.[23] To this end, songs were chosen that were already known and that were then given a new function. The reinterpretation of Pss 120–134 as songs of ascents is thus an element of the religio-political propaganda for the restoration of Zion as the central shrine on the return from exile in Babylon. This is most clear from the redactional references to Zion (e.g., Pss 122:2, 6; 125:1–2; 128:5–6; 134:3).

But where Crow focuses solely on the pilgrimage motif and the religio-political background, I have made the point in this essay that the songs of ascents do not stand alone but through their position and their imagery are linked to Ps 119. Our analysis of the imagery of Pss 119 and 121 has shown how it was possible for the redactors to see a link between the great psalm on the *torah* and the songs of ascents. By juxtaposing them, the redactors have created a distinctive center to the fifth book and provided not just one but two answers to the question that Micah formulated: "With what shall I come before the LORD and bow down before the exalted God?" (6:6). Micah's answer was to reject the sacrificial cult in favor of ethics, but the redactors of the fifth book of Psalms maintained the possibility of both—the way of *torah* and the way of pilgrimage.[24]

For Further Reading

Alter, Robert. *The Art of Biblical Poetry*. New York: Basic Books, 1985.

Berlin, Adele. *The Dynamics of Biblical Parallelism*. Bloomington: Indiana University Press, 1985.

Nielsen, Kirsten. "Sigmund Mowinckel—and Beyond." *SJOT* 11 (1997): 200–209.

Petersen, David L., and Kent Harold Richards. *Interpreting Hebrew Poetry*. GBS. Minneapolis: Fortress, 1992.

Watson, Wilfred G.E. *Classical Hebrew Poetry: A Guide to Its Techniques*. JSOTSup 26. Sheffield: JSOT Press, 1984.

Whybray, Norman. *Reading the Psalms as a Book*. JSOTSup 222. Sheffield: Sheffield Academic Press, 1996.

Notes

1. James Muilenburg, "Form Criticism and Beyond," *JBL* 88 (1969): 1–18.

2. Ibid., 8.

3. See Kirsten Nielsen, "Sigmund Mowinckel—and Beyond," *SJOT* 11 (1997): 200–209.

4. David L. Petersen and Kent Harold Richards, *Interpreting Hebrew Poetry* (GBS; Minneapolis: Fortress, 1992), 37. See also Wilfred G. E. Watson, *Classical*

Hebrew Poetry: A Guide to Its Techniques (JSOTSup 26; Sheffield: JSOT Press, 1984), 87–113.

5. Petersen and Richards, *Interpreting Hebrew Poetry*, 46.

6. Watson, *Classical Hebrew Poetry*, 222–50.

7. George Buchanan Gray, *The Forms of Hebrew Poetry: Considered with Special Reference to the Criticism and Interpretation of the Old Testament* (1915; prolegomena by David Noel Freedman; New York: Ktav, 1972), 50–51. See also Theodore H. Robinson, *The Poetry of the Old Testament* (London: Duckworth, 1947), 23–24.

8. James L. Kugel, *The Idea of Biblical Poetry: Parallelism and Its History* (New Haven: Yale University Press, 1981), 58.

9. Ibid., 53.

10. C. S. Lewis, *Reflections on the Psalms* (1961; Glasgow: Collins Fount, 1978), 12.

11. Adele Berlin, *The Dynamics of Biblical Parallelism* (Bloomington: Indiana University Press, 1985); Petersen and Richards, *Interpreting Biblical Poetry*, 27–34. See also Watson, *Classical Hebrew Poetry*, 114–59.

12. Robert Alter, *The Art of Biblical Poetry* (New York: Basic Books, 1985), 10–11.

13. Watson, *Classical Hebrew Poetry*, 160–200

14. Kirsten Nielsen, *There Is Hope for a Tree: The Tree as Metaphor in Isaiah* (JSOTSup 65; Sheffield: JSOT Press, 1989), 65–66.

15. On metaphors and intertexts, see further Kirsten Nielsen, "Intertextuality and Hebrew Bible," in *Congress Volume: Oslo, 1998* (ed. André Lemaire and Magne Sæbø; Leiden: Brill, 2000), 17–31.

16. The words *'zr* and *šmr* are also used in the account of Adam and Eve in the garden of Eden. In Gen 2:15, Adam's first task is to look after (*šmr*) the garden, while according to Gen 2:18–20 it is Eve who functions as Adam's *'ēzer*. With the expulsion from the garden, the role of guardian of the garden is surrendered to the cherubs. Nothing is said, however, about whether Eve loses her role in relation to Adam.

17. Norman Whybray, *Reading the Psalms as a Book* (JSOTSup 222; Sheffield: Sheffield Academic Press, 1996), 74–75.

18. See Ps 119:1, 3, 5, 14, 15, 26, 27, 29, 30, 32, 33, 35, 37, 59, 101, 104, 105, 128, 168.

19. Just as in Ps 121, the verb *šmr* is also in frequent use in Ps 119. But whereas in Ps 121 it is YHWH who watches and protects, in Ps 119 it is primarily the worshiper who is the subject of the verb. See Ps 119:4, 5, 8, 9, 17, 34, 44, 55, 57, 60, 63, 88, 101, 106, 134, 136, 146, 158, 167, 168.

20. James A. Sanders, *The Psalms Scroll of the Qumrân Cave 11 (11Qps^{a})* (DJD 4; Oxford: Clarendon, 1965), 5, 23–49.

21. In 11QPs^{a}, Ps 133:1–3 is placed between Pss 141:5–10 and 144:1–7, while Ps 134 is placed between Pss 140:1–5 and Ps 151A. See Matthias Millard, *Die Komposition des Psalters: Ein formgeschichtlicher Ansatz* (FAT 9; Tübingen: Mohr Siebeck, 1994), 219–27.

22. See further Kirsten Nielsen, "Why Not Plough with an Ox and an Ass Together? Or: Why Not Read Ps 119 Together with Pss 120–134?" *SJOT* 14 (2000): 56–66.

23. Loren D. Crow, *The Songs of Ascents (Psalms 120–134): Their Place in Israelite History and Religion* (Atlanta: Scholars Press, 1996).

24. This essay was translated by Edward Broadbridge.

Feminist Criticism: Sarah Laughs Last

Susan Brayford

Overhearing a conversation in which one of her husband's mysterious visitors predicts she would have a son, Sarah laughs to herself. Not only has she been barren her whole life, but both she and Abraham are too old to have children. As she reflects on the absurdity of conceiving a child, her thoughts wander, and she begins to wonder whether she could still have sexual pleasure, given Abraham's age. Her musings are cut short when the male visitors overhear her laughing at their overheard remarks. The spokesman for the group, whom we later learn is YHWH/God,[1] quickly criticizes her; he presumes that her laughter somehow indicates her lack of faith in his procreative capabilities. However, when Abraham had laughed earlier at the same prediction, he was not criticized by YHWH/God. In fact, he was rewarded. Why should Sarah's laughter indicate any less faith than that of Abraham? We readers are not told, but we might speculate. Perhaps Sarah's laughter was not primarily one of doubt, but one of delight. Perhaps she was ignoring or subverting the authority of the male characters. Perhaps she was forgetting the pain that YHWH/God earlier had built into childbearing and focusing instead on the pleasure associated with desire (Gen 3:16). If so, Sarah's laughing thoughts represent a woman's experience and serve to challenge the androcentric nature of the story and the patriarchal authority of its male characters. In short, Sarah's story foreshadows the social/ideological position of later feminists and, as such, offers an ideal text for feminist interpretation.

Forms of Feminist Biblical Criticism

In an article provocatively titled "Feminist Criticism of the Old Testament: Why Bother?" Deborah Rooke evaluates and ultimately rejects several interpretations of the garden story (Gen 2–3) that attempt to find in the text some good news for women.[2] Instead, she argues that the story is completely and irredeemably patriarchal; it originally intended to justify and reinforce the domination of women by men and has continued to do so for thousands of years. She points out that God lied to the humans with no consequences, but the snake was punished for telling the truth. Nevertheless, she maintains that feminist criticism does matter because it brings to light some unpleasant truths.

> The glimpse that feminist criticism gives us of the patriarchal world-order crumbling in the face of a women's desire for self-improvement remains as an after-image on our mental retina, pervading our picture of the world, relativizing patriarchy's absolutist authority claims, and enabling us to visualize and to work towards a very different future for both women and men.[3]

Rooke's pragmatic perspective on the significance of feminist criticism of Hebrew Bible texts reflects what Heather McKay characterizes as a rejectionist hermeneutic of feminist criticism. Although using the same "rejectionist" descriptor as did Carolyn Osiek in her often-cited 1985 essay characterizing the approaches that feminist critics used in interpreting biblical texts[4] (see below), McKay maintains that some rejectionists do not completely reject the Bible itself. Instead, they reject the authority and divine status of the Bible in order to preserve the authority and human status of women.[5]

In this essay I offer a feminist interpretation of the story of Sarah's voiceless laughter to provide a glimpse into the world in which laughter was her only option. By so doing, I leave my readers with an after-image—or better, an *after-chuckle*—that will, if not "relativize patriarchy's absolutist claims," at least suggest that Sarah might have the last laugh and thus offer a positive response to Rooke's challenging question: "Why bother?" Before proceeding with my feminist interpretation of Gen 18:1–15, I must first define and clarify the methodological objectives associated with feminist-critical approaches to biblical interpretation.

This task, however, is not so simple, because the term *feminist* has a wide range of meanings. Even when limiting definitions of the term to its use in biblical scholarship, one finds many opinions. The editors of one recent volume on feminist biblical interpretation define feminism as "a determined movement of women seeking to break free of the judicial and economic predominance of 'father' and from the psychic and ideological tutelage of men."[6] The editors of another anthology of essays in feminist biblical criticism refuse to hold their contributors to one definition of feminism.[7] Thus Phyllis Bird writes that feminism is a "critical and constructive stance that claims for women the full humanity accorded to men, insisting that women be represented equally in all attempts to describe and comprehend human nature and that they be full participants in the assignment and regulation of social roles, rights, and responsibilities."[8] In the same volume, Pamela Thimmes understands feminism as a political term describing a "liberation movement that not only critiques the oppressive structures of society but, by its various voices and approaches, works for transformation."[9] Because I take a feminist approach to my Women and Religion class, I have developed my own description of feminism as both an intellectual commitment and a political movement that seeks justice and equal rights for women and the end not just of sexism but of any type of discrimination.

Like feminism itself, feminist biblical criticism comes in many forms with different goals and objectives. In the essay referenced above, Bird follows her definition of feminism with a description of a feminist reading. Such a reading, Bird maintains, moves women from the margins to the center of analysis in order to show alternatives to "patriarchal and androcentric forms of thought and organization."[10] Thimmes argues that what makes a reading feminist is a particular methodological approach that "moves in a circular pattern, encompassing a number of ideas and presuppositions that find clarity only in partnership with the other elements contained in the circle."[11] These elements include feminism itself, women's experience, one's social location, and language. McKay, on the other hand, prefers to see feminist criticism not just as a particular methodology. Feminist readings can help "dissolve gendered false consciousness" if they are accompanied by other approaches and "standpoints, such as materialist and structuralist, or from other disciplines, such as sociology, psychology, and cultural anthropology."[12] Cheryl Exum, likewise, rejects the idea that feminist biblical criticism is either a discipline or a method. Instead, she understands it as "a variety of approaches, informed not so much by the biblical texts themselves as by the interests and concerns of feminism as a world view and political enterprise."[13]

Nevertheless, similar to the way in which most feminists can agree that feminism is a political stance that seeks to liberate women from oppression, most feminist biblical critics share a few common assumptions. They concur that biblical texts are androcentric, that is, male-centered.

Also, these texts reflect a patriarchal worldview, one in which males are dominant. In addition to acknowledging these biases, feminist critics also recognize the biases that underlie any and all interpretations of these texts. No text or interpretation is value-neutral; all reflect the experience, presuppositions, and prejudices of the interpreter. Most feminists and other socially located critics would also agree that texts and interpretations continue to shape the values of those who read and interpret them, and many advocate that the interpreter declare what she or he brings to the interpretation.[14] The interpreters' point of difference is the way in which they handle the Bible's inherent biases and how they evaluate the Bible's authority.

Contemporary feminist biblical criticism can trace its roots to the 1895 publication of *The Woman's Bible* by Elizabeth Cady Stanton.[15] A commentary on parts of the Bible "which directly refer to women and those also in which women are made prominent by exclusion,"[16] *The Woman's Bible* was as much, if not more, a political statement as a theological one. Stanton and her collaborators condemned the Bible's use as a weapon that legitimated the oppression of women. While finding a few biblical passages that offered some hope for women's liberation, Stanton concluded that one "cannot twist out of the Old or New Testaments a message of justice, liberty, or equality from God to the women of the nineteenth century."[17] As a result, other feminists and suffragists distanced themselves from Stanton, afraid that their political cause would be damaged by direct challenges to the Bible and its authority.

Feminist biblical critics were relatively silent until the 1970s, when scholars such as Phyllis Trible, Rosemary Ruether, and Elisabeth Schüssler Fiorenza began to challenge the exclusivity of "malestream" biblical scholarship. By 1985, the wide variety of perspectives found in publications by these and other feminists led Osiek to discern five major hermeneutical positions—rejectionist, loyalist, revisionist, sublimationist, and liberationist—that scholars find still applicable today. In what follows, I briefly discuss the assumptions, goals, and limitations of these approaches and offer examples of feminists who employ them.

Rejectionists, epitomized by Mary Daly and foreshadowed by Stanton, consider the Bible, the religions based on it, and the traditions that developed from it irredeemably corrupt. Their only option, per Osiek, is to reject the Bible entirely. As mentioned above, however, McKay and others envision other options for rejectionists who choose to abandon the integrity of the Bible but not the Bible itself. The goal of these partial-rejectionists is to preserve the integrity of women by rejecting the divine status of the Bible. As a historical and cultural product, the Bible provides access to voices from the past, voices that offer insight into women's roles—or lack thereof. Some rejectionists attempt to dig deeply into the texts to discover these muted voices and to bring these voices out of the margins for analysis and critique. Citing the work of Cheryl Exum as exemplary of a rejectionist approach, McKay comments that "any authority the biblical texts gains with readers has to be earned by relevance to their lives, not, *a priori*, as a matter of unthinking commitment."[18]

The proponents of the other four hermeneutic approaches attempt to preserve, at some level, the integrity of the text. Those adhering to a *loyalist* hermeneutic declare the essential goodness of the Bible and biblical tradition. As the Word of God, the Bible attests to God's ultimate authority and thus cannot be oppressive. If seen to be so, the problem lies with its fallible interpreters and the limited knowledge their interpretations reflect. Osiek applauds those loyalists whose determination in finding and focusing on the Bible's underlying message of love and human freedom allows them to make its texts central to their life and identity, yet she also acknowledges that loyalists are vulnerable "to the temptation to stretch history and the literal meaning of the texts" and have a tendency to ignore the political implications of what they see as inadequate interpretations of problematic texts.[19] McKay agrees that loyalists often give the Bible too much authority by overemphasizing the roles women play or by casting stories that are ambiguous in a positive light. Their need to defend the Bible to outsiders while keeping it central to members of their faith communities often demands complicity on the part of loyalists.[20]

Feminist biblical scholars with a *revisionist* hermeneutic adopt a stance midway between rejectionists and loyalists. While they do not consider the Bible to be virtually irredeemable, they do acknowledge that its texts are androcentric and often reflect, construct, and reinforce a patriarchal worldview. Revisionists fault the many different social and historical circumstances associated with the writing, reading, and interpretation of the Bible for corrupting its inherent goodness. They go on to argue that the tradition can be rehabilitated by delving more deeply into both the text and its contexts to find traces of the important and often subversive roles played by women.

The work of Phyllis Trible exemplifies the revisionist approach. Her thorough rhetorical analyses of biblical "love stories" and "texts of terror"[21] allow her to find kernels of good news in androcentric texts while also conceding their often misogynist grain. The texts and interpretations that have reinforced the abusive and oppressive patriarchal conditions that hinder women from being equal participants in society belong in the past. As such, she implores readers to respond to the affirmative messages she finds in the biblical texts by actively working to transform society in the present and future. Osiek admits that, despite the fact that revisionists attack the symptoms of the problems caused by patriarchal interpretation, rather than its causes, those "with historical patience and vision probably produce some long-lasting results."[22] McKay similarly points out that revised interpretations, while offering a temporary challenge to the tradition, nevertheless cannot change the text itself.

Those who employ a *sublimationist* hermeneutic focus on feminine imagery and symbolism to show the significance of difference between masculine and feminine qualities. Neither is to be displaced; both are to be celebrated. Nevertheless, many sublimationists focus their attention on—and deem superior—those symbols associated with feminine qualities such as nurturing, caring, and creating. As such, this approach risks merely reversing gender hierarchies. Both Osiek and McKay agree that the biggest problem with this approach is the tendency to ignore the political and social issues embedded in the texts in favor of a psychological realm where, in McKay's words, "no pain or slights can be felt."[23]

When she wrote in 1985, Osiek thought that the *liberationist* approach would offer the most promise for feminist biblical interpretation. Based on liberation theology, this approach recognized and continues to understand the oppression of women as part of a larger pattern of dominance-submission. As loyalists maintain the inherent goodness of the Bible, liberationists argue that the Bible's central message is human liberation from oppression, whether physical or spiritual, and maintain that the goal of biblical interpretation is transformation. If the biblical texts being interpreted do not promote the full equality of women, they cannot be considered the authentic word of God. This ideal, Osiek and others acknowledge, can easily result in the creation of "a canon within a canon," rejecting the texts that seem to contradict liberation and loyally adhering to those that reflect it. Trible goes further by commenting that abstracting liberating themes from texts "can even be dishonest, for the maneuver often ignores the particularities of texts."[24]

Feminist biblical criticism, while hardly monolithic and still regarded by some as a marginal enterprise, has nevertheless resulted in countless articles, monographs, and anthologies. These publications attest not only to the continued scholarly (and economic) significance of feminist criticism, but also to its evolving complexity and diversity. The *Women's Bible Commentary*, published originally in 1992 and updated in 1998,[25] represented one of the first appearances of a traditional biblical commentary that dealt exclusively with women's issues. Since then, other publishers have released women's commentaries, while traditional series have included articles on feminist interpretation.

Perhaps the most ambitious and significant contribution to and acknowledgement of the strength, diversity, and popularity of feminist biblical criticism is the Feminist Companion to the Bible series. As "companions" rather than commentaries, the volumes highlight biblical books and texts that address issues of importance to feminist criticism. In her review of the series, Adele Reinhartz observes that "the over 200 articles do not constitute a template for the field as a whole, nor do they claim to do so."[26] Instead, they reflect the varieties of feminist-critical approaches.

Future feminist exegetical strategies, McKay opines, should offer a "gender-friendly climate" that is both open to the attitudes and perspectives of scholars with varying perspectives and that is accompanied by approaches from other disciplines. Pamela Milne likewise advises feminist biblical scholars to move beyond the reactive approaches described above and to adopt strategies that are more in line with secular feminism. She argues that feminist biblical critics must not only mine the Bible for positive portrayals of women; they also must attend to the greater ideological issues and question whose interests are served by even positive images. Feminist critics should return to the position advocated by Cady Stanton and show the political and social implications of biblical gender ideology, "not only as it affects women characters in the text but as it has affected women in society through the millennia and in our own time."[27] Thus, feminist biblical scholarship should regain its edge and the political advocacy of its earlier days in which broader ethical issues were more important than apolitical and reader-centered methods. Instead of focusing attention on the reception of the Bible in confessional or theological contexts, feminist interpretation should address issues important in secular academic contexts.

Case Study: Sarah's Laughter in Genesis 18

For the purposes of this essay, I adopt the rejectionist approach as described by McKay and reflected in Rooke's provocative question about the value of feminist scholarship. In so doing, I do not regard the biblical text as the divine word of God but rather as a cultural product that provides a socially and historically conditioned description of a particular incident in the ongoing relationship between the God of Israel (YHWH/God) and his people. I discern the underlying assumptions about gender and gender roles by analyzing what the text says—and does not say—about Sarah and her laughing thoughts. I raise questions about why the characters are portrayed as they are and whose interests are being served. Finally, I use theories and models from other disciplines for feminist purposes and show how ancient and modern translators and interpreters have understood and often censored Sarah's laughing thoughts.

Before analyzing her (a)musing thoughts, I need to set the social, historical, and quite androcentric stage in which Sarah will play multiple roles. She is nowhere in sight when the story begins with a strange tale of her husband's hasty hospitality. Playing the perfect host, especially in the story's ancient context, was not merely a social nicety; it was a requirement of men, and by extension of their entire families, who lived in a culture informally governed by the anthropological code of honor and shame. This code served as a rudimentary system of social control and group identity and provided a simple set of rules about individual and group behavior. The complementarity of this code, that honor is most often associated with males and shame with females, makes it especially relevant for examining the function and significance of gender roles. In its most basic form, honor denotes esteem, respect, and prestige, both in one's own eyes and in the eyes of one's social group. All honor, however, is not equal. Vertical honor is unlimited and comes automatically to some men due to birthright, superior abilities, rank, and service. Horizontal honor, on the other hand, is in limited supply and can be won or lost. To acquire more honor, a man must take honor away from another man, who is then shamed. Thus, as an attribute of men, shame is negative and results in a state of disrespect. However, when attributed to women, shame is positive and indicates a woman's sexual modesty and propriety. Thus, in this system, a woman of shame is the status equivalent of a man of honor. At this point in the biblical narrative, the focus is on Abraham's honor. Sarah's place in the tent shows her in her rightful, that is, shameful position.

Unbeknownst to Abraham, God is about to appear to him for the third time. This time, however, God appears in disguise and arrives with two other men as Abraham is sitting by the entrance of his tent. Nevertheless, Abraham seems to sense the importance of these mysterious visitors. From the moment that he sees the three men standing above him, he rushes around to show them hospitality. First he runs to meet them and immediately bows down to greet them with deference and respect, a humble gesture that continues in his verbal greeting. Addressing the presumed leader of the group, he hails him as "my lord." Little does Abraham know that his greeting is not only respectful but also theologically correct. He continues his deferential manner by twice referring to himself in the third person as the guests' servant (Gen 18:3, 5). He begs them to stay and accept his hospitality, his humility especially evident when he three times uses the polite Hebrew particle *nā'* in his conversation with the group's leader. "If it *pleases* you," he begins, "that I have found favor, *please* do not pass by your servant" (18:3). He then continues, "if you *please*, let a little water be brought" (18:4).[28] Exactly who will bring the water is unclear. However, he himself offers to bring a "bit of food" while the guests are to refresh themselves under the tree. Only after they allow him as their servant to provide hospitality may they resume their journey. The visitors agree with his plan and likely deem him an honorable host.

Abraham quickly goes into action. He hurries to the tent and tells Sarah—without the politeness he extended to the visitors—to hurry her preparation of bread cakes. Then he runs to choose a tender young calf that his servant boy hurries to prepare. Then Abraham takes curds and milk and the calf that he, not the servant, is reported to have prepared and sets the meal before the guests, who eat the meal as he stands by. One wonders why he did not give them the bread cakes he ordered Sarah to make. Again, we readers are not told. Did she perhaps refuse, realizing that no amount of tasty bread cakes would compensate for a main course that had to be nearly raw? Or did Abraham think her contribution was not good enough for his guests? Most likely he just forgot, inasmuch as he seemed frantic throughout the entire scene. In any case, the guests ate and had no complaints. The real purpose of their visit was yet to come.

After eating the hastily prepared but incomplete meal, the visitors ask, "Where is your wife Sarah?" Abraham quickly answers but does not stop to wonder how they know his wife's name. Although he seems to be having a few "senior moments," he does remember she is in the tent and so informs the visitors. One of them makes a startling announcement that he would return the next year and that Sarah would have a son. This time Abraham does not laugh at the prediction of his unknown guest, as he had when God himself told Abraham the same thing earlier (Gen 17:17). For Abraham, this is old news, but news he likely had not shared with

Sarah. Perhaps he still hoped that God would acknowledge his firstborn son Ishmael as his rightful heir.

This time it is Sarah, overhearing the man's startling prediction, who laughs. Before reporting her laughter, however, the narrator interrupts the male conversation to remind the reader that Sarah and Abraham were getting old and that Sarah no longer has "the way of women" (Gen 18:11), that is, menstruation. Not only has she been barren her whole life, but it is now humanly impossible for her to bear children. Knowing this, Sarah realizes that she will be spared the punishing pains of childbirth. So she laughs to herself and wonders, "after my wearing out, can there be pleasure for me since my husband is old?" (18:12). Her musing thoughts differ from Abraham's earlier laughing skepticism in two ways. First, unlike Abraham, who bases his doubts on their *mutual* old age (17:17), Sarah's laughter focuses only on *Abraham's* old age. Although her self-described worn-out state could initially lessen the pleasure of sex, this would not be an issue if Abraham's age prevents him from pleasuring and impregnating Sarah. Second, while Abraham had distanced himself somewhat from the unlikelihood of paternity by expressing his procreative inability in the passive voice and a hypothetical tone (17:17), Sarah's remark about her husband's old age refers explicitly to Abraham's present and actual condition.

Her skepticism over her own ability to have sexual pleasure and Abraham's ability to provide her such pleasure is understandable. The word that Sarah uses to describe herself, *bĕlōtî*, is used most often in the Hebrew Bible to describe old sandals and clothes (e.g., Deut 8:4; 29:4 [MT]; Josh 9:13). This description, put into Sarah's mouth, is hardly a flattering self-image. Yet it provides a fitting parallel with her comment about Abraham's old age, as well as a stark and realistic basis for her thoughts about pleasure (*ʿednâ*). The kind of pleasure Sarah ponders is key to my feminist interpretation of her laughter and to my feminist critique of the subsequent censoring of her thoughts by later translators and commentators.

Inasmuch as the Hebrew word *ʿednâ* is a *hapax legomenon*, a brief discussion of its meaning is in order. The major Hebrew lexicons attest that *ʿednâ* refers to sexual pleasure or delight. BDB reports that the feminine noun *ʿednâ* means "delight" and that in its sole occurrence (Gen 18:12) that delight is sexual. *A Concise Hebrew and Aramaic Lexicon of the Old Testament* defines *ʿednâ* as "(sexual) pleasure." *HAL* defines *ʿednâ* as "Liebeslust" (thus "lust," according to *HALOT*) and refers the reader to an article by J. Hempel[29] in which he examines medical terms and equates *ʿednâ* with Ugaritic *ḥmḥmt*, meaning "orgasm."

Curiously, BDB does not include the reference to the *'ēden* garden as an attestation of the masculine noun. Instead, it suggests that the particular use of *'ēden* in Gen 2–3 is a proper noun that derives from a second root *'dn*, which is entymologically related to the Akkadian *edinu*, derived from the earlier Sumerian EDEN, meaning "steppe or plain."[30] In my opinion, the lushness of the garden and its association with fertility argues against BDB's classification from a semantic perspective. Alan R. Millard has also refuted BDB's classification on the basis of inscriptional evidence that relates the *'ēden* garden to the idea of abundance.[31] Furthermore, as Gary Anderson explains, the Septuagint translator did not translate *'ēden* as a proper noun in Gen 3:23–24. Instead, LXX treats it as a common noun, rendered "the garden of delight."[32]

Recent commentators have likewise acknowledged this relationship. Robert Alter, for example, maintains that the term *'ednâ* "is cognate with Eden and probably suggests sexual pleasure, or perhaps even sexual moistness."[33] Although not relating Sarah's *'ednâ* explicitly to Eden, Nahum Sarna writes that the "Hebrew *ednah* is now known to mean 'abundant moisture' and is an exact antonym of 'withered.' "[34] Lexical relationships aside, the physical aspect of "abundant moisture," from a woman's point of view, implies some level of sexual stimulation. Therefore, on the basis of the above discussion, I maintain that Sarah's thoughts are undoubtedly of the pleasures of sex.

Her thoughts of sexual pleasure are aborted, however, when YHWH/God criticizes her, presuming that her laughter indicates her lack of faith in *his* abilities (Gen 18:13–14), not Abraham's. Overhearing Sarah's laughter, YHWH/God asks Abraham why she laughed and (mis)reports her laughing thoughts as "can it really be true that I will bear a child since I am old?" His paraphrase shows that YHWH/God mistakenly attributes Sarah's laughter to the impossibility of bearing children. He further misrepresents her concerns as being due to *her* old age, not to *Abraham's* old age. YHWH/God refuses to acknowledge Sarah's thoughts of pleasure, refocuses the issue, and redefines the problem. It is Sarah's previous inability to bear children, rather than Abraham's potential inability to provide Sarah pleasure, that becomes central. YHWH/God relieves any "performance anxiety" on Abraham's part by omitting Sarah's concern about Abraham's age. He likewise relieves what should be Sarah's procreative performance anxiety by announcing that this previously barren woman will conceive within the year. Sarah's concerns, however, were not on *her* performance but on Abraham's.

In the language of honor/shame, Sarah's thoughts of the pleasures of sex characterize her as a shameless woman, a portrayal that takes away from Abraham's honor. Moreover, Sarah's questioning of Abraham's ability to provide her pleasure and/or progeny takes more honor away from him. Therefore, it is not Sarah's lack of faith that is the problem; it is her thoughts of experiencing sexual pleasure in her old age and worn-out state. These thoughts shame Abraham and make her shameless. Thoughts like these are hardly fitting or flattering for the earliest and most prominent matriarch of Israel.

YHWH/God was only the first to take exception to Sarah's laughter and help Abraham restore some lost honor and manly pride. Later translators and exegetes, as I discuss below, either ignored or condemned her laughter or explained it away. The Septuagint translator, however, denied even more than her laughter. Perhaps he also recognized the ambiguity associated with the reason for her laughter, since he omitted it from his otherwise rather literal translation. Refusing to acknowledge that Sarah, the elderly matriarch of Israel, would have thoughts of the pleasures associated with sex, he limits her musings only to the possibility of having children.

The reason for curbing her thoughts lies in the social and historical background of the LXX, the Greek translation of the Hebrew text. Drawing on a cultural-studies model of translation theory that acknowledges the complexities of gender and culture,[35] I maintain that the LXX, like all translations, both reflected and continued to shape its receiving culture. This culture, namely, third-century B.C.E. Alexandria, served as the contemporary center of the Hellenistic world and informed the social identity of its Jewish translators. From a religious perspective, they were Hellenistic Jews who valued their Hebrew Scriptures and wanted to make them accessible to their fellow Alexandrian Jews who could no longer read these stories in their original language. From a social perspective, they were one of several minority ethnic groups competing for status and influence in a cosmopolitan environment.

Furthermore, although translations of texts for commercial purposes were common in Alexandria, translations of religious texts had no precedent. With no explicit guidelines to follow, the translators made a rather literal exchange of Greek words for their Hebrew counterparts and chose to keep the paratactic Hebrew syntax. This resulted in a somewhat awkward-sounding Greek text. Nevertheless, they not only accomplished their goal of translating their Hebrew Scriptures; they also transformed these stories, consciously or unconsciously, to accommodate the dominant values of their cultural milieu. The fact that they were translating religious texts made their translation decisions even more susceptible to cultural influences, because religious texts address issues of utmost importance in human life.

One such issue is that of the socially constructed gender roles played by men and women in their particular cultures. Gender roles, as social scientists emphasize, vary between cultures. Emerging from specific social situations, gender roles are "both an outcome of and a rationale for various social arrangements and [function] as a means of legitimating one of the most fundamental divisions of society."[36] As opposed to the category of sex, which pertains to biological differences, the category of gender focuses on the behavioral aspects of being a woman or a man. Such behavior is defined "in light of normative conceptions of attitudes and activities appropriate for one's sex category."[37] The normative behavior for a Hellenistic matron was much more domesticated and positively shameful than that of Sarah, an outspoken Jewish matriarch who thought about sexual pleasure.

The stage on which the LXX story of Sarah's laughter takes place is just as androcentric as that in the Hebrew text and ends up being even more patriarchal. The LXX tells much the same story of hurried hospitality and overheard laughter, but it does so in a way that portrays Abraham as a more honorable host and Sarah as a more shameful wife. To emphasize Abraham's generous hospitality, the LXX does not limit Abraham's offer of water to his guests to only a "little water" (MT Gen 18:4). Similarly, the LXX Abraham does not restrict his guests to a "bit of food" (MT Gen 18:5). While they cool themselves under the tree, he will get an as-yet unspecified amount of food for them to eat. Furthermore, in the LXX Abraham does more than "give" (*ntn*; MT Gen 18:8) the meal to his guests; he "serves" (*parethēken*) them and stands by while they eat (LXX Gen 18:8).

Even more significant to improving the social reputation of the ancestors are the differences in the LXX description of Sarah's laughter. Following YHWH/God's lead in the Hebrew text, the Greek translation either ignores or misunderstands Sarah's musings about sexual pleasure and instead focuses her thoughts more appropriately on childbearing. The LXX of Gen 18:12 reads, *egelasen de Sarra en eautē legousa oupō men moi gegonen heōs tou nyn ho de kurios mou presbyteros*. At the beginning and end of verse 12, the LXX translation is literal: "so Sarah laughed to herself, saying," and "my lord is old." However, its translation of the middle part of the verse is anything but literal. LXX scholar John Wevers argues that the translator (mis)read the Hebrew *bělōtî*, not as "my being worn out," but as the negative particle *bēlet* meaning "not, except," and translated it as *oupō*, a translation permitted by the consonantal text. This removes Sarah's unflattering self-portrayal as a worn-out old woman. More problematic is *'ednâ*, the word denoting sexual pleasure. Inasmuch as the LXX translator might not have known this *hapax legomenon*, Wevers suggests that he read it as two Hebrew words, *hnh* and *'d* and translated it as *eōs tou nyn*: "until now." Thus, the LXX translation of the middle part of verse 12 might be rendered, "Never yet has it happened to me until now,"[38] with the referent of the pronoun "it" occurring in the previous verses: Sarah's inability to have children. Awkward as it is, the translation reflects its immediate literary context.

Thus, instead of pondering the possibility of sexual pleasure in her old age and withered state, the LXX Sarah merely reflects on her lifelong problem. Furthermore, by replacing Sarah's thoughts of pleasure with an allusion to her continued barrenness, the LXX has Sarah accept the blame for the couple's lack of progeny. Doing so downplays the significance of Abraham's age. His virility is less threatened, especially since he had earlier fathered a son through Hagar. Like a proper Hellenistic matron, Sarah thinks not of her own sexual pleasure. Rather, she reflects on her spousal duty of producing the required heir for Abraham. Thus, based in part on the notions of honor and shame, both Sarah and Abraham become model ancestors whose thoughts and deeds are more compatible with the appropriate Hellenized gendered identities that Diaspora Jews needed to adopt. But while the LXX merely *upgrades* Abraham's character by enhancing his social graces, it *redefines* Sarah's character by denying her her sexuality and refocusing her thoughts toward childbearing.

This apologetic representation of Sarah reflects the Platonic understanding of the authentic aim of the sexual act as well as traditional Greek descriptions of a wife's role. As a wife, Sarah is not kept for the sake of Abraham's pleasure. Her duty, to paraphrase Demosthenes, is to "bear legitimate children and be a faithful guardian of her household."[39] The LXX Sarah, like her Hellenistic role models, is portrayed as a woman whose value and fate are determined by her reproductive capacities. In refusing to be tainted by impure thoughts of sex, the LXX Sarah comes close to Perictione, an ideal Neopythagorean woman "who by controlling her desire and passion, becomes devout and harmonious, resulting in her not becoming a prey to impious love affairs."[40] Inasmuch as she no longer thinks about sex, the domesticated Sarah of the LXX also might resemble Semonides' good wife, who is "so chaste that she does not even like to listen to other women who talk about sex."[41] In other words, the process of translation has transformed Sarah into a model (i.e., shameful) Hellenistic lady and wife.

Her domestication continued about a century later in Jubilees, a retelling of the biblical stories between Gen 1 and Exod 16. The author whitewashed the blemishes of the Jewish ancestors and portrayed them as models of Torah obedience. Yet its account of the story of Sarah's laughter also addressed issues of social propriety and removed some of her questionable attributes. As in the original story, Sarah laughs when she hears that she herself would give Abraham a son. But there is no indication in Jubilees that her laughter suggests either a mistrust of God's abilities or skepticism about Abraham's. In fact, all the physical aspects of the Genesis story—Abraham's old age, Sarah's withered state, and her thoughts of pleasure—are missing. The primary focus of the story is her laughter itself. Jubilees omits the earlier biblical report of Abraham's laughter at God's promise of a son through Sarah, since he could hardly portray this paradigm of Torah faithfulness as doubting God. Instead, Abraham merely wondered whether such old parents could really have a son (Gen 15:17). It was necessary to acknowledge Sarah's laughter, an act that is theologically neutral and whose motivation is literary, so that the wordplay on Issac's name could be retained.

During the second century C.E., Jews in Palestine attempted several new and much more literal Greek translations of the Hebrew scripture. Neither Aquila nor Symmachus had the LXX's lexical and/or ideological problems with Sarah's *'ednâ*. Aquila's translation of Gen 18:12 showed Sarah pondering sexual tenderness (*trypheria*). Symmachus used a Greek word with physical connotations to render *'ednâ*. His choice of *akmē* produces a translation by which, according to Wevers, Sarah questions her stamina or vigor.[42] However, since *akmē* also can refer to the highest or culminating point of any condition or act, Sarah could be pondering whether she might reach a climax. Neither of these Palestinian revisers seemed particularly embarrassed about the physical aspects of Sarah's thoughts. Their goal of providing a more accurate and literal translation superseded any ideological or theological desire to domesticate Sarah.

However, these translators were the exception. Most other translations and retellings offered a more modest-thinking Sarah. The Targumim translators, like their LXX counterparts, were circumspect with regard to Sarah's sexuality. Michael Maher maintains that the translators did not translate the biblical phrase "shall I still have pleasure?" literally, because "they felt that this phrase had sexual connotations and that it was unworthy of Sarah."[43] Pseudo-Jonathan's "shall I become pregnant?" and Neofiti's "is it possible for me to return to the days of my youth and to have pregnancies?" censor Sarah's thoughts of sexual pleasure. The Babylonian Onqelos, however, removes not only the sexual connotations but also the physical condition of pregnancy in its translation, "shall I have youth again?" Moses Aberbach and Bernard Grossfeld suggest that this translation might represent "an attempt to avoid the sexual implications of *ʿednâ*, which may have been felt to be somewhat indelicate for Sarah to mention."[44]

The domestication of Sarah continued. Pseudo-Philo made no mention at all of Sarah's thoughts. His three references to Sarah all deal with her inability to conceive (*L.A.B.* 8:1; 23:5–7; 32:1). Josephus removes any reference to Sarah's thoughts of sex and ostensibly improves her character, like the LXX and the Targumim translators, by reporting that she merely "smiles" (*meidiasasēs*) because childbearing was impossible for a ninety-year-old woman with a hundred-year-old husband (*Ant.* 1.11.2 §198). By the time Sarah makes her appearance in the New Testament, she is quite tame and is remembered only for her miraculous motherhood. For Paul, she symbolizes the mother of the "children of the promise," who are the true descendants of Abraham (Rom 9:8–9; Gal 4). For the author of the Petrine epistles, Sarah models appropriate submissive spousal behavior. As the other holy women "used to adorn themselves by accepting the authority of their husbands," Sarah "obeyed Abraham and called him lord" (1 Pet 3:5–6 NRSV). The Petrine writer conveniently overlooks Abraham's earlier obedience to Sarah (Gen 16:3), and, although he correctly writes that Sarah did refer to Abraham as "lord," she did so in the context of his possible failure to provide her pleasure (Gen 18:12). Peter, of course, omits this possible denigration of Abraham. Thus, New Testament references to Sarah censored her thoughts of pleasure and focused on her role as a good (i.e., shameful) wife and mother whose thoughts and deeds would provide her husband honor and children.

Ancient translators and commentators were not the only ones who had problems with Sarah's thoughts of sexual pleasure. Although many commentators translate *ʿednâ* as "pleasure" or "enjoyment," they often add commentary that explains, or explains away, the text. Gerhard von Rad, for example, translates, "After I have grown old, and my husband is old, shall I have pleasure?" But, he adds a comment, "it has been considered a special nicety that Sarah's reflection is unexpectedly stripped of its bluntness when repeated by God; the expressions *bālā*, for the 'decay' of old clothes, and *'ednā*, 'sensual pleasure,' are not repeated."[45]

The KJV, RSV, and NRSV translate *'ednâ* as "pleasure," and the NJPS renders it as "enjoyment." Others translations, however, are less forthright. Like the reality brought into being for women as a result of the Greek translation, the reality hoped for among the readership of the following modern translations negates the reality of female sexuality and accentuates the more traditional female roles of procreation. The CEV describes itself in its welcome to the reader as a "user-friendly" and "mission-driven" translation that "takes into consideration the needs of the hearer, as well as those of the reader, who may not be familiar with the traditional biblical language."[46] It also claims that its text is faithful to the meaning of the original and its accuracy is assured by its direct translation from the *BHS*. Its translation of Gen 18:12 reads, "Now that I am worn out and my husband is old, will I really know such happiness?" The explanation of this verse is just as equivocal. It allows the reader to choose between two meanings for the phrase "know such happiness": either "the joy of making love" or "the joy of having children." Both the NEB and the REB are even more circumspect. The NEB purports to express no denominational or doctrinal viewpoint and claims it is not a revision of any previous translation; rather, it is a "fresh and authoritative translation." However, its translation, "Shall I indeed bear a child when I am out of my time, and my husband is old," is far from literal. Like the LXX and Targumim, the NEB takes away Sarah's "inappropriate" sexual thoughts. Its updated successor, the REB, continues the censoring of Sarah's thoughts in its rendering, "At my time of life, I am past bearing children, and my husband is old." These circumspect translations, I maintain, result from ideological, not philological, problems with Sarah's thoughts of *'ednâ*.

One could question whether my reading of Sarah's thoughts of sexual pleasure might be anachronistic. In other words, does Sarah's questioning of whether she might experience sexual pleasure reflect ancient ideas of the body and sexuality? Although it is impossible to penetrate the minds of the biblical writers or the later translators to determine their level of medical knowledge, I maintain that Sarah's thoughts of sexual pleasure, and my reading of this text, accords with ancient understandings of sexuality and reproduction.

Texts from ancient Ugarit provide evidence on several aspects of family life, including sexuality and reproduction. These texts suggest that, as in most ancient societies, the ultimate purpose in marriage was the procreation of legitimate sons.[47] Furthermore, as Adrianus van Selms notes, the people of Ugarit "shared the popular belief that pregnancy can only occur when the female has experienced orgasm."[48] He refers to Gen 18:12 as evidence that the ancient Hebrews also believed that sexual pleasure was necessary for conception.

Texts from the Hellenistic world similarly address issues of conception. While some reflect the idea of monogenesis in which the male parent is thought to be the only generative agent, others repudiate this idea and acknowledge that women also emit seed. Hippocrates even insisted that a woman's sexual pleasure was necessary for conception, because she will not ejaculate her seed unless she achieves orgasm.[49] Soranus, the prominent first-century C.E. gynecologist, denied the woman's seed a role in conception, since it is excreted outside the uterus.[50] However, like Hippocrates and the writers of the Ugaritic texts, he maintained that a woman's sexual pleasure, and resulting emission of seed, was necessary for conception. "Just as without appetite it is impossible for the seed to be discharged by the male, in the same manner, without appetite it cannot be conceived by the female.… neither can the seed be taken up or, if grasped, be carried through pregnancy, unless urge and appetite for intercourse have been present."[51]

With this in mind, I return one last time to Sarah's (a)musing question about the possibility of experiencing sexual pleasure since Abraham was old. Whether she *can*, in a physical sense, depends in part on Abraham. However, whether she *may*, in an ideological sense, depends entirely on the culturally conditioned translation in which her story is told. My feminist-conditioned translation allows, even demands, that Sarah gets the last laugh. And we feminist readers get an *after-chuckle* because we always remember the story of Sarah's *laughter*. And now we can remember that her laughing thoughts just might be about the sexual pleasure she is about to have—perhaps for the first time in her life.

For Further Reading

Exum, Cheryl. "Developing Strategies of Feminist Criticism/Developing Strategies for Commentating the Song of Songs." Pages 206–49 in *Auguries: The Jubilee Volume of the Sheffield Department of Biblical*

Studies. Edited by David Clines and Stephen Moore. JSOTSup 269. Sheffield: Sheffield Academic Press, 1989.

Newsom, Carol A., and Sharon H. Ringe, eds. *Women's Bible Commentary*. Expanded ed. Louisville: Westminster John Knox, 1992.

Rooke, Deborah. "Feminist Criticism of the Old Testament: Why Bother?" *Feminist Theology* 15 (2007): 160–74.

Schottroff, Luise, Silvia Schroer, and Marie-Theres Wacker, eds. *Feminist Interpretation: The Bible in Women's Perspective*. Translated by Martin and Barbara Rumscheidt. Minneapolis: Fortress, 1998.

Trible, Phyllis. *God and the Rhetoric of Sexuality*. OBT. Philadelphia: Fortress, 1974.

———. *Texts of Terror: Literary-Feminist Readings of Biblical Narratives*. OBT 13. Philadelphia: Fortress, 1984.

Washington, Harold, Susan Graham, and Pamela Thimmes, eds. *Escaping Eden: New Feminist Perspectives on the Bible*. New York: New York University Press, 1999.

Notes

1. Here and at points throughout this essay, I use the combined term "YHWH/God" to refer to Israel's god. Because I consider this god a male deity, I intentionally use the masculine pronoun.

2. Deborah Rooke, "Feminist Criticism of the Old Testament: Why Bother?" *Feminist Theology* 15 (2007): 160–74.

3. Ibid., 172.

4. Carolyn Osiek, "The Feminist and the Bible: Hermeneutical Alternatives," in *Feminist Perspectives on Biblical Scholarship* (ed. Adela Yarbro Collins; SBLCP; SBLBSNA 10; Chico, Calif.: Scholars Press, 1985), 93–105.

5. Heather McKay, "On the Future of Feminist Biblical Criticism," in *A Feminist Companion to Reading the Bible: Approaches, Methods, and Strategies* (ed. Athalya Brenner and Carole Fontaine; Sheffield: Sheffield Academic Press, 1997), 61–83.

6. Luise Schottroff, Silvia Schroer, and Marie-Theres Wacker, eds., *Feminist Interpretation: The Bible in Women's Perspective* (trans. Martin and Barbara Rumscheidt; Minneapolis: Fortress, 1998), 36.

7. Harold Washington, Susan Graham, and Pamela Thimmes, eds., *Escaping Eden: New Feminist Perspectives on the Bible* (New York: New York University Press, 1999), 13.

8. Phyllis Bird, "What Makes a Feminist Reading Feminist? A Qualified Answer," in Washington, Graham, and Thimmes, *Escaping Eden*, 124–31.

9. Pamela Thimmes, "What Makes a Feminist Reading Feminist? Another Perspective," in Washington, Graham, and Thimmes, *Escaping Eden*, 132–40.

10. Bird, "A Qualified Answer," 124.

11. Thimmes, "Another Perspective," 134–35.

12. McKay, "On the Future of Feminist Biblical Criticism," 81.

13. Cheryl Exum, "Developing Strategies of Feminist Criticism/Developing Strategies for Commentating the Song of Songs," in *Auguries: The Jubilee Volume of the Sheffield Department of Biblical Studies* (ed. David Clines and Stephen Moore; JSOTSup 269; Sheffield: Sheffield Academic Press, 1989), 207.

14. My interpretation is based on my experiences as a white, middle-class, second-career feminist who teaches in the Bible Belt and who has no children but a spouse and five cats.

15. Elizabeth Cady Stanton, *The Woman's Bible: A Classical Feminist Perspective* (Mineola, N.Y.: Dover, 2002).

16. As cited by Eileen Schuller, "Feminism and Biblical Hermeneutics: Genesis 1–3 as a Test Case," in *Gender Genre and Religion: Feminist Reflections* (ed. Morney Joy and Eva Neumaier-Dargyay; Waterloo, Ont.: Wilfrid Laurier University Press, 1995), 32.

17. Ibid., 33.

18. McKay, "On the Future of Feminist Biblical Criticism," 77.

19. Osiek, "The Feminist and the Bible," 100.

20. McKay, "On the Future of Feminist Biblical Criticism," 71–72.

21. Phyllis Trible, *God and the Rhetoric of Sexuality* (OBT; Philadelphia: Fortress, 1978); idem, *Texts of Terror: Literary-Feminist Readings of Biblical Narratives* (OBT 13; Philadelphia: Fortress, 1984).

22. Osiek, "The Feminist and the Bible," 101.

23. McKay, "On the Future of Feminist Biblical Criticism," 73.

24. Phyllis Trible, "Reflections on the 25th Anniversary of 'God and the Rhetoric of Sexuality,'" *LTQ* 38 (2003): 22.

25. Carol A. Newsom and Sharon H. Ringe, eds., *Women's Bible Commentary* (exp. ed.; Louisville: Westminster John Knox, 1992).

26. Adele Reinhartz, "Margins, Methods, and Metaphors: Reflections on 'A Feminist Companion to the Hebrew Bible,'" *Proof* 20 (2002): 44.

27. Pamela Milne, "Toward Feminist Companionship: The Future of Feminist Biblical Studies and Feminism," in Brenner and Fontaine, *A Feminst Companion*, 48.

28. All translations, unless otherwise indicated, are mine.

29. J. Hempel, "Ich bin der Herr, dein Arzt: Ex. 15, 26," *TLZ* 11 (1957): 814 n. 24.

30. The editors base this derivation on Friedlich Delitzsch's *Wo lag das Paradies? Eine Biblisch- Assyriologische Studie: Mit Zahlreichen Assyriologischen Beiträgen zur Biblischen Länder- und Völkerkunde und einer Karte Babyloniens* (Leipzig: Hinrichs, 1881), 4, 6, 79.

31. Alan R. Millard, "The Etymology of Eden," *VT* 34 (1984): 105.

32. Gary Anderson, "The Cosmic Mountain: Eden and Its Early Interpreters in Syriac Christianity," in *Genesis 1–3 in the History of Exegesis: Intrigue in the Garden* (ed. Gregory Robbins; Studies in Women and Religion 27; Lewiston, N.Y.: Mellen, 1988), 194–95. See also Anderson's discussion of the association of the Semitic root *ʿdn* with fertility and sexual intercourse, "The Garden of Eden and Sexuality in Early Judaism," in *People of the Body: Jews and Judaism from an Embodied Perspective* (ed.

Howard Eliberg-Schwartz; SUNY Series, The Body in Culture, History, and Religion; Albany: State University of New York Press, 1992), 60–62.

33. Robert Alter, *Genesis: Translation and Commentary* (New York: Norton, 1996), 79.

34. Nahum Sarna, *Genesis* (JPS Torah Commentary; Philadelphia: Jewish Publication Society, 1989), 130.

35. Sherry Simon, a cultural-studies theorist, writes that the model "allows us to situate linguistic transfer within the multiple 'post' realities of today: poststructuralism, postcolonialism, and postmodernism. To present these influences very schematically, it could be said that the first emphasizes the power of language to construct rather than simply reflect reality; the second highlights the power relations which inform contemporary cultural exchanges; and the third emphasizes that, in a universe where total novelty is a rare phenomenon, a great deal of cultural activity involves the recycling of already existing material. All three of these perspectives give heightened prominence to translation as an activity of cultural creation and exchange" (*Gender in Translation: Cultural Identity and the Politics of Transmission* [Translation Studies; London: Routledge, 1996], 135).

36. Candace West and Don Zimmerman, "Doing Gender," in *The Social Construction of Gender* (ed. Judith Lorber and Susan Farrell; Newbury Park, Calif.: SAGE Publications, 1991), 14.

37. West and Zimmerman, "Doing Gender," 14.

38. John Wevers, *Notes on the Greek Text of Genesis* (SBLSCS 35; Atlanta: Scholars Press, 1993), 252.

39. Demosthenes, *Against Neaera* 122 (*Speeches* 59.122).

40. Perictione, *On the Harmony of Women* 142–145.

41. Semonides of Amorgos, frg. 7 "On Women" (Diehl).

42. Wevers, *Notes on the Greek Text of Genesis*, 252.

43. Michael Maher, *Targum Pseudo-Jonathan: Genesis* (The Aramaic Bible 1B; Collegeville, Minn.: Liturgical Press, 1992), 67.

44. Moses Aberbach and Bernard Grossfeld, *Targum Onkelos to Genesis: A Critical Analysis Together with an English Translation of the Text* (The Aramaic Bible, The Targums; New York: Ktav, 1982), 106–7.

45. Gerhard von Rad, *Genesis* (rev. ed.; trans. John H. Marks; OTL; Philadelphia: Westminster, 1972), 204, 207.

46. CEV Youth Bible Global Edition (1995).

47. See, for example, Keret A.150–153 and Keret B.20–27, from "The Legend of King Keret," trans. H. L. Ginsburg (*ANET*, 144, 146).

48. Adrianus van Selms, *Marriage and Family Life in Ugaritic Literature* (Pretoria Oriental Series; London: Luzac, 1954), 83. See, e.g., Aqhat A.41–46, from "The Tale of Aqhat," trans. H. L. Ginsburg (*ANET*, 150).

49. See, e.g., Hippocrates, *On the Seed* 4–9, 12.

50. Soranus, *Gynecology* 1.12.

51. Soranus, *Gynecology*, 1.37.

Gender Analysis: Gender and Method in Biblical Studies

Beatrice Lawrence

Gender is not a method, but a lens. The distinction is subtle: a method provides the reader with a set of questions and the means to answer them. For example, a person reading biblical text with a historical-critical methodology (or, more accurately, methodologies) will ask a range of questions concerning the history of a given text: How did this text come into being? What can we learn about the authorship of this text? Does this text reflect the reality of ancient Israelite society? If so, during what time period? The historical-critical method provides the means to attempt to answer these questions, including (but not limited to) archaeology, source-critical examination, text-critical examination, and the study of comparative texts from the ancient Near East. All of these methodological tools enable the reader to ascertain (to some extent) *what happened* that resulted in the production of a given text.

Unlike a method, the lens of gender provides the reader with a set of questions to ask of a given text but does not dictate a singular methodology that must be used to answer those questions. A person reading with gender in mind can utilize historical-critical methodologies, literary criticism, reader-response criticism, and numerous other methodologies to answer her questions about the presentation of gender in a given text. Utilization of the lens of gender in biblical studies is, to some extent, a uniquely modern phenomenon. As feminist criticism and gender criticism have made their way into scholarly consciousness, readers have discovered a wealth of information worthy of analysis in the biblical text. Of course, we cannot assume that the biblical writers had gender specifically in mind when they wrote; rather, gender norms (which have always existed, whether stated openly or not) are portrayed in the text, sometimes explicitly, but more often implicitly. It is the reader, "wearing" the glasses of gender criticism, who brings the material to light and examines it to find evidence indicative of gender norms, practices, and conflicts in the Bible. This is an insight expressed by David J. A. Clines in his discussion of biblical and cultural studies: "it is not the Bible that sets the agenda but the culture in which its interpreters find themselves."[1] In other words, analyzing the Bible as an artifact concerning gender is an activity whose impetus lies almost[2] entirely with the reader and is a reflection of the reader's culture, beliefs, and worldview.

In order to determine the kinds of questions that are utilized in gender analysis, it is helpful to have a working definition of gender. This definition is, of course, subject to discussion and debate. Until the advent of postmodern perspectives, gender was seen as a biologically based, universal, binary aspect of humanity, comprising male and female. Men had masculine parts, and women had feminine parts. Certain characteristics were automatically attributed to males (strength, decisiveness), while others were automatically attributed to females (vulnerability, sensitivity). In the past few decades, however, the notion that gender is biological, binary, and universal has come under close scrutiny. Mary Ann Tolbert offers a definition that takes into account the results of postmodern analysis:

> Rather than describing innate natural traits, gender in the postmodernist perspective is most often asserted to be a socially constructed set of behaviors with deep political roots, and rather than being universal, it is enacted in multiple and different ways in each historical and local setting.... While gender is viewed by most postmodernists as still profoundly implicated in determinations of sex, the binary biological givenness of sex itself is challenged by recognizing it too as a fluctuating social and cultural construction written on the body. The postmodernist perspective on gender is built upon many bases: the insights of the feminist movement...; cognizance of the pervasive influence of ethnocentrism...; the awareness of the perspectival biases of all scientific theory; and most importantly, an acknowledgement of the great diversity of gender-appropriate performance in many cultures over time.[3]

In postmodern thought, gender has become increasingly complex. Biological sex is differentiated from gender; though body parts play a role in determining gender expectations, biology is not the sole determiner of gender roles. Tolbert points out that there are several elements that must be taken into account when analyzing gender: historical and geographical location, socioeconomic status, and race, among others. This means that gender is neither universal nor binary: every culture has its own norms for gender identity and performance; further, as proven by scholars who highlight multiple modes of sexuality (including but not limited to gay, lesbian, bisexual, and transsexual identities), gender exists on a spectrum, with vast diversity.

The kinds of questions motivated by gender analysis, therefore, are also diverse. One may ask of a biblical text: How is gender presented in this text? How are males and females identified, and what do they do? What do they want, and how do they achieve their goals? Typically masculine roles in the Bible include patriarch of a family, leader/judge, priest, and warrior. Female characters are usually limited to the roles of wife and mother.[4] However, there are notable exceptions that demand close examination, such as Deborah the judge (Judg 4), Yael the warrior (Judg 5), and Huldah the prophet (2 Kgs 22). In addition, some female characters engage in activities that are generally reserved for men: Hagar is the only woman in the Bible to *name* God (Gen 16:13), and Zipporah performs circumcision (Exod 4:24–26). Therefore, gender analysis also requires that we ask: Who "fits" the models of femininity and masculinity presented in the text? What about those characters who do not fit? Even if readers can ascertain with any level of certainty the expectations a text demonstrates for gender roles, the characters of the Bible generally defy easy categorization.[5]

A reader engaging in gender analysis must also take into account power dynamics. It is impossible to separate the category of "gender" from feminist thought, which highlights the ways in which hierarchy has resulted in social inequity. Awareness of gender construction developed alongside feminist thought. While the dominant mode of feminism up to the 1980s highlighted commonality among women struggling for equal rights, writers such as Elizabeth Spelman and bell hooks[6] argued against essentializing tendencies and pointed out the ways in which gender hierarchies affect different populations in different ways.[7] One of hooks's most important arguments pertains to the effect patriarchy has on men: "Like women, men have been socialized to passively accept sexist ideology.... Men are not exploited or oppressed by sexism, but there are ways in which they suffer as a result of it.... [T]hey benefit from patriarchy and yet are also hurt by it."[8] hooks cites Cellestine Ware, who argues that the ultimate focus of feminist work should be on power: "the domination of one human being by another is the basic evil in society."[9] According to these scholars, patriarchy is at its most basic form a hierarchy in which "male" members of society have power over "females." This inequity leads to injustice. This understanding of power has significant implications for gender analysis of the Bible: a reader engaging in gender analysis can and should question the text about the power dynamics displayed therein. Who has power, over whom? How is this power expressed?

It is not surprising that gender analysis has found multiple expressions in biblical studies. For some scholars, analysis of gender has taken place in commentaries written exclusively by women.[10] The impetus for these commentaries is the desire to elevate and highlight women's interpretations of women's stories, because of the understanding that the woman's voice has been marginalized, both in the text and in scholarly commentary. For other scholars, gender is explored through feminist exegesis that highlights violence and the abuse of power in biblical texts or, alternately, aspects of the text that can be viewed as paradigms for gender equality and healing.[11] Still others examine the Bible to develop a sense of how gender is *ideally* constructed and what the construction of gender can tell us about God and humanity.[12]

Literary criticism is the dominant methodology for these studies, because of its emphasis on final-form reading and the ease with which postmodern thought can find voice in literary analysis. Fewer studies have been published in this field that engage with historical-critical methodologies, in part because of the assumptions that patriarchy was the dominant mode in ancient Israel and that the biblical writers did not engage critically with the category of gender in their writings. Tikva Frymer-Kensky, however, has argued that a historical analysis of gender in the Bible can yield surprising results. In two major works, Frymer-Kensky argues that it is possible to ascertain from the text that the biblical writers had certain questions about gender.[13] Though the Bible is the product of a patriarchal society and deals primarily with public, communal concerns, the number and variety of stories about women leads the reader to wonder: "could the biblical stories about women have been written because of the desire of Israelite men to explore the nature of women and their role and to understand the question of gender?"[14] Frymer-Kensky finds that the biblical text offers no explanation or justification for the subordination of women, and there is no universal depiction of "womanhood": "There are no personality traits or psychological characteristics that are unique to women.... [E]ven though the Bible failed to eradicate or even notice patriarchy, it created a vision of humanity that is gender neutral."[15] To come to these conclusions, Frymer-Kensky utilizes philological analysis and also engages in comparative analysis of ancient Near Eastern texts.

It is clear that there are many ways to engage in gender analysis, with a variety of methodological underpinnings. Because of the unique nature of biblical text, there are challenges that confront any reader utilizing the lens of gender: this reader is attempting to access the treatment of gender in a text from a very different culture. There is obscurity, therefore, on several levels: (1) the text itself is not a clear pane of glass, affording easy access to its notions of gender;[16] (2) the text is from a time and place about which we know relatively little; (3) we do not know if the text is representing an ideal (construction) or a reflection of reality; and (4) every presentation of gender is obscured to some extent, as part of a culture that most likely does not name in an outright fashion what it is saying or doing with gender. In addition, the gendered nature of language itself is also a factor to be considered. Hebrew is a highly gendered language in which every noun has masculinity or femininity inscribed in it. Even if the gender of a word has little meaning in relation to the word's context or reception (by an ancient or contemporary audience), the impact of gendered language remains. Language reflects *and* shapes perceptions of reality, and as such, it is not possible to disregard the significance of the words used in text and in conversation about text.[17] Hence a thorough analysis of gender in any biblical text must incorporate exegesis of the text according to several methodologies, in order to bring light to the text by as many means as possible.

Proverbs 31:10–31: The Woman of Valor

The poem that constitutes the end of the book of Proverbs describes the tasks, characteristics, and abilities that make a good wife a rare and wonderful find. This is a somewhat problematic text to choose for a case study in gender analysis; because it emphasizes women (or, a woman), an analysis of the poem will result in a great deal to say about women but not as much about men. As discussed above, gender analysis is not synonymous with "analysis about women"; rather, constructions of masculinity and femininity are both of interest in this kind of study. In spite of the perceived one-sidedness of Prov 31:10–31, however, the poem reveals a great deal about both genders in relation to the domestic sphere and, as such, is worthy of close analysis.[18]

10. Who can find a woman of valor?
    Her worth is beyond rubies.
11. Her husband puts his confidence in her,[19]
    And he does not lack profit.
12. She is good to him, never bad,
    All the days of her life.
13. She looks for wool and flax,
    And sets her hand to them with pleasure.
14. She is like a merchant fleet,
    Bringing her food from afar.
15. She rises while it is still night,
    And supplies provisions for her household,
    The daily fare of her maids.
16. She sets her mind on an estate and acquires it;
    She plants a vineyard by her own labors.
17. She girds her loins with strength,
    And performs her tasks with vigor.[20]
18. She sees[21] that her business thrives;
    Her lamp never goes out at night.
19. She sets her hand to the distaff;
    Her palms grasp the spindle.
20. Her palm she opens to the poor;
    Her hands are stretched out to the needy.
21. She is not worried for her household because of snow,
    For her whole household is doubly clothed.[22]
22. She makes covers for herself;
    Her clothing is linen and purple.
23. Her husband is prominent in the gates,
    As he sits with the elders of the land.
24. She makes a garment and sells it,
    And offers a girdle to the merchant.
25. Strength and splendor are her clothing;
    She looks to the future cheerfully.[23]
26. She opens her mouth with wisdom,
    And a teaching of kindness is on her tongue.
27. She oversees the activities of her household
    And never eats the bread of idleness.
28. Her children rise and declare her happy;
    Her husband praises her:

29. "Many women have done valorously,
But you surpass them all."
30. Grace is deceptive,
Beauty is fleeting;
It is for her fear of YHWH
That a woman is to be praised.
31. Extol her for the fruit of her hand,
And let her works praise her in the gates.

Several methodological perspectives can be utilized to interpret this poem. The significance of the presentation of gender in the passage can vary according to the methodology. What follows is an examination of this text from a variety of perspectives, with a lens to the construction and reflection of gender.

Proverbs 31:10–31 must be understood in the context of wisdom literature. There is considerable difficulty in dating such texts, since wisdom traditions abound in the ancient Near East, and influence on Israelite wisdom literature could have come from several directions in several different time periods.[24] One of the most popular theories is that this poem, like much of wisdom literature, comes from postexilic Judah. This argument is based on linguistic evidence (features of Late Biblical Hebrew and Aramaic influence), as well as the fact that there is no mention of the monarchy or individual kings, and the household (rather than the temple) is the center of society.[25] If this text is indeed postexilic, then the recentering of the community around individual households makes sense: the people who experienced exile had to reorient themselves in the absence of the temple, and those who returned to the land of Israel found themselves part of a province that was not truly independent. The household as the center of Israelite life—incorporating values, education, and economic survival—would elevate the roles of members of the household.

An effective and dedicated wife/mother would be incredibly important to this reorganized society. Christine Roy Yoder proposes that the historical referent for the "woman of substance" is the socioeconomic reality of affluent women in Persian society.[26] According to epigraphical evidence, women of wealth frequently took charge of a household's economic production and engaged in public business dealings. Hence the poem can be seen as an actual representation of the lives of Jewish women in the Persian period.

The literary context of this poem also reveals a great deal. Proverbs as a whole deals with education, especially of young men. Though some of this education may have occurred in official schools,[27] several texts in Proverbs indicate that the home served as a locus of instruction: "My son, heed the discipline of your father, and do not forsake the instruction of your mother" (Prov 1:8). Throughout the book of Proverbs, the student is encouraged to seek the path of wisdom and to avoid folly, in order to grow in wealth, health, and good social standing.

Wisdom is depicted throughout the book as female. In some passages, Woman Wisdom is highly abstract (Prov 8), while in other passages wisdom is correlated with a lover, counselor, and wife. In Prov 9, Woman Wisdom builds a house, sets a table, and invites the many to come and eat. In Prov 4:5–9, the student is instructed to be faithful to wisdom, to "love" and "embrace" her in order to achieve honor. The words utilized in Prov 3:13–17 to describe the acquisition of wisdom are remarkably similar to the words used to describe the woman of valor:

13. Happy is the man who finds wisdom,
    The man who attains understanding.
14. Her value in trade is better than silver,
    Her yield, greater than gold,
15. She is more precious than rubies;
    All of your goods cannot equal her.
16. In her right hand is length of days,
    In her left, riches and honor.
17. Her ways are pleasant ways,
    And all her paths are peaceful. (NJPS)

Wisdom is further correlated with a good wife through the comparison set up in Prov 5–7. In these chapters, the "forbidden" woman is a seductive and conniving force that can cause a young man to go astray. He is drawn to her beauty and her sweet words; she is frequently out in public, dressed as a harlot, enticing young men to cavort with her in her bed. The antidote to the temptations of the forbidden woman is a loving, faithful wife: "Let your fountain[28] be blessed; find joy in the wife of your youth—a loving doe, a graceful mountain goat.[29] Let her breasts satisfy you at all times; be infatuated with love of her always" (Prov 6:18–19). Proverbs 18:22 instructs: "He who finds a wife has found happiness and has won the favor of YHWH," and 19:14 adds, "Property and riches are bequeathed by fathers, but an efficient wife comes from YHWH." Hence wisdom is linked to the acquisition of a lawful wife, while folly (the counterpart to wisdom) operates as a seductress, tempting men away from all that is good and decent.[30]

The immediate literary context for the poem of Prov 31:10–31 raises two important questions. First, what is the relationship of this text to Prov 31:1–9, in which Lemuel's mother instructs the king about the hazards of women? Second, why does "the woman of valor" serve as the end of the book of Proverbs? The first question can be addressed through textual criticism. In the Septuagint, the text of Prov 31:10–31 does not immediately follow 31:1–9. Rather, these two texts are separated by several passages from Prov 25–29. Hence, it is possible to argue that there is no immediately evident link between these two poems. However, the choice of the MT redactor to place these texts adjacent to one another requires explanation as well. One possibility is that the poem of 31:10–31 is the antidote to the warnings uttered by Lemuel's mother in 31:1–9; choosing the wrong woman can be disastrous, but choosing a woman of valor will enable a man to live in peace, prosperity, and honor.[31] In this way, the two poems that make up Prov 31 serve as an effective summary of the entire book of Proverbs: choose wisdom over folly.

To address the second question borne out of the literary context of this piece, that of the role of the poem at the end of the book of Proverbs, it is necessary to engage in close analysis of the language, themes, and ideas of the poem. There are several words used to describe the woman that are reminiscent of masculinity in the Bible.[32]

In 31:10, the woman is described as a woman of "valor" *ḥayil*. The word *ḥayil* is used elsewhere in the Bible to describe strength, military prowess, and power (both physical and economic).[33] The semantic range of this word is not one usually applied to women; in fact, of its multiple attestations throughout the Bible, it is only used to describe women two other times: Prov 12:4 ("a woman of valor is a crown for her husband"); and Ruth 3:11 ("all in the gates of my people know you are a valorous woman").

Another unusual word is used to describe this woman's deeds in 31:11: "he does not lack profit [*šālāl*]". The Hebrew word *šālāl* refers predominantly to booty, spoil, or goods that have been plundered.[34] Hence the woman of valor provides for her husband the way a victor brings home treasures from a conquest.[35]

In 31:15, we read that the woman of valor rises while it is still dark to provide "provisions" (*ṭerep*) for her household. In its verbal form, this word refers to beasts that have been torn or rent apart (purportedly by wild animals).[36] As a noun, the connotation of the word is primarily that of "prey"—animals eaten by other animals.[37] The woman of valor thus provides food for her household in a way analogous to a lioness providing food for her young by hunting and tearing apart the appropriate prey.

Verse 16 of our poem states that the woman of valor "sets her mind on an estate" in order to acquire it. The word translated here as "sets her mind" (*zāmĕmâ*) frequently bears the meaning "to scheme, to plot."[38] Hence, the woman of valor is crafty, capable of plotting to get what she wants.

The words of verse 17 are noteworthy as well. The woman of valor "girds her loins with strength" in preparation for her tasks. "Girding the loins" is an activity that represents preparation for physical toil, a difficult journey, or war.[39] This woman's tasks are daunting, indeed, to require such preparation. Since every other occurrence of this phrase in the Bible pertains to men, it is clear that in this text the woman of valor is not behaving in a typically female fashion. How ironic, then, that her loin-girding is in preparation for domestic duties. The fact that she girds her loins with *strength* only adds to this impression; while others in the Bible gird their loins with armor, special tunics, or regular clothing, this woman is literally enrobed with mightiness.

The composite effect of these word choices is clear: the woman of valor possesses great strength, power, and resourcefulness. She is an aggressive procurer of victuals and goods, one who, like a warrior, prepares for hard labor and executes it with zest (31:17).[40] It is noteworthy that the woman of valor is praised as a hero, mighty and cunning, but not as an erotic, romantic partner to her husband. Murphy notes that this poem is strikingly different from the Song of Songs, in which praise is offered for a lover's body. Not so in Prov 31: beauty is dismissed as transient (31:30), and the only body parts receiving attention are hands, palms, and arms, "but only in a frenzy of activity."[41] Al Wolters argues that traditionally masculine language is used to describe this woman, and the poem is devoid of romantic love, for form-critical reasons: the poem has been structured as a heroic hymn.[42] The requirements of this genre dictate the type of language utilized and prevent the poet from engaging in any other kind of praise.

Although Wolters's argument is compelling, there are elements of the poem that also "suit" a feminine object, such as the reference to ornate and beautiful clothing and the deft use of a spindle. In addition, the woman is praised for characteristics that are highlighted throughout wisdom literature: generosity, kindness, appropriate speech, and a strong work ethic. Hence no single theme dominates the praise offered the woman of valor. Instead, she is a composite of what is desirable in several categories.

It is not only the ideal woman who is constructed by this poem. The woman's husband is also described. His description is, perhaps, a description of absence: he is barely mentioned in the text. His task, apparently, is to benefit from his wife's work so that he can sit among the elders and serve as a community leader, arguably adjudicating disputes and making public decisions. As the public face of the family, he represents her labor, providing the tangible means for "her works to praise her in the gates." A man whose home is in disarray could not serve as a leader among the Israelites; his very presence in public attests to her skill and goodness. Murphy notes an irony inherent in this poem: although it is arguably written from a male perspective, highlighting those aspects of womanhood that enable a man to live an honorable life, the man's role in his household is remarkably limited: "He is reduced to hanging out with the crowd at the gates, while she is the effective power in the household."[43] The language used to describe the wife ascribes to her physical, emotional, and intellectual strength, while the male is a bystander, an observer of her abilities. His most important task in the poem is to praise his wife, to point out and honor the extent to which she is remarkable. Claudia V. Camp even suggests that the woman of this poem fulfills all the tasks usually accorded to *bêt-ʾāb*, "the leader/chieftain of the (ancestral) house."[44] What is consequently canonized by this text is a division of labor in which a man's task is to be the family's public face, while the woman's task is to do, literally, everything else.[45]

Although the portrayal of gender in Prov 31:10–31 discussed in this essay presents unequal responsibilities and expectations, it is also true that the poem is multivalent and multifaceted. The message of the poem—that the female head of household is important and worthy of praise—can be viewed positively, as evidence that the ancient Israelites valued the contributions of women. In addition, the use of traditionally masculine language for certain behaviors and characteristics of the woman of valor opens our eyes to the possibility that ancient Israelite literature demonstrates playfulness and flexibility in its use of gender. However, the overarching message of the poem highlights the ideal of a woman who handles the entire domestic sphere, as well as the family's economic health: she is relegated to the domestic realm, and the evidence of her valor is her husband's capacity to have a public life.

This portrayal of the ideal woman is not necessarily surprising when we contextualize it historically and literarily. It is possible to examine the presentation of gender in Prov 31:10–31 from historical-critical and literary perspectives, but this text is more than an artifact out of an ancient text. Traditionally, in Jewish households, this poem is read aloud every Sabbath eve by the male head of household, to honor his wife and the mother of his children. It is a time-honored tradition, held in high esteem even by progressive Jews. The ideals presented in the text are reiterated and reified weekly, as part of domestic Jewish culture. Even if it is possible to explain—or explain *away*—the unrealistic, idealistic aspects of this portrait, the portrait is still maintained and underscored every Sabbath. As a result, the image is of a superhero-like wife and mother who runs the household *and* provides for its economic security, all the while maintaining cheerfulness and kindness toward all she encounters. This is presented as a model for modern Jewish women.

This model is damaging, to say the least, because of its sheer unattainability. Carol R. Fontaine calls the woman of valor a "'SuperMom,' a picture of efficiency and approved domestic values to which few real human women are able to live up,"[46] and asks pointedly about her work ethic: "Is this a virtue or a symptom of dysfunction? Does she, like the Hebrew God (Ps. 121.4), suffer from sleep deprivation? Is her sleeplessness a sign of something to which we should be paying more attention?"[47] A gender-critical lens provides the reader with the sense that something is wrong with this poem, that its expectations are too high, that its values are rooted in outdated gender roles, and that a modern reader should not accept it too willingly. Perhaps modern communities have outgrown a family model in which one partner—male or female—handles the entire domestic sphere while the other provides the public face of the family. Perhaps analysis of this text can encourage modern readers to craft a new sense of what it means to be a woman—or man—of valor.

For Further Reading

Adam, A. K. M., ed. *Handbook of Postmodern Biblical Interpretation.* St. Louis: Chalice, 2000.

Bach, Alice. *The Pleasure of Her Text: Feminist Readings of Biblical and Historical Texts.* Philadelphia: Trinity Press International, 1990.

Day, Peggy Lynne, ed. *Gender and Difference.* Minneapolis: Fortress, 1989.

Frymer-Kensky, Tikva. *Reading the Women of the Bible: A New Interpretation of Their Stories.* New York: Schocken, 2002.
Newsom, Carol A., and Sharon H. Ringe, eds. *Women's Bible Commentary.* Exp. ed. Louisville: Westminster John Knox, 1998.
Spelman, Elizabeth. *Inessential Woman: Problems of Exclusion in Feminist Thought.* Boston: Beacon, 1988.
Trible, Phyllis. *God and the Rhetoric of Sexuality.* OBT. Philadelphia: Fortress, 1978.
———. *Texts of Terror: Literary-Feminist Readings of Biblical Narratives.* OBT 13. Philadelphia: Fortress, 1984.

Notes

1. David J. A. Clines, "Ecce Vir, or, Gendering the Son of Man," in *Biblical Studies/Cultural Studies: The Third Sheffield Colloquium* (ed. J. Cheryl Exum and Stephen D. Moore; JSOTSup 266; Sheffield: Sheffield Academic Press, 1998), 352–75, here 352.

2. I say "almost" because the biblical text itself does contain material that raises questions about gender; this material prompts gender-based exegesis. Of course, it is possible to ask if there is any form of biblical exegesis that does not spring forth from the culture of the reader.

3. Mary Ann Tolbert, "Gender," in *Handbook of Postmodern Biblical Interpretation* (ed. A. K. M. Adam; St. Louis: Chalice, 2000), 99–105.

4. Women in the Bible are so completely limited to the role of wife and mother that those women who suffer from barrenness endure not only the pain of childlessness but also a subsequent loss in social standing (Gen 16; 30; 1 Sam 1).

5. Clines has engaged in analysis of this phenomenon concerning models of masculinity in the Bible. In his study of David, he argues that at times in the biblical narrative, David veers away from typically masculine behavior (David J. A. Clines, "David the Man: The Construction of Masculinity in the Hebrew Bible" in idem, *Interested Parties: The Ideology of Writers and Readers of the Hebrew Bible* [JSOTSup 205; Sheffield: Sheffield Academic Press, 1995], 212–41). Although David is adept at several key components of masculinity, his struggles with his sons later in life, in which Absalom usurps a great deal of his power (and David does little, initially, to stop it), suggest that David is a "failure as a man, as a male" (232). Clines's argument is based upon the assumption that the text's construction of masculinity is uniform and that deviation from the constructed norm is a means of reifying the standard for masculine behavior. Although Clines himself notes that it is necessary to avoid the "intellectual sins" of "essentialism, reductionism and reification" (216 n. 11), it is possible that his portrayal of masculine norms in the text is too rigid and does not take into account the force of deconstruction in the narrative.

6. I want to honor hooks's decision to refrain from using capital letters in her name.

7. Elizabeth Spelman, *Inessential Woman: Problems of Exclusion in Feminist Thought* (Boston: Beacon, 1988).

8. bell hooks, *Feminist Theory from Margin to Center* (Boston: South End, 1984), 72.

9. Cellestine Ware, *Woman Power: The Movement for Women's Liberation* (New York: Tower, 1970), 16.

10. See, for example, Carol A. Newsom and Sharon H. Ringe, eds., *Women's Bible Commentary* (exp. ed.; Louisville: Westminster John Knox, 1998). Some of these commentaries focus on particular communities of women, such as Ellen Frankel's *The Five Books of Miriam: A Woman's Commentary on the Torah* (New York: HarperCollins, 1996), and, more recently, Tamara Cohn Eskenazi and Andrea L. Weiss, *The Torah: A Women's Commentary* (New York: URJ Press, 2008).

11. Phyllis Trible utilizes literary criticism to explore these issues in *God and the Rhetoric of Sexuality* (OBT; Philadelphia: Fortress, 1978), and *Texts of Terror: Literary-Feminist Readings of Biblical Narratives* (OBT 13; Philadelphia: Fortress, 1984). Literary criticism and postmodern theory are also utilized to explore the Bible in Cheryl A. Kirk-Duggan, ed., *Pregnant Passion: Gender, Sex, and Violence in the Bible* (SemeiaSt 44; Atlanta: Society of Biblical Literature, 2003).

12. Samuel Terrien, *Till the Heart Sings: A Biblical Theology of Manhood and Womanhood* (Grand Rapids: Eerdmans, 2004).

13. Tikva Frymer-Kensky, *In the Wake of the Goddesses: Women, Culture and the Biblical Transformation of Pagan Myth* (New York: Fawcett Columbine, 1992); idem, *Reading the Women of the Bible: A New Interpretation of Their Stories* (New York: Schocken, 2002).

14. Frymer-Kensky, *Reading the Women of the Bible*, xv.

15. Ibid., xv–xvi.

16. Alice Bach makes this point while discussing the arduous task of uncovering women's voices in the Bible; she notes that scholars are "reading the female voice as a palimpsest through the script of the dominant narrative." See Alice Bach, *The Pleasure of Her Text: Feminist Readings of Biblical and Historical Texts* (Philadelphia: Trinity Press International, 1990).

17. David E. S. Stein, ed., *The Contemporary Torah: A Gender-Sensitive Adaptation of the JPS Translation* (New York: Jewish Publication Society, 2006), is an interesting example of this problem. With the stated goal of presenting a "gender sensitive reading" of the Torah, David Stein argues that there is a distinction between social gender and grammatical gender. He sets about reconstructing the mindset of the original audience (xx) and subsequently presents a translation in which words such as *'îš* ("man") and male names for God are rendered without gender. The impetus for this project is admirable: Stein and his co-editors want to present a translation of the Torah that does not present as chauvinistic a theology as other translations. However, Stein's project of imagining the original audience merits further scrutiny, and he ignores the ontological function of gendered language, for ancient and modern readers.

18. Such close analysis, of course, begins with translating the text. The translation that follows is my own.

19. Literally, "entrusts his heart to her."

20. Literally, "strengthens her arms." Tzvi Novick suggests that this is a reference to fastening up shirtsleeves in order to free the arms for work ("'She Binds Her Arms': Rereading Proverbs 31:1," *JBL* 128 [2009]: 107–13). This works nicely with the first part of this verse; the woman must prepare herself for hard labor in a way that is reminiscent of men in the Bible preparing themselves for war or a long journey (2 Sam 20:8; 1 Kgs 2:5; Isa 5:27; Job 38:3; 40:7).

21. Literally, "tastes."

22. Though some translators render *šānîm* as "scarlet," I am translating according to the Septuagint and Vulgate.

23. Literally, "she laughs at a later day."

24. Glendon E. Bryce, *A Legacy of Wisdom: The Egyptian Contribution to the Wisdom of Israel* (Lewisburg, Pa.: Bucknell University Press, 1979); James L. Crenshaw, *Old Testament Wisdom* (Atlanta: John Knox, 1981); John G. Gammie and Leo G. Perdue, eds., *The Sage in Israel and the Ancient Near East* (Winona Lake, Ind.: Eisenbrauns, 1990); Edmund I. Gordon, *Sumerian Proverbs: Glimpses of Everyday Life in Ancient Mesopotamia* (Philadelphia: University Museum, University of Pennsylvania, 1959); John Day, R. P. Gordon, and H. G. M. Williamson, eds., *Wisdom in Ancient Israel: Essays in Honour of J. A. Emerton* (Cambridge: Cambridge University Press, 1995); Wilfred G. Lambert, *Babylonian Wisdom Literature* (Oxford: Clarendon, 1960).

25. Leo G. Perdue, *Proverbs* (Louisville: John Knox, 2000), 275. Tremper Longman III, *Proverbs* (Grand Rapids: Baker, 2006), 541–42. Christine Roy Yoder, *Wisdom as a Woman of Substance: A Socioeconomic Reading of Proverbs 1–9 and 31:10–31* (BZAW 304; Berlin: de Gruyter, 2001), 38. See also Yoder, "The Woman of Substance (אשת־חיל): A Socioeconomic Reading of Proverbs 31:10–31," *JBL* 122 (2003): 424–47.

26. See Yoder, "Woman of Substance," esp. 427 n. 1.

27. James L. Crenshaw, *Education in Ancient Israel: Across the Deadening Silence* (ABRL; New York: Doubleday, 1998).

28. A veiled reference to male genitalia and/or seminal emissions.

29. This is the only place in Proverbs where a woman is praised with erotic language reminiscent of Song of Songs.

30. See Carol A. Newsom, "Woman and the Discourse of Patriarchal Wisdom: A Study of Proverbs 1–9," in *Gender and Difference* (ed. Peggy Lynne Day; Minneapolis: Fortress, 1989), 146–49.

31. Victor A. Hurowitz, "The Seventh Pillar—Reconsidering the Literary Structure and Unity of Proverbs 31," *ZAW* 113 (2001): 209–18. Murray H. Lichtenstein, "Chiasm and Symmetry in Proverbs 31," *CBQ* 44 (1982): 202–11.

32. Some of the words and themes discussed in this essay are also examined by Longman, *Proverbs*, 542–48.

33. *HALOT* 1:311–12.

34. Ibid., 2:1531–32.

35. Yoder ("Woman of Substance," 434–36) argues for the translation "loot" not because the woman of valor has captured spoils for her household but because her husband avails himself of her dowry at will.

36. *HALOT* 1:380.

37. Ibid.; see Num 23:24; Isa 5:29, 31:4; Pss 104:21; 111:5.

38. *HALOT* 1:273.

39. Ibid., 1:291.

40. One can detect in certain translations of Prov 31:10–31 an attempt to render some of the language into more "feminine" (or at least, less "masculine") form. Thus NJPS and NRSV refer to the woman as "capable" rather than "valorous" or "mighty." In NJPS, the "booty" of 31:11b is translated as "good thing."

41. Roland E. Murphy, *Proverbs* (WBC 22; Nashville: Thomas Nelson, 1998), 249.

42. Al Wolters, "Proverbs XXXI 10–31 as a Heroic Hymn: A Form-Critical Analysis," *VT* 38 (1988): 446–57.

43. Murphy, *Proverbs*, 247.

44. Claudia V. Camp, *Wisdom and the Feminine in the Book of Proverbs* (Sheffield: JSOT Press, 1985), 91.

45. Longman suggests that Ps 112 is the male counterpoint to Prov 31:10–31, a suggestion worthy of further analysis (*Proverbs*, 541).

46. Carol R. Fontaine, "'Many Devices' (Qohelet 7.23–8.1): Qoheleth, Misogyny and the Malleus Maleficarum," in *Wisdom and Psalms* (ed. Athalya Brenner and Carol R. Fontaine; FCB 2/2; Sheffield: Sheffield Academic Press, 1998), 137–68.

47. Ibid., 148 n. 29.

Ecological Approaches: The Bible and the Land

Gene M. Tucker

Any doubt about the relevance of the Bible to the modern concern with the environment was erased in the fall of 2008 with the publication of *The Green Bible* by HarperOne, an imprint of HarperCollins. Publicity notes that the work was prepared in conjunction with The Sierra Club, the Humane Society of the United States, and the Eco Justice program of the National Council of Churches. The publication announcements emphasize, "The Green Bible is the definitive movement Bible that shows that God is green and how we can care for and protect God's creation."

This publication includes a number of articles on general issues related to the care of the earth, but its distinctive characteristic is that the verses and passages that speak to God's care for creation are highlighted in green. The reasons for the selection of texts to be printed in green indicate the basic hermeneutic of this project. Texts were highlighted that demonstrate: (1) how God and Jesus interact with, care for, and are intimately involved with all creation; (2) how all the elements of creation—land, water, air, plants, animals, humans—are interdependent; (3) how nature responds to God; and (4) how we are called to care for creation.[1]

The publication includes a selective concordance as well as a "green subject index." The editors hope *The Green Bible* will equip and encourage people to see God's vision for creation and help them engage in the work of healing and sustaining it. They point out that, with over 1,000 references to the earth in the Bible, compared to 490 references to heaven and 530 references to love, the Bible carries a powerful message about the earth.

To be sure, any publication that encourages concern for the earth is to be commended. But determining the teachings of the Bible on the basis of the number of references to a particular word, in this case "earth," is insufficient, if not superficial, and decisions about which texts should be in green often appear arbitrary. It is easy to highlight any and all texts that refer to the earth. Some of the texts in the plague stories of Exod 7–12 appear in green because they refer to natural phenomena and creatures, but how does that emphasis encourage care for the earth? The reader likely will be struck not by how "green" the New Testament is but by how much is printed in black. John 3:16 is green because it includes the word "world." But why is John 3:36 in green? "Whoever believes in the Son has eternal life; whoever disobeys the Son will not see life, but must endure God's wrath."

Clearly this publication is an environmental approach to the Bible, explicitly presented as a "movement" Bible, an expression of an ideology. In that regard, it takes its place in a long line of publications that mean to shape the Bible to a particular ideology or, more typically in the past, a theology. *The Green Bible* will remind some readers of such publications as the *Nave's Topical Bible*, which intends to make a theological point by printing the words attributed to Jesus in red. In the same category as *Nave's* are many other publications that include selective concordances and topical listings of texts designed to lead the reader in a particular theological direction.

1. Environmental Concerns and Biblical Interpretation

1.1. Context

It is important to locate environmental approaches to the Bible in the wider context of human attention to threats to the natural environment. Explicit concern with the environment and ecological issues is a relatively modern development, with its roots in the late nineteenth and early twentieth centuries. In important ways, it represents responses to the industrial revolution with its machines and technologies that have the capacity to wreak serious damage on the land, sea, and air, and all creatures that depend on the earth.

Throughout most of human history, the natural environment had been taken for granted. But expanding population, rampant urbanization, and the separation of most people from daily and immediate connections with the earth began to make it clear that human activity was doing damage. In many cases, the occupations and activities that took the lead in addressing the problems were farmers, ranchers, hunters, and fishermen.

In the early twentieth century in the United States, both federal and state laws were passed to control human activities seen to be destructive to land, water, and wildlife. These included the establishment of such agencies as the Soil Conservation Service (1935), The U.S. Fish and Wildlife Service, and game and fish agencies in every state. The Migratory Bird Treaty Act of 1918 came too late to save the passenger pigeon and millions of waterfowl killed by market hunters, but it has led to healthy populations of many species. The Endangered Species Act of 1973 carried that tradition to a new level, acknowledging the importance of all creatures for the health of the earth.

That there was a genuine measure of self-interest for many of those who promoted conservation—land for farmers and game populations for hunters—does not diminish their contributions.

The theme of the first half of the twentieth century was conservation, and its most articulate spokesperson was Aldo Leopold, acknowledged by many as the father of the modern environmental movement.[2] His leading thought was: "Conservation is a state of harmony between men and land." Another line, "The first rule of intelligent tinkering is to save all the pieces," set the tone for the preservation of species and the establishment of wilderness areas in national forests.

By the 1970s it became increasing clear to more and more people that an ecological crisis, if not a disaster, was on the horizon. The crisis was recognized as worse than the erosion of the land, the disappearance of species, or the pollution of the water. The very atmosphere was changing as a result of human activity. Some early harbingers of that crisis sounded a virtually apocalyptic warning.[3] A strong scientific consensus developed that the earth was warming, primarily because of the fluorocarbons being emitted into the atmosphere. By the beginning of the twenty-first century—despite denials from some quarters and political and economic opposition—majorities in most Western countries had come to recognize that the planet was in peril as a direct result of human behavior.[4]

1.2. Twentieth-Century Biblical Scholarship

Remarkably, one must look long and hard to find examples of biblical scholarship addressed directly to environmental issues until late in the twentieth century. To be sure, themes related to the environment were addressed frequently in works on the Bible and biblical theology. There were important contributions by Walther Zimmerli, Odil Hannes Steck, and Bernhard W. Anderson.[5] The concern was fundamentally to understand the Old Testament's view of the world and all its parts. On the other hand, the very influential work of George Ernest Wright revealed that the typical meaning of "environment" in the decades following World War II was not the world of nature or creation but the religious and cultural context, seen to be in conflict with ancient Israel's faith.[6]

But in the last two decades of the twentieth century, many biblical scholars began to focus their attention on environmental issues. This shift was stimulated by the growing public awareness of threats to the earth and all its creatures. Many scholars, however, responded directly to Lynn White's 1967 article, "The Historical Roots of our Ecological Crisis."[7] As is well known, he laid the blame for the human rape of the earth at the feet of God's instructions to the first couple in Gen 1:28. "Be fruitful and multiply, and fill the earth and subdue it; and have dominion over the fish of the sea and over the birds of the air and over every living thing that moves upon the earth" (NRSV).[8] In the West, he argued, this elevation of the human species over all creation had become a license to use and even use up the environment. While agreeing that ideas, including biblical ideas, have shaped behavior, many argued that to take this text as justification for the rape of the earth is to misread it.[9] The main lines of that response by biblical scholars were summarized by Norman Habel: (1) the term "rule" reflects royal language; (2) the first humans are thus depicted as ideal "kings"; (3) as rulers representing God, they should reflect God's just rule; (4) the ideals for God's rule through a chosen king are given in Ps 72; (5) those ideals include judging the poor with justice; (6) this is interpreted as taking care of the poor; and (7) "ruling" therefore means "taking care of the earth."[10] Although by no means did all interpreters of Gen 1:28 follow all those steps, most took the text to endorse stewardship of the earth.

In effect, the response by the biblical guild did not deny the force of White's major point about the influence of religious texts on human activity in relationship to the earth.[11] Most argued instead that it was not the Genesis text itself but the history of its interpretation that supported the rape of the earth. This issue remains at the heart of the present controversy. Is it the Bible or its (mainly Western) interpretation that supports human behavior that destroys the natural environment?[12] Whether that key text is taken as authorizing environmental despotism or ordaining stewardship, both alternatives assume that human beings have a role over the rest of creation.[13] In the tone of accusation, one writer observed, "The biblical concept of nature is strongly anthropomorphic."[14]

Soon the scholarly conversation concerning the Bible and the environment expanded far beyond that key text in Genesis. The leading concern was to learn what the Bible actually says about the world, its various parts, and the role of humans in that world. The traditional tools of modern criticism—philology, textual criticism, historical inquiry, literary criticism, form criticism, and so on—were brought into play. But shaping, if not driving, this inquiry was the conviction that the biblical tradition is authoritative, or if not, it is influential, even in modern culture. It remains the conviction of many if not most readers of the Bible that its teachings should shape how they live their lives in the world.

Many of the works produced in the 1980s and 1990s focused on the theme of creation. These included a major volume of essays edited by Richard J. Clifford and John J. Collins.[15] Some turned their attention to the Psalms and wisdom literature.[16] Terence Fretheim related ecological concerns to the theology of the Old Testament in a series of very sophisticated articles and books. Specifically, he reinterpreted the structure of the Pentateuch in terms of creation.[17] His work has shed new light on the older tensions between history as the "history of salvation" and the natural order.

Other important contributions to the discussion have come from the perspective of biblical ethics.[18] Although the works of both Carol Newsom and William Brown focus more on the moral sense of the cosmos, both have important implications, especially for the question of the role of humanity in the natural order.[19]

The understanding of land has long been recognized as a central issue in the Hebrew Scriptures, and sorting out its meanings in the Bible stands at the heart of environmental concerns. Walter Brueggemann's *The Land: Place as Gift, Promise and Challenge in Biblical Faith*, although not directly addressed to environmental issues, was a significant point of departure for more recent works.[20] Although Brueggemann is deeply aware of political, economic, and social issues, his book is essentially a work of theology. In fact, as the key terms of the subtitle reveal—gift, promise, and challenge—his approach is shaped by a particular historically oriented theology, the interpretation of Israel's relationship with its God *before*, *in*, and *exiled* from the land. Land functions for him mainly as an historical-theological symbol. He says, "land is indeed a prism through which biblical faith can be understood."[21] Thus the book has more to do with people and God than with land itself.

From the point of view of our questions concerning the meaning of land, Brueggemann makes two significant contributions. First, the Scriptures constantly view earth, land, and country in theological terms; that is, although they do not always claim that the land is the Lord's as such, they always presume that God created the earth and that human beings are accountable to that God for their relationship to the land. Second, it is indeed human stories that invest particular land with special significance, that transform space into place. Why else would so many call that area on the shore of the Mediterranean the "Holy Land"? It is the promised land of ancient (and modern) Israel, sacred to Muslims, the goal of the Crusades, the place of pilgrimages even to this day. Why this place, or any specific place, for that matter? Because dirt, particular ground, has symbolic force, primarily because of its stories.

"Space" is less significant in Brueggemann's work. But it is important to stress that at least some biblical traditions appreciate space as well, space in the sense of areas with no human stories. The poet of Ps 8 stands in awe before the heavens, Isa 40–55 is rich in the metaphors of space that contrast the divine with the human perspective, and the author of Job puts human beings in their place (!) by noting that God even brings "rain on a land where no one lives, on the desert, which is empty of human life" (Job 38:25–26 NRSV).[22]

One more small but important caveat: in his discussion of the land Sabbath of Lev 25, Brueggemann says, "land is not fully given over to our satiation. Land has its own rights over against us and even its own existence."[23] The only problem with that claim is the attribution of "rights" to land, or to anything or anyone, for that matter, in ancient Israel. Human rights, as commonly understood and as enshrined in the U.S. Constitution, are modern ideas, arising in the Enlightenment. The biblical emphasis is always on the other side, not individual rights but responsibilities to the other.

More directly related to concerns with the environment, and especially the intersection of those concerns with human rights, was Norman Habel's major project on land and justice.[24] Habel freely acknowledges that his concern with the biblical traditions and ideologies is shaped by conflicts over the land in his native Australia, conflicts between aboriginal peoples and European settlers. He is particularly concerned with claims to ownership, since "land claims and communal identity are often inextricably intertwined."[25] Habel frequently speaks of "land rights," but he knows that is a modern expression, particularly important in contemporary conflicts. He is more precise, and more faithful to the biblical texts, when he speaks of "entitlement to land." He is especially interested in the role that ideas of entitlement play in land ideologies. Thus, his "goal is to focus on the texts as social and political documents."[26] His analysis of these texts is rich and nuanced.

Habel demonstrates beyond question that there is not a single social and political understanding of land in the Bible. He recognizes at least six distinct ideologies, identified in different texts. He makes no effort to sort out these ideologies in terms of historical development, but he knows that some would have been contemporaneous and in competition with one another. Habel's work concentrates on the social, economic, and especially political understanding of land in the Hebrew Scriptures. It shows the ideological importance of land, but it reveals some theological and religious concerns as well. It also argues that a concern with justice drives virtually all biblical traditions. However, there were very different understandings of justice, especially distributive justice, depending upon which group was seen to be entitled to the land.

One of the most important works on the particular issue of land and the general topic of the Old Testament and the environment is Theodore Hiebert's *The Yahwist's Landscape: Nature and Religion in Early Israel*.[27] It focuses narrowly and deeply upon one particular text, the Yahwistic document of the Pentateuch, and unfolds that author's understanding of the natural environment, especially the land. Political considerations hardly come into view, but social and economic concerns are front and center. Hiebert shows convincingly that the Yahwistic document does not stem from the desert but reflects the mixed agricultural economy of the Judean hill country.[28]

The Yahwist uses both Hebrew words for land, but one of them is central: *'ădāmâ*. A major key to this interpretation of the Yahwist is Gen 2:5b: "For the LORD God had not caused it to rain upon the earth [*hā'āreṣ*], and there was no one [*'ādām*] to till the ground [*hā'ădāmâ*]." The account of the world before the Lord's creative action reveals the interdependence of the earth, humanity, and the deity. Hiebert demonstrates that in J *'ădāmâ* is a technical term for arable land,[29] and that is the case in other texts as well. The role of human beings is to serve the land, turning it into that which can support life, and God's role is to provide the rain. These two, argues Hiebert, are "the most fundamental facts of existence, the absence of which signify the state of the world before creation."[30] The real world, for the Yahwist, is the *'ădāmâ*, the life-giving arable land. The eyes that see the world in the Yahwistic narrative and many other texts are those of the farmer and the shepherd.[31] Hiebert concludes his analysis by arguing that the Yahwistic perspective endorses an environmental vision focused on small-scale agriculture, the human being as small farmer who nurtures the environment.[32]

1.3. The Earth Bible Project and Ecological Hermeneutics

Without a doubt, the most significant development with regard to the interpretation of the Bible from the perspective of concern for the environment is the Earth Bible project, under the leadership of Norman Habel. The roots of the project are in the soil of Australia, and many of the participating scholars are from Australia and New Zealand. However, participants and contributors come from around the globe.

Beginning in 2000, the project has published five volumes (see bibliography) addressing various parts of the Bible, from Genesis to the New Testament. The project has succeeded in generating a remarkable amount of research, reflection, insight, and public discourse on the Bible and the environment. In the process, it has shaped that discourse in new and often promising directions.

While earlier work on this topic had sought to understand and set out what biblical texts say about the earth and its various parts, or to examine various themes related to the environment, the Earth Bible means to be guided by a set of principles of interpretation and evaluation. These "eco-justice principles" are:

1. *The Principle of Intrinsic Worth.*
   The universe, Earth and all its components have intrinsic worth/value.
2. *The Principle of Interconnectedness.*
   Earth is a community of interconnected living things that are mutually dependent on each other for life and survival.
3. *The Principle of Voice.*
   Earth is a subject capable of raising its voice in celebration and against injustice.
4. *The Principle of Purpose.*
   The universe, Earth and all its components, are part of a dynamic cosmic design within which each piece has a place in the overall goal of that design.
5. *The Principle of Mutual Custodianship.*
   Earth is a balanced and diverse domain where responsible custodians can function as partners, rather than rulers, to sustain a balanced and diverse Earth community.

6. *The Principle of Resistance.*
   Earth and its components not only suffer from injustices at the hands of humans, but actively resist them in the struggle for justice.[33]

These principles are elaborated especially in the initial volume with an introduction by Habel and a further chapter by the Earth Bible team. Arguing that most previous biblical and theological scholarship has treated earth as an object, Habel states a major goal of the project:

> Our approach in this series attempts to move beyond a focus on ecological *themes* to a process of listening to, and identifying with, Earth as a presence or voice in the text. Our task is to take up the cause of Earth and the non-human members of the Earth community by sensing their presence in the text—whether their presence is suppressed, oppressed or celebrated. We seek to move beyond identifying ecological themes in creation theology to identifying with Earth in its ecojustice struggle.[34]

Any set of principles for interpretation should generate a respectful dialogue about their validity and usefulness.[35] First, there is the very idea of principles to guide a project of biblical interpretation; the need to set out such principles would not have come up as recently as three or four decades ago. Most scholars were taught to avoid imposing their preconceptions on the text or even deciding in advance what they wanted to discover. An inductive rather than a deductive approach was preferred; just read the text and see what comes out—that was the modern critical approach.

We were, of course, kidding ourselves. Principles of interpretation are both essential and inevitable. Until recently, our unacknowledged principles for the most part were Western, male, and historical. In the guild, theological and moral goals were suspect.

But one cannot enter new terrain—or even old terrain such as the biblical texts—without both a map and some idea of a destination or a goal. Many different kinds of maps may be useful, depending upon what one wants to find. Even geography includes physical geography, political geography, economic geography, and perhaps geology. Just what are we looking for as we head out into a strange—or even a supposedly familiar—country? Of course, the destination may of necessity change as we learn more about the land.

Some of the most hazardous principles—such as those that have guided so much of scholarship for the past century—are the ones that are unacknowledged and/or unexamined. It is not possible to know everything that shapes our journey or drives our exploration, for many of our principles are so close that we cannot see them. All the more reason to set out the principles as much as we can and to check them out in public. Principles, including principles of interpretation, can and must open up new problems and possibilities for understanding the terrain.

It would be preferable for "principles" to be stated in the interrogative rather than the indicative or any other mood, that is, as questions rather than statements or instructions. So each of the Earth Bible principles could be followed by a series of questions. To pose questions to the text does not mean that one abandons perspective or a structure of values, because particular questions lead in certain directions and not in others.

Moreover, it is important to acknowledge that principles of interpretation do not derive from the subject of inquiry—the biblical text—but they are accountable to it. To return to the metaphor of the map, we must be willing to adjust, to correct our map as we learn more about the territory. If we expect to discover anything new, we have to let the terrain guide us as we rewrite our maps.

Therefore, any principles need to be flexible and responsive to what is in or comes out of the texts; that is, they should facilitate a dialogue with the texts. With regard to the Earth Bible principles, it is obvious that there was no environmental science in antiquity, but there were attempts to understand the earth and all that dwells within, including some classifications of natural features and living things. For example, while *nature* and *culture* are important and useful categories, neither one is biblical. Asking questions in terms of those categories does reveal some of the relationships between human beings and the world. It also shows that "nature" does not fit the biblical tradition, which consistently uses the language of "creation."

The Earth Bible Project means to focus on understanding (and comprehending the biblical understanding) of the earth and all its components. In that process, some of the Earth Bible principles seem more fundamental than others. One could argue that the first two and the fifth would be sufficient. The first, the principle of intrinsic worth, is a moral claim.[36] The second, that all "living things … are mutually dependent on each other for life and survival," may be indebted to traditional religious beliefs, but it summarizes what earth, biological, and ecological science has taught us. Anyone who experiences and observes the world closely knows this to be true. Moreover, the only principles that make sense are those that see human beings as *part* of the natural order.

The exemplary questions following the principle in the Earth Bible, however, suggest that "hierarchy" is inconsistent with "community," "interconnection," and "mutual dependence." But in this community of living and even nonliving constituents, certain citizens at times inevitably rule over others. The most obvious of these hierarchical relationships is the food chain. All species seek to survive and to reproduce themselves, and they do so at the expense of other life. All life, at least all sentient life, lives on life. Lest we as *homo sapiens* believe we stand at the top of the food chain—except when a larger mammal meets us on the trail—even some of the smallest forms of life, such as viruses, can easily exercise dominion over us. For that matter, so can rocks and wind and water.

The fifth principle, regarding mutual custodianship, directly addresses the role and responsibility of human beings as partners with the earth, but not without tension. There is a fine line here, between custodian and ruler and between custodian and partner or citizen. Many will find it difficult to avoid linking responsibility with power and authority.

The two most problematic principles are numbers three and six, that the earth is capable of speaking and even of "voicing its cries against injustice" and that it "actively resists" human injustice. Is this language poetic or literal? Taken literally, it appears to personify the earth in human terms and thus move contrary to the other principles. It could be the most anthropocentric perspective of all. To be sure, there are biblical texts that speak poetically of the earth's voice.

On the other hand, the principle of voice could be turned around and taken as a summons to respect, that is, look again (re-spect) or listen again to the earth and all its wonderful features. In *Teaching a Stone to Talk*, Annie Dillard says, "Nature's silence is its one remark, and every flake of world is a chip off that old mute and immutable block."[37] But her essay invites us to pay attention to that and every stone. It is one matter to do one's best to identify with the earth and its components, another to argue that the earth and its parts can speak.

Is there a design and a will within the earth actively to resist human injustice? This is not unlike certain—for the most part theologically formulated—interpretations of disasters such as earthquake, flood, and drought. The best I can muster here is the recognition that actions have consequences, as set out in Hos 4:1–3: failure of faith leads to disorder within human society that leads to the suffering of the land and the disappearance of its creatures.[38] If we foul our nest, we will live in a foul nest. Houses built on fault lines or in the paths of hurricanes likely will fall, and their owners might think the earth is angry.

The Earth Bible principles are explicitly nontheological: "the specific terms 'God' and 'creation' are not employed in the wording of the principles." Two reasons are given for this decision: to facilitate dialogue with those who may not function with God or God's creation as an a priori assumption; and to force "the interpreter to focus on Earth itself as the object of investigation in the text, rather than on Earth as God's creation or property."[39]

The principle of purpose (number four), however, opens the door to explicit theological reflection. That is important but dangerous ground. Is that "dynamic cosmic design," in which we all participate, within or beyond the earth and all its components? Certainly the biblical texts affirm or assume that the world is good because it is God's creation and God's design, but it is not God. A continuing theme of the Hebrew Scriptures is the conflict between the Yahwistic faith and Canaanite religion. If one holds "nature" in high regard, is one in danger of worshiping it or the gods of nature? In short, the Hebrew Bible is essentially theocentric rather than anthropocentric or geocentric.

Clearly the various contributors have employed the Earth Bible principles with considerable flexibility. Some have used one of the principles as a lens through which to interpret a specific text or texts. Carol Newsom produces an alternative reading of Gen 2–3 as the human fall from God's original intention that human beings were created for harmony with the rest of creation.[40] Suzanne Boorer unfolds a very complex understanding of the land in P: sometimes it is property, sometimes a political entity, sometimes personified in destructive ways. But P shows respect for and appreciation of the intrinsic worth of the promised land.[41] Carole Fontaine takes seriously the principle of the voice of the earth and listens for it in Gen 49.[42] Taken as a body of research, these dozens of essays have made dramatic advances in "detecting features of the text that facilitate our retrieval of traditions about Earth or the Earth community that have been unnoticed, suppressed or hidden."[43]

A direct descendant of the Earth Bible Project is the work of the Consultations on Ecological Hermeneutics at the Annual Meetings of the Society of Biblical Literature in 2004, 2005, and 2006. Papers presented at those consultations were revised, edited by Norman Habel and Peter

Trudinger, and published in 2008.[44] While acknowledging that this hermeneutic is a work in process and that the papers are explorations of that hermeneutic, the editors set out a radical new approach to biblical interpretation. In an introductory chapter, Habel sets out and explains the three guiding principles of ecological hermeneutics: suspicion; identification; and retrieval.[45] The suspicion with which each reading begins is "that the text is likely to be inherently anthropocentric and/or has traditionally been read from an anthropocentric perspective."[46] Identification urges the interpreter, who naturally identifies with the human characters in the text, to "face the prior ecological reality of our kinship with Earth: that we are born of Earth, and that we are living expressions of the ecosystem that has emerged on this planet."[47] Retrieval refers to the process of hearing and articulating the nonhuman voices in the text as subjects and not as objects.[48]

Some aspects of this hermeneutic seem more problematic than others, but they are seen to be deeply connected to one another. The first, suspicion, is most fundamental to the approach. On the one hand, it would seem self-evident that texts written and read by human beings (as all texts obviously are) would favor their authors and readers. Habel, of course, recognizes this and is fundamentally concerned with the assumptions and effects of putting human beings center stage. To do so assumes that humanity has a special place in the world, distinct from all the rest, and leads to treating nature as "object." One could argue that many of the biblical texts are more theocentric than anthropocentric, but that "bias" would be equally problematic for a focus on the earth.

This project, like the Earth Bible, has generated a very significant body of research that, it is safe to say, would not have otherwise existed, bringing ecological concerns more and more into the consciousness of the readers of the Bible. As in the Earth Bible Project, various contributors have applied the hermeneutic differently. Theodore Hiebert's outstanding essay on air directs suspicion to the history of the interpretation of the texts in question.[49] Cameron Howard focuses on the actual reported animal speech in Gen 3 and Num 22 as revelation.[50] In his treatment of the voice of earth in the book of Amos, Hilary Marlow concentrates on the principles of identification and retrieval.[51]

2. Ecological Reflections on the Land in the Old Testament

What would we see if we viewed some of the biblical references to land through the eyes of Aldo Leopold and the ecologists who followed him?

His definition of land was broad and inclusive: "By land is meant all things on, over, or in the earth."[52] He said further: "The outstanding scientific discovery of the twentieth century is not television, or radio [had he lived long enough, he would have included computers as well], but rather the complexity of the land organism."[53] More poetically he said, "Land … is a fountain of energy flowing through a circuit of soils, plants, and animals. Food chains are the living channels which conduct energy upward; death and decay return it to the soil."[54]

The Old Testament has persistently been read as a story, a history of YHWH with a people, and too often this focus on history or story has blinded readers to the fact that the story happens in real places, on actual land. Moses was called to lead the people of Israel out of Egypt so they could enter "a land flowing with milk and honey" (Exod 3:8), and the spies sent from the wilderness said that is just what they found, "a land flowing with milk and honey" (Num 13:27). This description is common in the Hebrew Scriptures, occurring more than twenty times.

That is what land does. It flows with milk and honey. It produces food that sustains its inhabitants. Not always directly, of course. Honey is produced by bees from flowers that grow in the ground, and milk is produced by animals that eat the plants that grow in the ground. Leopold is right: it is virtually impossible to separate such things as milk and honey from land. In fact, all land flows with some kind of milk and honey, even the most barren terrain, the desert or the rocks. Mother earth always wants to cover herself, and as she does all living creatures, quite literally, reap the bounty. Land generates life that feeds life.

The sexual, life-giving force of the land is the foundation for all the others, for political power and economic survival. There is conflict in these arenas over land because so much is at stake, life itself. The awareness of this meaning of land can easily be lost when individuals and cultures become so divorced from the land, from the foundation for all life. Without life—survival—there is nothing to struggle over.

There is hardly a biblical book or document in which reflection on or assumptions about the earth and the land are not of vital importance. The biblical understanding cannot be reduced to a single point of view or even a single category, such as the political or economic or even theological dimension.[55] The perspectives are diverse, from texts that suggest domination of the land by human beings, to those that emphasize identification with it, to those that stress divine care, even for the desert. The land is known to be supportive, but the environment is experienced as hostile and dangerous as well. There are even deep tensions in attitudes toward the earth and the land. It brings forth its fruits, but it also bears thorns and thistles, and it must be worked with the sweat of one's brow (Gen 3:18–19). When one considers land in terms of that whole system of weather—Leopold's "all things on, over, or in the earth," and one must, for land needs rain—then it is indeed both supportive and threatening. This is the experience of farmers, from the time of ancient Israel to the present day. There is even in the Hebrew Scriptures the profound sense that, although it is solid ground, the earth is fragile and finite.[56]

Underneath it all is an awareness of the land as the symbol for life, for the interdependence of all living things as well as all nonliving things that sustain life. The understanding that human beings are seen to come from and return to the earth is not a curse so much as an observation: "until you return to the ground, for out of it you were taken; you are dust, and to dust you shall return" (Gen 3:19). The Bible teaches its readers to love life. "To live long on the land that the LORD your God gives you" is a blessing and a benediction (see Deut 25:15).

One need not worship the earth to be in love with it and to be aware of one's deep connection with it. In the Hebrew Scriptures, this is most explicit in the Yahwist's account of creation. Human beings consist of two parts, and one of them is ground, earth, dirt. The other is not "spirit," but life. Such an understanding is taken for granted throughout the Hebrew Bible, assuming a profound identification of humanity with the earth. Moreover, this understanding is both realistic and scientifically accurate: all life is made of the same matter as the earth, the land, the ground, indeed, the same as the rest of the universe.

There are many ways to approach the Bible "ecologically," particularly in the context of the present and continuing environmental crisis for the earth. These range from a *Green Bible* that seeks to highlight the Bible's positive understanding of creation, to more traditional historical, literary, and theological investigations, to the more radical principles of the Earth Bible Project and ecological hermeneutics. One may hope that any and all these approaches both illuminate corners of the biblical texts and lead to changed human behavior to prevent the destruction of our fragile environment.

For Further Reading

Anderson, Bernhard W. *From Creation to New Creation: Old Testament Perspectives*. OBT. Minneapolis: Fortress, 1994.

Clifford, Richard. J., and John J. Collins, eds. *Creation in the Biblical Traditions*. CBQMS 24. Washington, D.C.: Catholic Biblical Association of America, 1992.

Clines, David J. A. *The Bible and the Future of the Planet: An Ecology Reader*. Sheffield: Sheffield Academic Press, 1999.

Fretheim, Terence E. “Because the Whole Earth Is Mine.” *Int* 50 (1996): 229–39.

Habel, Norman C., ed. *Readings from the Perspective of the Earth*. The Earth Bible 1. Sheffield: Sheffield Academic Press, 2000.

Habel, Norman C., and Vicky Balabanski, eds. *The Earth Story in the New Testament*. The Earth Bible 5. Sheffield: Sheffield Academic Press; Cleveland: Pilgrim, 2002.

Habel, Norman C., and Peter Trudinger, eds. *Exploring Ecological Hermeneutics*. SBLSymS 46. Atlanta: Society of Biblical Literature, 2008.

Habel, Norman C., and Shirley Wurst, eds. *The Earth Story in Genesis*. The Earth Bible 2. Sheffield: Sheffield Academic Press, 2000.

———. *The Earth Story in the Psalms and the Prophets*. The Earth Bible 4. Sheffield: Sheffield Academic Press; Cleveland: Pilgrim, 2001.

———. *The Earth Story in Wisdom Traditions*. The Earth Bible 3. Sheffield: Sheffield Academic Press; Cleveland: Pilgrim, 2001.

Newsom, Carol A. “The Moral Sense of Nature: Ethics in the Light of God’s Speech to Job.” *PSB* 15 (1994): 9–27.

Olson, Dennis. “Biblical Perspectives on the Land.” *WW* 6 (1986): 18–27.

Tucker, Gene M. “Rain on a Land Where No One Lives: The Hebrew Bible on the Environment.” *JBL* 116 (1997): 3–17.

Notes

1. *The Green Bible: New Revised Standard Version* (San Francisco: HarperOne, 2008), I-16.

2. Aldo Leopold, *A Sand County Almanac* (New York: Oxford University Press, 1949).

3. See, e.g., Bill McKibben, *The End of Nature* (New York: Random House, 1989).

4. Alan Weisman’s *The World without Us* (New York: St. Martin’s Press, 2007) shows many of the effects of that human behavior by imagining what would happen to both the natural world and human constructions if suddenly all human beings disappeared from the earth.

5. Walther Zimmerli, *The Old Testament and the World* (Atlanta: John Knox, 1976), 5–7; Odil Hannes Steck, *World and Environment* (Nashville: Abingdon, 1980); Bernhard W. Anderson, *Creation in the Old Testament* (Philadelphia: Fortress, 1984), 4; idem, *Creation versus Chaos: The Reinterpretation of Mythical Symbolism in the*

Bible (New York: Association Press, 1967); idem, *From Creation to New Creation: Old Testament Perspectives* (OBT; Minneapolis: Fortress, 1994).

6. George Ernest Wright, *The Old Testament against Its Environment* (SBT 2; London: SCM, 1950).

7. Lynn White, "The Historical Roots of our Ecological Crisis," *Science* 155 (1967): 1203–7; repr. in *Ecology and Religion in History* (ed. David and Eileen Spring; New York: Harper & Row, 1974), 15–31.

8. One could argue that the divine command in the first part of that verse, "to be fruitful and multiply and fill the earth," has been even more destructive than the latter portion of the verse, given the explosion of the human population in modern times. But "multiplying" is what species do, or they disappear.

9. See, e.g., James Barr, "Man and Nature: The Ecological Controversy and the Old Testament," in Spring and Spring, *Ecology and Religion in History*, 48–75; Gene M. Tucker, "Creation and the Limits of the World: Nature and History in the Old Testament," *HBT* 15 (1993): 105–18; James Limburg, "The Responsibility of Royalty: Genesis 1–11 and the Care of the Earth" *WW* 11 (1991): 124–30; William Dryness, "Stewardship of the Earth in the Old Testament," in *Tending the Garden: Essays on the Gospel and the Earth* (ed. W. Granburg-Michaelson; Grand Rapids: Eerdmans, 1987), 50–65.

10. Norman C. Habel, *Readings from the Perspective of the Earth* (The Earth Bible 1; Sheffield: Sheffield Academic Press, 2000), 31.

11. White writes, "What people do about their ecology depends on what they think about themselves in relation to things around them. Human ecology is deeply conditioned by beliefs about our nature and destiny—that is, by religion" (White, "The Historical Roots," 23).

12. In fact, White argued that the problem lay more with the history of interpretation than with the Bible itself. Elaine Pagels shows how the interpretation of Gen 1–3 in the early Christian church fashioned so many of the fundamental perspectives that persist into the modern world: "What I intend to show in this book is how certain ideas—in particular, ideas concerning sexuality, moral freedom, and human value—took their definitive form during the first four centuries as interpretations of the Genesis creation stories, and how they have continued to affect our culture and everyone in it, Christian or not, ever since" (*Adam, Eve, and the Serpent* [New York: Vintage, 1988], xxviii).

13. Gene M. Tucker, "Rain on a Land Where No One Lives: The Hebrew Bible on the Environment," *JBL* 116 (1997): 5.

14. Jeanne Kay, "Concepts of Nature in the Hebrew Bible," *Environmental Ethics* 10 (1988): 313.

15. Richard J. Clifford and John J. Collins, eds., *Creation in the Biblical Traditions* (CBQMS 24; Washington, D.C.: Catholic Biblical Association of America, 1992). See also Ronald A. Simkins, *Creator and Creation: Nature in the Worldview of Ancient Israel* (Peabody, Mass.: Hendrickson, 1994).

16. James Limburg, "Who Cares for the Earth? Psalm Eight and the Environment," in *All Things New: Essays in Honor of Roy A. Harrisville* (ed. Arland J. Hultgren, Donald H. Juel, and Jack D. Kingsbury; Word and World Supplement Series 1; St.

Paul, Minn.: Luther Northwestern Theological Seminary Press, 1992), 43–52; James Limburg, "Down-to-Earth Theology: Psalm 104 and the Environment," *CurTM* 21 (1993): 340–46; James L. Mays, "What Is a Human Being? Reflections on Psalm 8" *ThTo* 50 (1994): 511–20; Robert Gordis, "Job and Ecology (and the Significance of Job 40:15)" *HAR* 9 (1985): 189–202.

17. Terence Fretheim, "Because the Whole Earth Is Mine," *Int* 50 (1996): 229–39; idem, "The Plagues as Ecological Signs of Historical Disaster," *JBL* 110 (1991): 385–96; idem, *The Pentateuch* (IBT; Nashville: Abingdon, 1996).

18. Bruce C. Birch, *Let Justice Roll Down: The Old Testament, Ethics, and Christian Life* (Louisville: Westminster John Knox, 1991).

19. Carol A. Newsom, "The Moral Sense of Nature: Ethics in the Light of God's Speech to Job," *PSB* 15 (1994): 9–27; William P. Brown, *The Ethos of the Cosmos: The Genesis of Moral Imagination in the Bible* (Grand Rapids: Eerdmans, 1999).

20. Walter Brueggemann, *The Land: Place as Gift, Promise and Challenge in Biblical Faith* (OBT; Philadelphia: Fortress, 1977).

21. Ibid., 184.

22. Gene M. Tucker, "Rain on a Land Where No One Lives," 3–17.

23. Brueggemann, *The Land*, 63–64.

24. Norman Habel, *The Land is Mine: Six Biblical Land Ideologies* (Minneapolis: Fortress, 1995).

25. Ibid., xi.

26. Ibid., 15.

27. Theodore Hiebert, *The Yahwist's Landscape: Nature and Religion in Early Israel* (New York: Oxford University Press, 1996).

28. Ibid., 61, 97, *et passim.*

29. Ibid., 34. He notes elsewhere, "As that from which all life is derived—plant, animal, human—arable soil is the key to the Yahwist's conception of the structure and essential character of the natural world" (63). He also notes, "In summary, J views the world of nature as a single metaphysical reality, the central and defining feature of which is *'ădāmâ*, arable land. Nature's constituent parts, the earth and soil and its various forms of life—plant, animal, human—are distinct features of the same organic system, sharing a common essence derived from the soil" (65).

30. Ibid., 72.

31. Tucker, "Rain on a Land Where No One Lives."

32. Hiebert, *The Yahwist's Landscape*, 149.

33. Habel, *Readings from the Perspective of the Earth*, 24. These principles are included in each subsequent volume of the Earth Bible.

34. Ibid., 35.

35. Many of the observations and comments that follow were published in "Conversations with Gene Tucker and Other Writers," in *The Earth Story in Genesis* (ed. Norman C. Habel and Shirley Wurst; The Earth Bible 2; Sheffield: Sheffield Academic Press; Cleveland: Pilgrim, 2000), 21–33.

36. An excellent guide to further reflection on this principle is Holmes Rolston's *Environmental Ethics: Duties to and Values in the Natural World* (Philadelphia: Temple

University Press, 1988). This work is a profound and poetic exploration of values inherent in the earth and all its components.

37. Annie Dillard, *Teaching a Stone to Talk: Expeditions and Encounters* (New York: Harper & Row, 1982), 69. See also Mays, "What Is a Human Being?"

38. Gene M. Tucker, "Sin and 'Judgment' in the Prophets," in *Problems in Biblical Theology: Essays in Honor of Rolf Knierim* (ed. Henry T. C. Sun and Keith L. Eades, with James M. Robinson and Garth I. Moller; Grand Rapids: Eerdmans, 1997), 373–88.

39. Habel, *Readings from the Perspective of the Earth*, 38.

40. Carol A. Newsom, "Common Ground: An Ecological Reading of Genesis 2–3," in *The Earth Story in Genesis* (ed. Norman C. Habel and Shirley Wurst; Sheffield: Sheffield Academic Press, 2000) 60–72.

41. Suzanne Boorer, "The Priestly Promise of the Land: Genesis 17:8 in the Context of P as a Whole," in Habel and Wurst, *The Earth Story in Genesis*, 175–86.

42. Carole Fontaine, "Forgotten Voices of the Earth: The Blessing Subjects in Genesis 49," in Habel and Wurst, *The Earth Story in Genesis*, 200–210.

43. Habel and Wurst, *The Earth Story in Genesis*, 39.

44. Norman C. Habel and Peter Trudinger, ed., *Exploring Ecological Hermeneutics* (SBLSymS 46; Atlanta: Society of Biblical Literature, 2008).

45. Norman C. Habel, "Introducing Ecological Hermeneutics," in Habel and Trudinger, *Exploring Ecological Hermeneutics*, 1–8.

46. Ibid., 4.

47. Ibid., 4–5.

48. Ibid., 5.

49. Theodore Hiebert, "Air, the First Sacred Thing: The Conception of רוח in the Hebrew Scriptures," in Habel and Trudinger, *Exploring Ecological Hermeneutics*, 9–20.

50. Cameron B. Howard, "Animal Speech as Revelation in Genesis 3 and Numbers 22," in Habel and Trudinger, *Exploring Ecological Hermeneutics*, 21–29.

51. Hilary Marlow, "The Other Prophet! The Voice of Earth in the Book of Amos," in Habel and Trudinger, *Exploring Ecological Hermeneutics*, 75–83.

52. This definition of land is not unlike the understanding of "Earth" in the Earth Bible Project.

53. From Aldo Leopold, "The Round River," cited in *Wyoming Wildlife* 52 (1998): 33.

54. Ibid., 27.

55. Habel, *The Land Is Mine*.

56. See Tucker, "Creation and the Limits of the World," 105–18.

Ethical Approaches: The Story of David as Moral Tale

Bruce C. Birch

It would be hard to think of an area in the study of the Hebrew Bible and its interpretation that has changed more dramatically during the span of David Petersen's career than the study of the relationship of ethics to the Bible in general and the Hebrew Bible in particular. In 1970, as Dr. Petersen and this author were just completing our graduate studies, our teacher, Brevard Childs, published his now much quoted comment: "In spite of the great interest in ethics, to our knowledge, there is no outstanding modern work written in English that even attempts to deal adequately with the biblical material as it relates to ethics."[1] Thirty-nine years have passed, and the situation has dramatically changed. There is a large bibliography of works, articles, and books that address the multifaceted relationship of ethics to the interpretation of the Bible. It is still probably the case that this bibliography is longer and more developed in relation to New Testament studies, yet there is a rich conversation with many voices relating ethics to the study of the Hebrew Bible as well, and it is to that conversation that this essay will attend.

It is not the purpose of this essay to give a detailed survey of the discussion and its many contributors or even to assess critically those contributions. Such critical surveys are available elsewhere.[2] It does, however, seem that the discussion of ethics and the Hebrew Bible is sufficiently developed at this point to allow for a snapshot of the state of the discussion. It would seem to me that areas of common agreement on defining and understanding major issues in the discussion have emerged, and we will begin with a brief discussion of this common ground. This, of course, allows for a discussion of work remaining to be done or issues still under significant contention, and we will turn to those areas next. Finally, we will focus on some dimensions of the story of David in 1 and 2 Samuel as a way of suggesting that fruitful gains might be made in considering the moral significance of biblical narrative texts through the lens of contemporary interest in character ethics.

Ethics and the Hebrew Bible: Common Ground in the Discussion

As the modern discussion of the Bible and ethics began in the 1970s, the terms of the discussion were still so undefined that individual scholars, wanting to discuss some dimension of the relation between ethics and the Bible (both Hebrew Bible and New Testament), seemed unaware that they sometimes chose completely separate arenas within which to frame their contribution. The simple phrase "Old Testament ethics" was used by some to discuss the moral dimensions of ancient Hebrew communities and by others to discuss the way in which texts from the Hebrew Bible function as moral resources for various contemporary communities of faith. Although there is a healthy diversity of opinion, it does seem that the discussion has moved to some common sets of categories for framing the questions.

Frameworks for Relating Ethics and Hebrew Bible

A significant number of scholars have been interested in describing and understanding the moral practices and assumptions of ancient Israel. The focus of this effort might be described as *the world behind the text*. While some early efforts sought to discover a unified or developmental pattern of morality, more recent efforts seem to understand that the complexity of ancient Israel will not allow this. Any given text will have a particular social location in the life of ancient Israel and will thus reflect the morality of a given social class or community, and the voice of the text might represent either a majority or minority voice within that context. However, the use of social-scientific methods alongside tools of moral and theological analysis is enriching our understanding of particular sets of texts and how they may have functioned morally in particular social and historical contexts for ancient Israel. This interaction of methods deepens our understanding of the moral dimensions of ancient Israelite life even if it does not allow a synthesis into some larger developmental treatment of ancient Israelite morality. The diversity of texts in the Hebrew Bible gives us glimpses into particular times and places and social structures. One text might reflect royal, noble classes, while another seems peasant-influenced.

One text may reflect tribal agrarian life, while another may be based in the community of struggling returned exiles. There will not be a single—even developing—system of morality recoverable in the world behind these texts, but a series of snapshots of the moral struggles of Israelite communities in their particularity.

Another framework which can be used to raise questions of ethics in relation to the Hebrew Bible is *the world of the text in the context of the canon*. The formation of the canon is a community process that now relates texts from disparate periods and contexts of Israel's experience. It is this collection that gets handed on to future generations with claims of theological and moral authority. Thus, witnesses from varied social contexts and differing literary genres can be considered as part of a rich conversation out of Israel's experience with God, community, and historical experience. The canon itself becomes a moral dialogue that can be studied and reflected upon completely apart from the existence of such a dialogue in any particular moment of Israel's experience. Redactors may have perspectives worth studying alongside the witness of particular texts, and all are a part of a larger canonical dialogue with moral and theological dimensions that transcend the contexts out of which individual texts may have come. The canon, of course, is then passed on in communities of faith (Jewish and Christian) that reflect on the ethical address of the text often apart from discovering much of the historical or social world behind the text. In recent times, an increasing number of scholars have found it fruitful to consider ethical dimensions of the canonical texts that are informed by but not dependent on discovery of the ancient Israelite context.[3]

Finally, ethics is a lens through which the *text as scripture through the generations to the present* may be read. There are still confessing communities in Judaism and Christianity that understand the canon of the Hebrew Bible to have moral authority. For these communities, the text can and should influence the faith and practice of the present generation as it has the generations between the present and biblical times. The emphasis in this framework is not simply on what the text says in its inherent diversity but how such texts are read in community and function as moral resource for contemporary moral character and conduct. The text invites readers into a process of moral discernment that is more than an adherence to ready-made rules, norms, or moral judgments. The history of reading the biblical text as ethical resource also informs our present reading. Contemporary communities of readers do not merely seek to emulate the moral example of the biblical communities but seek to be informed by the experience of ancient witnesses in their experience with God. Scripture thus becomes a key component—but not self-sufficient resource—for moral life today.

Foundations for Ethics in Community Witness

The texts of the Hebrew Bible are not isolated, individual witnesses. The text was formed in community and intended to give witness that shapes community for the future. The canon is the ultimate collection of this community effort. Every individual voice heard in the text was shaped by a community ethos and preserved by a communal decision to pass the witness of the text on to future generations of community. These communities were focused by testimony to experiences with divine reality and by the intent to shape and be shaped as moral agents in service of that divine reality.

> The OT assumes that all persons are moral agents. Who we are and how we act is considered to be a matter of moral accountability.... The Hebrew canon is not just the fortunately preserved literature of interesting ancient communities. It seeks to form communities of moral agency within which individuals are brought into relationship with the character, activity, and will of God as witnessed by these collected testimonies from ancient Israel. Such communities are then to understand themselves and to act, individually or corporately, as moral agents in the world. Furthermore, the formation, preservation and transmission of this literature as canon imply that its intention is to form communities of moral agency in relationship to God through succeeding generations.[4]

This recognition of the community context at every stage in the formation and transmission of the text can give renewed emphasis to efforts at descriptive ethics, those that focus on recovering insights into the ethics of particular voices in the canon and their social locations. To the older concern of form criticism for *Sitz im Leben* comes a fuller array of methodologies drawn from the social sciences to describe the moral concerns discernible in the situation out of which a particular text has been formed.

What is not acceptable is to operate as if this is the only meaningful level to attempt to describe the moral dimensions and meanings of the text. Texts take on new meanings, morally and theologically, as they are handed on to subsequent communities that have preserved them in the formation of an authoritative canon. Previously separate and discreet moral voices are now brought into conversation with a collection of voices. For example, with respect to the opening creation accounts in Gen 1–2, it becomes legitimate to ask how the moral address of originally separate testimonies to God as creator is transformed by juxtaposing them (not even in chronological order) at the beginning of the canon.

Finally, through the generations until the present, communities of faith have gone to these texts as a resource for moral deliberation, for their shaping as moral agents, and for their efforts to live morally in the world. Although individuals may read the canonical texts and ponder these matters, they do not do so without relationship to the communities that continue to claim these texts as scripture, whether an individual reader/moral-agent is fully aware of this or not. The Hebrew Bible is the book of the synagogue and the church, not of individuals in isolation. Thus, contemporary readers of these texts and the generations before them are readers in community with differing degrees of self-conscious and critical awareness of this.[5] How the text functions in this reading is multifaceted, affecting both character and conduct and witnessing to constructive and destructive exercise of moral agency in the witness of biblical communities to their experience before God and within history.[6] No single pattern of moral address will emerge from the texts of the Hebrew Bible—not in their formation, nor in their collection into canon, nor in the reading and appropriation of that canon by historic or contemporary communities.

Foundations for Ethics in Divine Reality

The texts of the Hebrew Bible and the ongoing communities that recognize that it has some sort of authoritative status are in agreement: the focus at the heart of these texts is a response to the reality of God as experienced by individual witnesses and communities, both ancient and modern. Israel understands itself as formed in response to divine initiative ("You have seen what I did to the Egyptians, and how I bore you on eagle's wings and brought you to myself"; Exod 19:4) that now requires their moral response ("if you obey my voice and keep my covenant"; 19:5) and leads to formation as a special people related to God ("treasured possession … kingdom of priests … holy nation"; 19:6). Even the wisdom literature understands the pursuit of wisdom as related to a divinely created order.

Any attention to ethics in ancient Israel or to the ethical address of the canon requires prior attention to the character and conduct of God as witnessed in the canonical texts. Ethics is dependent on "knowing" God; in the rich Hebrew understanding of the term, knowing implies an entering into the very life of God. Moral agency, whether of individuals or communities, is relational and arises out of lived relationship with the God who creates, promises, and makes covenant. Notions of morality cannot be abstracted from the texts of the Hebrew Bible as universal codes of conduct or abstract qualities of moral character. As Barton argued, the Old Testament is not a moral guide but testimony to a way of life lived in the presence of God.[7]

At present there seems to be a broad-based agreement on the bases of moral norms in the Hebrew Bible. The reality of God and the way in which moral claims might arise from "knowing" God can be seen in at least three modes.

The first of these is the *imitation of God* (*imitatio Dei*). There is a growing body of scholarship reflecting on the importance of *imitatio Dei* as a source for moral norms.[8] The life of God serves as a model for the moral life of the community of God's people. For those who choose to live in relationship as God's people, God's own character and conduct serve to shape the identity and actions of those seeking to live faithfully in that relationship.

Micah 6:8 seems to make such a moral claim. The context of the verse is a trial, in which God has just testified to divine graciousness (6:1–4). Now the prophet gives a verdict. "He has shown you, O mortal, what is good…" What follows are qualities of life that seem less like commandments than qualities God has already demonstrated or revealed in God's own life with Israel: justice, steadfast love, humility.

Even in the context of explicit commandment, the motivation for ethical behavior is sometimes claimed as imitation of God rather than mere obedience to divine authority. Even as God "executes justice for the orphan and the widow, and … loves the strangers, providing them with food and clothing, you shall also love the stranger for you were strangers in the land of Egypt" (Deut 10:18–19).

Imitation of God includes not only moral actions but qualities of life. "You shall be holy, for I the Lord your God am holy" (Lev 19:2). Israel is challenged to love God (Deut 6:4) and the neighbor (Lev 19:18) because God has already loved Israel (Deut 7:8). Psalm 82 suggests that this is one of the features that distinguishes Israel's God from the gods and goddesses of other ancient Near Eastern cultures. These deities may demand some sort of moral behavior from their human subjects but are themselves often depicted as willful and self-centered. Israel's God stands in their midst to declare the divine life as a model of justice and compassion, and by that standard other gods are not gods at all.

There are, however, limits to *imitatio Dei* because Israel (and we) are human and not gods. For example, we cannot imitate God's sovereign power and may create moral chaos when we try to do so (Gen 3). Put simply, we cannot perfectly embody the qualities of character and action that we seek to imitate. It is perhaps because of these limits that the moral life lived in relation to God also requires texts of explicit moral guidance.

Indeed, most of the attention to the Hebrew Bible and its relation to ethics has come in regard to texts that express explicit moral admonitions related to ethical conduct. Thus, many appeals to the Hebrew Bible for ethical resources focus almost entirely on law (especially the Decalogue), prophetic address, and pedagogical texts. The emphasis here is upon *God's revealed will* as the basis for ethics in the people of God.

Attention to God's revealed will must certainly be a major part of any consideration of the relationship of the Hebrew Bible to ethics. This centers in the understanding of Israel that God had made promises of relationship from Abraham onward that resulted in the eventual establishment of a covenant relationship between God and Israel. This covenant relationship entailed mutual obligations for both God and Israel, and Israel's obligations were expressed in the giving of the law. Obedience was expected but was not an end in itself. Indeed, covenant represented a divine-human partnership in relation to God's larger mission for the wholeness of creation and the final redemption of history. Israel's obligations for moral behavior were expressed in law codes and commandments, through the guidance and admonition of priests and prophets, and through the direction of leaders raised up by God for particular moments in Israel's history. These do not function autonomously but point to the God who gave the laws and raised up leaders. Even the wisdom literature, which lacks a true covenantal understanding, regards wisdom as inherent in God's creation of the world, discoverable by sound teaching and practice.

At its best, emphasis on God's revealed will has led to the claim that ethics in the Hebrew Bible are distinctively and primarily deontological.[9] At its worst, the emphasis on God's revealed will has led to the caricature of a rigid, legalistic Old Testament over against the freedom of the gospel in the New Testament. But obedience to God's revealed will never functions in the Hebrew Bible as admonition to blind obedience, nor is it the fulfillment of some inherent human purpose. Obedience is part of a reciprocal relationship defined on God's side by expressions of justice, steadfast love, righteousness, and compassion. Israel's obedience to the law and response to prophetic calls for renewed obedience made its claim in relationship to God's activity of moral grace. Even the Decalogue begins with a reference to God's deliverance of Israel out of bondage as a preface to the first commandment (Exod 20:2). The relational character even of commandment is made evident by the appearance, especially in the prophets, of a continual process of commitment, accountability, and renewal that plays itself out through Israel's story in relation to God. Since God's commitment to the partnership with Israel is ongoing, Israel's obedience is never measured over against a static legal reality or an implacable order of creation that can be adhered to or violated (the wisdom of Proverbs comes closer to this view). Obedience is relational. As such, God loves, holds accountable, forgives, and renews, and God does not give up on partnership with Israel in the ongoing divine mission and purposes. "Thus, even obedience to divine will in the OT has both deontological (duty oriented) and teleological (purpose oriented) elements, and both are encompassed in a theology of shared relationship and moral agency."[10]

Alongside imitation of God and obedience to revealed divine will it is widely recognized that a third basis for ethics in the Hebrew Bible is a concept of created divine order that is akin to *natural law*. John Barton has argued convincingly for such a position.[11]

It has always been notable that the various witnesses to creation in the Hebrew Bible understand Israel's God as Creator. Yet Israel does not claim a special relationship to creation. All people, indeed all things, are the creation of God and, as such, are related to the created order of things. Inherent in this creaturely relation is the possibility of moral life without respect for revealed divine character or conduct. Creation is good (Gen 1), all humans have the created capacity for moral choice (Gen 2), and human participation in creation can be corrupted by seeking status beyond created human limitations (Gen 3). All humans are created a little lower than the angels (Ps 8:5). God sustains the complexities of creation without reference to specific relationship with human partners (Job 38–41).

It is the wisdom literature that also appeals to a standard of moral behavior that rests in a divinely created order without regard to the experience of Israel in relationship to God or a divinely revealed will of God.

Moral agency is dependent on seeking the wisdom/righteousness that comes from learning to live in ways that are harmonious with God's creation and its human and natural realities. Job 31, also part of the wisdom tradition, appeals to patterns of behavior that make the "good person" and denote moral behaviors that are not dependent on any tradition of revealed will or experience with a God to be emulated.

Even outside of wisdom literature there are occasional appeals to moral standards that do not seem dependent on any particular revealed tradition but seem to appeal to moral standards that should be common to all humanity. For example, Amos's indictment of the surrounding nations in Amos 1–2 appeals to commonly understood moral behaviors and their violation.

A basis in the Hebrew Bible for dimensions of ethics that are rooted in creation and universal humanity may not be the full equivalent of later Western philosophical notions of natural law, but the evidence needs fuller exploration. It certainly seems there is evidence for an appeal to moral agency that is not dependent on knowledge of particular experience with God or the revealed will of God.

Ethics and the Hebrew Bible: Present Discussions

Although there is growing common ground in the discussion of ethics related to the Hebrew Bible, the present discussion is relatively new, with many areas for further exploration and development. This essay will highlight two of these interrelated areas.

Character and Conduct in Moral Discourse

One of the significant developments in the last decades of the twentieth century was renewed attention in Protestant Christian ethics to the importance of understanding ethics in terms of *both* character and conduct, that is, identity and action. The tendency had been to think of ethics in terms of moral action to address the significant moral issues and challenges of any given time. Catholic moral theology had retained an interest in the moral virtues that emphasized acquiring traits of identity and values that could influence the taking of right action. New conversations among Protestant and Catholic ethicists and moral theologians created a lively new conversation reemphasizing the ethics of being alongside the ethics of doing. Governing questions include: How are identity and character formed? What sort of ethical resources do communities of moral discourse bring to any conversation about ethical conduct and action directed to a particular issue?[12]

In this climate, new interest was kindled in exploring the relationship between Scripture and ethics. Among the first books to discuss this relationship in this renewed conversation was *Bible and Ethics in the Christian Life*, by Bruce Birch and Larry Rasmussen. One of our strongest conclusions was that almost all of the writing on the relationship of the Bible to ethics began with issues; that is, scholars explored biblical passages and perspectives in an attempt to answer the question: What should we do about X? The result was that only those parts of the canon that explicitly make admonitions to moral conduct were considered worthwhile in thinking about ethics. For the Hebrew Bible, this limited attention to the law codes (where all but the Decalogue was considered superseded for Christians by the teachings of Jesus and Paul) and the prophets. Much of the Hebrew canon was ignored as having little value for reflections on ethics.

Our discussion of moral agency proposed taking seriously both character and conduct as dimensions of ethical life. The formation of identity—with its values, perspectives, obligations, and vision—was as important as the shaping of conduct—with its decision-making and plans for action. We believed and argued that with this broadened understanding of moral agency the entire canon became a moral resource. We are shaped as a people of God by the stories we tell, the songs we sing, the liturgies we intone, the apocalyptic visions we take hope from, the histories we preserve. These help make the community of God what it is; these are formational for the character of this distinctive people throughout the generations. There are, of course, those particular texts that inform and inspire our conduct and claim our obedience as revealing of God's will. But attention to both character and conduct is necessary to engage the whole of God's word in both of the Testaments for the sake of a faithful, moral life.

By the time a revised edition of *Bible and Ethics* was published in 1989, a somewhat limited conversation in 1976 had become a lively discussion with many voices. Unfortunately, most of these dealt more fully with the New Testament but many notable new voices joined the Old Testament discussion.[13]

Twenty years later, at this present writing, the interdisciplinary discussion between scripture and ethics is thriving. Interestingly, many of the liveliest elements of this discussion have focused on the ethics of character rather than the ethics of conduct. For over ten years there has been a section in the Society of Biblical Literature on Character Ethics and Biblical Interpretation. Its sessions have been rich and lively, and in 2007 they published two volumes of papers from the deliberations of the section, one for Old Testament and one for New Testament.[14] One of the founders of this section, William Brown, has published several volumes looking at biblical texts through the perspective of character ethics, and he is now joined in this interest by many others.[15]

It is not possible to summarize all the results of this new interest in looking at biblical texts in relation to character ethics. The most general result of this line of inquiry is the realization that possible perspectives on moral character are as broad and rich as the diversity of texts themselves. We are formed by hearing multiple voices that testify to the experience of Israel with God. Then we are brought into conversation with them by the process that gathered these testimonies into canon. Finally, we are shaped as moral agents—both our character and conduct—by reading and interpreting these texts in the diversity of ecclesiastical communities that have handed the texts on to us.

The Moral Significance of Biblical Narrative

In spite of renewed attention to the ethics of character, there remains a distressing tendency to devalue narrative as a genre in the Hebrew Bible that contributes to the dialogue between Scripture and ethics. A large portion of the Hebrew Bible is storytelling material, and even some of the nonnarrative texts are placed in a storytelling context; most notably, the law itself is given during the encampment at Sinai in the journey from Egypt to the promised land. We miss the significance of this narration if we think that Israel's stories are simply for entertainment or informational purposes. These stories have shaped Israel into a peculiar and complex community, a community whose identity has been formed by its relationship to God, and these stories have been handed on to shape future generations.

The moral significance of narrative traditions in the Hebrew Bible has simply not been fully considered.[16] The 1994 publication of a magisterial work on Old Testament ethics by Eckart Otto illustrates this.[17] It is widely regarded as a masterful work, but it deals only with legal and wisdom texts because Otto regards these as the major concentrations of texts that deal with explicit systems of moral norms. He defends this narrowing of focus by saying that he is guarding against the collapse of Old Testament ethics into the history of Israelite religion or the theology of the Old Testament. One wonders if he is guarding against something that the Old Testament itself has not been concerned to do. Otto also adamantly argues against any sort of "application" of insights from Old Testament ethics into the concern for ethical issues today. This ignores the continuous function of these texts as moral resources in Jewish and Christian communities from ancient time to the present. Barton, in criticizing Otto, acknowledges that the moral address of biblical narrative has yet to be fully explored.[18]

As only a beginning to such a discussion, I offer here three suggestions on how narrative texts function as moral resource.[19] First, the stories approximate the moral complexities of human life. Life is not experienced in the neat, compartmentalized categories of laws or proverbs. Moral challenges overlap in the messy complexity of life, and the narrative storytellers often capture that complexity in ways that allow a reader, even centuries removed, to experience his or her own story intersected by the biblical story. We identify with the moments of faithfulness and faithlessness alike in the characters of these stories. We see triumphs and tragedies and also the living-out of a moral vision that, though imperfect, has integrity and dignity.

Second, the complexity of ethics in the midst of life is not lived alone but in relationship to a God who is engaged in the processes of historical experience with us. Far better than legal or sapiential texts, the narratives present the unique testimony of Israel: God is in the story with them. Further, readers of these canonical texts hear the testimony that God lives in this moral complexity with those faith communities. Multiple narrative traditions tell this story of God in partnership with human life, revealing multiple facets of this relationship with multiple implications for the moral life. Some texts show leaders and people rising to the challenge to be God's people in ways that are inspiring and encouraging to our best efforts to be moral agents in the world. In other texts, the narrative tells of Israel's failure—or the failure of a particular leader—and of God's exacting accountability for such failures of moral courage and integrity.

Third, the narratives have a power to transform and call persons and communities beyond the minimum ethical standards that might be defined by law codes or wise teachings. Narratives unfold with the rich complexity of all relationships, and partnership between God and Israel is complex, marked as it is by particularity: promise, righteousness, commitment, sin, judgment, compassion, forgiveness, renewal, and redemption.

These and more are reflected in the character and actions of both God and Israel in the ongoing story of their relationship and its moral consequences for life in the world. We read these stories and are encouraged, convicted, inspired, and repentant as they shape our own moral possibilities. Israel often falls short of its moral goals only to find God reaching beyond a narrow enforcement of moral law for the sake of renewal and redemption. Characters sometimes surprise us with moral courage only to disappoint us by later moral failure. We are called and inspired by such stories to reach beyond the moral minimums of legal precepts or proverbs. We are chastened by such stories to recognize our moral failures and the willingness of God to grant us forgiveness and renewal. The narrative complexity of biblical story resonates with the narrative complexity of our lives and allows for a moral dialogue that can inform our own character and conduct.

The Story of David as a Moral Tale

The editors of this volume hoped that each essay would give example to the interpretive methods highlighted by considering some specific text or segment of texts. Although it may seem ambitious, the issues related to the moral address of biblical narrative may best be considered over against the whole story of David, one of the most substantial pieces of Hebrew storytelling. Here, of course, there is only time to lift up key points in relation to this story of David rather than to give it a close reading (which I have done elsewhere).[20]

The story of David in the books of Samuel (1 Sam 16–2 Sam 24) has long been recognized as one of the finest examples of narrative storytelling in the Bible. However, to think of this story in relation to ethics has always posed a challenge. His story is too morally complex and challenging. With the tendency mentioned above to think of biblical ethics primarily in terms of moral commandment or admonition, the primary way of allowing narrative traditions into the ethical arena was through the moral tale, namely, a tale only featuring an exemplar of one who lived up to moral commandment and admonition. A few such characters can be found, with the story of Joseph (Gen 37–50) as the best example (a story often considered a wisdom teaching story). When a character in all his or her complexity cannot serve as a moral exemplar, one can find individual narrative episodes that function as moral tales, such as Abraham's obedience in Gen 22.

When considered as a moral tale, the story of David seems at first so promising but then so frustrating. He begins as the "man after God's own heart" (1 Sam 13:14), only to be singled out by Nathan's condemnation: "You are the man!" (2 Sam 12:7). We cannot make the whole of David's story into a moral tale, if we understand such a story to be a presentation of a character who models only what we are to do as moral agents.

I would argue for a broadening of the category of moral tale. What if such stories were considered for their power to present and shape moral character and not only to model a feature of moral conduct? What if the power of the story to shape us lay in its own presentation of the complex and multifaceted shaping of David's moral character in spite of the successes and failures of David as an agent of moral conduct? In this light, David's story becomes a moral tale that has the power to mirror the messiness of our own moral journeys, and perhaps teach us something about ourselves as well as about David.

Here I offer only some elements of David's story worthy of fuller exploration and visible in new ways if we consider his story one dominated by the ethics of character and its power to shape our own moral character.

(1) Does the shaping of our character in an encounter with God's character begin with a convergence of "heart"? God seeks one "after [his] own heart" and, through the prophet Samuel, finds David by going beyond appearances to "look on the heart" (1 Sam 16:8).

(2) What does it mean that David is constantly affirmed and related to divine providence by the affirmation that "God was with him" (1 Sam 16:18; 17:37; 18:12, 14, 28; 20:13; and the great summation in 2 Sam 5:10)? Despite the numerous appearances of this phrase, God does not appear in these stories as an overt character as in the narratives in Genesis or Exodus. If God is not overtly visible, to what in David's character does this affirmation point? What do people see that is interpreted as "God with him"? In 1 Sam 18, this affirmation appears three times alongside four affirmations that David is loved. Is the ability to evoke love from others a sign of God's presence?

(3) In 1 Samuel, David prays constantly, often offering up the outcome of his own ventures to the will of God. Are these acts of piety attempts to manipulate divine favor, or do they reflect a genuine willingness to receive what God's providence may bring (e.g., the encounter with Goliath in 1 Sam 17)? When David enters the period of his own royal power and then begins to abuse that power (2 Sam 11), prayer disappears from his mouth.

Following Nathan's announcement of God's judgment, David responds with confession and repentance and prays only for the life of his first child with Bathsheba (2 Sam 12:16). Prayer does not again cross his lips until his penitential retreat from Jerusalem, when he first confesses that his future is in God's hands (2 Sam 15:25–26) and then prays for God to confuse the counsel of Ahithophel (2 Sam 15:31). How does prayer both shape the moral character of David and reflect his moral character?

(4) The account of David's friendship with Jonathan begins in 1 Sam 18:1–4 but finds full and moving expression in 1 Sam 20. The full scope of their friendship tells us something about the moral character of both men and their capacity to give concrete human expression to *ḥesed*, "steadfast love." This term is most frequently found in covenant contexts and used of God's love for Israel. Thus it is a remarkable testimony to the capacity of David and Jonathan that they seek the welfare of the other in a situation fraught with danger for both. It is also a comment on David's character when the term *ḥesed* reappears to explain his kindness to Jonathan's surviving and lame son, Mephibosheth (Meribaal) in 2 Sam 9. Some read this kindness as cynical coopting of an heir of Saul, but one wonders if this act would be described as showing *ḥesed* if the narrative itself took that view.

(5) The honesty with which the narrative details the failings of David from his sin with Bathsheba through his lack of judgment during the tragedies that consumed his family demonstrates that the narrative presentation of moral character can fearlessly include the detailing of failures of moral character. In these stories David is a negative moral example multiple times, as he indulges his sons and their grasping for desires and power, even as he had done with Bathsheba and Uriah. David's story becomes a prime example of a moral tale as something more than stories of actions to emulate. The power in David's story lies in part in its ability to show the whole of David, his moments of moral courage and his failures of moral vision. The community sees itself in both dimensions of David's story.

The story of David, composed of narratives from differing sources, edited together over time, now presents a multifaceted narrative with the power to model the character of a life lived as an exemplary moral agent serving God's larger purpose and as a failed moral agent whose own grasp has brought moral chaos on many. In all of this, it is clear that God, though not an overt actor, is the providential power behind all events. God does not overtly manipulate, but God makes moral judgments ("But it was evil in the eyes of the Lord"; 2 Sam 11:27b) and actively seeks out those who may serve as agents of God's purposes (Samuel, Saul, and David in the books of Samuel). God's primary way of working is through empowering and trusting human moral agents in these stories—even working through their failures.

Much more could be said of the rich and renewed discussion of ethics and Hebrew Bible and of the role of moral character in David's story, but time and space do not permit, and others will carry on the conversation.

For Further Reading

Barton, John. *Understanding Old Testament Ethics: Approaches and Explorations*. Louisville: Westminster John Knox, 2003.

Birch, Bruce C. "Ethics in the OT." *NIDB* 2:338–48.

———. *Let Justice Roll Down: Old Testament, Ethics, and Christian Life*. Louisville: Westminster John Knox, 1991.

Birch, Bruce C., and Larry L. Rasmussen. *Bible and Ethics in the Christian Life*. Rev. ed. Minneapolis: Augsburg, 1989.

Brawley, Robert, ed. *Character Ethics and the New Testament: Moral Dimensions of Scripture*. Louisville: Westminster John Knox, 2007.

Brown, William P. *Character in Crisis: A Fresh Approach to the Wisdom Literature of the Old Testament*. Grand Rapids: Eerdmans, 1996.

Wilson, Robert R. "Sources and Methods in the Study of Ancient Israelite Ethics." *Semeia* 66 (1994): 55–63.

Notes

1. Brevard S. Childs, *Biblical Theology in Crisis* (Philadelphia: Westminster, 1970), 124.

2. See Bruce C. Birch, "Old Testament Ethics," in *The Blackwell Companion to the Hebrew Bible* (ed. Leo G. Perdue; Malden, Mass.: Blackwell, 2001), 293–307; idem, "Ethics in the OT," *NIDB* 2:338–48; John Barton, *Understanding Old Testament Ethics: Approaches and Explorations* (Louisville: Westminster John Knox, 2003).

3. See Bruce C. Birch, *Let Justice Roll Down: The Old Testament, Ethics, and Christian Life* (Louisville: Westminster John Knox, 1991); Christopher J. H. Wright, *An Eye for an Eye: The Place of Old Testament Ethics Today* (Downers Grove, Ill.: InterVarsity Press, 1983); Waldemar Janzen, *Old Testament Ethics: A Paradigmatic Approach* (Louisville: Westminster John Knox, 1994)

4. Birch, "Ethics in the OT," 340.

5. See Stephen E. Fowl and L. Gregory Jones, *Reading in Communion: Scripture and Ethics in Christian Life* (Grand Rapids: Eerdmans, 1991).

6. See Bruce C. Birch and Larry L. Rasmussen, *Bible and Ethics in the Christian Life* (rev. ed.; Minneapolis: Augsburg, 1989).

7. John Barton, "Approaches to Ethics in the Old Testament," in *Beginning Old Testament Study* (ed. John Rogerson; Philadelphia: Westminster, 1982).

8. See John Barton, "Understanding Old Testament Ethics," *JSOT* 9 (1978): 44–64; idem, "The Basis of Ethics in the Hebrew Bible," *Semeia* 66 (1994):11–22; idem, *Ethics and the Old Testament* (London: SCM, 1998); idem, "The Messiah in Old Testament Theology," in *King and Messiah in Israel and the Ancient Near East* (ed. John Day; JSOTSup 270; Sheffield: Sheffield Academic Press, 1998); idem, *Understanding Old Testament Ethics: Approaches and Exploration* (Louisville: Westminster John Knox, 2003); Harry P. Nasuti, "Identity, Identification, and Imitation: The Narrative Hermeneutics of Israelite Law," *Journal of Law and Religion* 4 (1986): 9–23; Birch, *Let Justice Roll Down*; idem, "Moral Agency, Community, and the Character of God in the Hebrew Bible," *Semeia* 66 (1994): 23–41; idem, "Divine Character and the Formation of Moral Community in the Book of Exodus," in *The Bible in Ethics: The Second Sheffield Colloquium* (ed. John W. Rogerson, Margaret Davies, and M. Daniel Carroll R.; Sheffield: Sheffield Academic Press, 1995); idem, "Old Testament Ethics"; idem, "Ethics in the OT."

9. Thomas W. Ogletree, *The Use of the Bible in Christian Ethics* (Philadelphia: Fortress, 1983).

10. Birch, "Ethics in the OT," 343.

11. Barton, "Approaches to Ethics in the Old Testament"; idem, *Understanding Old Testament Ethics.*

12. See Stanley Hauerwas, *A Community of Character: Toward a Constructive Christian Ethic* (Notre Dame, Ind.: University of Notre Dame Press, 1981).

13. Janzen, *Old Testament Ethics*; Ogletree, *The Use of the Bible.*

14. M. Daniel Carroll R. and Jacqueline E. Lapsley, eds. *Character Ethics and the Old Testament*; Robert Brawley, ed., *Character Ethics and the NewTestament: Moral Dimensions of Scripture* (Louisville: Westminster John Knox, 2007).

15. William P. Brown, *Character in Crisis: A Fresh Approach to Wisdom Literature of the Old Testament* (Grand Rapids: Eerdmans, 1996).

16. Bruce C. Birch, "Old Testament Narrative and Moral Address," in *Canon, Theology, and Old Testament Interpretation: Essays in Honor of Brevard S. Childs* (ed. Gene M. Tucker, David L. Petersen, and Robert R. Wilson; Philadelphia: Fortress, 1988); John Barton, *Understanding Old Testament Ethics.*

17. Eckhart Otto, *Theologische Ethik des Alten Testaments* (Stuttgart: Kohlhammer, 1994).

18. John Barton, *Understanding Old Testament Ethics.*

19. This is drawn from a longer treatment in Birch, "Ethics in the OT," 346.

20. Bruce C. Birch, "1 and 2 Samuel," *NIB* 2:1094–1383.

Theological Interpretation: A Proposal*

William P. Brown

In a discipline bursting with new approaches, David Petersen's call for methodological clarity rings loud and clear. His writings on everything from Genesis to the prophets are presented with characteristic rigor and judiciousness, a model of scholarly inquiry.[1] It is only appropriate, then, that an attempt at such clarity be made in an area of biblical studies that has been anything but clear. To wit: the theological interpretation of Scripture is scarcely addressed in most introductions to exegesis, and with good reason.[2] It lacks the precision that other "criticisms" enjoy, since theological reflection is typically deemed more confessional than textual, a product more of the interpreter's faith tradition or religious context than of the biblical text's meaning and context.[3] Whenever theological interpretation does manage to find its way into the discussion, it most often appears as an afterthought.

It must be said at the outset that a theological interpretation of Scripture does not typically follow a step-by-step, meticulously laid out method so much as adopt an approach to the text that exercises the interpreter's creativity and imagination, as well as rigor and discipline. Theological interpretation is a matter of textual orientation. It begins by looking for something in the text that other modes of inquiry may not find particularly significant or interesting, namely, what the text says about God.

---

* I had the pleasure of writing much of this essay at one of David's favorite retreats, Ring Lake Ranch. Perhaps it was providential that throughout my week-long stay a daily reading of Ps 95 was included in morning prayer.

In addition, I want to thank my colleagues who graciously took the time to read and comment on an earlier draft of this essay: Christine Roy Yoder, Kathleen O'Connor, Elizabeth Johnson, David Bartlett, and Walter Brueggemann. Of course, I alone am responsible for all errors and opinions in this essay.

While theological interpretation acknowledges the constructive role of the interpreter, particularly in relation to her view of God and the world, it begins by carefully attending to all that the text, not the interpreter, has to say about God. And so it must, for otherwise the text would be nothing more than a Rorschach figure.

But as the theological interpreter embeds herself in the world of the text and draws from what little can be reconstructed about the sociohistorical world behind the ancient text, she conducts her interpretive work as one who remains fully within her own world. In the hermeneutical venture, the interpreter encounters the text as a strange new world whose otherness is never lost even as the text's world becomes part of the interpreter's world, and in the joining of these two worlds, the text becomes a lens through which to view (i.e., interpret) the interpreter's world. Put theologically, the God inscribed by the text points to the God beyond the text. Put methodologically, instead of conducting only a "bottom-up" approach to exegesis by focusing exclusively on the grammatical, literary, and rhetorical contours of the text, a theological interpretation adds a "top-down" layer to the hermeneutical enterprise, one that reorients and integrates the various foundational exegetical methods toward addressing the question of God's identity and relationship to the interpreter's world. Far from being an afterthought, theological discernment is operative from the very outset.

Because of its distinctive mode and focus, theological interpretation does not simply provide a description of what the text says about God. Indeed, it cannot. Theological interpretation, by definition, involves the exercise of reason (*logos*): the text's own "theo-logic" provides the beginning point and basis for the interpreter to make sense of God and the world vis-à-vis the text. The definition coined by Anselm of Canterbury remains apt: theology is "faith seeking understanding."[4] The theologically attuned reader interprets the text in order to better understand God, the world, and herself.

For persons of faith, God is a definitive, encompassing source of meaning that informs and forms their lives, here and now. In God, the past is linked to the present and to the future. And because knowledge of God and knowledge of the self are inextricably linked, a distinctly theological interpretation fully acknowledges the context and role of the interpretive self in the exegetical process, from beginning to end. A theological interpretation seeks to discern the text's impact upon the interpreter while acknowledging its otherness or strangeness, that is, its ancient roots, peculiar content, and particular ways of communicating.[5] Theological interpretation bears relevance, and as such it addresses issues of contemporary urgency. It is as descriptive as it is constructive. The text is not simply an artifact buried beneath layers of history and tradition that await the interpreter's trowel. It is also a voice that engages the interpreter's mind and heart. Theologically, the text informs, shapes, and challenges the interpreter who seeks theological understanding. He or she does not stand aloof from the text as a dispassionate observer, let alone as a machine going through the exegetical motions. To the contrary, the theological interpreter has a vested interest in the text, for it is out of the impulse of faith seeking understanding that one treats the ancient text more as a partner than as an object.

Theological interpreters, thus, are boundary-crossers. According to James Mead, biblical theologians walk a "tightrope" between history and theology, between ancient text and contemporary reflection.[6] I would, however, replace "tightrope," which signals only danger, with "interface." Theological interpreters thrive on the interface between biblical scholarship and theological inquiry, between ancient text and contemporary context. As much as they are focused on the biblical text and its ancient context to be biblical, they are also engaged with traditional and contemporary theological discourse in order to be theological.

A Proposal

Theological interpretation begins, as do most interpretive approaches, with careful exegetical work. The investigative work of exegesis includes developing a translation that relies upon the tools of text criticism, philological study, and grammatical and syntactical analysis. In addition, discerning the design of the text, including its boundaries, form, and genre, is also essential. Such analysis helps to determine how the text is put together, how its various parts are organized or arranged in such a way that communication is achieved through, for example, conventional patterns of rhetoric, literary devices, and overall structure or movement. Exegetical study, moreover, helps distinguish what is central to the text and what is, by comparison, peripheral. But perhaps most important, a close reading of the text helps to distinguish the world of the text from the interpreter's; it highlights the otherness of the text, an integrity that lies beyond the interpreter's own prejudices and projections. Exegesis requires becoming honest with the text.

Especially important for theological interpretation is the text's context in all its nuances: historical, literary, and canonical. The text's historical context reflects both its cultural particularity and its dynamic background. The biblical text is the product of a particular community whose turbulent history involved the painful struggle for theological discernment, not to mention survival. In so far as theological discernment is a process, it is historical, and historical study reveals, however vaguely and partially, something of the sociohistorical dynamics that led to the text's literary and theological development.

Attention to the literary context places the text and its perspective(s) about God and the world in relation to the surrounding texts, which offer comparable or competing perspectives. The integrative, reasoning work of theology engages the variety of theological perspectives that the scriptural texts themselves bear. No text is an island—literarily, much less theologically. Hence, the text's position in relation to other texts invites lively interaction with the surrounding material. As the neighboring texts contribute to the meaning of the text in question, the text contributes to the larger network of meaning conveyed by the surrounding material. As the interpretive net is cast ever more widely, the literary context shifts to canonical context once the entirety of Scripture is caught up in the hermeneutical venture.

Orienting Questions

As the interpreter explores the exegetical contours and contexts of the text, from the philological to the structural, from the historical to the canonical, two tightly interrelated questions "from the top" need to be posed from the outset: (1) What is the text's "theo-logic"; that is, what can be ascertained from the text about *God's character* and *relationship to the world*? (2) Intimately related to the first question, what is the text's "cosmo-logic"; that is, what can be ascertained from the text about the *world in its relationship to God* and *humanity's place within it*? Exploring the text's "theo-logic" is preferable to encapsulating the text's "theology." The latter suggests something monolithic that suspends itself, as it were, above the text rather than is embedded within it. The same applies to the text's cosmo-logic. Far from being something distant and otherworldly, the text's cosmo-logic inscribes the interpreter's world in a certain way and, in so doing, imparts a view of human identity and condition, in other words, a particular anthropology. As God and world are inextricably related in Scripture, so the text's theo-logic and cosmo-logic are bound together in the overall logic of the text, that is, in its manner of discourse and construction as determined by the various contours, accents, interconnections, transitions, and movements that give the text its form and content. As the logic of the text is disclosed in the way the text crafts its message, it in turn determines how the text unfolds before the reader in the very process of reading. Invariably, the text's various elements and accents, its structure and movement, constitute a network of interconnections that evoke something about God and the world. A text's theo-logic, in short, points to the text's reasoning about, or making sense of, God and the world that invites the reader's reasoning to do the same.

Articulating the text's theo-logic acknowledges not only the text's contextuality but also the interpreter's. It attempts to make theological sense of the text in ways that are, in the end, understandable and relevant to the interpreter and, at least in principle, to any reader. It explores how the passage constructs a coherent depiction of God and the world that bridges the past and the present. Bound up with the text's theological dimensions are its cosmological aspects, which render, *inter alia*, a profile of human identity in relation to God and the world, including that of the interpreter in relation to the text.

These two overarching questions guide all other questions concerning the text's context and meaning. For example, how does an understanding of the historical, social, and cultural aspects of the text inform one's theological interpretation? What are the theological threads and tensions that both connect and distinguish the text vis-à-vis neighboring texts? Is there evidence of the text's literary growth that reflects a process of theological discernment? As part of Scripture, how does the text contribute to the theological and cosmological scope of the canon? Conversely, how does the canon contribute to the meaning of the text?

Constructive Engagement

The "final" step of a theological interpretation of the biblical text involves the interpreter's explicit *meditatio* on the text, a reflective lingering over the text's significance for the life of faith, a process of appropriation. Again, theological engagement is more than descriptive. It involves conveying what the text means *for* the interpreter and her audience. This provisionally final step is to articulate a message from the text that, according to the interpreter's determination, needs to be heard at this time. This message should arise naturally from the text but also in response to the needs and concerns of people today. No interpretation is final; one's theological understanding of the text is always developing, itself reflecting a process of discernment. But for now, the interpreter presents with clarity and conviction a message that she has gained from the text and desires others to hear. In so doing, the otherness of the ancient text becomes an integral part of the interpreter's own world. Again, to draw from the visual metaphor, the text is not made in the interpreter's image; it is an image distinct from the interpreter's projections. But this culminating step transforms the distinct image of the text into a lens through which the world, God, and the interpreter come to be viewed anew. In the end, theological exegesis is about "putting on" the text, as with a pair of glasses, seeing through it, and figuring out what looks concretely, indeed contextually, different. Theological exegesis is, in short, the work of the analogical imagination.

A Theological Interpretation of Psalm 95

By way of illustration, I present a theological interpretation of Ps 95. First, a translation:

1. Come, let us shout aloud in joy to YHWH!
   Let us raise a joyful cry to the rock of our salvation!
2. Let us come before his face with thanksgiving!
   With songs of joy we shall raise a joyful shout to him!
3. For YHWH is a great God,
   A great king above all the gods,
4. In whose hands are the depth[7] of the earth;
   The heights[8] of the mountains belong to him,
5. To whom also belongs the sea, which he has made,
   And the dry land, which his hands have formed.
6. Come, let us bow down, bending the knee!
   Let us kneel before YHWH, our maker!
7. For he is our God, and we are the people of his pasture,
   The flock of his hand.

If you would only heed his voice today!

8. "Do not harden your hearts as at Meribah,
   As in the day of Massah in the wilderness,
9. Where your ancestors put me to the test,

(And) tried me, even though they had beheld my works.[9]
10. For forty years I detested (this) generation,
For I said, "They are a people wayward of heart;
They do not acknowledge[10] my ways."
11. So I swore to them in my anger,
"They shall never enter into my rest."

Design

From its style and content, the psalm easily divides itself into two sections: 95:1–7a revels in ecstatic praise; 95:7b–11 adopts the harsh tone of admonition. Further divisions are evident. Praise consists of two brief hymns (95:1–5 and 6–7a), each of which consists of an opening call to praise (95:1–2, 3–5, and 6, 7a) followed by an expressed reason (95:3–5 and 7a). The second section opens with an exhortation from the speaker, which introduces God's admonition to the worshipers (95:7b and 8–11).

I. Praise, 95:1–7a
- A. Hymn 1, 95:1–5
  - 1. Call to praise, 95:1–2
  - 2. Reason, 95:3–5
    - a. God's majesty, 95:3
    - b. God's ownership of creation, 95:4–5
- B. Hymn 2, 95:6–7a
  - 1. Call to praise, 95:6
  - 2. Reason, 95:7a
    - a. Identity of "our God," 95:7aα
    - b. Identity of God's people, 95:7aβ

II. Admonition, 95:7b–11
- A. Opening exhortation, 95:7b
- B. Divine address, 95:8–11
  - 1. Negative command, 95:8aα
  - 2. Historical basis, 95:8aβ–11
    - a. People's testing of God, 95:8aβ–9
      - 1) Geographical location, 95:8aβ
      - 2) Test, 95:9
    - b. YHWH's response, 95:10–11
      - 1) Reason/indictment, 95:10
      - 2) Oath of rejection, 95:11

Outlining the psalm's structure helps identify its central elements, including the theological, which are primarily lodged in the reasons for praise (95:3–5 and 7) and in YHWH's own address (95:8–11). In each of these sections, the deity is profiled in a distinctive way.

As the outline above illustrates, there is no single center in the psalm. Instead, the psalm exhibits an overarching movement that strikes several theological chords in concert. The psalm's transition from praise to admonition is facilitated theologically by a shift in the possessive pronouns featured at the end of several verses: from "our salvation" (95:1b) and "our maker" (95:6b) to "my works" (95:9b), "my ways" (95:10b), and "my rest" (95:11b). In addition to indicating a shift in speaker, from the worshiping community to God, each of these phrases points to one of the psalm's interrelated theological themes.

The Text's Theo-logic

What, then, is the psalm's unfolding theo-logic? To answer this question, one begins by noting the language and form of the discourse employed, its way of communication. Next, the various units within the psalm are to be considered (as indicated in the outline above). Each requires examination in its own right but always in relation to the others. Each unit stresses something different about the character of the divine. Only by examining the various units of the psalm can one explore how these discrete sections interact in offering a coherent, multifaceted depiction of God.

Manner of Discourse

The language of praise (95:1–7a) depicts a God who is not simply worthy of worship but who elicits worship as a natural complement to the deity's character. The rhetoric of praise does more than express the worshipers' gratitude to God, which it clearly does. It also conveys their wholehearted, exuberant faithfulness. The very act of praise binds the worshiper to God and, in turn, God to the worshiper.

The language of admonition that follows (95:7b–11) makes clear that YHWH has a specific claim upon the audience addressed. The worshiper who renders praise to God is also accountable to God. This second section provides a negative example drawn from Israel's narrative history to illustrate how the community is to conduct itself apart from the legacy of its past. The admonition serves as a warning to the present. Together, praise and admonition render a profile of the God who is both worthy of worship and commanding in character, a God who elicits praise *and* enjoins a certain way of life. What precisely makes YHWH worthy of praise is indicated by the content of the first half of the psalm. The content of the second half specifies, in turn, YHWH's claim of accountability upon the community.

The Content of the Parts

With regard to content, the initial call to praise calls YHWH the "rock of our salvation" (95:1b). Such an image, as found elsewhere in the psalms, connotes stability, strength, and protection.[11] In Ps 95 YHWH is depicted as the steadfast agent of salvation and source of strength, imparting protection in the face of distress and adversity. In the first reason given for praise (95:3), YHWH is deemed incomparably "great" among all other deities. Such greatness is fully rooted in divine kingship. Although the statement makes no claim to monotheism, it does stress the totalizing scope of YHWH's reign: all the world belongs to YHWH.[12] The universal breadth of YHWH's reign is expressed through two pairs of contrasting images: impenetrable depths and towering mountains, the sea and dry land (95:4–5). Such juxtaposed opposites constitute a merismus, which renders a picture of totality—in this case, the totality of divine ownership. Precisely how divine ownership is justified marks a crucial step in the psalm's theo-logic. Its warrant is found in the text's cosmologic, that is, in its references to the divine work of establishing creation. What belongs to YHWH is what YHWH has created. All creation lies in YHWH's "hands" (95:4a) because it was formed by YHWH's "hands" (95:5b).

The following passage of praise narrows the focus from YHWH's reign over all creation to YHWH's rule over a particular people. Here, theology and anthropology are tightly bound. The creator of the cosmos is also "*our* maker," "*our* God" (95:6b, 7a). The move toward particularity is matched by a shift to pastoral imagery: "pasture" and "flock" (95:7a). The community of praise is likened to domestic animals (e.g., sheep, goats, cattle) that enjoy a select part of creation for their well-being. YHWH, in turn, is likened to a pastoralist, a common metaphor for king, consonant with 95:3. Whereas the initials calls to praise in 95:1–2 solicit shouts of joy to the creator king, the call to praise in the second section enjoins gestures of allegiance to the God who claims the worshiping community (95:6), even as the community claims YHWH as their God (95:7a), the "rock" of their "salvation" (95:1).

This entire first section is linked by two anthropomorphic references to the deity: "face" (95:2a) and "hand(s)" (95:4a, 5b, 7b). The speaker exhorts his audience to approach YHWH's "face with thanksgiving" (95:2a). Face signifies presence, and it is before YHWH's presence that the community performs its praise. Worship, according to the psalm, is directed *to* God; it is done *coram deo*.[13] Given YHWH's distinctly royal presence, the picture the psalmist paints is that of the community oriented toward YHWH's throne. The imagery shifts from "face" to "hand" as the psalm moves from royal presence to divine ownership: all creation lies "in his hands" (95:4a); YHWH's "hands" have "formed" the land (95:5b); the worshiping community is the "flock of his hand" (95:7b). Through such language, the psalm does not focus on divine presence alone. YHWH is shown to be a "hands-on" deity with respect to both creation and a people, cosmologically and anthropologically. The hands that fashioned the earth are the same ones that constitute a people.

The second half of the psalm (95:7b–11) opens with a form of direct address that matches the exhortatory tone of the first half (95:1–2, 6). But instead of an invitational command, the opening line of the second half begins with a protasis or conditional phrase (*'îm*, "if"), effectively introducing the admonition that follows. The imagery also shifts: no longer is the focus on the work of YHWH's "hands," namely, creation and community. Rather, it is the discourse of YHWH's "voice" that takes center stage (95:7a), raising issues of history and accountability. Once the worshipers have sung their songs of praise and thanksgiving, God speaks, matching the exuberance of the worshipers' praise with the harshness of admonition. The psalm's climactic section leaves the scene of creation by recalling the scene of a crime. Creation gives way to history, from world to word. Specifically, the "flock" of YHWH's "hand" set amid a lush pastoral vista is admonished by a lesson from history drawn from the inhospitable wilderness.

The specific references to Meribah and Massah are not explicated in the psalm itself. Mentioned two other times in the Psalter, Meribah refers to a time of testing (Ps 81:7) when Israel provoked YHWH's anger (106:32). In the pentateuchal wilderness narrative, Meribah and Massah[14] designate the twin sites where the Israelites "contended with and tested" YHWH over the lack of water in the wilderness, bespeaking their lack of trust in YHWH (Exod 17:7). Paired elsewhere, Massah and Meribah are in Israel's collective memory emblematic of faithlessness (see also Deut

6:16; 9:22; 33:8). In the post-Sinai wilderness narrative, such lack of trust is also displayed by Moses and Aaron, which by way of divine judgment prevents them from leading their people into the promised land (Num 20:12–13). The psalm heightens the reproachful tone with reference to "hardening the heart" (Ps 95:8), applied most famously to Pharaoh in the Exodus narrative but by no means limited to him.[15] Such language accuses Israel's ancestors of recalcitrance and defiance.

Instead of referring to YHWH's "hand(s)" in the first half of the psalm, the divine address speaks of "my works" (95:9b), "my ways" (95:10b), and "my rest" (95:11). In the context of the wilderness accounts, YHWH's "works" include the miracles of sustenance in the wilderness, namely, purified water (Exod 15:23–25), food (16:1–36), and water out of the rock (17:1–7), each of which is occasioned by the people's complaint. In Ps 95, YHWH complains of the people's lack of faith despite many instances of deliverance and sustenance (95:9b), beginning with the Red Sea. In the post-Sinai narratives in Numbers, Israel's persistent complaints—ten, no less, according to Num 14:22—warrant divine judgment (Num 11:1–35; 20:1–13; 21:4–9), including the prevention of the present generation from entering the land, a sentence of forty years in the wilderness (Num 14:22–23, 28–34; see also 32:13). God's resolve to let the present generation die in the wilderness is cast as an oath in Numbers (14:28–34). So also in Ps 95, though in different form. Indeed, the conditional particle *ʾîm* in 95:11, which introduces the oath (literally, "*if* they ever enter into my rest"), corresponds to the exhortation that opens the admonition ("*if* you would only heed my voice today"), which also features the conditional particle (95:7b), thereby rounding out the admonition as a whole.

The opening warning against adopting the intransigence of an earlier generation leads to divine complaint, whose center is found in the indictment in 95:10b: "they are a people wayward of heart; they do not know my ways." Although the "ways" of YHWH remain undefined in the psalm, they clearly draw from negative examples given in the wilderness narratives that highlight the people's lack of trust in YHWH's guidance, as manifested in the desire to assimilate with other peoples and worship other gods, particularly Baal of Peor (Num 25:1–5). YHWH's "ways," by contrast, include trust and allegiance, as indicated in true worship.

YHWH's "rest," the last word in the psalm, points to both land and sanctuary. Psalm 132, for example, makes repeated reference to Zion as YHWH's "habitation" and "resting place" (132:8, 13–14). The pentateuchal narrative tells of YHWH dwelling with a people by means of a portable tabernacle constructed in the wilderness (see Exod 35–40). In the Deuteronomistic historiography, the "ark of God" contained in the tabernacle becomes settled in Jerusalem under the reign of David (2 Sam 6:1–15), whose son Solomon builds the temple for YHWH's permanent habitation (see 1 Kgs 6:1–38). According to Ps 95, the wilderness generation is excluded from such "rest" (95:11), which binds together the settlement of a people in the land of Canaan and the permanent establishment of God's habitation, a sanctuary.[16] The admonition, of course, warns the present generation, which *is* settled in the land and does have a temple, against repeating the sins of the past, and it does so by lifting up the dire prospect of exile, the stark antithesis of rest in the land.

So far we have examined Ps 95 theologically according to its various units with only an occasional glance at their interconnections. Among these units, YHWH takes on various roles: king, creator, pastoralist, admonisher, and guide. Regardless of whether 95:1–7a and 7b–11 were originally independent, the pressing question for the theological interpreter would not be so much *why* and *how* these units were joined together—a question reserved primarily for the redaction critic—but *what* their final juxtaposition contributes to the literary and, ultimately, theological coherence of the psalm. That is, in what ways do the parts inform each other? How do they fit together to create something new, something more than the mere sum of the parts? So begins the integrative work of theological interpretation.

Constructing Coherence

Taken together, the two halves of the psalm bind together creation and history, the universal and the particular, with YHWH deemed the author of both. The God whose "hands" fashioned the earth is the same God whose "voice" indicts and pronounces judgment against a generation. The reference to "our salvation" in the opening verse anticipates the reference to YHWH's "works" in 95:9. Both refer to specific acts of divine intervention on behalf of a people, beginning with the exodus. But there is more. In the context of the whole, the "works" that a past generation failed to behold also include the work of creation itself. The first half of the psalm broadens the horizon of divine activity referenced historically in the second half, specifically regarding 95:9. The history of a people, specifically of God's punishment of a "wayward" generation, takes on cosmic significance in view of the God whose handiwork includes *all* of creation. The "rock of our salvation" (95:1) is also the agent of "our" creation (95:6), indeed, of the earth and sea (95:4–5). The psalm blurs the boundary between salvation and creation. Soteriology stands beside cosmology.

Anthropologically, the psalm acknowledges Israel as an indispensable part of God's creation, as the "people of [YHWH's] pasture" (95:7). The creator of the cosmos is also "our maker" (95:6). As YHWH lays claim to the sea and dry land as essential elements of divinely wrought creation, so YHWH claims a people first and foremost because they, too, are created; they are the "flock of his hand" (95:7b). But the psalm presses further: Israel is not simply held in ownership by YHWH, as sheep are to a shepherd; Israel is also held accountable (95:10b). By analogy, Israel is not to test its maker by distrusting YHWH, by dismissing YHWH's works of creation and deliverance, and thereby longing for the fleshpots of Egypt.

Literary Context

A number of connections can be discerned between the themes of this psalm and the larger canon. Close to home, Ps 95 is positioned within a series of enthronement psalms that highlight YHWH's kingship over Israel, the nations, and creation, beginning with Ps 93 and extending to Ps 100 (with the exception of Ps 94). In several psalms, YHWH is proclaimed king by universal acclamation (93:1a; 96:10a; 97:1a; 99:1; cf. 95:3b). God's royal majesty is measured against the mighty roar of the seas (Ps 93:4). YHWH's greatness is consistently lauded (94:3; 96:4; 99:2), sometimes in comparison to the other gods. As in Ps 95, YHWH is "above all gods" (96:4); "all gods bow before [YHWH]" (97:7b); YHWH is "exalted far above all gods" (97:9). At the same time, however, this cluster relegates the gods to "worthless idols" (97:7; see also 96:5), a point that is missing in Ps 95 (cf. 95:3b).

As for the relationship between kingship and creation, the opening of Ps 93:1–2, the first psalm in the series, is telling:

1. YHWH is king!
  With majesty he is robed; robed is YHWH;
    With strength he girds himself.
  Yes, the world is well-established;[17]
    It shall not be shaken.

> 2. Well-established is your throne from of old;
> From everlasting you are [God].[18] (Ps 93:1–2)

YHWH's majesty is evinced in the establishment of the world. The parallel between the world and YHWH's throne suggests that creation itself has a hand in undergirding YHWH's "everlasting" majesty. By theological necessity, then, the world is firmly established. With YHWH as king, stability reigns over creation (see also Ps 96:10a). Creation and kingship are bound seamlessly together in other ways throughout these psalms; not only does creation's stability testify to YHWH's everlasting majesty; creation also renders praise to God, the judge of all the earth (Pss 96:11–12; 97:1, 6; 98:7–9). Even the "roar" of the sea gives praise, along with the inhabited world, the floods, and the hills (Ps 98:7; see also Ps 93:3–4). Creation as agent of praise, object of God's creativity, and the vehicle of divine majesty theologically expands the way Ps 95 views the relationship between God and creation. Nevertheless, Ps 95 adds its own distinctive cadence to the cosmic chorale; creation is God's possession (95:4–5), as metaphorically inscribed by the image of YHWH's "hand." The image of hand, in fact, figures nowhere else in this group of psalms within a creational context (see Ps 98:1).[19] Thus Ps 95 makes its own theological contribution to the series of enthronement psalms.

On the anthropological level, there is only one parallel to the image of Israel as a flock among the enthronement psalms, namely in Ps 100:3.

> Know that YHWH is God—
> It is he who made us, not we ourselves;[20]
> His people (we are), the flock of his pasture.

Here, too, YHWH is acknowledged as sole creator. Moreover, as in Ps 95, the pastoral context evokes a relationship of utter dependency upon God: the "flock of his pasture" (Ps 100:3), the "flock of his hand" (Ps 95:7b) refers to a people.

Also unique to Ps 95 vis-à-vis the enthronement psalms is the divine discourse it features. Ps 95 is the only psalm that delivers an oracular admonition. Its closest parallel lies outside this series, in Ps 81. It, too, begins with a call to praise but quickly leads to a divine admonishment (Ps 82:6–16) set in the context of Israel's history beginning with the exodus. The warning given in Ps 95 not to "harden your hearts" (95:8) is matched by the statement in Ps 81 that God "gave [the Israelites] over to the stubbornness of their hearts" (81:12). Psalm 81, in short, broadens the historical purview of Ps 95. In addition, Ps 81 renders God's "ways," referenced also in Ps 95:10b, with greater specificity: Israel is to worship no other god but YHWH (81:9). While the historical frame is significantly broadened in Ps 81, missing is any reference to creation. Except in Ps 95, nowhere else in the Psalter is the theme of creation paired so tightly with historical admonition.

Canonical Context

Casting the interpretive net even wider, one finds the pairing of creation and history evocatively attested in Isa 40–55 (Deutero-Isaiah). From this anonymous prophet of the late exile, the creation of the cosmos fits hand in glove with the deliverance of Israel in exile, an act of new creation. The exilic voice declares God's incomparability within the context of creation (Isa 40:25–26). Israel is both "chosen" and "made" by YHWH (44:1). The God who "created the heavens and stretched them out" is also the God who has "called" Israel "in righteousness" (42:5a, 6a), the one who both "formed" Israel "in the womb" and "made all things" (44:24). As in Ps 95, creation is the work of YHWH's "hands" (Isa 45:11–12). In the "hollow of [YHWH's] hand" the waters are "measured" (40:12), and it is by God's hand that Israel was sent into exile and now will be redeemed (40:2; 41:10). Israel, in short, is the product of God's creative work, and because of this, "You are my people," announces YHWH (51:16), just as Israel is the "the people of his pasture, the flock of his hand" (Ps 95:7). As YHWH's chosen servant, Israel is appropriately admonished for not living up to its divinely ordained calling: "You have forgotten YHWH, your maker, who stretched out the heavens and laid the earth's foundations. You fear continually all day long because of the fury of the oppressor" (Isa 51:13). Warranting admonishment from God, fear is a cardinal sin in Deutero-Isaiah, a symptom, the psalmist would suggest, of a lack of trust in YHWH. It is Meribah and Massah all over again.

Comparing Ps 95 and Deutero-Isaiah also reveals a certain process of theological discernment. YHWH's majestic reign over the gods in Ps 95 is tantamount to the absence of all deities other than YHWH in Deutero-Isaiah.

> I am YHWH, and there is no other;
> besides me there is no god....

> I am YHWH, and there is no other.
> I form light and create darkness,
> I make weal and create woe;
> I YHWH do all these things. (Isa 45:5–7[21])

The theo-logic is clear: because YHWH has created everything, including darkness (see Gen 1:1–3), there is nothing left for the other deities to do or to claim; indeed, there is no other deity at all! The gods attested in the earlier biblical traditions are now mere idols, made by human hands (see Isa 44:9–20; cf. Pss 96:5; 97:7). The totalizing scope of God's creation undercuts all other claims to divinity. YHWH's exaltation in the psalm is pressed to its theo-logical conclusion in Deutero-Isaiah: as consummate creator and sovereign Lord, YHWH stands alone in the divine realm.

Gleaning Relevance

Psalm 95 has much to say to communities of faith today: the sovereignty of God; the life of praise and faithfulness; our dependence upon God; the worthlessness of idols, to name only a few. However, by viewing my own context and concerns through the lens of this psalm, I see the prospect of another interpretation, one that addresses a crisis that all communities face, albeit in varying degrees, and it is environmental, or better creational, in scope. How does the mounting degradation of the earth look through the lens of Ps 95? The psalmist praises the God whose "hands" fashioned the earth and hold all creation (95:4a, 5b). To behold God's "works" is not only to acknowledge that God acts on behalf of a particular people, delivering and sustaining them against insurmountable odds (95:9), but also to bear witness to the wonder of creation itself—its impenetrable depths and towering heights, the sea and the land—and in so doing, to testify to the creator's sovereign majesty (95:3–5).

The psalm's emphasis on God as creator in no way diminishes God's other roles as savior, liberator, and redeemer, all well-attested in ancient Israel's historiography and psalmic poetry. Such titles, however, lack the tactile activity the psalmist lifts up regarding God's way in the world, as one can see already in Gen 2: YHWH God forms the *ʾādām* from the "dust of the ground" and plants a garden (Gen 2:7–8), both hands-on activities. The image of God's "hands" in the psalm suggests an intimate, indeed organic, connection between God and creation. By contrast, verbs such as "save," "deliver," "redeem," and "liberate" all involve separation: to save is to save *from*, to deliver *from*, to liberate *from*, to redeem *from*. Such actions involve distancing the sufferer from the suffering, and appropriately so. But there is another side of divine agency to which the psalm vividly bears witness, namely, the God who works *with* creation, who fashions creation with "hands."

The God who gets down and dirty with creation, grubbing about in the soil to create and sustain life, validates creation's worth. Creation's integrity comes from the God who fashioned creation by hand, as well as by word, and holds it all in the hollow of the hand. Such an intimately tactile image is violated by the ongoing destruction of creation wrought by human hands. Taking a cue from Ps 95, God's admonition for today would highlight our destructive disregard of creation as we continue to test and try God's forbearance through our imperious, exploitative practices. We have "hardened" ourselves through our consumptive greed, leaving a legacy of destruction for future generations. The hope is that a future generation will repent and marshal the moral wherewithal to reverse the sins of its forbearers so that it may truly enter into "rest" with creation, so that it may serve and preserve creation's integrity. Perhaps. Regardless, that generation is not ours.

For Further Reading

Barr, James. *The Concept of Biblical Theology: An Old Testament Perspective*. Minneapolis: Fortress, 1999.

Brueggemann, Walter. "Biblical Theology Appropriately Postmodern." Pages 97–108 in *Jews, Christians, and the Theology of the Hebrew Scriptures*. Edited by Alice Ogden Bellis and Joel S. Kaminsky. SBLSymS 8. Atlanta: Society of Biblical Literature, 2000.

Childs, Brevard S. *Biblical Theology of the Old and New Testaments: Theological Reflection on the Christian Bible*. Minneapolis: Fortress, 1992.

Collins, John J. "Is a Critical Biblical Theology Possible?" Pages 1–17 in *The Hebrew Bible and Its Interpreters*. Edited by William H. Propp, Baruch Halpern, and David Noel Freedman. Biblical and Judaic Studies 1. Winona Lake, Ind.: Eisenbrauns, 1990.

Levenson, Jon D. *The Hebrew Bible, the Old Testament, and Historical Criticism: Jews and Christians in Biblical Studies*. Louisville: Westminster John Knox, 1993.

Mead, James K. *Biblical Theology: Issues, Methods, and Themes*. Louisville: Westminster John Knox, 2007.

Newsom, Carol A. "Bakhtin, the Bible, and Dialogic Truth." *JR* 76 (1996): 290–306.

Tsevat, Matitiahu. "Theology of the Old Testament—A Jewish View." *HBT* 8/2 (1986): 33–50.

Notes

1. At the same time, much of his work reflects a passion for theological creativity and ethical discernment. See most recently his SBL presidential address, "Genesis and Family Values," *JBL* 124 (2005): 5–23; idem, "Shaking the World of Family Values," in *Shaking Heaven and Earth: Essays in Honor of Walter Brueggemann and Charles B. Cousar* (ed. Christine Roy Yoder et al.; Louisville: Westminster John Knox, 2005), 23–32.

2. For example, among the various criticisms and approaches featured in Odil Steck's classic guide to Old Testament exegesis, theological interpretation is nowhere to be found. Any mention of theological reflection is found only in the final step ("Considering the Text's Historical Meaning in Light of the Present"), brief as it is (*Old Testament Exegesis: A Guide to the Methodology* [2nd ed.; trans. James D. Nogalski; SBLRBS 39; Atlanta: Scholars Press, 1998], 166; cf. 201–2). In the user-friendly guide by Mary H. Schertz and Perry B. Yoder, that final step is called "Integrating Text and Life" (*Seeing the Text: Exegesis for Students of Greek and Hebrew* [Nashville: Abingdon, 2001], 149–62), comparable to the "sixth element" or "Reflection … The Text Today" in Michael J. Gorman, *Elements of Biblical Exegesis: A Basic Guide for Students and Ministers* (Peabody, Mass.: Hendrickson, 2001), 123–34, suggesting that anything theological is almost exclusively a matter of contemporary reflection, an afterthought entertained after most or all other exegetical steps are fulfilled. To their credit, John H. Hayes and Carl R. Holladay, in their *Biblical Exegesis: A Beginner's Handbook* (2nd ed.; Louisville: Westminster John Knox, 2007), lodge theological concerns in the chapters on "Redaction Criticism: The Final Viewpoint and Theology" (127–38) and "Canonical Criticism" (152–66). The final chapter contains a brief section on "Doing Theology" under "Employing the Fruits of Biblical Exegesis" (196–99). Of final note: absent in the useful series Guides to Biblical Scholarship (Fortress, 1971–2002), which includes even "psychological biblical criticism," is an entry on theological interpretation.

3. Moreover, any explicitly theological engagement with the biblical text has been largely deemed a Christian enterprise. See Jon D. Levenson, "Why Jews Are Not Interested in Biblical Theology," in idem, *The Hebrew Bible, the Old Testament, and Historical Criticism* (Louisville: Westminster John Knox, 1993), 33–61; repr. from *Judaic Perspectives on Ancient Israel* (ed. Baruch A. Levine et al.; Philadelphia: Fortress, 1987). See, however, the more nuanced discussion in Walter Brueggemann, "Biblical Theology Appropriately Postmodern," in *Jews, Christians, and the Theology of the Hebrew Scriptures* (ed. Alice Ogden Bellis and Joel S. Kaminsky; SBLSymS 8; Atlanta: Society of Biblical Literature, 2000), 97–108.

4. *Fides quaerens intellectum*, the original title to Anselm's *Proslogion* as found in

his preface (see Anselm of Canterbury: *The Major Works* [ed. Brian Davies and G. R. Evans; Oxford World's Classics; Oxford: Oxford University Press, 1998], 83, 87).

5. Brueggemann calls this the "thematization" of the text, that is, "an attempt to notice claims … that are larger than the individual text" ("Biblical Theology Appropriately Postmodern," 99).

6. James K. Mead, *Biblical Theology: Issues, Methods, and Themes* (Louisville: Westminster John Knox, 2007), 93.

7. From the root *ḥqr*, meaning "investigate" or "explore." Cf. the use of the related term *ḥēqer* in Job 11:7; 38:16; Sir 42:16. One Hebrew manuscript and the Septuagint read *merḥaqqê* ("ends, extremities").

8. For various senses of this enigmatic term, see Num 23:22; 24:8 with reference to "horns." The ancient versions of this verse consistently render the sense of "height." See *HALOT*, 1705–6.

9. Singular in the Hebrew but with collective voice. See LXX and Peshitta.

10. Or "know" (*ydh*). The more active sense fits the context better.

11. See, e.g., Pss 18:2; 31:2–3; 62:2, 6; 89:26; 144:2.

12. Cf. Deut 32:8–9, in which YHWH is one among many deities, each of whom is allotted a people by the "Most High" (*'elyôn*). YHWH's allotted people is Israel.

13. As signified by the repeated use of the *lamed* preposition (*lĕ*) in 95:1a, 1b, 2b.

14. The geographical names are etymologically related to the verbal roots *ryb* ("contend") and *nsh* ("test"), respectively.

15. E.g., from Exod 4:21 to 14:17. Elsewhere, this expression of defiance against YHWH is applied to others: Deut 2:30 (the "spirit" of King Sihon); Josh 11:20 (the kings of Canaan); 1 Sam 6:6 (Israelites like the Egyptians); 2 Chr 36:13 (Zedekiah); Isa 63:17 (supplicants lamenting to YHWH); Dan 5:20 (Nebuchadnezzar).

16. Not unlike Ezekiel's vision of the restored temple and land (40:1–48:35).

17. *BHS* and *HALOT* suggest *tikkēn* ("Indeed, you steadied the earth"), which makes equally good sense. Did the MT morphologically harmonize an originally active (*pi'el*) verb with the following *niph'al* (*timmôt*), or is the parallel originally deliberate? The question remains open.

18. Targum adds "God" and is proposed by *BHS* for metrical reasons.

19. In Ps 98:1, YHWH's "hand" is the instrument of "victory." The closest parallel to Ps 95:5 lies outside this cluster in Ps 102:25.

20. So Kethib, the more provocative meaning. For syntactical parallels whereby the negative particle + personal pronoun stands alone and elliptically so, see Job 15:6; 34:33; Gen 45:8; 1 Kgs 18:18; Isa 45:12. The Qere ("to him") is more conventional, and even banal, in context: it summarizes generically what is further developed later in the verse. It is more likely that a copyist changed this elliptical clause to a more familiar formula than the reverse. The Kethib highlights the aspect of God as creator and that human beings are not autonomous beings, contrary to what the "wicked" or "fools" think (see, e.g., Pss 10:4; 14:1).

21. See also, e.g., Isa 43:10; 46:9.

Homiletical Appropriation of the Hebrew Bible

Gail R. O'Day

As any of David Petersen's students and colleagues can confirm, one can always count on David Petersen to ask a penetrating question about method in his assessment of any paper or thesis and in his review of any project subjected to his editorial eye. Doctoral students in Hebrew Bible and New Testament at Emory University quiz each other with the question, "What is your method?" before they present anything to a faculty group that includes David Petersen, knowing that they will need to have a good answer to that question if their prospective project is to pass muster. David has saved many a student and colleague from careless thinking and methodological haziness by his astute sense that the method by which one approaches a biblical text determines the answers that one will discover, and that initial clarity about method is essential for clarity of the subsequent interpretation. The theme of the present volume reflects and is shaped by this dimension of David's work.

I accepted the assignment to write an essay on homiletical approaches to the Hebrew Bible for this volume with great trepidation, because this is not a topic that is inherently methodological. Preaching the Hebrew Bible in the context of Christian proclamation is primarily a hermeneutical and theological question. The determination of the locus of theological meaning in the Hebrew Bible takes precedence for preaching over the method one then uses to draw out that meaning. David, of course, would say that a theological approach is a particular method, so perhaps he will indulge an essay that does not immediately answer the "What is your method?" question.

In keeping with the format of this volume, the essay that follows is in two parts. The first part discusses the hermeneutical and theological issues that are involved in approaching a Hebrew Bible text homiletically. The second part provides a specific example of a homiletical approach to a Hebrew Bible text.

Part 1: Hermeneutical Considerations

Framing the Question

The parable of the rich man and Lazarus (Luke 16:19–31) is among the most richly imagined and narrated parables in the New Testament. Its narrative setting is vividly described (16:20–22), with a level of detail about the rich man's clothing and Lazarus's sores that is unusual for the normally lean and allusive narrative style of parables. Equally richly narrated is the evocation of the afterlife, in which the poor man finds solace in the bosom of Abraham and the rich man is tormented in Hades (16:22–23). Both of these vivid scenes—the descriptions of the rich man and Lazarus pre- and postdeath—are only the backdrop for the center of the story, however, which is the imagined afterlife conversation between Abraham and the rich man (16:24–31).

This conversation is remarkable in the New Testament for the way in which it uses the figure of Abraham. Abraham is held up not as an exemplar of faith, spoken about indirectly (e.g., John 8:56–58; Heb 12), but Abraham is an actual character whose direct speech is the lynchpin of the parable. The general drift of the conversation between Abraham and the rich man is well-known: the rich man asks "Father Abraham" to send Lazarus to serve him so that his torment in Hades can be lessened. Abraham refuses (16:25–26), so the rich man asks instead that Lazarus be sent to his father's house so that Lazarus can warn them about the torment of Hades (16:27–28). Abraham responds to this second request with words that befit his standing as the great patriarch of the faith, "They have Moses and the prophets; they should listen to them" (16:29). The rich man again rebuffs Abraham's words, which leads to a final exchange between the rich man and Abraham (16:30–31):

> He [the rich man] said, "No, father Abraham, but if someone goes to them from the dead, they will repent. He said to him, "If they do not listen to Moses and the prophets, neither will they be convinced even if someone rises from the dead."

Abraham's teaching in 16:31 underscores that no additional type of revelation is needed to supplement the call to repentance that is found in the totality of the Law and the Prophets. Within the immediate narrative setting of the parable, a story told by Jesus during his lifetime to a Jewish audience, Abraham's words censure the rich man for thinking that anything more than the Law and Prophets could lead to a life of repentance. When the rich man requests a revelation by someone who "goes to them from the dead," his request makes sense as an appeal to necromancy, a practice explicitly prohibited by the law (Deut 18:10–11; Lev 19:31; 20:6, 27). Violations of this prohibition are recorded in the Hebrew Bible (Isa 8:19: 2 Kgs 21:6), most dramatically in Saul's séance with the medium of Endor (1 Sam 28:1–25). To appeal to necromancy is to show one's lack of fidelity and loyalty to God (e.g., Deut 18:13), so in the very speaking of this request the rich man shows that he does not heed Moses and the prophets.

Yet to the reader of Luke's Gospel, Abraham's words in 16:31 obviously carry an additional resonance. It would be impossible for a Christian audience to hear the phrase "someone rises from the dead" and not associate it with the resurrection of Jesus. In that context, Abraham's words in 16:31 confront the Gospel reader with this assertion: if one does not hear the call to repentance in Moses and the prophets, then one will not hear that call through the person of Jesus either.

I have used Luke 16:19–31 to frame the hermeneutical considerations involved in Christian appropriation of the Hebrew Bible for preaching because the conversation between Abraham and the rich man provides a vivid example of the crucial interpretive question: Can the gospel, the good news of God, be fully preached out of the Hebrew Bible?

The Gospel Beforehand

Luke 16:31 answers this question affirmatively. Abraham's words in 16:31 frame the response in terms of a negative contrast ("If they do not listen to Moses and the prophets, neither will they be convinced even if someone rises from the dead"), but nonetheless affirm the sufficiency of the revelation contained in the Law and the Prophets. A positive articulation of this hermeneutical conviction casts the choices involved in Christian preaching of the Hebrew Bible even more starkly: all the revelation of God that is needed for a faithful life is contained in Moses and the prophets.

This is also the theological conviction of the New Testament more broadly. There is a dialectical component to the conviction that the gospel, the good news of God, is fully contained in the Hebrew Bible (although in this context the confessional designation, "Old Testament," may be more apt). Christians affirm that God's self-revelation in Jesus is the defining and decisive lens through which to interpret God's words and works in the world, yet God's self-revelation in Jesus makes no sense unless Christians see it as a piece of God's ongoing righteousness toward God's people.

Paul is perhaps Christians' most helpful conversation partner in thinking through the hermeneutical and theological decisions involved in preaching the Hebrew Bible. Paul writes to interpret the meaning of God as revealed in Jesus to communities of faith, and he does this not by *telling* the Jesus story, as, for example, the Gospels do, but by *interpreting* this story. Paul's primary interpretive lens is Paul's Bible and the God of this Bible. As in Luke 16:19–31, Abraham figures prominently in Paul's theological work and in particular for Paul, Abraham's faith in God. Two Pauline texts are especially important in this regard: Gal 3:8–9 and Rom 4:16–17.

Galatians 3:8–9. In these verses, Paul describes Abraham as a model of relationship to God based on faith and says, "And the scripture, foreseeing that God would justify the Gentiles by faith, declared the gospel beforehand to Abraham, saying, 'All the Gentiles shall be blessed in you.' For this reason, those who believe are blessed with Abraham who believed" (Gal 3:8–9). A more literal translation would read, "and the scripture … proclaimed the good news beforehand" (*proeuangelizomai*). The Scripture Paul has in view here is Gen 12:3, which makes known in advance the good news of God, that is, as Paul writes being made known again among the Galatians, Gentiles who share in the faith of Abraham. The promise of Gen 12:3 contains fully within it the truth of the Galatians' experience of God—that the inclusiveness of God's offer of salvation has always been a part of God's story with Israel.

The offer of faith that the Jesus story makes available to the Galatians was already there in the Genesis story. In Genesis, one gets a glimpse of the gospel beforehand, so that when one gets a glimpse of the gospel at hand, one recognizes the presence of God in it. The God of Abraham and the God of the Galatians are one and the same, and when one proclaims the God of Genesis, one proclaims the fullness of God. To proclaim the Hebrew Bible from the perspective of the gospel beforehand is to recognize that the theological meaning of the Hebrew Bible for Christians rests not in the ways in which the Hebrew Bible points forward to its eventual fulfillment in Jesus but in the ways in which the New Testament recapitulates God's earlier and continuing promises. The Christian preacher's task is to give voice to those promises on their own terms, so that the gospel beforehand can be heard.

Romans 4:16–17. The model of Abraham's faith also provides the context for Paul's words in Rom 4:16–17, where he says:

> For this reason it depends on faith, in order that the promise may rest on grace and be guaranteed to all his [Abraham's] descendants, not only to the adherents of the law but also to those who share the faith of Abraham (for he is the father of all of us, as it is written, "I have made you the father of many nations")—in the presence of the God in whom he believed, who gives life to the dead and calls into existence things that do not exist.

What is important here, however, for homiletical appropriations of the Hebrew Bible, is not the fact of Abraham's faith but the object of Abraham's faith.

The God in whom Abraham believes is described by Paul in language that simultaneously makes clear the continuity between the God of Abraham and the God revealed in Jesus, but more importantly, that the heart of the gospel of God's grace as revealed in Jesus is already the heart of the gospel in which Abraham believes. Abraham's God is one who gives life to the dead and calls into existence things that do not exist. This pattern—life out of death, existence out of nonexistence—can be seen as a theological condensation of the good news of God revealed in the death and resurrection of Jesus. God's power for life is decisively revealed in the death and resurrection of Jesus, but these verses from Paul are an essential reminder that this same power of God for life has characterized God and God's dealings with God's people throughout the Hebrew Bible.

The God Who Gives Life to the Dead

Paul helps Christians to see that the way God is known in Jesus is consistent with the way that God was known before Jesus. Paul's words in Rom 4:16–17 provide the necessary hermeneutical starting point for Christian homiletical use of the Hebrew Bible, because they locate the conversation between Christians and the Hebrew Bible on the common ground of the character of God. From this starting point, the Hebrew Bible is not simply a precursor to the "real" story of Jesus but is an essential element in the Christian story, since the Jesus story makes no sense without this previous story of God. Christians can only recognize and celebrate God in Jesus because they have already come to know the story of God in the Hebrew Bible. Jesus did not spring *de novo* (like Athena emerging fully grown from Zeus's head), but his life continues a story and revelation of God that began centuries before. In naming Abraham's God as the one who "gives life to the dead" and "calls into existence things that do not exist," Paul identifies the character of God in a way that names the essentials of the Christian gospel and captures the essentials of Israel's experience of God.

The decisive instance of God giving life to the dead for Christians is the crucifixion-resurrection of Jesus. This is the quintessential moment of life-giving for Christians that determines how Jesus' story is understood and appropriated for the community's story. Yet as Paul reminds the Romans, this pattern of God's actions has characterized God for much longer than the time of Jesus. This pattern of "life to the dead/existence to things that do not exist" can be laid as a grid over all of the Hebrew Bible in hermeneutically and theologically suggestive ways:

Things That Do Not Exist/Death	God Gives Life/ Calls into Existence	Example Hebrew Bible Texts
Void	Creation	Gen 1
Barrenness	Birth	Gen 18, 21; 1 Sam 1–2
Slavery/Captivity	Exodus	Exodus
Landlessness	Land	Deuteronomy, Joshua
Exile	Restoration	Isaiah, Jeremiah, Ezekiel
Sin	Judgment and Forgiveness	Hosea
Despair	Rescue	Lament Psalms

This list could be added to endlessly as one reads through the Hebrew Bible, because the characteristics with which Paul identifies Abraham's God do indeed define the core of the character of the God of Israel. This is an essential hermeneutical starting point for Christian proclamation of the Hebrew Bible because it begins by affirming the integrity and totality of the Hebrew Bible's revelation of God and God in the world.

Romans 4:16–17 is hermeneutically essential because it is a reminder that the Jesus story does not add anything new to the character of God: God was life-giving before God raised Jesus from the dead, and indeed, God's decisive act in Jesus was a bold reminder of this truth of God's character. When the God-and-Jesus story is read this way, the Hebrew Bible becomes the theological resource for deepening Christian understanding of the God who is revealed in Jesus, rather than an incomplete revelation waiting for its fulfillment. What Christians learn of God through Jesus provides the lens for them to discover previous instances of God's life-giving activities in the Hebrew Bible and so to deepen their understanding of who their God is.

The understanding of Christian preaching of the Hebrew Bible advocated here depends in large measure on the presuppositions and gains of the historical-critical method and on a canonical approach to the Bible (and here we return to David Petersen's overarching attention to methodological clarity). This understanding of the use of the Hebrew Bible in and for Christian preaching depends on the presuppositions of the historical-critical method because it assumes that one can locate the Hebrew Bible in its own historical and theological world and that this world has its own historical and theological integrity. The ability to investigate and interrogate the world of ancient Israel—its history, its literary forms and conventions, its social dynamics—enables the interpreter to speak concretely about a range of historical and theological possibilities that are not dependent on a Christian worldview. Historical criticism and its corollary methods have freed ancient Israel and the Hebrew Bible from the defining lens of Christian doctrine and its attendant presuppositions.

Yet this understanding of Christian preaching of the Hebrew Bible also assumes that the Hebrew Bible and the New Testament form a continuous canon and as such reflects and assumes a Christian appropriation of the Hebrew Bible. A contemporary Jewish faith community would not take Rom 4:16–17 as the decisive lens for reading the story of its God, and the very language that Paul uses, "gives life to the dead and calls into existence the things that do not exist," reflects a hermeneutic grounded in the Christian experience. Paul's language provides a hermeneutical lens for reading the Hebrew Bible and the Jesus story as part of a continuous story and so gives the Hebrew Bible a voice for Christian faith communities as more than prophecy or precursor. Nonetheless, that continuity is read through the story of the death and resurrection of Jesus and reflects a Christian canonical approach to Scripture.

At the center of these reflections on the homiletical appropriation of the Hebrew Bible stands the conviction that the same God is revealed in the Hebrew Bible and the New Testament. The Hebrew Bible enriches and deepens Christians' ability to speak of God and to know God, because its stories and other writings present the full range of a community's efforts through time to be faithful to its God.

Part 2: An Example

The best way to provide an example of a homiletical approach to a text from the Hebrew Bible is to include a sermon on a Hebrew Bible text that reflects the hermeneutical considerations discussed in part 1. The second part of this essay, then, is a sermon on Gen 32:22–32, accompanied by hermeneutical reflections and annotations.

The governing hermeneutical assumption that shapes the sermon that follows is that the God of Gen 32 is the God of Christian proclamation and that careful exegetical work on a Hebrew Bible text can and will yield a gospel proclamation in and of itself. Reference to the death and resurrection of Jesus is not necessary to validate the gospel proclamation found in Gen 32; proclamation of the God who "gives life to the dead and calls into existence the things that do not exist" can be made on the basis of a Hebrew Bible text alone.

For the sermon, I have chosen a very well-known Hebrew Bible text. As the sermon introduction makes clear, I first approached this text the way the majority of preachers seem to approach this text: with the assumption that the wrestling match at the center of this text is a central metaphor for defining life with God. Yet my exegetical work soon led me in another direction. After working carefully through the text, I turned to some Genesis commentaries and read one observation in *The New Interpreter's Bible* that led me to think about the wrestling match in a new way. In the *NIB* volume on Genesis, Terence Fretheim observes how this story occurs at a time when Jacob's "brother's anger once again focuses all of his energies," that "Jacob remains filled with fear and distress (Gen 32:7,11); for all he knows, Esau still plans to kill him."[1]

This observation led me to think not only about Jacob's frame of mind at Gen 32 but about Jacob's entire story, Jacob's character, and how Jacob in particular would encounter a stranger in the dark at a moment when he expects to be attacked by his brother. Attention to Jacob's character changed my way of looking at the story and of thinking about the wrestling match. Genesis 32 does not say who started the wrestling match, simply that "Jacob was left alone and a man wrestled with him until daybreak" (32:24). The wording allows for the possibility that Jacob was the aggressor, something wholly consistent with Jacob's character throughout Genesis. If for a moment I thought of Jacob as the aggressor, on the offensive to defend his life, then the story would start to look quite different, and the meaning of the dialogue would change. From this perspective, it becomes possible to ask the question, What if God did not want to wrestle with Jacob but could not get Jacob to let go, because Jacob understood himself to be fighting for his life?

The dominant interpretive method that emerged from my exegetical work was literary critical, namely, a character study. Asking about Jacob's character changed the rest of my work with the text and thinking about the sermon, because attention to Jacob's character led to a fresh perspective on the wrestling match and, indeed, on the larger theological metaphor of wrestling with God.

A second interpretive method also informed my homiletical appropriation of Gen 32, attention to its form and setting (i.e., form criticism). Genesis 32:22–32 is a recognition story, and I wondered if there were other recognition stories in the Bible where someone meets God in the darkness right before dawn. John 21 suggested itself to me, and the similarities between these two stories was striking: two stories set at a liminal time, just before daybreak, and at a liminal place, the water's edge; two stories of struggle, followed by blessing and abundance; two stories of unknown identity and divine revelation. In both, the central characters have been described as full of fear immediately before the story begins (Gen 32:7, 11; John 20:19). Could John 21 be used as a conversation partner for Gen 32, not to show that the resolution of the tension in Gen 32 was found in the New Testament, but to cast Jacob's situation into even clearer relief through the parallels between the two stories? Connecting two stories that are not usually associated with one another, but that nonetheless have much in common, provided a way to highlight the counternarrative that this sermon constructs about Gen 32.

The Sermon[2]

> This story of Jacob wrestling with God is one of the most well-known in the Old Testament and is the source of countless theological metaphors of human-divine interaction. Indeed, my sense is that this Jacob story may be the source of our most dominant metaphor for our relationship with God. As part of my sermon preparation, I Googled "wrestling with God," and my Google search yielded 579,000 results. 579,000—I think it is fair to say that "wrestling with God" is a popular phrase.
>
> And I suppose that makes sense. The United States is an inherently competitive culture, and we are somewhat sports obsessed—so the Jacob story provides us with theological language that draws on and is fed by both of these cultural preferences. Wrestling is an Olympic sport, after

> all, and I am sure that in those 579,000 hits there is at least one sermon reflecting on who got the gold medal in wrestling—Jacob or God. And for most of my life, I have been captivated by this metaphor, nodding happily as our wrestling match with God is held up as a theological good, accepting that I can't get anything from God without a struggle, that everything worth receiving is worth struggling for, and on and on. A very prominent preacher even entitled a recent article about preaching, "The Weekly Wrestling Match," [3] and when I first read the article, I thought, "How clever." But on further reflection, I thought, "Enough." I am tired of my life with God, my engagement with the biblical text being described primarily in agonistic terms, as a battle, a competition that I have to win in order to get anything from God, that I have to earn whatever God has to give. So I have returned to the Jabbok to see if there is another, a better way.

The introduction makes a promise that derives directly from the exegetical analysis of Gen 32 and the dominant way the story is appropriated by scholars and preachers. The promise, or hunch, of the sermon, is that there is another and better way to think about life with God than the dominant theological image of wrestling with God; a fresh reading of the story of Jacob at the Jabbok may provide that better way.

> The Jacob whom we meet in this story is not a happy man. He is alone because he has sent his family and entire household away to safety in anticipation of his dreaded reunion with his brother Esau. Jacob is afraid, Jacob is defensive, Jacob is working the odds (as always), Jacob is out to prove that, by God, he can stand up for himself. And so when he meets the unknown man in the dark, alone, already primed for a fight, Jacob does what Jacob does best—he gives his all for his own survival. Never mind if maybe a marathon wrestling match was not the reason the stranger appeared to Jacob—Jacob will not be taken advantage of by anyone, by God.

The description of Jacob as an unhappy man reflects my exegetical work and the possibilities that Fretheim's passing allusion to Jacob's fear and distress has suggested. My sense of Jacob's character—as evidenced in this passage and throughout the Jacob story—and the impact that Jacob's character would have on the course of the wrestling match determines how I shape the presentation of the text in the sermon. Jacob's character also leads to the first hint of a possible counternarrative to the dominant way of reading the passage, that perhaps Jacob's character has made it impossible for him to see the true purpose of the encounter by the Jabbok.

> One of the wonders of this story is that it begins as a recognition story—Jacob does not know the identity of the man with whom he wrestles, and the storyteller tells the story so that we join Jacob in this lack of recognition, even though all the listeners already know the story and know exactly with whom Jacob wrestles. The two wrestlers are evenly matched, and no wonder. Jacob wrestles as if he were fighting for his life, empowered by his fear of Esau. The man strikes Jacob on the hip, but that wound does not stop Jacob or lead him to loosen his grasp on the man he takes to be his opponent. And this exegetical detail is to me the first clue that maybe we have been reading the wrestling metaphor wrong. This encounter between Jacob and the "man" is only a battle because Jacob makes it a battle, only a struggle because Jacob won't let go. The man tries to get his attention, tries to bring the match to a conclusion by distracting Jacob with an injury—but Jacob will have none of it. Jacob is so absorbed in the struggle, so intent on not being beaten, that he has not noticed that the sky is growing lighter and that daybreak is approaching. Jacob is so intent on being the victor, on not being pinned by his opponent,that he has not noticed who his opponent is.[4]

An additional key exegetical detail is the identification of the form of the story as a recognition story. It is important to make this element of the story explicit, because it provides a connection to other recognition stories, including John 21, and also hints at what really is at stake for Jacob in the wrestling match. My sense of Jacob's character is crucial to the retelling of the story here. My central homiletical conviction is that Jacob's anger, fear, determination, and self-protectiveness, in evidence throughout the Jacob story, here interfere with his experience of God. If one grants, as is exegetically possible, that the man wounds Jacob to get him to stop wrestling and notice with whom he wrestles, then the good news of this story starts to look very different. This perspective is summed up in the line, "Jacob is so intent on being the victor, on not being pinned by his opponent, that he has not noticed who his opponent is." This line is the lynchpin to the counternarrative, as it picks up on clues in the story itself that Jacob is missing something in the wrestling match. This is a significant rereading of the wounding of Jacob and a homiletical gamble.

> Daybreak matters, because Old Testament tradition holds that no human can look on the face of God and survive. So in Jacob's intense drive not

> to let go of the man who has come to him in the dark, when he was vulnerable and alone, Jacob now risks two things: he risks his life by seeing God face to face, and perhaps more important, he risks the moment of recognition altogether. He risks winning the wrestling match and losing the chance to be knowingly in the presence of God.

In the final line of this paragraph, the conventional narrative and the counternarrative come together. The readers of Gen 32, the listening community, think they know what is going on and who is going to win the wrestling match, but that turns out to be beside the point.

> The injury did not do the trick, so the man says directly to Jacob, "Let me go, for the day is breaking." "You are so busy wrestling to win, Jacob, that you do not see that time is running short." But even in the face of those words, Jacob is so set on the struggle, so set on victory—or avoiding defeat—that Jacob continues to set the terms of the encounter, "I will not let you go, unless you bless me." Instead of a blessing, the man gives Jacob a new name, a name that acknowledges what this story illustrates, that Jacob is a man who is defined by struggle and that Jacob is a man who prevails in the struggle. This new name does not change who Jacob is—Jacob is still called Jacob for the rest of his life—but provides a shorthand for the central plot of Jacob's life. Jacob strives with God and with humans, and Jacob prevails.

The conventional narrative reads the naming as a high point of the story. This way of reading suggests that something else is going on here. The name changes nothing but only provides explicit confirmation of Jacob's character, and Jacob's character completely takes over how the wrestling match is presented: Jacob is a fighter who answers to no one.

> And to show that this new name is indeed the right name, even this name does not get Jacob to cease from the struggle. Instead, Jacob shows that he still wants to win on his terms, "Please tell me your name." I can only imagine God's frustration at this moment. Jacob has a singular opportunity—he stands alone, face to face with the divine—and all he wants is to win. He wants the spoils of the struggle—he wants God's name.
>
> But our God, brothers and sisters, has had enough. Our God has played on Jacob's terms long enough—all night, in fact—and so God ignores Jacob's agonistic question and instead gives Jacob his blessing. Then—and only then—does Jacob let go of his drive to win and recognize that he is in the presence of divine grace and divine love, "For I

> have seen God face to face, and yet my life is preserved." Jacob no longer speaks in terms of winning and losing but simply of being alive in the presence of God.

These two paragraphs tell the story of Gen 32 from the perspective of the counternarrative. It creates the possibility for the congregation to look at the story from the perspective of a God of grace and presence rather than from Jacob's perspective. When God gives Jacob the blessing, Jacob's storyline and his perspective of getting what is his due comes to an end. The storyline of God's grace takes over.

> And the sun rises, day breaks, and Jacob walks away, limping, wounded because of his own need to fight to his last breath instead of allowing himself to notice that he spent the evening in the presence of God. Jacob wrestled with God all right, but his insistence on wrestling was a hindrance, not an aid, to being in the presence of God. His desire to win and not to be vanquished became an obstacle to the offer of love and grace that was before him all the time.

As Jacob exits the story, the tension of the conventional narrative is resolved—Jacob limps away—but the gain of the counternarrative, of reading Gen 32 as God's story and not Jacob's story, is not yet fully revealed. This is the point at which I make a move to a New Testament text, John 21. Importantly, this move is not made to "complete" the Hebrew Bible story, but by setting up the two stories as parallels, a fresh homiletical perspective is possible for both stories. The juxtaposition with John 21 brings the counternarrative of God's grace at the Jabbok to the fore by giving a glimpse of another story of grace and by shifting the focus decisively from Jacob's character to God's character. The good news of this sermon comes in recognizing the character of God who met Jacob on Jacob's own terms at the Jabbok. The John 21 story shows that the God who was present at the Jabbok is also present to the disciples.

> On another dark night, a group of men set their boats into the water and struggle mightily to catch some fish. And at dawn, just as day breaks—just as in the Jacob story—the love of God incarnate stands on the water's edge, acknowledges their struggle, and offers a blessing, "Cast the net to the right side of the boat, and you will find some." And just as Jacob recognized God in the blessing, the disciples recognize Jesus in the superabundant catch of fish, "It is the Lord." And Jesus invites them to have breakfast with him on the beach, charcoal-grilled fish and bread.

"Jesus came and took the bread and gave it to them, and the same with the fish." And so the disciples feasted on the love of God, in the presence of the love of God.

This is what Jacob almost missed but what God did not allow Jacob to miss—Jacob was in the full presence of God, arm in arm with the love and grace of God, and all he could think about was winning and losing. But there was no way Jacob could have lost that wrestling match—how can you lose when you are already in the presence of the love and grace of God, so Jacob did not have to fight to win.

The statement that there was no way Jacob could have lost the wrestling match is the theological and pastoral resolution of the sermon and the definitive statement of the perspective of the counternarrative I have been probing. There is no winning and losing in a wrestling match with God, because to be arm in arm with God is to be in the full presence of God's grace. The sermon has built to this resolution inductively so that the congregation can experience—and not simply be told—this new way of recognizing and finding the grace of God. The sermon's form and movement is built on the redirection of the perspective of the Jacob story and follows the movement of the counternarrative on which I as exegete and preacher have wagered.

Charles Wesley understood this about the Jacob story, understood it better than perhaps anyone before or since. In his poem "Wrestling Jacob" (four stanzas of which provide the words for the hymn "Come, O Thou Traveler Unknown"), Wesley moves inside the story of Jacob's wrestling and reveals the name of Jacob's "opponent":

The morning breaks, the shadows flee
pure Universal Love thou art:
to me, to all, thy mercies move—
thy nature and thy name is Love.

The poem—and hymn—are written so that the poet and the community that sings the hymn is the "I" of the Jacob story. We are the ones locked arm in arm with God's love. In the poem's final stanza, not part of the hymn, Wesley invites us to celebrate God's love as revealed in the Jacob story:

Lame as I am, I take the prey
hell, earth, and sin with ease overcome;
I leap for joy, pursue my way,

> and as a bounding hart fly home,
> through all eternity to prove
> thy nature and thy name is Love.
>
> There is no losing, and there is no winning, because it is not a contest. God is not our opponent; we are not God's prey. There is only the love and grace of God—always available to us, always ready to bless us, to feed us, even when we are alone by the river at night or fishing in vain until dawn.

Charles Wesley's famous poem on Gen 32 provides the perfect mediating voice for the good news offered by the sermon's counternarrative for Jacob's wrestling. The poem makes clear that the grace that the disciples find in John 21 is already there in Gen 32, only Jacob almost did not see it. Charles Wesley saw and named what the sermon sees and names—that at the Jabbok Jacob stands in the presence of the love of God. At the Jabbok, God called Jacob from nonexistence to existence, with a name and a blessing.

For Further Reading

Allen, Ronald J., and John C. Holbert. *Holy Root, Holy Branches: Christian Preaching from the Old Testament*. Nashville: Abingdon, 1995.

Davis, Ellen F. *Wondrous Depth: Preaching the Old Testament*. Louisville: Westminster John Knox, 2005.

Holbert, John C. *Preaching Old Testament: Proclamation and Narrative in the Hebrew Bible*. Nashville: Abingdon, 1991.

Turner, Mary Donovan. *Old Testament Words: Reflections for Preaching*. St. Louis: Chalice, 2003.

Wolff, Hans Walter. *Old Testament and Christian Preaching*. Philadelphia: Fortress, 1986.

Notes

1. Terence Fretheim, "Genesis," *NIB* 1:565–66.

2. Throughout the sermon, which is presented in block quotes and a smaller font, detailed commentary on the homiletical appropriation of Gen 32:22–32 is provided.

3. Barbara Brown Taylor, "The Weekly Wrestling Match," in *What's the Matter with Preaching Today* (ed. Michael Graves; Louisville: Westminster John Knox, 2004), 171–82.

4. This same counternarrative is found in a fresco by Eugene Delacroix, "Jacob Wrestling with the Angel" (1854–61) in St. Sulpice Church in Paris. In this painting, Jacob's intensity in wrestling the angel is in stark contrast to the angel's more relaxed grip on Jacob.

Latin American Approaches: A Liberationist Reading of the "Day of the Lord" Tradition in Joel

Pablo R. Andiñach

It is difficult to establish how it all began, but it may be said that a combination of a growing social awareness, support for popular struggle, a sense of revolutionary expectations, and the work of thousands of Christians involved in those processes produced in Latin America what would later be called the theology of liberation. It was not born as academic theology, nor did it originally nourish itself with the philosophical trends of the day. Liberation theology found its nourishment in social praxis and the basic needs of humans. It seeks its raw materials from the questions that emerge through the struggles for political liberation, in the defense of life, and in the struggle for human rights. Cold, hard reality is what establishes its agenda, and only then follows theological reflection on this reality. This theology, as would be expected, developed hand-in-hand with a new way of reading the Bible, since issues emerging from social praxis question our traditional methods of reading Scripture. The origin of Latin American hermeneutics is thus nothing more than the readings that men and women make of the Bible while they struggle for justice and equality in a context of poverty and in a society that despises life. Later readers discovered that the structures of oppression cannot be reduced to a merely economic expression; rather, oppression is far more complex, involving almost all aspects of life. This discovery was the birth of feminist, indigenous, ecological, and other hermeneutics. Each one began from a particular area of society where some form of oppression could be perceived and readers sought to find illumination to overcome this situation and construct the justice that the Bible promises.

Preliminary Observations

In the strictest sense, there is no Latin American method for reading the Bible. What does exist is Latin American *reading.*[1] For this reading, the methods that the discipline of biblical criticism developed continue to be used. What is particular to Latin American reading is an intuition. Readings that emerge from these lands suspect that every reading that justifies any sort of oppression is a doubtful reading. If the reading does not unmask the unequal relation of white over indigenous, men over women, rich over poor, capital over people and nature, it can be presumed that something has gone wrong. While there is no prejudice here against academic research or university sophistication, Latin American readers seek to remain alert that those tools not be used against the poor and the marginalized. As a matter of fact, Latin American hermeneutics turn to historical-critical methods as often as they turn to synchronic methods such as linguistics, narratology, and stylistics.

In Latin America, two lines of work can be recognized that also happen to exist in many other parts of the world. One of these privileges sociopolitical reading and makes extensive use of historical-critical methods. It seeks to reconstruct the conditions of the text's production and then analyze it from four different perspectives: ideological; economic; political; and social. It has been called the "the four sides reading" and has at times produced excellent results. The other line of work privileges the text as such and turns to linguistics, rhetoric, and literary analysis for its resources. The best work generally takes advantage of a certain convergence of both currents.

Currently it is common in biblical studies and theology to characterize the work produced in the global South as "postcolonial." I would like to point out that this is not, however, an expression derived from our own political vocabulary in Latin America. The wars for South American independence occurred early in the nineteenth century, and most of our countries are close to celebrating their bicentennials in the next ten years. As such, we do not feel that the concept of postcolonialism expresses anything relevant to our current political reality. Furthermore, the "us/them" structure mentioned by Sugirtharajah does not really work for Latin America.[2] We never felt a radical difference between Spain, Portugal, or Europe and ourselves in cultural terms. We currently read Marx or Heidegger (or Barth or Pannenberg) as part of our own culture, even when we understand that they are part of their own particular realities. We do not feel that there is a cultural distance between them and us, at least no more of a distance than an American from the U.S. can feel between herself and a British person. We share the same languages and the same Christian religion and a long history of intellectual relationships with Europe. In any case, the troubles we are currently facing—ones that look very much the same as those faced by the U.S.—are economic and political rather than truly cultural. There is, however, an increasing challenge to this particular framing of the problem, especially from the perspective of the indigenous cultures of Latin America, who did and still do experience a tremendous cultural difference between themselves and the Europeans. But, for the moment, the concept of liberation looks rather useful, in light of our political situations, as a tool with which we may enter into dialogue with the biblical text.

The Day of YHWH in Joel: The Language of Resistance Confronting Imperial Power

The opening verses of the book of Joel demand that tragedy described in this book must be bequeathed to future generations in the fullness of its realism and truth and, at the same time, in a language that will avoid the ravages of time or the forgetfulness (whether wilful or merely neglectful) of memory: "Hear this, O elders; give ear, all inhabitants of the land! Has such a thing happened in your days or in the days of your ancestors? Tell your children of it, and let your children tell their children, and their children another generation" (1:2–3). Joel does not deliver a superficial version of events, a dry chronicle that we can dismiss as an antique and thus inadequate for new situations. On the contrary, the book of Joel is interested in presenting and interpreting the facts it describes, and it does so in a way that establishes the connections of an invasion of an imperial army (Persian? Hellenic?[3]) with other oppressive situations that the people may suffer in the future. The text from Joel provides an example of language built to resist imperial power and offer alternative constructions of reality.

Two dominant semantic axes are held in tension throughout the book of Joel: language concerning the day of YHWH; and language concerning concrete nations and peoples. The former axis indicates a transcendental dimension to the narrative that opens itself out upon the horizon of history. The latter axis indicates the material histories of people, presenting nations so that they can be geographically identified and recognized as political entities. This axis relates to texts that present some degree of reference toward factual reality. In this tension between the two axes, a powerful dynamic emerges in which the transcendental dimension becomes involved in the human history of oppression. At the same time, the pain of a weak people subject to imperial powers is lifted up to show how its suffering will be valued by God at the time "when all nations are gathered" (3:2) and to demonstrate how oppression is judged by God.

The theme of the Day of YHWH has been studied in depth and continues to be an open-ended issue.[4] Research has concentrated on trying to unveil the origin of this expression rather than analyze its textual signification. Authors seem to agree that the expression goes back to the preexilic period and gradually absorbed new meaning in the frame of Judean theology during the restoration period (post 539 B.C.E.). It has been pointed out that the Day of YHWH describes an act of ultimate power on YHWH's part, who on a certain day conquers all enemies and liberates the people.[5]

We will follow this expression, the "Day of YHWH," throughout the book of Joel,[6] studying its contribution to the particular meaning of each passage in which it occurs and the semantic tension created by its juxtaposition of the transcendental dimension to the parallel axis of the "historical world." From our perspective, this dialogue between semantic axes provides the clue for interpreting the Day of YHWH within the text of Joel. We begin with the first occurrence of the theme in 1:15:

> Alas for the day!
> For the day of the LORD is near,
> And as destruction from the Almighty it comes.

The Day of the Lord theme initiates the textual unit 1:15–20, though the particular vocabulary and message associated with this occurrence are quite unique within Joel. This discrepancy has led many interpreters to suggest that this verse is a late addition. However, this distinctive language does not necessarily require its late insertion. In fact, taken as part of the original text, this verse contributes significantly to the overall interpretation of the Day of YHWH in Joel in three ways: (1) what it says about such a day; (2) its relation to other passages about the day; (3) its interaction with 1:16–20.

First, 1:15 says that the Day of the Lord "is near," which is another way to indicate that the invasion close at hand is not the actual Day of YHWH; the people must still wait longer. What must be clarified, then, is if the foreign invasion is a model for or an omen of the Day of YHWH. In the first case, that future event will be understood as a judgment against Israel itself—following the invasion paradigm, which at times is interpreted as God's judgment on his people (2:12–17). In the second case, the invasion that destroys the land directs us toward that Day in which YHWH will avenge all injustice and will destroy the enemy of the people.

The answer to this dilemma can be found in the text itself when it indicates that the Day of YHWH is a future event, further along in history. The characteristics of this future event are described in 2:18–27, which detail God's response to the violations suffered: YHWH *speaks* (2:19–27) and promises the restitution of all that was lost as well as judgment on oppressors. Joel 1:15 also points to the other occurrences of the Day of the Lord theme (2:28–32 [MT 3:1–5]; 3:14–17 [MT 4:14–17]), which describe Israel's salvation and the definitive judgment of all enemies. In light of these passages, the nearness of the Day of YHWH does not announce an eschatological vision of an invasion that destroys the economic and religious life of Israel. Quite the contrary, it announces the realization of absent justice, salvation of the condemned of history, and the return of liberated slaves (3:7 [MT 4:7]).

Joel 1:15 also affirms that that Day comes "as destruction [*šōd*] from the Almighty [*šadday*]." The Hebrew word *šōd* means "destruction," "devastation," or "ruin" and communicates the human activities of "oppression" and "exploitation" (see Isa 16:4). Our text plays on the phonological similarities between YHWH's nickname (*šadday*) and this word, suggesting that YHWH's action is related to—in this case, in opposition to—the actions of the people that have brought devastation on Judah, actions that are likewise material and human. The devastation of YHWH can be confused in this first instance with the action described against Judah. Yet after reading the complete book, it is clear enough that YHWH's "destruction" refers to judgment that will be executed against those who oppressed Israel. The same phrase can be found in Isa 13:6 applied against Babylon.

How does one semantically link Joel 1:15 with the other texts on the Day of YHWH? In this sense, our text acts as an introduction. It draws our attention to the need to "read" in the text more than a mere historical description. It opens the interpretive horizon to new spaces that can be accessed from historical events through extending their signification. This effect allows the transformation of the invasion account from a tragedy to a message of hope and justice, considering that from the very first moment foreign devastation is preannounced in God's answer: oppression is not God's final word for the people.

Joel 1:15 helps interpret 1:16–20, an extremely crude and realistic text, by balancing its historical sense with a dimension that exceeds that context: the transcendental dimension. The text anticipates the message that will be revealed further on and works as an anticipation of God's action, in such a way as to diminish the effect of oppression and strengthen the promise of liberation from injustice. The present lack of food and the sadness in the temple will later be compensated, even though the text does not present such an alternative until YHWH's answer in 2:18–27. The destruction of land and the lack of water do not possess the same powerful effect that YHWH's actions will have on the day of judgment—in not too distant times—on those responsible for such an aggression.

Joel 2:1–2a and 2:10–11 contain the next occurrences of the Day of the Lord theme:

> 1. Blow the trumpet in Zion;
>   sound the alarm on my holy mountain!
> Let all the inhabitants of the land tremble,
>   for the day of the LORD is coming, it is near—
> 2. a day of darkness and gloom,
>   a day of clouds and thick darkness!
>
> 10. The earth quakes before them,
>   the heavens tremble.
> The sun and the moon are darkened,
>   and the stars withdraw their shining.
> 11. The LORD utters his voice
>   at the head of his army;
> how vast is his host!
>   Numberless are those who obey his command.
> Truly the day of the LORD is great;
>   terrible indeed; who can endure it?

In this text, our theme frames the poetic unit, clearly drawing attention to the motif of the Day by its function as an inclusio. At this point in Joel, the Day of the Lord represents foreign invasion (2:2–9) and the siege of the city. Similar to the previous case, these verses are clearly distinguished from the rest of the passage that they yet frame. Their conspicuous presence, rendered in profile due to differences in style and theme, allow us to suspect a specific semantic function for these verses. In the following pages, we are interested in exploring this presence. For this reason, we will subject the text to the same questions that we addressed to Joel 1:15.

What do these verses tell us about the Day of YHWH? In its first occurrence, it is announced with an invitation "to blow the trumpet in Zion," which is a sign used repeatedly in the Old Testament in various senses.[7] The trumpet sound may point to the fact that the city is in danger; in that case, 2:1 addresses the imminent invasion of Jerusalem by a foreign army. Yet it is also used to announce war against other nations, and in this case it would foretell the defeat of the enemy. In this latter case, the sound would make YHWH remember his people and spur him on to free them from oppression (Num 10:9). I feel inclined toward reading in light of the second possibility. Blowing the trumpet is motivated by the nearness of the Day of YHWH, not because of military invasion. From this literary point of view, a semantic consequence can be appreciated: the sound of the trumpet can be heard as hope for the oppressed and judgment for the invaders. This is the sense of the Day of the Lord in this passage.

It is "all the inhabitants of the land" who are called to hear the message in Joel 2:1. We also find these words at the beginning of the book (1:2). It is clear that the phrase refers to *all* who inhabit Judah,[8] though it is difficult to discern if this includes foreign residents or the Israelites, since during the Persian period Jerusalem was part of a rigorous administrative system directed by foreign civil servants who at the same time acted as political representatives and emissaries of military power.[9] If the expression "all inhabitants of the land" included these civil servants—which could explain the subtle ambiguity of the term—Joel 2:1 would then be announcing a warning to the invaders and their local allies. Whatever the case, faced with YHWH's imminent action, all inhabitants without exception will tremble.

To suggest that the darkness designated in verse 2a is produced by the proximity of a cloud of locusts seems inadequate and impoverishes the sense of the text. In Zeph 1:15 we find the same phrase in the context of the "Day of YHWH" with no relation to the cloud of locusts. On the other hand, in Joel 2:31 (MT 3:4), darkness is again mentioned as a characteristic of the events described, without locusts being part of the narrative. The idea of darkness can relate to deeper experiences beyond the historical event of a plague, namely, creation stories. There, darkness is a state that

YHWH modifies to the effect of creating an adequate environment for life.[10] If light is a gift from God, the loss of it then refers to a moment in which the habitable spaces of creation will be lost. The Day of YHWH evokes unknown spaces, spheres in which only the creator dominates.

In Joel 2:10–11 we find the closing of the literary unit. The theme of fear is repeated, juxtaposed to the announcement that the day draws close (2:10a). Through what follows (2:10b), we once again know that the fear refers to the day of YHWH. This fear eclipses the fear that the invading army inspires in Joel 2:6. As in 2:1, the language of fear in 2:10a relatives the power of occupying forces and has the effect of transcending the military event, anticipating divine judgment.

Descriptions of natural phenomena again appear in 2:10, considerably enlarging a theme introduced in 2:2b. The trembling heavens signal the difference between this divine event and a merely human invasion. In this announcement that the sun, moon, and stars will lose their brightness,[11] once again we see an allusion to the moment of creation. Genesis 1:16 speaks of the creation of the "greater light [the sun] and the lesser light [the moon]" and "the stars"—in the same order as Joel 2:10b—so as to separate light from darkness. The various lights' brightness has not ceased until now, though the end of all brightness will be found in the day that quickly approaches. In 2:3 we find a reference to a powerful and destructive force: as the army passes, what looked like the "garden of Eden" is reduced to a "desolate desert." This description proves ironic, given the ultimate fate of the aggressor. What we had noted concerning 2:2a is now more clearly drawn: the Day of the Lord will inaugurate a new era. The coordinates established at the beginning of creation will be deactivated. On the Day of the Lord—as it was on the day of creation—the only one who will have power to act and decide will be YHWH.

Joel 2:11 introduces a new element that can further clarify the nature of the Day of the Lord: YHWH's army. It is worth noting at the outset that interpretation of this verse is in dispute. The general tendency is to see in this reference the same army whose invasion is mentioned in 2:3–9. This proposal is sustained by appeal to 2:25, in which YHWH refers to the locusts as "my army," establishing a connection among locusts, destruction/invasion, and YHWH's army. This interpretation is consistent with the classical understanding of Joel's compositional process, in which the verses on the Day of YHWH are understood as later insertions to the primitive narrative of a natural locust plague. In this way, the later author would have "reread" the original narrative of a drought or locust plague in an eschatological or even apocalyptical sense, establishing a link between the action of locusts and a divine action involving the armies of God. There is a contrast in the semantic dimensions of these texts: an oppositional relationship exists between the Day of YHWH in 1:1–2:17 and the Day of YHWH in 2:18–3:21 (a narrative of the destruction of the social and religious life of Jerusalem). This opposition means that the texts resist being read as simply a history of the oppression and subjection of a weak people. The texts resist the implication that deportations and death, humiliation and suffering would be considered part of YHWH's redeeming action, even when it is understood in an eschatological sense.

Joel 2:11 presents YHWH's army in contrast to the army of 2:3–9. This army comes to execute YHWH's word, not to destroy Jerusalem and the life of its inhabitants. Its power comes from YHWH who leads, from YHWH's commanding voice that directs these actions. The army of YHWH will be more powerful and larger than the greatest human army in history (2:2b). Verse 11 closes with a question: "Who can endure it?" This is a rhetorical question that includes a degree of irony, particularly if one considers that it may have been addressed to those residents of Judah who were somehow related to the invading power, whose security depended on the strength of the occupying army and its reputation of invincibility.

What is the function of these verses in the development of the semantic axis concerning the Day of YHWH? The concept of the Day of YHWH has been expanded inasmuch as it provides more information about that event. While Joel 1:15 presents the idea that the Day will be a day of devastation, Joel 2:1–2a and 10–11 both specify the cosmic and re-creational character of YHWH's actions. Once this dimension has been introduced, no one is excluded from facing this day. It is not about Israel avenging against its oppressors nor about the expectations to strengthen militarily to conquer its enemies and repair the injustices suffered. This would not make any sense within the social and political reality of the Persian Empire, in which Judah was only a small portion of the satrapy called "Beyond the River." What the reader of Joel now knows is that the Day of YHWH will be a definitive time in which the action of God will oppose at root level the enemies of God's people.

I have already pointed out some of the aspects of the relation of 2:1–2a and 2:10–11 with the literary unit of which they are a part. I would like to be specific at this point because it is of great importance for understanding the internal sense of the text. The texts that open and close a unit are granted a position of privilege that these particular texts effectively exploit.

In this case, these texts connote two different events that also carry different meanings. On one hand, the Day of YHWH is placed in the future, even though it is emphasized that the future is imminent by repeating the phrase "is near" (1:15; 2:1b). On the other hand, the central body of the passage is described as a currently developing action in the present, utilizing verbs in the imperfect aspect. This dynamic reflects the tension between two semantic axes that we have described. One axis presents the historical invasion and destruction. It is the cruel reality of a weak people, a tragedy that cannot be avoided and that must be remembered as testimony and memory of oppression. The other axis announces a specific signification for these events and suggests that God will not leave them unpunished. The text then introduces a transcendent dimension by which the power of the oppressor will cease and in which the God of the oppressed will be the one that judges. So far this message of hope has been given as a word that counters the dominant axis of destruction.

The theme of the Day of the Lord continues its development in Joel 2:28–32 (MT 3:1–5). It is to these verses we now turn.

> 28. Then afterward
> I will pour out my Spirit on all flesh;
> your sons and your daughters shall prophesy,
> your old men shall dream dreams,
> and your young men shall see visions.
> 29. Even on the male and female slaves,
> in those days, I will pour out my Spirit.
>
> 30. I will show portents in the heavens and on the earth, blood and fire and columns of smoke. 31. The sun shall be turned to darkness, and the moon to blood, before the great and terrible day of the LORD comes. 32. Then everyone who calls on the name of the LORD shall be saved; for in Mount Zion and in Jerusalem there shall be those who escape, as the LORD has said, and among the survivors shall be those whom the LORD calls.

The delimitation of the unit is established in 2:28 (MT 3:1) with the formulation "then afterward," which serves as an introduction to a new section. We find this formulation often in the historical books (2 Sam 2:1; 8:1; 10:1; 12:1; 21:18; 2 Kgs 6:24), although it is rare in prophetic literature, with the exception of Jeremiah (16:12; 21:7; 49:6).[12] The temporal accent of Joel 2:28 (MT 3:1; "then afterward") initiates a series of two other units headed by temporal formulations (3:1 [MT 4:1] "in those days"; 3:18 [MT 4:18] "in that day"), all of which refer to the same point in time in the future. The closing of the unit is marked by the beginning of the next (3:1 [MT 4:1]) with a new theme and the "in those days" formula. As in previous cases, it is necessary to point out that the delimitation of the unit does not signify that the two units are semantically isolated. There are many elements that point to the interrelatedness of these units, including the continued use of the first-person voice in 3:1 (MT 4:1).

There is only one text-critical issue in Joel 2:28–32 (MT 3:1–5) that deserves consideration here. In the last line of the pericope (2:32), we find the expression "among the survivors," which is not morphologically coherent. There have been various attempts to reconstruct the original version, of which the version "the survivors of Jerusalem" seems to be the most convincing.[13] The word "survivor" is typical of historical literature; we find it in numerous narratives on acts of war, signifying those who have survived devastation.[14] In Isa 1:9, it carries the sense of the "rest" or the "remnant." In this sense, considering the dark tone of the passage, we have the sense that this word refers to those who escape being murdered.

The literary structure is linear and presents a natural linkage among the subunits. After the introductory formulation it continues with the announcement in the first person of the pouring out of the Spirit on "all flesh." It continues (2:28b–29 [MT 3:1b–2]) by enumerating the beneficiaries of this pouring out of the Spirit and concludes by repeating the first words "I will pour out my Spirit," constituting something of a small chiasm. Verses 30–31 introduce the announcement of the cosmic phenomena and the Day of YHWH. Verse 32 abandons the first-person voice to introduce another speaker who talks in the third person. Here we are at the climax of the unit. On the Day of judgment, those who call on the name of YHWH will be rescued, making explicit that the final decision concerning this remnant remains in YHWH's hands. This announced salvation will also take place physically in Zion.

In 2:28–32 (MT 3:1–5) thematic elements present in previous units converge. If the events described so far have been creating tension between a historical dimension and a transcendent one, in this new unit once again this tension is encountered, although here it is taken to a new level. The text occurs as a part of YHWH's answer to his people (cf. Joel 2:19). Joel 2:18–27 describes YHWH's response mostly within the context of agricultural renewal. The announcement of fertility and peace concludes with the affirmation of YHWH's presence in the midst of the people (2:27). God's presence enables the unity among the people described in 2:28–32 (MT 3:1–5): YHWH's presence will create a new situation in the midst of the believing community in which many will be able to imagine a new reality different from their current situation, and particularly the young, the elderly, and the servants, both male and female, will discover this imaginative power.[15] In the context of a military invasion, destruction of the land and deportation of youth—when impotence before the arrogance of the powerful is clearly felt—the announcement of the possibility of a different society sounds to the ears of Israelites like a wonderful act of liberation. However, this liberation does not refer only to liberation from foreign powers. It refers to the internal situation, too. The undervalued sectors of society are the ones that will transmit the word of God. Women, servants, youth, and the elderly will be the vehicle through which it will be possible to outline a new world according to God's will. From a sociological perspective, one can suspect that this "democratization" of the prophetic gift supposes a critique of the distribution of power, particularly concerning the political projection of the temple-related circles.[16] It is probable that behind our text there existed power struggles in Jerusalem.[17] However, we must proceed with a high degree of caution on this point because it is a difficult to justify this interpretation in light of the text itself. In any case, it is noteworthy that Joel, who is so apt to classify the inhabitants of Judah in sectors, this time avoids sectarian divisions to trace a line that runs through them, distinguishing within them the undervalued, possibly in opposition to those inhabitants considered important: chiefs ("elders," 1:2), priests (1:8, 13; 2:17); small scale farmers (1:11).

Verse 28 begins with an announcement of the pouring out of the Spirit on "all flesh." This universal affirmation will be limited in the following lines, yet it remains open to future rereadings. The early Christian community will realize how to interpret this text in light of its own Pentecostal experience (Acts 2). The use of the verb "to pour out" is also significant.[18] It is used for water (Exod 4:9) and blood (Gen 9:6), as well as other liquids. It is related to the pouring out of feelings (Ps 62:9; Lam 2:19), as for the relief of one's soul (1 Sam 1:15, Ps 42:5). We must look to Ezek 39:29 to find another reference to the "out-pouring" of the Spirit, a text with which Joel 2:28 (MT 3:1) seems to resonate. The choice of the verb suggests the novelty of the event and at the same time plays with the image of water that is poured without container or the image of rain that falls on all things and everybody without limitation.

Male and female slaves will be part of YHWH's chosen. The ancient laws had afforded a modicum of protection for slaves, but in this new situation a special value is afforded in the terms of God's plan that they had never had before.[19] They will not only be definitively free, but they will also speak in God's name, a privilege that not all masters had enjoyed. The environment in Joel 2:29 (MT 3:2) seems to affirm that justice will burst through in that day and at the same time refers to the existence of Hebrew slaves in Judah, who were by definition excluded from the circle of the chosen by YHWH. If the differences of age and gender would be overcome in this new time, so would be the categories of social standing. What is outstanding is that this declaration of dignity and liberation of slaves emerges as a consequence of a new experience of exploitation and pain of all the people of Judah. The memory of ancestors' slavery (Deut 6:10–13) is a repeated theme of the Old Testament. In this case, this memory is brought alive by the direct action of a foreign force acting in their midst and destroying their land. This devastating reality sensitizes them to the fate of the poorest and the most excluded members of society.

Verses 30–31 detail the cosmic phenomena that will be produced due to the advent of the Day of YHWH. They are an extension of what had been announced in 2:2 and 2:10–11. It will be a theophany in which YHWH will appear, producing a marvelous set of events in heaven and on earth. Primary elements are invoked: "blood, fire, columns of smoke" and the sun and the moon will alter their appearance due to the coming of the Day of YHWH. But these things should not be confused with their signification. The "great and terrible" thing is the Day itself, not the phenomena that announce it.[20] The word "signs" (*mōpĕtîm*) is charged with enormous meaning, which forces this translation inevitably to be poor and incapable of transmitting the essence of its full meaning. In the Hebrew language we have another word that means "sign" in its dry and prosaic form without denoting any special attribute (*'ōt*), but "signs" (*mōpĕtîm*) point us to YHWH's acts at the time of liberation from Egypt.[21] It is in this sense that they are "signs," though with a specific content: they announce YHWH's acts in favor of God's people. This lexicographic option of the author is not naïve and is aligned with a whole series of allusions to the founding acts in the history of the people of Israel and their traditions (e.g., creation and exodus). The signs of liberation from Egypt will again be seen on that day in which YHWH will call the people to judgment.

Verse 32 closes the unit by introducing a geographic element that seems not to fit in the picture being described. The reference to "Mount

Zion and Jerusalem" seems out of place in an event that has acquired cosmological dimensions and that seems to want to escape the coordinates of human reality. Nevertheless, once again we are in the presence of a tension that covers the whole book: the elements that connote transcendence and those that emphasize the concrete and factual events. The Day of the Lord may be in the future, in an uncertain time, but Mount Zion and Jerusalem are there to testify to the reality of the promise. Since the summons was to blow the trumpet on Mount Zion (2:1, 15) there they will gather to await the appointed time. Jerusalem is placed at the crossroad of the coordinates between an indefinite time and factual space. Moreover, this same place where they are suffering the dishonor of foreign humiliation will bear witness to YHWH's act of salvation, giving dignity to the people. In short, the text has a concrete and real understanding of the events that are expected for that Day of YHWH. The eschatological is not something indefinite or unnamed. Rather, it is conceived as an extension of the present reality, where we find the marks that orient us in the understanding of what will happen. The future will not consist of a break from human reality, but a just resolution of conflicts.

Resolution, that is, salvation, will come to those who call on the name of YHWH. It is the acceptance of God's project that makes the difference, not simply an oral declaration. What other name can be called on that Day? Surely, in the mind of the biblical author, there is no other possible name than YHWH. There are however, different practices that are undertaken before that Day arrives, and it is the nature of those practices that indicate whether one actually accepts God's project.

In sum, Joel 2:28–32 (MT 3:1–5) provides a magnificent description of the Day of YHWH as an answer to the reality of oppression to which Israel has been subject. The symbolic language invites us to read that future event in a semantic relation with the historical events, namely, the foreign invasion. Yet the language also transcends all the forms of oppression that the people have suffered as subjects of imperial powers.

Toward the end of Joel, we find the last mention of the Day of YHWH in 3:14–17 (MT 4:14–17). This text is neither mere concluding formula nor elegant literary closure. The text completes and clarifies the meaning of the Day of the Lord theme in Joel, even considering the ambiguity inherent in the symbolic language that prevails in these texts.

14. Multitudes, multitudes,
in the valley of decision!

For the day of the Lord is near
in the valley of decision.
15. The sun and the moon are darkened,
and the stars withdraw their shining.
16. The Lord roars from Zion,
and utters his voice from Jerusalem,
and the heavens and the earth shake.
But the Lord is a refuge for his people,
a stronghold for the people of Israel.
17. So you shall know that I, the Lord your God,
dwell in Zion, my holy mountain.
And Jerusalem shall be holy,
and strangers shall never again pass through it.

What do these verses say about the Day of YHWH? In accordance with the complete unit 3:1–17 (MT 4:1–17), of which it is part, 3:14–17 make it clear that there will be "multitudes" called. This formulation reveals the all-embracing character of the event, the implications of which are not limited to revenge for the invasion, that is, that which originated the text in the first place. The expressions "multitudes" in verse 14 could be interpreted as an allusion to the size and grandeur of the invading army. Yet, within the "Day of YHWH" tradition in Joel, in which the eschatological space predominates as a final referent, the text is clearer if we understand it as referring to all those who have oppressed and attacked Israel—both past and future. Because of the symbolic element of the message, the historic experience overflows its own particular significance and can illumine the experiences of the past and future.

Verse 17 announces that strangers shall never again pass through Jerusalem—a way to testify to the presence and protection of God for God's people. In this case, the meaning of the word "strangers" is clear; it points to those who have committed the crimes described throughout the book. The expression "shall never pass through" means that these criminals will not govern over Israel. Israel will be free from foreign subjection at the arrival of a new era or an eschatological time. There is a clear emphasis in verse 17 on geographical precision (Zion/mountain/Jerusalem), which once again counterbalances the eschatological with elements of historical reality. It is this persistent interplay of the eschatological and the historical that functions to resist understandings of God's actions that tend to disconnect the hope of the coming Day of the Lord from the domain of real-life injustices and inequalities. Thus, to those who have—and are still—experiencing the very real effects of oppression, Joel's concept of the Day of the Lord offers the refuge of coming justice and peace.

For Further Reading

Carroll R., M. Daniel. *Contexts for Amos: Prophetic Poetics in Latin American Perspective.* JSOTSup 132. Sheffield: JSOT Press, 1992.

Gutiérrez, Gustavo. *On Job: God-Talk and the Suffering of the Innocent.* Translated by Matthew J. O'Connell. Maryknoll, N.Y.: Orbis, 1987.

Míguez, Néstor. "Latin American Reading of the Bible: Experiences, Challenges and Its Practice." *ExpTim* 118 (2006): 120–29.

Ruiz, Jean-Pierre. "Biblical Interpretation from a U.S. Hispanic American Perspective: A Reading of the Apocalypse." Pages 78–105 in *Cuerpo de Cristo: The Hispanic Presence in the U.S. Catholic Church.* Edited by Peter Casarella and Raul Gomez. New York: Crossroad, 1998.

Segovia, Fernando F. *Decolonizing Biblical Studies: A View from the Margins.* Maryknoll, N.Y.: Orbis, 2000.

Sugirtharajah, R. S. "Charting the Aftermath: A Review of Postcolonial Criticism." Pages 7–32 in *The Postcolonial Biblical Reader.* Edited by R. S. Sugirtharajah. Malden, Mass.: Blackwell, 2006.

Notes

1. There are many articles written on this topic: J. Severino Croatto, "Las nuevas hermenéuticas de la lectura bíblica," in *Nuevas hermenéuticas bíblicas* (ed. José Luis Burguet and Rafael Aragón M.; Managua: Lascasiana, 1998), 15–36; Pablo Richards, "Interpretación latinoamericana de la Biblia: Realidad, método, prospectiva," in *Comentario Bíblico Latinoamericano III* (ed. Armando Levoratti; Estella: Verbo Divino, 2003), 11–18; Néstor Míguez, "Latin American Reading of the Bible: Experiences, Challenges and Its Practice," *ExpTim* 118 (2006): 120–29; also in *Journal of Latin American Hermeneutics* (*JOLAH*), 2004– (Instituto Universitario ISEDET, www.isedet.edu.ar); Pablo R. Andiñach, "Liberation in the Latin American Biblical Hermeneutics," in *The Future of the Biblical Past* (ed. Ronald Boer and Fernando F. Segovia; SemeiaSt, Atlanta: Society of Biblical Literature, forthcoming).

2. R. S. Sugirtharajah, "Charting the Aftermath: A Review of Postcolonial Criticism," in *The Postcolonial Biblical Reader* (ed. R. S. Sugirtharajah; Malden, Mass.: Blackwell, 2006), 27 *et passim*.

3. The identity of this particular empire is not a crucial aspect for my argument.

4. Gerhard von Rad, "The Origin of the Concept of the Day of YHWH," *JSS* 4

(1959): 97–108; A. Joseph Everson, "The Days of YHWH," *JBL* 3 (1974): 330; Yair Hoffmann, "The Day of the Lord as Concept and a Term in the Prophetic Literature," *ZAW* 93 (1981): 37–50; Moshe Weinfeld, "They Fought from Heaven: Divine Intervention in War in Ancient Israel and in the Ancient Near East" [Hebrew], *ErIsr* 14 (1978): 23–30.

5. See Douglas Stuart, "The Sovereign's Day of Conquest," *BASOR* 220/221 (1975/6): 59–164. However, the interpretation of the Day of YHWH as an ultimate act of God is complicated by the fact that all YHWH's appearances clearly take place in prophetic writings: Isa 13:6, 9; Ezek 30:2–3; Joel 1:15; 2:1, 11; 2:31; 3:14; Amos 5:18, 20; Obad 15; Zeph 1:14; Mal 3:23.

6. See William Cannon, "The Day of the Lord in Joel," *CQR* 103 (1927): 32–63; Ferdinand Deist, "Parallels and Reinterpretation in the Book of Joel: A Theology of the Yom YHWH?" in *Text and Context: Old Testament Semitic Studies for F. C. Fensham* (ed. Walter Claassen; Sheffield: JSOT Press, 1988), 63–79; John Bourke, "Le Jour de Yahve dans Joel," *RB* 56 (1959): 5–31, 191–212.

7. See Amos 3:6; Ezek 33:3, 6; Hos 8:1; Zeph 1:16, where its sound announces destruction; in Isa 27:13 it is a call to the nations, while in Num 10:1–10 it announces war against the enemies.

8. See Luís Alonso-Schökel and José Luís Sicre, *Profetas I–II* (Madrid: Cristiandad, 1980), 932.

9. See Israel Eph'al, "Syria Palestine under Achaemenid Rule," *CAH* 4:139–64.

10. The word "darkness" is mentioned four times in the primeval narrative of Gen 1:1–2:4.

11. See Amos 8:9; Zeph 1:15; Isa 13:10; Ezek 32:7–8.

12. Prophetic literature has preferred other structural formulations similar to the ones found scattered in different books. See Hans Kosmala, "At the End of the Days," *ASTI* 2 (1963): 27–37.

13. See textual variants in Hans Walter Wolff, *Joel and Amos: A Commentary on the Books of the Prophets Joel and Amos* (Hermeneia; Philadelphia: Fortress, 1977), 57 n. z, 68; Avrid Schou Kapelrud, *Joel Studies* (Uppsala: Almqvist & Wiksell, 1948), 142–43; Wilheim Rudolph, *Joel, Amos, Obadja, Jona* (Stuttgart: Gütersloher, 1971), 70–71.

14. See also Num 21:35; Deut 2:34; 3:3; Isa 8:22; 10:20, 28, 30, 33, 37, 39; 2 Kgs 10:11.

15. But see a different approach in Marvin Sweeney, *The Twelve Prophets I* (Berit Olam; Collegeville, Minn.: Liturgical Press, 2000).

16. Cf. the roll of Levites during the Second Temple period in David Petersen, *Late Israelite Prophecy: Studies in Deutero-Prophetic Literature and in Chronicles* (SBLMS 23; Missoula, Mont.: Scholars Press, 1977), 55–87.

17. See Paul Hanson, *The Dawn of Apocalyptic* (Philadelphia: Fortress, 1972); Osvaldo D. Vena, "Visionarios vs. Establishment en la comunidad judea post-exílica," *Cuadernos de Teología* 9 (1988): 85–98.

18. See Wolff, *Joel and Amos*, 65–66; Alonso Schökel and Sicre, *Profetas II*, 943–44.

19. See Exod 21:2–4, 7, 20, 26, 32.

20. See Hans-Peter Müller, "Prophetie und Apokalyptik bei Joel," *ThViat* 10 (1965): 231–52.

21. See Exod 7:3; Deut 6:22; Jer 32:20; Neh 9:10; John Holladay, "The Day(s) the Moon Stood Still," *JBL* 87 (1968): 187–98; and Wolff, *Joel and Amos*, 68.

Midrash and Exegesis: Insights from Genesis Rabbah on the Binding of Isaac*

Alan J. Avery-Peck

Much has been made in recent scholarship of the value of using ancient commentary in the contemporary interpretation of Scripture. At issue is the extent to which ancient commentators' depth of knowledge, social and cultural location, and relative proximity to the text being examined have the potential for opening new avenues of explanation otherwise invisible to the contemporary scholar. The question is whether or not the text's meaning is better revealed when we avail ourselves of the history of interpretation. Of course, if it is, the question of the methodology by which we can turn to ancient commentaries must be clarified.

The call for sensitivity to traditional commentary has been especially prominent in relation to classical Jewish biblical interpretation, both that found in the early rabbinic literature of the first six centuries C.E. and that of medieval Jewish biblical commentators. The call for attention to tra-

---

* This study is appropriately dedicated to David Petersen for reasons that go beyond David's current scholarly focus on the book of Genesis. Thirty-five years after he was my biblical Hebrew and Scripture professor at the University of Illinois, the story of God's testing of Abraham continues to bring David to my mind. It's not just my memory of the weekly Hebrew quizzes that suggested David's willingness to sacrifice even his beloved students on the altar of advanced wisdom. More to the point, David taught us continually to challenge ourselves. He showed us through his own example that the kind of critical learning that begins in the academy is fulfilled, and is truly fulfilling, only when we test our talents in all of life's activities, social, athletic, and intellectual. I learned from David that, as much as the learning and the critical study are important, what you do with your life overall, the extent to which you challenge yourself, is what really counts. In recognition of this lesson and of all that David Petersen has given me, I am honored to be able to recognize and thank him.

ditional Jewish exegetical sources has two foundations. The first focuses on the source and content of classical Judaic commentary, on the premise that the rabbis of the talmudic and midrashic literature stand directly within the unfolding Jewish traditions that had led to the formation of the Hebrew Scripture in the first place. Emerging from a linguistic and social world close to Scripture's own, rabbinic understandings are seen as valuable keys to the meanings of biblical texts. The second impetus for a focus on the Jewish interpretative tradition is essentially political. Christian hegemony within biblical studies has long meant the imposition upon the text of the Hebrew Bible of attitudes, ideologies, and specific interpretations shaped by Christian theology and the worldview developed in the New Testament and later Christian thinking.[1] Now Jews—and increasingly Christians—are demanding greater awareness of the impact of this theological and cultural bias on the reading of the Hebrew Bible. So both Jewish and Christian scholars more and more have joined in a call to include the previously ignored rabbinic tradition and thus correct past sins.

There is no disagreeing with this general trend. The academy's recognition of its historical bias in favor of Christian readings of the Hebrew Scriptures is a significant step in our improved understanding of that ancient text. Further, the idea that rabbinic commentary might provide special insights, whether they be into the meaning of words, sentences, passages, or overall biblical redaction, appropriately gives the ancient scholarship represented in the talmudic and midrashic literatures a deserved place at the table.

At the same time, my point, for those who do not yet have a clear picture of the overall interests and workings of the rabbinic literature, is that the potential use of rabbinic texts in biblical interpretation must take into account those texts' own biases, presuppositions, and interests. The readings of the Hebrew Bible found in the New Testament and subsequent Christian readings of the Hebrew Bible cannot be taken at face value as revealing something about the authorial meaning of the earlier text. Likewise, rabbinic commentaries should not be understood first and foremost as exegeses in the contemporary academic sense of the term. Rather, as we shall see in detail in the examples given below, rabbinic biblical interpretation generally uses the Hebrew Bible as a foundation for explaining and making sense of the contemporaneous experience of the Jewish communities out of which the rabbinic literature itself emerged. Put simply, this mode of interpretation is a mode of eisegesis, a far cry from the search for authorial or redactional meaning that is at the heart of contemporary academic interpretation of Scripture. To exemplify this point, I explore below a selection of rabbinic passages on the binding of Isaac, Gen 22.

The Focus and Goal of the Midrashic Literature

The problem for the rabbis of the Talmud and midrash, as for all faith communities, is the seeming distance between contemporary experiences and the expectations established by the community's canonical literature. For the Jews in late antiquity, the problem was clear: How does one comprehend the idea of divine chosenness and promise amidst the historical reality of political and economic subservience first to a series of pagan powers and then to a triumphant Christianity? This question dominated the first through sixth centuries C.E. The destruction of the Second Temple in 70 C.E., the failed Bar Kokhba revolt of 133–135, and the rise of Christianity, with its claim to supplant Judaism as the true successor to God's covenantal promise, brutally challenged the canonical legacy of Jewish self-understanding and beliefs about the nature and direction of history.

If the problem was how to uphold the self-comprehension that emerged from Scripture, the solution would be a distinctive rabbinic reading of Scripture, a reading in which the rabbis could identify the way Scripture applied to and, indeed, explained the Jews' current circumstances. Seen in this light, the resulting midrashic literature is not so much exegetical as polemical. It has at its heart the comprehension that Scripture speaks to an age other than the one in which it was written. Scripture explains a history and, indeed, a historical trajectory, that could not have been known to or expected by its own authors and redactors. Thus, if rabbinic midrash does have the potential for uncovering the authorial meaning of the biblical text, it does so only unsystematically—and, indeed, accidentally—for midrash's purpose is not to explain Scripture in the sense of modern exegesis. Rather, it is to explain how Scripture foretells and makes sense of the experience of later Jews, proving that what they are going through is but a prelude to the fulfillment of their covenantal destiny set out in Scripture.

Central to understanding the midrashic approach is the rabbis' conviction that Scripture's relevance and value is, in the first place, the result of its having been written by God. For this reason and for this reason alone, Scripture answers *all* questions and contains *all* truth. Indeed, at the core of the midrashic enterprise is, as Herbert Basser has explained, the evaluation of "every event in Israel's 'experienced' history ... by reference to three categories of faith: namely, Israel's election, Israel's suffering, and Israel's final redemption. God's existence and revelation are accepted as givens in the Rabbinic evaluation of reality and are not open to speculation."[2] Basser's work focuses on the juxtaposition within early midrash of these three interrelated aspects of faith. My goal here is more general, to show how the rabbis used central theological themes of Scripture to explain events experienced throughout Israelite history, including in their own day. The effect of the rabbis' comprehension of Scripture is seen in their belief that, again in Basser's words, "Nothing happens except that which was expected; and once experienced it proves the 'correctness' of the 'Midrashic understanding of reality.' "[3]

Genesis Rabbah

The examples before us derive from Genesis Rabbah, a product of rabbis in the land of Israel. The text dates as early as the middle of the third century C.E. but, in its final redaction, is placed between the beginning of the fifth and middle of the seventh centuries. This is the earliest, longest, and most important of the Amoraic haggadic midrashim (i.e., midrashic texts produced by rabbis of the period of the Talmud that are focused on nonlegal sections of Scripture). The overall theological premise of this document is in line with the purpose of midrash stated above. The rabbis see in the book of Genesis a single, coherent statement regarding not just the past history of the people of Israel but, rather, their future. The rabbis, that is, hold that what happened to and what was accomplished by Israel's patriarchs and matriarchs, Abraham and Sarah, Isaac and Rebekah, Jacob, Rachel, and Leah, speaks not only nor primarily of these ancestors' history and faith. Rather, the patriarchs' actions in the past—the way they responded to each other and to God's demands of them—shapes and foretells the entire future of the Israelite nation. The book of Genesis thus does more than detail what has happened to the Israelite nation in its history up to contemporary times. It provides the contemporary reader access to the future story of Israel, up to God's ultimate fulfillment of the original promises to Abraham. In a period of deep questioning regarding the meaning of Jewish history and the future prospects of the Jewish nation, Genesis Rabbah finds in the book of Genesis a plan and blueprint for a future very different from the present.[4]

Let us examine how this theory of Scripture and of Israelite history is expressed in the rabbis' distinctive readings of Gen 22. I begin with Gen. Rab. 55 on Gen 22:1–3.[5]

LV:I

1.A. "And it came to pass after these things God tested [Heb.: *nsh*] Abraham" (Gen. 22:1):

B. "You have given a banner [Heb.: *ns*] to those that fear you, that it may be displayed because of the truth, selah" (Ps. 60:6 [Eng. 60:4]).[6]

C. [Since the word for "banner" shares the consonants of the word for "test," we interpret Gen. 22:1 to mean:] test after test, one attainment of greatness after another, so as to test them in the world and so as to endow them with greatness in the world, like the ensign of a ship.

D. And all this why? "...because of the truth [Heb.: *kst*], selah" (Ps 60:6).

E. [Since the word for "truth" and the word for "validate" share the same consonants, we interpret:] it is so that [God's] attribute of justice may be validated [Heb.: *kst*] in the world.

F. For if someone should say, "He gives riches to whomever he wishes, and he impoverishes whomever he wishes, and whomever he wishes he makes king [all this without justice], and so too as to Abraham, when he wanted, he made him rich, and when he wanted, he made him king [and all this without justice], you may reply to him, saying, "Can you do what Abraham did?"

G. "Abraham was a hundred years old when Isaac, his son, was born to him" (Gen. 21:5). And after all that anguish, it was stated to him, "Take your son" (Gen. 22:2).

H. And he did not demur.

I. Accordingly: "You have given a banner to those that fear you, that it may be displayed because of the truth, selah" (Ps 60:6).

J. "And it came to pass after these things God tested [i.e., "made a banner of;" displayed] Abraham" (Gen. 22:1).

The midrashic reading of Gen 22:1 is on the surface fanciful, making a number of exegetical moves that no modern commentator could find legitimate. At its foundation is the (erroneous) association of the Hebrew root *nsh* found in Gen 22:1, referring to God's testing of Abraham, with the distinct root *nss*, the source of the word *nēs*, "banner," at Ps 60:6. While the congruence of two of the root letters of the different words lends at least some credence to the rabbinic reading, the next interpretative jump is beyond what a critical exegete would propose. Having identified a similarity between a word in two different verses, the midrashic authors read the second verse in its entirety as a reflection of the meaning of the first. Thus Ps 60's notion that God provides his followers with a symbol of his truth suggests the deeper meaning and broader historical impact of the Akedah (Gen 22). God did not "test" Abraham simply or primarily to discover the depth of Abraham's faith. The "test," rather, was an opportunity for Abraham to respond to God in a way that merited the special treatment God would subsequently give him and his descendants. The Akedah narrative thus teaches more than about God's interactions with Abraham. It offers insight into God's character, God's justice, and the justification for God's covenantal relationship with Abraham's descendants.

We have no firm knowledge of the extent to which rabbis in the period of the composition of Genesis Rabbah were familiar with Christian readings of Scripture, let alone with the New Testament texts in which those readings already were being transmitted. Be this as it may, we immediately see in the rabbis' interpretation of Gen 22:1 a possible response to what was, by the period of this text's composition, a key Christian understanding of God's selection of and covenant with Abraham. The rabbinic interpretation directly refutes Paul's rejection of the law, found in Rom 4:19–22. Paul denies the efficacy of observance of the law as a path to righteousness, by pointing to Abraham, who, Paul asserts, was selected for God's promise as a reward for faith alone. But the rabbis here reject the idea of a reward for those who have not in a concrete way earned God's beneficence. Abraham was rewarded because of what he did. In the face of Paul's claim, the end of line F is particularly pointed. Action, contrary to what Paul asserts, is what counts, and anyone who questions this need only reflect on the question, "Can you do what Abraham did?"

What is at first glance a fanciful interpretation turns out to respond to a rather deep theological challenge that Jews faced in the period of this text's composition and beyond. The rabbinic reading continues in our own day to represent a necessary corrective to an ongoing line of Christian interpretation of the Akedah narrative that asserts that Paul's understanding is intrinsic to Scripture's sense. Thus, in his commentary on Genesis, Bruce Vawter writes:

> This is without any doubt whatsoever the most important contribution that the Elohist has made to the story of Abraham. In Romans 4:19–22 Paul rhapsodizes on Abraham's faith which never questioned or doubted God's promise; and although he does not allude to this passage it cannot fail to have been in his mind, for it exactly epitomizes a faith of this kind which the Bible so confidently ascribes to Abraham.[7]

Certainly, as Vawter points out, the passage "epitomizes" Abraham's absolute and unwavering faith. But to refer here to Paul's focus on that faith is to add a level of meaning—faith, not works—that is far from what the passage at least on the surface wishes to express. Whether or not we wish to assert that the rabbis' reading is implicit in the Genesis text, it should be clear that any reading that takes into account the later Pauline reading adds to the text an idea that is not explicit there. The rabbinic reading thus provides a corrective to the early Christian, anti-Judaic assertion that invalidated the Jews' theory of Torah by asserting that "works" have no place in the establishment of one's relationship with God.[8] The rabbinic reading, by contrast, provides a quite different approach: it asserts that God is just and, therefore, that what people do matters.[9] Abraham passed God's test and so was to be rewarded. The implications of this interpretation are significant and are expressed in the following passage of Genesis Rabbah.

LV:2

1.A. "The Lord tries the righteous, but the wicked and him who loves violence his soul hates" (Ps. 11:5):

B. Said R. Jonathan, "A potter does not test a weak utensil, for if he hits it just once, he will break it. What does the potter test? He tests the strong ones, for even if he strikes them repeatedly, they will not break. So the Holy One, blessed be he, does not try the wicked but the righteous: 'The Lord tries the righteous' (Ps. 11:5)."

C. Said R. Yose bar Haninah, "When a flax maker knows that the flax is in good shape, then the more he beats it, the more it will improve and glisten. When it is not of good quality, if he beats it just once, he will split it. So the Holy

One, blessed be he, does not try the wicked but the righteous: 'The Lord tries the righteous' (Ps. 11:5)."

D. Said R. Eleazar, "The matter may be compared to a householder who has two heifers, one strong, one weak. On which does he place the yoke? On the one that is strong! So the Holy One, blessed be he, does not try the wicked but the righteous: 'The Lord tries the righteous' (Ps. 11:5).

God selected Abraham for this trial because God already knew that Abraham would pass the test. This idea is developed through the passage's focus on Ps 11:5, which, while verbally unrelated, is explicit in its statement that, "The Lord tries the righteous."

As with the preceding passage, the relevance of this point to the passage's rabbinic authorship should be clear: the persecution the people of Israel now are experiencing indicates not abandonment by God but God's love, not a punishment for sin but a sign of righteousness. Again we discern here a rather direct response to Christian ideology, which held that the Jews' degraded condition signified their being cut off from God's covenant. The rabbis, by contrast, argue implicitly through the text that accepting and passing God's test earns God's favor.

The relevance of this passage for modern readings of the text should also be made clear. The announcement in Gen 22:1 that this is, in fact, a test is a frequent focus of contemporary interpretation of the Akedah narrative—understood to imply that God in fact never wished to have Abraham sacrifice Isaac. Ephraim A. Speiser puts it this way:

> The reader's anxiety, to be sure, is allayed at the very outset by the underscored notice that this is to be only a test, however heroic the scale and the stakes. The suspense thus is shifted from the viewers to the actors, yet the transfer does little to relieve the tension. There is no way of assuring the father that he need have no fear about the final result; one can only suffer with him in helpless silence.[10]

Similarly, Nahum Sarna writes:

> This information is imparted to the reader, not divulged to Abraham, in order to remove any possible misunderstanding that God required human sacrifice as such. Therefore, the purely probative nature of the divine request is emphasized. As a result, the focus of tension shifts from Isaac to Abraham. Now the reader knows that the son will not be

> slaughtered. But is the father's faith in God of such transcendent quality as to overcome his natural love for his heir in full consciousness that obedience to God's cruel request would mean the end of all his hopes and dreams, the nullification of the promises he had so often heard from the mouth of this selfsame god?[11]

Exactly like these contemporary commentators, the rabbis focus on the biblical text's explicit declaration that this is a test, and they propose that beyond meaning that Isaac will not be sacrificed, this suggests God's foreknowledge of Abraham's strength and ability to withstand the test. At the same time, even as it gets to the heart of one aspect of the biblical narrative, the rabbis' overall point is polemical: what the Israelite nation is experiencing in the rabbis' own day is but a divine trial, a trial that suggests that God knows the people's strength and destines them for future redemption.

We skip to paragraph 8 of this section of Genesis Rabbah.

LV:8

1.A. "And Abraham rose early in the morning, [saddled his ass, and took two of his young men with him, and his son Isaac, and he cut the wood for the burnt offering and arose and went to the place which God had told him]" (Gen. 22:3):

B. Said R. Simeon b. Yohai, "Love disrupts the natural order of things, and hatred disrupts the natural order of things.

C. "Love disrupts the natural order of things we learn from the case of Abraham: '…he saddled his ass.' But did he not have any number of servants? [Why then did a servant not saddle the ass for him? Out of his dedication to his son, Abraham performed that menial task.] That proves love disrupts the natural order of things.

D. "Hatred disrupts the natural order of things we learn from the case of Balaam: 'And Balaam rose up early in the morning and saddled his ass' (Num. 22:21). But did he not have any number of servants? That proves hatred disrupts the natural order of things.

E. "Love disrupts the natural order of things we learn from the case of Joseph: 'And Joseph made his chariot ready' (Gen. 46:29). But did he not have any number of servants? But that proves love disrupts the natural order of things.

F. "Hatred disrupts the natural order of things we learn from the case of Pharaoh: 'And he made his chariot ready' (Ex. 14:6). But did he not have any number of servants? But that proves hatred disrupts the natural order of things."

2.A. Said R. Simeon b. Yohai, "Let one act of saddling an ass come and counteract another act of saddling the ass. May the act of saddling the ass done by our father Abraham, so as to go and carry out the will of him who spoke and brought the world into being, counteract the act of saddling that was carried out by Balaam when he went to curse Israel.

B. "Let one act of preparing counteract another act of preparing. Let Joseph's act of preparing his chariot so as to meet his father serve to counteract Pharaoh's act of preparing to go and pursue Israel."

C. R. Ishmael taught on Tannaite authority, "Let the sword held in the hand serve to counteract the sword held in the hand.

D. "Let the sword held in the hand of Abraham, as it is said, 'Then Abraham put forth his hand and took the knife to slay his son' (Gen. 22:10), serve to counteract the sword taken by Pharaoh in hand: 'I will draw my sword, my hand shall destroy them' (Ex. 15:9)."

...

4.A. "...and he cut the wood for the burnt offering [and arose and went to the place which God had told him]" (Gen. 22:3):

B. R. Hiyya bar Yose said the following in the name of R. Miasha, while it has been taught on Tannaite authority in the name of R. Benaiah, "[Since the word for wood is written in the plural, we know that Abraham cut up two logs. Hence] on account of the reward of the two acts of woodcutting that our father, Abraham, carried out in preparing wood for the burnt offering, he received the merit that the Holy One, blessed be he, would cut the Sea in half before his children, as it is said: 'And the waters were divided' (Ex. 14:21)."

C. Said R. Levi, "Enough for you. This is as far [as we can go]. In point of fact, Abraham did what he could do, and the Holy One, blessed be he, did what he could do. [The two acts are not on a par.]"

No detail of the Akedah story is without particular significance, both in reflecting Abraham's individual motivations and consciousness and in prefiguring the later history and salvation of the Israelite nation. Thus, in response to each of Abraham's acts, God produced a corresponding action to rescue Israel from its enemies.[12] Within this interpretative framework, Levi's statement in unit 4 is striking. It sees the parting of the Red Sea, the ultimate act of redemption, as totally beyond anything anyone could expect or predict as a response to human actions. Even as he asserts a limitation to the rabbinic theory of history, Levi thus insists that God retains his ultimate power and self-will. God's actions are not totally predictable nor based exclusively on the merit of Israel's ancestors. Clearly what the rabbis are discussing here is extrinsic to the biblical texts from which this ideology is said to emerge. Our next example is from Gen. Rab. 56 on Gen 22:4.

LVI:1

1.A. "On the third day Abraham lifted up his eyes and saw the place afar off" (Gen. 22:4):

B. "After two days he will revive us, on the third day he will raise us up, that we may live in his presence" (Hos. 6:2).

C. On the third day of the tribes: "And Joseph said to them on the third day, 'This do and live'" (Gen. 42:18).

D. On the third day of the giving of the Torah: "And it came to pass on the third day when it was morning" (Ex. 19:16).

E. On the third day of the spies: "And hide yourselves there for three days" (Josh. 2:16).

F. On the third day of Jonah: "And Jonah was in the belly of the fish three days and three nights" (Jonah 2:1).

G. On the third day of the return from the Exile: "And we abode there three days" (Ezra 8:32).

H. On the third day of the resurrection of the dead: "After two days he will revive us, on the third day he will raise us up, that we may live in his presence" (Hos. 16:2).

I. On the third day of Esther: "Now it came to pass on the third day that Esther put on her royal apparel" (Est. 5:1).

J. She put on the monarchy of the house of her fathers.

K. On account of what sort of merit?

L. Rabbis say, "On account of the third day of the giving of the Torah."

M. R. Levi said, "It is on account of the merit of the third day of Abraham: 'On the third day Abraham lifted up his eyes and saw the place afar off' (Gen. 22:4)."

While consciousness of repeating themes marks modern as much as rabbinic interpretation, here the authors of Genesis Rabbah take that approach to an extreme beyond anything explicit in the text before us. The third day marks the time of fulfillment of promise, and this means that Abraham's act of obedience to God is directly related to Israel's redemption, the end of time, and the eventual resurrection of the dead. In the rabbinic view of the cogency of God's plan for Israel, the reference to the third day at Gen 22:2, that is, evokes the entirety of God's plan for Israel, including the certainty of Israel's redemption, seen here not as so far in the future but, rather, simply as a matter of "the third day."

LVI:2

5.A. Said R. Isaac, "And all was on account of the merit attained by the act of prostration.

B. "Abraham returned in peace from Mount Moriah only on account of the merit owing to the act of prostration: '…and we will worship [the Hebrew word refers to an act of prostration] and come [on that account] again to you' (Gen. 22:5).

C. "The Israelites were redeemed only on account of the merit owing to the act of prostration: 'And [when told by Aaron what God had promised] the people believed, … then they bowed their heads and prostrated themselves' (Ex. 4:31).

D. "The Torah was given only on account of the merit owing to the act of prostration: 'And [before giving the Torah to Moses, God instructs Aaron and the elders of Israel to] worship [prostrate themselves] afar off' (Ex. 24:1).

E. "Hannah was remembered [with a child] only on account of the merit owing to the act of prostration: 'And [Hannah and her husband] worshipped before the Lord' (1 Sam. 1:19).

F. "The exiles will be brought back only on account of the merit owing to the act of prostration: 'And it shall come to pass in that day that a great horn shall be blown and they shall come that were lost … and that were dispersed

... and they shall worship the Lord in the holy mountain at Jerusalem' (Is. 27:13).

G. "The Temple was built only on account of the merit owing to the act of prostration: 'Exalt you the Lord our God and worship at his holy hill' (Ps. 99:9).

H. "The dead will live only on account of the merit owing to the act of prostration: 'Come let us worship and bend the knee, let us kneel before the Lord our maker' (Ps. 95:6)."

Again, the similarity of a word in different contexts is understood to establish a paradigm, suggesting the cogency of the entire history of Israel, seen as flowing from a series of acts of worship ("prostration"). These acts earned merit, from which all the generations of Israel benefited and will benefit again, in the eventual resurrection of the dead. As Jacob Neusner notes,[13] at stake here is not simply the meaning of the passage at hand but the way in which the passage contributes to an encompassing "law of history." While following from and expressing the rabbis' theory of history and God's justice, and while providing a hopeful message for the Israelite people in the period of the composition of Genesis Rabbah, the rabbis have moved beyond anything that is intrinsic to the biblical text.

We conclude by turning to Gen. Rab. 56:9.

LVI:9

1.A. "And Abraham lifted up his eyes and looked, and behold, behind him was a ram, [caught in a thicket by his horns. And Abraham went and took the ram and offered it up as a burnt offering instead of his son]" (Gen. 22:13):

B. What is the meaning of the word for "behind"?

C. Said R. Yudan, "'Behind' in the sense of 'after,' that is, after all that happens, Israel nonetheless will be embroiled in transgressions and perplexed by sorrows. But in the end, they will be redeemed by the horns of a ram: 'And the Lord will blow the horn' (Zech. 9:14)."

Our final sample text again links the life of an individual, Abraham, to the history of the entire Israelite nation. Like Abraham, the people are caught up in a trial from God. In line with the rabbis' theory of history, in their case, as in Abraham's, the ram's horn will indicate redemption. So, for the rabbis, the meaning of Gen 22 flows well beyond the immediate implications of the biblical text. The Akedah is not just or primarily about Abraham and God. It is about the pattern of history that assures the eventual fulfillment of God's promise to the people of Israel.

Conclusion

Genesis Rabbah explains the Akedah by asserting and then examining its significance within the entire span of Jewish history. For the midrash's authors, each detail of the biblical story represents a paradigmatic act that epitomizes the special relationship between the people of Israel and God and that establishes the fact of the Israelites' ultimate redemption. The Akedah in this reading elucidates the adversity the Jews face, viewed as a test God imposes exclusively on those he loves and knows to be able to withstand whatever hardship they are made to face. The testing of Abraham thus stands for the trials of Israel in general. Israel's being subjected to such a test marks the people as special and holy. They are the true victors in the context of God's relationships with the nations of the world and God's determination of who ultimately will experience salvation.

At the heart of this rabbinic reading stands an implicit challenge to early Christian ideology. The covenant, the rabbis argue, is the reward the people of Israel were granted for specific actions. This is because God, in his justice, repays what people concretely do as aspects of their faith and commitment to God. For each action of faith by the people, a specific act of salvation by God is forthcoming, leading finally to national redemption and resurrection of the dead.

In many ways, this rabbinic perspective hits at the heart of the theological issues raised by the text of Genesis: the meaning of faith and the nature of the relationship between humankind and God. At the same time, it is clear that the rabbis' specific interpretations—reading disparate biblical verses in light of each other, finding meaning in the consonantal tally between words that in fact are unrelated, seeing in this story an explanation of the circumstances of Jews well beyond the period of Genesis's authors—read as much rabbinic ideology into the biblical text as they identify in it the Bible's own author's meanings.

The conclusions to be drawn from this brief sample of rabbinic interpretation thus tally with the overall results reached, for instance, by Lieve Teugels, whose 2004 study examined the midrashic treatment of Gen 24.[14] Teugels finds that "[k]nowledge of rabbinic literature, its contents, history and hermeneutics, is extremely useful for a biblical scholar. It is even mandatory for a scholar of the New Testament."[15] In support of this position, Teugels notes the extent of the rabbinic exegetes' knowledge of Hebrew and the rabbis' deep focus on the biblical storyline. This, he notes, leads them to identify the significance of the redactional ordering of stories, a matter that, he says, sometimes is "overlooked by a too narrow historical-critical focus on the text."[16] Teugels further notes the particular importance of rabbinic interpretation for the study of the New Testament. Rabbinic exegesis reveals a great deal about the Judaic world and the theological and literary setting out of which the New Testament emerged. In this context, Teugels correctly chastens us against the sometimes "hidden agenda of certain theologians who are 'interested' in the Jewish tradition" but who, he notes, use the rabbinic literature only to show the correctness of Christianity's message as against that of the rabbis.[17]

Even as Teugels points out the significance of rabbinic midrash both in the interpretation of the Hebrew Bible and in contributing to our understanding of the world of the New Testament, he is clear that midrash is not biblical exegesis in the contemporary sense of the word. "Biblical exegesis and traditional rabbinic exegesis," he notes, are "different enterprises that should not be mixed up."[18] This fact has two implications. First, while midrashic texts may, on occasion, enhance our comprehension of biblical themes and motifs, the meaning of individual words, and the implications of the redactional ordering of biblical passages, the rabbis do not present objective, critical interpretations that modern biblical scholars seek. This fact leads to a second matter that biblical scholars who turn to midrash must keep in mind. Unlike contemporary exegetes, midrash's rabbinic authors have no conception of and are not attempting to understand the perspective of the biblical authors. As we have seen, the rabbis wish, rather, to find the meaning that the biblical texts hold for their own much later Jewish communities. This means that, as wrong as it is to replace contemporary critical scholarship with midrashic interpretation, so it is wrong and even absurd to compare midrashic readings with contemporary interpretations or to criticize midrashic interpretations as somehow not up to contemporary standards.[19] Such criticism misses the point of the rabbis' distinctive method and purpose.

Through midrash, the rabbis put their own experience in the perspective of the history of the Israelite people, God's absolute justice, and the covenantal relationship that assures the Jewish people's ultimate redemption. Pursuing a careful and intense program of identifying the meaning of every aspect of Scripture, these rabbis are astute interpreters of the biblical text and have much to teach modern readers. But founding their interpretations on interests and perspectives distinctive to their own theology and worldview, the midrashic texts that emerge do not always add to, and never replace, the work of the contemporary critical exegete intent on identifying the viewpoint from which Scripture's own authors wrote and the point of view those authors wished to present.

For Further Reading

Basser, Herbert W. *Midrashic Interpretations of the Song of Songs.* New York: Lang, 1984.

Ginsburg, Louis, ed. *Legends of the Jews.* 10th ed. 7 vols. New York: Jewish Publication Society, 1954.

Neusner, Jacob. *The Midrash: An Introduction.* Northvale: Aronson, 1990.

Neusner , Jacob, and Alan J. Avery-Peck, eds. *Encyclopedia of Midrash.* 2 vols. Leiden: Brill, 2005.

Strack, Hermann, and Günter Stemberger. *Introduction to the Talmud and the Midrash.* Translated by Markus Bockmuehl. Minneapolis: Fortress, 1992.

Teugels, Lieve. *Bible and Midrash: The Story of 'The Wooing of Rebekah' (Gen. 24).* CBET 35. Leuven: Peters, 2004.

Notes

1. Among many scholars who have pointed out and offered correctives to this approach, the pioneering work of E. P. Sanders on this topic deserves note. See his *Paul and Palestinian Judaism: A Comparison of Patterns of Religion* (Minneapolis: Fortress, 1977), 1–12, 33–59.

2. Herbert W. Basser, *Midrashic Interpretations of the Song of Songs* (New York: Lang, 1984), 6–7.

3. Ibid., 9.

4. See Jacob Neusner, *The Midrash: An Introduction* (Northvale, N.J.: Aronson, 1990), 141–42. See also Jacob Neusner, "Genesis Rabbah, Theology of," in *Encyclopedia of Midrash* (ed. Jacob Neusner and Alan J. Avery-Peck; 2 vols.; Leiden: Brill, 2005), 1:105–21.

5. Translation adapted from Jacob Neusner, *Genesis Rabbah: The Judaic Commentary to the Book of Genesis, A New American Translation* (3 vols.; BJS 104–6; Atlanta: Scholars Press, 1985), 2:267–85.

6. The verse is difficult and variously translated. JPS has: "Give those who fear

You because of Your truth a banner for rallying." The NIV has: "But for those who fear you, you have raised a banner to be unfurled against the bow" (Eng. 60:4).

7. Bruce Vawter, *On Genesis: A New Reading* (Garden City, N.Y.: Doubleday, 1977), 254.

8. Note that Gen 22:15–18 offers internal evidence that, at the earliest stages of its composition, the story was read as having the implications the rabbis attribute to it, with Abraham's blessings here "presented as a reward of a *particular* virtuous act" (Robert Daly, "The Soteriological Significance of the Sacrifice of Isaac," *CBQ* 39 [1977]: 47, cited in Carol Delaney, *Abraham on Trial: The Social Legacy of Biblical Myth* [Princeton: Princeton University Press, 1998], 112).

9. Neusner, *Genesis Rabbah*, 2:267–68.

10. Ephraim A. Speiser. *Genesis: Introduction, Translation, and Notes* (AB 1: Garden City, N.Y.: Doubleday, 1964), 164.

11. The *JPS Torah Commentary: Genesis* (Philadelphia: Jewish Publication Society, 1989), 151.

12. Neusner, *Genesis Rabbah*, 2:275.

13. Neusner, *Genesis Rabbah*, 2:279–80.

14. Lieve Teugels, *Bible and Midrash: The Story of 'The Wooing of Rebekah' (Gen. 24)* (CBET 35; Leuven: Peters, 2004), 148.

15. Ibid. Regarding this position, Teugels refers to John F. A. Sawyer, "History of Interpretation," in *A Dictionary of Biblical Interpretation* (ed. R. J. Coggins and J. C. Houlden; London: Trinity Press International, 1990), 139–52.

16. Teugels, *Bible and Midrash*, 148.

17. Ibid.

18. Ibid.

19. Such criticism often emerges within a Christian polemic against Judaism. Teugels points by way of example to André Robert, *Guide to the Bible* (Paris: Desclee, 1960), whose derision of rabbinic interpretation emerges from what Teugels refers to as Christian triumphalism.

Postmodern Literary Criticism: The Impossibility of Method

Mark K. George

Challenges

One of the notable aspects of David Petersen's teaching and scholarship is its clarity in both organization and argumentation. I regularly hear students and scholars alike express appreciation for this aspect of his work. In honor of this clarity, it is appropriate to refine the focus of this chapter on the assigned topic of "postmodern literary criticism." As a topic, postmodern literary criticism requires refinement because, technically speaking, it is not a method or even a single unified approach, notwithstanding its inclusion in a volume whose theme is "methods." Its inclusion in this book, therefore, presents certain challenges, and those challenges, in turn, merit discussion. For the time being, let us defer a definition of "postmodernism"; perhaps an exploration of the problems inherent in the concept of "method" will prepare some space for its careful explanation.

A "method" is usually defined as a systematic, orderly series of steps a scholar follows in order to analyze a text from a particular vantage point. The purpose of following these steps is to identify and articulate the interpretation or meaning of the text being read. Used properly, a method achieves a proper interpretation of the text's meaning—at least in principle, if not in fact. As long as the interpreter has the appropriate skills with which to use a method (in Hebrew Bible scholarship, this includes knowledge of appropriate languages and other such skills), that individual can use the method to identify the text's meaning. In this line of thought, a method is a means to the truth (or, ideally, the Truth) of the text. This concept of "method" seems to adumbrate a number of principles of "modernity"—above all, the ability of rational thought guided by proper technique to overcome in due time the prejudices and traditions that would otherwise skew objective thought. Such a principle can be seen to operate in the thought of Descartes and Kant as well as many, if not most, current scholars.

Postmodern thought seeks to move beyond this modern paradigm. Thus, postmodern interpreters challenge a number of assumptions and claims at work in such an understanding of method. One such assumption is that scholars may be largely, if not entirely, objective, in the sense of being uninfluenced by particular social or cultural biases derived from the interpreter's context. Postmodern interpreters, in general, do not accept this assumption. New Historicists, for example, argue that no interpreter is uninterested or objective in reading a text, because every interpreter is located in a particular context, and that context is unavoidably caught up within the interpretive process.[1] Jean-Francois Lyotard famously defined postmodernism as "incredulity toward metanarratives."[2] Primary among rejected metanarratives is the modernist project of unending progress based on rational objectivity assured by proper technique. In contrast, postmodern critics assert that the interests of a reader influence and shape the use of a method in a variety of ways, and self-styled objective rationalists are no exception. Any reading of a scholar from the past supposedly practicing proper technique and rational disinterestedness will, in time, doubtless reflect certain quirks that can be explained only with recourse to his or her particular cultural time and place. The decision to read and interpret the Hebrew Bible, for example, reflects a particular interest, because it values the Hebrew Bible as something worth interpreting. The interests of an interpreter also are influenced and shaped by the larger social, economic, political, theological, historical, and cultural context within which she or he is situated. Which method(s) is chosen, how it is employed in relation to the text, which questions are asked of the texts, in what order, what evidence is considered relevant, and how evidence is organized into a larger argument are aspects of the interpretive act that these larger contextual influences shape.

So, for example, if an interpreter works in a denominationally related seminary, that social context will in some way influence the interpreter's work. Theological aspects of the text, and especially their relevance for particular faith communities, may be highly valued by the seminary, and elucidating these aspects may, in turn, influence hiring and promotion decisions affecting that interpreter. An interpreter located in a department of religion at a major U.S. research university, in contrast, might be influenced to avoid such theological issues in favor of social and historical ones. These are quite simple examples of how context influences interpreters, and we may be assured that there are countless other influences also at work on interpreters. Both the seminary and the university professor, for example, live in a culture that configures secondary and postsecondary education in a particular manner that is more or less arbitrary (with summer breaks, a tenure system, private and public schools) and radically different from educational systems have been configured in the past (rabbinic schools in the Middle Ages, for example, or scribal education in ancient Sumer). These countless differences will influence the boundaries of "rational" thought and the choices of proper (or improper) techniques to analyze texts. For this reason, the assumption that an individual can be largely, if not entirely, objective in reading a text is impossible from a postmodern perspective.

Another assumption challenged by postmodern interpreters is the supposedly systematic nature of any given method. As Jacques Derrida argues, systems of thought, whether philosophical, political, theological, social, or otherwise, tend to structure themselves on binary opposites in which one term is privileged over the other (such as "male" over "female," "straight" over "gay," or "ethnically normal" over "foreigner"); these structures and privileges seem to most people within them as "natural" and thus unimpeachable. Derrida's deconstructive theory consists of questioning both the necessity of the given opposition and the arbitrariness of the privileged term.

As systems of interpretation, methods inherently and unconsciously privilege certain evidence, material, texts, political or social ideas, religious claims, and other cultural artifacts over others merely by selecting the steps they follow. The steps prescribed by any method are rather like a guided bus tour of a text, where the bus moves quickly through those areas deemed (by the method) as unsuitable or inappropriate for tourists to examine and experience, so as to arrive quickly at the "important" areas. The steps of a method ignore, pass over, and thereby repress ideas, evidence, and voices in the texts that are present in the text but incompatible with the method. Methods, in other words, exercise power in the interpretive process, shaping what is possible in interpretation, both in terms of what the texts are allowed to mean and over the routes interpreters may take through the material.

A related problem is that methods create an illusion about how meaning is produced. Methods hold forth the promise that scholars need only follow a particular system of steps to obtain the text's meaning. For postmodern interpreters, this promise is illusory, since texts are made up of language, and language is inherently ambiguous. In addition, texts cannot define every word and term they use, since every definition or explanation will only introduce more words that need definition and explanation. Postmodern critics also have introduced the idea that authors do not even understand everything they "mean to say": they are unwittingly a part of their own ideological system and will be unaware of some of their own text's meanings. Thus, every text can be read in numerous ways. The modern concept of method ignores the gaps, inconsistencies, and alternative meanings that are a part of any text, that undermine and threaten any meaning asserted for it. It also ignores the role interpreters play in creating meaning for a text. Furthermore, it fails to recognize how methods privilege certain terms and repress others and the way in which those alternative terms are inherent in the privileged ones. Due to its supposedly systematic nature, a method exercises a particular kind of power over a text because it predetermines the possible meanings of a text. Postmodern interpreters seek to counter that exercise of power and allow multiple meanings of a text to emerge.

For these reasons, among others, postmodern readers eschew both calling their approaches "methods" and proposing systematic steps for others to follow. This is not to say postmodern readers claim there are no steps or assumptions in their own readings. On the contrary, they do. New Historicists, for example, readily acknowledge they make assumptions about texts, use critical tools for analysis in their readings, and therefore their own readings repress and exclude certain voices and perspectives. As H. Aram Veeser comments, "every act of unmasking, critique, and opposition uses the tools it condemns and risks falling prey to the practice it exposes."[3] Yet postmodern interpreters seek to be honest and self-critical about the problematic nature of their interpretations.

The nature of the Hebrew Bible as an object of study is another assumption challenged by postmodern interpreters. Complementing the assumption that the interpreter approaches the text largely independent of bias or other influence is the assumption that the Hebrew Bible is separate and distinct from its context, whether that context be understood as ancient or contemporary. New Historicists, in contrast, view writers of texts as inextricably bound up in their social, cultural, and historical contexts, incapable of separating themselves or their texts from them. Texts and other cultural products are instances of larger cultural energies, forces, and influences—ranging from words and phrases to power strategies and technologies—that circulate through societies and writers. The interpretive task is to investigate those social energies, to determine how they are present in texts, and therefore to trace the multiple connections between texts such as the Hebrew Bible and the cultural web of which they are an integral part.

The question of meaning, particularly absolute or ultimate meaning, is a final challenge postmodern interpreters make to the concept of method. For texts (or anything else) to convey absolute or ultimate Truth, the foundational claim of that text must be immediately available to anyone who reads it. Such an understanding involves metaphysics, or what Jacques Derrida calls "logocentrism."[4] Logocentrism signals the overlap between *logos*/Logos (historically, the Word of God) and presence, which is, in short, the idea that meaning may be immediately available to an individual.[5] Language, the supposed bearer of meaning, is composed of signs, and signs are notoriously tricky things to understand. Building on the work of Ferdinand de Saussure's *Course in General Linguistics*, Derrida shows that the unending referentiality of signs renders impossible the immediacy of the Logos.[6] Saussure defines the linguistic sign as an irreducible relationship of signifiers (i.e., the ideal sound-pattern of a spoken word) and signifieds (i.e., the particular concept associated with that sound-pattern). For example, with the sign "dog," the signifier refers to the idea of a four-legged domesticated animal that barks; this idea is the signified. "Dog," however, is simply the arbitrary English sign for this animal; the French sign is "chien." In neither case does the signifier ("dog," "chien") express the inherent nature or meaning of such an animal.

For Saussure, the "meaning" of a signifier is the signified. In turn, Derrida asks about the nature of the signified: What is it, and where do we find it? When we want to produce signifieds (that is, "meanings"), we must resort to "explaining" the signifier using a series of other words. That is, to give a meaning of a signifier, we must instead give more signifiers. A definition is simply more signs substituted for the initial sign. This process, Derrida notes, never produces anything other than more signifiers in varying patterns. There are only moments of relative stability when the signifiers arrange in particular patterns so that one signifier occupies something of a unique space among the other signifiers.

Given the temporary nature of the meaning of signifiers, Derrida argues there is no single, privileged signifier that represents Truth. There is no way to escape words and language in order to gain access into the world of "True Being" or "Real Things." This is why Derrida famously claims, "*There is nothing outside of the text* [there is no outside-text; *il n'y a pas de hors-texte*]."[7] That is, there is nothing that escapes this textual condition by simply containing pure meaning in and of itself. Likewise, there is no text that has one and only one Meaning. Interpretation cannot convey ultimate Truth; it can merely participate in the referential condition through its ongoing process of creating new interpretations.

In terms of methods for reading the Hebrew Bible, what this means is that using a particular method to ascertain "the meaning" of a text is impossible. Claims for an absolute meaning in a text (what someone once described as "the shining white rod of Truth behind the text") are unsustainable by an interpreter, because such meaning is always deferred, both by the text itself and by the interpreter, who uses language to express it. To be fair, many modern scholars assume that their methods do not reveal such secrets. But all of these scholars share an idea that their combined efforts are in some way shedding increasing light upon the true Meaning of the Hebrew Bible. From a postmodern perspective, because it is expressed in language, any meaning proposed for the Hebrew Bible is always provisional, limited, and contextual.

Four Postmodern Criticisms

If "postmodern literary criticism" is not a method, then what is it? Once again the challenge of writing about this topic becomes apparent, because there is no single entity, criticism, interrogation, investigation, reading, or approach that *is* postmodern literary criticism. There are, rather, a range of theories that qualify as "postmodern" or that move beyond (without completely negating) modernist modes of thought. In light of this fact, it is more appropriate to speak of postmodern literary *criticisms* and to think in terms of a class of objects than to think singularly of an object or topic. It also is important to recognize that this class of objects is not predicated on a monothetic classificatory system. It is, instead, a polythetic classificatory system. As Jonathan Z. Smith explains, a monothetic mode of classification seeks a single item as the basis upon which to make distinctions between each member of a taxonomic system, such that the members of a particular class within that system all share at least one feature in common. A polythetic mode of classification, by comparison, determines membership in a class by means of a set of properties, and each member of that class contains a large, if ultimately unspecified, number of them. Possession of any single property by each member of this class of objects is not required for membership.[8] This way of thinking about postmodern literary criticisms is consonant with certain commitments of postmodernism itself, in which the fixed boundaries of classificatory systems are problematic because of what they exclude. A polythetic mode of classification does not fix the boundaries, leaving open the possibility of movement within and between classes of objects.

What, then, constitutes the set of properties for the polythetic class of objects included in the category "postmodern literary criticisms"? Some of those properties have been indicated above, but there are others, including:

- a resistance to attributing absolute meaning to anything supposedly found or conveyed in texts or other cultural artifacts;
- a realization that every text, interpretation, system, or other social construction contains gaps, inconsistencies, and other lacks that betray and undermine them, despite efforts to obscure such gaps;
- an assertion that the gaps and inconsistencies in texts produce a surfeit of meanings, despite authorial attempts to restrict a text's meaning;
- the methodological stance that interpreters should seek to demonstrate the limited nature of all interpretive productions by revealing the gaps, inconsistencies, repressed voices, and other forms of discursive and political power each (including their own) seeks to exert, so as to create opportunities for alternative interpretations;
- from the linguistic turn, an interest in the intertextual nature of texts (that is, each and every "text" is composed of word-signs that derive from earlier texts and find their way into later texts, which calls into question authorial originality as well as the boundaries of any particular text);
- skepticism to systematic approaches to texts (i.e., methods) that exercise power over those texts, repress and obscure voices, perspectives, views, and ideas contrary to the assumptions and privileged terms of that method and its underlying social biases;
- an opposition to the act of privileging certain texts over others (e.g., canonical texts over archival texts), since this very act is

the result of social constructs, based on social assumptions and biases;

- an observation that interpreters are deeply implicated and entwined in the construction and production of meaning from "texts", and that interpreters are shaped by the social, political, economic, religious and theological, and other cultural realities of their context, which, in turn, shape their interpretations; and
- commitment to the impossibility of one interpretation dominating all others; therefore, interpretations may be meaningful within the interpreter's particular context, but not necessarily beyond it, which encourages other interpretations to be offered.

Labeling thinkers and modes of thought as "postmodern" is notoriously difficult, since many possible suspects, such as Derrida, Foucault, and Lacan, have rejected the label. However, using a very inclusive set of criteria, several objects, among others, can be said to share these properties: these include poststructuralism, deconstruction, Foucauldian studies, New Historicism, Lacanian psychoanalysis, critical spatial theory, feminist criticism, narratology, gender studies, intertextuality, womanist criticism, postcolonial criticism, ideological criticism, and culture studies (see *The Postmodern Bible*, which suggests something of the range of objects within this class).[9] Each of these theoretical perspectives shares a number of the properties listed above, yet there is no expectation that any single property is shared by all of them. Each investigates the Hebrew Bible differently, due to the different assumptions and lenses of their analytics.

Because postmodern literary criticisms constitute a class of theoretical perspectives, each of which could fill a chapter's discussion of its objectives, use in biblical studies, and implications for Hebrew Bible scholarship, I will discuss a smaller subset of them. This subset consists of deconstruction, the work of Michel Foucault, New Historicism, and postcolonial theory, and it suggests both the diversity of this class of objects as well as why they can be grouped together.

Deconstruction, which is closely linked with the work of Jacques Derrida, is an approach to texts and their interpretations that has thrilled and terrified many, both within and without biblical studies. Of particular concern in deconstruction is the demonstration that texts, their interpretation, and those who interpret them are not the stable objects they have been presumed to be. Such assumptions are understood as characteristics of modernism, the era in Western society and culture that is predominantly marked by Enlightenment ideas about human progress, human reason and justice, the ability of science and the scientific method to explain all aspects of existence and know it, confidence in the ability of technology and technological advances to aid in those explanations, and the autonomy of the human subject (the self). In biblical studies, this led to the view that texts such as the Hebrew Bible could be read and understood in their historical, social, and cultural contexts, the meaning of the texts in those contexts could be identified, and that meaning, once extracted, could be (re)interpreted for the modern context and community. Interpreters were thought to be objective and able to understand the nuances and vagaries of the ancient contexts out of which the biblical texts arose (assuming they could identify them correctly). As a result, interpreters assumed they could identify the particular and univocal meaning of the texts under study. This work was important because identifying the meaning meant identifying divine truth, the unchanging Word (Logos) of God contained in the biblical text.

Deconstruction undertakes very close readings of texts; in fact, Derrida himself is a model of rigorous exegesis. Through the course of his readings, Derrida deconstructed the above-mentioned modernist assumptions about texts, reading, and the interpretive process. These readings trace the logic of texts in order to reveal their instability, the result of inevitable jumps in logic, the surplus meanings of language, and other inconsistencies. The goal of such readings is not nihilism or the end of civilization, critics notwithstanding. At its best, deconstruction of the interpretive edifices built around the Hebrew Bible and other texts makes room for other interpretations to emerge from them. The effect of deconstructing the Hebrew Bible, such an important text in Western civilization and culture, is to allow more voices to be heard, not only within the text, but among those interpreting it. However, as critics such as Terry Eagleton have argued, demonstrating the instability of texts and interpretations does not leave one much to work with. In the end, deconstruction leaves a situation that Eagleton finds unpalatable, given the ongoing suffering and oppression in the world.[10] Deconstruction is a powerful tool of interpretation, but it leaves open the question of how to move forward from its conclusions, in however limited a way.

A number of biblical scholars have used deconstruction over the years. Early work with it spent time introducing and explaining it (e.g., Patriquin, Detweiler, Greenstein).[11] Much of this work used the insights from deconstruction in reading texts from the Writings, particularly wisdom texts and Psalms. Other readings followed in which scholars used deconstruction more fully as an investigative tool to open up texts (and their later interpretations), revealing new ways of understanding and interpreting Hebrew Bible texts, in more parts of it (e.g., Jobling, Clines, Sherwood).[12]

The work of Michel Foucault is difficult to classify, given that Foucault worked on a number of topics, from the history of science to prisons, sexuality, sociology, philosophy, and political science. Nevertheless, his work shares with other postmodern literary criticisms a rejection of absolute meaning, a denunciation of the assumption of any autonomy of texts or interpreters, support for the notion that interpreters are deeply shaped by their contexts, and the belief that "texts" are entwined in a larger social and cultural milieu. While he worked on a number of topics, the underlying concerns of Foucault focused on a society's "discourses." In Foucault's thinking, institutionally authorized patterns of speech and thought (called "discourses") shape the way all people perceive of their self and the world. For example, the rise of a scientific worldview radically changed the ways in which humans conceived of the human body (and mind) and interacted with their surroundings. These discourses, at certain times and places, define and effect what he calls "power/knowledge" and the ability to produce governable subjects in society. Since the possibilities of what one may do or think are in some way limited and shaped by discursive structures, what is defined as "knowledge" is simultaneously a form of power. It is the intimate connection between power and knowledge that Foucault signals in "power/knowledge." As a result, the subjects that are the object of social control are not autonomous selves. On the contrary, Foucault argues that the individual ("man") is a relatively recent creation in Western society, one that will disappear in the not too distant future.[13] In place of the autonomous individual is a human body shot through with multiple social discourses, the combination of which make possible a sense of self-awareness, because these discourses create identity, establish the range of possible behaviors, gender, speech patterns for that person, and so on. These discourses are the formal and informal ways whereby specific topics and areas of knowledge are discussed, the terminology used within them, determination of who gets to speak authoritatively about them, where and when they are discussed, and other ways in which social knowledge is produced. An individual's sense of self is determined by these discourses, which provide knowledge of the self and of what it consists (e.g., gender, socioeconomic status, education, family, abilities, religion or religious identity). Foucault sought to identify and explain how different discourses emerged, developed, and combined as mechanisms of political strategies attempting to govern societies and populations.

Direct engagement with Foucault's work among Hebrew Bible scholars has been less frequent than deconstruction. New Testament scholars have done more of this work, in part because of Foucault's work on human sexuality, the first volume of which begins in the Greek period.[14] Neither has there been as much engagement with New Historicism, which depends on Foucault's work in important ways for how such analyses are undertaken. This may well be because New Historicism, which emerged in English literature departments in the 1980s, marked a return to situating literature and literary texts within their social, cultural, and historical contexts, while the study of the Hebrew Bible never turned away from history and historical interpretation. New Historicism differs from the ways Hebrew Bible scholars pursue the study of history in that, like other postmodern approaches, it does not view texts as independent from their larger social, cultural contexts. Rather, texts are inextricably caught up in a larger web of ideas, behaviors, politics, economics, and other social forces, which weave themselves through any and every cultural production of a society. Consciously and unconsciously, authors of texts borrow, appropriate, acquire, reflect, and use words, themes, ideas, metaphors, and other social energies of their larger context in their works. New Historicism seeks to trace how those larger cultural contexts are present in texts, by identifying the social concerns, aspirations, and conflicts that shape and inform those texts. They also seek to explain how texts themselves participate in the creation of society and culture, in turn becoming part of that larger web of social energies and relations. Like Foucault's work, New Historicism is interested in larger social and cultural questions, so that the investigation of texts provides a means of studying societies and cultures in particular periods, rather than simply focusing on texts as isolated from those contexts. Several Hebrew Bible scholars explicitly have pursued New Historical interpretations and attempted to introduce and explain it in the field (e.g., Washington, Rowlett).[15]

Postcolonial criticism shares certain properties with deconstruction, Foucault, and New Historicism. It is overtly political, because it is concerned with the social, economic, cultural, and psychological impacts of imperialism and colonialism on colonized peoples, territories, and civilizations. This overt political focus stems in part from a perception that deconstruction, Foucauldian studies, and other poststructuralist and postmodern approaches to texts give too little attention to such matters. Postcolonial criticism aims to reconsider texts from the standpoint of the colonized, to examine the social, economic, cultural, and political impact of colonialism on both the colonized and the colonizer, to examine the process of decolonization, and to seek liberatory interpretations of texts, so that texts may be available to all and marginalized voices and cultural identities may be given expression vis-à-vis those texts.[16] This work attempts to understand the discursive images of the colonized that were created by the colonizers and how the colonized used and subverted such images, moving beyond them to create their own self-understandings, identities, and images. Interpretations of the Bible have played an important role in colonial practices, whether in the historical period of European colonization or in the neo-colonialism of the early twenty-first century, expressed in terms of globalization, multiculturalism, and cultural imperialism (see, e.g., the *Semeia* volumes dedicated to these issues).[17] Postcolonial criticism also works through what R. S. Sugirtharajah terms "cognate disciplines," which he broadly identifies as "liberative movements," an example of which is feminism.[18] These cognate disciplines share with postcolonial criticism the task of revealing "the subjugation of both men and women in colonial texts, and the modes of resistance of the subjugated, and expose the use of gender in both colonial discourse and social reality."[19] It should be noted, finally, that there is contention and disagreement among postcolonial scholars and their readings over terminology, the scope of the work, how it proceeds, the object(s) of its study(-ies), and other matters. Rather than producing *angst* or despair, such contention is taken as part and parcel of this critical approach and therefore encouraged.

Josiah, the Deuteronomic Code, and the Disciplinary State

> If anyone secretly entices you—even if it is your brother, your father's son or your mother's son, or your own son or daughter, or the wife you embrace, or your most intimate friend—saying, "Let us go worship other gods," whom neither you nor your ancestors have known, any of the gods of the peoples that are around you, whether near you or far away from you, from one end of the earth to the other, you must not yield to or heed any such persons. Show them no pity or compassion and do not shield them. But you shall surely kill them; your own hand shall be first against them to execute them, and afterwards the hand of all the people.

> Stone them to death for trying to turn you away from the LORD your God, who brought you out of the land of Egypt, out of the house of slavery. Then all Israel shall hear and be afraid, and never again do any such wickedness. (Deut 13:6–11 NRSV [13:7–12 MT])

In the Deuteronomistic History, Josiah receives a positive evaluation by the Historian (2 Kgs 22:2) because of his religious reforms. He restored the Jerusalem temple, where the book of the law was found and, from the Deuteronomist's viewpoint, acted appropriately after hearing it (2 Kgs 22:3–20). Josiah shut down all the high places, removed all the objects associated with other deities from the temple in Jerusalem and throughout Judah, deposed or killed priests and diviners of other gods, commanded observance of Passover, and performed other religious and social reforms (2 Kgs 23:4–25). Apart from his reforms, however, the Deuteronomist has almost no interest in Josiah. The rest of Josiah's life and reign is summarized in a few sentences (2 Kgs 22:1–2; 23:28) before being quickly ended with his death at the hands of Pharaoh Neco (2 Kgs 23:29–30).

The Deuteronomist's focus on Josiah's religious reforms creates the impression that he exercised political power exclusively in the public domain, where he acted in dramatic ways. From the moment when he has the book of the law read to the population of Judah and Jerusalem at the temple (2 Kgs 23:1–2), to his removal of the mediums, wizards, teraphim, idols, and all other objects considered to be abominations (2 Kgs 23:24), Josiah acts in public. His purpose through these actions are, according to the Deuteronomist, to "[establish] the words of the law that were written in the book that the priest Hilkiah had found in the house of the LORD" (2 Kgs 23:24), which also is part of the drama of his actions.

Josiah's actions are part of how he, and through him the state, governs the populations of Judah and Jerusalem. As Jean-Louis Ska notes, religious centralization "was accompanied by judicial centralization. The extended family had to relinquish a large part of its power to the central authority in Jerusalem."[20] That judicial centralization, however, was not limited to actions that occurred in the public domain. Those public actions—centralizing worship and cultic practices in Jerusalem (Deut 12), killing diviners and others who enable communication with "other gods" (Deut 18), and observance of Passover (Deut 16)—correspond with behaviors explicitly commanded in the Deuteronomic Code (Deut 12–26). It is quickly apparent when reading the Code, however, that public displays of political power are not all that it commands. On the contrary, its common form of address, to an unspecified second-person masculine singular subject, indicates that the Code is as concerned with the population of Judah and Jerusalem as it is with the king and the exercise of royal power.[21] This suggests that the Deuteronomic Code enabled Josiah to exercise power over the population in ways other than by dramatic public actions. That he did so is indicated through his public actions: the book is read to all the people (i.e., population) at the temple, and Josiah and the population enter into a covenant with YHWH immediately after hearing it (2 Kgs 23:1–2).

How, then, is power exercised over the population, assuming the Deuteronomic Code provided the basis for Josiah's efforts at centralizing in Jerusalem (and the state) control over that population? For this, Foucault's understanding of power, especially judicial power, is important. Power functions in various ways in a society, beyond its ability to tax, conscript, adjudicate, kill, and pardon. It also is found in more subtle social mechanisms. The judicial centralization that Ska notes Josiah and his government introduced in Judah, by which the central government assumed power once held by the extended family, is one example of the subtle mechanisms of power over a population.[22] More is at work in Judean society, according to Deut 12–26, than simply (re)introducing the Decalogue and the laws based on it.

The Decalogue (Deut 5:6–21) is what Foucault describes as a judicial mechanism. It operates on a system of binaries, classifying actions and behaviors of that population as permissible or prohibited, and thus acceptable or unacceptable: "you shall have no other gods before me" (5:7); "neither shall you steal" (5:19). But the Code also is a judicial mechanism, operating in addition to that of the Decalogue: "you must not yield to or heed anyone who secretly entices you to follow other gods" (see 13:8); "you shall not boil a kid in its mother's milk" (14:21). The judicial mechanism is accompanied by spectacular punishments: death by stoning; imposition of the ban; banishment. The Decalogue implies such punishments (by means of its form), and the Code either implies them or spells them out ("show them no pity or compassion and do not shield them. But you shall surely kill them"; 13:8–9).

In addition to the public spectacle of the judicial mechanism, the Code makes use of a disciplinary mechanism as a political strategy. This disciplinary mechanism uses punishment to bring about a corrective effect, if not on the one who violates the law (because he is killed), then on those who watch the punishment being carried out: "Stone them to death for trying to turn you away from the LORD your God.… Then all Israel shall hear and be afraid, and never again do any such wickedness" (Deut 13:10–11); "As for anyone who presumes to disobey the priest ... or the judge, that person shall die.... All the people will hear and be afraid, and will not act presumptuously again" (17:12–13). The disciplinary mechanism thus seeks to effect a change in the behavior of the population and, in doing so, controls and directs that behavior to those actions the state finds acceptable. This mechanism leads to a third, the mechanism of security, whereby the state seeks to anticipate probable violations of the law: "You must demolish completely all the places where the nations whom you are about to dispossess served their gods" (12:2); "When you come into the land the LORD your God is giving you, you must not learn to imitate the abhorrent practices of those nations" (18:9).[23]

Recognizing there are various mechanisms at work in the Deuteronomic Code enables a more nuanced understanding of how Josiah's use of it as the basis for his centralization efforts permitted him to exercise power over the population. A series of judicial mechanisms, verified by the prophetess Huldah as being the authentic word of YHWH (2 Kgs 22:18–19), laid out for the people permissible and prohibited actions. They established a range of behaviors, including how and where they should worship their god, what meat they should eat (or not) and how they should slaughter it, what festival times they must observe, the ways of the king, property rights, warfare and the treatment of captives, the treatment of slaves, sexual and marital behavior, and membership in the assembly. A series of punishments accompanied those judicial mechanisms, many of which were dramatic. Indeed, Josiah's request when sending his servants to verify the words of the book concerns those punishments, "for great is the wrath of the LORD that is kindled against us, because our ancestors did not obey the words of the book, to do according to all that is written concerning us" (2 Kgs 22:13). Punishment for failure to observe the words of the book are especially dire: the loss of the city and nation as the deity turns against the people. But other dramatic, if less apocalyptic, punishments also appear with the judicial mechanisms of the Code: stoning; death by hanging; cutting off of body parts; and death by other, unspecified, means.

The Code also contains disciplinary mechanisms. Four times in the Code, for example, punishment by death is prescribed for specific actions: enticing a person to follow other gods (Deut 13:12); not obeying the judgment of a priest or prophet (17:13); bearing false witness (19:20); and being a rebellious son (21:21). The purpose of enforcing the death penalty is so that others will "hear and be afraid" (19:20). The importance of others hearing and being afraid is that they should not engage in such actions again (13:12; 17:13; 19:20). As a punishment, death is severe and dramatic, but it can have a corrective effect on the population, discouraging others from engaging in the same actions and suffering the same fate. Other disciplinary mechanisms are found in the repeated calls that the people "diligently observe" the commandments (12:1, 32; 16:12; 19:9), that they remember they were slaves in Egypt (24:18, 22), that they not add or reduce the commandments or turn to the left or the right (12:32; 17:11, 20; 24:19, 21), and that they be careful to obey the commandments (12:28; 13:4, 18; 15:5; 26:7). By taking heed of these disciplinary mechanisms, the population will avoid the fate of those who violate the judicial mechanisms and suffer the punishments.

The security mechanism also is in evidence in the Deuteronomic Code. The judicial mechanisms occasionally are framed by anticipatory statements: "when you come into the land" (Deut 17:14; 18:9; 26:1, 3); "when you cross over the Jordan" (12:10); "there will be no one in need among you because the LORD is sure to bless you in the land" (15:4); "when the LORD your God has cut off the nations whose land the LORD your God is giving you, and you have dispossesd them" (19:1). Possible violations of the law are anticipated even before the people enter the land.

Identification of the various social mechanisms at work in the Deuteronomic Code helps explain how Josiah's centralization worked to effect itself even beyond the dramatic, public actions he performed. Judicial and disciplinary mechanisms are prominent in the Code, and they were effective because they did not require royal action in order to be effective. Instead, responsibility for observing and enacting the commandments of the Code was the responsibility of each member (or at least each male) of the population. They implicitly became agents of the state and enforcers of its Code because of the explicit commandments that they be vigilant against violating that Code, whether that violation be of their own doing or of the actions of another. In Deut 13:6–11, for example, the Code clearly spells out the judicial mechanism—do not entice someone in secret to worship other gods—and the accompanying punishment: stoning. The person who is approached by the family member or friend is authorized to act immediately against that individual: "your own hand shall be first against them to execute them, and afterwards the hand of all the people" (Deut 13:9). The king need not be consulted, nor even a priest, prophet, or elder. Responsibility for obeying the commandment lies with each member of the population, who are urged repeatedly to observe and keep the commands (12:1, 32; 13:4, 18; 16:12; 19:9; 26:7, 16) without adding to them or taking away from them (12:32) or turning to the right or the left (17:11, 20). By placing this responsibility on each person, power becomes more diffuse in Israel, even while being centralized. The state (i.e., Josiah and the royal administration) legitimates the legal code (the Deuteronomic Code), but the agents who maintain and enforce it are the people.

Foucault's work provides a different way of analyzing Hebrew Bible texts. His arguments about the ways in which political systems exert their influence and control over populations make that "different way" possible. Josiah's use of the Deuteronomic Code enabled him to establish a disciplinary state, one whose effects were multiplied by the self-regulation of the population. The Deuteronomistic Historian praised him for his public actions to centralize Israel's religious practices, but the judicial centralization he achieved with the help of the Code, while less dramatic, was an even more important effort to transform Judah and Jerusalem.

For Further Reading

The Bible and Culture Collective. *The Postmodern Bible*. New Haven: Yale University Press, 1995.

Clines, David J. A. "What Remains of the Hebrew Bible? Its Text and Language in a Postmodern Age." *ST* 56 (2002): 76–95.

Detweiler, Robert. *Derrida and Biblical Studies*. *Semeia* 23 (1982).

Greenstein, Edward L. "Deconstruction and Biblical Narrative." *Proof* 9 (1989): 43–71.

Habib, M. A. R. *Modern Literary Criticism and Theory: A History*. Malden, Mass.: Blackwell, 2008.

Hens-Piazza, Gina. *The New Historicism*. GBS. Minneapolis: Fortress, 2002.

Jobling, David. "Deconstruction and the Political Analysis of Biblical Texts: A Jamesonian Reading of Psalm 72." *Semeia* 59 (1992): 95–127.

Sherwood, Yvonne, ed. *Derrida's Bible (Reading a Page of Scripture with a Little Help from Derrida)*. Religion/culture/critique. New York: Palgrave Macmillan, 2004.

Sugirtharajah, R. S. *Postcolonial Criticism and Biblical Interpretation*. Oxford: Oxford University Press, 2002.

Notes

1. Gina Hens-Piazza, *The New Historicism* (GBS; Minneapolis: Fortress, 2002), 7.

2. Jean-Francois Lyotard, *The Postmodern Condition: A Report on Knowledge* (trans. Geoff Bennington and Brian Massumi; Manchester: Manchester University Press, 1984), xxiv.

3. H. Aram Veeser, *The New Historicism* (New York: Routledge, 1989), xi.

4. While Derrida is generally considered "poststructuralist," or moving beyond the claims of structuralism that were initiated by Ferdinand de Saussure's thought, his work resonates with many of the claims attributed to postmodernism in general.

5. Jacques Derrida, *Of Grammatology* (trans. Gayatri Chakravorty Spivak; Baltimore: Johns Hopkins University Press, 1997), 3. See also Peggy Kamuf, ed., *A Derrida Reader: Between the Blinds* (New York: Columbia University Press, 1991), 31–33, M. A. R. Habib, *Modern Literary Criticism and Theory: A History* (Malden, Mass.: Blackwell, 2008), 101.

6. Ferdinand de Saussure, *Course in General Linguistics* (ed. Charles Bally et al.; trans. Roy Harris; LaSalle, Ill.: Open Court, 1986).

7. Derrida, *Of Grammatology*, 158, emphasis original.

8. Jonathan Z. Smith, "Fences and Neighbors: Some Contours of Early Judaism," in idem, *Imagining Religion: From Babylon to Jonestown* (CSHJ; Chicago: University of Chicago Press, 1982), 1–18.

9. The Bible and Culture Collective, *The Postmodern Bible* (New Haven: Yale University Press, 1995).

10. Terry Eagleton, *Literary Theory: An Introduction* (2nd. ed.; Minneapolis: University of Minnesota Press, 1996), 125.

11. Allan Patriquin, "Deconstruction, Plurivocity, and Silence," *Semeia* 19 (1981): 121–23; Robert Detweiler, ed., *Derrida and Biblical Studies*, *Semeia* 23 (1982); idem, "What Is a Sacred Text," *Semeia* 31 (1985): 213–30; Edward L. Greenstein, "Deconstruction and Biblical Narrative," *Proof* 9 (1989): 43–71.

12. David Jobling, "Deconstruction and the Political Analysis of Biblical Texts: A Jamesonian Reading of Psalm 72," *Semeia* 59 (1992): 95–127; David J. A. Clines, "What Remains of the Hebrew Bible? Its Text and Language in a Postmodern Age," *ST* 56 (2002): 76–95; Yvonne Sherwood, ed., *Derrida's Bible: Reading a Page of Scripture with a Little Help from Derrida* (Religion/culture/critique; New York: Palgrave Macmillan, 2004).

13. Michel Foucault, *The Order of Things: An Archaeology of the Human Sciences* (New York: Pantheon, 1971), xxiii.

14. Michel Foucault, *The History of Sexuality* (New York: Pantheon, 1978).

15. Harold C. Washington, "Violence and the Construction of Gender in the Hebrew Bible: A New Historicist Approach," *BibInt* 5 (1997): 324–63; Lori L. Rowlett, *Joshua and the Rhetoric of Violence: A New Historicist Analysis* (JSOTSup 226; Sheffield: Sheffield Academic Press, 1996).

16. See the helpful explanation of postcolonial criticism and several of its central practitioners in Habib, *Modern Literary Criticism*, 159–71.

17. Roland Boer, ed., *A Vanishing Mediator? The Presence/Absence of the Bible*

in Postcolonialism, *Semeia* 88 (2001); and Laura Donaldson, ed., *Postcolonialism and Scriptural Reading*, *Semeia* 75 (1996).

18. R. S. Sugirtharajah, *Postcolonial Criticism and Biblical Interpretation* (Oxford: Oxford University Press, 2002), 28.

19. Sugirtharajah, *Postcolonial Criticism and Biblical Interpretation*, 29. Sugirtharajah's work has given important shape to postcolonial criticism in biblical studies; see also idem, *The Postcolonial Bible* (Bible and Postcolonialism 1; Sheffield: Sheffield Academic Press, 1998); idem, *The Bible and Empire: Postcolonial Explorations* (Cambridge: Cambridge University Press, 2005); idem, *The Postcolonial Biblical Reader* (Malden, Mass.: Blackwell, 2006).

20. Jean-Louis Ska, *Introduction to Reading the Pentateuch* (trans. Pascale Dominique; Winona Lake, Ind.: Eisenbrauns, 2006), 188–89.

21. I assume this second masculine singular form is the collective singular, used to address the entire population; see Richard D. Nelson, *Deuteronomy: A Commentary* (OTL; Louisville: Westminster John Knox, 2002), 6.

22. Ska, *Introduction to Reading the Pentateuch*, 188–89.

23. See Foucault's descriptions of the judicial, disciplinary, and security mechanisms and how they function are part of his analysis of "bio-power," the mechanisms by which Western societies made humanity an object of political strategies. See Michel Foucault, *Security, Territory, Population: Lectures at the Collège de France, 1977–78* (ed. Michel Senellart et al.; trans. Graham Burchell; Basingstoke, U.K.: Palgrave Macmillan, 2007), 4–7. While his analyses are concerned with Western societies from the eighteenth century onward, he recognized that societies before that time used these same mechanisms, albeit in different ways.

Reflections on the "Historical-Critical" Method: Historical Criticism and Critical Historicism

Martti Nissinen

"Die Liebe ist hier wie bei jeder Interpretation die beste Lehrmeisterin des Forschers."[1] (Hugo Greßmann)

Lamenting Historical Criticism?

Historical criticism, once considered the one and only legitimate scholarly method of investigating the biblical text, toward the end of the second millennium has been deprived of its status as *the* academic approach to the Bible. Itself a product of history and the so-called Enlightenment in particular, historical criticism is undergoing a redefinition under the influence of the post-Enlightenment mood of the emerging third millennium. It has never been a fixed and unaltered entity, though; Hugo Greßmann maintained already in 1924 that, while there is a unanimity to some degree about historical understanding being the actual purpose of Old Testament studies, a living scholarship will always produce new ways of attaining such understanding.[2] Greßmann was right, even though he could hardly imagine the course historical scholarship would take along with the "linguistic turn," that is, the idea that reality is constituted by language, which dismisses the ideal of historical objectivity not only as unreachable but as entirely impossible.[3] Moreover, the heterogeneous set of approaches coined as postmodernism has by its very elusiveness put the traditional self-image of historical criticism as an objective and disinterested scholarly pursuit in a melting pot.

The postmodern contention that there is no reality outside the text itself has challenged biblical criticism, as historical studies in general, throughout the latter part of the twentieth century. Since the radical antihistoricism of some postmodernist and poststructuralist theories attempts to render history as an awkward endeavor leading to an epistemological impasse, it has, therefore, not attracted the majority of (biblical) historians. As a result, new ways of formulating the task of historical criticism, refuting the objectivist and foundationalist assumptions, have been developed. Many scholars who would not carry the torch of postmodernism, at least not in its most radical appearance, are ready to admit that the challenge of postmodernism has forced historians to interrogate their methods of interpretation and encounter their own subjectivity.[4] Historical approaches inspired by poststructuralist theories, such as the New Historicism,[5] which turns away from theory and moves back toward the social contexts of the production of the texts, have been welcomed by a fair number of biblical critics, especially those whose research focuses on the biblical text itself as a historical product.[6]

Reading the biblical text as a literary product of history is one thing, while reconstructing history on its basis is another. Historical methodology has been a matter of controversy also in recent discussions concerning the possibility of reconstruction of past events using the biblical text as a historical source. The issues of writing the history of Israel[7] and chronology of the late Iron Age Palestine[8] have stirred heated debates among biblical scholars and archaeologists, produced a significant number of publications, and guaranteed big audiences for sessions where the debates have taken place, not to mention the public interest evident on television and in the press more generally.

No less than three decades ago, Leander Keck asked whether the historical-critical method would survive.[9] When David Clines presented an outspokenly critical review of historical criticism in Helsinki in 2007 with the title "Historical Criticism: Are Its Days Numbered?"[10] his answer was rather in the negative: historical biblical studies still seem to be well alive and going strong. Thus, in the absence of the corpse, there seems to be no reason for lamenting historical biblical criticism. This, however, should not grant its practitioners the luxury of resting on their laurels—at least not if the designation "critical" is supposed to do any justice to its meaning. Far from being in a state of endangerment, historical biblical studies should not let themselves be lulled into the idea that "the postmodernist challenge will eventually go away,"[11] thus missing the opportunity of self-critical reflection.

"Historical-critical method" may not be the best possible designation for what it conventionally represents. Not all biblical studies placed under this heading are specifically historical, whereas studies that come forward as historical cannot always be considered critical. It is also worth asking whether all this should be called hypothesis, approach, or orientation but not a "method,"[12] which sounds more like a technical procedure than an interpretive intellectual pursuit. A further difficulty with the designation "historical-critical method" is its implied reference to a certain *Methodenkanon* of biblical studies—that is, the compound of textual criticism, source criticism, form criticism, and redaction criticism—which no longer constitutes the full agenda of historical biblical criticism. Nevertheless, taken as such, both "historical" and "critical" are genuinely descriptive of a broad range of approaches to the biblical text; therefore, it suggests itself to reflect their meaning and significance—indeed, their necessity—in the landscape of contemporary biblical studies.

I want to begin my reflections with a personal note. That biblical studies ought to be driven by a historical interest is far less self-evident today than it was at the University of Helsinki in the early 1980s, when I took my basic courses in biblical studies (or "exegetics," as the discipline was called) under the guidance of such well-known masters of historical criticism as Heikki Räisänen, the "fair-player" who programmatically transgresses the boundaries of biblical canon and theology,[13] and Timo Veijola, whose approach was as pointedly historical as it was theological—and, toward the sudden end of his life, increasingly canonical.[14] "New" methodologies, even though no longer new, played a minor role in my scholarly upbringing, although I came to witness my teachers' opening up toward the challenges coming from outside of the conventional *Methodenkanon*.[15] Instead of new methodologies, my scope was broadened toward ancient Near Eastern texts—and not primarily as the "context of Scripture," for that matter—when I continued my studies with Oswald Loretz the Ugaritologist[16] and Simo Parpola the Assyriologist, both known as rigid and enthusiastic philologists whose interest has never been restricted to their narrowly defined fields of scholarship. Later on, I became interested in gender studies (needless to say, mainly from a historical perspective) and learned valuable lessons of archaeological practice in the excavations of the Iron Age city of Kinneret.[17]

I relate all this, not to demonstrate any sense of a sovereign stewardship of the field, but to show where I come from and how proud I am to be the student of my teachers—and, at the same time, to give the reader an idea about where the limits of my own objectivity may be found, what kind of subjectivity I am accountable for, and where my blindspots might be found.[18]

Why *Historical*? The Necessity of Historical Criticism

Why *historical*? To me, the question of the necessity of historical criticism implies not so much a need for an apology, let alone a reactionary defense of historical biblical studies against inimical incursions of postmodernism, as a reflection of my own work. Therefore, I would not like to frame the question as a binary opposition between historical criticism and its postmodern/poststructuralist/post-Enlightenment critics. The historical/nonhistorical divide does not appear to me as particularly useful in describing the current methodological agenda of biblical criticism. Whether one understands historical criticism mainly as a literary paradigm or sees its aim in historical reconstruction, what matters is *the relatedness and otherness between the critic and the source*, ancient or modern, the interplay between times and spaces in the hermeneutical process, in which "scholars should seek to understand the differing cultural and moral views of past and present societies—and to recognize the limited and often provincial quality of their own."[19] I have learned a lot from scholars who are persuaded by approaches other than historical but who are still familiar with the traditional historical-critical practice,[20] and I hope to be able to make this visible in what follows.

Having reached the point where historical criticism has been taken down from its pedestal of objectivity and the relativity of the historical knowledge is acknowledged, it is time to formulate the question positively: Why is historical criticism necessary, anyway? The following points are neither exhaustive nor presented in any particular order but represent my idea of why historical criticism should be praticed in the present-day social reality as I perceive it as a male, white, Finnish, Lutheran, heterosexual, and middle-aged member of the guild of biblical and ancient Near Eastern scholars.[21]

(1) Because it helps us to understand our own time and culture. Historical criticism can be seen as the (grand)mother or the midwife of most critical approaches to the Bible that have come to the fore in the twentieth century, at the very least in the sense that nonhistorical biblical studies have often emerged as a rebellion against the hegemony of the dominant paradigm. One could say that, for the purposes of the present-day society, it is more important to teach how this text is read and used today,[22] but even the present day is history tomorrow, and remembering the past is an important constituent element in perceiving the present.[23]

While not being more foundational than other approaches, historical criticism is necessary to develop an understanding that the phenomena of the present world are the result of historical developments. As Dobbs-Allsopp poignantly remarks, "By studying the past we learn that the direction which history takes is contingent rather than absolute.... This knowledge of the contingency in the past can then make us aware of the changeability of the present."[24] Therefore, the interest of historical criticism is not only and narrowly antiquarian but ultimately hermeneutical.[25]

(2) Because historical questions require historical criticism. To have a job properly done, appropriate tools have to be used;[26] cutting the lawn with an axe simply does not work. Historical questions require historical criticism, but not all relevant questions are historical. There are significant areas of biblical scholarship where historical issues are of little or no relevance. Theological and lingustic studies, even though usually done under the label of the historical-critical method, need not be primarily concerned with historical issues, let alone methods related to literary criticism, such as rhetorical or reader-response criticism, or those related to ideological criticism, such as cultural or postcolonial criticism, or many other approaches, such as psychological reading of the Bible. The relevance of different approaches should always be interrogated, but the worst one can do is to resort to historical criticism in order to avoid important but discomforting issues raised by, say, feminist or postcolonial approaches, by declaring them irrelevant because they are not historical (and, by implication, not critical either)—which is not true. There is a historical dimension even to studies that deal with contemporary issues.

Biblical studies are done in time and space and are, therefore, always related to communities and readerships in history, ancient or modern. Indeed, many of the practitioners of, say, feminist and postcolonial studies necessarily work on historical themes that are not necessarily inspired by postmodernism. Colonialism, if anything, is a historical phenomenon;[27] reception criticism can be characterized as "a reader-response criticism cast on a historical plane";[28] the study of the modern construction of gender is greatly indebted to the Foucauldian concept of the "history of sexuality";[29] feminist criticism is often deconstruction and/or interpretation of ideologies of the past.[30]

(3) Because the Bible is a representative of ancient Near Eastern literature. As important as it is to understand the role of the Bible as a book that is printed, sold, read, and imposed upon in the present-day world in countless languages and different contexts, it is also necessary to appreciate its otherness as an ancient text produced in a world alien to us. Biblical

studies need to be pursued in interaction and mutual appreciation with archaeology, Assyriology, Egyptology, Semitic philology, studies in classical antiquity, history of religion, and other fields of scholarship in which the relatedness and otherness between the critic and source has a historical dimension. This is important, both to be able to recognize the cultural situatedness of the producers of the biblical texts and to prevent the "biblical world," whether historical or literary, to become a virtual world on its own terms. Moreover, colleagues in these fields deserve to have discussion partners among biblical scholars who understand their language. As a matter of fact, many biblical scholars have expertise not only in biblical texts but also in one or more of the above-mentioned areas.

(4) Because historical criticism serves the public. This easily entices the biblical scholar to enjoy the rare opportunity of basking in the spotlight of publicity, but it is nevertheless vitally important that biblical scholars realize their responsibility for informing the public about their scholarship, often sponsored by taxpayers who have the right to know how public funds are spent. A typical situation for a biblical critic to be approached by mass media is when public attention is captured by sensational news concerning a newly discovered or publicized text or artifact. Historical critics render a good service by providing the general public with informed and critical, even media-savvy, assessments of the object in question.[31] The media are often on the move for goal-oriented answers of the type "… and the Bible is thus (not) true." Thus, is the task of the historical critic to refute uncritical historizing, to relativize biblicist or antibiblicist claims to the truth or untruth of the biblical text, to point out the potential exploitation of scholarship as continuation of politics,[32] and to assess critically the significance (or lack thereof) of the matter at issue for contemporary concerns, not retiring behind the screen of purportedly disinterested detachment. Doing so, the scholar fulfills his or her duty as a responsible citizen, which brings us to the next point.

(5) Because it is politically relevant. As the self-image of "objectivity" of biblical scholarship has turned out to be false, "to acknowledge that the critic is inextricably bound to and influenced by his or her own cultural-historical context is by default to acknowledge that the critic's interpretations and reconstructions of texts from the past must have relevance in the present as well."[33] This acknowledgement inevitably means that the different historical reconstructions and their alleged relevance cannot be presented as a historically ascertained truth. Their relevance is always at issue and has to be evaluated against the background of contemporary concerns.

This becomes very clear when one compares the contrasting strategies of assessing the present-day relevance of the historical knowledge of same-sex eroticism in two recent books written by two biblical historians coming from similar academic background but different traditions of biblical interpretation[34] and their critical reception from the point of view of, for example, gender theories[35] and historical scholarship.[36]

(6) Because it is relevant for theology and for religious communities. Historical critics have often been seen as hostile toward faith-based readings of the Bible, which, therefore, should be reclaimed for the church.[37] In contrast to this, however, some would regard most of the contemporary biblical scholarship as theological practice under the camouflage of historical criticism.[38]

The relationship between historical criticism and theology is a complex one and is understood in a variety of ways. Many would opt for "history of Israelite religion" instead of "theology of the Old/New Testament,"[39] while others would consider both categories to be legitimate but methodologically incompatible,[40] and yet others take the antithesis to be mistaken altogether.[41] Evidently, the discussion is impaired by different sensitivities of the scholars toward the concept of "theology" and the equally different meanings they give to it. When reading biblical texts as historical literary products, it can be reasonably argued that texts communicating religious experiences always have a theological horizon that deserves to be understood as a part of the historian's encounter with the text.[42] On the other hand, it is equally justified to argue that, when biblical texts are used as a source of information on ancient history, this should not be influenced by any kind of theological recontextualization, ancient or modern.[43]

Now if "theology" in itself implies a confessional bias, the biblical critic should indeed be on the alert about what he or she is doing. In those academic settings, however, where biblical studies are housed in faculties of theology together with church history, systematic theology, practical theology, and even religious studies, biblical scholars *are* theologians by virtue of their education, and this title does not imply that their study is driven by a confessional commitment. What is (or at least should be) practiced as "theology" in these contexts is critical study of religious texts, traditions, and communities in conversation and cooperation with other disciplines in a mutually understandable language and methodology.[44] In this interdisciplinary enterprise, historical criticism of the Bible is a necessary discussion partner, and the benefit is mutual:

much of the work of biblical critics is analyzing how the theological discourse works in their sources. On the other hand, historical critics can help to recognize what kind of transformations of meaning take place when theologians, ancient or modern, recontextualize texts that are already de- and recontextualized in the biblical canon.[45]

(7) Because it is fun. I am not joking. Few of us would do historical studies out of mere responsibility or sheer boredom. Many of us are simply fascinated by history, but this fascination ridicules all disciplined explanations, all objectivity, hence the epigraphic motto of this article, and hence the lack of a footnote at this point.

Why *Critical*? Toward a Critical Historicism

If the quest for an objective—that is, a single and complete—description of the full and authentic past is to be rejected as a foundationalist project that neither does justice to the multiple perspectives of the sources nor to the present-day diversity of relevant research questions, what kind of historical approach could still be called *critical*? I attempt an approach I would like to call "critical historicism" by reflecting upon the following four topics.

History Is Relatedness

Both the historian and the sources are historically situated, hence history is a relation between historically contingent representations of reality at both ends. Therefore, historical criticism requires a "wholehearted embrace of historical contingency, both with respect to the texts which are the object of study and to the people who are doing the studying."[46] The situatedness of the historian means that all study is done and all questions asked within a social, academic, and personal context, which is always reflected by the researcher's list of priorities and the hierarchy of relevant questions. The situatedness of the objects of study, again, means that, while being socially determined products of their own environment, they at the same time contribute to constructing their own time and culture instead of merely presenting photographic snapshots of it.

History, whether ancient or contemporary, is all about distance, otherness, and interpretation. There is an inevitable temporal and cultural distance between the historian and the past, between the context of the researcher and that of the source. Coping with this distance requires the establishment of a relation that is possible only when the otherness of the source in relation to the historian is recognized. Historical scholarship has been well aware of the *historicity of texts*, that is, their cultural specificity and social embeddedness. What may not have been fully acknowledged is the *textuality of history*, that is, that the past is accessible to us only through the mediation of textual remains, themselves subject to subsequent textual mediations.[47]

The otherness also means that the historian remains an outsider; where there is no direct access to the object of study, the only way to make sense of it is interpretation. In spite of the distance between the historian and the source, the objects of study "can never be wholly other from the interpreting self over against which they stand."[48] To come to terms with a textualized history in spite of the inevitable distance with the source and otherness it reflects, the text must be taken up into the researcher's consciousness, which, again, is historically situated, socially determined, personal, and subjective. But the very textuality of the source means that it has an existence independent of the reader. The distance between the text and the reader remains there; the otherness cannot be chased away.[49]

History Is a Construction

The slogan "wie es eigentlich gewesen" (how things really were) seems to be all that is remembered of Leopold von Ranke, one of the founding fathers of modern historiography, to whom all historical studies owe much of their source-based critical approach.[50] Von Ranke's ghost is usually conjured up as a caricature of the idea of historical objectivity,[51] "that noble dream" that was challenged long before postmodernism.[52] Very few (biblical) historians would stand up to defend a naïve objectivity today, yet there is a certain "reluctance among practicing historians to give up the idea that there is some connection between what they write and past reality."[53] This attitude could be called "reasonable objectivity,"[54] which acknowledges the otherness of the text and its world in relation to the world and experience of the reader. It is the referential illusion, that is, the idea of a direct referentiality between the source and historical factuality, that should be at issue rather than the straw man of objectivity,[55] for if the modern historians are subjective, so were the authors of written sources.

History is not a sequence of past events that the historian discovers but the intellectual construction that the historian creates on the basis of the available evidence; every history is the creative product of the human mind.[56] It is only the historian's creative (and ultimately subjective) process of collecting, selecting, arranging, contextualizing, and interpreting the available sources that gives a meaning to the pluriform historical data. This process makes the historical narrative possible—a narrative that is not a neutral description of past events but something that "serves to impose coherence, continuity, and closure on the messiness of life and of the historian's sources."[57] This means that historical studies of any kind, including biblical studies, are not likely to produce assured results; moreover, there is no more room for the "genetic fallacy," that is, the quest for "original" meanings as potentially superior to secondary interpretations.[58] Nevertheless, inquiring into the history of the emergence of texts and other cultural products (or, for instance, one's own mind) is often illuminating, even though the claim to provide a full and definitive explanation is, without any doubt, a fallacy.

The most immediate relation is not between the historian and the past but between the historian and the sources. The sources, again, disallow access to a full and authentic past. This is because the sources, too, are constructions of their authors and tell in the first place how they perceived and represented the things they describe. While referring to past events, the sources do not imply a direct link to the past. Especially in narrative sources, the past is a constituent in the construct of "cultural memory"[59] that does not simply represent the past but also provides identity. This, in fact, applies to modern historiography as well—especially if the sources form a significant part of the modern cultural memory, as is the case in biblical studies.[60] Memory is not an archive of information of the past but a part of the cognitive system that adapts present experiences to previous ones and, hence, a prominent constituent of our construction of reality.[61]

The primary question, thus, cannot be what really happened but what kind of secondary reconstructions of the past are enabled by the primary reconstructions of the past, that is, the available set of sources. This inevitably restricts the scope of relevant research questions, the relevance of which, again, is dependent on the agenda of the researcher and the academic community where he or she is situated. The question to be asked is what degree of plausibility can be given to these reconstructions (or, rather, reconfigurations) with regard to the questions they attempt to answer.

By establishing a relation between a modern concept and ancient documents—prophecy and homosexuality come to my mind because of my own occupation with these concepts—we already start building our construction of history. This construction work begins when the historian decides which questions can be considered relevant and makes a choice between available objects of study. It is far from self-evident what is meant with the concept of "prophecy," hence the historian must decide what he or she means with it, since there is no single word inherent in the ancient Near Eastern texts that would be adequate for scholarly purposes. To quote myself, "[t]he definition is necessary first and foremost as an aid of communication between people who work on different fields with cognate materials. It should not be understood as a static image of truth; rather, it should be seen from the point of view of the sociology of knowledge as a methodical process that emerges from concrete needs of the scholarly community and develops along with its application."[62] The definition of "prophecy" is not an independent entity but a methodological tool necessary for constructing the image of the ancient phenomenon thus defined. "Homosexuality," again, is a term that has been used since the very late nineteenth century only, and it is not very useful when we try to construct the image of same-sex interaction in the ancient world. But it is certainly a concept inherent in the world and language of the modern historical critic, who must decide whether the study of ancient same-sex eroticism should be driven by modern concerns, and, if not, whether it is possible at all to create a "neutral" image of ancient homoeroticism without positioning oneself somehow in the contemporary discussion. This, I think, is a good example of the otherness of the object of study, which, nevertheless, cannot be totally other from the interpreting self.

History Is Interpretation

The situatedness of the historical critic, at least if internalized to any degree, naturally leads to situations where the academic "objective" detachment is impossible, if not irresponsible, with regard to issues that concern people's lives in the contemporary social reality. This makes the so-called "advocacy readings" such as feminist, postcolonial, or queer readings necessary and natural. There is no reason why a historical critic could not practice such readings, as if they were inherently alien to historical criticism; as we have seen, there is a historical aspect to these readings, too. It is true that one should avoid "the deliberate overriding of proper historical judgement by promoting a particular point of view because it suits certain needs beyond academic interpretation and reconstruction of history,"[63] and a good deal of criticism is in place when the academic interpretation is designed to serve nonacademic needs. But whose needs are the academic needs anyway? The voices from the margins that remind the (historical) critics of the consequences of their own situatedness may help the historian to look in the mirror.[64] They also revive the question: For whom is the scholarship written, if not exclusively for fellow academics?[65]

One prominent aspect of many biblical historians' situatedness is their present or former context in religious communities; it is true, after all, that the majority of biblical scholars are somehow religiously affiliated. Many Christian and Jewish scholars take part in the life of religious communities as laypersons or as ordained ministers. It does not follow from this by any logical necessity that their scholarship is religiously motivated or that it is of inferior quality. Scholars have different commitments, and claims that a *religious* commitment in particular prevents the historian from being critical sounds like invoking the phantom of "objectivity" again. Since "[n]o-one is really 'disinterested'; everyone has an axe to grind,"[66] a nonbeliever (so-called) is not necessarily better equipped as a biblical critic than a believer (so-called).[67] It is exactly at this point the distance and the otherness between the source and the historian must be acknowledged; otherwise, we end up cutting the lawn of history with our own axes, which would only result in bad scholarship.

If history is all about interpretation, what is it that we are supposed to understand? When reading texts written in human language, we interpret culturally constructed signs that are inevitably historical regardless of their age, immersed in time and place, contextualized in particular societies, and determined by their cultural memory and ideology. To understand these signs, the historian has to acknowledge the distance, otherness, and relation between her or him and the source and, in Lee Patterson's words, to refuse to "reduce difference and opposition to sameness by collapsing together subject and object."[68] This collapse easily happens if the otherness of the sources is forgotten and they are fused together with the historian's mindset to fuel his or her favorite ideas, be they motivated by religious commitment, a particular theory, or anything else. This, I believe, can be avoided by recognizing the correlations and discrepancies between the *textual worlds*, *symbolic worlds*, and *real worlds* of the texts and their interpreters.[69] The text, ostensibly the same regardless of the time when it is read, has multiple contexts, ancient as well as modern.[70] Any reconstruction of the past begins with making a difference between the symbolic world (or cultural specificity, or ideology) and the real world (or social embeddedness, or social reality) of each source and the researcher. This requires sensitivity toward the purpose, function, context, and ideology of the variety of texts and artifacts.

Historical Factuality Exists

The very idea of a sociohistorical contextualization inevitably presupposes that the textual world is not entirely self-contained but reflects past social realities. There is such a thing as a historical factuality and real people involved in it (and dinosaurs, for that matter); this cannot be eliminated by any theory.[71] This does not deprive history of its constructedness. On the contrary, the extremely fragmentary set of available sources from antiquity (not only texts but also archaeological remains) and the difficulty of determining the actual historical context of most of the biblical writings should convince every historical critic of the Bible of the impossibility of reaching the full and authentic past.[72] A sherd of ancient pottery is not a construction of the modern mind (unless it is a forgery, of course), but every theory built upon it is.

It is more evident today than ever before that no serious historical criticism of the Bible can be done without the data provided by archaeology and ancient Near Eastern texts[73]—which, however, cannot be used as "hard data" over against the biased presentation of the Bible but as culture-specific products that require exactly the same degree of criticism as the biblical texts. Even archaeological evidence requires the same critical process of interpretation as textual sources, hence archaeology is a scholarly construct to the very same extent as text-based history, involving the issues of understanding, construction, and ideology.[74] As Elizabeth Bloch-Smith notes, "Biblical Israel is an ancient literary construct given form more than 2000 years ago, while historical/archaeological Israel is a modern construct, a composite picture grounded in material remains, informed through biblical testimony, and fleshed out through insights produced by the social sciences."[75]

The present-day exploitation of archaeology of the southern Levant, Palestine, or Israel will convince anyone that there are interested parties with distinct ideologies involved in interpreting the archaeological data. This is also true in fields such as Assyriology, Egyptology, or Ugaritic studies, where the situatedness of the scholars can be seen either in an outspoken intention of using the Near Eastern evidence to buttress the "reliability" of the Bible[76] or in more subtle ways of endorsing the historical accuracy of the Bible via interpretation of Near Eastern sources.

The limits of historical reconstruction correspond to the availability of evidence, on the one hand, and to the nature of sources, on the other hand. The perspective to the past opens itself differently depending on what kind of source is used as the gateway to the past. Sometimes the texts or artifacts are close enough to the events they describe to be interpreted as reflecting certain aspects of historical factuality (primary sources), while in other cases, there is a significant gap between the event and the sources that come to us through several recontextualizations (secondary sources).[77] An economical document such as a contract or a decree of expenditures; the pottery collected from an archaeological site; a letter written to the king by an official; a royal inscription; or a biblical prophetic book—all these are culture-specific products that are related to their past contexts each in their own way. Economical texts, without being overtly ideological, speak volumes about the structure and hierarchy of the society, distribution of wealth, and the agency of women; pottery is indicative of the construction of the social world of its users. Royal inscriptions, again, while retelling events of political history from the ruling king's point of view, are primarily to be read as representations of the royal ideology.

The biblical texts have gone through several de- and recontextualizations during their long history of emergence and interpretation and, therefore, virtually always fall into the category of secondary sources. A biblical text cannot simply be accepted as a historically accurate source unless it is proved wrong; rather, every reconstruction based on it must be argued for.[78] It is the historian's task to find out which purposes the texts once served and which kind of questions they are supposed to answer now, being on the alert for his or her own preferences in transferring meanings from sources to the construction of history.[79] This implies both the hermeneutical question of what the text meant and what it means[80] (supposing that texts continue to have meanings to their readers) and the search for the "interested parties" and their ideologies,[81] ancient and modern (supposing that there are no value-free meanings of a text).

Historical factuality exists; something has really happened in the past, and there are texts and artifacts that allow us to see glimpses of the past, "whose very disappearance authorizes the historian's work."[82] "What actually happened" becomes a legitimate question again when the naïve referentialism is abandoned, the constructed nature of knowledge is acknowledged, and the answer to that question in each case is given in awareness that, as far as historical factuality can be reached, every attempt to communicate it is interpretation.

Case Study: Prophecy

I have never considered myself a man of theory, so it has been an exciting effort to formulate the above thoughts on historical criticism in a way that would satisfy those more experienced in theoretical reflection. To convince at least myself—and, I hope, also David Petersen, a true historical critic to whom this *Versuch* is dedicated with much pleasure—that there is a correlation between my epistemological cogitations and source-based work, I close this essay with a case study of my own field of study, ancient Near Eastern prophecy.[83]

The sources on which our knowledge of the phenomenon of prophecy is based are well known: two textual corpora from eighteenth-century B.C.E. Mari and seventh-century B.C.E. Assyria, supplemented by miscellaneous cuneiform and West Semitic texts from different times and places, representing a variety of textual genres.[84] The Hebrew Bible, however, is the text where the issue of prophecy is more prominent than anywhere else and which is also important as a historical source, albeit a very different one from the other ancient sources. The difference between the Near Eastern sources and the Hebrew Bible lies mainly in the textual transmission. In the former, the information about prophets and prophecy is embedded in written oracles, letters, administrative documents, and so on, written usually by officials of the king or a temple and filed away in archives where they have been found by archaeologists of our times. In these cases, the chronological and cultural distance between the source and the event is usually not very long. The Hebrew Bible, again, is a collection of canonized writings that derive from different times and have been selected, edited, collected, and transmitted by several generations of scribes mostly in the time of the Second Temple of Jerusalem, that is, in the Persian and Hellenistic periods from the sixth until the second century B.C.E.

In both cases, all the information that we can gain of prophets and prophecy is dependent on the type of textual transmission. There is no direct access to the prophets as historical personalities; even the first-hand documents of their appearances come to us only to the extent the scribal filters between us and them allows us to perceive. Especially in the case of the Bible, this means that to identify the symbolic world or social embeddedness of, say, a prophetic book, the historical critic has to dig through countless layers of interpretation and recontextualization.

In the Hebrew Bible, texts concerned with prophets or prophecy are included in two different kinds of literature: the narrative and the prophetic books. The prophetic appearances narrated in the books of Samuel and Kings, not to mention Chronicles, are precarious evidence with regard to actual prophetic activities in the kingdoms of Judah and Israel. This is not only because of the significant chronological gap between the stories and the time they describe, but also because these narratives primarily function within their present literary contexts and may be multilayered or fictitious altogether, serving the ends of their editors. Therefore, our principal question should concern the *constructs* of prophecy in these texts, since it is only through the dark glass of these multiple and often deconstructable constructs that we have access to the eventual historical factualities that may be dimly visible as building material of these constructs.

If anything, the narratives in the Former Prophets and in Chronicles show what their authors and editors, predominantly living in the Second Temple communities, took for granted with regard to prophets and their activities in the times that these literary compositions describe (which is not necessarily compatible with the image they have of the prophets in their own time). It is reasonable to assume that a part of the image of the ancient prophets in these writings is based on older documents and thus contain indirect information of the prophetic goings-on in the ninth–seventh centuries B.C.E.; however, it is equally clear that all this material is reread and adapted to a secondary context. In other words, the primary context of, say, the stories about Elijah and Elisha (1 Kgs 17–2 Kgs 9) is their present literary context within the composition scholars call the Deuteronomistic History. They are not first-hand evidence of prophecy in the kingdom of Israel in the ninth century, even though they are still often used as if they were.

The prophetic books of the Hebrew Bible represent yet another kind of literature, which presents itself for the most part as divine words transmitted by the prophets to whom each book is ascribed, that is, the so-called writing prophets. However, the prophetic books are not primarily the work of these prophets but scribal compilations with a long editorial history. The books are likely to contain passages originating from written records based on actual prophetic performances, and there has been a more serious concentration on the "original" writer here than in any other part of the Hebrew Bible. The authors of the prophetic books are personalized to a higher degree than any other books of the Hebrew Bible. The very issue of the *ipsissima verba* of the prophets concerns exclusively the prophetic books (who would break a lance for the *ipsissima verba* of David or Job?), hence the whole concept of authorship is discussed differently from other books of the Hebrew Bible.

In their present contexts, however, even the passages that might go back to prophetic words once pronounced by the mouth of Isaiah, Jeremiah, Amos, and Hosea are completely decontextualized. They are edited from the point of view of communities that have read and reused them according to their own needs and preferences, creating their own constructs of prophets and prophecy. Reading the books of the "classical" prophets as providing direct historical data from the eighth and seventh centuries often means forgetting that "[t]exts are not photographs of social reality but are imaginative creations of their writers."[85] This easily introduces a procedural error of transferring meanings from texts to a historical reality, which may lead to serious misconceptions, not only of the prophets as persons, but of prophecy as an ancient phenomenon.

Does the situation get any different when we move to the evidence of prophecy in nonbiblical texts? To a certain extent, yes. Most of the texts of archaeological provenance, such as letters and administrative texts, do not usually have a long editorial history behind them and are, therefore, of less interpretive nature than the biblical texts. But the bad news is that even here we are entirely dependent on scribal control: the interests of the writers of these texts and the officials who have selected the material to be included in the archives—not to mention the accidental nature of archaeological finds. Therefore, the ancient Near Eastern texts are no photographs of social reality either.

To what extent this picture concurs with historical factualities must be judged with regard to the nature of the sources, their purposes and eventual biases.[86] The purpose of, say, a food-ration list is primarily administrative, for example, to keep record of how much barley had been delivered to whom.[87] Misleading records are unlikely to have ended up in the archives, so if prophets are mentioned among recipients of food rations, it is as good as certain that they actually were there. In the letters, the interest of the letter-writer plays a more significant role: when a temple official gives an account of a prophecy he has either witnessed or otherwise become aware of, he may manipulate the contents of the prophecy to correspond to his own purposes of citing it.[88] The problem is that the fragmentary condition and uneven distribution of the sources disallows us from seeing the whole picture. Why did some prophecies end up in archives, while the vast majority of them did not? Why are most prophecies known to us concerned with royal affairs, while the perspective of a private citizen is almost totally lacking? While we can be rather confident that many details in the general picture of the social reality of prophecy in the ancient Near East are not far from the historical reality, it is also possible that the picture is unproportional and that many local variations are not visible at all. Details that we do know may not be the most important details that we *should* know.

All that said, it is also true that every text is written by someone somewhere; thus, not reading them as photographs of social reality does not mean that they do not tell anything at all about the past. Texts are not isolated from the world in which they are written and interpreted, even though we have to be careful not to make straightforward moves from text to history and engage in illegitimate transfers of meaning. The point is that the information discernible from each text, biblical or extrabiblical, depends on its writer and on its purpose (as far as these can be known), on its temporal distance from what it describes, on its genre and on the process of transmission.[89]

When drawing the picture of prophets in the ancient Near East, we should begin by paying attention to the constructs of prophecy within the sources we have at our disposal. If we can observe a similar construct occurring in different contexts, we can assume that it is shared by more than one writer and serves more than one episodic purpose. These observations are like pieces of a puzzle: when they fit together, they contribute to constructing a bigger picture that, as such, is not a photograph of historical reality but an interpretation of it, not the full and authentic past but fragments of different constructs of the past.

For Further Reading

Barton, John. *The Nature of Biblical Criticism*. Louisville: Westminster John Knox, 2007.

Carroll, Robert P. "Poststructuralist Approaches: New Historicism and Postmodernism." Pages 50–66 in *The Cambridge Companion to Biblical Interpretation*. Edited by John Barton. Cambridge: Cambridge University Press, 1998.

Clines, David J. A. "Historical Criticism: Are Its Days Numbered?" *Teologinen Aikakauskirja* 114 (forthcoming 2009).

Dobbs-Allsopp, F. W. "Rethinking Historical Criticism." *BibInt* 7 (1999): 235–71.

Iggers, Georg G. *Historiography in the Twentieth Century: From Scientific Objectivity to the Postmodern Challenge*. Hanover, N.H.: Wesleyan University Press, 1997.

Stichele, Caroline van der, and Todd Penner. "Mastering the Tools or Retooling the Masters: The Legacy of Historical-Critical Discourse." Pages 1–29 in *Her Master's Tools? Feminist and Postcolonial Engagements of Historical-Critical Discourse*. Edited by Caroline van der Stichele and Todd Penner. SBLGPBS 9. Atlanta: Society of Biblical Literature, 2005.

Zagorin, Perez. "History, the Referent, and Narrative: Reflections on Postmodernism Now," *History and Theory* 38 (1999): 1–24.

Notes

1. "Here, as with each interpretation, love is the best teacher of the researcher." Hugo Greßmann, "Die Aufgaben der alttestamentlichen Forschung," *ZAW* 42 (1924): 1-33 (12).

2. Ibid., 1: "Bis zu einem gewissen Grade sind die Aufgaben der alttestamentlichen Forschung natürlich immer dieselben und haben alle nur ein einziges Ziel: das geschichtliche Verständnis des AT. Und noch kann man mit demselben Recht das Gegenteil behaupten: Wo die Wissenschaft in lebendigem Fluß bleibt, da wechseln die Aufgaben mit jedem Forschergeschlecht, wei sich neben den alten neue Wege zeigen, die demselben Ziel zuführen wollen." For Greßmann, this meant, among other things, the movement from source criticism to ancient Near Eastern studies: "Auf das literarkritische ist das vorderorientalische Zeitalter gefolgt" (8–9).

3. For the challenge of "linguistic turn" and postmodernism in historical studies, see, e.g., Peter Novick, *That Noble Dream: The "Objectivity Question" and the American Historical Profession* (Cambridge: Cambridge University Press, 1988); Georg G. Iggers, *Geschichtswissenschaft im 20. Jahrhundert: Ein kritischer Überblick im internationalen Zusammenhang* (Göttingen: Vandenhoeck & Ruprecht, 1993); idem, *Historiography in the Twentieth Century: From Scientific Objectivity to the Postmodern Challenge* (Hanover, N.H.: Wesleyan University Press, 1997); Perez Zagorin, "History, the Referent, and Narrative: Reflections on Postmodernism Now," *History and Theory* 38 (1999): 1–24; Hans-Jürgen Goertz, *Unsichere Geschichte: Zur Theorie historischer Referentialität* (Stuttgart: Philipp Reclam, 2001), 11–31; Elizabeth A. Clark, *History, Theory, Text: Historians and the Linguistic Turn* (Cambridge: Harvard University Press, 2004).

4. See, e.g., Richard J. Evans, *In Defence of History* (London: Granta, 1997), 248.

5. For New Historicism, see, e.g., Gina Henz-Piazza, *The New Historicism* (GBS; Minneapolis: Fortress, 2002); and the contributions collected in H. Aram Veeser, ed., *The New Historicism* (New York: Routledge, 1989), especially those of Stephen Greenblatt ("Towards a Poetic of Culture," 1–14), Louis Montrose ("Professing the Renaissance: The Poetics and Politics of Culture," 15–36), and Hayden White ("New Historicism: A Comment," 293–302).

6. See, e.g., the issue on New Historicism in *BibInt* 5/4 (1997), with contributions by Stephen D. Moore, Robert P. Carroll, Harold C. Washington, Yvonne Sherwood, Clive Marsh, Susan Lochrie Graham, and R. Adam Veeser; see also F. W. Dobbs-Allsopp, "Rethinking Historical Criticism," *BibInt* 7 (1999): 235–71.

7. That is, the debate prompted by, e.g., Niels Peter Lemche, *Early Israel: Anthropological and Historical Studies on the Israelite Society before the Monarchy* (VTSup 37; Leiden: Brill, 1985); idem, *The Old Testament between Theology and History: A Critical Survey* (Louisville: Westminster John Knox, 2008); Thomas L. Thompson, *Early History of the Israelite People: From the Written and Archaeological Sources* (SHANE 4; Leiden: Brill, 1992); Philip R. Davies, *In Search of "Ancient Israel"* (JSOTSup 148; Sheffield: Sheffield Academic Press, 1992); idem, *The Origins of Biblical Israel* (LHBOTS 485; London: T&T Clark, 2007); idem, *Memories of Ancient Israel: An Introduction to Biblical History—Ancient and Modern* (Louisville: Westminster John Knox, 2008); see also the counterreactions by, e.g., William G. Dever, *What Did the Biblical Writers Know and When Did They Know It? What Archaeology Can Tell Us about the Reality of Ancient Israel* (Grand Rapids: Eerdmans, 2001); Iain V. Provan, Philips Long, and Tremper Longman, *A Biblical History of Israel* (Louisville: Westminster John Knox, 2003); Jens Bruun Kofoed, *Text and History: Historiography and the Study of Biblical Texts* (Winona Lake, Ind.: Eisenbrauns, 2005). For a recent overview of this discussion, see Thomas Krüger, "Theoretische und methodische Probleme der Geschichte des alten Israel in der neueren Diskussion," *VF* 53 (2008): 4–22.

8. That is, the low chronology suggested by Israel Finkelstein; see, e.g., "High or Low: Megiddo and Rehov," in *The Bible and Radiocarbon Dating: Archaeology, Text, and Science* (ed. Thomas E. Levy and Thomas Higham; London: Equinox, 2005), 302–9; and the criticism of Amihai Mazar, "The Debate over the Chronology of the Iron Age in the Southern Levant: Its History, the Current Situation, and a Suggested Resolution," in Levy and Higham, *The Bible and Radiocarbon Dating*, 15–30.

9. Leander E. Keck, "Will the Historical-Critical Method Survive? Some Observations," in *Orientation by Disorientation: Studies in Literary Criticism and Biblical Literary Criticism, Presented in Honor of William A. Beardslee* (ed. Richard A. Spencer; Pittsburgh: Pickwick, 1980), 115–27.

10. David J. A. Clines, "Historical Criticism: Are Its Days Numbered?" forthcoming in *Teologinen Aikakauskirja* 114 (2009).

11. Zagorin, "History, the Referent, and Narrative," 2.

12. See John Barton, *The Nature of Biblical Criticism* (Louisville: Westminster John Knox, 2007), 31–68.

13. See Heikki Räisänen, *Beyond New Testament Theology: A Story and a Programme* (London: SCM, 2000); for Räisänen's program, see also the articles collected in *Moving beyond New Testament Theology? Essays in Conversation with Heikki*

Räisänen (ed. Todd Penner and Caroline van der Stichele; Publications of the Finnish Exegetical Society 88; Helsinki: Finnish Exegetical Society, 2005).

14. See, e.g., Timo Veijola, *Leben nach der Weisung: Exegetisch-historische Studien zum Alten Testament* (FRLANT 224; Göttingen: Vandenhoeck & Ruprecht, 2008); idem, "Text, Wissenschaft und Glaube: Überlegungen eines Alttestamentlers zur Lösung des Grundproblems der biblischen Hermeneutik," *JBTh* 15 (2000): 313–39.

15. E.g., Heikki Räisänen, "Biblical Critics in the Global Village," in *Reading the Bible in the Global Village: Helsinki* (ed. Heikki Räisänen; SBLGPBS 6; Atlanta: Society of Biblical Literature, 2000), 9–28; idem, "Matthew in Bibliodrama," in *Neutestamentliche Exegese im Dialog: Hermeneutik—Wirkungsgeschichte—Matthäusevangelium, Festschrift für Ulrich Luz zum 70. Geburtstag* (ed. Peter Lampe, Moisés Mayordomo, and Migaku Sato; Neukirchen-Vluyn: Neukirchener, 2008), 183–95; Timo Veijola, "Depression als menschliche und biblische Erfahrung," in idem, *Offenbarung und Anfechtung: Hermeneutisch-theologische Studien zum Alten Testament* (ed. Walter Dietrich and Marko Marttila; BibS(N) 89; Neukirchen-Vluyn: Neukirchener, 2007), 158–90.

16. I am happy to be listed among his students by Mark S. Smith, *Untold Stories: The Bible and Ugaritic Studies in the Twentieth Century* (Peabody, Mass.: Hendrickson, 2001), 44, even though there is very little I have done in the field of Ugaritic studies.

17. For the excavations at Kinneret, see Juha Pakkala, Stefan Münger, and Jürgen Zangenberg, *Kinneret Regional Project: Tel Kinrot Excavations* (Proceedings of the Finnish Institute in the Middle East, Report 2/2004; Vantaa: The Finnish Institute in the Middle East, 2004); available at www.kinneret-excavations.org.

18. This paper is written while enjoying the William D. Loughlin Membership at the Institute for Advanced Study in Princeton, New Jersey. I would like to express my heartfelt thanks to my colleagues in Princeton who have read the manuscript with a critical eye: Pamela Barmash, David Moon, and Peter Holquist, co-members at the Institute, and especially F. W. "Chip" Dobbs-Allsopp at the Princeton Theological Seminary. The remaining blindspots are all mine, not theirs.

19. Clark, *History, Theory, Text*, 157.

20. In particular, I would like to mention Clines, "Historical Criticism."

21. Greatly startled by Elisabeth Schüssler Fiorenza's fierce criticism against Räisänen's attempt to read the Bible in the global village ("Defending the Center, Trivializing the Margins," in Räisänen, *Reading the Bible in the Global Village*, 29–48), I would like to emphasize that, having this background, it is not a conscious part of my scholarly agenda to partisan the case of the center over against the margins, to prefer Finnish for foreign, or to bolster heteronormativity or male dominance. If I am caught in the very act of doing so, I can only plead guilty, with explanation: I consciously strive for distancing myself from such positions.

22. See David J. A. Clines, *The Bible in the Modern World* (Sheffield: Sheffield Academic Press, 1997).

23. For the concept of cultural memory, see especially Jan Assmann, *Religion and Cultural Memory: Ten Studies* (trans. Rodney Livingstone; Stanford, Calif.: Stanford University Press, 2006); trans. of *Religion und kulturelles Gedächtnis: Zehn Studien* (3rd ed.; Munich: Beck, 2007); for an application of this concept in biblical studies, see Davies, *Memories of Ancient Israel*, 105–23.

24. Dobbs-Allsopp, "Rethinking Historical Criticism," 270.

25. Robert P. Carroll, "Poststructuralist Approaches: New Historicism and Postmodernism," in *The Cambridge Companion to Biblical Interpretation* (ed. John Barton; Cambridge: Cambridge University Press, 1998), 50–66, esp. 57: "Yet both the categories of history and literature when used in relation to the Bible are equally in need of interpretation, so the old-fashioned category of hermeneutics remains as ever the fundamentally necessary approach to any reading of the Bible (whatever the intellectual basis of that approach)." See also Hans-Jürgen Goertz, *Umgang mit Geschichte: Eine Einführung in die Geschichtstheorie* (Rowohlts Enzyklopädie; Reinbek bei Hamburg: Rowohlt, 1995), 105–17.

26. See the editors' introductory essay, "Mastering the Tools or Retooling the Masters: The Legacy of Historical-Critical Discourse," in *Her Master's Tools? Feminist and Postcolonial Engagements of Historical-Critical Discourse* (ed. Caroline van der Stichele and Todd Penner; SBLGPBS 9; Atlanta: Society of Biblical Literature, 2005), 1–29.

27. For an attempt at "historical-critical postcolonialism," see John W. Marshall, "Postcolonialism and the Practice of History," in van der Stichele and Penner, *Her Master's Tools*, 93–108.

28. Clines, "Historical Criticism," n. 10.

29. Michel Foucault, *The History of Sexuality* (trans. Robert Hurley; 3 vols.; New York: Vintage, 1988–1990).

30. See Esther Fuchs, "The History of Women in Ancient Israel: Theory, Method, and the Book of Ruth," in van der Stichele and Penner, *Her Master's Tools*, 211–31.

31. E.g., the Nag Hammadi specialists who have ably and elegantly responded to the public interest in assessing the significance of the Gospel of Judas for audiences domestic (Antti Marjanen and Ismo Dunderberg, *Juudaksen evankeliumi* [Helsinki: WSOY, 2006]) and international (Elaine Pagels and Karen L. King, *Reading Judas: The Gospel of Judas and the Shaping of Christianity* [New York: Viking, 2007]).

32. See especially Robert P. Carroll, "Clio and Canons: In Search of a Cultural Poetics of the Hebrew Bible," *BibInt* 5 (1997): 300–323, esp. 308–15.

33. Dobbs-Allsopp, "Rethinking Historical Criticism," 255.

34. I.e., the "pro-gay" Martti Nissinen, *Homoeroticism in the Biblical World: A Historical Perspective* (trans. Kirsi Stjerna; Minneapolis: Fortress, 1998); and the "anti-gay" Robert A. J. Gagnon, *The Bible and Homosexual Practice: Texts and Hermeneutics* (Nashville: Abingdon, 2001).

35. E.g., Ken Stone, "Homosexuality and the Bible or Queer Reading? A Response to Martti Nissinen," *Theology and Sexuality* 7 (2001): 107–18; Anthony Heacock, "Wrongly Framed? The 'David and Jonathan Narrative' and the Writing of Biblical Homosexuality [*sic*]," *The Bible and Critical Theory* 3/2 (2007).

36. Cf. the contrary opinions of Jean-Fabrice Nardelli, *Homosexuality and Liminality in the Gilgameš and Samuel* (Amsterdam: Hakkert, 2007); and Markus Zehnder, "Observations on the Relationship between David and Jonathan and the Debate on Homosexuality," *WTJ* 69 (2007): 127–74.

37. See Carl E. Braaten and Robert W. Jenson, eds., *Reclaiming the Bible for the Church* (Edinburgh: T&T Clark, 1996).

38. See Barton, *The Nature of Biblical Criticism*, 167–71, referring to David J. A. Clines, *Interested Parties: The Ideology of the Writers and Readers of the Hebrew Bible* (Sheffield: Sheffield Academic Press, 1995); Philip R. Davies, *Whose Bible Is It Anyway?* (Sheffield: Sheffield Academic Press, 1995; 2nd ed., London: T&T Clark, 2004); Fernando Segovia, *Decolonizing Biblical Studies: A View from the Margins* (Maryknoll, N.Y.: Orbis, 2000); and Jacques Berlinerblau, "The Unspeakable in Biblical Scholarship," *SBL Forum* (March 2006); online: http://www.sbl-site.org/publications/article.aspx?articleId=503.

39. So, in different ways, e.g., Rainer Albertz, "Religionsgeschichte Israels statt Theologie des Alten Testaments!" *JBTh* 10 (1995): 3–24; Niels Peter Lemche, "Warum die Theologie des Alten Testaments einen Irrweg darstellt," *JBTh* 10 (1995): 79–92; idem, *The Old Testament between Theology and History* (Louisville: Westminster John Knox, 2008); Räisänen, *Beyond New Testament Theology*.

40. E.g., Isaac Kalimi, "Religionsgeschichte Israels oder Theologie des Alten Testaments: Das jüdische Interesse an der biblischen Theologie," *JBTh* 10 (1995): 45–68.

41. E.g., Frank Crüsemann, "Religionsgeschichte oder Theologie? Elementare Überlegungen zu einer falschen Alternative," *JBTh* 10 (1995): 69–77.

42. This point has most recently been made by Samuel Byrskog, "När gamla texter talar: Om att tolka det förgångna," *STK* 84 (2008): 49–57, esp. 55; see also Veijola, "Text, Wissenschaft und Glaube."

43. So most recently Emanuel Pfoh, "Más allá del círculo hermenéutico: El pasado de Israel entre la teología del Antiguo Testamento y la historia de Palestina," *Revista Bíblica* 69 (2007): 65–82.

44. This, I believe, is close to the "critical theology" advocated by Barton, *The Nature of Biblical Criticism*, 185.

45. See Carroll, "Clio and Canons," 316.

46. Dobbs-Allsopp, "Rethinking Historical Criticism," 241.

47. The reciprocal concern between the historicity of the texts and the textuality of history is introduced by Montrose, "Professing the Renaissance," 20; so also White, "New Historicism: A Comment," 297: "every approach to the study of the past presupposes or entails some version of a textualist theory of historical reality of some kind."

48. Lee Patterson, *Negotiating the Past: The Historical Understanding of Medieval Literature* (Madison: University of Wisconsin Press, 1987), 42.

49. See Dobbs-Allsopp, "Rethinking Historical Criticism," 265.

50. See Georg G. Iggers and James M. Powell, eds., *Leopold von Ranke and the Shaping of the Historical Discipline* (Syracuse, N.Y.: Syracuse University Press, 1990).

51. In fact, von Ranke's paradigm was not based on a strictly positivistic attitude but an aesthetic and religious experience of the past. "Ranke *did* insist on critical method, but unless his reasons for doing so and the creative-imaginative way in which he pursued critical research is taken into account, the 'paradigm' remains a mere shadow of Ranke's thought" (J. D. Braw, "Vision as Revision: Ranke and the Beginning of Modern History," *History and Theory* 46/4 [2007]: 45–60, esp. 59, emphasis original).

52. See Novick, *That Noble Dream*; Georg G. Iggers, "The Crisis of the Rankean Paradigm in the Nineteenth Century," in Iggers and Powell, *Leopold von Ranke*, 170–79; Clark, *History, Theory, Text*, 9–17.

53. Lester L. Grabbe, *Ancient Israel: What Do We Know and How Do We Know It?* (New York: T&T Clark, 2007), 29.

54. Barton, *The Nature of Biblical Criticism*, 49; cf. Ernst-Axel Knauf, "From History to Interpretation," in *The Fabric of History: Texts, Artifact and Israel's Past* (ed. Diana V. Edelman; JSOTSup 127; Sheffield: Sheffield Academic Press, 1991), 26–64, esp. 30–31: "The difference between an objective, scientific history and a nonscientific history is not that the scientific historian is without presuppositions. The difference is that in scientific history the theory is as disputable as the facts are; the presuppositions are conceived to be debatable to the same extent that any statement derived from them is." See also Krüger, "Theoretische und methodische Probleme," 18–22.

55. See Goertz, *Unsichere Geschichte*, 15.

56. See Knauf, "From History to Interpretation," 26–27; and Goertz, *Umgang mit Geschichte*, 103–4, who underscores the importance of a "disciplined fantasy" in history writing.

57. Clark, *History, Theory, Text*, 86, referring to the theorists who emphasized the imaginary and ideological nature of the historical narrative; see, e.g., Hayden V. White, *Metahistory: The Historical Imagination in Nineteenth-Century Europe* (Baltimore: Johns Hopkins University Press, 1973); idem, *Tropics of Discourse: Essays in Cultural Criticism* (Baltimore: Johns Hopkins University Press, 1978); idem, *The Content of the Form: Narrative Discourse and Historical Representation* (Baltimore: Johns Hopkins University Press, 1987).

58. The "genetic fallacy" and the absence of assured results are among the weaknesses David Clines has found in historical criticism; see "Historical Criticism."

59. See above, n. 25.

60. See Philip R. Davies, "The History of Ancient Israel and Judah," *ExpTim* 119 (2007): 15–21, esp. 19–20.

61. See Goertz, *Unsichere Geschichte*, 96.

62. Martti Nissinen, "What Is Prophecy: An Ancient Near Eastern Perspective," in *Inspired Speech: Prophecy in the Ancient Near East, Essays in Honor of Herbert B. Huffmon* (ed. John Kaltner and Louis Stulman; JSOTSup 378; London: T&T Clark, 2004), 17–37, esp. 20.

63. Lester L. Grabbe, *Ezra–Nehemiah* (Old Testament Readings; London: Routledge, 1998), 6.

64. See R. S. Sugirtharajah, "Critics, Tools, and the Global Arena," in Räisänen, *Reading the Bible in the Global Village*, 49–60.

65. On the moral and political responsibility of the historian, see Knauf, "From History to Interpretation," 32–33; for the need of dialogue with participating communitites and the wider implications of scholarship from the point of view of archaeology, see Ian Hodder, *Archaeology beyond Dialogue* (Foundations of Archaeological Inquiry; Salt Lake City: University of Utah Press, 2003).

66. Barton, *The Nature of Biblical Criticism*, 13.

67. For the issue of faith-commitment and biblical criticism, see James Barr, "Evaluation, Commitment, and Objectivity in Biblical Theology," in Räisänen, *Reading the Bible in the Global Village*, 127–52; Barton, *The Nature of Biblical Criticism*, 173–75. For a nonbeliever perspective, see Jacques Berlinerblau, *The Secular Bible:*

Why Nonbelievers Must Take Religion Seriously (New York: Cambridge University Press, 2005).

68. Patterson, *Negotiating the Past*, 72. Dobbs-Allsopp ("Rethinking Historical Criticism," 252) writes: "Critical historicism wants to ally a poststructuralist reading strategy with the historicist respect for the other and belief that the cultural and social milieu in which past literary works originated is likely to be relevant for understanding those works."

69. This three-world model is developed by Kari Syreeni; see "Wonderlands: A Beginner's Guide to Three Worlds," *SEÅ* 64 (1999): 33–46.

70. Carroll, "Clio and Canons," 312: "The Bible is not just a book read and revered by thousands [*sic*!] of generations of Jews and Christians. It is deeply formative of belief and behaviour in its readers.... It is also a book read into and out of whatever cultural context the readers may find themselves situated in at any time of reading."

71. See Iggers, *Historiography in the Twentieth Century*, 119.

72. See Carroll, "Prophecy and Society," in *The World of Ancient Israel: Sociological, Anthropological and Political Perspectives* (ed. R. E. Clements; Cambridge: Cambridge University Press, 1989), 203–25.

73. So already Greßmann, "Die Aufgaben der alttestamentlichen Forschung," 11, 15.

74. See Colin Renfrew and Paul Bahn, *Archaeology: Theories, Methods and Praxis* (4th ed.; London: Thames & Hudson, 2004), 405–34; Michael Shanks and Ian Hodder, "Processual, Postprocessual and Interpretive Archaeologies," in *Interpreting Archaeology: Finding Meaning in the Past* (ed. Ian Hodder et al.; London: Routledge), 3–29.

75. Elizabeth Bloch-Smith, "Bible, Archaeology, and the Social Sciences: The Next Generation," in *The Hebrew Bible: New Insights and Scholarship* (ed. Frederick E. Greenspahn; New York: New York University Press, 2008), 24–42, esp. 37.

76. E.g., Kenneth A. Kitchen, *On the Reliability of the Old Testament* (Grand Rapids: Eerdmans, 2003).

77. See Grabbe, *Ancient Israel*, 35.

78. Ibid., 35–36.

79. For the risk of illegitimate transfers of meaning, see Carroll, "Prophecy and Society," 206–9.

80. This dichotomy was coined by Krister Stendahl; see his comments in "Dethroning Biblical Imperialism in Theology," in Räisänen, *Reading the Bible in the Global Village*, 61–66.

81. See Clines, *Interested Parties*.

82. Clark, *History, Theory, Text*, 156.

83. This section is based on a lecture given at the University of Lausanne on 17 October 2008 on the occasion of the colloquium "Les rédactions des livres prophétiques de la Bible hébraïque" organized by Thomas Römer and Jean-Daniel Macchi. I take this opportunity to thank the organizers as well as the co-lecturers Dominique Charpin and George Brooke for a most rewarding discussion.

84. The sources are collected in Martti Nissinen, with contributions by Choon-Leong Seow and Robert K. Ritner, *Prophets and Prophecy in the Ancient Near East* (SBLWAW 12; Atlanta: Society of Biblical Literature, 2003).

85. Carroll, "Prophecy and Society," 207.

86. I fully subscribe to the principles of historical reconstruction as presented by Grabbe, *Ancient Israel*, 35–36.

87. E.g., the Middle-Assyrian list VS 19 1 i 37–39 (Nissinen, *Prophets and Prophecy*, 185, no. 123): "Ten homers four seah five liters of barley for Aššur-apla-iddina on the second day, for the food rations of the prophets, prophetesses and the *assinnus* of the Ištar temple."

88. This may be the reason why one prophet wanted a scribe to write a letter to the king from his own dictation: "Atamrum, prophet of Šamaš, came to me and spoke to me as follows: 'Send me a discreet scribe! I will have him write down the message which Šamaš has sent me for the king'" (ARM 26 414:29–33; Nissinen, *Prophets and Prophecy*, 75, no. 48). The letter of the prophet is probably known to us (ARM 26 194; Nissinen, *Prophets and Prophecy*, 24–25, no. 4); see Dominique Charpin, "Prophètes et rois dans le Proche-Orient amorrite: Nouvelles données, nouvelles perspectives," in *Florilegium Marianum 6: Recueil d'études à la mémoire d'André Parrot* (Mémoires de NABU 7; Paris: Societe pour l'Etude du Proche-Orient Ancien, 2002), 7–38, esp. 29–31.

89. See Grabbe, *Ancient Israel*, 220.

Reflections on Social-Scientific Criticism

Robert R. Wilson

Social-scientific criticism is a label that contemporary biblical scholars often apply to interpretive approaches that employ techniques from the social sciences or that focus on the social dimensions of the biblical text and the world out of which it came. Biblical interpreters did not begin to employ the social sciences (sociology, economics, anthropology, political science, and psychology) until the middle of the nineteenth century, when those academic disciplines began to develop. However, as early as the Middle Ages, commentators on both the Old and New Testaments sometimes attempted to illuminate difficult texts by setting them into their social contexts. Odd social customs were explained, and psychological motives were suggested for the actions of biblical characters. Particularly the medieval interpreters who were interested in what would later be called the "plain sense" of the text would sometimes set biblical passages into a reconstructed social setting or would appeal to contemporary social behavior in order to explain the biblical material.[1]

By the nineteenth century, scholars had become increasingly conscious of the historical gap that separated them from the biblical text and its world, and thus they began to look for extrabiblical resources that would aid in the interpretive process. In addition to using ancient Near Eastern textual material that was beginning to be discovered and deciphered, they also began to explore the newly emerging social sciences as possible aids to biblical interpretation. Archaeology, which was beginning to develop as a branch of anthropology, encouraged scholars to excavate biblical sites in the hope of discovering texts or artifacts that could shed light on Israelite history and religion and on the biblical text itself. In the newly developing field of sociology, the work of Max Weber (1864–1920) provided the first effort by a sociologist to describe ancient Israel as a coherent society. Reacting against the dialectical materialism of Karl

Marx (1818–1883), who had seen economic interests driving the development of societies, Weber held that societies were shaped by commonly held value orientations. In order to test this thesis, he studied several societies in detail, including the ancient Israelites. Weber saw early Israel as a loose assembly of seminomadic and settled agricultural groups that occasionally acted in unity in times of crisis and grounded that unity in a religiously oriented covenant. The Israelite confederation was led by charismatic leaders until the rise of the monarchy, when power shifted from the people to the central government and the wealthy landowners and merchants who supported it. These abuses of power were criticized by the prophets, who advocated a return to the older system. Weber's views were enormously influential among Old Testament scholars, and accounts of Israelite society by Adolphe Lods (1867–1948), Antonin Causse (1877–1947), and Louis Wallis (b. 1876; d. after 1950) clearly depended on Weber's reconstructions.[2]

At the same time that sociological theories were having an impact on biblical scholarship, anthropologists at the end of the nineteenth century were collecting ethnographic information, much of it from so-called primitive societies that were thought to be comparable to ancient Israel. Much of this material was not systematically collected, and its relevance to Israelite society was not always clear. However, this early interest in ethnography did lead biblical scholars to broaden their interpretive approaches to include more intercultural comparisons. Furthermore, the rapidly growing accumulation of ethnographic data provided the foundation for two new subfields that would soon become influential in biblical studies: comparative mythology and folklore studies. The best example of the first subfield is the massive collection of material published by James George Frazer (1854–1941) under the title *The Golden Bough*.[3] Frazer later extracted some of this material and applied it explicitly to the Old Testament, and in this form it became an influential source of comparisons for biblical scholars. In the second subfield, the work of Jacob and Wilhelm Grim eventually led to the development of the discipline of folklore studies, which focuses on the collection, analysis, and classification of folktales. The pioneering work of the Grim brothers made a major impact on Hermann Gunkel (1862–1932), whose development of the form-critical approach to the Old Testament was heavily indebted to folklore research. Gunkel's interest in oral literature, in standard literary forms, and in the social setting of those forms was in fact an early form of social-scientific criticism. Later form critics and tradition critics who were influenced by

Gunkel were, in a sense, using social-scientific approaches to the study of ancient Israel and its literature, although they were not always aware of the sociological dimensions of their work.

Nineteenth-century biblical scholars sometimes also made use of the overarching theoretical frameworks into which the social sciences set their collected data. Particularly influential was the work of the anthropologist Edward B. Tylor (1832–1917), who developed an evolutionary theory of human culture that could easily be applied to the development of ancient Israelite religion and to Old Testament literature itself. Biblical scholars who followed Tylor's lead traced Israel's religion from its "primitive" roots to the highly developed ethical monotheism of the prophets and ultimately of the New Testament. In the same way, biblical scholars understood Israelite literature to exhibit an evolutionary development from short oral sayings to more complex written literary forms.[4]

However, in spite of the apparent early success of these explorations into social-scientific criticism, the field of biblical studies gradually began to lose interest in the approach, and by the end of World War I only a few examples of it remained in the scholarly literature. The reasons for this loss of interest are difficult to determine, but several factors were probably involved. First, as a result of the war, biblical studies seems to have taken a more theological turn and, at least in Germany, was heavily influenced by the work of Karl Barth. The theological approaches that came to dominate the field were not particularly interested in the sociological methods that had previously attracted biblical scholars. Second, early social-scientific research exhibited some methodological weaknesses, which were soon recognized by social scientists themselves and which tainted the use that biblical scholars made of this research. Sociological and anthropological data were often collected unsystematically, or the collection of material and its interpretation were influenced by scholarly assumptions that could not be justified. When biblical scholars recognized these difficulties, they began to question the use of this flawed data in biblical interpretation. Finally, biblical scholars began to realize that social scientists sometimes took comparative material out of its original context and set it in theoretical frameworks that in fact were not well supported by the data. To the extent that these frameworks were questionable, biblical scholars who had tried to use them had in fact jeopardized the integrity of their own work. This situation was particularly obvious in the case of evolutionary sociological and anthropological schemas. After the two World Wars, scholarship in general began to doubt the evolutionary nature of the development of society and culture. Biblical scholars therefore began to reject earlier evolutionary approaches to ancient Israel and its literature.

The "Second Wave" of Social-Scientific Approaches

No matter what factors led biblical scholars to reject early efforts at social-scientific criticism, by the middle of the twentieth century there was renewed scholarly interest in social-scientific approaches both in New Testament and in Old Testament studies. This "second wave" cannot be traced to a single source, and it was not well-coordinated enough to be considered a movement.[5] Scholars in the United States were particularly interested in reviving some sort of social-scientific approach to the Bible, but it is worth noting that at about the same time there was also a flurry of interest in England and Germany.

The causes of this renewed interest are difficult to identify with any precision, but since the scholars initially involved in the "second wave" expressed various reasons for trying a social-scientific approach, it is apparent that a combination of factors was involved.

First, by the 1960s some Old Testament scholars began to be dissatisfied with the methods generally being used to study ancient Israel's religion and literature. The general historical-critical approach to the field was still largely unquestioned, but there was a growing feeling that standard methods such as source criticism, form criticism, tradition criticism, redaction criticism, and traditional archaeological research were limited in their ability to provide a comprehensive picture of the Old Testament and the people who produced it. The traditional methods were still considered valid and useful, but they were increasingly thought to be producing incomplete results. Something more was needed, although there were differences of opinion about what might be required. Some scholars thought that the traditional methods had simply not been pushed far enough and that more detailed applications were needed. Scholars with theological interests became convinced that the traditional methods were obscuring the theological dimensions of the biblical text and that some means needed to be devised to correct this situation.[6] Still others noted that the traditional methods had still not been able to produce a comprehensive picture of Israel's everyday life, with the result that histories of Israel were still largely written as political histories, and literary studies of the biblical text often ignored the social context within which the literature itself was generated. This latter group of scholars was particularly interested in reviving some sort of social-scientific approach.

Second, just as biblical scholars were beginning to become dissatisfied with the traditional approaches, new developments were taking place in the fields of history, sociology, and anthropology, including the subfield of archaeology. Among historians of all sorts there was in the 1950s and 1960s a general drift away from concentrating solely on writing political history, and scholars developed a new interest in social history, which focused not on states and their leaders but on individuals and the way they lived in particular social contexts. This shift of interest is often connected with the French *Annales* tradition of history writing, which stressed the long-term relationships of people to their environment, the relationships of people to their social contexts, and the ways in which people related to particular events. Historians influenced by the *Annales* tradition therefore tended to be interdisciplinary in their approaches and in particular to look to the social sciences for help in understanding how particular people in particular societies related to particular events. This new sort of social history served as a stimulus for some biblical scholars and encouraged them to explore the sociological dimension of biblical history.[7]

The new emphasis on social history was particularly influential among archaeologists concentrating on Israel in the biblical period; as a result, they began to ask more sociologically oriented questions of their data and to employ more interpretive models from the social sciences. This shift to a new approach to presenting archaeological data in turn provided additional raw material for biblical scholars interested in enriching their own studies of Israelite history and literature.[8]

From the standpoint of the social sciences, the period after World War II saw an effort among anthropologists to correct the methodological flaws in earlier approaches to their field. Particularly influential during this period in England and in the United States was the rise to prominence of social anthropology, which focused on social organization rather than on social customs. Building on earlier work by Bronislaw Malinowski (1884–1942) and A. R. Radcliffe-Brown (1881–1955), British social anthropologists such as E. E. Evans-Pritchard and his students suggested that societies are best understood by seeing them as organic units with interdependent and interacting parts. The result of this approach was the production of a large number of ethnographic studies of individual societies that stressed the ways in which all of the components of particular social systems functioned as organic wholes. For biblical scholars in search of sociological approaches, social anthropology provided detailed studies of actual societies. Thus it avoided the problems caused by earlier research that extracted isolated data from context or that overlooked the particularity of data by incorporating it in general interpretive theories. However, on the negative side, by using social-anthropological data for comparative purposes and for model building, biblical scholars also often unwittingly inherited social anthropology's tendency to overlook the importance of studying social development over time.[9]

Finally, at least in the United States, some of the scholars involved in the second wave were influenced by the social ferment taking place during the 1950s and 1960s. The Civil Rights Movement and the antiwar movement focused public attention on issues of political power and social hierarchy, while the emergence of women's studies called attention to gender issues. Although postmodernist approaches were still on the horizon, there was a genuine hermeneutical debate beginning to take place about the role of social location in the interpretation of data and in the reading of texts.[10]

In contrast to the situation in the United States, where interest in social-scientific criticism appeared primarily among biblical scholars and historians of ancient Israel, in England the second wave seems to have been stimulated by the work of social scientists who became interested in applying their own approaches to the Bible and to ancient Israel. Particularly influential in this regard was the early work of the social anthropologist Mary Douglas, who published *Purity and Danger* in 1966. In it, she applied her anthropological theories about purity and pollution to the Bible, which she used as a source of ethnographic data.[11] Somewhat later, the anthropologist Edmund R. Leach began to apply structural analysis to biblical narratives and to the descriptions of religious practices that they contained.[12] Still later the social anthropologist Julian Pitt-Rivers published an enlightening analysis of the stories in Genesis from an anthropological perspective.[13] This interest in the Bible on the part of social scientists seems to have stimulated a renewed appreciation of the usefulness of social-scientific criticism among biblical scholars in England and in the United States as well. In Germany, scholars of the second wave seem to have been influenced initially by older theoretical approaches, particularly those of Marx and Weber, although more recent German work has participated fully in the American discussion and shows a clear interest in the use of data from social anthropology.[14]

In the United States, the second wave initially involved scholarly work in two general areas of study: the social history of early Israel; and the study of prophecy and apocalyptic. In the first area, second-wave studies are usually thought to have begun with the work of George Mendenhall, who in 1962 challenged traditional views of the Israelite conquest of Canaan by suggesting that biblical scholars should apply recent anthropological research on tribes and state formation to a reconstruction of the conquest period.[15] Rather than accepting traditional scholarly views that early Israelites as a group entered Canaan from the outside, either violently or peacefully, Mendenhall suggested that early Israel was composed of groups of peasants who had revolted against the oppression of the Canaanite cities and then formed a confederation that was united in covenant with a God who was Israel's only ruler. The unity of the confederation was celebrated by common worship at a central shrine. This situation existed until the rise of the monarchy, which eventually was able to shift power from the people to the central government.

The basic model proposed by Mendenhall was later taken up and elaborated enormously by Norman Gottwald, whose mammoth study *The Tribes of Yahweh* applied a thorough-going social-scientific approach to the ancient Israelite data.[16] Gottwald did not follow a single sociological approach but instead drew upon a number of comparative sources. The influences of Karl Marx and Gerhard Lenski are particularly visible, but Gottwald also used the work of social anthropologists, social historians, and the "new" archaeologists. Moving beyond the work of Mendenhall, Gottwald saw early Israel as a collection of egalitarian bands or tribes unified by common worship but acting together politically only in the face of outside military pressure. These bands were particularly attractive to peasants fleeing the oppression of the Canaanite cities and also eventually incorporated the groups that had experienced the exodus from Egypt. The growing Israelite groups eventually became powerful enough to take over the Cannanite cities and then to take over the whole land, although they were still able to maintain their egalitarian form of government, at least until the rise of the monarchy. Gottwald's reconstruction of the history of early Israel was enormously influential and was later developed further by a number of scholars, including Marvin Chaney, Frank Frick, Robert Coote, Keith Whitelam, and James Flanagan.[17]

At about the same time that Gottwald was developing his views on early Israel, Abraham Malamat proposed using social-anthropological studies of lineage-based societies to understand the social structure of early Israel.[18] This proposal was developed extensively by Robert Wilson in a study of the form and function of the biblical genealogies.[19] Like

Gottwald, Wilson also discussed the methodological issues involved in the use of social-scientific criticism and proposed methodological guidelines for the use of this sort of comparative approach.

The second area of study in the "new wave" involved the use of a social-scientific approach to better understand Israelite prophecy and apocalyptic. The pioneer in this area of research was Thomas Overholt, who attempted to cast light on biblical prophecy by looking at Native American prophets. Beginning with the Ghost Dance of 1890 and later extending his work into other American prophet movements, he provided a thorough study of the ethnographic material before attempting any sort of comparison with the biblical texts. Out of this study came a useful model for understanding the complex interaction between the prophet and the deity as well as between the prophet and the audience. Overholt later expanded his comparative interests to include cultures outside of North America, and he also collected a number of important ethnographic studies for the use of biblical scholars.[20]

Not long after Overholt began his comparative research into Native American ethnography, Robert Wilson began to publish a series of studies on biblical prophecy against the background of ethnographic treatments of religious figures closely resembling the Israelite prophets. Synthesizing material from a wide range of cultures, Wilson identified general patterns in the way that prophetic figures behaved, interacted with their audiences, talked about their experiences, and functioned within their social contexts. This ethnographic material was then used to explore ancient Near Eastern prophetic figures and those from ancient Israel. Wilson's work stressed the way in which the prophetic experience related to prophetic behavior in Israel as well as the various locations within which prophetic activity took place and the various social functions that it served. Finally, he expanded Overholt's work on the interaction between prophet and audience and tried to set stereotypical prophetic behavior into that context.[21]

Shortly after Wilson's monograph appeared, David Petersen suggested a different social-scientific approach to the study of Israel's prophets. Rather than using ethnographic studies as Overholt and Wilson had done, Petersen used sociological role theory to try to identify the various functions associated with the different labels attached to the Bible's prophetic figures. He concluded that Israelite prophets performed a variety of social roles and that biblical prophecy was a more complex phenomenon than scholars had previously thought.[22] A theoretical comparative approach was also used by Robert Carroll, who appealed to cognitive dissonance theory to study the way in which Israelite prophets reacted to the nonfulfillment of their predictions. Carroll concluded that, when the prophets and their audiences were troubled by problems of nonfulfillment, they edited their prophecies or created new ones in order to resolve the dissonance they experienced. In this way cognitive dissonance became a factor in the development of prophetic literature.[23]

Approaches based on sociological theory were also being used to study other issues during this period. Particularly prominent was the work of Paul Hanson on apocalyptic religion and literature. Hanson noted that scholars had increasingly identified the existence of social conflict in Israel's apocalyptic literature, and he set out to explore the nature of this conflict as well as the origins of apocalyptic itself. Using the work of Max Weber, Karl Mannheim, and Ernst Troeltsch, Hanson argued that apocalyptic was an internal Israelite phenomenon that grew primarily out of sociological and religious conflicts between prophets and priests.[24]

Although much of the initial work of the "second wave" was done by people who consciously identified themselves as biblical scholars, it is important to remember that some archaeologists during this period were also raising sociological questions about their material. As a result, the gap between archaeology and biblical studies began to narrow as archaeologists began to use their data to reconstruct the social life of biblical Israel. A good example of this phenomenon is the sociologically oriented work of Lawrence Stager and John S. Holladay, particularly their early work on types of housing in Israel. Both drew on contemporary anthropological studies of the way in which living space relates to daily activities, and in the process both enriched scholarly understanding of daily life in Israel.[25]

Even this brief description of the work of some of the early participants in the second wave of social-scientific criticism suggests several features of the approach that need to be noted. First, it appears that the participants were, at least initially, not in conversation with each other about their work. They had different motives for undertaking their research, and they went about their tasks in different ways. They did not share a single method but rather a general area of interest. However, after publications began to appear, scholarly interactions did begin to take place, although these interactions did not always lead to agreement. Still, there was a growing sense of a shared area of discourse that has continued to mark the practitioners of social-scientific criticism. Two factors were particularly important in facilitating the scholarly conversation. Beginning in the

1970s, working groups and seminars in the Society of Biblical Literature brought together scholars having similar interests, and out of these conversations new scholarly directions began to emerge.[26] Beyond personal interaction, two journals in particular, *Semeia* and *Journal for the Study of the Old Testament*, encouraged both new approaches and the subsequent debate that later arose about them. The literary foundation that these publications laid became the basis for much later research.[27]

Second, early participants in the second wave were still working in the context of the historical-critical method. It is therefore unlikely that many of them believed that they were developing a new method of any sort. Rather, they seem to have thought that they were practicing a sort of social history of the kind that was beginning to develop among historians and archaeologists.

Finally, all of the early participants were comparative in their approach to their subjects. Material was being imported from the social sciences and then applied to texts and artifacts from the biblical world. In that sense, there was not much new in the second wave, since biblical scholars of the period had traditionally used comparative material from the ancient Near East. However, the source of the comparative data was new, and the direction of scholarly inquiry therefore changed.

The Swelling of the Wave

Since the beginning of the second wave, a large number of studies have appeared that identify themselves as applying some sort of social-scientific criticism to the Old Testament. An online bibliography that covers only publications through the year 1998 lists almost five hundred such items.[28] However, it is not complete, and it includes nothing from the past ten years. Those familiar with recent research in the field of Old Testament will recognize that the number of publications in the area of social-scientific approaches is only a small fraction of the total, but the number is still significant enough that it is impossible in a short essay to describe all of it. It would even be unfair to single out individual items as being particularly important. In general, however, these publications can be loosely grouped into two categories.

First, a number of the publications explore some aspect of social history by using comparative material from the social sciences or by applying social-scientific theories to the Bible and its world. Some of these studies are in continuity with work done early in the second wave and are in conversation with it, while others apply social-scientific criticism to new areas of study. Examples of the former would be Lester Grabbe's study of religious officials in Israel, Richard Horsley's exploration of religion and politics in the Second Temple period, and Wilda Gafney's treatment of women prophets in Israel.[29] Particularly important examples of the latter are the efforts undertaken by Victor H. Matthews, Don C. Benjamin, and Rainer Kessler to write comprehensive social histories of Israel.[30] These works are important not only because of the syntheses of data that they provide but because of the useful comprehensive bibliographies that they contain. On the theoretical side, there has been renewed interest in the work of Max Weber, both in Germany and in the United States, and the applicability of his theories to biblical studies has been reassessed.[31]

Second, growing numbers of studies are focusing on specific aspects of the social system of ancient Israel. Particularly important have been studies of the roles of women and gender in Israel, a topic first treated in detail by Carol Meyers and taken up later by other scholars.[32] Significant work has also been done on the Israelite family by Naomi Steinberg, and a number of studies of Israelite ritual have been produced. In the latter category, the work of Saul Olyan has been particularly visible, as has the study of biblical sacrifice by the sociologist Nancy Jay.[33] Finally, the social dimensions of law are beginning to be explored in order to set Israel's legal traditions into a concrete social setting.[34] These examples are only a small sample of the wide variety of studies that have been undertaken, but they do serve to illustrate the range of work currently being done.

The Critics of Social-Scientific Criticism

Although social-scientific criticism seems now to be generally accepted and broadly applied in the field of biblical studies, there have always been strong criticisms of the approach. These criticisms reach beyond normal learned arguments about the results of scholarly inquiry and challenge fundamental aspects of the approach itself. The complexity of some of these critiques prevents dealing with them briefly, but in general the following claims have been made.

First, some scholars have argued that applying social-scientific criticism to an ancient society or to an ancient text is virtually impossible because the methods of social science depend on participant observation and an ability to test results by interacting with the subjects being studied. While such testing is possible in contemporary societies, it is obviously impossible in the case of ancient ones.[35] This is a fundamental criticism of the social-scientific approach; carried to an extreme, it would raise questions about the ability of modern scholars to write a social history of antiquity. Most modern historians would not carry the argument this far, but it is clear that scholars engaging in social-scientific criticism must consider in great detail the methodological problems raised by their enterprise.[36]

Second, some critics have felt that the application of social-scientific criticism can lead to a social reductionism that ignores all nonsocial forces in the shaping of history and literature.[37] A variant of this criticism focuses in particular on the way in which social-scientific criticism can cause scholars to overlook the theological dimensions of the text. While social reductionism is indeed always a danger to the interpreter, it is not a necessary result of using social-scientific criticism, and most practitioners of the approach have guarded against reductionism by using other interpretive methods as well.

Third, critics have sometimes objected to the use of models and reconstructions in the application of social-scientific criticism, although it is difficult to see how the writing of ancient social history could take place at all without reconstructions of some sort, and their use is not limited to social-scientific approaches. Still, it is important to recognize models and reconstructions for what they are and not to claim too much certainty for them. If nothing else, models and reconstructions can help scholars to expand their understandings of historical and literary problems and to suggest new questions to ask of their subject matter.[38]

Fourth, there has been some criticism of the comparative use of ethnographic data on the grounds that the data is not representative of similar data in other cultures. This issue has been raised particularly when biblical scholars have adopted a segmentary lineage model of social organization from anthropological research on the Nuer, a large confederation of tribes in western Ethiopia and southern Sudan, and then used that material to reconstruct the social organization of early Israel.[39] The use of atypical comparative material is always a danger, as is the failure to recognize cultural uniqueness, but the danger can be avoided by understanding the comparative data first in its own context and then by comparing it with data in analogous cultures before any application is made to ancient Israel.

Finally, recent debates about the dating of the biblical texts have raised questions about the possibility of applying social-scientific approaches to those texts. If the texts that describe preexilic Israel are in fact late creations, as some scholars claim, then they cannot be used for any sort of sociological reconstruction of an earlier period unless it can be shown that the late texts accurately preserve early material. Faced with these uncertainties, some scholars have gone so far as to suggest that no historical reconstruction of any kind can take place solely on the basis of the Bible and that scholars should simply confine their work to literary analyses of texts.[40] The question of the dating of the biblical texts is a genuine problem for any attempt to use those texts in historical reconstruction, and this issue must be faced and resolved in any attempt to apply social-scientific criticism. Extreme solutions on either side are not likely to win the day, but the basic problem cannot be ignored.

The Future of Social-Scientific Criticism

Given the widespread use of social-scientific criticism, it is difficult to predict the directions it may take in the future. The approach has already been used in so many diverse ways that questions may eventually have to be raised about whether the designation itself any longer has any utility. However that may be, it is fairly clear that most of the directions that this approach has taken in the past will be continued in the future and that new directions will be explored. In addition, there are several areas of study that would benefit from further exploration.

First, it is clear that major methodological problems are still associated with social-scientific criticism. Some of these issues are discussed above, and future researchers must refine the analysis of the difficulties and seek working solutions for them, if this sort of criticism is to continue to be useful.

Second, in recent years biblical scholars have begun to focus increasingly on the issue of how the Old Testament came to be in the form in which we now have it. To be sure, this issue has been on the scholarly agenda for a long time, but recent work has concentrated on the mechanics of text production in a much more concrete way than in the past and has highlighted the role that scribes played in the creation of the text.[41] This concentration on text production raises a number of sociological issues, which social-scientific criticism is well equipped to address. To date, much of the sociological discussion has focused on issues of hierarchy and the power of elites, but much more about the actual life of scribes remains to be explored. Such an exploration may well change the way that scholars think about the formation of biblical literature and may move the discussion onto different ground.

Finally, in the past, practitioners of social-scientific criticism have occasionally referred to the importance of understanding the social location of the interpreter, not just the social location of the text. For the most part, however, little attention has been paid to the sociology of interpretation outside of postmodernist circles, and it remains one of the unexplored dimensions of the social-scientific approach. Such an undertaking is difficult, particularly when it involves interpreters who are still alive, but if it is responsibly done it might provide a clearer understanding of the nature of scholarship and the directions that it takes.[42] For the moment, however, this area of research is largely untouched and remains an open field for future research.

For Further Reading

Carter, Charles E., and Carol L. Meyers, eds. *Community, Identity, and Ideology: Social Science Approaches to the Hebrew Bible*. Winona Lake, Ind.: Eisenbrauns, 1996.

Chalcraft, David J., ed. *Social-Scientific Old Testament Criticism*. Biblical Seminar 47. Sheffield: Sheffield Academic Press, 1997.

Esler, Philip F., and Anselm C. Hagedorn. "Social-Scientific Analysis of the Old Testament: A Brief History and Overview." Pages 15–24 in *Ancient Israel: The Old Testament in Its Social Context*. Edited by Philip F. Esler. Minneapolis: Augsburg Fortress, 2006.

Frick, Frank S. "Norman Gottwald's *The Tribes of Yahweh* in the Context of 'Second-Wave' Social-Scientific Biblical Criticism." Pages 17–34 in *Tracking* The Tribes of Yahweh*: On the Trail of a Classic*. Edited by Roland Boer. JSOTSup 351. London: Continuum, 2002.

Mayes, Andrew D. H. *The Old Testament in Sociological Perspective*. London: Marshall Pickering, 1989.

Petersen, David L. *The Roles of Israel's Prophets*. JSOTSup 17. Sheffield: JSOT Press, 1981.

Steinberg, Naomi. "Social-Scientific Criticism." *DBI* 2:480–81.

Wilson, Robert R. *Sociological Approaches to the Old Testament*. GBS 9. Philadelphia: Fortress, 1984.

Notes

1. For examples of this sort of interpretation, see Robert R. Wilson, *Sociological Approaches to the Old Testament* (GBS 9; Philadelphia: Fortress, 1984), 1–3 and the literature cited there.

2. Accounts of the influence of Weber and the use of sociological approaches by biblical scholars in general are provided by Andrew D. H. Mayes, *The Old Testament in Sociological Perspective* (London: Marshall Pickering, 1989). See also Wilson, *Sociological Approaches*, 15–16, 23–24.

3. James George Frazer, *The Golden Bough* (3rd ed.; 12 vols.; New York: Macmillan, 1935); idem, *Folk-Lore in the Old Testament* (3 vols.; London: Macmillan, 1918).

4. For a discussion of anthropological influences on Old Testament scholarship in the nineteenth and early twentieth centuries, see John W. Rogerson, *Anthropology and the Old Testament* (Oxford: Basil Blackwell, 1978); idem, *Old Testament Criticism in the Nineteenth Century: England and Germany* (London: SPCK, 1984); and idem, *The Bible and Criticism in Victorian Britain: Profiles of F. D. Maurice and W. Robertson Smith* (Sheffield: Sheffield Academic Press, 1995).

5. The term "second wave" seems to have been coined by Frank S. Frick in his "Norman Gottwald's *The Tribes of Yahweh* in the Context of 'Second-Wave' Social-Scientific Biblical Criticism," in *Tracking The Tribes of Yahweh: On the Trail of a Classic* (ed. Roland Boer; JSOTSup 351; London: Continuum, 2002), 17–34. Although the "second wave" appeared in both Old Testament and New Testament scholarship, the discussion that follows focuses on the Old Testament. For a discussion of the New Testament applications of the approach, see Philip F. Esler, "Social-Scientific Models in Biblical Interpretation," in *Ancient Israel: The Old Testament in Its Social Context* (ed. Philip F. Esler; Minneapolis: Augsburg Fortress, 2006), 3–14.

6. A particularly vocal advocate of this position was Brevard S. Childs, who had become convinced that the "Biblical Theology Movement" that was influential in the United States in mid-century could not in fact deliver on its claim to be able to unite historical-critical scholarship with a theological understanding of the biblical text. See, in particular, his *Biblical Theology in Crisis* (Philadelphia: Westminster, 1970). Childs would later find problems with most historical-critical approaches, including social-scientific perspectives. See, for example, his discussion in *Biblical Theology of the Old and New Testaments* (Minneapolis: Fortress, 1992), 22–25, 666–68, 675–76.

7. For a discussion of this new form of history writing and its influence on biblical scholars, see Hans M. Barstad, "The History of Ancient Israel: What Directions Should We Take," in *Understanding the History of Ancient Israel* (ed. H. G. M. Williamson; Proceedings of the British Academy 143; Oxford: Oxford University Press, 2007), 25–29.

8. For a discussion of the influence of the Annales tradition on archaeologists, see Thomas E. Levy and Augustin F. C. Holl, "Social Change and the Archaeology of the Holy Land," in *The Archaeology of Society in the Holy Land* (ed. Thomas E. Levy; London: Leicester University Press, 1998), 2–8.

9. For a discussion of the influence of social anthropology on "second wave" social-scientific criticism, see Wilson, *Sociological Approaches*, 19–21; and Philip F.

Esler and Anselm C. Hagedorn, "Social-Scientific Analysis of the Old Testament: A Brief History and Overview," in Esler, *Ancient Israel*, 15–24.

10. The influence of current social events is particularly marked in the early work of Norman Gottwald, and the beginnings of postmodernist influences can already be seen in the work of Frank Frick, among others. See, e.g., Frank S. Frick, "Sociological Criticism and Its Relation to Political and Social Hermeneutics, With a Special Look at Biblical Hermeneutics in South African Liberation Theology," in *The Bible and the Politics of Exegesis* (ed. David Jobling, Peggy L. Day, and Gerald T. Sheppard; Cleveland: Pilgrim, 1991), 225–38. On the role of women's studies in the discussion, see Naomi Steinberg, "Social-Scientific Criticism," *DBI* 2:480–81.

11. Mary Douglas, *Purity and Danger: An Analysis of Concepts of Pollution and Taboo* (London: Routledge & Kegan Paul, 1966). In her later work she engaged more fully in a conversation with biblical scholars and made many helpful suggestions about literary and religious issues in the biblical field. See, e.g., *In the Wilderness: The Doctrine of Defilement in the Book of Numbers* (JSOTSup 158; Sheffield: Sheffield Academic Press, 1993); idem, *Leviticus as Literature* (Oxford: Oxford University Press, 1999); and idem, *Jacob's Tears: The Priestly Work of Reconciliation* (Oxford: Oxford University Press, 2004).

12. Edmund R. Leach, "The Legitimacy of Solomon," in *Genesis as Myth and Other Essays* (ed. Edmund Leach; London: Jonathan Cape, 1969), 25–83.

13. Julian Pitt-Rivers, *The Fate of Shechem or the Politics of Sex: Essays in the Anthropology of the Mediterranean* (Cambridge: Cambridge University Press, 1977). On the development of the "second wave" in England, see John W. Rogerson, "Anthropology and the Old Testament," in *The World of Ancient Israel: Sociological, Anthropological and Political Perspectives* (ed. R. E. Clements; Cambridge: Cambridge University Press, 1989), 19–20; and Esler and Hagedorn, "Social-Scientific Analysis," 21–22.

14. For a discussion of the "second wave" in Germany, see Rainer Albertz, "Social History of Ancient Israel," in Williamson, *Understanding the History of Ancient Israel*, 347–54; and Rainer Kessler, *The Social History of Ancient Israel: An Introduction* (Minneapolis: Fortress, 2008), 5–12.

15. George E. Mendenhall, "The Hebrew Conquest of Canaan," *BA* 25 (1962): 66–87.

16. Norman K. Gottwald, *The Tribes of Yahweh: A Sociology of the Religion of Liberated Israel 1250–1050 B.C.E.* (Maryknoll, N.Y.: Orbis, 1979).

17. Marvin L. Chaney, "Ancient Palestinian Peasant Movements and the Formation of Premonarchic Israel," in *Palestine in Transition: The Emergence of Ancient Israel* (ed. David Noel Freedman and David Frank Graf; Sheffield: Almond, 1983); Frank S. Frick, *The Formation of the State in Ancient Israel: A Survey of Models and Theories* (Decatur, Ga.: Almond, 1985); Robert B. Coote and Keith W. Whitelam, *The Emergence of Early Israel in Historical Perspective* (Sheffield: Almond, 1987); James W. Flanagan, "Chiefs in Israel," *JSOT* 20 (1981): 47–73. For an insider's view of the early phase of the discussion, see Frank S. Frick, "Social Science Methods and Theories of Significance for the Study of the Israelite Monarchy: A Critical Review Essay," *Semeia* 37 (1986): 9–52; and Marvin L. Chaney, "Systemic Study of the Israelite Monarchy," *Semeia* 37 (1986): 53–76.

18. Abraham Malamat, "King Lists of the Old Babylonian Period and Biblical Genealogies," *JAOS* 88 (1968): 163–73.

19. Robert R. Wilson, *Genealogy and History in the Biblical World* (New Haven: Yale University Press, 1977).

20. Thomas W. Overholt, "The Ghost Dance of 1890 and the Nature of the Prophetic Process," *Ethnohistory* 21 (1974): 37–63; idem, "Prophecy: The Problem of Cross-Cultural Comparison," *Semeia* 21 (1982): 55–78; idem, *Prophecy in Cross-Cultural Perspective: A Sourcebook for Biblical Researchers* (SBLSBS 17; Atlanta: Scholars Press, 1986); idem, *Channels of Prophecy: The Social Dynamics of Prophetic Activity* (Minneapolis: Fortress, 1989).

21. Robert R. Wilson, "Early Israelite Prophecy," *Int* 32 (1978): 3–16; idem, "Prophecy and Ecstasy: A Reexamination," *JBL* 98 (1979): 321–37; idem, *Prophecy and Society in Ancient Israel* (Philadelphia: Fortress, 1980).

22. David L. Petersen, *The Roles of Israel's Prophets* (JSOTSup 17; Sheffield: JSOT Press, 1981).

23. Robert P. Carroll, *When Prophecy Failed* (New York: Seabury, 1979).

24. Paul D. Hanson, *The Dawn of Apocalyptic* (Philadelphia: Fortress, 1975).

25. Lawrence E. Stager, "The Archaeology of the Family in Ancient Israel," *BASOR* 260 (1985): 1–35; John S. Holladay, "House, Israelite," *ABD* 3:308–18.

26. For an account of the role of the scholarly working groups, see James W. Flanagan, "New Constructs in Social World Studies," in Jobling, Day, and Sheppard, *The Bible and the Politics of Exegesis*, 210–15.

27. Many of the sociologically oriented articles that appeared in *JSOT* have been reprinted in David J. Chalcraft, ed., *Social-Scientific Old Testament Criticism* (Sheffield: Sheffield Academic Press, 1997). Other relevant work from the "second wave" has been collected in Charles E. Carter and Carol L. Meyers, eds., *Community, Identity, and Ideology: Social Science Approaches to the Hebrew Bible* (Winona Lake, Ind.: Eisenbrauns, 1996).

28. K. C. Hanson, "The Old Testament: Social Sciences and Social Description"; online: http://www.kchanson.com/CLASSIFIEDBIB/otsocsci.html.

29. Lester L. Grabbe, *Priests, Prophets, Diviners, Sages: A Socio-historical Study of Religious Specialists in Ancient Israel* (Valley Forge, Pa.: Trinity Press International, 1995); Richard A. Horsley, *Scribes, Visionaries, and the Politics of Second Temple Judea* (Louisville: Westminster John Knox, 2007); Wilda C. Gafney, *Daughters of Miriam: Women Prophets in Ancient Israel* (Minneapolis: Fortress, 2008).

30. Victor Matthews and Don C. Benjamin, *Social World of Ancient Israel: 1250–587 B.C.E.* (Peabody, Mass.: Hendrickson, 1993); Kessler, *Social History*.

31. David L. Petersen, "Max Weber and the Sociological Study of Ancient Israel," *Sociological Inquiry* 49 (1979): 117–49. On recent applications of Weber in Germany, see Kessler, *Social History*, 5–12.

32. Carol Meyers, *Discovering Eve: Ancient Israelite Women in Context* (New York: Oxford University Press, 1988). Note also Phyllis A. Bird, *Missing Persons and Mistaken Identities: Women and Gender in Ancient Israel* (Minneapolis: Fortress, 1997).

33. Naomi Steinberg, *Kinship and Marriage in Genesis: A Household Economics Approach* (Minneapolis: Fortress, 1993); Saul M. Olyan, *Rites and Rank: Hierarchy in*

Biblical Representations of Cult (Princeton: Princeton University Press, 2000); idem, *Biblical Mourning: Ritual and Social Dimensions* (New York: Oxford University Press, 2004); Nancy Jay, *Throughout Your Generations Forever: Sacrifice, Religion, and Paternity* (Chicago: University of Chicago Press, 1992).

34. Herbert Niehr, *Rechtsprechung in Israel: Untersuchungen zur Geschichte der Gerichtsorganisation in Alten Testament* (Stuttgart: Katholisches Bibelwerk, 1987); Bernard S. Jackson, "Law in the Ninth Century: Jehoshaphat's 'Judicial Reform,'" in Williamson, *Understanding the History of Ancient Israel*, 369–97.

35. For an example of this position, see Cyril S. Rodd, "On Applying a Sociological Theory to Biblical Studies," *JSOT* 19 (1981): 95–106.

36. For a helpful discussion of the methodological issues, see Albertz, "Social History of Ancient Israel," 347–67.

37. See, e.g., the remarks of Gary A. Herion, "The Impact of Modern and Social Science Assumptions on the Reconstruction of Israelite History," *JSOT* 34 (1986): 3–33.

38. See the criticisms of Herion (ibid.) and the reply of Mark G. Brett, "Literacy and Domination: G. A. Herion's Sociology of History Writing," *JSOT* 37 (1987): 15–40.

39. David Fiensy, "Using the Nuer Culture of Africa in Understanding the Old Testament: An Evaluation," *JSOT* 38 (1987): 73–83; J. W. Rogerson, "Was Early Israel a Segmentary Society?" *JSOT* 36 (1986): 17–26.

40. Note, for example, the remarks of Robert P. Carroll, "Poets Not Prophets," *JSOT* 27 (1983): 25–31. Carroll thought that any attempt to reconstruct the phenomenon of Israelite prophecy on the basis of the biblical texts was impossible. A similar skeptical approach is taken by Philip R. Davies, *Scribes and Schools: The Canonization of the Hebrew Scriptures* (Louisville: Westminster John Knox, 1998).

41. See, e.g., Davies, *Scribes and Schools*; William M. Schniedewind, *How the Bible Became a Book* (Cambridge: Cambridge University Press, 2004); David M. Carr, *Writing on the Tablet of the Heart: Origins of Scripture and Literature* (Oxford: Oxford University Press, 2005); and Karel van der Toorn, *Scribal Culture and the Making of the Hebrew Bible* (Cambridge: Harvard University Press, 2007).

42. For an example of an attempt to study the sociology of the interpreter, see Burke O. Long, *Planting and Reaping Albright: Politics, Ideology, and Interpreting the Bible* (University Park: Pennsylvania State University Press, 1997). The difficulties involved in this sort of undertaking can be seen in the enormous amount of criticism that was provoked by Long's book.

Reflections on Literary Criticism

John Barton

The term *literary criticism* has had a complicated history in biblical studies. It has been used to designate two quite different movements in biblical criticism, often regarded as polar opposites. In older scholarship it was a translation of the German *Literarkritik*, whereas in contemporary usage it refers to a range of interpretative approaches having affinities with what is called "literary criticism" in the wider literary and cultural world. Examining these two usages can be instructive, since, as I shall argue, they are not so far apart as they seem at first glance.

Literarkritik means what used to be called "the higher criticism." Whereas textual (or "lower") criticism attempts to establish the earliest written version of a given text by comparing manuscripts and reasoning back to an *Urtext*, *Literarkritik* operates by asking how the text came to be in the first place and whether it is made up from a diversity of underlying sources. The most common term for *Literarkritik* in English is now no longer "literary criticism" but "source criticism." The standard example of such criticism would be the source analysis of the Pentateuch into J, E, D, and P according to the classic Graf-Wellhausen hypothesis. The approach involved is "literary" rather than merely textual in that it is concerned with the original composition, rather than the technical transmission, of the texts in question.

Although one thinks first of the Pentateuch in reflecting on literary criticism in this sense, a great deal of this kind of criticism has been done, and continues to be done, on other texts. For example, when we speak of the Succession Narrative or Court History of David in 2 Sam 9–20; 1 Kgs 1–2, we are practicing *Literarkritik*, because we are isolating a particular section of the books of Samuel and putting forward a hypothesis about its original writing. It was crucial to this hypothesis, as originally put forward by Leonhard Rost,[1] that there was a break in the text of Samuel just before 2 Sam 9, so that what followed could be construed as an originally independent literary work. What preceded it, according to him, belonged to the History of David's Rise, which once existed as a separate work. *Literarkritik* has also been central to the study of the prophetic books. It is to this approach, for example, that we owe the theory that there are three independent collections in the book of Isaiah—First, Second, and Third Isaiah—and within them other separable passages, such as the Isaiah Apocalypse (Isa 24–27). Even in the wisdom literature scholars have hypothesized earlier collections underlying the present text, as in the almost universal acceptance that the Egyptian Instruction of Amen-em-opet forms the basis of Prov 22:17–24:34, which is therefore a separate unit within the book of Proverbs.

Literary criticism in this sense of the word continues to be practiced by biblical scholars especially (though not exclusively) in the German-speaking world. In recent years it has tended to take the form of what is sometimes called "composition criticism." In this, interest centers not so much on reconstructing originally independent sources as on tracing the stages by which the finished work came into being. One may think of William McKane's hypothesis about the book of Jeremiah; it is not a collection or anthology of materials with discrete origins that a redactor or editor has then assembled but rather what he calls a "rolling corpus"—a snowball that gathers more and more material as it rolls downhill.[2] Whereas in the Pentateuch the majority of scholars probably still detect several (or at least two) underlying works that had an independent existence before they were collected by "R," the pentateuchal redactor, the "rolling corpus" model implies that books had an original core that has been supplemented successively as scribes copied and recopied it (in pentateuchal studies this would correspond to the old Supplementary Hypothesis of the first half of the nineteenth century, elaborated by Heinrich Ewald). Such a model may indeed be more plausible once we start to think of the technology of ancient book production. To weave together four separate sources, each on its own scroll, is prodigiously difficult, but to copy out a text and supplement it as one goes is a much easier task. One of the earliest examples of such composition criticism would be Jacques Vermeylen's *Du prophète Isaïe à l'apocalyptique*,[3] which suggests many successive stages in the production of the book of Isaiah, from the eighth century B.C.E. to the second. On Vermeylen's view, there was a continuous tradition of copying out "Isaiah," and at each stage it was augmented and given a new slant by the scribes, some of whom had distinct theological concerns of their own that they conveyed both by what they added to the text they had inherited and by the way they shaped the material.

But in the last few decades there has been a radical shift in biblical studies, particularly outside the German world, toward a new sense of "literary criticism," the sense it has in general literary studies: a form of aesthetic appreciation of texts. In its current North American and British form, this seems as far removed as it could be from the "reconstructive" tendency of *Literarkritik*. It works with the text as it now lies before us and self-consciously rejects as irrelevant (or even historically inaccurate) hypotheses of earlier stages underlying the present text. One of the main proponents of a literary approach to the Bible in this sense is Robert Alter, Professor of Hebrew and Comparative Literature at the University of California, Berkeley, author of works on modern European and American literature as well as on the Bible. In a series of works he has outlined a literary approach to the Hebrew Bible that takes its norms from the "close reading" of texts usual in the world of English and comparative literary studies.[4] Alter contrasts his work with *Literarkritik* by describing the latter as "excavative," a kind of literary archaeology. His description is a useful way of pointing to the tendency to look at earlier strata in the text rather than at the text that has come down to us.

One may also contrast a modern literary reading (in the British and American sense) with traditional "higher criticism" by deploying the terms *synchronic* and *diachronic*, much used in linguistics. A diachronic (through time) reading of a text is one concerned with how the text came to be, whereas a synchronic (contemporaneous) reading looks at the text just as it meets us in the present. Alter's work is certainly in this sense synchronic. That does not mean that it ignores the historical context of the text, reading it as though it had been written yesterday. On the contrary, Alter locates the text carefully in an ancient literary context. Alter's synchronic analysis does entail eschewing any concern for how the biblical text came into being and any stages it may have passed through on the way to its present form.

The clearest example of Alter's synchronic reading is his discussion of Gen 38. Alter tries to show how Gen 38, the story of Tamar and Judah, is not the erratic block within the Joseph story that generations of commentators have believed but can be read as perfectly well-integrated into its narrative context. The clue is the theme of recognition: Judah "recognizes" (in a technical, legal sense) the items he left with Tamar, just as he forced his own father Jacob to "recognize" Joseph's blood-stained coat.[5]

The theme of the brothers getting what they deserve through the way events unfold is thus present here just as much as in the rest of the story of Joseph, and there is no need to posit an interpolator who has inserted Gen 38 after the Joseph narrative was complete.

But this kind of argument, which depends on verbal connections as well as on connections of theme, need not stop at the level of the (supposed) "Joseph narrative." It can be applied, and Alter does apply it, to Genesis as a whole or to the historical books as a whole. Thus he traces connections between widely separated narrative texts, established by identifying *Leitwörter* and "type scenes." For example, there are several stories of a meeting at a well (Gen 24:10–27; 29:1–12; Exod 2:15–22) in which a wife is secured for a great figure in Israel's history. There is a significant "intertextuality" among the stories, such that we can interpret one in the light of the others. They are not "doublets" as in the classic source-critical interpretation, which concerns itself with which is the earliest example (see, e.g., critical discussions of the "wife-sister" stories in Gen 12:10–20; 20:1–18; 26:6–11). Rather, they belong to the careful construction of narrative echoes, intended to lead the reader to see connections over a wide textual span. Alter is not interested in the old questions about the historical origins of texts and is quite happy to detect intertextual allusion between texts that do not come from the same period, historically speaking.

Alter's work represents the transfer into biblical studies of the sorts of method and interests current in "secular" literary criticism, especially in the Anglo-American tradition, with its concern for "richness" of meaning requiring close and detailed reading of the text to become aware of it. A comparable example from New Testament studies is Frank Kermode's book *The Genesis of Secrecy*,[6] a close reading of the Gospel of Mark. Kermode and Alter collaborated in editing *The Literary Guide to the Bible*,[7] in which a range of scholars seek to read all the books of the (Protestant) Bible as literary works, even insisting on using the King James Version because that is the translation that is iconic for English-speaking readers. In a way, this is to treat the Bible as an English literary classic rather than as a collection of ancient Hebrew, Aramaic, and Greek books, and to a traditionally trained biblical scholar it can easily appear anachronistic. It represents, however, a serious shift in the style of biblical scholarship and interpretation, and one that shows every sign of vigorous growth in recent years. Even someone who approaches it with some skepticism cannot fail to see that it has resulted in a whole generation of people becoming interested in the Bible who might otherwise have regarded it merely as an ancient document to be studied only by specialists. There is no overt religious agenda in Alter's work, and many literary-critical readers of the Bible deliberately set themselves against a theological interpretation of the text; however, the idea that the Bible is somehow our contemporary, in a way that is not true of classical or other ancient texts, perhaps owes something to its traditional religious authority. Treating the Bible as a "classic" is a kind of secularized version of seeing it as "inspired." Critics such as Alter say, in effect: never mind that these texts are regarded as authoritative Scripture by Jews and Christians; even considered simply as literature, they are great works.

Such an approach goes back, in a way, to a critic such as Robert Lowth in the seventeenth century, whose aim was to convince his readers that the Bible was not *only* a book of religious authority but actually just as great in literary terms as the Greek and Latin classics.[8] He was confronted with people who thought the Bible divinely inspired—for they were religious—but would not have wanted to read it on any other basis, since they did not think of it as in the same aesthetic league with great works of literature, such as Homer. Lowth's object was to show that the Bible had its own literary excellence, which emerged once one had learned the conventions of Hebrew writing, such as the parallelism that characterizes Hebrew verse. Alter is in many ways the heir of Lowth, and so are all modern literary critics of the Bible. It seems to them, rather paradoxically, as though the very status of the Bible in believing circles has blinkered readers to its literary excellence. In Alter's careful reading of the story of David, for example, we find that this is a work that can take its place without shame beside the stories of Achilles or Odysseus, even beside modern literary classics.

This view of the Bible's literary merits represents an interesting shift, because there is another twentieth-century tradition of refusing to allow that it is literature in a modern sense. C. S. Lewis was particularly scathing about the "Bible as Literature" movement in Britain between the wars, which had issued in the publication of *The Bible Designed to be Read as Literature*.[9] He thought that to treat the Bible as literature was to ignore its peculiarly religious claim—as it were, deliberately to look away from what it was really trying to tell us.

> There is a certain sense in which "the Bible as literature" does not exist. It is a collection of books so widely different in period, kind, language, and aesthetic value that no common criticism can be passed on them. In uniting these heterogeneous texts the Church was not guided by literary

> principles, and the literary critic might regard their inclusion between the same boards as a theological and historical accident irrelevant to his own branch of study.... Unless the religious claims of the Bible are again acknowledged, its literary claims will, I think, be given only "mouth honour" and that decreasingly. For it is, through and through, a sacred book. Most of its component parts were written, and all of them were brought together, for a purely religious purpose.... In most parts of the Bible everything is implicitly or explicitly introduced with "Thus saith the Lord." It is, if you like to put it that way, not merely a sacred book but a book so remorselessly and continuously sacred that it does not invite, it excludes or repels, the merely aesthetic approach. You can read it as literature only by a tour de force. You are cutting the wood against the grain, using the tool for a purpose it was not intended to serve. It demands incessantly to be taken on its own terms: it will not continue to give literary delight very long except to those who go to it for something quite different. I predict that it will in the future be read, as it always has been read, almost exclusively by Christians.[10]

There is an echo of this same sentiment in a work that does treat the Bible from a literary point of view, Gabriel Josipovici's *The Book of God*, which argues that in the Hebrew Bible literary expectations are often defeated; the Bible is literature that subverts literature.[11] As Benjamin Jowett argued, we should read the Bible "like any other book," but when we do so, we find that it is *not* like any other book but has its own unique (he would have said, "uniquely inspired") character.[12] On the whole, however, biblical study by the end of the twentieth century was persuaded that treating the Bible as literature was appropriate, and for many critics the kind of close reading practiced by Alter represents an ideal style in which to approach the biblical text.

There are other kinds of literary criticism on offer. Alter inherits the Anglo-American tradition of literary criticism that found its main theoretical expression in the so-called New Criticism, associated with W. K. Wimsatt Jr., M. C. Beardsley, Cleanth Brooks, R. Wellek, A. Warren, and Allen Tate, and aligned in many ways also with T. S. Eliot. As against an older Romantic criticism that concerned itself with the biography and psychology of the author, New Critics focused austerely on "the text itself" and permitted no reference to authorial biography or even intention. I have argued that there are parallels to the New Criticism in the so-called "canonical approach" of Brevard S. Childs, though Childs denies this.[13] But this focus on the text itself was also characteristic of other strains of criticism in the twentieth century, which may be described in general terms as *formalist*. Formalist approaches are even further than was New Criticism from asking about the author's intention, since they concerned themselves with the text almost as a free-floating entity, to be assessed in and of itself.

The Russian version of formalism, influential during the first half of the twentieth century in the world of secular criticism but arriving in biblical studies in the 1960s and 1970s, began by studying "authorless" texts—such things as folktales and other traditional literature. Very influential here was Vladimir Propp. His work on the morphology of the folktale was mediated in the West through the structuralist school in France. One of its concerns was "narratology." Narratology, as the art or science of understanding how written narratives work, is by general consent a product of the structuralism of the 1970s, associated with such names as Algirdas Greimas, Gérard Genette, and Roland Barthes, but its ultimate inspiration was certainly Propp's *Morphology of the Folktale* (published in 1928 but not translated into English until 1958).[14] Propp's work was a study of oral forms, traditional stories transmitted by word of mouth. It argued that each character in a folktale belongs to one of a restricted number of classes, such as the originator of a quest, the hero, the helper, and so on, and that one can work out a set of algorithms that determine how these characters can be combined into a finite set of basic plots, which can then be set out using symbols that look rather like the symbols used in symbolic logic. Narratology began when it occurred to critics, mostly in France, that such an analysis could also be applied to written narratives. It was all part of the attempt by structuralists to move away from a more humanistic analysis of literature as the expression of profound thoughts and toward a quasi-scientific approach in which, in a sense, literature writes itself, given certain conditions.

Structuralism thus reconfigured literary criticism as the pursuit of objective meaning in texts, dependent on neither the author nor the reader but only on the structures the text itself exhibits. It was quite influential for a time in biblical studies. The classic structuralist study of a biblical text is Roland Barthes's article on Jacob wrestling with the mysterious being at the ford of the Jabbok in Gen 32:22–32.[15] In the story Jacob has been sent on a journey to his relatives in Mesopotamia. After many years he returns, feeling that the God who sent him on his journey is about to complete his quest by granting him a peaceful life back in the land that would become Israel. Just before he crosses over into the promised land, however, he encounters during the night a being, called simply "a man" in the Hebrew text, who wrestles with him all night but whom he overcomes. As the man is fleeing from him before daybreak (possibly there is an old folktale motif here of a kind of troll that cannot survive in daylight), he touches Jacob and injures him, yet at the same time he gives Jacob a new name, "Israel," marking him out as the ancestor of a great nation.

Now in the Bible the only person who can give someone a new name is God, and it is clear that the mysterious "man" is either God himself or at least his appointed representative—an angel, as we might say. But if we analyze the story in Proppean terms, we find something very strange. God is, according to such an analysis, the originator of the quest and the one who presides over its fulfillment and eventually rewards Jacob by giving him the promised land. Yet in this story he is also Jacob's opponent. This, in terms of narratological analysis, is improper, a confusion of roles. It shows that the story cannot be a real folktale, even though it may ultimately rest on one and has certain obvious folktale features. As it stands, the story subverts the normal rules of folktale. It cannot therefore be an oral tale that has been later committed to writing but must be some kind of deliberate exploitation or parody of a folktale. It is using the themes and motifs of folklore to make a point that folklore would never make.

A Proppian analysis thus has the paradoxical effect of identifying in Gen 32 a story that is not really susceptible of such an analysis but rather breaks the mold. One could move in two directions from this conclusion, and I would say that the two directions have been determinative for subsequent study of narrative texts in the Hebrew Bible. Barthes himself, strangely, drew theological conclusions from his analysis. He argued that it was Hebrew monotheism that was responsible for the strange turn in the story. For a monotheistic culture, the one God must be the source of all that happens: hence he must be the opponent as well as the originator of the quest. This accords with a general tendency in the Hebrew Bible to acknowledge no sources of power beyond the one God, YHWH. Even when, in rather late texts, a kind of devil appears, the being known as Satan, he is clearly subordinate to the one God and sometimes even his agent, a kind of hit man appointed by God himself to do his dirty work. In general, dualism is avoided in the Hebrew Bible, and that has the consequence, unpleasant as it may seem, that evil as well as good has to be traced back to God. So for Barthes, Hebrew culture turns out to be one in which Propp's laws do not really hold. This remarkable conclusion that made the Bible unique commended structuralism to some very conservative Jews and Christians who would otherwise have been put off it by structuralism's generally Marxist-atheist style.

But Barthes's narratological analysis could also move in a more strictly literary direction. One need not make a point about the extreme uniqueness of Hebrew literature but could instead focus on the way in which narratology can, as it were, in spite of itself, point to literary skill. When we talk about someone as a great writer we mean that the person has an ability to take commonplace conventions and use them to deliver an unconventional message. We admire stories that have "a sting in the tail," where things do not turn out as we expected. Identifying "the opponent" with "the originator" turns the story of Jacob from a commonplace folktale into great literature, or at least potentially so. We realize this, I would argue, at a subliminal level; most readers of the story experience a sort of shiver down the spine when they read it. Only knowing about Propp's laws makes it possible to articulate just what it is that gives the story this spine-tingling effect. But the story also shows that Propp's laws are not deterministic; rather, they tell us how conventional literature works and thereby open up the possibility that we shall recognize literature that is unconventional. Structuralists were very interested in detective stories, and one can easily see why; they are governed by very strict rules about what is and is not allowed to happen within the genre. But one can have subversive detective stories, as in Agatha Christie's *The Murder of Roger Ackroyd*,[16] where the murderer turns out to be the first-person narrator, or Alain Robbe-Grillet's *Les Gommes*,[17] where a detective arrives in a town to investigate a murder that has not in fact happened and ends up committing it himself. The story of Jacob is like these, a story that undercuts the rules for stories. Barthes's analysis does not, I think, really show that it requires a culture of a wholly unique religious character but rather that it comes from a culture that was sophisticated in its literary abilities.

Structuralism has ceased to be a major force in the literary world, where it has been replaced by various forms of poststructuralism, deconstruction, and postmodernism. But for a time it promised a kind of literary criticism that was not a subjective aesthetic response to the biblical text but based on entirely objective criteria—just as objective, in fact, as *Literarkritik* had usually claimed to be. There is still interesting formalist work being undertaken, especially in the Netherlands, where one thinks of Jan Fokkelman and Eep Talstra,[18] who are concerned with the internal structuring of texts, as the structuralists were, but without the high ideological commitment to a "science" of the text. Fokkelman's analysis of the structures of the books of Samuel, for example, show how it is possible, through detailed investigation, to show how the text "works" to produce the literary effect it does.

A related movement that may also be called formalist can be found in the work of scholars who practice what is variously known as text-linguistics or discourse analysis. Here attention is paid to extremely minute details of the text in order to show how the text flows: how, for example, change of speaker is marked in a text, or when word order varies from the normal default order.[19]

In all these approaches, which I have lumped together as "formalist," emphasis falls on the text itself as the object for investigation; no interest is or should be paid to the author, the historical circumstances of the text's production, or how it is or has been read or received by its readers. Another major branch in modern biblical criticism, however, concentrates precisely on these matters. I have in mind reader-response criticism and reception history.

In reader-response criticism, whose main "secular" exponent is Stanley Fish, the leading idea is that meaning does not reside in either the text or its author, but only in the interplay between text and reader. The author provides the words, but it is the reader who supplies the interpretation. In his classic *Is There a Text in This Class?*[20] Fish showed how a series of names left written up on a board in a classroom could be construed by the next class as some kind of poem. This was because the second class was a class in English literature, whereas the original readers had been a group of history students concerned simply to list some important figures in the period they were studying. The second class tended to construe the list as a poem because, within the context of a course in English literature, they expected anything displayed on the board to be relevant to their own concerns, and the only way to make sense of the list in that context was to read it as a poem. This highlights two points that are equally important in Fish's theory: first, that we bring our own concerns to the reading of texts, which have no meaning apart from the reader; but, second, that the context of reading is important, too. Fish talks of "interpretive communities" that look for particular sorts of meaning in texts. Where the Bible is concerned, it is obvious that the church or synagogue constitutes such an interpretive community, which tends to push readers to find certain meanings in the biblical texts and to avoid others. Whereas traditional biblical criticism (the "historical-critical method," as it is sometimes called) deliberately sets out to discount the meanings that religious people tend to ascribe to the biblical text and instead to establish an "objective" meaning valid for all, reader-response criticism makes a virtue of necessity by arguing that there is no such thing as an objective reading. Further, there is no objection at all to believing readers finding in the Bible the kind of religious message they are looking for.

Reader-response criticism partakes of the general stance often called postmodern, which opposes "modernity," that is, the values of the European Enlightenment with its stress on the progress of objective knowledge. It sees conventional critical biblical study as in thrall to "the Enlightenment project," ignoring the fact (which is accepted now even by some scientists) that there are no neutral observers, only people with commitments to this or that ideology. We cannot, it urges, stand outside our own interests when we approach a text; always we bring ourselves to the text, and this is not a drawback to be avoided if possible, but the only way we have, as humans, of knowing anything. Consequently it is perfectly acceptable (because there is in fact no alternative) to read the Bible through the eyes of a believer—equally, of course, to read it through the eyes of an unbeliever. We shall find there what we are looking for. People committed either to traditional biblical criticism or to the "close reading" tradition tend to think this rather nihilistic and ask why we should bother with the biblical (or any other) text at all, if we necessarily see in it only the reflection of our own faces. My own sympathies lie very much with that objection. But there is no doubt that reader-response criticism is an important movement in the literary criticism of the Bible.

Reader-response criticism can take either a "soft" or a "hard" form. The hard form is represented by Fish, for whom the text has no meaning except as it is activated by the reader; a text in an unknown language, for example, is not merely unreadable but actually has no meaning so long as the language remains undeciphered. In a much-quoted saying, the text is like a picnic to which the author brings the words and the reader the meaning. However, there is also a softer kind of reader-response criticism in which it is not denied that texts have meanings, but it is stressed that the meaning only takes on an active life when a reader interprets it and that there can be many equally valid interpretations. The chief theoretician of this softer form of reader-response criticism is Wolfgang Iser.[21] To use a musical analogy, a symphony cannot validly have absolutely any conceivable interpretation, yet a great deal in our understanding of it does depend on the conductor. The same is true of a play; we can recognize that some "readings" of a play do violence to the text, yet we do allow that there can be ever-new interpretations by inventive producers and actors, and we recognize "Ian McKellen's King Lear," for example, as one possible meaning of Shakespeare's play. The same, we may argue, is true for literary (including biblical) texts; we as readers contribute to their meaning when we read them creatively and sensitively.

But if we are concerned with how readers (including ourselves) read the Bible *now*, then it makes sense also to be concerned for how it was read in the past. One of the fastest-growing areas in biblical studies today is reception history. The theory of this movement was worked out by a colleague of Wolfgang Iser's at the University of Konstanz, Hans Robert Jauss, under the catchword *Wirkungsgeschichte*, "the history of [a texts's] effect," or *Rezeptionsgeschichte*, "the history of [a text's] reception," sometimes rendered in English, rather jarringly, as "effective history"; "reception history" is a better translation.[22] The idea is to discover what the text has been taken to mean down the generations in which it has been read. This is potentially an enormous task, since one would theoretically need to be expert in each of the periods in which the text was "received," and where the biblical text is concerned that means every century—and within every culture that has had contact with the Bible! Nevertheless, the magnitude of the task has not deterred scholars from undertaking it, and there is a major series of commentaries just now appearing in which each biblical book is examined from a reception-historical point of view.[23]

If we link reception history with reader-response interpretation, the following question arises: Is any one stage in a text's interpretation privileged above the others? For example, it was normal in historical criticism to argue that there had been many interpretations of the text in the past, some of which might even be surveyed,[24] but that the meaning established by the historical-critical method was the "real" meaning of the text. But in a reception-historical commentary, the interpretations of historical-critical scholars simply take their place alongside more traditional, or even interestingly idiosyncratic, interpretations as yet another possible way of reading the text. This has a strongly relativizing tendency where historical-critical interpretation is concerned. Like reader-response approaches, it suggests that the text means whatever it has been taken to mean—and therefore means something different in each period, in each culture, potentially to each individual reader. There may be reception historians who do not press the matter to this conclusion but are content simply to register how the biblical book in question has been read in various contexts. But as a general movement, reception history does tend to encourage the view that all interpretations are valid interpretations. If one interpretation is to be preferred over another, this will not be because it is somehow "truer" to the text but rather because it is desirable in itself as promoting some value taken to be worthwhile. Thus one may depreciate readings of the text that promote politically unacceptable points of view, not because they are "false" to the text (a meaningless category, from this point of view) but because they are wrong from a philosophical, religious, or social standpoint. To take an example, the reception history of the book of Joshua is bound to note how important it was in the mentality of supporters of apartheid in South Africa. The book provided a model for the settlement of a land of promise and the subjugation of the native inhabitants. But the reception history will express disapproval of such an interpretation, not on the grounds that that is not what Joshua "really means" (a vacuous concept), but on the grounds that one ought not to use the Bible as a tool of oppression—this being argued on nonbiblical, general theological grounds.

With reader-response and reception history we are a long way from *Literarkritik*, and it must seem strange that all the movements we have surveyed can come under the general rubric "literary criticism." All the movements of the twentieth and twenty-first centuries seem in their various ways to be opposed to the "excavative" and reconstructive tendencies of "historical criticism"; they are all concerned to read texts holistically and synchronically and to dissent from the idea of a "correct" interpretation. Yet in concluding I should like to argue that the contrast between *Literarkritik* and the many approaches we now call "literary criticism" of the Bible is exaggerated; there is more in common than one might think. What unites them all is the act that we may call *construing* the biblical text. This term is in origin a grammatical one. It means working out the grammar and syntax of a sentence, particularly in a classical language such as Latin, where for the speaker of a modern language it is often necessary to parse individual words and work out the construction of the sentence—though even in Latin one may become so fluent that the process is unconscious, just as it is in one's own native tongue. But we can use the term by extension to mean grasping the overall flow (what in German is called the *Duktus*) of the text in question. The "close-reading" method is in a way the basic technique here: attending to each word, but doing so in order to see how it relates to all the other words in the text and contributes to what the text as a whole means. When we read a text, we are not satisfied as readers until we have grasped the text as a whole and come to see how the parts relate to this whole. Then we can return to the parts and understand them better in the light of the whole. This process is formalized in the idea of the hermeneutic circle, as formulated by Wilhelm Dilthey,[25] where the understanding of the parts relates to the understanding of the whole and vice versa, and the reader goes around this circle again and again, gaining ever more insight into the text.

Now this process of interpretation is clear enough, indeed transparent, in the case of modern literary readings such as those of Robert Alter; one gains a sense of understanding the whole portion of text he is interpreting, such as the David or the Joseph story. But it is also present, though less obviously so, in more formalistic approaches that require the reader to scrutinize the text very closely and to grasp how the parts relate to the whole. One sees it, for example, in text-linguistics/discourse analysis, where attention to the detail of the text is so intense that some of its critics even think it guilty of overinterpretation—taking tiny details as more significant than they really are. But—and this is perhaps the more surprising conclusion—the desire to construe the text as a whole also lies at the root of *Literarkritik*. Source criticism does not in principle begin with a prejudice in favor of seeing the text as composite. It begins with an attempt to read the text as coherent, just like all other modes of interpretation. The conclusion that the text is *not* fully coherent arises when it turns out to resist a holistic reading. Thus the early proponents of a source-critical solution to the problem of the Pentateuch, such as Jean Astruc,[26] did not have a prior theory that the Pentateuch was likely to be the product of weaving together several separate sources. They began by trying to read it "straight," but like many previous readers they found that it was quite resistant to such a reading because of repetitions, inconsistencies, and incoherence. Astruc then made the novel suggestion that some of these problems could be explained if the text was seen as the product of joining together more than one original document, and this conclusion has sustained itself ever since, at least until the recent past. Source criticism (*Literarkritik*) differs from more recent types of literary criticism in being willing to accept the fact of inconsistency and try to explain it, whereas most of the movements surveyed in this essay regard it as the task of criticism to ignore or bypass the problem. But the initial impulse to read the text as a coherent whole is common to historical criticism and to later literary criticism. None of this has to do, incidentally, with the application of a "method" to the text; source criticism is, rather, a set of hunches. As I have written elsewhere:

> As now taught, source criticism is often presented as though it were a rational procedure like a scientific method, which can be (and ought to be) applied in principle to any text. But in origin source criticism is not a method but a hypothesis. And the way in which the hypothesis is tested is not scientific, but humanistic: its truth or falsity depends on whether the individual sources isolated by the hypothesis can be read with understanding. If they cannot, then the "solution" is no solution at all but leaves us back where we began, with incoherent texts. The characteristic way of trying to refute source criticism then consists precisely in seeking to show, on the one hand, that the Pentateuch is perfectly coherent as it stands or, on the other, that the hypothesized sources are not themselves internally coherent—or, of course, both. Nowhere in this process, so far as I can see, is any particular "method" involved. There is no set of procedures one can apply to the text that will yield the classic four-source hypothesis about the Pentateuch. It results from *noticing* certain things about the text which others had overlooked or explained away too quickly. We may fully grant that now, when source criticism has been established for a couple of centuries, students can be preconditioned to see the inconsistencies which form the basis of the theory, even coerced into seeing them: and in this way source criticism can be turned into a kind of method that anyone can practice. But it did not originate as a method, but as a series of observations made by people who, *ex hypothesi*, did not till then believe in a source-critical method! Source analysis began, as we might put it, from the bottom up, not from the top down. It was not a method arrived at prior to being applied, but a theory generated from the frustrating experience of trying to understand a text and failing to do so.[27]

If we go back to an issue that was referred to briefly at the beginning of this essay, the question of where the Succession Narrative begins, we can see how intricately interwoven are source-critical and literary-aesthetic perceptions, *Literarkritik* and "literary criticism." For the idea that a new narrative begins in 2 Sam 9, which sounds like a classic piece of "source criticism," in fact rests on a subtle literary perception about the nature, purpose, and scope of the story of David. There are no objective techniques that will determine that a new source begins just here, but only a careful reading of the text with an eye to unity and coherence of theme and purpose. The literary observations that lead Alter, for example, to treat the story of David as a single, unified narrative are no different *in kind* from those that led Rost to hypothesize a break after 2 Sam 8, even though the conclusions arrived at happen, in this case, to be opposite.

Thus all the approaches I have examined in this essay are in the same boat, and that includes *Literarkritik*, the translation of which as "literary criticism" is perhaps not so misleading as it seems. "Literary criticism" of the Bible is any way of reading the biblical text that is interested in it as "literature," that is, as words on paper, rather than (say) in the underlying history, or the social setting from which it comes, or the religious or theological significance of its contents for today. If one approaches the Bible "as literature" in this sense, one may generate a wide range of questions that need answers. How did the text come to be, and why? How is it structured? What is its overall meaning and purpose? Through what techniques does it convey its "message"? How important is the reader's role in understanding it? How has it been read in the past? How ought it to be read in the present? All these questions are asked in the study of "secular" literature, and it would be surprising if they were not asked in the case of the Bible. To isolate any one of them as the only genuinely "literary" question is understandable. Any critic likes to make his or her preferred question look as though it was the only one that truly matters. But criticism is a broad church and encompasses many questions that critical readers may ask. The wise reader of the Bible will be open to all of them.

For Further Reading

Alter, Robert. *The Art of Biblical Narrative*. New York: Basic Books, 1981.

———. *The Art of Biblical Poetry*, Edinburgh: T&T Clark, 1990.

Alter, Robert, and Frank Kermode, eds. *The Literary Guide to the Bible*. Cambridge: Harvard University Press, 1987.

Barton, John. *The Nature of Biblical Criticism*. Louisville: Westminster John Knox, 2007.

Fewell, Danna Nolan, and David M. Gunn. *Narrative in the Hebrew Bible*. New York: Oxford University Press, 1993.

Jobling, David, and Stephen D. Moore, eds. *Poststructuralism as Exegesis*. *Semeia* 54 (1991).

Powell, Mark Allan, Cecile G. Gray, and Melissa C. Curtis, eds. *The Bible and Modern Literary Criticism: A Critical Assessment and Annotated Bibliography*. Bibliographies and Indexes in Religious Studies 22. Westport, Conn.: Greenwood, 1992.

Notes

1. Leonhard Rost, *The Succession to the Throne of David* (trans. Michael D. Rutter and David M. Gunn; Sheffield: Almond, 1982); translation of *Die Überlieferung von der Thronnachfolge Davids* (Stuttgart: Kohlhammer, 1926).

2. William McKane, *A Critical and Exegetical Commentary on Jeremiah* (ICC; 2 vols.; Edinburgh: T&T Clark, 1986–1996).

3. Jacques Vermeylen, *Du prophète Isaïe à l'apocalyptique: Isaïe I–XXXV, miroir d'un demi-millénaire d'expérience religieuse en Israël* (Paris: Gabalda, 1977–1978).

4. Robert Alter, *The Art of Biblical Narrative* (New York: Basic Books, 1981); idem, *The Art of Biblical Poetry* (Edinburgh: T&T Clark, 1990); idem, *The World of Biblical Literature* (New York: Basic Books, 1992); idem, *The David Story: A Translation with Commentary of 1 and 2 Samuel* (New York: Norton, 1999); idem, *The Five Books of Moses: A Translation with Commentary* (New York: Norton, 2004); idem, *The Book of Psalms* (New York: Norton, 2007).

5. Alter, *The Art of Biblical Narrative*, 9–10.

6. Frank Kermode, *The Genesis of Secrecy: On the Interpretation of Narrative* (Cambridge: Harvard University Press, 1979).

7. Robert Alter and Frank Kermode, eds., *The Literary Guide to the Bible* (Cambridge: Harvard University Press, 1987).

8. Robert Lowth, *Lectures on the Sacred Poetry of the Hebrews* (trans. G. Gregory; London: Routledge/Thoemmes Press, 1995); translation of *De Sacra Poesi Hebraeorum*, 1753. See the essays on Lowth and Astruc in John Jarick, ed., *Sacred Conjectures: The Context and Legacy of Robert Lowth and Jean Astruc* (New York: T&T Clark, 2007).

9. Ernest S. Bates, *The Bible: Designed to be Read as Literature* (London: Heinemann, 1937).

10. Clive S. Lewis, *The Literary Impact of the Authorised Version: The Ethel M. Wood Lecture Delivered before the University of London on 20 March 1950* (London: Athlone, 1950).

11. Gabriel Josipovici, *The Book of God: A Response to the Bible* (New Haven: Yale University Press, 1988).

12. Benjamin Jowett, "On the Interpretation of Scripture," in Frederick Temple et al., *Essays and Reviews* (6th edition; London: Longman, Green, Longman, & Roberts, 1861).

13. See my discussion in John Barton, *Reading the Old Testament: Method in Biblical Study* (2nd ed.; London: Darton, Longman & Todd, 1996), 140–79.

14. Vladimir Propp, *Morphology of the Folktale* (2nd ed.; Austin: University of Texas Press, 1968); translation of *Morfologija skazki* (Leningrad: Academia, 1928).

15. Roland Barthes, "La lutte avec l'ange: analyze textuelle de Genèse 32.23–33," in *Analyse structurale et exégèse biblique* (ed. Roland Barthes et al.; Neuchâtel: Delachaux et Niestlé, 1971), 27–40; translated as *Structural Analysis and Biblical Exegesis* (trans. Alfred M. Johnson Jr.; Pittsburgh: Pickwick, 1974).

16. Agatha Christie, *The Murder of Roger Ackroyd* (London: William Collins & Sons, 1926).

17. Alain Robbe-Grillet, *Les Gommes* (Paris: Les editions de minuit, 1953); translated as *The Erasers* (trans. Richard Howard; London: Calder & Boyars, 1966).

18. Jan P. Fokkelman, *Reading Biblical Narratives: An Introductory Guide* (Louisville: Westminster John Knox, 2001); idem, *Literary Structure and Rhetorical Strategies in the Hebrew Bible* (Assen: Van Gorcum, 1996); *Narrative Art and Poetry in the Books of Samuel: A Full Interpretation Based on Stylistic and Structural Analyses* (4 vols.; Assen: Van Gorcum, 1981–1993); Epp Talstra, *Solomon's Prayer: Synchrony and Diachrony in the Composition of 1 Kings 8.14–61* (Kampen: Kok Pharos, 1993).

19. See, e.g., Walter R. Bodine, "Discourse Analysis of Biblical Hebrew: What It Is and What It Offers," in *Discourse Analysis of Biblical Literature* (ed. Walter R. Bodine; Winona Lake, Ind.: Eisenbrauns, 1992); Gillian Brown and George Yule, *Discourse Analysis* (Cambridge: Cambridge University Press, 1983); David A. Dawson, *Text-Linguistics and Biblical Hebrew* (JSOTSup 177; Sheffield: Sheffield Academic Press, 1994); Jean-Marc Heimerdinger, *Topic, Focus and Foreground in Ancient Hebrew Narrative* (JSOTSup 295; Sheffield: Sheffield Academic Press, 1999); Michael Stubbs, *Discourse Analysis: The Sociolinguistic Analysis of Natural Language* (Oxford: Blackwell, 1983).

20. Stanley E. Fish, *Is There a Text in This Class? The Authority of Interpretive Communities* (Cambridge: Harvard University Press, 1980).

21. Wolfgang Iser, *The Act of Reading: A Theory of Aesthetic Response* (London: Routledge & Kegan Paul, 1978), translation of *Der Akt des Lesens: Theorie ästhetischer Wirkung* (Munich: Fink, 1976).

22. See Hans R. Jauss, *Towards an Aesthetic of Reception* (Minneapolis: University of Minnesota Press, 1982).

23. The series is called Blackwell Bible Commentaries. At the time of writing, the most recent example was Susan E. Gillingham, *Psalms through the Centuries* (Malden, Mass.: Blackwell, 2008). See also the massive *Encyclopedia of the Bible and Its Reception* (ed. Hans-Josef Klauck et al.; Berlin: de Gruyter, 2009–).

24. A very early example of a survey of the reception of a biblical text can be found in Adalbert Merx, *Die Prophetie des Joel und ihre Ausleger von den ältesten Zeiten bis zu den Reformatoren* (Halle: Waisenhauses, 1879).

25. See, e.g., Wilhelm Dilthey, *Introduction to the Human Sciences* (Princeton: Princeton University Press, 1989). Dilthey lived from 1833 to 1911.

26. Jean Astruc, *Conjectures sur les mémoires originaux don't it paroit que Moyse s'est servi pour composer le livre de la Genèse* (Brussels: Fricx, 1753).

27. John Barton, *The Nature of Biblical Criticism* (Louisville: Westminster John Knox, 2007), 63.

Reflections on Ideological Criticism and Postcritical Perspectives

Carol A. Newsom

That ideological criticism and postcritical perspectives should appear in the same essay may strike many readers as peculiar, if not incoherent. While it is undoubtedly true that these two approaches to biblical studies occupy very different positions in the spectrum of biblical interpretation, they are in many respects complementary opposites. That is to say, their very differences arise from distinct responses to issues that they both perceive to be important and yet that tend to be invisible to certain classic forms of biblical scholarship. Two parallel phrases that show up in many articles on each perspective will illustrate this phenomenon. In discussions of ideological criticism, it is commonplace to say that one of the distinguishing features of this approach is that it self-consciously reads "against the grain" of the biblical text. In discussions of postcritical biblical studies, one often finds the claim that this approach intentionally reads "with the grain" of the biblical text. Juxtaposition of these two phrases prompts one to ask: What is meant by "grain"? The metaphor apparently comes from the field of woodworking, though its actual origin is somewhat uncertain. The grain in a piece of wood is the direction of the long fibers. To cut with the grain is to leave the directionality of the fibers more or less undisturbed. To cut across the grain, however, is to reveal the existence of the many fibers that constitute the piece of wood and to risk a fraying of the fibers by a force that works directionally across their natural inclination. The use of this metaphor both by ideological and by postcritical biblical studies suggests that these two approaches take their starting point from a recognition that biblical texts have a vivid "directionality" that requires an engaged response from the reader. In this regard, these two approaches both distance themselves from what they posit to be the stance of classical historical-critical scholarship, which they perceive as a scientific/objective orientation toward the biblical texts that construes them as neutral objects of dispassionate study. Whether that is an adequate characterization of the work of classical biblical studies might be questioned, but both approaches take pains to dissociate themselves from what they see as the objectivist stance of historical-critical studies and to attempt to close the hermeneutical gap opened up by this method.

In several other respects one might draw attention to the common ground of ideological criticism and postcritical biblical studies. Both approaches are self-consciously postmodern. While it is true that ideological criticism in general begins as a phenomenon of high modernism (in its early Marxist forms), it is now practiced with a deep sense of the contextualized nature of truths and of the way in which all texts can be deconstructed to reveal conflicting claims and implicit contestations for power. Postcritical biblical studies, as a kind of radical return to forms of communitarian truth, also finds in postmodernism a warrant for its assertion of the legitimacy of its own difference. Both of these perspectives see themselves as counterhegemonic, with the hegemonic discourse identified as the material and ideological forms of modernity, though that way of putting things is to use the idiom of ideological criticism. Finally, an emerging element of commonality between ideological and postcritical approaches is a mutual interest in reception history or the "history of effects" of the biblical text. Here, however, noting a shared focus again leads to a perception of the great differences between these approaches. Whereas postcritical biblical studies looks to certain traditional forms of biblical interpretation as a model and even a norm, ideological criticism is intrigued by the protean forms that interpretive activity can take. If ideological criticism and postcritical biblical studies are strange bedfellows, then these are some of the covers that they are likely to snatch back and forth in their close quarters.

In the essay that follows, I will first discuss the nature and development of ideological criticism and of postcritical biblical studies, then bring them back into conversation at the end. What they have to say to one another may suggest important directions for the future of biblical studies in general.

Ideological Criticism: What Is It?

Ideological criticism is one of those terms that simultaneously begs and defies definition. In part, this definitional problem is inherited by biblical studies from the conflicted nature of the term in the humanities and social sciences in general.[1] But in particular within biblical studies there has been a decided reluctance to make a definition that would foreclose what some see as its fruitfully diffuse boundaries. The fluidity of what counts as ideological criticism is also helpful in situating it in relation to postcritical biblical studies. The term "ideology" originates in the eighteenth century, when it was proposed as a term—as its etymology suggests—for the study of ideas. Early on, however, the term developed a somewhat pejorative air, though what made it pejorative might be differently understood. In Marxist thought, a distinction was made between the "real conditions" of existence, as these are embodied in the modes of production in a society, and the false consciousness that is engendered by the way in which ideas are produced to justify the rightness of such a mode of production in the interests of those who benefit from the economic relations. This is not to suggest that writers and artists know what is real and intentionally set out to present a false account of things. Instead, the system of ideas corresponding to the mode of production is perceived as natural, commonsensical, and true. Thus all of culture is ideological in a distorted sense, and the task of ideological criticism is demystification.

Another understanding of ideology equates it with propaganda. Here again, the issue is false description of reality, though the mechanism is somewhat different. In this understanding of the category, ideologies may not arise simply out of economic relations, as epiphenomena. They may be more intentionally constructed distortions of reality to reflect the interests of those who have or who wish to have power, as in the propagandistic efforts of National Socialism and other overt programs of cultural and political dominance. Here, too, the task of ideological criticism is to unmask the falsification of reality by ideology.

The puzzles set for ideological critics by either of these kinds of analysis include the assumptions encoded in the terms "false consciousness" and "reality." By what means does one know what kind of consciousness is false and what is true? What is reality, and what is not? Classical Marxist theory, of course, had its own confidence about such matters, but that very claim to incontestable truth subjected it to the reciprocal accusation that it was simply another form of ideological mystification. In reaction to overly simplistic contrasts between ideology and reality, some critics, influenced by certain strands of postmodernism, have argued that all constructions of reality are simply that—constructions. There is no "real." Rather, all that there "is" is representation. It is ideology, all the way down. There is no foundation-only representation. While there is much that is ethically as well as conceptually problematic in this view of ideology, it does serve to remind one how utterly persuasive certain totalizing ideological systems can be for persons who live within them, no matter how outrageous they may seem from the outside. They can and do constitute what is taken for reality by their participants. A more benign version of this understanding of ideology is one that equates ideology more or less with worldview. Ideology is a term for the symbolic structures of meaning by means of which a society or segment of society constructs its understanding of the meaningful nature of things. Thus ideologies are an essential element of human culture. There is no "view from nowhere." In this perspective, the task of ideological criticism is description and analysis of a cultural symbolic system, so that its constructed quality is made evident.

These thumbnail descriptions of various options for understanding ideology and ideological criticism identify various poles of thought. Many ideological critics operate with an understanding of ideology, culture, and truth that owes something to each of the alternatives outlined above. But although ideological criticism takes many diverse forms, at its heart is a concern for the relation between language (and other forms of symbolic representation) and power. All cultural constructions, no matter how natural or commonsensical they present themselves, are understood as encoding the interests of some elements of a society. Indeed, one of the primary functions of ideology is to naturalize a particular state of power and economic relations. Ideology in this sense functions as a kind of theodicy (either secular or religious), allowing both those who benefit from the given social arrangements and those who are disadvantaged by them to see the state of affairs as just or natural or simply inevitable. Ideology provides persuasive explanations for what is experienced, and in this way it continually reproduces the reality that it justifies. While this interested perspective may sometimes be quite self-conscious, it more often operates at an unconscious level, so that persons are unaware of the effects of the ideological discourse they unknowingly use. The situation is rather like what Foucault described: "People know what they do; they frequently know why they do what they do; but what they don't know is what what they do does."[2]

The task of ideological criticism is thus to disclose "what what they do does." It operates as a hermeneutic of suspicion. However, given the pervasive and hidden nature of ideology and the problematic nature of "reality," how is ideological criticism even possible? For one thing, all ideological systems contain internal contradictions that can be used to expose the interests encoded in them. In an oft-cited example, the Declaration of Independence's assertion that "all men are created equal," with a right to "life, liberty, and the pursuit of happiness," speaks in universal terms, yet was contradicted by the existence of racially based slavery. Moreover, the term "men" contained an unstable ambiguity, since it might refer to "males" or to "persons generally." A second foothold for ideological criticism resides in the fact that societies (and, indeed, individuals) are always interpenetrated by multiple ideological systems that can provide alternative perspectives from which to observe and critique any particular ideological construction. Third, it is not the case that ideology is wholly constitutive of reality. The material conditions of existence and the innate sense of justice that is characteristic not only of humans but even of certain other species provides a fundamental point of resistance to ideologically justified imbalances of power. At the same time, since there is no "view from nowhere," no wholly disinterested perspective, any act of ideological criticism should contain a self-reflexive moment, when the interests encoded in the critique are also rendered visible and contestable.

No single method of doing ideological criticism exists. While certain practitioners, especially in the Marxist tradition, have developed detailed procedures for analysis,[3] ideological criticism in general tends to be eclectic and polymorphous. As one survey remarked, "it comes in many voices, speaks many languages, and resides in many different disciplines and critical approaches, including psychoanalytic theory, cultural criticism, sociolinguistics, subaltern studies, feminist theory, and deconstruction, to name a few."[4] The common thread is the concern for raising to consciousness the workings of power in discourse. Consequently, the practice of ideological criticism is often seen as a form of resistance to unacknowledged and oppressive power and thus as raising issues of the ethics of interpretation. One chooses to interpret in a way that supports or opposes the power dynamics at work in the text.

Ideological Criticism and Biblical Studies

Historically speaking, ideological criticism emerged into biblical studies in the late 1970s and early 1980s from several different but not unrelated new perspectives. The earliest and in some ways the most determinative was the impact of Latin American liberation theology, with its intellectual indebtedness to Marxist/materialist forms of analysis. This trajectory of influence was mediated in Hebrew Bible studies above all by Norman Gottwald's work, in particular *The Tribes of Yahweh: A Sociology of the Religion of Liberated Israel, 1250–1050 B.C.E.*[5] Although primarily concerned with a reconstruction of a peasant revolt model for the formation of the nation of Israel, it analyzed a historical series of "horizons" of interpretation, recoverable from the biblical text, that delineated different ideological construals of the events of the Late Bronze/Early Iron Age. Although in many ways independent of Gottwald, both African (Itumeleng Mosala, *Biblical Hermeneutics and Black Theology in South Africa*) and feminist (Gale Yee, *Poor Banished Children of Eve*) Marxist/materialist forms of interpretation have been significant in ideological criticism of the Hebrew Bible.[6]

The sociological appropriation of Marxist/materialist approaches was soon matched by emerging trends in literary criticism. As biblical studies moved rapidly through its New Critical phase and its even briefer encounter with structuralism in the mid 1970s, it quickly found itself sorting through the variety of poststructuralist options in interpretation. Some of these were themselves in conversation with developments in Marxist literary theory (e.g., Terry Eagleton, *Criticism and Ideology: A Study in Marxist Literary Theory*; Fredric Jameson, *The Political Unconscious*) and sought to interpret literary phenomena in relation to material conditions of experience. These influences on biblical ideological criticism can be seen not only in the *Semeia* 59 issue devoted to ideological criticism but also in the recent work of Gale Yee, referred to in the preceding paragraph. Among non-Marxist approaches, deconstruction, Lacanian psychoanalysis and Foucault's complex theories about power and discourse have all become part of the equipment of biblical ideological critics (e.g., Carol Newsom, "Woman and the Discourse of Patriarchal Wisdom: A Study of Proverbs"; David Clines, "Deconstructing the Book of Job"; Yvonne Sherwood, ed., *Derrida's Bible*; Elizabeth Castelli, *Imitating Paul: A Discourse of Power*).[7] It should be noted, however, that some of these postmodern approaches are not *intrinsically* connected to ideological criticism, and there has been significant concern on the part of Marxist-influenced critics that these perspectives can be used in ways that lack adequate concern for the ethical dimensions of interpretation (e.g., Terry Eagleton, *The Illusions of Postmodernism*).[8]

One of the most important confluences between literary perspectives and ideological criticism can be located in reader-response criticism. Although reader-response theory per se was a fairly short-lived phenomenon in literary studies, the shift of attention from the author and/or the text to the reader has had profound implications for ideological criticism. Prior to reader-response theory, the act of reading was assumed to be a matter of competence in decoding a symbolic script. Reader-response theory began by emphasizing the active (and somewhat subjective) role of the individual reader, who was not otherwise defined. Both feminist criticism and the varieties of ethnically based hermeneutical approaches (starting with African American biblical hermeneutics), which initially articulated their critical approaches independently of literary theory, have nevertheless found the shift of attention to the reader to be fertile ground for identifying the distinctive perspective of marginalized readers as critical to ideological analysis. Much the same can be said with respect to postcolonial biblical studies. Although this approach to biblical interpretation draws on many different theoretical perspectives, it is the very precise and noninterchangeable location of readers that has come to be a central focus in postcolonial hermeneutics (see Fernando Segovia and Mary Ann Tolbert, eds., *Reading from This Place*; R. S. Sugirtharajah, *Postcolonial Criticism and Biblical Interpretation*; Gerald O. West, ed., *Reading Other-wise: Socially Engaged Biblical Scholars Reading with Their Local Communities*).[9]

As might be expected, one of the primary consequences of the emergence of ideological criticism in biblical studies is the loss of unself-consciousness. The ideological assumptions embedded in historical criticism have been explored and endlessly discussed. Interpreters have become increasingly aware of how their own biographies, genders, ethnicities, nationalities, religious and institutional affiliations, and much more are part and parcel of their interpretive work. Meanwhile, the object of interpretation—the Bible—has been examined and scrutinized for the variety of ways in which contestations for power and influence have left their undeniable traces in the ideological configurations of its texts. But in the presence of so much acute awareness of what are, broadly speaking, political dimensions, what becomes of the Bible's traditional roles as the narrative of faith and locus of religious encounter? These are questions raised by postcritical approaches to biblical studies.

Postcritical Biblical Studies

The postcritical turn in biblical studies is directed not so much at ideological criticism in particular as at the historical-critical project in general. Indeed, in exposing the specific ideological commitments of the historical-critical method, ideological criticism and postcritical biblical studies can sometimes sound quite similar. Historical criticism was developed in light of the Enlightenment ideal of objective scientific inquiry, independent of the authoritative claims of tradition. It is, as one critic has argued, "*methodologically* atheistic."[10] Moreover, as a historical discipline, it has been interested in uncovering matters that lie behind the text, whether they be historical events to which biblical texts refer or the stages of the development of the text itself. In this regard, historical criticism is a form of a hermeneutics of suspicion, since it puts in question the surface or plain meaning of the text and sees historical truth as residing in the reconstructed events or processes that led to the production of the text. At the same time, historical criticism can be seen to have a profoundly ethical motivation: to hear in all their otherness the disparate human voices that speak in the biblical texts, freed from tradition's tendency to harmonize and recast them in the voice of a later time with different concerns. Even the advocates of postcritical approaches acknowledge the stunning success of historical criticism in accomplishing the goals that it set for itself—but that very success is seen as the source of the major problem.

Biblical scholarship's historicizing of the Bible created the sense of a gap between the world of the text and the world of the reader. Yet because it situated itself as an autonomous form of inquiry, historical criticism had no logical way to relate its findings to the specifically religious claims of the Bible as Scripture or to the forms of interpretation used by the church and the synagogue in the centuries before the Enlightenment. This is not to say that biblical scholars who were also devout members of religious communities did not attempt to connect the results of their scholarship to the needs of the church and synagogue. Indeed, the program of biblical theology may be seen as just such an effort. In the eyes of postcritical interpreters, however, various attempts at discerning the theological significance of the historical content and modes of ancient Israelite and early Christian writings simply disclose the intrinsic problems. The comments of Luke Johnson are telling:

> The many attempts at constructing a satisfactory biblical theology have succeeded mainly in revealing the contradictions inherent to the enterprise. Efforts to transcend history reveal how profoundly pervasive the historical perspective is. The desire to unify diverse witnesses almost inevitably leads to eliminating some of Scripture's voices while

> privileging others, and to imposing a false harmony by means of some abstract category or principle. Most of all, Biblical Theology manages to keep the world of Scripture firmly in the past, with its own mediational role alone emphasizing the distance between the world imagined by Scripture and the world inhabited by contemporary investigators.[11]

Brevard Childs's "canonical method" was one attempt to articulate an alternative. By focusing on the text in its canonical form as the locus of interpretation and understanding the canon as a whole to form the context and intertext for any particular passage, Childs attempted to forge a normative means of reading Scripture as Scripture, rather than as texts relevant to the history of Israelite and early Christian religion. The context of the canon and the meaningful coherence of the canon as a whole thus set the horizon for interpretation. Despite considerable appreciation for what he was attempting to do, Childs's project has been aggressively critiqued as finally an incoherent attempt to bridge the gap between historical criticism and scriptural interpretation.[12] The very term *canon* is used in several somewhat inconsistent ways, confusing the nature of what Childs attempts to do. Moreover, the "canonical intentionality" he ascribes to the final form of the text is often asserted rather than demonstrated, though there is ample evidence that the final stages of scribal activity frequently had no particular hermeneutical purpose. Most significantly, Childs rather arbitrarily defines the Christian Old Testament canon as the Masoretic Text (rather than the Septuagint or at least the larger Roman Catholic canon) because it provides common ground with Judaism. But he does not deal adequately with the radical difference of the meaning of the canon as it appears in the Jewish Bible and as it appears in the Old Testament in Christian contexts. While Childs attempted to defend his approach against the dangers of harmonization and so explicitly rejected the traditional church's use of figurative, typological, and allegorical exegesis, this restriction oddly cut off canonical interpretation from a significant part of the church's traditional engagement with Scripture, despite Childs's own deep knowledge of early church exegesis.

Other forms of postcritical scriptural interpretation have taken a somewhat different route. The fountainhead of these approaches in the Christian tradition is to be found in Hans Frei's *The Eclipse of Biblical Narrative* and in George Lindbeck's *The Nature of Doctrine*.[13] While explicitly scriptural, ecclesial, and theological in orientation and motivation, the approach founded in their work is also deeply literary, specifically narrative. Both authors make the case that, in the precritical period, the normative way of reading the Gospels in the church was the "literal sense," that is, a reading of the Gospels as realistic narrative. The Old Testament was a part of this story both by means of the narrative flow of the biblical narrative from Genesis to Revelation and through various forms of literary appropriation in which the Old Testament figures and events might be related as "shadow and reality, prophecy and fulfillment, metaphorical type and literal antitype."[14] What makes the narrative approach to Scripture so important is that it effectively brackets historical questions and so makes the postcritical approach independent of the project of historical criticism. As Lindbeck puts it, "it is as if the Bible were a 'vast, loosely-structured, non-fictional novel.' "[15] Equally important, the narrative approach is also independent of the complex but ultimately problematic project of philosophical hermeneutics. In Frei's understanding, meaning does not lie "behind" the text in some historical reconstruction of the events to which it ostensibly points. Nor, as Paul Ricoeur's hermeneutical theory would have it, does it lie in some space "in front of" the text. Frei himself drew the analogy to Anglo-American "New Criticism," which insists that the textual narrative constructs a world of meaning "quite apart from any factual reference it may have, and apart from its author's intention or its reader's reception."[16] The meaning of Scripture resides in the story that it tells.

The story that Scripture tells, of course, is not simply *a* story but a grand narrative. That is to say, it is a narrative within which persons live and by means of which they understand reality. As Lindbeck says, "For those who are steeped in [the canonical writings of religious communities], no world is more real than the ones they create. A scriptural world is thus able to absorb the universe."[17] The fundamentally aesthetic orientation of the postcritical understanding of Scripture and its effects is recognizable in the frequency with which the terminology of imagination appears, as in the title of Luke Johnson's essay, "Imagining the World Scripture Imagines." Similarly, one might point to the postcritical understanding of Scripture at the heart of Hans Urs von Balthasar's *The Glory of the Lord: A Theological Aesthetics*.[18] In this respect postcritical biblical studies is both a product of postmodernism and a challenge to some of its assumptions. It is thoroughly antifoundational, making no claim to some kind of objective or independent verification of its imagined world. Rather, with other forms of postmodernism it understands all possible worlds to be imagined or figured worlds.[19] Postcritical biblical studies, however, properly challenges one of postmodernism's truisms, which is a skepticism toward all grand narratives. What it recognizes is that postmodernism's antifoundationalism opens up the space within which the meaningfulness of grand narratives and the alternative realities they construct once again becomes possible.[20]

What prevents this embrace of Scripture's grand narrative from being simply an idiosyncratic exercise of the imagination is its grounding in communal practice. One cannot imagine the world that Scripture imagines apart from participation in a religious community. Thus it is important to recognize postcritical biblical studies' grounding not only in literary models but, more importantly, in the kind of ethnography practiced by anthropologists such as Clifford Geertz. This orientation is captured in George Lindbeck's characterization of his approach as "cultural-linguistic."[21] One learns to enter into the world of Scripture as one learns a language or as one learns how to live in another culture. Such understanding does not require a complex theory so much as it is made intelligible by participating in the practices and using the words and symbols of the culture. By this analogy, religious conversion is a matter of "going native."

A variety of postcritical approaches to biblical studies exist, but one of the common features of this type of biblical interpretation (in contrast to the canonical criticism of Brevard Childs) is the intentional recovery and appropriation of precritical forms of interpretation. Whereas historical criticism largely rejected such hermeneutical methods as typology, allegory, and midrash as fanciful eisegesis, postcritical biblical studies argues that they are ways of producing knowledge that have their own legitimacy. Moreover, at least in the perspective of Peter Ochs, the task is to seek in the biblical text itself and in the forms of early interpretation the normative rules or practices of biblical interpretation. This means a privileging not just of the biblical text itself but *"in particular as it is read in the primordial communities of rabbinic or of Christian interpreters."*[22] The contrast with historical biblical studies is evident. Even for biblical scholars who are interested in the final form of a biblical book, the horizon of understanding is set by the time at which the book in question was composed or finally redacted (i.e., the late monarchic and early Second Temple periods of most of the Hebrew Bible, the mid- to late first century for most of the New Testament writings). But for Ochs and many other postcritical interpreters, it is not the period of composition that is privileged but the Tannaitic and Amoraic periods for Judaism and the early patristic period for Christianity, for these are the horizons within which the classical forms of interpretation are developed, though they have some precursors in the biblical texts themselves. Thus, in an odd sense, it appears that the Bible *as composed* is displaced in favor of a Bible *as read* by a somewhat later community of interpreters. But perhaps this is not so odd as it first appears. To read the Bible *as Scripture* does imply a function that the texts for the most part did not play when they were first composed but only later came to hold as they took on the distinctive authority of Scripture and canon.

But what does it mean to learn the rules and patterns of biblical interpretation from the biblical text and its early interpreters? In *The Return to Scripture in Judaism and Christianity*, Ochs collects three examples of such interpretation in the Jewish tradition, by Steven Fraade, David Halivni, and Michael Fishbane, in which the authors variously attempt to discern the ways in which rabbinic interpretation functioned and to reappropriate these as models for contemporary biblical interpretation. Ochs is clear, however, that what happens in such an engagement can never be a simple recapitulation of the hermeneutics of a classical past. Drawing on Fishbane's *The Garments of Torah*, Ochs observes that "to enter [the Bible's inner life], modern exegetes may first study the various patterns and then seek to imitate them as rules for their own, postmodern exegesis.… This 'imitation' is not literal: it means learning from the various patterns that were displayed in the biblical context comparable ways of rereading Scripture in this contemporary context."[23] Where historical criticism's break with traditional modes of scriptural hermeneutics created an unbridgeable gulf between the interpreting communities of modernity and the classical past, postcritical biblical interpretation attempts self-consciously to build in continuity with those patterns of interpretation.

While postcritical biblical interpreters are sometimes accused of a nostalgic desire to return to a precritical era, they are quite articulate about the difference between precritical and postcritical. In making the case for the world imagined by Scripture as an alternative reality, Johnson states the issue clearly. To speak in terms of alternatives is to acknowledge "our loss of that world imagined by Scripture, for if we really inhabited it wholly, we could not speak of it as one world among others.… it would be, if we inhabited it wholly, simply our world."[24] Whether a postcritical return to the world imagined by Scripture is indeed possible is a difficult question. The discussion of these issues has taken place largely in the academy, even as the participants in the conversation acknowledge that the critical loci are the practicing religious communities in general. Yet in both

Judaism and Christianity the role of Scripture and the familiarity with the narrative of the Bible appears to decline steadily even among those who profess that the Bible is central to their faith. The loss of the precritical sense of the symbolic world of Scripture is less the direct consequence of academic historical-critical scholarship than the effect of modernity itself, with the emergence of a variety of secular grand narratives that gradually came to displace the religious ones, such that religious discourse began to reconfigure itself so as to fit within the canopy of these construals of reality. Whether a postmodern mentality opens up the possibility for a renewal of the role of Scripture in constructing reality remains to be seen.

"Plywood": Or, the Conversation between Ideological Criticism and Postcritical Perspectives

I began this essay by musing over the complementary figures of speech by which scholars representing these fields of biblical interpretation describe their reading habits as either "against the grain" or "with the grain." As woodworkers know, wood is stronger against the grain than parallel to the grain, though furniture is more beautiful if cut with the grain. Already in the second millennium B.C.E., Egyptian carpenters developed techniques to compensate for this phenomenon. They cut thin strips of wood and glued them with the grain running in perpendicular directions to produce an early form of plywood. Thus plywood is a cultured form of wood that combines in one board the features of both cross and parallel grain. Is it possible to contemplate a form of biblical interpretation that combines both ideological and postcritical perspectives? Or are they simply too incompatible to be joined together? Whether or not they can be envisioned as different moves in a single form of interpretation, each does need to be informed by the critique of the other.

In postcritical biblical interpretation, an assumption that is fundamental but rarely made explicit is that the Bible is "the Good Book." It seems to be taken as self-evident that the Bible's narrative is redemptive and liberative. To be sure, the religious movements founded on the Bible would not have existed and persisted if this were not largely experienced to be the case. What one rarely encounters in postcritical discussions, however, are the very things that ideological criticism has been so adept at uncovering, namely, the ways in which the Bible itself has been a force of resistance against redemption and liberation. These issues are taken up in a brief but perceptive essay by Sandra Schneiders, who comes as close as anyone can to embodying both interpretive stances. The essay is entitled "Does the Bible Have a Postmodern Message?"[25] Schneiders answers this question with a "yes" and a "maybe." The "yes" is her affirmation of the possibilities of a postmodern biblical hermeneutics that incorporates both historical-critical and postcritical forms of interpretation as complementary ways of knowing and understanding. Her "maybe" has to do with what ideological criticism has disclosed in recent years: "the oppressive content of much of the Bible and the ideological uses of the Bible throughout history to legitimate and support the domination of the weak by the strong."[26] Schneiders considers the problem of the ideological use of the Bible to be "soluble and … slowly being solved,"[27] largely through the efforts of various forms of liberation theologies. But the problem of the ideological content of the Bible, specifically its patriarchal ideology, is a much more serious one. Her forceful critique requires to be quoted in full:

> [The Bible] assumes that history is the story of important men and their exploits and so to a large extent it omits, obscures, and distorts the participation of women in sacred history. It assumes the human and moral inferiority of women and so regularly reduces them to their biological roles in relation to men and demonizes their initiatives. It assumes male superiority and so legitimates the sexual double standard within and outside of marriage and winks at male violence against women. And this says nothing of such explicitly oppressive injunctions as that wives submit to their husbands (compare Ephesians 5:22-24) and keep silent in the churches (compare 1 Corinthians 15:34-35). We are not speaking of an occasional text that could be explained or explained away but of a pervasive patriarchy, androcentrism, and overt sexism that directly and indirectly, by what it says and what it fails to say, lends the authority of sacred scripture to the age-old oppressions of patriarchy and particularly to the oppression of women by men."[28]

This, Schneiders suggests, is also the world that Scripture imagines.

While the problem of developing the grounds for an intrinsic critique of Scripture has not yet been widely developed within postcritical biblical studies, there are some indications of how it would unfold. In "Critical Traditioning: Seeking an Inner Biblical Hermeneutic," Ellen Davis makes use of the rubrics of Michael Fishbane's inner-biblical exegesis in order to show how the biblical text itself often undermines one ethically problematic voice through the emergence of other voices.[29] In the final form of the text, the voices compete for allegiance in an unresolved conversation that she refers to as "critical traditioning." The term refers to the Bible's own tendency not to jettison an old *traditum* but to contextualize it by means of scribal *traditio*. This process provides Davis with a model for the way in which the religious community can continue to engage in such a process without resorting simply to excising the ethically offensive texts from the biblical canon. One might also note Luke Johnson's *Scripture and Discernment: Decision Making in the Church* as an attempt to combine both historical-critical and postcritical perspectives in modeling the way in which the biblical text and the interpretive process can lead to transformation in ethical perspectives within the church, in this case concerning the status of homosexual relations.

If ideological criticism raises the question of the necessity of an internal critique for postcritical biblical interpretation, the opposite is the case for the issue that postcritical perspectives raise for ideological criticism: its positioning of its critique exclusively from the outside. Johnson frames the issue sharply. "The development of ideological criticism among biblical scholars only makes explicit the way in which they assume the moral superiority of the world they inhabit to the world imagined by Scripture."[30] Schneiders might reply that the assumption is in some instances amply justified. But the broader point is a significant one, and the externality of ideological criticism's stance is often frankly acknowledged by its practitioners. David Clines makes the point explicitly:

> "Critique" does not of course imply *negative* evaluation, but it does imply evaluation of the texts by a standard of reference outside themselves—which usually means, for practical purposes, by the standards to which we ourselves are committed.... We have a responsibility, I believe, to evaluate the Bible's claims and assumptions, and if we abdicate that responsibility, whether as scholars or as readers-in-general of the Bible, we are in my opinion guilty of an ethical fault.[31]

For ideological critics who locate themselves outside of religious communities, external critique presents no problem. Moreover, since ideological criticism does not assume a nonideological reader, the process of reading may be an occasion for mutual critique. But construed in this fashion, the encounter is still posed as the meeting of two worlds of value external to one another.

Many ideological critics in biblical studies, however, do belong to religious communities, and their embrace of ideological criticism is motivated precisely out of that passionate commitment. How such readers negotiate the tensions of a dual hermeneutics of assent and of suspicion varies considerably and is perhaps one of the issues requiring more explicit attention from ideological criticism. An element of what postcritical scholars see as the intransigence of ideological criticism certainly comes from the deep concern not to be complicit with the ethical oppressiveness of the Bible. Elisabeth Schüssler Fiorenza stakes out a strong position: "Biblical revelation and truth can today be found only in those texts and traditions that transcend and criticize the patriarchal culture and religion of their times."[32] But not all ideological critics are so certain that the texts and traditions can be sorted out so clearly or the issues posed so simply. A particularly nuanced view is articulated by postcolonial biblical scholar R. S. Sugirtharajah. As he reflects on the unfinished work of Third World hermeneutics and postcolonial theology, he argues for the need to move its work away from the largely secular and liberal frameworks of academia and to focus on "the theological and religious beliefs of peoples,"[33] that is, on the ways in which religion in postcolonial contexts provides the encompassing narratives within which people live. He critiques postmodern assumptions that denigrate narrative, observing that "at a time when postcolonial theorists are trying to recover subaltern histories and stories, we are informed that there is no history to be narrated or stories to be told."[34] Yet the very nature of postcolonial religious experience would significantly complicate the attempt by Western Christian postcritical scholars to posit the reading culture of the patristic period as an unproblematic touchstone for future biblical interpretation. Sugirtharajah also exposes the parochialism of the postcritical scholars who assume that *the* problem is the hermeneutical gap, whereas, he points out, too easy an identification between the reader and the biblical narrative can lead both to pastoral and ethical misuses of the text, against which the historical-critical method provides a welcome "hermeneutics of distance."[35] At the conclusion of "Getting the Mixture Right," Sugirtharajah discusses two stories. In one, the character is certain that narrative is salvific, if only she can find the right one. In the other, a character on the edge of a violent criminal culture is given a Bible but quickly tosses it in a river, seeing it as a book that would be of no use in negotiating the world he is entering. "This is the choice we have—either to embrace the book or discard it. Or, is there a third, in-between way?"[36] Sugirtharajah suggests that the very hybridity of postcolonial identity, its irreducible "in-betweenness" provides a crucial hermeneutical perspective as it defies a simple alternative choice between inside and outside, embrace or rejection, a hermeneutics of assent or a hermeneutics of suspicion. In this way, perhaps, postcolonial biblical studies may provide a means of mediating future conversations, not only between ideological criticism and postcritical biblical interpretation but also between these two approaches and their mutual intellectual adversary, historical criticism.

For Further Reading

Clines, David. J. A. *Interested Parties: The Ideology of Writers and Readers of the Hebrew Bible*. JSOTSup 205. Sheffield: Sheffield Academic Press, 1995.

Davis, Ellen F., and Richard B. Hays, eds. *The Art of Reading Scripture*. Grand Rapids: Eerdmans, 2003.

Frei, Hans. W. *The Eclipse of Biblical Narrative: A Study in Eighteenth and Nineteenth Century Hermeneutics*. New Haven: Yale University Press, 1974.

Gottwald, Norman K. *The Tribes of Yahweh: A Sociology of the Religion of Liberated Israel, 1250–1050 BCE*. Maryknoll, N.Y.: Orbis, 1979.

Mosala, Itumeleng. *Biblical Hermeneutics and Black Theology in South Africa*. Grand Rapids: Eerdmans, 1989.

Newsom, Carol A. "Woman and the Discourse of Patriarchal Wisdom: A Study of Proverbs." Pages 142–60 in *Gender and Difference in Ancient Israel*. Edited by Peggy L. Day. Philadelphia: Augsburg Fortress, 1989.

Ochs, Peter. *The Return to Scripture in Judaism and Christianity: Essays in Postcritical Scriptural Interpretation*. New York: Paulist, 1993.

Schüssler Fiorenza, Elisabeth. *Bread, Not Stone: The Challenge of Feminist Biblical Interpretation*. Boston: Beacon, 1984.

Sugirtharajah, R. S. *Postcolonial Reconfigurations: An Alternative Way of Reading the Bible and Doing Theology*. St. Louis: Chalice, 2003.

Yee, Gale A. *Poor Banished Children of Eve: Woman as Evil in the Hebrew Bible*. Minneapolis: Fortress, 2003.

Journals: Many of the issues of *Semeia*, published by the Society of Biblical Literature from 1974 to 2002, concern issues related to aspects of ideological criticism. See especially issue 59 (1992). In addition, the online *Journal of Scriptural Reasoning* (etext.virginia.edu/journals/ssr) is devoted to postcritical scriptural interpretation.

Notes

1. See the discussion of Terry Eagleton, *Ideology: An Introduction* (New York: Verso, 1991).

2. Quoted in Hubert L. Dreyfus and Paul Rabinow, *Michel Foucault: Beyond Structuralism and Hermeneutics* (2nd ed.; Chicago: University of Chicago Press, 1983), 187.

3. See, e.g., Fredric Jameson, *The Political Unconscious: Narrative as a Socially Symbolic Act* (Ithaca, N.Y.: Cornell University Press, 1981).

4. The Bible and Culture Collective, *The Postmodern Bible* (New Haven: Yale University Press, 1995), 209.

5. Norman Gottwald. *The Tribes of Yahweh: A Sociology of the Religion of Liberated Israel, 1250–1050 B.C.E.* (Maryknoll, N.Y.: Orbis, 1979).

6. Itumeleng Mosala, *Biblical Hermeneutics and Black Theology in South Africa* (Grand Rapids: Eerdmans, 1989); Gale Yee, *Poor Banished Children of Eve: Woman as Evil in the Hebrew Bible* (Minneapolis: Augsburg Fortress, 2003).

7. Carol Newsom, "Woman and the Discourse of Patriarchal Wisdom: A Study of Proverbs," in *Gender and Difference in Ancient Israel* (ed. Peggy L. Day; Minneapolis: Fortress, 2000), 142–60; David J. A. Clines, "Deconstructing the Book of Job," in *The Bible as Rhetoric: Studies in Biblical Persuasion and Credibility* (ed. Martin Warner; London: Routledge, 1990), 65–80; Yvonne Sherwood, ed., *Derrida's Bible* (New York: Palgrave Macmillan, 2004); Elizabeth Castelli, *Imitating Paul: A Discourse of Power* (Louisville: Westminster John Knox, 1991).

8. Terry Eagleton, *The Illusions of Postmodernism* (Oxford: Wiley-Blackwell, 1996).

9. Fernando Segovia and Mary Ann Tolbert, eds., *Reading from This Place* (2 vols.; Minneapolis: Augsburg Fortress,1995–2000); R. S. Sugirtharajah, *Postcolonial Criticism and Biblical Interpretation* (Oxford: Oxford University Press, 2002); Gerald O. West, ed., *Reading Other-wise: Socially Engaged Biblical Scholars Reading with Their Local Communities* (SemeiaSt 62; Atlanta: Society of Biblical Literature, 2007).

10. Brian E. Daley, "Is Patristic Exegesis Still Usable? Some Reflections on Early Christian Interpretation of the Psalms," in *The Art of Reading Scripture* (ed. Ellen F. Davis and Richard B. Hays; Grand Rapids: Eerdmans, 2003), 72, emphasis original.

11. Luke Timothy Johnson, "Imagining the World Scripture Imagines," *Modern Theology* 14 (1998): 171.

12. See, e.g., the critiques raised by various scholars in the May 1980 issue of *JSOT*, devoted to a consideration of Childs's *Introduction to the Old Testament as Scripture*. See also John Barton, *Reading the Old Testament: Method in Biblical Study* (rev. ed.; Louisville: Westminster John Knox, 1996), 77–103.

13. The term "postcritical" is often used interchangeably with "postliberal." Both terms posit a historical sequence of approaches to Scripture and theology. "Postcritical" acknowledges the decisive break introduced into biblical interpretation by the emergence and dominance of the historical-critical method. Postcritical biblical interpretation is thus not a simple return to an interpretive status quo ante but an alternative form of interpretation that could emerge only in the wake of historical

criticism. Similarly, a "postliberal" theology, and the biblical interpretation associated with it, posits a history in which traditionalist orthodoxy was challenged by forms of liberal theology from Schliermacher onwards. Postliberal theology is thus an alternative that emerges in conscious response to the preceding theological debate.

14. Hans W. Frei, *The Eclipse of Biblical Narrative: A Study in Eighteenth and Nineteenth Century Hermeneutics* (New Haven: Yale University Press, 1974), 58.

15. George A. Lindbeck, *The Nature of Doctrine: Religion and Theology in a Postliberal Age* (Philadelphia: Westminster, 1984), 120–21.

16. Frei, *The Eclipse of Biblical Narrative*, 72.

17. George A. Lindbeck, "Toward a Postliberal Theology," in *The Return to Scripture in Judaism and Christianity: Essays in Postcritical Scriptural Interpretation* (ed. Peter Ochs; New York: Paulist, 1993), 90.

18. See the recent study by W. T. Dickins, *Hans Urs von Balthasar's Theological Aesthetics: A Model for Post-critical Biblical Interpretation* (Notre Dame, Ind.: University of Notre Dame Press, 2003).

19. Johnson, "Imagining the World Scripture Imagines," 166.

20. See Richard Bauckham, "Reading Scripture as a Coherent Story," in Davis and Hays, *The Art of Reading Scripture*, 38–53, for an attempt to distinguish the biblical metanarrative from those that have received critique from postmodernism.

21. Lindbeck, *The Nature of Doctrine*, 32–42.

22. Peter Ochs, "An Introduction to Postcritical Scriptural Interpretation," in Ochs, *The Return to Scripture*, 14, emphasis original.

23. Peter Ochs, "Returning to Scripture: Trends in Postcritical Interpretation," *Cross Currents* 44 (1994–1995), 446.

24. Johnson, "Imagining the World Scripture Imagines," 167.

25. Sandra M. Schneiders, "Does the Bible Have a Postmodern Message?" in *Postmodern Theology: Christian Faith in a Pluralist World* (ed. Frederic B. Burnham; San Francisco: Harper & Row, 1989), 56–73.

26. Ibid., 63–64.

27. Ibid., 64.

28. Ibid., 68.

29. Davis, "Critical Traditioning: Seeking an Inner Biblical Hermeneutic" in Davis and Hays, *The Art of Reading Scripture*, 163–80.

30. Johnson, "Imagining the World Scripture Imagines," 171.

31. David J. A. Clines, *Interested Parties: The Ideology of Writers and Readers of the Hebrew Bible* (JSOTSup 205; Sheffield: Sheffield Academic Press, 1995), 21.

32. Elisabeth Schüssler Fiorenza, *Bread, Not Stone: The Challenge of Feminist Biblical Interpretation* (Boston: Beacon, 1984), 41.

33. Sugirtharajah, *Postcolonial Criticism and Biblical Interpretation*, 111.

34. Ibid., 94.

35. Ibid., 88.

36. Ibid., 113.

Reflections on the History of Consequences: The Case of Job

C. L. Seow

Several ongoing projects signal a sharp rise in interest among scholars in the afterlife of the Bible: *The Hebrew Bible/Old Testament: The History of Interpretation*;[1] the Blackwell Bible Commentaries;[2] the Church's Bible;[3] the Ancient Christian Commentary on Scripture;[4] and the *Encyclopedia of the Bible and Its Reception*,[5] to name only the most important examples. Yet interest in earlier exegesis is not new. It is evident already in the catenae of the early church from the fourth century C.E. onwards, sporadically in medieval Jewish and Christian commentaries, and in reference works such as the *Glossa Ordinaria* and the *Miqra'ot Gedolot* that have the "standard" commentaries surrounding the biblical text at the center of each page, the Latin Vulgate in the former, the Hebrew text in the latter. Commentators in the nineteenth century sometimes included surveys of earlier exegesis,[6] and a few in the twentieth have done so as well, most notably Brevard Childs, whose *The Book of Exodus* was published in 1974.[7]

Until recently, efforts to document interpretations have been largely confined to commentaries. Methodologically, they belong to the "history of interpretation" (*Auslegungeschichte*), although that discipline includes also various theological writings. Indeed, in a programmatic essay published in 1947, Gerhard Ebeling argued that the term "interpretation" (*Auslegung*) should encompass all manners of encounter with Scripture: "not only explicit but also implicit, not only conscious but also unconscious, not only positive but also negative."[8] To Ebeling, therefore, the history of interpretation must consider also ritual and prayer, ecclesiastical pretensions and politics, works of mercy, justification for wars, martyrdoms and witch hunts, and so on. Ebeling's concern in the essay is with the relationship of the history of interpretation and the history of the Christian church, but he also recognizes encounters with the Bible beyond the church. Hence, one also might consider the interpretation and effects of the Bible in Judaism, Islam, and other religions, as well as in the secular contexts.[9] In any case, Ebeling sowed seeds of what would later be variously called the "history of influence," "history of effects," or "reception history."

The first two of these labels are attempts to translate the German term *Wirkungsgeschichte*, employed by Hans-Georg Gadamer, who also provided the most substantial philosophical underpinnings for the enterprise.[10] The third formulation, "reception history" (*Rezeptionsgeschichte*), which comes from Hans Robert Jauss's development of a literary theory under the influence of Gadamer,[11] is more at home in the anglophone world than the awkward "history of influence" or "history of effects," though the term "reception" does not quite convey all that is implied by Gadamer's "*Wirkung*."[12] Gadamer's conception of *Wirkungsgeschichte* calls for an account of how a text is worked out in reality. This is an important undertaking for every interpreter, since one cannot transpose oneself into the author's mind and thought world, and thereby achieve objectivity, when seeking to understand an ancient text. One must delve into the transmission process, in which "present and past are constantly mediated."[13] What Gadamer calls for is not simply a historicist mapping of the realization of a text or tradition. Rather, he speaks of an interpreter's awareness of the effects of that text or tradition in history and of one being affected by that history.

In his commentary on Matthew, Ulrich Luz attempts to distinguish *Wirkungsgeschichte* from *Auslegungsgeschichte* in biblical studies.[14] To Luz, *Auslegungsgeschichte* concerns what is in commentaries and theological writings, whereas *Wirkungsgeschichte* involves works in other media, such as homilies, visual arts, music, and action. Framed this way, however, the distinction appears to be between scholarly explications of and other encounters with the Bible, as if scholars interpret but others only use or are influenced or impacted by it. Yet, to cite only examples of works on Job, Chrysostom's commentary consists of notes for sermons, and neither its method nor its content may be distinguished from his homilies that are based on Job. Moreover, commentaries may be philological and historical, or they may also be largely or entirely allegorical or mystical. The works of Christian art known from the first five centuries C.E. all contain elements found also in the commentaries and theological writings. Indeed, every element in these early artistic renderings may be corroborated by exegesis in the commentaries, homilies, and theological works. In short, the distinction between *Auslegungsgeschichte* and *Wirkungsgeschichte*, if one has to be drawn, cannot be made on the basis of genre and media.

Luz's intention is perhaps to distinguish those works whose purpose is to explicate the Bible, such as commentaries and theological writings, and those that expound only implicitly or, indeed, those that reimagine the text as something radically different from, even contrary to, what a face-value reading might yield. Even so, a rigid dichotomy between interpretation, on the one hand, and the use, influence, and impact of the text, on the other, is problematic. Indeed, Luz does not want to isolate one history from the other. Hence, immediately after trying to define the purview of each area, he subsumes *Auslegungsgeschichte* under *Wirkungsgeschichte*, arguing that the latter necessarily includes the former: "'history of influence' is inclusive of 'history of interpretation.'"[15] Luz is correct that "interpretation" and "influence" cannot always be equated. Thus, Prudentius's allegorical poem *Psychomachia*, which is clearly influenced by Job, is not strictly an interpretation of the book. Similarly, Christopher Marlowe's many allusions to Job in his *Jew of Malta* cannot meaningfully be called an interpretation of Job. *Auslegungsgeschichte* and *Wirkungsgeschichte* overlap with another as in a Venn diagram. One may indeed speak meaningfully of "interpretation," "reception," "influence," "effects," and "use," but none of these terms suffices as a rubric for all the types of engagements of and encounters with the Bible. I prefer to speak, therefore, of the "history of consequences," using "consequences" to connote *what comes after* (as in the history of interpretation and reception) as well as *impact* and *effects*.

To illustrate what a history of consequences might entail and the challenges and the promises that such an investigation poses, I would like to consider, if only selectively, the case of Job.[16]

Jewish, Christian, and Muslim Consequences[17]

Jewish Consequences

The history of Jewish consequences of Job begins in the Second Temple period.[18] It includes the Old Greek (OG), the book of Tobit,[19] Ben Sira (49:9),[20] a fragment by Aristeas the Historian,[21] four biblical manuscripts from Qumran,[22] an Aramaic version of the book (11Q10), 1QH^a from Qumran,[23] and the Testament of Job (T. Job). The early rabbinic period includes the debates and legends of the Tannaim and the Amoraim,[24] the Targum, and a few *piyyûṭîm* that interact with the Joban text. In the medieval period, Jews living under Muslim or Christian rule wrote nearly eighty commentaries on Job. From this period, too, come the earliest extant Jewish music based on Job, more *piyyûṭîm*, chronicles of the crusades that contain allusions to Job, literary fiction, and a few manuscript illustrations. The modern period begins with Spinoza in the seventeenth century. Until the Haskalah of the late eighteenth century, however, works produced on Job, apart from Spinoza, were aligned more with the approach of the medieval period than with modernity. The Haskalah ushered in a new era of Jewish scholarly writings on Job that were conversant with the methods of exegesis adopted by modern Christian interpreters. The twentieth century brought some of the most profound Jewish interactions with Job, primarily in the form of philosophical works by a host of writers: Hermann Cohen, Franz Rosenzweig, Leo Baeck, and, after the Shoah, Elie Wiesel, Martin Buber, Margarete Sussman, André Neher, Ernst Bloch, Richard Rubenstein, and Abraham Heschel. Jewish consequences of Job in the modern period are evident as well in literary works, beginning with a number of seventeenth-century works by Marrrano poets and dramatists Antonio Enríquez Gómez, Diego Enríquez Basurto, and Felipe Godínez, all survivors of the Spanish inquisitions. These were followed by others, including literary luminaries, including Goethe, Heine, and Kafka. There are as well musical compositions by Chaim Adler, Lehman Engel, and Herman Berlinski and visual art by Max Liebermann and Marc Chagall.

Jewish consequences of Job in most of the last two millennia have been focused on the reason for human suffering and the role of God therein. Unlike Christians and Muslims, Jewish interpreters did not presume that Job's afflictions were undeserved. Indeed, a majority assumed that Job's suffering was either a punishment for his sins or for some deficiency that must be corrected or a test of his faith. Divine justice is not questioned, and, in fact, interpreters tended to see suffering as part of divine providence, "chastisements of love" (*yissūrîn šel ʾahăbâ*). Accordingly, Job's suffering had a redemptive value. This view continued its dominance through the early decades of the twentieth century, as manifest in the writings of Cohen, Rosenzweig, and Baeck. The Shoah, however, brought about a sharp change in perspective, even though the traditional view continued to be held by a few interpreters.[25] With the Shoah, the earlier theodic readings gave way to antitheodic ones, as interpreters: (1) accentuated the notion of innocent suffering; (2) rejected the assumption of divine providence in suffering; and (3) identified with the voice of protest against God in the poetry of Job.

Christian Consequences

The earliest Christian interaction with Job is found in two passages of the New Testament. The first, alluding to a *written* text, is in 1 Cor 3:19, taken from the OG of Job 5:13. The second, Jas 5:11, refers to something that the recipient of James's epistle *heard*, namely, about "the patience of Job," likely an allusion to the Testament of Job.[26]

The OG version of Job is a sixth shorter than Masoretic Text;[27] the result is a version that in substance is at variance with the Hebrew.[28] The speeches of Job are less vitriolic than in the Hebrew, and Job comes across as a patient man. Furthermore, divine intention in permitting the trials of Job is seen as benign: the trials are a God-given opportunity to prove the righteousness of Job (40:8). There are also additions to the story, most significantly in an expansion of the speech of Job's wife (2:9; cf. T. Job 24:1–3). She speaks not out of impulse but only after a long time, thus showing patience as well, and she does not tell Job to curse God and die but simply to "say something to the Lord." Also, the conclusion of the book is expanded and affirms the possibility of life after death. Thus, OG is already engaged in both interpretation and retelling.

Most scholars would not regard the Testament of Job as belonging to the history of interpretation of Job, since it is not an explication of the book. In fact, one cannot even be sure that the story is a reception of the biblical story or if it is based on an alternate version.[29] Yet, for the earliest Christian interpreters, OG was the authoritative version, and the Testament of Job had a quasi-canonical status until it was explicitly rejected as such in the Gelasian Decree. Hence Christian interpreters consistently represented Job as an example of patience, a term that never occurs in the book but recurs in the Testament of Job. Moreover, among the most common analogies of Job's persistence in early Christian exegesis is that of an athlete or a wrestler[30] an analogy derived from the Testament of Job (4:12; 26:3).

For Christians, the "golden age" in the interpretation of Job was the patristic period. The rival exegetical traditions of the Alexandrian and Antiochene schools are both amply represented in the interpretation of Job. The Alexandrian school favored an allegorical approach to the text, while the tradition identified with Antioch stressed the literal-historical meaning, though even the allegorists took the prose prologue at face value (since Job is a moral example), while the literalists could not read the poetry without resorting to figurative explanations.[31] Whether writing in Greek, Syriac, or Latin, these interpreters found support for their various doctrinal positions in Job, regardless of whether their perspectives were Arian or anti-Arian, Nestorian or anti-Nestorian, Pelagian or anti-Pelagian. Christian interpreters found in Job polemics against those with whom they disagreed—heretics, pagan philosophers, and especially Jews.

Job was engaged not only in commentaries, theological writings, and homilies; Job was also invoked in liturgy. A second-century example of the *Commendatio animae* includes the words, "Deliver us as you have delivered Job."[32] On the Brescia Casket from the fourth century one finds the prayer, "Deliver, Lord, his soul, just as you delivered Job from suffering."[33] By the fourth century, Job 1:1–3:3 provided the readings for Holy Week or for Lent. Furthermore, certain passages (Job 1:21; 14:4–10; 40:23) were invoked with the rite of baptism.

Job is explicated through the medium of poetry by Ephrem the Syrian and Jacob of Sarug, and he is also cited in a literary fiction found in the Apocalypse of Paul and in Prudentius's *Psychomachia*. In addition to such literary reception, Job is often depicted in Christian art, typically as a Stoic, sitting nobly on the ash-heap or a pedestal. This is seen on frescoes in the catacombs and on sarcophagi.[34] Importantly, of the nearly thirty examples of Joban iconography in the first five centuries, about a third recalls the Testament of Job.

Medieval Christian consequences of Job are marked by a lively engagement in the Latin West, where Gregory's *Moralia in Iob* held nearly absolute sway until the thirteenth century.[35] Indeed, commentaries on Job in this period are largely commentaries on or abridgments of the *Moralia*.[36] Gregorian interpretation is evident as well in other genres, such as the homilies of the Anglo-Saxon ecclesiast Aelfric[37] and Peter Riga's paraphrase in his hexametric poem, *Aurora*. Gregory's dominance was broken only by the burst of scholastic exegesis in the thirteenth century led by Thomas Aquinas.

Another turning point came in the fourteenth century through Nicholas of Lyra's *Postilla litteralis in vetus et novum testamentum*.[38] Whereas the interpreters before him had at best superficial knowledge of Hebrew, Nicholas was sufficiently proficient in the language to use not only the Hebrew text but also the early rabbinic sources as well as contemporary

Jewish exegetes. The importance of Nicholas's work also lies in the fact that it became a standard commentary in the *Glossa Ordinaria*.

Apart from these writings, Job was known through the *Office of the Dead*, which typically consisted of nine lessons comprising portions of the Psalter and Job. In the latter case all the passages are from Job's protests against God (Job 7:16b-21; 10:1–7; 10:8–12; 13:23–28; 14:13–16; 17:1–3, 11–15; 19:20–27; 19:25–27). Yet these texts are understood in the liturgy in light of Gregory's *Moralia*, which takes these to be the mournful words of a penitent.

Works of visual art depicting the consequences of Job from this period are found in the hundreds of manuscript illuminations, sculptures, stained glass, ivory, enamel, and mosaic.[39] Mirroring the commentaries and homilies, the artistic illustrations of Job in the West are heavily influenced by the interpretation of Gregory. In addition, there are fifteen extant illustrations of Job in the *Psychomachia* and about one hundred illuminations of Job in the *Office of the Dead*.

Literary engagements with Job in this period are vast.[40] These include Cynewulf's *Ascension* and a 677-line poem, *The Phoenix*, once also attributed to Cynewulf, Hartmann von Aue's *Der arme Heinrich*, the *Legend of Saint Eustace*, best known in Jacobus de Voraigne's *Legenda Sanctorum, Liber de Antichristo* by an anonymous author in the thirteenth century, Geoffrey la Tour Landry's *Le livre du chevalier de La Tour Landry*, Petrarch's translation and retelling of the story of Patient Griselda (the hundredth novella in Boccacio's *Decameron*), Chaucer's *Canterbury Tales*, Dante's *Divine Comedy*, and William Langland's *Piers Plowman*.

Little by way of musical reception of Job is extant in the medieval period, though we may assume that the *Office of the Dead* was chanted, for these became the basis of numerous musical compositions during the Renaissance and Reformation. Already in some motets by Guillaume de Machaut in the fourteenth century, however, we find music based upon liturgical renderings of Job.[41]

The same lively interaction with Job is evident during the Renaissance and the Reformation. There are some twenty extant commentaries from this period, yet commentaries were by no means the only site of exegesis. Luther, for instance, did not write a commentary, but his exegesis of Job is evident in scores of comments scattered through his commentaries on other books of the Bible, letters, treatises, polemical writings, and homilies. Similarly, Savonarola and Calvin expressed their views of Job primarily through their sermons, but they did not write commentaries.

As in earlier periods, Job is engaged not only in the expositions of the clergy but also in popular culture. The *Office of the Dead* was popularized through the fifteenth-century poem known as *Pety Job*, but also in a poem by Pierre Nesson, *Vigillus de la Mort* or *Paraphrase de neufs leçon de Job*, as well as two plays that draw on the *Office of the Dead*, the anonymous *Mystère de la pacience de Job* and *Le Mistère du Viel Testament*. Other literary works include a metrical poem called *The Life of Job*, Johann von Tepl's *Der Ackermann aus Böhmen*, Hans Sach's *Hiob, der Geduldige*, and Shakespeare's *King Lear*.

In visual art, the Job story is depicted in a variety of media and styles by artists such as the Master of the Legend of St. Barbara, Jan Mandyn, Giovanni Bellini, Vittore Carpaccio, Bernard van Orley, Albrecht Dürer, and Hans Holbein.[42] Notable in the iconography of Job in this period is the frequent depiction of Job as a patron saint and protector of outcasts and those vulnerable to deadly diseases such as brought on by the Black Death. One may also point to several hospitals established in this period in the name of Job, such as those in Bologna, Venice,[43] and Utrecht to combat syphilis, which came to be known as "Saint Job's disease." Job is also for the first time, and frequently, associated with musicians, and indeed some regard him as having been patron saint of musicians.[44] It is perhaps not a coincidence, therefore, that this period witnesses an outburst of musical compositions based on Job.

In the modern period, Job is engaged not only by translations, paraphrases, and poetic renderings of the book but also by literally hundreds of commentaries, philosophical and theological writings, psychological readings, and throughout literature and the visual arts. Among the most prominent engagements of Job in literature are poems by John Milton, Robert Frost, and the Taiwanese poet Siren (Xie Shude); novels by Fyodor Dostoevsky, Emile Baumann, Wolfgang Borchert, Flannery O'Connor, and Japanese writer Ayako Sono; and plays by Samuel Beckett, Archibald Macleish, Robert Heinlein, Neil Simon, and Chinese playwright Lao She.

In the visual arts, one might mention just a few samples, such as the paintings of Rubens, la Tour, and Decamps; the etchings of Delcloche and Blake; the sculptures of Ivan Mestrovic and Goro Kakei; and the modern manuscript illuminations of Jamaican poet and artist Anna Ruth Henriques. Musical consequences of Job in the modern period include oratorios by Carrisimi, Händel, Parry, and Nabokov; the cantata of J. S. Bach, Dallapiccola, and Kósa; the organ composition of Eben; the soft rock of Joni Mitchell and the hard rock of Bad Religion; and the hip-hop musical of Jerome Saibil and Eli Batalion. Blake's illustrations provided the inspiration for Ralph Vaughn William's musical score for ballet, *Job: A Masque for Dancing*, a piece that was choreographed by Ninette de Valois in 1931, cued by the movements in Blake's etchings. Also composed to be choreographed is the poetic opera *Las Danzas de Job*, by Costa Rican poet Fernando Centeno Güell.

Nearly two thousand years of Christian encounter with the story of Job have resulted in a tremendously vibrant collage of images in a vast array of media, mostly in Europe, but within the last five centuries also in the Americas, Asia, and Africa. Unlike their Jewish counterparts, Christians have discerned in Job an example of virtue and a symbol of hope and renewal, tropes picked up from OG and the Testament of Job that, once lifted up, took lives of their own. These perspectives persisted despite Jerome's expressed return to *Hebraica veritas*,[45] even long after exegetes beginning with Nicholas of Lyra in the fourteenth century relied on the Hebrew text. The OG has a profound impact as well in Christian theology, for it consistently renders Hebrew *haśśāṭān* (the adversary) as *ho diabolos* (the devil). It speaks, too, of God's death sentence on "the apostate dragon" (LXX Job 26:13), even as "dragon" translates Leviathan in 40:25, part of a passage (in OG) that came to be interpreted as relating God's redemption for humanity through Christ by the defeat of the devil. Coupled with the conceit of resurrection in the appendix of the OG (42:17), which inevitably colors the interpretation of 19:25 as a text about Christ as Redeemer, Christians have understood Job to predict redemption through Christ. Regardless of what the author of the Hebrew book might have meant, all these views have become part and parcel of what Job has come to mean for Christians.

Muslim Consequences

Job (*'ayyūb*) is mentioned in four passages in the Qur'an (4:163–164; 6:84; 21:83–84; 38:41–44), where he is a prophet.[46] The qur'anic accounts are supplemented by narratives known as *Qiṣaṣ al-Anbiya'* ("Stories of the Prophets"), which survive in different versions and languages. Drawn mostly from Jewish legends, with many elements traceable to the Testament of Job, the *Qiṣaṣ* provide in midrashic fashion many details of Job, his family, and his suffering. In accordance with the Testament of Job, the protagonist of the story is a patient man whose trials were brought upon him by Satan—known as Iblis, "the enemy of God"—out of jealousy for

Job's relationship with God. As in the Testament of Job and Christian interpretation, but in contrast to much of Jewish tradition, Job's suffering is undeserved. Thus, suffering serves as a test for Job. Hence the only limit placed upon Iblis at the outset is that he must not hurt Job's tongue, presumably so that Job may either praise or curse God. Iblis is also not allowed to harm Job's wife, whose name, according to a strong tradition, is Raḥma, the name being also the Arabic term used for divine mercy. The term is in fact the one used of God's response to Job's cry for divine intervention (Qur'an 21:84; 38:43). Like Sitidos in the Testament of Job, Raḥma is viewed more positively than in the Hebrew version. She is the one who sustains him with food and supports him physically, emotionally, and spiritually.

It is perhaps no coincidence, therefore, that she is portrayed in a very positive light in the Aljamiado version of the *Qiṣaṣ*, which was secretly preserved among the Moriscos in al-Andalus in the sixteenth century.[47] In the wake of Christian persecutions, when the Morisco men were killed or in hiding, the women were the ones who kept faith and sustained their families.[48] In contrast to the stereotypical Christian view that she is Satan's assistant, this version of the Muslim tradition holds that she is the agent of divine succor for Job. Unlike Christians who argued that she was left unharmed by Satan in order that she might tempt Job to sin, the Muslims discerned a salvific purpose in her preservation.

Among the most interesting Islamic theological reflections on Job are by the Sufi mystic, Ibn al-ʿArabī (1165–1240) whose *Fuṣūṣ al-ḥikam* ("Bezels of Wisdom") contains a section on Job.[49] He portrays Job as a model of a good Muslim. Job's appeal to God for relief does not make him any less patient and faithful. On the contrary, supplication is appropriate when one suffers, for it is acknowledgement that God alone can deliver. Referring to Sura 22:37 ("those who hurt God and his Apostle"), Ibn al-ʿArabī concludes that God, too, can be hurt, so that when a human being suffers, God also suffers. But God afflicts suffering on people so that they might realize their needy state. In fact, failure to come to God to seek relief is tantamount to disregarding divine reality.

"Patient Job" becomes a model of faith throughout the Islamic world, and the legends of his excellence, his suffering, and God's restoration of him reverberate in Islamic commentaries, theological writings, sermons, and literature from the medieval period to the present. In modern Arabic poetry, Job remains a frequent referent and an inspiration.[50] Interestingly, while the allusions to Job in earlier Islamic literature have been entirely to the versions of Job's tale found in the Qur'an and the *Qiṣaṣ al-Anbiya'*, modern poets occasionally engage the Job of the Bible. As for other media, Job is occasionally represented in Islamic art from Turkey and Persia,[51] and there is a film based on the Islamic traditions of Job, *Ayoub* (1983), starring Omar Shariff.

Consequential Contributions

Modern interpreters who have paid attention to the history of interpretation have done so because earlier exegeses, even the so-called "precritical" ones, often offer insights that anticipate or are missed altogether by later interpreters, and they regularly point to alternate ways a text might mean.[52] That is true not only of the commentaries, treatises, and sermons; it is true as well of other modes of interaction with the text. A few examples from the history of consequences of Job will suffice to make this point.

Job 3:3–5

Job's reference to the conception of *geber* (3:3b) has troubled modern interpreters who recognize that the term is more properly used of an adult male than of an embryo or infant.[53] Hence scholars sometimes emend to read *zākār* "male" (Jer 20:15).[54] Early interpreters, however, recognized that Job is speaking here not of himself but humanity as a whole. Origen judged that Job's problem is not so much with his own existence but with human existence (PG 12:495), and Didymus the Blind concurred that Job was speaking "concerning the entire human race."[55] For Hesychius of Jerusalem, Job was alluding to the creation of the first human being (PO 42.1:170). The Targum of Job may imply this view as well when it reads, *ʾtbrʾ gbr* "a man is created."

In light of such views, one might note that *geber* appears fifteen times in the book, most often as a synonym for *ʾĕnôš* (4:17; 10:5) or *ʾādām* (14:10; 16:21; 33:17), and it refers to a human, as opposed to God (3:21; 14:14; 22:2; 33:29; 34:7, 9). It may seem odd that the poet should use such a term when it is Job who is the subject of the preceding line, yet parallelism, as recent studies of Hebrew poetry have amply demonstrated, is not the mere repetition of ideas. On the contrary, the second line may heighten the stakes.[56] In this case, the poet moves from an impersonal day in which Job was born to a personal night that speaks, and, in a move that modern literary critics call "defamiliarization,"[57] it momentarily disorients the reader with the unexpected sequence of birth followed by strange notion of the conception of a *geber*. Afterwards, the reader is reoriented by the allusion to creation of the cosmos, except that the undoing of creation is in view. Insofar as ancient readers were able to cope poetically and theologically with the disorientation, they prove to be sensitive readers of Joban poetry.

In his exegesis of this passage, Hesychius of Jerusalem proceeds to associate the light in 3:4c with Christ and Darkness in 3:5a with "the Enemy," also called "the Traitor" (PO 42.1:170). Modern critics may dismiss this christological reading as anachronistic and fanciful. What is important, though, is that Hesychius recognizes the integral relationship between verses 4 and 5 and the personification that is at work. His exposition reflects the liturgy for Christian initiation. A candidate for baptism would face west, which represents Darkness, and renounce all ties with "the Enemy" and "Traitor," and then turn east to acknowledge allegiance to Christ, the Light. Hesychius recognizes the tension between personified Light and Darkness in Job's poem, although Job seems ironically to be calling for the opposite of what Christian baptismal liturgy performed. Job calls for the abandonment of claim by God and the absence of light, on the one hand, and the claim of darkness, on the other. Some illustrations of Job 3:4–5 in an early twelfth-century manuscript from Cyprus may reflect an exegesis similar to that of Hesychius. In these, Job is shown cursing the day of his birth, while personified Darkness stands nearby in a mandorla (Bib. Vat., MS gr. 1231, fols. 97v, 99v, 101v).[58] Job is shown in these illustrations with his hand extended toward personified Darkness, as if reaching out to it. This representation of personified Darkness is unusual, since elsewhere typically it is Christ who is depicted in a mandorla. The manuscripts portray personified Darkness as an ominous counterredeemer to whom Job is reaching out through his malediction. These early Christian interpreters have appropriately called attention to the relationship between verses 4 and 5,[59] understood verse 4c as an allusion to divine presence, which in light of the usage of the *hip'il* of *yp'* it surely is, and emphasized the tension between redemption by God in verse 4 and the counterredemption by Darkness in verse 5. These ancient exegetes, including the artistic ones, prove once again to be perceptive close-readers of the text who have much to contribute to their modern counterparts.

Job 6:6–7

It bears reiterating that artistic representations cannot be simply classified as "reception," as opposed to "interpretation." The artist of MS gr. 1231 in the Vatican represents the interpretation in the catena it accompanies. The same manuscript also illustrates Job 6:6–7, where Job speaks of his refusal to partake of unpalatable food, a metaphor for his partaking of suffering. It shows Job sitting before a table of unappetizing food. Job's left hand covers his mouth, indicating his refusal to take the food. Eliphaz is with him, his right hand raised in an argumentative posture, and a lion is next to him. The artist thus connects this passage with 4:10–11, where Eliphaz speaks of the roar of leonine predators, probably alluding to Job's outburst (see *šaʾăgōtay* in 3:24). The artist suggests that Job's argument at this point is with Eliphaz's comparison of Job's outburst with the roar of the lion. Thus, whereas Eliphaz associates Job with predators, Job sees his outcry more like that of the wild ass and the ox (MS gr. 1231, fol. 135r), vulnerable and needy animals that have not been properly treated.

Job 3:24

Interestingly, a very similar scene in the manuscript illustrates 3:24, where Job speaks of his suffering coming before his food (Bib. Vat., MS gr. 1231, fol. 109v). While modern critics have tried to emend the text[60] or impute meanings for *lipnê* that cannot be defended, namely, *lipnê* meaning "as," "like," "instead of," or "more than," the artist understands "bread" as a metaphor for the experience of suffering, an attractive interpretation in light of Job's references in the poem to the bitterness of the *nepeš*, literally, the bitterness of throat (3:5c, 20b). The artistic interpreter is sensitive to the poetry, whereas modern interpreters have been much too prosaic.

Job 2:9–10

At times the benefit of a history of consequences comes not so much by the insights of a single interpretive tradition but from the tension of alternate viewpoints. Such is the case with the reception of Job's wife. The dominant view of her is negative; among Christians she is usually seen as a shrew, a temptress, and a tool of the devil. This perspective is found also among Jewish interpreters, for whom she, along with Satan, symbolized the evil inclination. In Islam, however, she is viewed largely in positive terms. She is faithfully patient and selflessly supportive of her husband. She is the ideal Muslim wife. Even more, she is the earthly embodiment of divine mercy. That perspective is not unique to Islam, however. Already in the Testament of Job she is seen as a sustainer of her husband. In Christian iconography from the earliest period onwards, she is sometimes represented as one who delivers food and drink to her husband,[61] sustenance that in Christian liturgy is symbolized by bread and wine. In literary works as well, such as the medieval Life of Job[62] and in la Tour Landry's *Le livre du Chevalier*,[63] she is presented positively. To the German mystic Hermann von Fritzlar, she is an ideal wife, like the wife of Eustace.[64]

In the history of consequences, therefore, we find not just one view of Job but two or more. The minority position can challenge the exegesis of the majority, thereby pointing to the ambiguity of the text to which the reader is invited to return. The ambiguity lies in the fact that of the six Hebrew forms that constitute Jobs wife's only words in the book, three echo the divine affirmation of Job in 2:3 and three echo the Adversary's prediction in 2:5. Duly cued by the history of consequences, the interpreter may realize that the role of Job's wife in her single contribution in the book is to give voice on earth to Job of divine confidence as well as divine doubt. Furthermore, that tension is played out in the ambiguity of the imperative, *bārēk*. Is it to be taken as an antiphrasis meaning, "curse," as those who read Job's wife negatively presumed? Or ought one to take her words at face value, meaning, "bless"? Some medieval Jewish interpreters in fact take the imperative literally, thus giving Job's wife the benefit of doubt.[65] The exegetical effect of this ambiguity is to put Job's rebuke of his wife in 2:10 in question. Job seems to have taken her words as outrageous, but he does not after all have access to the celestial goings on to this point. The omniscient narrator is, however, much more nuanced. Indeed, read in the light of the rest of the book, Job's rebuke is ironic, for Job proceeds to do precisely what he tells his wife not to do. The alternative interpretations proffered in that history prompts one to a richer engagement of the text.[66]

Cross-Cultural Consequences

A history of consequences will uncover not only the insightful and delightful. It underscores as well the contextuality of every interpretation and brings to light the sometimes-nefarious consequences of the biblical traditions that are shared and contested. Such an investigation must, therefore, be concerned not just with the conversations that take place within a single religious tradition. It must be ever-attentive to wider cross-cultural effects.

Job was a contested narrative for Christians and Jews from the very beginning of their encounter with one another. The hermeneutical parting of ways is inevitable because both communities had different starting points. For Christians, Job was known largely through the OG and the Testament of Job, whereas for Jews the book of Job was the Hebrew version. To Christians, therefore, Job was an example of faithful conduct, a prefiguration of Christ, and an antetype of the Christian sufferer. Moreover, the protagonist was a Gentile. Beginning with Justin Martyr in the second century, Job's Gentile origin was held up and given theological significance by Christians, since Job supposedly lived before the law and even performed a sacerdotal function (1:5). Furthermore, if Job is a figure for Christ, then Job's enemies must be Christ's enemies. Thus Hippolytus in the third century read Job 6:27b as a direct address by Christ to the Jews accusing them of bartering him away and approaching him "like a robber in the garden" (PG 10:791). The friends of Job are thus linked with Judas, who betrayed Jesus in the Garden of Gethsemane. A similar linkage appears in one of his *Catechetical Lectures* (14:5). Patristic writings on Job are replete with such anti-Jewish interpretations.

None, however, was more vehement and far-ranging in anti-Jewish polemics than Gregory in his *Moralia in Iob*.[67] There are scores of references to the Jews in this commentary, mostly in characterizations of Jews as arrogant about the law and their initial relationship with God, cruel in rejecting and persecuting Christ and the church, stubborn and blind to the truth of Christianity. There are suggestions as well that the church has replaced the Jews. Gregory's views would have tremendous consequences during the crusades. His anti-Jewish readings were all the more pernicious because of his exegesis of Job 7:1 and 14:14. Merging the view in the Old Latin (based on OG) that life on earth is a *temptatio* (7:1) with Jerome's new translation (Vulgate) of the same verse to mean that life is a *militia*, Gregory sees the righteous sufferer as a soldier—a soldier of God (*Moral.* 31.41.82; 31.43.84), a soldier of Christ (31.39.72, 80), a heavenly soldier (31.40.80; 31.51.82) going through the trial of warfare to the end. The warfare has the effect of revealing the soul's weakness, prompting one to be humble and penitent. Suffering adversities in that warfare, therefore, one might ironically be liberated. Gregory makes it clear, though, that the warfare he means is a spiritual one, a struggle against temptation to surrender one's faith (6.33.52; 30.25.75–77). Yet his exegesis would later be used for the encouragement of crusaders. Even as Job called life a *militia*, the layperson may call life a *militia*, in the sense of a crusade, at once a pilgrimage and an act of penitence. Though the ultimate end of the crusades was the liberation of Jerusalem from Muslims, the Jews were the first to suffer the consequences, in no small part because of Gregory's anti-Jewish interpretation of Job.

There were fewer Christian polemics against Muslims stemming from the book of Job. Nevertheless, in the wake of Muslim persecution of Christians in Cordova in 852, Paulus Albarus invoked Gregory's association of Behemoth and Leviathan with the Antichrist (PL 121:542, 548). To Albarus, that "prophecy" in Job has meaning in every age, and he suggests that Muhammad—at once Muhammad the founder of Islam and Muhammad I, the emir of Cordova who was responsible for the massacre of Christians in 852—was a forerunner of the antichrist. Accordingly, Behemoth's moving of its tail like cedar (40:18) and Leviathan's breathing out fire and belching smoke (41:19–20) point to the persecuting forces that Christians must resist. The Muslims of Iberia pressed north until Charles Martel stopped them at Tours in France in 732. The twelfth-century English historian William of Newburgh later offered that Christian victory at Tours was by divine will, citing Job 38:11. Thus, William explains, the Arabians were unable to proceed further and were driven back into Spain.[68]

As with Christian interpreters, Jews also read Job polemically. In fact, many of the negative attitudes of the rabbis toward Job may have been prompted by Christian appropriation of Job. Thus, whereas Rabbi Joḥanan of Tiberius of the third century suggested that Job was praised more than Abraham—since Job was "blameless and upright, a fearer of God and one who turned away from evil" (Job 1:1, 8; 2:3), whereas Abraham was said only to have feared God (Gen 22:12; see b. B. Bat. 15a)—a countertradition presents Job as decisively inferior to Abraham, fearing God though not loving him and accusing God of destroying the good with the wicked (Job 9:22; see Gen. Rab. 49:9).[69] Jewish interpreters reading Job after Christianity had become a state-recognized religion under Constantine reacted to Christian triumphalism. Meanwhile in the East, where Shapur II of the Sassanid Empire distrusted Christians as potential allies of the Romans and favored the Jews, Jewish exegesis bolstered the Jewish position as they sought to convert Christians. It was here that the Amora Rava suggested in the fourth century that Job was rebellious, blasphemed against God, and denied the resurrection (b. B. Bat. 16a), a perspective that was perhaps deliberately set against the interpretation of Job by Rava's Christian contemporary Aphrahat.[70]

Jewish exegesis of Job in the medieval period was shaped to a large extent by Islamic exegetical methods, with its distinction between the "apparent meaning" (*ẓāhir*) and the "intrinsic-meaning" (*bāṭin*) of the text, and by its philosophical-theological debates. In fact, the first extant Jewish commentaries, by Saadiah in the tenth century and by his Karaite contemporary, Japhet ben Ali, are structured in the style of an Islamic commentary. Saadiah took advantage of the book's dialogical form to explore various Muslim theological positions.[71] One may occasionally detect in Saadiah's work as well a subtle anti-Muslim polemic. Thus, in 9:24, where the Hebrew has "the land is given into the hand of the wicked," he translates with the Arabic verb *salima*, thus making a wordplay: "the land is surrendered [*tusallamu*] into the hand of an oppressor" (*ẓallām*, my translation). Similarly, in a gloss on 10:22, he speaks of an aggressive ruler who "subjugated" (*yusallim*) the country and then proceeded to destroy its social structures. As Goodman notes, Saadiah's language "suggests his restiveness with Islamic triumphalism."[72] Along with such animosity directed at the Muslim rulers, however, one also finds attempts to accommodate the idioms of Islam. Thus, whereas the Hebrew speaks of God favoring Job, Saadiah interprets it to mean "God accepted Job's intercession" (my translation).[73] That view accords with the Islamic perception of Job as one whose prayers were heard by God (Qur'an 21:83–84; 38:41–41). Saadiah concludes that God gave Job and his friends "blessings in this world prior to the great reward in the hereafter, and God caused their history to be written as a lesson to all creation, so that we may bear sufferings with fortitude when they befall us and not hasten to impugn God's judgment but submit [*yusallimûn*] to God." Embedded here is an *apologia* about what it means to be true "Muslims." Thus, the faithful Jew is already a "Muslim."

One may only speculate about the reasons for the abundance of Jewish commentaries in the medieval period. No doubt the relevance of the book's subject matter during the period when Jews suffered in lands ruled by Muslims or Christians was a factor. The dialogical nature of the book, too, appears to encapsulate competing theological discourses. One suspects that the number of commentaries especially coming out of Europe might also have been generated in response to the popularity of Christian works produced under the influence of Christian allegorical readings that supported the crusades and fomented animosity against the Jews. We cannot read Naḥmanides' writings on Job without thinking of the Disputation of Barcelona of 1264 in which he was forced to participate and as a result of which he was expelled from Spain.[74] In fact, Naḥmanides reflected on Job in his sermon delivered on the eve of his departure.[75] Neither can one read Rabbenu Tam's commentary without recalling that he witnessed the massacre of Jews at the beginning of the Second Crusade and was himself stabbed several times when Christians plundered his home.[76] Riqam, who wrote a commentary on Job, fled Spain in the wake of Muslim persecution by the Almohads in 1148, only to face persecution in France by Christians.[77] Though emphasizing the plain sense in his commentary, Riqam was not above allegorical readings in his use of Job in anti-Christian polemics. So Job 14:1 is used against the notion of a deity supposedly born of woman.[78] In this, Riqam was not alone, for in the anonymous anti-Christian polemical work called *Sēper Niṣṣāḥôn Yāšān* ("Old Book of Polemics"), he also refers to the same text in an attack against Christian theology of incarnation, suggesting that Job had "already prophesied that he [Jesus] is of no use."[79] When Job says in 14:3 that God has "opened his eyes on this," it is taken to mean that God knew "that the world will err with regard to this man and [God] prepared to bring to judgment all who follow him."[80] Riqam's interpretation of Job 14:1 in his polemical work does not in fact reflect his preferred exegetical approach, which is to give the plain sense of the text. Still, he uses the allegorical approach of Christian interpreters in polemics against them, for medieval Christian interpreters in France, by following Gregorian exegesis, employed the passage to speak of the uniqueness of Jesus.

Conclusion

The value of a history of consequences may be illustrated in some ways by the valuation of Chinese landscape paintings. Such paintings are typically found with a number of stamps on them—as few as two or three and, and for particularly important and valuable paintings, as many as thirty stamps. Along with these stamps are poems and epigrams by the artist, subsequent scholars and poets, and owners of the work, each offering an interpretive cue or a critical judgment, often at variance with other views expressed on the work. The value and the meaning of the painting thus reside not in what the original artist might have intended but in the many ways the work has been engaged. Unless the viewer participates in the "conversation" that the piece encapsulates, he or she would miss out on the true depth and meaning of that living work of art. In the same sense, then, Job is not simply an artifact from the ancient past. "Job" is a tradition that has been encountered and realized through the ages in many contexts and by many different constituencies.

For Further Reading

Gadamer, Hans G. *Truth and Method.* 2nd ed. Translated and revised by Joel Weinsheimer and Donald G. Marshall. New York: Crossroads, 1989.

Ginsburg, Louis, ed. *Legends of the Jews.* 10th ed. 7 vols. New York: Jewish Publication Society, 1954.

Hayes, John L., ed. *A Dictionary of Biblical Interpretation.* 2 vols. Abingdon: Nashville, 1999.

Saebø, Magne, ed. *Hebrew Bible/Old Testament: The History of Interpretation.* 2 vols. Göttingen: Vandenhoeck & Ruprecht, 1996–2008.

Sawyer, John. *A Concise Dictionary of the Bible and Its Reception.* Westminster John Knox, 2009.

Sherwood, Yvonne. *A Biblical Text and Its Afterlives: The Survival of Jonah in Western Culture.* Cambridge: Cambridge University Press, 2000.

Spieckermann, Hermann, Choon-Leong Seow, Hans-Josef Klauck, Bernard McGinn, and Barry Dov Walfish, eds. *Encyclopedia of the Bible and Its Reception.* Berlin: de Gruyter, 2009–.

Terrien, Samuel L. *The Iconography of Job through the Centuries: Artists as Biblical Interpreters.* University Park: Pennsylvania State University Press, 1996.

Notes

1. Magne Saebø, ed., *Hebrew Bible/Old Testament: The History of Interpretation* (2 vols.; Göttingen: Vandenhoeck & Ruprecht, 1996–2008). A third volume is now in progress.

2. Published by Blackwell under the editorship of John Sawyer et al. With eight volumes released since 2004, the series attempts to document broadly the reception history of every book of the Bible.

3. Published by Eerdmans under the editorship of Robert L. Wilkens. Three volumes have been published since 2005. The volumes consist in the main of translations of a selection of Christian commentaries.

4. Published by InterVarsity Press under the general editorship of Thomas C. Oden. Twenty-six volumes have been published since 1998. Each volume includes translations of a selection of Christian commentaries.

5. To be published by Walter de Gruyter under the editorship of C. L. Seow et al. The first volumes have now appeared.

6. See, e.g., Christian D. Ginsburg. *Song of Songs* (London: Longman, Brown, Green & Roberts, 1857); idem, *Coheleth* (London: Longman, 1861).

7. Brevard S. Childs, *The Book of Exodus* (OTL; Philadelphia: Westminster, 1974).

8. Gerhard Ebeling, *Kirchengeschichte als Geschichte der Auslegung der heiligen Schrift* (Tübingen: Mohr Siebeck, 1947), 24.

9. Ebeling uses the term "profane" to describe the interactions with the Bible beyond the church, which are to him not properly within the purview of church history. The term is unsatisfactory, as is his implication that the consequences of the Bible outside the church are not within the domain of church history.

10. Hans-Georg Gadamer, *Truth and Method* (German ed. 1960; 2nd ed.; trans. and rev. Joel Weinsheimer and Donald G. Marshall; New York: Crossroads, 1989), 265–307.

11. Hans R. Jauss, *Literaturegeschichte als Provokation der Literaturwissenschaft* (Konstanzer Universitätsreden 3; Konstanz: Universitätsverlag, 1967).

12. Martydom (so Ebeling), for instance, can hardly be called "reception."

13. Gadamer, *Truth and Method*, 290.

14. Ulrich Luz, *Matthew 1–7* (German ed. 1985; trans. Wilhelm C. Linss; Minneapolis: Augsburg, 1989), 95–99.

15. Ibid., 95. Ebeling, however, concludes the opposite, that the history of interpretation includes the various modes of actualization of the text.

16. The most ambitious attempt to gather the different views and uses of Job is in Stephen J. Vicchio, *The Image of the Biblical Job: A History* (3 vols.; Eugene, Oreg.: Wipf & Stock, 2006). Though containing an impressive wealth of material, however, the usefulness of the volumes is diminished by a lack of methodological discipline, numerous factual errors (including works that are incorrectly attributed and even a few works that do not exist), and inadequate documentation.

17. These are the principal constituencies that interact with or are impacted by the use of Job, though research on the history of consequences must not be limited to them. One might, for instance, find allusions to Job in other religions, perhaps Buddhist interaction with the notion of suffering in Job. There are also purely secular engagements of Job. For the purposes of this essay, however, my focus will be the consequences of Job among Jews, Christians, and Muslims.

18. For a survey of Jewish consequences of Job, see Gabrielle Oberhänsli-Widmer, *Hiob in jüdischer Antike und Moderne: Die Wirkungsgeschichte Hiobs in der Jüdischer Literatur* (Neukirchener-Vluyn: Neukirchener, 1998).

19. The affinities between Tobit and Job are obvious. Both Job and Tobit are men of piety and charity (Job 1:1–5; 29:12–17; Tob 1:3, 8, 17). Both lost their possessions and otherwise suffered, though not due to sinfulness. In fact, Tobit's suffering came precisely because he had been pious, just as Job in Testament of Job suffered because he acted faithfully. Both are confronted by their wives, and both rebuke their wives out of their own sense of righteousness (Job 2:9; Tob 2:14). Just as Job says he prefers strangulation and death and loathes his life (Job 7:15), so Tobit says he prefers death to the excessive distress in his life (Tob 3:6). In fact, Jerome, claiming an Aramaic *Vorlage* for his translation of Tobit, explicitly relates Tobit to Job (Vulgate Tob 2:12–18).

20. On affinities between Job and Ben Sira, see Friedrich V. Reiterer, "Das Verhältnis Ijobs und Ben Siras," in *The Book of Job* (ed. Wim A. M. Beuken; BETL 114; Leuven: Leuven University Press, 1994), 403–29.

21. See Carl R. Holladay, *Fragments from Hellenistic Jewish Authors* (SBLTT Pseudipigrapha Series 10; Chico, Calif.: Scholars Press, 1983), 261–75.

22. It is obvious that all translations belong to the history of consequences, but even the extant Hebrew texts are part of that history. The earliest Hebrew manuscript known is 4QPaleoJob[c] from Qumran, which is written for the most part without internal matres. If the conservative orthography is secondary, the archaism is part of the book's reception history, in this case corroborating the tradition that Moses was the author of the book, a tradition found later in the Talmud. If, however, the archaistic orthography reflects the original, the other biblical Job manuscripts from Qumran (4QJob[a], 4QJob[b], 2QJob) must be seen as already contributing to the book's interpretation, for the introduction of the vowel letters is itself interpretive.

23. See Heidi Szpek, "On the Influence of Job in Jewish Hellenistic Literature," in *Seeking Out the Wisdom of the Ancients: Essays Offered to Michael V. Fox* (ed. Ronald L. Troxel, Kelvin G. Friebel, and Dennis R. Magary; Winona Lake, Ind.: Eisenbrauns, 2005), 357–70.

24. See Irving Jacobs, "The Book of Job in Rabbinic Thought" (Ph.D. diss., London University, 1971); Judith R. Baskin, *Pharaoh's Counsellors: Job, Jethro, and Balaam in Rabbinic and Patristic Tradition* (BJS 47; Chico, Calif.: Scholars Press, 1983), Joseph H. Leibowitz, "The Image of Job as Reflected in Rabbinic Writings" (Ph. D. diss., University of California, Berkeley, 1987).

25. So, e.g., Joseph B. Soloveitchik, "Kol Dodi Dofek: It Is the Voice of My Beloved That Knocketh," in *Theological and Halakhic Reflections on the Holocaust* (ed. Bernhard H. Rosenberg and Fred Heuman; Hoboken, N.Y.: Rabbinical Council of America/Ktav, 1992), 51–117. See Jason Kalman, "Biblical Criticism in the Service of Jewish Theology: A Case Study in Post-Holocaust Biblical Exegesis," *OTE* 18 (2005): 93–108.

26. The Greek term *hypomonē* in Jas 5:11 is closer to the usage in Testament of Job than to OG-Job, where it appears only once, in 14:19, translating Hebrew *tiqwâ* "hope." For the term in the former, see Cees Haas, "Job's Perseverance in the Testament of Job," in *Studies on the Testament of Job* (ed. Michael A. Knibb and Pieter W. van der Horst; SNTSMS 66; Cambridge: Cambridge University Press, 1989), 117–54.

27. Noticing this discrepancy, Origen in the third century supplied the missing texts from Theodotion, marking each addition with asterisk. The resultant text became the standard ecclesiastical text that came to be known as "LXX-Job." By then, Christian views of Job's character had already been shaped to a large extent.

28. The shortening of OG is a result of the omission of parallel lines in numerous couplets, the paraphrasing of couplets and triplets in single prosaic lines, and larger scale elimination of lines (as many as twenty lines at one) as the book progresses. The distribution of the omissions, with the largest concentration in chs. 22–31 (25 percent) and 32–37 (35 percent), suggest that they may have been done in consideration of the wearying of the reader, that is, to make the book more readable. The intent is, therefore, not interpretive. This is not *Auslegung*, though the result, at least in part, affects the interpretation of the Greek text.

29. Ezekiel knew of a tradition of Job as a man from antiquity who was renowned for his righteousness, which, the prophet implies, saved not just Job himself but others

as well (Ezek 14:14, 20), a version clearly different from that told in the book of Job. See Shalom Spiegel, "Noah, Danel, and Job," in *Louis Ginzberg Jubilee Volume* (New York: The American Academy of Jewish Research, 1945), 305–55. The protagonist of Testament of Job seems closer to this version of the story than the one told in the biblical book.

30. Thus, for example, Origen, Didymus the Blind, Chysostom, Gregory of Nazianzus, Ambrose of Milan, Pelagius, Jerome, Theodoret of Cyrus, John Cassian, Mar Aba, and Leontius the Presbyter.

31. Literal exegesis recognized the poetic and theological nature of much of Job. Thus, even Theodore of Mopsuestia, according to his defenders, read Job with an awareness of its "spiritual sense." See Jean B. Chabot, *Synodicon orientale ou recueil des synods nestoriens* (Paris: Imprimerie Nationale, 1902), 137–38, 399.

32. Ludovico A. Muratori, ed., *Liturgia romana vetus* (2 vols.; Venice: Pasquali, 1748), 1:750.

33. See Catherine B. Tkacz, *The Key to the Brescia Casket: Typology and the Early Christian Imagination* (Collection des Études Augustiniennes, Série Antiqué 165; Paris: Institut d'Études Augustiniennes; Notre Dame, Ind.: University of Notre Dame, 2001), 114–17.

34. All of these are found in the Princeton Index of Christian Art (http://ica.princeton.edu/).

35. By contrast, there is a dearth of commentaries in the East, save a few works in Syriac (by Jacob of Edessa in the late seventh or early eighth century, Ishodad of Merv in the mid-ninth, and Bar Hebraeus in the thirteenth) and several Greek catenae, mostly of Chrysostom, Olympiodorus, and the Cappadocian fathers.

36. See René Wasselynck, "Les compilations des 'Moralia in Job' du VIIe au XIIe siècle," *RTAM* 29 (1962): 5–32; idem, "Les 'Moralia in Job' dans les overages de morale du haut moyen âge latin," *RTAM* 31 (1964): 5–31; idem, "L'influence de l'exégèse de S. Grégoire le Grand sur les commentaries bibliques médiévaux (VIIe –XIIe s.)," *RTAM* 32 (1965): 157–204.

37. See Peter Clemoes, ed., *Aelfric's Catholic Homilies: The First Series* (Early English Text Society 17; Oxford: Oxford University Press, 1997) I, 31.472–74; II, 19.242–59, 30; Walter W. Skeat, ed., *Aelfric's Lives of Saints* (Early English Text Society 76, 82, 94, 114; London: Early English Text Society, 1881–1900), 16.36–54; Malcolm Godden, *Aelfric's Catholic Homilies: Introduction, Commentary and Glossary* (Oxford: Oxford University Press, 2000), 592–600. Aelfric also produced the first English translation and interpretation of Job, albeit only of the prologue and epilogue. See Edward Thwaites, ed., *Heptateuchus, Liber Job, et Evangelium Nicodemi* (Oxford: Theatro Sheldoniano, 1698), 164–68; Benjamin Thorpe, ed., *Analecta Anglo-Saxonica* (London: Smith, Elder, 1844), 159–64. The translation is also available in the West Midland dialect as "Forbisne of Job [The Example of Job]" in a twelfth-century manuscript. See Rubie D-N. Warner, ed., *Early English Homilies from the Twelfth Century MS. Vesp. D. XIV* (London: Paul, Trench, Trübner, 1917), 123–29.

38. For a recent facsimile based on an edition printed in Strassburg in 1492, see Nicolaus de Lyra, *Postilla super totam Bibliam* (4 vols.; Frankfurt: Minerva, 1971), vol. 3.

39. See Paul Hüber, *Hiob: Dulder oder Rebell? Byzantinische Miniaturen zum Buche Hiob in Patmos, Rom, Venedig, Sinai, Jerusalem und Athos* (Dusseldorf: Patmos, 1986); Samuel Terrien, *The Iconography of Job through the Centuries: Artists as Biblical Interpreters* (University Park: Pennsylvania State University Press, 1996), 33–104.

40. For fuller discussions, see Margaret J. Allen, "The Book of Job in Middle English Literature (1100–1500)" (Ph.D. diss., University of London, 1970).

41. See Jan Nelson, "Guillaume de Machaut as Job: Access to the Poet as Individual through His Source," *Romance Notes* 23 (1982): 185–90; Sylvia Huot, "Patience in Adversity: The Courtly Lover and Job in Machaut's Motets 2 and 3," *Medium Ævum* 58 (1994): 222–38.

42. There also a number of illustrations of Job according to the Office of the Dead in various Books of Hours.

43. The Church of San Giobbe in Venice was founded in the fifteenth century as a chapel for the hospital in the wake of the plague in 1478.

44. See Valentin Denis, "Saint Job, patron des musiciens," *Revue belge d'archéologie et d'histoire d'art* 21 (1951): 253–303; Kathi Meyer, "St. Job as Patron of Music," *Art Bulletin* 36 (1954): 21–31.

45. Jerome himself continued to cite the Old Latin (based on OG) even after the translation of the Vulgate.

46. The view of Job as a prophet is continuous with Jewish and Christian interpretation going back at least to Ben Sira and is emphasized especially by Christian Syriac interpreters.

47. See F. Guillén Robles, *Leyendas moriscas sacadas de varios manuscritos existente en las Bibliotecas Nacional, Real, y de D. P. de Gayangos* (3 vols.; Madrid: Tello, 1885), 1:225–63; Antonio Verpertino Rodríguez, *Leyendas aljamiadas y moriscas sobre personajes biblicos* (Madrid: Editorial Gredos, 1983), 272–99.

48. See Mary E. Perry, "Patience and Pluck: Job's Wife, Conflicts and Resistance in Morisco Manuscripts Hidden in the Sixteenth Century," in *Women, Texts, and Authority in the Early Modern Spanish World* (ed. Marta V. Vicente and Luis R. Corteguera; Hampshire: Ashgate, 2003), 91–106; idem, *The Handless Maiden: Moriscos and the Politics of Religion in Early Modern Spain* (Princeton: Princeton University Press, 2005), 109–32.

49. Shaykh Muḥyi al-Din ibn ʿArabī, Fuṣūṣ al-ḥikam (ed. Abū al-ʿlā ʿAfifi; Iran: Intisharāt al-Zahrā, 1987), 170–76; English trans. in Ibn al-ʿArabī, *The Bezels of Wisdom* (Classics of Western Spirituality; trans. Ralph W. J. Austin; New York: Paulist, 1980), 212–17.

50. See Jeries N. Khouri, "The Figure of Job (Ayyub) in Modern Arabic Poetry," *Journal of Arabic Literature* 38 (1987): 166–95.

51. See, e.g., Rachel Milstein, Karin Rührdanz, and Barbara Schmitz, *Stories of the Prophets: Illustrated Manuscripts of the Qiṣaṣ al-Anbiyā'* (Costa Mesa: Calif.: Mazda, 1999), MS B, fol. 148a; MS L, fol. 91a, MS N, fol. 109a; MS T-7, fol. 126a; Stephen J. Vicchio and Lucinda D. Edinburg, *The Sweet Uses of Adversity: Images of the Biblical Job* (Annapolis, Md.: St. John's College, 2002), 56.

52. See David C. Steinmetz, "The Superiority of Pre-critical Exegesis," *TT* 37 (1980): 27–38.

53. This struggle is evident in the varied ways the text is translated: "a man child" (KJV, NRSV), "a male child" (NKJV), "a boy" (NIV, NJB, NASB, REB; cf. the revised Luther Bible, "ein Knabe"), "a male" (NJPS), "a man" (NEB; cf. the German translation of the Roman Catholic liturgical Bible *Einheitsübersetzung*, "ein Mann"), and NAB's "the child is a boy!"

54. Thus, for example, Georg Beer, *Der Text der Buches Hiob* (Marburg: Elswertsche, 1897) 14; Arnold B. Ehrlich, *Psalmen, Sprüche und Hiob* (Ranglossen zur hebräischen Bibel 16; Leipzig: Hinrichs, 1918), 189. The OG is usually cited in support of this emendation, although OG is clearly harmonizing with Jer 20:15. Symmachus and *ho hebraios* more properly have *anthrōpos*.

55. Didymus the Blind, *Kommentar zu Hiob (Tura-Papyrus): Teil 1, Kommentatar zu Hiob Kap. 1–4* (PTA 1; ed. and trans. Albert Henrichs; Bonn: Habelt, 1968), 180–81.

56. See Robert Alter, The Art of Biblical Poetry (New York: Basic Books, 1985), 76–84.

57. See Alex Preminger et al., eds., *The New Princeton Encyclopedia of Poetry and Poetics* (Princeton: Princeton University Press, 1993), 1101–2 and the literature cited there.

58. See the Princeton Index of Christian Art (http://ica.princeton.edu/).

59. Note that *ʾal-yidrĕšēhû* (v. 4b) chimes with *yigʾālūhû* (v. 5a), while *nĕhārâ* (v. 4c) rhymes with *ʿănānâ* (v. 5b), both forms being unique in Hebrew. Moreover, *tiškon-ʿālâw* (v. 5b) matches *ʾal-tôpaʿ ʿālâw* (v. 4c), so that *ḥōšek wĕṣalmōt* (v. 5a) matches *ʾĕlôah* (v. 4b). Thus, we have a chiasm of four lines:

ʾal-yidrĕšēhû ʾĕlôah mimmaʿal	Let Eloah above not seek it;
wĕʾal-tôpaʿ ʿālâw nĕhārâ	Let no light shine upon it.
yigʾālūhû ḥōšek wĕṣalmōt	Let darkness and pall redeem/defile it;
tiškōn-ʿālâw ʿănānâ	Let a cloud settle over it.

60. Commentators have proposed, *inter alia*, *kĕpî*, *lĕpî*, *kĕlaḥmî*, and *lĕpānay*.

61. See, e.g., Hüber, *Hiob, Dulder oder Rebell*, 158, 189, pls. 111, 141; I. Hutter, *Corpus der byzantinischen Miniaturenhandschriften* (Stuttgart: Hiersemann, 1977), 2:135, pl. 163; Jules Leroy, "Les peintures des couvents du Ouadi Natroun," in idem, *La Peinture murale chez les Coptes* (3 vols.; Cairo: Institut français d'archéologie orientale du Caire, 1982) 2:39–40, pls. 60, 71–72; Sirarpie D. Nersessian, *L'Illustration des psautiers grec du Moyen-âge* (Paris: Klincksieck, 1970), 2, fig. 248; Henri Omont, *Miniatures des plus anciens manuscripts grecs de la Bibliothèque Nationale du Ve au XIVe siècle* (Paris: Librairie ancienne Honoré Champion, 1929), 17, pl. 27; Kurt Weitzmann and George Galavaris, *The Monastery of Saint Catherine at Mount Sinai: The Illuminated Greek Manuscripts* (Princeton: Princeton University Press, 1991), 103, fig. 317.

62. G. N. Garmonsway and R. R. Raymo, "Middle English Metrical Life of Job," in *Early English and Norse Studies Presented to Hugh Smith in Honour of his Sixtieth Birthday* (ed. Arthur Brown and Peter Foote; London: Methuen, 1963), 7–98.

63. Geoffrey de La Tour Landy, *Le livre du chevalier de La Tour Landry, pour l'enseignement de ses filles: Pub. d'aprés les manuscrits de Paris et de Londres* (ed. M.

Anatole de Montaiglon; Paris: Jannet, 1854). The relevant portion on Job's wife is on pp. 159–61.

64. See Franz Pfeiffer, ed., *Die deutscher Mystiker des vierzehnten Jahrhunderts: Herrmann von Fritzlar, Nicholaus von Strassburg, David von Augsburg* (Göttingen: Vandenhoeck & Ruprecht, 1907), 233, lines 26–27; Karl Reissenberger, ed., *Das Väterbuch aus der Leipziger, Hildesheimer und Strassburger Handschrift* (Deutsche Texte des Mittelalters 22; Berlin: Weidman, 1914), vv. 37098–99 and 37385; and the discussion in Ulf Wielandt, *Hiob in der Alt- und Mittelhochdeutschen Literatur* (Bamberg: Rodenbusch, n.d.), 89–91.

65. See Moses Kimḥi, *Commentary on the Book of Job* (ed. Herbert Basser and Barry D. Walfish; South Florida Studies in the History of Judaism 69; Atlanta: Scholars Press, 1992), 6 [Hebrew]. Joseph Kimḥi, too, reports that several of his contemporaries took the imperative at face value. See *Tiqwat Enosch*, 81. A similar position was adopted by Moshe Alschich in the sixteenth century.

66. See further, C. L. Seow, "Job's Wife, with Due Respect," in *Das Buch Hiob und seine Interpretationen: Beiträge zum Hiob-Symposiu, auf dem Monte Verità vom 14.–19. August 2005* (ed. Thomas Krüger et al.; ATANT 88; Zürich: Theologischer Verlag Zürich, 2007), 351–73.

67. Gregory the Great, *Moralia in Iob* (ed. Marc Adriaen; CCSL 143, 143A, 143B; Turnholt: Brepols, 1979–1985).

68. Hans C. Hamilton, ed., *Historia rerum Anglicarum Wilhelmi Parvi* (London: Suptibus Societas, 1856), 162 (5.14).

69. For all these, see Jacobs, "Book of Job in Rabbinic Thought"; Baskin, *Pharaoh's Counsellors*, 7–43; Leibowitz, "The Image of Job"; Joanna Weinberg, "Job Versus Abraham: The Quest for the Perfect God-Fearer in Rabbinic Tradition," in Beuken, *The Book of Job*, 281–96.

70. Jason Kalman, "With Friends Like These: Turning Points in the Jewish Exegesis of the Biblical Book of Job" (Ph.D. diss., McGill University, 2005), 124–51.

71. See the excellent introduction to Saadiah's exegesis of Job in Lenn Evan Goodman's translation of Saadiah's commentary, *The Book of Theodicy: Translation and Commentary on the Book of Job* (New Haven: Yale University Press, 1988), 3–92. For the text and a Modern Hebrew translation of Saadiah's work, see *ʾIyyôb ʿim targum ûpêyrûš haggāʾôn rabbēnû saʿadyāh ben yôsēp payyûmî* (ed. and trans. Josef Kafiḥ; Jerusalem: Maqor, 1973).

72. Saadiah, *Book of Theodicy*, 238 n 16.

73. Goodman emends the text to read *šafā* "healed," which aligns well with the Qur'an's account, but such an emendation seems unnecessary. I take the form to be *šaffaʿa*, which in the second form means "to accept intercession" (Edward William Lane, "*šaffaʿa*," *Arabic-English Lexicon* 4:1572). This is related to the noun *muštaffaʿ* "one whose intercession is accepted."

74. See Charles B. Chavel, *Kitbê Rabbēnu Mōšeh ben Naḥmān* (2 vols.; Jerusalem: Mosad Rav Kook, 1963), 1:9–118; idem, *Ramban (Naḥmanides): Writings and Discourses* (2 vols.; New York: Shiloh, 1978), 2:454–68.

75. Chavel, *Kitbê*, 1:143–231, esp. 191–200.

76. See Israel M. Ta-Shma, "A Commentary on the Book of Job" [Hebrew], *Kove*

ʻal-Yad 13 (1996): 191–33.

77. There are two versions of a Job commentary by him, a shorter one published in Israel Schwartz, *Tikwath Enosch* (Berlin: Gerschel, 1868), 147–66; and a longer recension surviving in two manuscripts. The manuscript from Munich, comprising 24:17–42:16, was published in S. Eppenstein, "Un fragment du commentaire de Joseph Kimḥî sur Job," *Revue des études juives* 37 (1898): 86–102. There is an unpublished manuscript containing 10:1–41:22 in the Jewish Theological Seminary of America (ms L865).

78. Joseph Kimḥî, *The Book of the Covenant* (ed. and trans. Frank Talmage; Toronto: Pontifical Institute of Mediaeval Studies, 1972), 30.

79. See David Berger, *The Jewish-Christian Debate in the High Middle Ages: A Critical Edition of the Niṣṣaḥon Vetus* (Philadelphia: Jewish Publication Society, 1979), 131.

80. The polemist in the *Niṣṣaḥon* also suggests that Eliphaz's assertion that one who is born of woman cannot be pure (Job 15:14) is a reference to Jesus, who is said to be son of a woman, Mary, not a man. Jesus could not be righteous because he was born *only* of a woman.

Contributors

Yairah Amit is full professor of Hebrew Bible in the department of Hebrew Culture Studies and the head of the Training Program for Teachers of Hebrew Bible in the School of education at Tel Aviv University in Israel. Her research focuses on poetics, editing, and ideology in biblical historiography. Her recent publications in English include *History and Ideology: An Introduction to Historiography in the Hebrew Bible* (Sheffield Academic Press, 1999); *Hidden Polemics in Biblical Narrative* (Brill, 2000); and *Reading Biblical Narratives: Literary Criticism and the Hebrew Bible* (Augsburg Fortress, 2001).

Pablo R. Andiñach is Professor of Old Testament and President at Instituto Universitario ISEDET, Buenos Aires, Argentina. His recent books include *Cantar de los Canares: El fuego y la ternura* (Editorial Lumen, 1997); *El libro del Éxodo* (Ediciones Sígueme, 2006); and *Ser Iglesia* (Lumen Humanitas, 2007). He is also a contributing co-editor of *Comentario Bíblico Latinoamericano: Antiguo Testamento* (Editorial Verbo Divino, 2005).

Alan J. Avery-Peck is Kraft-Hiatt Professor of Judaic Studies and chair of the Department of Religious Studies at the College of the Holy Cross, Worcester, Massachusetts. Specializing in Jewish history and religion in the first six centuries C.E., he is, most recently, a co-author and editor of *The Encyclopaedia of Judaism* (2nd ed.; 4 vols.; Brill, 2005) and *The Mishnah in Contemporary Perspective, Part 2* (Brill, 2006). He is editor of the journal *The Review of Rabbinic Judaism.*

John Barton is Oriel and Laing Professor of the Interpretation of Holy Scripture, University of Oxford. His recent publications include *The Nature of Biblical Criticism* (Westminster John Knox, 2007).

Bruce C. Birch is Emeritus Dean and Professor of Old Testament at Wesley Theological Seminary in Washington, D.C. He is currently serving as Chair of Council for the Society of Biblical Literature. He is the author of numerous books and articles, including *A Theological Introduction to the Old Testament* (2nd ed.; Abingdon, 2005), co-authored with Walter Brueggemann, Terence Fretheim, and David Petersen.

Susan A. Brayford is Associate Professor of Religious Studies at Centenary College in Shreveport, Louisiana, and has served several years as Associate Academic Dean of the College. Her research centers on the ways in which biblical writers, translators, and interpreters have portrayed women and women's issues. She recently published the first English-language commentary on the Greek translation of Genesis (LXX Commentary Series; Brill, 2007).

William P. Brown is Professor of Old Testament Language, Literature, and Exegesis at Columbia Theological Seminary in Decatur, Georgia. His recent publications include *Engaging Biblical Authority* (editor; Westminster John Knox, 2007) and *Seeing the Psalms* (Westminster John Knox, 2002), as well as his forthcoming book *The Seven Pillars of Creation: The Bible, Science, and the Ecology of Wonder* (Oxford University Press, 2010).

Walter Brueggemann is William Marcellus McPheeters Professor Emeritus of Old Testament at Columbia Theological Seminary in Decatur, Georgia. He has recently authored *Mandate to Difference: An Invitation to the Contemporary Church* (Westminster John Knox, 2007) and *An Unsettling God: The Heart of the Hebrew Bible* (Fortress, 2009).

Mark K. George is Associate Professor of Hebrew Bible at the Iliff School of Theology in Denver, Colorado. He recently published *Israel's Tabernacle as Social Space* (Society of Biblical Literature, 2009) and is chair of the Space, Place, and Lived Experience in Antiquity section at the SBL Annual Meeting.

William K. Gilders is Associate Professor of Hebrew Bible at Emory University. His publications include *Blood Ritual in the Hebrew Bible: Meaning and Power* (Johns Hopkins University Press, 2004). His research focuses on ritual (especially sacrifice) in the Hebrew Bible and early Jewish literature. He is working on a new commentary on Leviticus for the Old Testament Library (Westminster John Knox) and a study of how ancient Jewish texts represent and interpret temple sacrifice.

John H. Hayes is the Franklin N. Parker Professor of Old Testament Emeritus of Candler School of Theology, Emory University in Atlanta, Georgia. His recent works include *A History of Ancient Israel and Judah* (co-authored with J. Maxwell Miller; 2nd ed.; Westminster John Knox, 2006) and *Biblical Exegesis: A Beginner's Handbook* (co-authored with Carl Holladay; 3rd ed.; Westminster John Knox, 2007). He is the general editor of the *Dictionary of Biblical Interpretation* (Abingdon, 1999).

Christopher B. Hays is D. Wilson Moore Assistant Professor of Ancient Near Eastern Studies at Fuller Theological Seminary in Pasadena, California. His research focuses on prophecy, particularly the book of Isaiah, and on religion in the ancient Near East, particularly death and afterlife.

Ralph W. Klein is Christ Seminary Seminex Professor of Old Testament Emeritus at the Lutheran School of Theology at Chicago. He was editor of *Currents in Theology and Mission* from 1974 to 2009. He is also the author of the Hermeneia commentary on the books of Chronicles (Fortress, 2006, 2011). Presently he serves as the Curator of the LSTC Rare Books Collection.

Douglas A. Knight is the Drucilla Moore Buffington Professor of Hebrew Bible and Professor of Jewish Studies at Vanderbilt University, Nashville, Tennessee. In addition to having published numerous articles and edited volumes, he is the author of *Rediscovering the Traditions of Israel* (3rd ed.; Society of Biblical Literature, 2006) and the forthcoming *Law, Power, and Justice in Ancient Israel* (2010). He is also editor of the Library of Ancient Israel series (Westminster John Knox).

Beatrice Lawrence is Assistant Professor of Hebrew Bible at Hebrew Union College-Jewish Institute of Religion in Los Angeles, California. She completed her Ph.D. in 2009 with a dissertation on the presentation of Jethro in postbiblical Jewish interpretation. Her research interests include gender, the role of non-Israelites in the Bible, and rabbinic hermeneutics.

Joel M. LeMon is Assistant Professor of Old Testament at Candler School of Theology, Emory University in Atlanta, Georgia. His research focuses on Hebrew poetry and ancient Near Eastern iconography. He is the author of *Yahweh's Winged Form in the Psalms: Exploring Congruent Iconography and Texts* (Academic Press, 2009).

Christoph Levin is Ordinary Professor of Old Testament Studies at the University of Munich, Germany. He has published on the history of Old Testament covenant theology; the redaction history of the Pentateuch as well as of the Historical Books, especially Judges and Kings; the history of Old Testament prophecy, especially Jeremiah and Amos; and the literary history of the Psalms. His publications in English include *The Old Testament: A Brief Introduction* (Princeton University Press, 2001).

James Luther Mays is Professor Emeritus of Hebrew and Old Testament Interpretation at Union Theological Seminary and Presbyterian School of Christian Education in Richmond, Virginia. His recent publications include *Preaching and Teaching the Psalms* (Westminster John Knox, 2006).

S. Dean McBride Jr. is professor emeritus of Hebrew and Old Testament Interpretation at Union Theological Seminary and Presbyterian School of Christian

Education in Richmond, Virginia. His recent publications include *God Who Creates: Essays in Honor of W. Sibley Towner* (co-edited with William P. Brown, Eerdmans, 2000). He is a member of the editorial board of the commentary series Hermeneia.

Gene M. Tucker is Professor of Old Testament Emeritus of Candler School of Theology, Emory University. He is the author, co-author, or editor of nineteen books, including the commentary on Isaiah 1–39 in the *New Interpreter's Bible* (vol. 6; Abingdon, 2001). He is also the series editor of some thirty-five books and the author of numerous articles, including several on issues concerning the Bible and the environment.

Kirsten Nielsen is Professor Emerita, Aarhus University, Denmark. Her main field is the Bible as literature, with a special focus on metaphors and intertextuality. Her publications include *Ruth: A Commentary* (Westminster John Knox, 1997) and *Satan: The Prodigal Son? A Family Problem in the Bible* (Sheffield Academic Press, 1998). She is co-editor and co-author of a Danish three-volume commentary on Psalms (Anis, 2002). Most recently she is the editor of *Receptions and Transformations of the Bible* (Aarhus University Press, 2009).

Martti Nissinen is Professor of Old Testament Studies at the University of Helsinki, Finland. He has published extensively on prophecy as well as on gender issues in the ancient Near East, including *References to Prophecy in Neo-Assyrian Sources* (Neo-Assyrian Text Corpus Project, 1998); *Homoeroticism in the Biblical World* (Augsburg Fortress, 1998); and *Prophets and Prophecy in the Ancient Near East* (Society of Biblical Literature, 2003).

Carol Newsom is Charles Howard Candler Professor of Old Testament at Candler School of Theology, Emory University, in Atlanta, Georgia. Her recent work includes *The Book of Job: A Contest of Moral Imaginations* (Oxford University Press, 2003); *The Self as Symbolic Space: Constructing Identity and Community at Qumran* (Brill, 2004), and the translation of the *hodayot* for volume 40 of Discoveries in the Judaean Desert (Oxford University Press, 2009).

Gail O'Day is the Senior Associate Dean of Faculty and Academic Affairs at Candler School of Theology, Emory University, in Atlanta, Georgia. She is the author of numerous books and articles on the Gospel of John, including *The Word Disclosed: Preaching the Gospel of John* (Chalice, 2002) and *John* (Westminster John Knox, 2006). Her additional research and teaching interests include literary criticism and biblical studies, history of biblical interpretation, and biblical hermeneutics and preaching. She has served as the general editor of the *Journal of Biblical Literature.*

Kent Harold Richards is Professor of Old Testament and Executive Director of the Society of Biblical Literature. He is the co-author of *Interpreting Hebrew Poetry* (Augsburg Fortress, 1992) and co-editor of *Second Temple Studies 2: Temple Community in the Persian Period* (Sheffield Academic Press, 1994) and *Old Testament Interpretation: Past, Present, and Future: Essays in Honor of Gene M. Tucker* (Abingdon, 1995).

Naomi Steinberg is Associate Professor of Religious Studies at DePaul University in Chicago, Illinois. She has published numerous works on the family in ancient Israel, including *Kinship and Marriage in Genesis: A Household Economics Perspective* (Fortress, 1993). Her research on children in the Hebrew Bible is informed by her recent volunteer work at a Guatemalan orphanage and her present service as a court-appointed Special Advocate for children in Illinois.

Thomas Römer is Ordinary Professor of Hebrew Bible at the University of Lausanne, Switzerland, and holds a chair of Bible and its contexts in Paris at the College de France. His recent publications include *The So-Called Deuteronomistic History* (2nd ed.; T&T Clark, 2007,) translated into French, Italian, Portugese and Japanese; and *The Books of Leviticus and Numbers* (Peeters, 2008). He is currently working on a commentary about the Abraham narrative.

C. L. Seow is the Henry Snyder Gehman Professor of Old Testament Language and Literature at Princeton Theological Seminary. He is the co-general editor of *The Encyclopedia of the Bible and Its Reception* (de Gruyter, 2009–), the first two volumes of which have just been published. He has published many articles and books, including *Ecclesiastes* in the Anchor Bible commentary series (Doubleday, 1997), and is co-editor of *Hebrew Inscriptions: Texts from the Biblical Period of the Monarchy* (Yale University Press, 2005).

Brent A. Strawn is Associate Professor of Old Testament at Candler School of Theology and in the Graduate Division of Religion at Emory University, where he is also associated professor in the Department of Middle Eastern and South Asian Studies. He is author of *What Is Stronger Than a Lion? Leonine Image and Metaphor in the Hebrew Bible and the Ancient Near East* (2005) and co-editor of *Qumran Studies: New Approaches, New Questions* (Eerdmans, 2007) and the Old Testament Theology series (Cambridge University Press).

Marvin Sweeney is Professor of Religion in the Claremont Graduate University School of Religion in Claremont, California. His recent publications include *Reading the Hebrew Bible after the Shoah: Engaging Holocaust Theology* (Fortress, 2008); *1 and 2 Kings: A Commentary* (Westminster John Knox, 2007); and *Form and Intertextuality in Prophetic and Apocalyptic Literature* (Mohr Siebeck, 2005). His editorial work includes editing the journal *Hebrew Studies* and co-editing the Forms of the Old Testament Literature commentary series (Eerdmans).

Robert R. Wilson is Hoober Professor of Religious Studies and Professor of Old Testament at Yale University. He has published numerous articles and three books on the sociological dimensions of the Old Testament and has recently been writing on the sociological aspects of Israel's exile in Babylon.

Scripture Index

Apocryphal/Deuterocanonical Literature

New Testament

Name Index